Time-Limited Interests in Land

A comprehensive comparative treatment of six instances of time-limited interests in land as encountered in fourteen European jurisdictions. The survey explores the commercial or social origins of each legal institution concerned and highlights their enforceability against third parties, their content and their role in land development. The commercial purpose of residential and agricultural leases is contrasted with the social aim of personal servitudes (and its common-law equivalent liferent) to provide sustenance for life to mostly family members, making the latter an important estate planning device. Whereas the ingrained principles of leases and personal servitudes restrain the full exploitation of land, it is indicated that public authorities and private capital could combine to turn the old-fashioned time-limited institutions of hereditary building lease (*superficies*) and hereditary land lease (*emphyteusis*) into pivotal devices in alleviating the acute shortage of social housing and in promoting the fullest exploitation of pristine agricultural land.

CORNELIUS VAN DER MERWE read law at Bloemfontein and Oxford and obtained an LLD from the University of South Africa. He held chairs in Private Law at the Universities of South Africa and Stellenbosch, in Civil Law at the University of Aberdeen and is presently a Senior Research Fellow at the University of Stellenbosch. He is the main author of the South African 'Property and Trust Law' in the *International Encyclopedia of Laws* (2002) and the co-editor of *Introduction to the Law of South Africa* (2004).

ALAIN-LAURENT VERBEKE is Professor of Law at the Universities of Leuven and Tilburg, teaching contracts, property, estate planning, private international law, comparative law, negotiation and mediation. He is also a Visiting Professor of Law at Harvard Law School and at UCP Global School of Law, Lisbon. In addition to his teaching, he is also a founding partner with Greenille, a private client law firm with attorneys in Brussels and Antwerp and notaries and attorneys in Amsterdam and Rotterdam. He has vast experience in negotiating large inheritance, divorce and contract cases and is regularly acting as an arbitrator in national and international contract and inheritance cases.

The Common Core of European Private Law

For the transnational lawyer the present European situation is equivalent to that of a traveller compelled to cross legal Europe using a number of different local maps. To assist lawyers in the journey beyond their own locality *The Common Core of European Private Law Project* was launched in 1993 at the University of Trento under the auspices of the late Professor Rudolf B. Schlesinger.

The aim of this collective scholarly enterprise is to unearth what is already common to the legal systems of European Union member states. Case studies widely circulated and discussed between lawyers of different traditions are employed to draw at least the main lines of a reliable map of the law of Europe.

Time-Limited Interests in Land

Edited by

Cornelius van der Merwe

and

Alain-Laurent Verbeke

CAMBRIDGE
UNIVERSITY PRESS

CAMBRIDGE UNIVERSITY PRESS
Cambridge, New York, Melbourne, Madrid, Cape Town,
Singapore, São Paulo, Delhi, Mexico City

Cambridge University Press
The Edinburgh Building, Cambridge CB2 8RU, UK

Published in the United States of America by Cambridge University Press, New York

www.cambridge.org
Information on this title: www.cambridge.org/9781107026124

First published 2012

Printed in the United Kingdom at the University Press, Cambridge

A catalogue record for this publication is available from the British Library

Library of Congress Cataloguing in Publication data
Time limited interests in land / Edited by Cornelius Van Der Merwe and Alain-Laurent Verbeke.
p. cm. – (The common core of European private law ; 12)
Includes bibliographical references.
ISBN 978-1-107-02612-4
1. Land use – Law and legislation – Europe. 2. Time (Law) – Europe. 3. Landlord and tenant – Europe. 4. Land titles – Registration and transfer – Europe. 5. Servitudes – Europe. 6. Leases – Law and legislation – Europe. 7. Usufruct – Europe. I. Van der Merwe, C. G. II. Verbeke, Alain.
KJC6127.T56 2012
346.404′32–dc23

2012015502

ISBN 978-1-107-02612-4 Hardback

Contents

General editors' preface

This is the twelfth book in the *Common Core of European Private Law* series. The project was launched in 1993 at the University of Trento under the auspices of the late Professor Rudolf B. Schlesinger.

The methodology used in the Trento project is novel. By making use of case studies it goes beyond mere description to detailed inquiry into how most European Union legal systems resolve specific legal questions in practice, and provides a thorough comparison between those systems. It is our hope that these volumes will provide scholars with a valuable tool for research in comparative law and in their own national legal systems. The collection of materials that the *Common Core* project is offering to the scholarly community is already quite extensive and will become even more so when more volumes are published. The availability of materials attempting a genuine analysis of how things are is, in our opinion, a prerequisite for an intelligent and critical discussion on how they should be. Perhaps in the future European private law will be authoritatively restated or even codified. The analytical work carried on today by the almost 200 scholars involved in the *Common Core* project is also a precious asset of knowledge and legitimisation for any such normative enterprise.

We must thank the editors and contributors to these first published results. With a sense of deep gratitude we also wish to recall our late Honorary Editor, Professor Rudolf B. Schlesinger. We are sad that we have not been able to present him with the results of a project in which he believed so firmly.

No scholarly project can survive without committed sponsors. The Italian Ministry of Scientific Research is funding the project, having recognised it as a 'research of national interest'. The International University College of Turin with the Compagnia di San Paolo and the

Consiglio Nazionale del Notariato allow us to organise the general meetings. The European Commission has partially sponsored some of our past general meetings, having included them in their High Level Conferences Programme. The University of Turin, the University of Trieste, the Fromm Chair in International and Comparative Law at the University of California and the Hastings College of Law, and the Centro Studi di Diritto Comparato of Trieste have all contributed to the funding of this project. Last but not least, we must thank all those involved in our ongoing projects in contract law, property, tort and other areas, whose results will be the subject of future published volumes.

Our home page on the internet is at www.iuctorino.it There you can follow our progress in mapping the common core of European private law.

General Editors
Mauro Bussani, University of Trieste
Ugo Mattei, University of Turin and University of California, Hastings College of Law

Honorary Editor
Rudolfo Sacco, University of Turin

Late Honorary Editor
Rudolf B. Schlesinger, Cornell University and University of California, Hastings

Preface

This book has a fairly long history. Following the approval of the topic at a Trento meeting in 2002, several important issues had to be discussed in preliminary meetings which pre-dated the preparation of an official questionnaire. Initially we had to satisfy ourselves that real rights limited in time actually constitute a special category of property rights that is sufficiently important to discuss as such. We then had to decide on the title of the project. We were torn between a number of potential titles, including 'Real Rights Limited in Time'; 'Real Rights of Limited Duration'; or 'Proprietary Rights Limited in Time'. Our eventual choice of the title 'Time-Limited Interests in Land' was closely connected to the decision to confine ourselves to the discussion of the most important time-limited rights with regard to land, and not to include a discussion of time-limited rights in movable property and incorporeal property. Furthermore, confining our analysis in this way not only allowed us to focus in more detail on the relevant legal institutions but allowed us to avoid an overlap with another simultaneous study that concentrated on time-limited interests in incorporeals.

A further preliminary issue was the question of whether we should confine ourselves to a discussion of the two most important time-limited interests in land, namely leases and personal servitudes (common law liferent) or whether the more obscure real interests in land of hereditary building rights (*superficies*) and hereditary land leases (*emphyteusis*) should also be considered. Additionally, we had to resolve whether to include the less important institutions of loan (*commodatum*) and precarious loan (*precarium*). The wider approach was favoured not only for the sake of comprehensiveness but also because we noted that in the past the little-known institutions of hereditary building rights (*superficies*) and hereditary land lease (*emphyteusis*) played an important role in land-development programmes initiated by public authorities to improve the exploitation of uncultivated land (*emphyteusis*) and the provision of housing for the homeless (*superficies*). It is our belief that even today these institutions could play a pivotal role in achieving these ends.

Owing to the fact that the project is within the sphere of property law, the editors agreed to concentrate on the proprietary rather than the obligational aspects of leases. Since commercial leases are mostly extensively regulated by special legislation, they restricted the project to the proprietary aspects of residential and agricultural leases. Finally, a decision was taken to make the first question a general one, in response to which reporters could give a fairly detailed account of the characteristics and content of the various time-limited interests in land encountered in their respective jurisdictions.

The three appointed editors, Cornelius van der Merwe, Alain Verbeke and Raffaele Caterina met in Aberdeen in December 2002 and together with Roderick Paisley of the School of Law, University of Aberdeen, prepared a provisional questionnaire to be presented at the next annual meeting of the Trento project. This questionnaire was accepted with a few minor amendments and the national reporters of fifteen jurisdictions were given the opportunity to provide answers to the various case studies dealt with in the questionnaire.

The book is arranged in three main sections, entitled 'Introduction and context', 'Case studies' and 'Concluding remarks'. The case studies themselves are also arranged in three sections dealing with: the enforceability of time-limited interests against third parties, the content of time-limited interests and the role of time-limited interests in land development. The book is distinguished by two special features. First, the comparative observations containing a summary of the various reports are placed at the beginning instead of at the end of each case study, and are followed by the various responses of the national reporters of the jurisdictions represented. Secondly, tables indicating the practical importance of each of the time-limited interests in the jurisdiction concerned are included in an Appendix.

Unfortunately, the completion of the project was delayed because of difficulty experienced in recruiting national reporters for France, Austria and eventually for Scotland. Fortunately we were able to persuade Odile Roy of the Université Paris Ouest Nanterre La Défense to write the French report in French. We are very grateful to Professor Lionel Smith, the James McGill Professor of Law, McGill University,

Montreal, Canada who assisted us in having the French report translated into English, a task primarily undertaken by Edmund Coates of the Quebec Research Centre of Private and Comparative Law, Faculty of Law, McGill University. Judith Schacherreiter of the University of Vienna and Dr Peter Webster, presently Judicial Assistant at the Supreme Court of the United Kingdom, kindly agreed to write the national reports for Austria and Scotland respectively.

The editors wish to thank Raffaele Caterina, Paul du Plessis and the combination of Alain Verbeke, Nicholas Carette and Bart Verdict for writing the three chapters in Part I, entitled 'Setting the scene', 'Historical evolution of the maxim "sale breaks hire"' and 'The many faces of usufruct'. Our main gratitude is, however, due to the national reporters for furnishing us with the national reports of their jurisdictions and for their patience in waiting for the project to reach its completion. We owe a particular debt of gratitude to Ilse van der Merwe of Stellenbosch and the Cambridge University Press team consisting of Helen Francis, Daniel Dunlavey, Paul Smith and Geoff Bailey for the linguistic and technical editing of the final manuscript and for compiling the various lists and the index. We gratefully acknowledge the assistance of research assistants Ryan Hartley of the University of Stellenbosch and John Townsend of the University of Aberdeen for linguistic editing of the national reports. We wish to thank Carla Boninsegna and Manuela Amsler for organising the discussion groups at the yearly meetings of the Trento Project at Trento and subsequently at Turin. We also thank Sinead Moloney for her unwavering encouragement and support, together with Professor Antonio Gambaro and the anonymous referee of this volume, whose advice helped to improve the final manuscript.

Cornelius van der Merwe acknowledges with gratitude the financial support of the National Research Foundation of South Africa and the Law School Research Committee of the School of Law of the University of Aberdeen. Without their generous assistance the volume would never have come to fruition.

The editors wish to note that most of the reports have been written between 2005 and 2009 and that a very few have been updated after 2009. Because of this, a small number of important recent developments have not been included, the most important being the reintroduction of the hereditary building right (*superficies*) by the Greek parliament in 2011 for the better development of public parcels of land.

Contributors

NICOLAS CARETTE, Professor of Law, University of Antwerp, Attorney at the Brussels Bar (Greenille) (co-author of Belgian report)

RAFFAELE CATERINA, Professor of Private Law, University of Turin (Italian report, Prologue)

EDMUND COATES, Quebec Research Centre of Private and Comparative Law, Faculty of Law, McGill University (translator of French report into English)

EUGENIA DACORONIA, Associate Professor of Civil Law, University of Athens, Department of Law (Greek report)

PAUL DU PLESSIS, Senior lecturer, University of Edinburgh (Historical essay)

HANS HENRIK EDLUND, Professor of Private Law, Aarhus School of Business and Social Sciences, University of Aarhus (Danish report)

MAGDALENA HABDAS, Assistant Professor of Private Law, Department of Civil Law and Private International Law, Faculty of Law and Administration, University of Silesia (Polish report)

DIRK-JAN MAASLAND, Candidate Civil Law Notary in Rotterdam (Greenille) (co-author of Chapter 4)

CSONGOR ISTVAN NAGY, Adjunct Professor of Law, University of Szeged, Department of Private International Law and Budapest University of Technology and Economics, Department of Business Law (Hungarian report)

SANDRA PASSINHAS, Professor of Civil Law, University of Coimbra (Portuguese report)

OLIVER RADLEY-GARDNER, Barrister, Falcon Chambers, London (English report)

ODILE ROY, Maître de Conférences en droit privé, Centre d'Études Juridiques Européennes et Comparées, Université Paris Ouest Nanterre La Défense (French report)

JACOBIEN RUTGERS, Professor of Private Law, University of Amsterdam (co-author of Dutch report)

ELENA SANCHEZ JORDAN, Professor of Private Law, University of La Laguna (Spanish report)

JUDITH SCHACHERREITER, Research Assistant, Faculty of Law, University of Vienna; Visiting Researcher, University of Oaxaca, Mexico (Austrian report)

CORNELIUS G. VAN DER MERWE, Emeritus Professor of Civil Law, University of Aberdeen, Research Fellow, University of Stellenbosch (South African report, Comparative observations, Introduction, Concluding remarks)

LARS VAN VLIET, Professor of Private Law, University of Maastricht (co-author of Dutch report)

ALAIN-LAURENT VERBEKE, Professor of Law, Universities of Leuven and Tilburg, Visiting Professor of Law, Harvard Law School, and UCP Global School of Law, Lisbon, Attorney at the Brussels Bar (Greenille) (co-author of Belgian report, Chapter 4 and Tables)

BART VERDICKT, Research Assistant at University of Leuven, Attorney at the Brussels Bar (Greenille) (co-author of Chapter 4)

MICHAEL VON HINDEN, Civil law notary, Hamburg, Lecturer at Bucerius Law School, Hamburg (German report)

PETER WEBSTER, Solicitor, Judicial Assistant at the Supreme Court of the United Kingdom (2010–11) (Scottish report)

Abbreviations

ABGB	*Allgemeinen bürgerlichen Gesetzbuch*
AD	Appellate Division [of the Supreme Court of South Africa]
AH(S)A 03	Agricultural Holdings (Scotland) Act 2003
AH(S)A 91	Agricultural Holdings (Scotland) Act 1991
ALR	*Allgemeines Landrecht*
AP	*Areios Pagos*
App Cas	Law Reports: Appeal Cases, House of Lords
APR	*Algemene Practische Rechtsverzameling*
Arr Cass	*Arresten van het Hof van Cassatie*
B. & Ad.	*Barnewall & Adolphus' King's Bench Reports*
BauRG	*Baurechtsgesetz*
BCC	Belgian Civil Code
BGB	*Bürgerliches Gesetzbuch*
BGBl	*Bundesgesetzblatt*
BGHZ	*Entscheidungen des Bundesgerichtshofs in Zivilsachen*
Bing.	*Bingham's Common Pleas Reports*
BTVG	*Bauträgervertragsgesetz*
Bull. civ. I–IV	*Bulletin des arrêts de Chambres civiles de la Cour de cassation* [1st, 2nd, 3rd and Commercial Civil Chamber]
BW	*Burgerlijk Wetboek* (Dutch Civil Code)
C. & P.	*Carrington & Payne's Nisi Prius Reports*
Cass. civ.	Civil chamber of the *Cour de cassation*
Cass.	*Cour de cassation*
CFR	Common Frames of Reference
Ch	Law Reports: Chancery Division (1891 onwards)
ChD	Law Reports: Chancery Division 1875–90
Civ. 1	First Civil Chamber of the *Cour de cassation*

Civ. 2	Second Civil Chamber of the *Cour de cassation*
Civ. 3	Third Civil Chamber of the *Cour de cassation*
Co. Rep.	Cokes King's Bench Reports
Constr. urb.	*Construction urbaine*
CPD	Common Pleas Division
CSIH	Court of Session (Scotland), Inner House
CSOH	Court of Session (Scotland), Outer House
D	*Recueil Dalloz*
Dz.U.	*Dziennik Ustaw*
EDL	Eastern Districts Local Division [of the Supreme Court of South Africa]
EEN	*Efimeris Ellinon Nomikon*
EllDni	*Elliniki Dikaiossyni*
EvBl	*Evidenzblatt der Rechtsmittelentscheidungen*
FCC	French Civil Code
GCC	Greek Civil Code
GlUNF	*Glaser/Unger Neue Folge, Sammlung zivilrechtlicher Entscheidungen des OGH*
GWD	Green's Weekly Digest
H(S)A 88	Housing (Scotland) Act 1988
HS	*Sammlung handelsrechtlicher Entscheidungen*
Int and Comp LQR	International Comparative Law Quarterly
JAP	*Juristische Ausbildung und Praxisvorbereitung*
JBl	*Juristische Blätter*
KBB	*Kommentar zum Allgemeinen bürgerlichen Gesetzbuch*
LAWSA	The Law of South Africa
LDT	limited duration tenancy
LoH	Law on Hypothecs
LP(MP)A	Law of Property (Miscellaneous Provisions) Act 1989
LPA	Law of Property Act
LR(S)A 79	Land Registration (Scotland) Act 1979
LRA	Land Registration Act 2002
LRL	Legislative Reference Library
LTR(S)A 74	Land Tenure Reform (Scotland) Act 1974
M. & W.	Megarry and Wade: The Law of Real Property
MietSlg	*Mietrechtliche Entscheidungen*
NJ	*Netherlandse Jurisprudentie*
NJW	*Neue Juristische Wochenschrift*

Not Fisc M	*Notarieel en Fiscaal Maandblad*
NoV	*Nomiko Vima*
NPD	Natal Provincial Division [of the Supreme Court of South Africa]
NRAU	*Novo Regime do Arrendamento Urbano*
NZ	*Notariatszeitung*
Ob	*Oberster*
ÖJZ	*Österreichische Juristen-Zeitung*
Pas.	*Pasicrisie belge*
PPP	Public Private Partnership
Rev Dr ULB	*Revue de Droit de l'Université libre de Bruxelles*
ROW(S)A 95	Requirements of Writing (Scotland) Act 1995
RTDciv	*Revue trimestrielle de droit civil*
RW	*Rechtskundig weekblad*
SA	[High Court of] South Africa
SAFER	*Société d'aménagement foncier et d'établissement rural*
SALJ	South African Law Journal
Sh Ct Rep	Sheriff Court Report
Sh Ct	Sheriff Court
SLDT	short limited duration tenancy
SLT	*Scots Law Times*
Stb	*Staatsblad*
SZ	*Entscheidungen des österreichischen Obersten Gerichtshofes in Zivilsachen*
T Not	*Tijdschrift voor Notarissen*
TBBR	*Tijdschrift voor Belgisch Burgerlijk Recht*
TC(S)A	Title Conditions (Scotland) Act 2003
THRHR	*Tydskrif vir Hedendaagse Romeins-Holandse Reg*
TPD	Transvaal Provincial Division [of the Supreme Court of South Africa]
TPR	*Tijdschrift voor Privaatrecht*
TvR	*Tijdschrift voor Rechtsgeschiedenis*
U Toronto LJ	University of Toronto Law Journal
UfR	*Ugeskrift for Retsvæsen*
WEG	*Wohnungseigentumsgesetz*
wobl	*Wohnrechtliche Blätter*
WPNR	*Weekblad voor privaatrecht, notariaat en registratie*
ZEuP	*Zeitschrift für Europäisches Privatrecht*

PART I

Introduction and context

1 Setting the scene

RAFFAELE CATERINA

1. The scene

Every modern legal system recognises, besides perpetual ownership rights, time-limited interests in land. There are many reasons why people may wish to deal in rights that are limited in time as opposed to dealing in perpetual rights. The acquirer might simply not be interested in a perpetual right, for instance, because he/she knows that he/she is going to leave for another country in a few years or because financially he/she may not be able to afford to buy a perpetual right.

Looking at things from the perspective of the grantor, he/she may be interested in realising financially some of the value of the land without giving up his/her right to live there until his/her death. Alternatively, the grantor may be inspired by his/her concern for his/her family. For instance, the grantor may wish for his/her younger sister to live comfortably in his/her house until her death, but the grantor may also want to ensure that at her death all of his/her property will go to the grantor's son.

Simplifying all of this, one may see two fundamental rationales for creating time-limited interests in land: first, ensuring a more efficient exploitation of land and second, providing for the personal needs of the creator or for someone he/she cares for. The first rationale usually requires that the limited interest's duration is fixed in time. The latter is more compatible with lifelong limited interests. Lease, *superficies* and *emphyteusis* can be seen as examples of how to achieve more efficient exploitation of the land, whereas usufruct and life estate (liferent) are good examples of how to facilitate the personal needs or wishes of the creator.

Recognition of the fact that most of these needs can be met to some extent by the law of contract is important. However, the contractual solution is not entirely satisfactory, since contracts create only personal rights. This introduces an element of risk: if the land is alienated, the personal time-limited interest will not be enforceable against the new owner.

On the other hand, creating real time-limited interests in land can be problematic. It makes the circulation of land more difficult. This is especially true for lifelong time-limited interests. The time-limited interest holder cannot transfer any better title than he/she has himself/herself. Thus alienation of his interest is very difficult because the acquirer will have an interest measured by the life of the original holder. This is certainly a precarious (and somewhat illogical) position. It is evident that an interest measured by someone else's life is not very appealing to anyone. Consequently, the time-limited interest's holder will encounter great difficulties in trying to sell it or use it as a security to borrow money. Furthermore, any agreement with the future holder is particularly difficult because there is an element of uncertainty about the duration and thus the value of their respective rights, and negotiation tends to be easier when the rights involved are clear.

These needs and problems more or less define the outlook of time-limited interests in land in all contemporary legal systems. What is very much different is the theoretical conceptualisation of the different rights. Some legal systems see absolute ownership as something radically and qualitatively different from time-limited interests, which are, together with praedial servitudes, considered as *iura in re aliena*. This is generally considered to be the Roman law solution, and is the prevailing view in modern civil law jurisdictions. Other legal systems put perpetual and time-limited rights in the same class.

A different conceptualisation was adopted by English law, which has divorced ownership from land itself and attached it to an imaginary thing called an estate, which entitles the owner to use the land for a longer or shorter period of time. The time-limited interest is thus seen as an estate in land, which differs from the perpetual fee simple only in quantity.

It should be noted that a partially similar solution was adopted by the continental legal systems in the age of the *ius commune*, when *emphyteusis*, *superficies* and *locatio ad longum tempus* were considered *dominia utilia*. The *summa divisio* between absolute ownership and limited real rights is largely the product of the rebirth of the Roman law doctrine of ownership. However, the reality that the scholars of the *ius commune* tried to put into the Roman schemes was substantially common to all European countries. It has been said that 'la Common law a résisté à l'influence romaine; son droit de la propriété foncière, construit sur la base des structures féodales et des institutions normandes, rappelle l'organisation complexe du droit médiéval français'.[1]

A second, more specific point of theoretical difference concerns lease. While universally it has experienced a sort of 'realification' process through the abandonment of the principle *emptio tollit locatum*, lease of land in England began life as a mere personal right, but by the close of the Middle Ages the leaseholder had a fully protected interest in the land, being able to recover the land against all persons who evicted him. In Scotland, the Leases Act 1449 conferred security of tenure on lessees by permitting them to remain on the land until the end of their leases, even if the landlord sold the property. In continental Europe, the principle 'sale does not break hire' triumphed with the great codifications at the turn of the nineteenth century, but it was already widely accepted in Roman-Dutch law. However, not all legal systems came to the logical conclusion of recognising lease as a real right in land. In many legal systems the right of the lessee is still commonly classified as a mere personal right, or at least is considered as a sort of 'hybrid'.

In any case, legal systems invariably seem to recognise the need for real rights (enforceable against third parties) that have a fixed duration. Sometimes the same tool answers all needs: in England, a lease of land may be from year to year or for ninety-nine or even for 300 years. In other countries, leases are used for creating short-time interests (in Italy, for instance, a contract of lease cannot be stipulated for a period exceeding thirty years (Civil Code, art. 1573)) and thus the functional equivalents of the English lease include lease and *superficies* as well as *emphyteusis*.

The real point of difference concerns lifelong time-limited interests. In England, the common law (in the narrow sense in which it is contrasted with equity) has since 1925 recognised only two estates, namely the perpetual fee simple and the lease.

> The problem with settlement of land was that the splitting up of the fee simple estate over time meant that there was no one person for the time being who was independently capable of giving an absolute title and thus being able to effectively manage that land. In a well-drawn settlement, these difficulties were often overcome by the grantor using a trust, under which he would convey the fee simple to trustees with a direction or power to sell, lease, mortgage and

[1] Patault, *Introduction historique*, p. 33.

so on and to allow the family members to take an equivalent benefit from the proceeds of sale, a process known as 'overreaching'. It was this device that the draftsman of the 1925 legislation adopted. Indeed, all that the statute did was to make good conveyancing practice compulsory. Thus from 1925 onwards the splitting up of the enjoyment of land over time was still a possibility. The only difference was that it now had to be done behind a trust containing powers for the beneficial interests to be overreached.[2]

The functional equivalent of the civilian usufruct, life estate, can now exist only behind the curtain of a trust. The English story is an instructive lesson for civil law countries. Usufruct may be a problem for effective management of the land. This may be an explanation for the relative decline in the use of usufruct in many civil law systems. The idea of giving the usufructuary the right to sell, thus transferring the nude owner's interest on the proceeds of sale, is seen as problematic in some civil law countries. This is because the classical notion of usufruct includes the duty to preserve the substance of the property. This kind of resistance may condemn usufruct to be abandoned as too rigid a tool.

2. Balancing the interests: a handful of common problems

Whenever a time-limited interest in land is created, the law has an important role to play in reconciling the competing interests of the parties involved. Different legal systems face substantially the same problems.

A 'stylistic' divergence between civil law and common law systems has been rightly emphasised. Many civil law systems 'define what is owned by the usufructuary by explicitly relying on the idea of a right to do certain acts': 'the usufructuary has the right to use and to draw the fruits of the thing subject to the usufruct'.

Turning now to the English law of property, it is fair to say that the problem of how to split ownership among successive holders of an asset has seldom been addressed in England by asking the question of what *rights* the holder *pro tempore* gets while in possession. English courts have more often dealt with the converse question, i.e., under what circumstances does a limited owner face liability in torts for acts he should have refrained from doing? The difference in the two starting points may reflect a general English preference for framing legal issues without recourse to the ubiquitous and amorphous notion of a legal right.[3]

[2] Swadling, 'Property: General Principles', p. 231. [3] Graziadei, 'Tuttifrutti', pp. 130–1.

While civilian systems often use the language of rights and duties, the relevant English rules were shaped through the tort of waste. The practical divergences must not be overemphasised. This is even more evident when one considers that some key cases on the liability of limited interest holders for waste make free use of various civilian resources. In a case concerning the cutting of timber by a life tenant, Bowen LJ went so far as to say that in a case which has no direct precedent, 'it is desirable to refer to the law of usufruct, on which the English law of waste is, to a great extent, based'.[4] Whether or not this is true, it highlights the fact that English judges and scholars did not see a radical, qualitative discontinuity between Roman law and English law with regard to the law concerning time-limited rights.

The time-limited interest holder is entitled to exploit the land. He/she can use it directly and take its produce, as was said by Lord Blackburn in a Scottish case:

> the law of England, and, I believe, of every country, the feudal law, and the civil law, too, would say that in that case the person who has the limited interest takes, beyond all doubt, the annual produce, the grass, the apples, and things of that sort, and applies them to his own use as he pleases, as long as his interest lasts.[5]

In any legal system, however, the time-limited interest holder's rights of exploitation meet some limitations, which can easily be explained. A time-limited interest holder 'will have an incentive to maximize not the value of the property, that is, the present value of the earnings stream obtainable from it, but only the present value of the earnings stream obtainable' during his interest's expected lifetime. He/she may, for instance, 'want to cut the timber before it has attained its mature growth – even though the present value of the timber would be greater if the cutting of some or all of it were postponed', if the added value will enure to the future interest holder.[6] A time-limited interest holder may want to exploit the land intensively even if, in the long run, this is detrimental to the land itself. There is a clear potential for conflicts of interest here.

Every legal system has developed a body of rules in order to regulate the possible conflicts of interest. In the common law this role is played by the law of waste. In the civil law tradition, with regard to usufruct, the relevant rules were developed starting from the *salva rei substantia*

[4] *Dashwood* v. *Magniac* [1891] 3 Ch 306, 362.

[5] *Campbell* v. *Wardlaw* (1883) 8 App Cas 641, 645.

[6] Posner, *Economic Analysis*, p. 73.

limit and the *cautio fructuaria* already present in Roman law and are expressed through different formulas. In general terms, the usufructuary has the duty to preserve the substance of the property and has to use the diligence of a good *paterfamilias* with regard to the enjoyment of the property. These rules are designed to prevent the property being depleted as a source of income.

Many legal systems go further and forbid radical modifications of the property even if their effect is not directly detrimental. With regard to usufruct, the general idea is well expressed by the German Civil Code: the usufructuary is not entitled to transform the property or substantially change it (§ 1037) and in exercising his/her right of use, the usufructuary cannot alter the economic destination of the property (§ 1036). This idea is not unknown to English law: alterations in the physical characteristics of the premises by an unauthorised act of the tenant that increased the value of the property were considered ameliorating waste, and were prohibited. It is uncertain whether this is still the law today.[7] There may be a legitimate interest in the land being returned substantially unchanged: even if a change of destination is not detrimental *per se*, it may be incompatible with the personal plans of the future interest holder. This must nevertheless be balanced against the need to avoid the land being locked into an inefficient use.

Some legal systems have developed lesser time-limited rights, which limit the power of the holder to use the property and appropriate its fruits and usually do not entitle the holder to lease the property. These more-limited rights (which include the Roman *usus* and *habitatio*) are not always clearly distinguished from irregular servitudes, which confer a limited right of use (for example, a right of way) upon a particular person.

A time-limited interest holder will not necessarily have an incentive to keep the property in a good state of repair. It is highly unlikely that he will be bothered about the long-term effects of disrepair. In many civil law systems the usufructuary and the lessee are obliged to carry out repairs and maintenance. The extent of this duty has not always been entirely clear. In the common law tradition, this kind of problem has been tackled through the law of permissive waste. In Coke's times, it seemed clear that 'to doe or make waste . . . includes as well permissive

[7] An injunction against ameliorating waste may still be awarded at least where the whole character of the property will be changed. See e.g. Megarry and Wade, *Real Property*, p. 81.

waste, which is waste by reason of omission, or not doing, as for want of reparation'.[8] In English law, the liability of the life tenant for permissive waste is now excluded while the position of the lessee is more uncertain.

A more general problem concerns the extent to which the statutory regime can be modified when a time-limited interest is created and whether these modifications simply give rise to a bundle of personal rights and obligations between the parties or to rights which are fully enforceable against third parties.

While these problems can be met with different solutions, it must be noted that this variation does not respect the *summa divisio* between common law and civil law, nor does it seem strictly related to the different theoretical conceptions of time-limited interests in land. Only time will tell how particular legal systems choose to deal with these problems. It is submitted that whatever varying methods are adopted by different systems, they will simply be balancing the same goals in a different manner.

3. Time-limited interests arising by operation of law

The need to provide for one's widow or widower without putting at risk the children's right to inherit is an obvious explanation for the creation of lifelong time-limited interests in land. This may be traced to the origins of the Roman usufruct: the normal method of creating a usufruct was by legacy, and the most common case was the legacy of usufruct by the testator to his widow.

In the civil law tradition, usufruct has remained one of the common tools for providing for the widow's needs. In many cases, the surviving spouse is granted a usufruct (or another similar right) by operation of law over the deceased spouse's property, either as an intestate successor or as a forced heir.

In various versions, usufruct is still a common solution in the civil law countries. In France, the rules have changed several times. Since 2001, if a deceased dies intestate, leaving a spouse and children or descendants, the surviving spouse will take, at his/her option, either the usufruct of the whole of the existing property or the ownership of one quarter of the existing property (Civil Code, art. 757). In the absence of an intention to the contrary expressed by the deceased, a spouse, entitled

[8] Coke, *Laws of England 1590–1640*, p. 145.

to inherit and who occupied as his/her main habitation at the time of the deceased's death a lodging belonging to the deceased, has until his/her death a right of habitation in the lodging and a right of use of its furnishings (Civil Code, art. 764). In Spain, the surviving spouse receives a usufruct over one-third of the estate if there are descendants (Civil Code, art. 834).

In Italy, the Civil Code originally reserved to the surviving spouse a usufruct over a variable share of the deceased spouse's property. Since 1975, the surviving spouse takes a share (between one-quarter and one-half) of the deceased spouse's patrimony (in full ownership and not in usufruct). He/she is, however, also granted the right of habitation of the house used as a family home and the right of use of its furnishings (Civil Code, art. 540). This has resulted in the diminishing importance of the usufruct with a counterpart increase in importance of the right of habitation.

A new system has been introduced in the Netherlands with the new Book 4 of the Civil Code. If no will has been made, the spouse acquires the assets of the deceased's estate by operation of law. The children, however, have pecuniary claims against the surviving spouse. If the latter declares an intention to remarry, he/she is obliged, on request, to make over to the child assets to the value of the pecuniary claim, subject to a reserved right of usufruct (art. 19). Where, as a result of any testamentary disposition, the deceased's spouse is not entitled to the dwelling and household effects which form part of the deceased's estate and in which the surviving spouse was living at the time of the deceased's death, the heirs have to co-operate to establish a usufruct on behalf of the surviving spouse to that dwelling and those household effects to whatever extent the latter requires them to do so (art. 29). Thus, in the rather complex system introduced by the new Dutch law of succession, the creation of a usufruct in favour of the surviving spouse over some portion of the deceased's property is still a probable result.

The idea of a life estate of the widow or widower on the deceased's land is not foreign to the common law tradition. The common law recognised the marital life estate of dower to protect a widow from disinheritance by her husband. In most instances, the life estate of curtesy protected the widower from disinheritance by his wife. The lifetime protection afforded a widow extended to an interest in only one-third of the estate which her husband acquired during their marriage. The lifetime protection afforded the widower covered all of his wife's inheritable freehold estates. On the other hand, the husband was required to have issue that could inherit in order to obtain the curtesy interest, while no such requirement was present for a surviving wife in order to receive dower. After 1833, curtesy and dower were abolished in England. Today a few American states recognise dower by statute, although a survivor's rights under such a statute are frequently quite different from those found at common law.[9]

While interests in land for a fixed period of time are important tools for its efficient exploitation, the practical importance of lifelong time-limited interests (in their various incarnations) is strongly related to the law of succession. They are useful tools for estate planning but they are also one of the basic instruments in the legislator's arsenal, especially for regulating the hereditary rights of the surviving spouse. The usufruct (or some other similar right) remains, in the eyes of many legislators, a useful mechanism to provide financial support to a widow for the rest of her life.

[9] See Bashier, 'Disinheritance and the Modern Family', p. 83.

2 General introduction

CORNELIUS VAN DER MERWE

1. Overview

The topic of time-limited interests in land has never been the subject of thorough research. Although there are voluminous works on the law pertaining to leases and to a lesser extent on personal servitudes and liferents, the combination of these two mainstreams of time-limited interests in land has rarely been the subject of academic investigation. This is perhaps the main reason why the Common Core Project has chosen this topic as one of its later sub-topics to be examined after the well-known topics of security rights in movable property and trusts were completed.

Part II of this book will deal with the presentation and comparative overview of thirteen case studies by various national reporters on significant issues in the law relating to time-limited interests. The aim of this short introduction is to explain the hybrid character of the topic and the specific approach of the present study that not only differs from the usual type of comparative investigation but also deviates, albeit to a lesser extent, from other studies within the Common Core Project. The genesis of the project on time-limited interests will then be discussed before the structure of the book will be laid out.

2. The hybrid character of time-limited interests in land

Time-limited interests in land straddle both the law of property and the law of contract. From the law of contract it draws the second most important specific contract after the contract of sale, namely the contract of lease and in particular the lease of land into its ambit. The main thrust is, however, not the contractual aspects of the law of lease, but those aspects of the lease of land which endows the tenant with certain proprietary entitlements even in those civil law jurisdictions which do not recognise a lease as a limited or subordinate real right. In this regard, two historical developments in the law of lease are important. The first is the replacement of the rule of *emptio tollit conductionem* (sale breaks lease) with the maxim *emptio non tollit conductionem* (sale does not break lease). This entails that the purchaser of land has to respect the entitlements of an existing lease and allow the tenant to stay on the land for the duration of the lease. The history of this remarkable turnaround of the maxim is explained in the following chapter. The second aspect is the historical development of a distinction between two kinds of leases of land, namely residential leases and agricultural leases. This distinction has been received in most of the continental jurisdictions and today agricultural and residential leases are generally regulated by specific legislation applicable to each.

The topic of time-limited interests in land is of great relevance to many areas of property law. The ambit of time-limited interests in land is far reaching and can be said to encompass, with the exception of praedial servitudes and mineral rights, the most important categories of limited real rights. These include the personal servitudes of usufruct (liferent); use; habitation; *superficies* or hereditary building lease (the right to erect buildings on land); and *emphyteusis*[1] or hereditary land lease (the right to improve the land by buildings or otherwise). Some jurisdictions such as Poland treat usufruct as a separate real right and distinguish it from the personal servitudes of use and habitation. Poland has also developed the interesting distinct personal servitude of lifetime habitation which has evolved into a useful estate planning device. Other jurisdictions such as Greece have tried to categorise the so-called irregular praedial servitudes under the personal servitude of use. These are servitudes created in favour of a particular person instead of the dominant land, for instance, the right to graze, draw water or pass over land to reach a family graveyard. Moreover, certain jurisdictions have adapted or modernised the Roman-law institutions to suit their own peculiar circumstances, while others have combined the institutions of *superficies* and

[1] The noun *emphyteusis* is derived from the Greek verb meaning 'to cultivate'. The institution was developed around 400 BC in Greece and appeared in Roman cities not later than the third century BC. See Yiannopoulos, *Louisiana Civil Law*, p. 343, § 225; Johnston, 'Emphyteusis', p. 323; Rome, 'An Elegy for Emphyteusis', p. 4.

emphyteusis into one institution. A few jurisdictions have developed new categories of time-limited interests in land.

3. The approach and purpose of this study

3.1. Background

This project forms part of a larger project initiated by Ugo Mattei and Mauro Bussani entitled 'The Common Core of European Private Law'. Building on the results of the methods and investigations of Rudolf Schlesinger and his followers at the Cornell Law School in the 1960s, the main aim of the project is to unearth what is common (or indeed uncommon) among the private law systems of the member states of the European Union. The project envisages the demarcation of a legal map of Europe by unearthing similarities without imposing new rules or different categories. A unique characteristic of the Common Core Project is that national reporters are asked to discuss hypothetical situations instead of presenting their legal systems in an abstract way by the formulation of principles, rules and exceptions to the rules. This so-called functional approach aims to prove that the answers to specific hypothetical situations are broadly similar irrespective of the reasoning and dogmas used to arrive at the answer.

Since the aim of the project is to find out how the law of a particular system deals with problems raised by factual situations, the editors are asked to make use of as little legal terminology as possible in selecting and formulating the cases. The beneficial aspect of such an approach is that it avoids the difficulties that dogmatic rigidity can pose. The dangers inherent in classical comparative studies (focusing on concepts, principles and rules) are greater than in other branches of property law. If one concentrates primarily on, for instance, the important dividing lines between whether a lease gives rise to a right *in rem* or a right *in personam*, or on general principles of registration as the overriding factor for making time-limited rights enforceable against third parties, one may probably attribute more weight than is justified to these conceptual differences. The present research shows that these conceptual dividing lines and differences matter less for the practical outcome of cases than the mode of analysis adopted that one might expect.

The more problematic aspect of this approach is that in contrast to projects concerning the law of contract and delict such as 'Good Faith in European Contract Law' and 'Pure Economic Loss', it is not easy to formulate factual situations on time-limited interests without using legal terminology. This is illustrated by the way in which most of the cases are presented. A good example is the issue in Case 2: whether and in what circumstances a previously created time-limited interest will be enforceable against a successor-in-title to the land. In order to request reporters to answer this question with regard to each time-limited interest recognised in that particular jurisdiction, it was necessary to start from a neutral factual situation. The same is true of the rest of the Cases dealing with the effect of attachment of the property, the insolvency of the owner of the burdened property and the dispossession or disturbance of the factual hold which the holder has on the property. In Cases 5–10 on the content of the time-limited right, the editors were able to formulate the factual situations in a less dogmatic manner. Similarly, Cases 11–13 on land development succeeded to a large extent in formulating pure factual situations with little dogmatic veneer.

3.2. *Drawing a geographical map of the law of Europe*

The aim of the Common Core Project is to draw at least 'the main lines of a reliable geographical map of the law of Europe'. In other words, the goal is to paint a general picture of the different rules in different jurisdictions across the continent. According to the general editors, the use of this map is of little 'concern to the cartographers who are drafting it'. In actual fact their aim is not to force the diverse reality of the law which exists in practice into one single map in order to obtain uniformity. Such an endeavour will be fruitless. The project is directed neither at the preservation of traditional legal rules nor as a movement to achieve a higher measure of harmonisation of European private law. Nor is it designed to be a stepping stone towards the realisation of a European Civil Code. In contrast to the activities of the Lando Commission and the European trend to write case books on European law, the Common Core Project is not engaging in city planning but rather in agnostic legal cartography. In the present study, the various legal formants shaping the outcomes of legal disputes have been intermingled without any sharp demarcation.

The main goal of the editors and national contributors to the present study is to provide methodical and reliable information in an objective way without forcing uniformity where it does not exist. We are, however, also interested in what lies ahead after stock has been taken. We are of the opinion that the summary of similarities and differences in the final chapter of this book may be useful with a view to possible future trends towards the harmonisation or codification of the law concerned with time-limited interests. However, as has been stressed, this is not a stepping stone towards a Civil Code. Rather, it is a tentative first step towards the eventual possibility of harmonisation across Europe.

4. The genesis of the book

4.1. *Narrowing down the topic*

The present sub-topic was initiated by the editors as a second-generation topic of the Common Core Project on Property. The questionnaire containing the twelve cases was discussed at several meetings in Trento and eventually approved in its present form. Originally it did not include cases 10–13 on land development, but after consideration of case law on this matter (and in particular English case law) it was decided to include these cases to supply a commercial real estate development angle to the project. At the outset it was decided that commercial leases should be avoided because this area of the law is primarily regulated by special statutes. Instead, the project has been designed to concentrate on residential and agricultural leases. In the field of personal servitudes, it was decided (upon the suggestion of the late Professor Peter Birks) that the position with regard to the usufruct of intangibles such as shares in a company would not be included in this project but should be dealt with in a separate project. Unfortunately, this project was subsequently abandoned owing to the emergence of a comprehensive thesis, later published as a book on the subject.[2] The main reason for the extraordinary time length of the project is the late introduction of the national reports from Eastern Europe and the difficulty in finding a French and an Austrian reporter in the initial stages of the project.

4.2. *Terminology*

From the beginning, the terminology to be used in the project presented problems. In the sphere of lease, we had to decide between the term 'tenant' and 'lessee' and settled for the term 'tenant', owing to the fact that a lessee is not considered a tenant before he/she enters into possession of the premises.[3] Whereas the distinction between agricultural and residential leases is fairly clear, several mainly civil law

[2] See Pretto-Sakmann, *Boundaries of Personal Property*.
[3] See Guerts, 'Historical Development of Leases', p. 357.

jurisdictions employ the terms 'income-producing', 'usufructuary' and 'fruendi' leases to distinguish ordinary leases from other leases. Here we preferred the term 'income-producing' leases. To overcome the difficulty of the English institution of liferent being embedded in the English law of trust giving rise to a mere personal right with little proprietary effect, the more familiar term 'usufruct' received from Roman law in the continental civilian jurisdictions and the mixed jurisdictions of Scotland and South Africa is used. The politically incorrect term 'personal servitude' is used to encompass the institutions of usufruct, the right of use and the right of habitation, despite its vivid reminder of the services owed by vassals under the abhorrent medieval feudal system of landownership. The term now signifies the inextricable connection of these rights with the life of the holders of these rights. Real difficulty was also experienced in finding an English equivalent for the institutions of *superficies* and *emphyteusis*. Since *superficies* essentially entitles its holder to improve the land by the construction of buildings,[4] the term 'hereditary building right' has been settled for. The concept of *emphyteusis* was the hardest nut to crack. Since it entails a transferable and transmissible right, akin to ownership, to improve and exploit the land for a longer period of time, the term 'hereditary land lease' was decided upon.

4.3. *Classification of the national reports represented*

This study contains three reports from jurisdictions following the German approach; six reports from jurisdictions modelled on French law origins; the English report from the prime common law jurisdiction; the Scottish and South African reports representing mixed jurisdictions; the Danish report from the Scandinavian legal family and two reports from the Eastern European jurisdictions of Poland and Hungary. In the Case studies in Part II, the reports are arranged in alphabetical order.

5. Structure of the book

This work comprises three parts. Part I consists of four chapters. Chapter 1 sets the scene in the Prologue. Chapter 2 provides a general introduction explaining the legal context of time-limited interests in land. This is followed by Chapter 3, which contains a historical review of the evolution of the maxim 'sale breaks hire' – which gradually led to

[4] In some jurisdictions planting and sowing are also allowed.

the sitting tenant acquiring some kind of proprietary interest in the leased land. Chapter 4 examines the many faces of usufruct, especially when utilised as an estate-planning mechanism.

Part II consists of twelve case studies. Case 1 requests the enumeration of the various instances of time-limited interests in land that are recognised in the various jurisdictions. Cases 2–4 deal with the enforcement of time-limited interests against third parties. These cases examine the instances where the land subject to the time-limited interest is conveyed to a third party, attached and sold in execution by the creditors of the landowner or where the landowner becomes insolvent. It also examines the cases where the holder of a time-limited right is dispossessed. Cases 5–9 assess the content of the various instances of time-limited interests. These cases consider the obligation of the holder of a time-limited interest to repair, replace or renew the object of his/her interest; the entitlements of the holder to the fruits of agricultural property; the question whether a holder may convert his/her interest in the land to make it more profitable; the remedies of the landowner against misconduct by the holder of the time-limited interest; and the entitlement of the holder to transfer his/her time-limited interest. Cases 10–12 are concerned with the role of various forms of time-limited interests in land development, the options to purchase and the maintenance obligations that may arise from the use of these mechanisms. These are followed by a consideration of how a developer can commercialise existing buildings and how public institutions can use time-limited mechanisms to give a new lease of life to unimproved land.

Part III contains an enumeration of the similarities and differences between the various instances of time-limited interests, a summary of the main conclusions of this study and a brief indication of the modern practical significance of each of these legal institutions.

3 Historical evolution of the maxim 'sale breaks hire'

PAUL J. DU PLESSIS

1. Introduction

The maxim *emptio tollit locatum* (sale lifts/breaks hire) is a shorthand way of describing the legal effect of the transfer of ownership of the object of lease on sitting tenants. It is a construction of the historical *ius commune* and has had an enduring impact on the development of the law of letting and hiring in the civilian tradition. The aim of this chapter is to trace a history of this maxim from its roots to its current incarnation against the backdrop of the history of the European *ius commune*, that is the *corpus* of Roman, canon and feudal law which developed during the late medieval period and which provided the intellectual foundations from which the legal systems of (mainly, but not exclusively) western Europe arose. As the *ius commune* in a historical sense is a broad and controversial concept, an element of delimitation is required to give focus to this discussion.[1] At the end of the medieval period, this body of 'common law' fragmented as different nation states formed. During the early modern period which followed, through the process of 'reception', different legal systems engaged with the terms and concepts comprising the *ius commune* in different ways. From this process three distinct legal families (Germanic, Francophile and Italianate) arose in western Europe. This chapter will focus solely on the Germanic legal family as it provides a comprehensive analytical account of the second life of this maxim. Since this chapter is concerned with the history of a specific legal maxim, a doctrinal approach is required. While doctrinal legal history is a good starting point, detractors of this method have pointed out that investigations of this kind are too narrowly focused,

[1] For criticisms of modern understanding of the historical *ius commune*, see Osler, 'Myth of European Legal History', pp. 393–410; 'Fantasy Men', pp. 169–93.

take law out of context and do not take other factors such as macro-level narratives surrounding European legal history into account.[2] Whether these criticisms are valid is a subject for a different chapter, but it is worth pointing out that European legal culture is largely based on (re)interpretations of a fixed canon of mostly Roman legal texts. Since there is undoubtedly much value in doctrinal investigations, this chapter will utilise this method as a starting point, but will also employ the Ewald approach,[3] which emphasises 'law in the mind', that is structures of thought that past jurists may have employed in relation to this topic.

2. The Roman-law approach

The Roman-law foundations of this maxim have been discussed extensively by Mayer-Maly, Thomas and Zimmermann.[4] The following is largely a summary of their findings. The two Roman legal texts on which this maxim is founded are:

D.19.2.25.1 Gaius, Provincial Edict, book 10. When a man leases out to someone the enjoyment of a farm or a dwelling, and he then for some reason sells the farm or building, he should, in the same agreement with the buyer, provide that the tenant farmer is permitted to enjoy and the urban tenant to dwell; otherwise he (the tenant farmer), if forbidden (to enjoy or dwell), may sue him on hire. [Watson translation]

C.4.65.9 The Emperor Alexander Severus to Aurelius Fuscus, a soldier. It is not necessary for a purchaser of a farm to retain a tenant to whom the former owner let it, unless he bought it with that condition; but if it is shown that he in some manner, though not in writing, agreed that the lease should continue, he will be compelled in an equitable action to comply with the agreement (AD 234). [Blume translation]

The textual infelicities surrounding these texts are well documented and need not detain us here.[5] They present a snapshot of classical Roman law spanning the period from the mid-second to the mid-third century AD. Given the paucity of textual evidence, it is impossible to

[2] On this matter, see generally the contributions collected in Caroni and Dilcher, *Norm und Geschichte*.

[3] Ewald, 'Legal History', pp. 553–9.

[4] Mayer-Maly, *Locatio Conductio*, p. 45; Thomas, 'Sitting Tenant', pp. 35–44; Zimmermann, *Obligations*, pp. 379–80. See also de Wet, 'Huur Gaat voor Koop', pp. 74–87.

[5] Thomas, 'Sitting Tenant', pp. 35–6. For a discussion of a related problem relating to the death of the landlord during the course of the tenant's term of lease, see Du Plessis, 'Hereditability of *Locatio Conductio*', pp. 139–53 with the caveat that this piece did not fully address the issue of novation.

determine when the rule explained by Gaius arose. The tone of the (later) Imperial rescript suggests a degree of legal uncertainty (probably owing to the absence of a written contract), which the petitioner expected the Imperial chancery to correct in an authoritative manner. Since both texts have a provincial context, it is plausible that the uncertainty may be related to the enactment of the *Constitutio Antoniniana* in 212 AD, which gave most inhabitants of the Empire citizenship and must therefore also have had an impact on the different forms of ownership in existence at the time, but these matters are best left for another time.

A collective reading of these two texts generates the following three scenarios:

(a) A landlord sells a property with sitting tenants and in the sale agrees a *pactum* with the purchaser to tolerate the tenants for the remainder of their term of lease. The purchaser abides by the *pactum*.
(b) A landlord sells a property with sitting tenants and in the sale agrees a *pactum* with the purchaser to tolerate the tenants for the remainder of their term of lease. The purchaser contravenes the *pactum* and evicts or threatens to evict the tenants.
(c) A landlord sells a property with sitting tenants and does not make any special provision in the sale to protect them. The purchaser evicts or threatens to evict the tenants.

From the three scenarios outlined above, it would appear that the rule which existed in classical Roman law may be formulated in the following manner. When a landlord decided to sell a property (whether urban or agricultural) during the course of a tenant's term of lease, the purchaser did not have to accommodate the sitting tenants unless the seller and purchaser had made an agreement to that effect when the object was sold. Where such an agreement existed and the purchaser contravened it (scenario b), the sitting tenants had no direct recourse against him, but had to sue their former landlord (the seller) under the now defunct contract of lease. The seller could then seek recourse against the purchaser on the basis of the contravention of their agreement. Thomas[6] has suggested that contractual provisions of this kind would have been fairly common as they served to protect landlords from lawsuits brought by former tenants when selling the property. The Imperial rescript suggests that the new owner could be compelled to endure the tenant for the remainder of his term of lease and one can imagine that

[6] Thomas, 'Sitting Tenant', p. 38.

this would be crucial in the case of agricultural tenancy where, for example, the harvesting of agricultural produce was at stake. This may explain the use of the term 'enjoyment' (*frui*) in D.19.2.25.1 and the agricultural context of the Imperial rescript where it concerns the renting of a *fundus*.

Suffice it to say that both texts presuppose a smooth handover from seller to purchaser in order to satisfy the requirements of conveyance without the sitting tenants objecting. As Thomas has shown,[7] it must not be assumed that this was necessarily always the case, and two texts, D.43.16.12 and D.43.16.18, discuss circumstances where the sitting tenants were less than willing to vacate the property.

Much attention has been paid by modern scholars to the motivations for the existence of this rule in Roman law. While the sitting tenant is not left entirely without remedy, he does not have any legal recourse against eviction by the new owner and must instead seek recourse by suing the former owner (his landlord) *ex conducto* for his *interesse*.[8] On a strict interpretation of the distinction between real and personal rights in Roman law, this rule makes perfect sense. Letting and hiring in Roman law only generated personal (contractual) rights between landlord and tenant. The tenant merely had *possessio naturalis* (*detentio*) under the contract of letting and hiring and therefore could not defend himself/herself against the real right of the owner.[9] It has been suggested that this rule is an example of the Roman legal bias in favour of ownership at the expense of lesser contractual rights.[10] While there may be some elements of truth in this statement, it does not convey the full complexity of the situation. As Zimmermann has demonstrated,[11] this rule is an example of the complex relationship between real and personal rights in Roman law. In his view, it was not the sale which 'terminated' the pre-existing contract of letting and hiring. Rather, the 'real' effect of the sale made the continued existence of the contract impossible. Schrage[12] has identified two further reasons for the existence of this rule. First, since letting and hiring only ever generated personal rights (with the exception of *emphyteusis* and *superficies*, which were only grudgingly classified as related to letting and hiring), the

[7] *Ibid.* 36–7. For associated complexities such as the division of rent and subletting, see *ibid.* 38–9.

[8] *Ibid.* 44. [9] Zimmermann, *Obligations*, pp. 379–80.

[10] See Frier, *Landlords and Tenants*, p. 64. [11] Zimmermann, *Obligations*, pp. 370–80.

[12] Schrage, 'Emptio (nondum) tollit locatum', pp. 1–2. See also De Wet, 'Huur Gaat voor Koop', pp. 75–7.

ability of the tenant to protect his holding of the property was restricted to contractual measures in Roman law. Secondly, and perhaps most importantly, Roman contract law was fundamentally opposed to the creation of contracts in favour of third parties and therefore the ability to create a contractual arrangement binding both sitting tenants and new owner was limited.

Two final points deserve mention. We do not know whether the rule as articulated by Gaius, and in the Imperial rescript, applied to movable objects or not. The texts are silent on the matter. Furthermore, there is no evidence that the new owner had to notify the sitting tenants of the eviction and whether such eviction had to take place within the confines of a legal process.

3. The *ius commune* position

3.1. *Medieval learned law*

The rise of the historical *ius commune*, an amalgam of Roman, canon and feudal law created during the period 1100–1400, is traditionally linked to the intellectual endeavours of three different groups of jurists, namely the Glossators, the *Ultramontani* and the Commentators.[13] The majority of the works referred to in this section are juristic commentaries on the Justinianic Code, initially a more fertile source for commentary than other parts of the Justinianic compilation of Roman law.[14] As Schrage has pointed out,[15] C.4.65.9 became the *sedes materiae* around which most medieval jurists focused their discussions of this maxim. Much of the groundwork regarding the medieval interpretations of these texts has been done by de Wet[16] and Schrage and what follows is merely a summary of their findings, together with a few additional comments.

Two initial observations are required. First, the contract of letting and hiring does not appear to have attracted much juristic comment in classical canon law of the late medieval period.[17] While this may create the impression that medieval scholars of canon law were not interested in leases, it seems more plausible, in the absence of any specific comments, that the Roman law of letting and hiring was absorbed into canon law *en masse*. This would account for the widespread use of the

[13] Stein, *Roman Law*, pp. 38–71. [14] But see Radding, 'Justinian's Corpus', pp. 35–50.
[15] Schrage, 'Sale Breaks Hire', pp. 287–96. [16] De Wet, 'Huur Gaat voor Koop', p. 74.
[17] For a survey of the possible influences of pre-classical canon law on this topic, see *ibid.* 77–80.

Roman law of letting and hiring in canonic courts in the early modern period. Secondly, there does not appear to be much discussion about the Roman law of letting and hiring prior to the thirteenth century. In Schrage's view,[18] this may be explained by the fact that prior to this time most arrangements subsequently classified as letting and hiring under Roman law would have been governed by feudal law.

Despite the paucity of information about the contract of letting and hiring prior to the thirteenth century, one of the influential twelfth-century anonymous summaries of the Justinianic Code, *Lo Codi*, a summary of the Justinianic Code written in what would later be southern France, mentions the Roman-law rule.[19] Since this work, possibly compiled by more than one author, was written as an instruction manual for lay-judges, it demonstrates that the Roman-law rule was not entirely unknown prior to the thirteenth century, even though in practice feudal arrangements may have been more common.

The Glossators, the first group of (mainly Italian) jurists engaged in the teaching of Roman law during the twelfth and thirteenth centuries, introduced a number of innovations in the understanding of the Roman-law texts. The most important of these were in relation to the extent of the application of this maxim. First, Johannes Bassianus, a student of Bulgarus, one of the *quattuor doctores* who studied under Irnerius, argued that the original scope of the maxim had to be extended to include tenants of both urban and agricultural property.[20] This argument was supported by Bassianus' pupil Azo and thus was included in the Accursian Gloss. Secondly, Otto Papiensis (and following him Azo) argued that the maxim should apply not only to cases where a third party had purchased the leased property with sitting tenants, but to all cases where a third party acquired a real right over the leased property, that is, any *successor singularis*.[21] Since these two reinterpretations of the original Roman-law texts created a maxim with a rather extensive application, and given the textual contradictions, it comes as little surprise that the Glossators also devoted much time to introducing exceptions to this rule. The main exception which they developed was concerned with those forms of letting and hiring such as *emphyteusis* and *superficies*, which granted the tenant a real right.[22] Given the long

[18] Schrage, 'Sale Breaks Hire', 293. On the nature and content of these arrangements, see De Wet, 'Huur Gaat voor Koop', p. 82.

[19] Fitting, 'Lo Codi', pp. 144–5.

[20] Schrage, 'Sale Breaks Hire', p. 288.

[21] *Ibid.*

[22] *Ibid.* 288–90.

periods of time associated with especially *emphyteusis*, the Glossators developed this idea further by drawing a distinction between a short-term lease and a lease for a longer term (variously defined as a lease for a period of ten years or longer).[23] A short-term lease only granted the tenant a personal right and therefore 'sale broke hire', but a long-term lease gave the tenant a real right, *dominium utile*, and therefore the *singularis successor* was bound to tolerate the tenant until the end of his tenancy. He could protect his possession against the *singularis successor* using an *actio in rem* or an *exceptio*.[24] Thus, in the culmination of the glossatorial endeavours, the Accursian Gloss, a distinction was drawn between a short-term lease, where the maxim applied, and a long-term lease, where it did not and where the tenant could not defend his contractual rights arising from the lease against the new owner.

The scientific approach of the School of Orleans (*Ultramontani*), which had a profound impact on legal science during much of the thirteenth century, continued the work of the Glossators when it came to the interpretation of this maxim. One of the prominent French jurists associated with this movement, Jacques de Revigny, essentially followed Accursius' views.

The most prominent Commentators of the fourteenth century, Bartolus de Saxoferrato and Baldus de Ubaldis, supported the Accursian position and expanded it.[25] Bartolus' view is particularly significant as he argued in a *consilium* that the protection enjoyed by the tenant under a long-term lease should be extended to a short-term tenant.[26] This was done using a rather ingenious construction involving a pledge without possession, better known as a hypothec. Bartolus argued that a tenant in a short-term lease should secure a hypothec over the (mostly immovable) property of the landlord to ensure the continuation of the tenancy for the full term. Thus, should the landlord sell or dispose in another way of the leased property, the sitting tenant could secure the continuation of the lease against the *singularis successor* by invoking the hypothec.[27] Since a hypothec generated real rights

[23] This distinction between short-term and long-term leases appears to have originated in the feudal and canon-law traditions; see De Wet, 'Huur Gaat voor Koop', pp. 79–80. See also generally Grossi, *Locatio ad longum tempus*.

[24] Schrage, 'Emptio (nondum) tollit locatum', pp. 8–11.

[25] De Wet, 'Huur Gaat voor Koop', p. 87; Schrage, 'Sale Breaks Hire', p. 291.

[26] De Wet, 'Huur Gaat voor Koop', pp. 86–7; Schrage, 'Sale Breaks Hire', pp. 291–2.

[27] This construction may also cast light on Bartolus' conception of letting and hiring as a 'real' contract, but this matter requires further investigation.

enforceable against any third party, the tenant could therefore effectively resist the *singularis successor*. While Bartolus' invention is a clever one, Schrage[28] has rightly pointed out that this construction is 'artificial' and 'unsatisfactory'. A hypothec was an ancillary agreement designed to secure performance of a primary agreement (usually the repayment of debt) and one cannot help but feel that the extension attempted here was doctrinally unsound.

Zimmermann[29] has suggested that the manifold extensions identified and elaborated upon by medieval jurists rendered the Roman-law rule meaningless. While on some level this statement is correct, it would seem that there is more to the matter. For it has to be asked why the medieval jurists were so intent on transforming the rights of the tenant under the contract of letting and hiring into real rights.[30] The answer must lie both in the context of medieval agricultural arrangements where long-term leases were the norm and where vestiges of feudal tenure remained, and in the desire to protect the interests of the tenant, whether humble or noble, against those of the propertied classes. This requires a more detailed investigation which cannot be undertaken here.

3.2. From medieval learned law to the Prussian Civil Code

The period from the start of the fifteenth century to the end of the eighteenth century is usually described in terms of the 'reception' of (mostly, but not exclusively) Roman legal principles and the rise of the Germanic legal family within the context of the Holy Roman Empire.[31] The reception process gained momentum during the fifteenth century when local Germanic customary laws began to be influenced by *ius commune* principles distilled mainly from Roman law. The reception in the Germanic lands comprising the Holy Roman Empire was comprehensive.

Schrage[32] has demonstrated that in leases based on early medieval Germanic customs sitting tenants were protected against a new owner. Most of these customs had a feudal background and they provided the tenant with a measure of protection against eviction by the new owner through the remedy of *Gewere*, but this position was by no means

[28] Schrage, 'Sale Breaks Hire', pp. 288–9. [29] Zimmermann, *Obligations*, pp. 379–81.
[30] See De Wet, 'Huur Gaat voor Koop', p. 84.
[31] See on this matter generally Wieacker, *Privatrechtsgeschichte*; Stein, *Roman Law*, pp. 75–103.
[32] Schrage, 'Sale Breaks Hire', pp. 293–4.

universally held. The plurality of customary views on the protection of the sitting tenant together with the feudal heritage of these leases in many cases prevented the wholesale reception of the *ius commune* maxim.[33] The interaction between the Roman-law rule, its *ius commune* incarnation and Germanic customary law is a key aspect of this section of our discussion.

De Wet[34] has shown that the historical development of this maxim in (what would later become) the Netherlands was similar to that in the Germanic lands comprising the Holy Roman Empire. A comparative analysis may yield important results from which conclusions concerning the development in the Germanic legal family may be drawn. The picture emerging from the Spanish Netherlands (then still part of the Holy Roman Empire) during the sixteenth century is a varied one. In certain regions, leases were based on (feudal) customary law which prevented the *ius commune* maxim from taking root. As mentioned above, leases based on custom tended to provide the tenant with protection against the *singularis successor*. In other regions, feudal customs were replaced by the *ius commune* maxim which gave a tenant of a long-term lease a real right and therefore protected him against the *successor singularis*, while a tenant of a short-term lease could still only protect his tenancy in a roundabout way by using the hypothec construction created by Bartolus de Saxoferrato. In the northern regions, in what was to become the United States of the Netherlands, a similar patchwork of legal opinions existed.[35] In some regions the Roman-law rule prevailed, in others the *ius commune* maxim was followed. Some jurists even advocated that the hypothec construction provided inadequate protection for short-term tenants and that all tenants (according to the famous Dutch natural-law scholar, Hugo Grotius) acquired a real right by virtue of the contract of letting and hiring and could therefore protect themselves against a *singularis successor* irrespective of the period of the lease.[36] This was a simplified version of the medieval position which essentially did away with the medieval distinction between short-term and long-term leases and which also disposed of the Bartolus construction in cases of short-term leases.

Given the similar historical development of this *ius commune* maxim in the Germanic legal family, it comes as little surprise that the same

[33] De Wet, 'Huur Gaat voor Koop', pp. 167–73. [34] *Ibid*. 174–8.
[35] *Ibid*. 179–94. See also Schrage, 'Sale Breaks Hire', pp. 294–6.
[36] For a summary of the Roman-Dutch position, see Schrage, 'Sale Breaks Hire', pp. 294–6.

line of development can be traced through the works of jurists of the sixteenth and seventeenth centuries. Jurists of the sixteenth century follow the *ius commune* maxim, while some of those of the seventeenth century, probably under the influence of the natural-law doctrine, grant all tenants a real right by virtue of the contract of letting and hiring.[37] It is well documented that 'Germanic' legal scholarship of the seventeenth and eighteenth centuries came under the influence of the secularised natural-law doctrine. This legal-philosophical current had a particular impact on the drafter of the Prussian Civil Code, Carl Gottlieb Svarez (Schwarz), who was a student of one of the most famous natural-law scholars of the eighteenth century, Christian Wolff.

Thus, prior to the enactment of the Prussian Civil Code towards the end of the eighteenth century, the Roman-law maxim 'sale breaks hire' had undergone a considerable transformation. The author of this Code had a variety of juristic constructions on which to base his article and these ranged in complexity from, on the one hand, the rejection of the *ius commune* maxim (in favour of the Roman-law or the customary-law position) to, on the other hand, an acceptance of it, but with the interpretations and accretions added onto it, especially those arising from the natural-law supporters. What is remarkable about these different positions is that (with the exception of the Roman-law position) they actually seem to have converged by the eighteenth century to the extent that both the *ius commune* maxim and customary law advocated the protection of the tenant against the *singularis successor* irrespective of the time-period of the lease.

The Prussian Civil Code contains one article on the topic (ALR I.21.358). This article encapsulates the essence of the European development up to this point. According to Enneccerus,[38] this article gave all sitting tenants a real right over the leased property. In formulating the article in this manner, the Prussian Civil Code broke with the Roman-law maxim. The acquisition of this real right through tenancy was linked to the sitting tenant's possession of the leased property and, though admirable, it created various problems and academic debates, especially in relation to loss of possession and scenarios where the sitting tenant was unwilling to relinquish possession to the new owner.[39] The reason for this is that the Prussian Civil Code, following Roman law, emphasised the legal function of possession. For all its

[37] De Wet, 'Huur Gaat voor Koop', pp. 177–8. [38] Enneccerus, *Lehrbuch*, § 355.
[39] Otte, 'Rechtsstellung des Mieters', pp. 464–6.

lucidity, this article also did not resolve the legal basis of the relationship between the *singularis successor* and the sitting tenants and the rights/duties which they had towards one another. Since the drafter of the Prussian Civil Code did not provide a comprehensive overview of his 'motives' for framing articles of the Code in a specific manner, the true reasoning behind it may never be known in full. At best it may be speculated that he was influenced by natural-law doctrine in this regard.

3.3. *From the Prussian Civil Code to the German Civil Code*

Germanic legal scholarship of the nineteenth century leading up to the codification of German civil law in 1900 was dominated by two juristic movements.[40] The German Historical School dominated roughly the first half of the nineteenth century and followed methods not dissimilar to those of the Humanists of the sixteenth century in the sense that they were mainly concerned with uncovering the true state of classical Roman law with a view to providing a solid doctrinal foundation for contemporary law. Evidence of this may be seen in the works of scholars such as Mackeldey[41] and Mühlenbruch.[42] During the mid-nineteenth century, an offshoot of the Historical School, known as Pandectism, gained prominence. Jurists of the Pandectist movement held various views on the subject.[43]

As was the case prior to the enactment of the Prussian Civil Code, the drafters had a number of potentially different options before them. It is interesting to note that later works setting out the process of decision-making regarding the German Civil Code, like the *Motive* and the work by Enneccerus, present the 'common' law as if it were the Roman-law position with only the briefest mention of customary law or the *ius commune* position.[44]

The drafters of the German Civil Code were influenced by the Prussian Civil Code, but did not follow it in all respects. The most important deviation from the Prussian position was to deny that letting and hiring created a real right while at the same time providing sitting tenants with legal recourse where they were threatened with eviction by the new owner. According to commentators of the time, the motivation for this hybrid was neither legal-philosophical nor based on a class bias. Rather, it seems to have been driven by a socio-political motive

[40] Stein, *Roman Law*, pp. 115–22. [41] *Lehrbüch*, § 379. [42] *Ibid.*, § 413.
[43] Zimmermann, *Obligations*, p. 380.
[44] The reality is far more complex; see Mugdan, *Gesammten Materialen*, §§ 509–11.

taking the large proportion of the German population, which lived in rented accommodation, into account.[45]

In dealing with this matter, the German Civil Code distinguishes between letting and hiring of movables and immovables. In the case of movables, the sitting tenant is not given any specific protection. The *singularis successor* becomes owner and acquires the owner's vindication through *cessio* and the only remedy open to the sitting tenant is to raise an objection (by virtue of his possession) that he is entitled to it when threatened with eviction (art. 986, Abs. 2). In the case of immovables, the *singularis successor* steps into the shoes of the former landlord and acquires the rights and duties of the former landlord for the remainder of the lease (originally art. 571, since renamed art. 566). Part 2 of article 571 also provides the sitting tenant with a remedy against his former landlord where the *singularis successor* fails to honour the lease. If evicted, the tenant must first seek recourse against the *singularis successor*. The former landlord is liable in a subsidiary capacity (as a guarantor), unless the tenant had been notified of the transfer of ownership.

It is not the purpose of this chapter to discuss the modern developments after the enactment of the *Bürgerliches Gesetzbuch* (BGB) as this can be traced in one of the authoritative expositions such as the Munich commentary. It is worth noting, however, that the recently published model rules on European Private Law, the Common Frames of Reference (CFR), contains a section on lease of movables (lease of immovables is yet to be tackled). Much like in German law, the CFR states explicitly that lease only generates personal rights. Under the CFR rules, the *singularis successor* steps into the shoes of the landlord, provided the tenant is in possession of the leased movable (CFR B-7.101). This is an indication of the continued importance of possession in case of movables. The former landlord remains liable in a subsidiary capacity akin to a provider of security should the *singularis successor* fail to fulfil his duties under the lease. The effect of this is similar to the position regarding immovables in the German Civil Code. The rules do not explicitly mention what the consequences would be for a *singularis successor* who does not wish to continue with the lease. Presumably, he will be bound to tolerate the sitting tenant until the earliest possible time when notice to quit can be given under the contract.

[45] See *Motive*, §§ 509–11. The various comments by the different commissions may be traced in the *Beratungen*.

4. Conclusions

In his now celebrated work on obligations, Zimmermann identified three reasons for the demise of the Roman-law rule 'sale breaks hire' in the history of the *ius commune*.[46] In his view, these reasons were the textual inconsistencies in the Roman law, the force of local customary law as is visible, for example, in Roman-Dutch law of the seventeenth century, and the pervasive influence of secularised natural-law doctrine in the eighteenth century. While these factors undoubtedly played an important role in the history of this maxim, there are a number of additional factors which need to be highlighted. The first of these is the rigidity of the distinction between real and personal rights in Roman law and the Roman jurists' unwillingness to accept the principle of contracts in favour of third parties. The second important factor is the interplay in the works of medieval jurists between the intellectual ideal of the Roman-law rule and the reality of leases based on feudal custom. It seems plausible that the reason why the medieval jurists were so intent on extending protection to sitting tenants was because of the realities of feudal tenure with which they would have been familiar in daily practice. The development of *dominium directum* and *dominium utile* must not be underestimated in this context. The third important factor is the interaction between Germanic custom and the Roman-legal rule and the manner in which the strength of Germanic customs resisted the adoption of it. Although this led to a host of different legal positions, there appears to have been a convergence between the customary and by now *ius commune* position regarding sitting tenants in the sense that both regimes favoured protecting the sitting tenant against the *singularis successor* of the landlord. This convergence seems to have been noticed by the supporters of the natural-law doctrine and it therefore comes as little surprise that the drafter of the Prussian Civil Code opted to award the sitting tenant a real right in lease which enabled him to resist the *singularis successor*. Although there is no direct evidence that the changes in the structure of the law of contract in the *ius commune* had an impact on this maxim, it is worth pointing out that the mid-seventeenth century also witnessed the abandoning of the closed Roman system of contracts in favour of a general principle of contract based on consent and it is conceivable, though as yet unproven, that this may have influenced juristic perceptions regarding the Roman prohibition

[46] Zimmermann, *Obligations*, pp. 377–80.

against contracts in favour of third parties. While the real-right construction offered by the Prussian Civil Code was an interesting conceptual leap forward, it was held back by the drafter's attempt to link the real right with possession. By linking the real-right construction to possession, it is also clear that the drafter of the Prussian Civil Code was not yet prepared fully to entertain the notion of party substitution in contract. The period between the enactment of the Prussian Civil Code at the end of the eighteenth century and the codification of German civil law in 1900 was dominated by differing points of view. On the one hand, the supporters of the Historical School favoured a return to the Roman-law position, while on the other hand, supporters of the Pandectist movement held different opinions. The construction eventually chosen by the drafters of the German Civil Code is a compromise. On the one hand, it was made explicit that a lease would only ever generate a personal right for the tenant, but on the other, the sitting tenant was given a level of protection by permitting the *successor singularis* to step into the shoes of the former landlord. By playing down the link between the sitting tenant's protection and possession, this construction has removed many of the infelicities which plagued the Prussian approach. The model rules for a harmonised European private law which to date have only dealt with the lease of movable property, have mimicked the German approach in relation to immovable property almost entirely. Whether these rules truly reflect the rich historical past of this institution in European legal culture is debatable, but at least they resolve some of the historical complexities.

4 The many faces of usufruct

ALAIN-LAURENT VERBEKE, BART VERDICKT AND DIRK-JAN MAASLAND

1. Usufruct in tax and estate planning

The various national reports demonstrate that the institution of usufruct has always been and still is a popular legal mechanism that offers a broad range of options that can be employed in many diverse situations. It is, however, not merely its application that is manifold. The concept itself is not as unequivocal as it appears at first glance. The area of continental estate planning in particular, reveals several nuances of the concept of usufruct.

1.1. Transferring assets yet retaining control and income

Estate planning is a complex process aimed at organising and transferring an estate to one's partner, the next generation, or to charity.[1] Transfers can be made after death, but also during the transferor's lifetime. Most people prefer to retain (at least indirect) control over their estate and gain income therefrom for as long as they live. In Anglo-American jurisdictions, trusts are the obvious device for realising such aspirations. Continental jurisdictions lack this tradition, although foundations and other trust-like vehicles have become increasingly popular in recent years.

In several civil law jurisdictions, gifts and donations function as typical estate planning tools. They allow the transfer of assets during a person's lifetime to the next generation, while still retaining some control over the assets and income therefrom through several modalities and conditions. This can be in the interest of the donor who needs the income to maintain a certain standard of living. The donor may also wish to retain substantial direct or indirect control and management

[1] See in general Verbeke, Buyssens and Derycke, *Handboek Estate Planning*.

over the donated assets. This can serve the interests of both the donor and the beneficiary. For example, the managerial expertise of the donor may allow the assets to be put to their most efficient use. This allows the donor to realise his aspiration of managing the property, while the beneficiary is protected against unwise management and can in fact reap the benefits of skilful management.

In most jurisdictions, there are no real tax incentives to donate. Generally, donation and inheritance tax (estate duty) are treated alike,[2] and in several European jurisdictions, inheritance and donation tax between spouses and children have been abolished or the rates of taxation have been reduced substantially.[3] In Belgium, gifts and donations are very popular for tax reasons. It is possible to donate goods to a partner, children or even third parties without being taxed or at least with substantially reduced rates of taxation (except for real estate located in Belgium). Donations of movables, if registered in Belgium, are taxed at 3 per cent for spouses, certain cohabitants and children and 7 per cent for others, while inheritance taxes go up to 27 per cent for spouses, certain cohabitants and children and 65 per cent for others.[4] Since 1 January 2012, donations of shares are taxed in Flanders at 0 per cent subject to certain conditions (Flemish Registration Tax Code, art. 140bis). Donations not registered in Belgium are not taxed and will also not incur inheritance tax if the donor dies more than three or seven years respectively after the donation was made (Inheritance Tax Code, art. 7).

In spite of the identical treatment of inheritance and donation tax in the Netherlands (10 per cent (up to EUR 115,708) to 20 per cent (for anything over EUR 115,709) to children), one can reduce inheritance tax[5] by making staggered donations or gifts during one's lifetime. Parents can donate assets up to a value of EUR 115,708 to each child annually at a rate of 10 per cent.[6] A similar technique is permitted under

[2] E.g. the Netherlands (Dutch Gift and Inheritance Tax Code, art. 24) and France (General Tax Code, art. 777).

[3] E.g. Denmark: no inheritance or gift tax between spouses, 15 per cent to children; France: no inheritance tax between spouses; Italy: 4 per cent on the net value exceeding 1 million euro per beneficiary; Luxemburg: up to maximum 5 per cent inheritance tax or death duties and maximum 4.8 per cent between spouses and direct heirs; the Netherlands: spouses exempted up to 600,000 euro; Portugal: no inheritance nor gift taxes between spouses and direct line; Spain: regional regulations with huge exemptions between spouses and direct line; Switzerland: cantonal regulations with no taxation between spouses and in most cantons also for direct line (see www.ibfd.org).

[4] On inheritance taxes, see Verbeke and Van Zantbeek, 'Succession Law', pp. 68–78.

[5] See above for exemptions.

[6] Successiewet 1956 (Dutch Inheritance Tax Code), art. 24.

French law where donations up to a value of EUR 159,325 (2012) per child are tax exempted.[7] However, contrary to the position in the Netherlands, there has to be a time lapse of six years between each gift in order to benefit from the exemption. In the case of donations with reservation of a usufruct, the tax exemption is calculated on the value of the nude ownership of the property.[8] As usufruct can have a substantial value, donations with reservation of usufruct are often favoured as an estate planning mechanism in France.

These tax benefits do not, however, prevent the goods donated from immediately and irrevocably leaving the estate of the donor, which often militates against his/her objective to keep control over the property and its income. It is precisely this concern that explains the popularity of the 'reservation of usufruct' clauses in deeds of donation. The usufruct seems to offer a sound compromise between the desire to transfer goods to the next generation during a person's lifetime and yet not to lose all control over the property or the income from the property.

Usufruct comes in different forms and shapes which determine the powers and competences of the donor-usufructuary. The more extensive these powers are, the better the compromise between transferring assets (and resultant tax benefits) and maintaining a strong position for the donor. In this chapter, we briefly discuss these different faces of usufruct, an instrument which is often used as a tool in tax and estate planning in some continental jurisdictions.

1.2. Overview

The concept of usufruct is explained in section 2 below. We shall see how the traditional concept of usufruct (referring back to Roman Law) offered rather limited entitlements to the usufructuary in relation to both the issues of control and income (section 3 below). In a more modern approach (section 4 below), but still in line with the *ratio legis* of the traditional approach, the situation appears to be somewhat ameliorated with regard to the issue of control. This modern face of usufruct was introduced in French and Belgian law through the application of usufruct in new contexts such as shares and stocks, or 'universalities' such as an investment portfolio or a commercial enterprise (not incorporated as a company).

In the discussion of the Janus face of usufruct (section 5 below), the usufructuary's position appears to be quite powerful. Indeed, the

[7] Code Général des Impôts (General French Tax Code), art. 779.

[8] Following General French Tax Code, art. 669.

concept of *quasi*-usufruct allows him/her to control the assets donated and to receive the income as if he/she were a *quasi*-owner. However, this *quasi*-usufruct, appearing quite different in its application at first glance, is – at least in its conceptual nature – still very much compatible with the traditional concept of usufruct.

This, however, is not the case for the final face of usufruct, namely the new Dutch usufruct (section 6 below). Since the New Civil Code of 1992, the very concept of usufruct has changed substantially. Control and income may be fully vested in the hands of the usufructuary. The new Dutch usufruct may in appropriate circumstances entail the power of disposing and even consuming the assets subject to the usufruct. This has created a totally new, and perhaps even twisted, face of usufruct.

2. The concept of usufruct

The English word 'usufruct' derives from the Latin *usus et fructus* (use and enjoyment). Usufruct is a real right over movable and immovable property that is owned by another. Under Roman law, the usufructuary had the right to use and enjoy the property and its fruits, while preserving the substance of the property.[9] The owner retained nude ownership, that is, ownership burdened with a real right of enjoyment and use. Both the French and Belgian Civil Codes (henceforth FCC and BCC) employ a similar description, namely *usufruit* and *vruchtgebruik* respectively (FCC/BCC, art. 578).[10] In German law, property may be similarly burdened with a *Niessbrauch* (BGB, § 1030). Comparable descriptions are encountered in Austria, Portugal, Spain and Poland.

Usufruct is a real right, that is, a right on the property itself and not merely a right in relation to the property's profits.[11] In spite of this characterisation, usufruct remains a right with personal and temporal features[12] since it is linked to the life of the usufructuary.[13] This intensely personal character does not prevent the right of usufruct

[9] Gaius, 2.30; D.7.1.1; D.6.1.33; D.7.1.72; D.7.4.2; D.23.37.8.3. References from Scott, *Civil Law*, p. 286.

[10] The description in Old Dutch Civil Code, art. 803 (in force until 1992) was derived from Civil Code, art. 578 (Mijnssen, Van Velten and Bartels, *Asser*, *Eigendom*, p. 261).

[11] Zenati-Castaing and Revet, *Les Biens*, p. 494; de Page, *Traité élémentaire*, p. 153.

[12] More comprehensive: Verbeke, 'Creatief met vruchtgebruik', pp. 532–8.

[13] Cass. 3 July 1879; Pas. 1879 I 342; Borkowski and Du Plessis, *Roman Law*, p. 172; Baudry-Lacantinerie, *Précis de droit civil*, p. 770; de Page, *Traité élémentaire*, p. 258; Prutting, *Sachenrecht*, p. 364; Verbeke, 'Quasi-vruchtgebruik', p. 37.

from being alienated but merely limits the time frame of the transferred usufruct to the life of the original usufructuary (FCC, art. 617). It is, however, possible to establish the usufruct for a fixed term. Nevertheless, here too the usufruct will expire upon the death of the person on whose life the right was based, irrespective of the contracted term.[14] It is not possible to constitute a usufruct which is permanent or unlimited in time.[15] Its temporary quality is a rule of law which cannot be challenged.[16]

All kinds of property[17] such as movable and immovable property (FCC/BCC, art. 581; BGB, § 1031–3); corporal and incorporeal property; factual and judicial collections of different kinds of property (universalities); shares; intellectual property; and fungibles (perishable property) (FCC/BCC, art. 589), can be burdened with a usufruct.[18] Under French and Belgian law, an existing usufruct can also be subject to a usufruct.[19] Since the usufructuary has the obligation to preserve the substance of the property, one can argue that, in principle, consumable or perishable goods cannot be burdened with a usufruct.[20] After all, how is preservation possible in the case of goods which are consumed or which perish because of wear and tear? However, already in Roman law, and followed in current law, a specific regime was created for such goods, namely *quasi*-usufruct. Since the goods may be consumed, the principle of restitution in kind is replaced by restitution by equivalent (FCC/BCC, art. 587; BGB, § 1067). This offers an interesting perspective

[14] See Belgian report, Case 1.

[15] De Brabandere, 'Usufruit, Usage, Habitation', p. 30; de Page, *Traité élémentaire*, p. 157.

[16] Vandenberghe, 'Actuele problemen', p. 54. The temporal aspect also applies to the common law life interest (McClean, 'Common Law Life Estate', p. 655; Lawson and Rudden, *Property*, p. 97).

[17] Baudry-Lacantinerie, *Précis de droit civil*, p. 774.

[18] Bougle and Gouthiere, 'Patrimoine', p. 134; Du Mongh, *De erfovergang van aandelen*, p. 227; Vieweg and Werner, *Sachenrecht*, p. 553; Zenati-Castaing and Revet, *Les Biens*, p. 484. More comprehensive: Verbeke and Vanhove, 'Spelen met vruchtgebruik', pp. 174 ff. Between the civil law usufruct and the common law legal life interest, there is no substantial difference as to the nature of the property on which both rights can be vested. It is certain that a legal life estate can subsist over real property. The question whether movable property can be the object of a legal life estate is more difficult to answer, but the common law jurisdiction will to a large extent uphold in one form or another a legal life estate in movable property (McClean, 'Common Law Life Estate', p. 653).

[19] Borkowski and Du Plessis, *Roman Law*, p. 169; de Page, *Traité élémentaire*, p. 217; Hansenne, *Les Biens*, p. 1025; Zenati-Castaing and Revet, *Les Biens*, p. 483.

[20] Verbeke and Vanhove, 'Spelen met vruchtgebruik', p. 174.

from a tax and estate planning point of view (cf. The Janus Face, section 5 below).

Although the nude owner and the usufructuary do not co-own the property in undivided shares, and each party has independent rights over the property, the actual powers of each party are determined and limited. Neither the usufructuary nor the nude owner can act as if he/she were the full owner. Each party must respect the interests of the other party while exercising his/her own rights. In this sense, there exists a fiduciary relationship between the two parties.[21]

Usufruct, as a typical civil law institution, is as such unknown in Anglo-American jurisdictions. Civil law is structured on the basis of ownership as the most extensive right with regard to property and more than one person can have real rights over the same property, as in the case of undivided full ownership of property being burdened with a usufruct, *superficies*, *emphytheusis* or a servitude.[22] Common law, on the other hand, is based on a system of estates or tenures without full ownership, except for ownership held by the Crown. There is no room for real rights such as usufruct and personal servitudes. In spite of the different conceptual framework, a comparable pragmatic result is achieved by way of a life interest on property.[23] A life interest or life estate confers the right on a person to enjoy the property for his/her lifetime. The legal life tenant has the right to use the property and to receive the profits directly.[24] The equitable life tenant, however, does not have the right to enjoy the property *in specie*. He obtains his right via payments or distributions by a third person such as the trustee under the life estate.[25]

3. The traditional face

3.1. Control

Although the usufructuary has a strong right conferring the enjoyment and use of the property on him/her, the obligation to preserve the substance of the property imposes serious limits on his/her control and use of the property.[26]

[21] Verbeke, 'Creatief met vruchtgebruik', p. 537; cf. Nudelholc and Karadsheh, 'Réflexions', p. 424.

[22] Bougle and Gouthiere, 'Patrimoine', p. 135; Ferid, 'Review of the Louisiana Practice', p. 584; Gordley, *Foundations*, p. 50.

[23] McClean, 'Common Law Life Estate', pp. 649–50. [24] *Ibid.* 651. [25] *Ibid.* 652.

[26] Verbeke, 'Creatief met vruchtgebruik', p. 542.

Some jurisdictions hold that a usufruct as such can be transferred by the usufructuary while others hold that it is only the rights under a usufruct that can be transferred. The latter means that the usufructuary who transferred the rights under a usufruct remains liable to the nude owner. Roman law held that the usufructuary could rent out, pledge and even sell or donate the usufruct. Under Polish law, the rights under the usufruct are transferable, although the usufruct as such cannot be transferred. The transferred right cannot last beyond the term of the initial usufruct or the life of the initial usufructuary.[27] The position is similar under German law (BGB, § 1059).[28] Under French and Belgian law, the usufructuary can alienate his/her usufructuary rights (FCC/BCC, art. 595): they can be sold, leased or mortgaged[29] but the transferred rights expire with the death of the original usufructuary (FCC/BCC, art. 617).[30]

The obligation to preserve the substance of the property encompasses the duty of care,[31] the duty to draw up an inventory and the duty to provide security against damage to the property (FCC/BCC, arts. 600–1; BGB, § 1037). The usufructuary can be exempted from these obligations, but the nude owner may always insist that they should be complied with at his/her own cost. The exemption is automatic in the case of a donation with reservation of a usufruct which legally exempts the usufructuary from these obligations.

The usufructuary cannot transform the property or make substantial changes.[32] The substance must be maintained at all times. This holds true even if the intention of the usufructuary is to upgrade the property by replacing it with something of a higher quality, or to prevent the decrease of income or revenues.[33] Repairs and renovations are allowed only to the extent that they are considered normal maintenance of the property (BGB, § 1041). The usufructuary is, however, not responsible for alteration or deterioration of the property that arises from the proper exercise of the usufruct (BGB, § 1050). This is the position in Germany, Australia, Greece, Belgium, Portugal, Italy, South Africa and Poland. Under Portuguese and Spanish law, the usufructuary can

[27] Belgian report, Case 1. [28] Prutting, *Sachenrecht*, p. 362.

[29] Cass. 30 May 1995; Bull. Civ. 1995 IV, no. 161; de Page, 'Les Donations', p. 261; Hansenne, *Les Biens*, p. 1043; Zenati-Castaing and Revet, *Les Biens*, p. 496.

[30] Hansenne, *Les Biens*, p. 1043. [31] de Page, 'Les Donations', p. 271.

[32] Belgian report, Case 7; Planiol and Ripert, *Traité pratique*, p. 822. The life tenant has a similar obligation. He is under an obligation not to cause lasting or permanent damage to the property (McClean, 'Common Law Life Estate', p. 662).

[33] de Page, 'Les Donations', p. 372.

improve the property as long as he does not change its economic destiny.[34]

On the same line of reasoning, the traditional view holds that the usufructuary cannot dispose of the usufructuary property.[35] Upon extinction of the usufruct, the owner has to regain a similar use and enjoyment to that existing at the outset of the usufruct.[36] Consequently, restoration in kind is impossible if the usufructuary has disposed of the usufructuary property. '*L'obligation de conserver la substance et le pouvoir de disposer sont deux choses incompatibles.*'[37] The consent of both the nude owner and the usufructuary are required to dispose of the usufructuary property in its entirety, even in the case where disposal is necessary to counter decrease in the value of the property.[38] Disposal without consent can lead to a forced expiration of the right of usufruct (FCC/BCC, art. 618).

It is clear that the donor who reserves for himself/herself a traditional usufruct, loses his/her absolute control over the assets which he/she donated.[39] If the donor donated shares and bonds (investment portfolios), he/she cannot arbitrate, trade or sell the stocks of the portfolio even if this can be construed as sound economic management of the portfolio or be justified or even needed for preserving the value of the portfolio. The donor requires the nude owner's permission to carry out any such act, which usually means obtaining the consent of his/her children. Consent, however, cuts both ways. Hence the nude owner cannot alienate without the consent of the usufructuary. Consequently, a donation with reservation of even traditional usufruct may be a balanced mechanism for realising a tax optimised transfer of property (see section 1) without transferring full powers of alienation to the children.

The same issues exist concerning voting rights based on shares in companies and partnerships.[40] Some argue that voting rights are exercised by the usufructuary, while others plead for them to be exercised by the nude owner. A third view is that it depends on the particular

[34] See Comparative observations, Case 7.

[35] Aynès, 'Observation', p. 168; Bougle and Gouthiere, 'Patrimoine', p. 134; de Page, 'Les Donations', p. 263; Fiorina, 'L'usufruitier', pp. 48 ff.; Hansenne, *Les Biens*, p. 1028; Planiol and Ripert, *Traité pratique*, p. 769; Prutting, *Sachenrecht*, p. 364; Raynaud, *Les Biens*, p. 107. See Verbeke, 'Creatief met vruchtgebruik', p. 545.

[36] Jamar, *Les Novelles*, p. 160; Laurent, *Principes*, pp. 419, 478.

[37] Laurent, *Principes*, pp. 419, 478.

[38] de Page, 'Les Donations', p. 372.

[39] Verbeke, 'Creatief met vruchtgebruik', pp. 545 ff.

[40] See Du Mongh, *De erfovergang van aandelen*, pp. 258 ff.

decision to be taken by the organisation in question. The best solution is to determine the voting rights of each party explicitly in the by-laws of the organisation. In the absence of such specification it is, according to the traditional view, uncertain whether the usufructuary is entitled to vote. This is a significant impediment when the shares of a family company are transferred with reservation of a usufruct. The new Dutch Civil Code provides a legal framework for shares burdened with a usufruct (DCC, art. 2: 88–9).

We may conclude that, with regard to the traditional face of usufruct, the possibility to retain control is rather limited. The donor (nude owner) or the usufructuary cannot dispose of the usufructuary assets without the consent of the other. The consent of the nude owner is required for disposal by the usufructuary, which constitutes a serious impediment from an estate planning point of view.

3.2. *Income*

The usufructuary takes over the owner's rights of use and enjoyment of the property,[41] which is a rather extensive entitlement.[42] He/she enjoys the whole of the property, including accessories,[43] possesses the asset (BGB, § 1036; cf. FCC/BCC, art. 2228),[44] and consequently receives the fruits gained from the property (FCC/BCC, arts. 582–4; BGB, § 954).[45] In the case of usufruct, fruits are assets created by, and separable from, the property in accordance with the intended purpose (destination) of that property.[46] Hence the qualification as a fruit requires causality, separation and conformity.[47] Recurrence of fruits at regular intervals is not required.[48]

The first element of causality requires that the usufructuary asset must be the direct or indirect cause or source of the alleged fruit.[49] Natural fruits are spontaneous products of the earth – in other words, the ordinary, natural products of the property (FCC/BCC, art. 585).[50] Industrial or civil fruits are obtained by cultivation (FCC/BCC, art. 583).

[41] See Belgian report, Case 1. [42] Prutting, *Sachenrecht*, p. 361.

[43] Zenati-Castaing and Revet, *Les Biens*, p. 491.

[44] Derine, Vanneste and Vandenberghe, *Zakenrecht*, p. 247; McClean, 'Common Law Life Estate', p. 653; Prutting, *Sachenrecht*, p. 361; Zenati-Castaing and Revet, *Les Biens*, p. 488.

[45] See Belgian report, Case 1; Prutting, *Sachenrecht*, p. 362.

[46] Dockes, 'Essai', p. 493; Verbeke, 'Creatief met vruchtgebruik', p. 570.

[47] Verbeke, 'Creatief met vruchtgebruik', p. 570.

[48] Dockes, 'Essai', p. 485; Verbeke, 'Creatief met vruchtgebruik', p. 570.

[49] Dockes, 'Essai', p. 482; Borkowski and Du Plessis, *Roman Law*, p. 174.

[50] Borkowski and Du Plessis, *Roman Law*, p. 174.

Civil fruits consist of the income and revenues from hiring out the property such as the rent from letting real estate (FCC/BCC, art. 584), interest on sums due and yearly income from annuities.

Secondly, the fruits must be separable from the asset for the usufructuary only becomes the owner of the fruits once they are separated from the principal property.[51] Natural fruits belong to the usufructuary upon their harvest. Shares can only provide fruits if separation from the share is possible, for example, the distribution of dividends.[52] When the articles of association of a company provide that profits are reserved or at least not distributable, separation is not possible. The profits are then integrated into the capital. Hence fruits which are reserved for the company are not distributable but belong to the owner.[53] The usufructuary can, however, exercise his usufructuary rights on shares of a company which declares dividends.[54] If such distribution is a monetary distribution, it will qualify as *quasi*-usufruct (see section 5, below). This situation is also comparable to capital shares of a trust fund,[55] where the profits are reinvested systematically. Hence the profits cannot be separated from the capital shares. The usufructuary can, however, claim his/her usufructuary rights upon sale of the capital shares. As the proceeds are of a monetary nature, the usufruct can arguably qualify as a *quasi*-usufruct in such a case.

The third requirement of conformity relates to the difference between fruits and products.[56] The collection of fruits can neither change nor diminish the substance of the usufructuary property whereas the collection of products gathered from the principal property can cause or result in deterioration of the property.[57] Consequently, products belong to the nude owner. Gold bars, for example, do not in principle produce fruits. The usufructuary is therefore not entitled to rings or necklaces produced from gold bars which have been melted down.[58] He does, however, have the right to use these rings or necklaces by virtue of the application of real subrogation in appropriate

[51] See Belgian report, Case 1; de Page, 'Les Donations', p. 213; Dockes, 'Essai', p. 490.
[52] Cass. 1 Dec. 1960; Pas. 1961 I 355; Dockes, 'Essai', p. 484; Verbeke, 'Creatief met vruchtgebruik', p. 571.
[53] Planiol and Ripert, *Traité pratique*, p. 783.
[54] Verbeke, 'Creatief met vruchtgebruik', p. 573.
[55] Dockes, 'Essai', p. 484.
[56] Verbeke, 'Creatief met vruchtgebruik', p. 571; cf. Dockes, 'Essai', p. 490.
[57] van Neste, *Beginselen, Zakenrecht*, p. 20.
[58] Verbeke, 'Creatief met vruchtgebruik', p. 578.

circumstances. There is no automatic *quasi*-usufruct here, unless contractually agreed.

In conclusion, one can argue that from the perspective of the donor who reserves a usufruct over the property and who wishes to retain the income from the donated assets, reservation of traditional usufruct only partially achieves this purpose. The receipt of rent, dividends and interest can provide him/her with the desired income. In the case of shares, however, the usufructuary is not entitled to the excess value or the profits if reserved in the articles of association of the organisation. The same problem exists in relation to capital shares. It is, however, possible to obtain some income by a contractual redefinition of the concept of fruits.[59]

4. The modern face of usufruct

This reasoning is in full accordance with the basic characteristics of the institution of usufruct. It is a mere adaptation of the basic rules of usufruct in respect of the intended purpose or destination of the property.[60] It is now clear that even the traditional concept of usufruct takes the destination or intended purpose of the property into account to determine the position of the usufructuary. For usufruct to be adapted to the needs of modern society, one simply has to extend this reasoning beyond fungible assets to all assets over which a usufruct is reserved, such as investment portfolios and art collections, while taking into account the intended purpose or specific destination of the assets. This destination is often more closely related to their economic value than to the substance of the assets,[61] which is obvious in the case of an investment portfolio where the destination of the shares which is subject to the usufruct is probably not the shares themselves but their economic value. The traditional limitation on the entitlements of the usufructuary seems to prevent the efficient management of the usufructuary property in many instances where maximising the economic value of the property will require an extension of the entitlements of the usufructuary.[62]

The French Court of Cassation has therefore advanced the concept that a usufruct over an investment portfolio is a usufruct over a

[59] *Ibid*. 573. [60] *Ibid*. 550.

[61] Aynès, 'Observation', p. 168; Verbeke, 'Creatief met vruchtgebruik', p. 546.

[62] See Verbeke and Vanhove, 'Spelen met vruchtgebruik', p. 191.

collection of different kinds of assets (*universitas iuris*).[63] In such a case, the object of the usufruct is not every single individual share or stock, but the portfolio in its entirety (*in globo*). The consequence is that the usufructuary can dispose of the usufructuary assets in the collection and can sell and reinvest shares.[64] He/she cannot, however, impair the usufruct asset itself, which is the portfolio as such. The duty of restoration on expiry of the usufruct relates to the asset, namely the portfolio. Hence he can restore a portfolio, of whatever composition, to the nude owner by real subrogation of all the rights to the assets in the portfolio.[65]

Although this approach is useful, it still remains a mere application of the traditional concept of usufruct. The trick here is to re-define the object of usufruct, the portfolio as a universality of assets in lieu of concentrating on the individual shares as the object of the usufruct. In a more modern approach, it is not merely the object of the usufruct but also the legal status of the usufructuary and his/her entitlements that are re-defined. The key then is to assess the position of the usufructuary in view of the intended purpose or destination of the usufructuary property.[66] We shall see how the position of the usufructuary becomes more opportune in relation to both retention of control and the provision of income.

4.1. *Control*

With the emphasis on the destination or intended purpose of a usufructuary asset and its role in modern commerce, the obligation of the usufructuary to preserve the substance of the property is re-defined as an obligation to preserve the property in accordance with its destination.[67] The destination of the property thus becomes the seminal criterion for shaping the management of the usufructuary property and determining the competence and powers of the donor-usufructuary. He can now, within the framework of his/her entitlement to use and enjoy the property, perform any act, including an act of disposal and/or

[63] Aynès, 'Observation', p. 167; Van Sinay, 'Vruchtgebruik op een algemeenheid', pp. 729–46.

[64] Verbeke and Vanhove, 'Spelen met vruchtgebruik', p. 192.

[65] Sagaert, 'Oude zakenrechtelijke figuren', p. 240.

[66] Aynès, 'Observation', pp. 168–9; Dockes, 'Essai', pp. 487–94; Verbeke, 'Creatief met vruchtgebruik', p. 547; Verbeke and Vanhove, 'Spelen met vruchtgebruik', p. 181.

[67] Dockes, 'Essai', p. 493; Verbeke, 'Creatief met vruchtgebruik', p. 547.

alienation, in so far as it corresponds with the destination of the property.[68]

If the identity and destination of the usufructuary asset is closely linked to economic value, fungibility, exchangeability and quick circulation, as in the case of stocks and bonds, alienation is not only in line with, but can even be required, in the interests of good management.[69] The destination of an investment portfolio is not the individual shares and other assets of the portfolio, but the value of the portfolio as a whole:[70] the shares are merely the means by which the objective of maximising the value of the portfolio can be achieved. Consequently, the donor-usufructuary who reserved the usufruct can dispose of and alienate shares which form part of the portfolio. He/she can sell shares and reinvest in other shares that seem more profitable or appear to represent a better investment in the long run. The donor will be preserving the substance of the usufructuary property as long as he/she acts with prudent and sound judgement in accordance with the destination of the usufructuary property.[71] His right of disposal and exchange of the assets comprising the usufructuary property is inherent in the nature of the property and in tandem with the interests of the usufructuary who will benefit from the maximisation of the value of the usufructuary asset.

The same reasoning applies to the question whether the usufructuary can exercise the voting rights bestowed on the shareholder of a partnership or company (see section 3, above). Since the usufructuary can perform all acts that fall within the ambit of the destination of the usufructuary property, the voting rights with regard to transactions in respect of the usufructuary property will probably vest in the usufructuary because the exercise of voting rights is a part of the right to use the property and is necessary for the use and enjoyment of the property as (temporary) owner.[72]

It is equally clear that a house or a farm as usufructuary property is destined for a different purpose than stocks and bonds, namely to remain part of the estate for a longer period. Alienation is not compatible with the destination of such property and does not fall within the competence of the usufructuary. The usufructuary can therefore only

[68] Dockes, 'Essai', pp. 493–4; Fiorina, 'L'usufrutier', p. 51.

[69] See Verbeke and Vanhove, 'Spelen met vruchtgebruik', p. 191.

[70] Verbeke, 'Schenking met voorbehoud vruchtgebruik', p. 264. [71] *Ibid.* 276.

[72] Du Mongh, *De erfovergang van aandelen*, pp. 248; Verbeke, 'Creatief met vruchtge bruik', 560.

dispose of the property with the consent of the nude owner.[73] The modern face of usufruct is thus characterised by a relative and functional prohibition against alienation of the property.[74]

The criteria for such 'teleological' (purposive) management (in line with the destination of the property) are twofold.[75] First, in the abstract, the usufructuary must behave as a prudent and reasonable man and bear in mind that he must return the property to the owner upon extinction of the usufruct without impairment of its substance. Secondly, and more concretely, the owner can pertinently determine the destination of the property. The usufructuary can use mines and quarries in the same way as the owner had previously used them if working the mines commenced at the outset of the usufruct (FCC/BCC, art. 598). A painting, art collection or a special quantity of wine produced in a particular year can be bought for investment purposes. The same applies to a house, apartment or farm. If the real estate is clearly identified as a mere investment asset, the usufructuary may have the power to dispose of the property to increase the value of the investment.

4.2. *Income*

Based on the destination of the usufructuary asset as the key criterion, the scope of the term 'fruits' can be increased under a modern approach. Products or proceeds gained from the usufructuary property can be considered fruits, even when the collection thereof affects the substance of the property, provided that the collection of the gains corresponds to the destination of the property. As explained above, this destination is determined *in abstracto* according to the criterion of the prudent man and concretised by the existing use and enjoyment of the owner. Hence certain products can be considered fruits if it was the intended purpose of the owner to accord that particular destination to the usufructuary property. The intention of the donor/owner is decisive. The usufructuary can continue to exploit the property as the owner did and enjoy the products as if they were fruits, if this was intended by the owner.[76] Rings or necklaces produced from a gold bar which was melted down can be considered fruits if the owner had given the gold bar such a destination. One can argue that the products of logging down a plantation donated with reservation of a usufruct

[73] Verbeke, 'Creatief met vruchtgebruik', p. 547.
[74] Sagaert, 'Oude zakenrechtelijke figuren', p. 231.
[75] More comprehensive: Verbeke, 'Creatief met vruchtgebruik', p. 548.
[76] *Ibid.* 572.

are not considered fruits. This argument does not hold true where the owner has given a clear indication that the trees in the plantation are destined to be felled and thus have to be classified as fruits when cut down (cf. BCC, art. 590).

If the general meeting of a company decides to incorporate profits in the reserves, these profits become an integral part of the capital. Hence, reserves generated in the company cannot be considered fruits to be distributed to the shareholders in the company and to the person to whom these shares have been granted in usufruct (see section 3, above). We explained that the nude owner is entitled to these reserves and that the usufructuary is not allowed to contend that his/her usufruct (or even *quasi*-usufruct) entitles him/her to enjoy the reserves as fruits.[77] However, it can be argued that if the articles of association of a company sanction the distribution of dividends with the specific objective of providing an income to the shareholders in the absence of profits, it may be considered a collection of the fruits of the property. This is an application of the principle that the destination or intended purpose of the usufructuary property must be taken into account.[78]

We discussed the position of the usufructuary concerning the capitalisation of the shares of a company. Normally the shares subject to the usufruct are not considered to generate fruits which can be enjoyed by the usufructuary. However, if the original object of the usufruct are shares from which dividends and profits can be expected and, subsequently, the general meeting decides to capitalise the profits derived from trading in shares, one may argue differently. This is especially the case if the decision to capitalise the profits is not taken by the owner, but by a general meeting where the owner has no decisive voting power. If the donor has indicated from the outset in the constitutive deed of the usufruct that the income derived from the shares will be distributed, it can be argued that the entire excess value of the shares can be considered fruits.[79]

We may conclude that the modern approach as to both control and income offers substantially more leeway to the donor-usufructuary. The modern interpretation of usufructuary rights, entitlements and competences is more in line with the commercial needs and context of today's society, while respecting the basic characteristics of the notion of usufruct to the greatest possible extent.

[77] Hansenne, *Les Biens*, 1048. [78] Verbeke, 'Creatief met vruchtgebruik', p. 578.
[79] *Ibid.*

5. The Janus face

A strict application of the requirement that restitution of the property must be in kind, makes it impossible to create a usufruct on property such as money, wine or grain, consumed directly by its use, as it is impossible to restore something that is consumed by its use. The problem is comparable to the more extreme case of the usufruct of perishable property which eventually perishes on account of wear and tear (see section 4, above). The Romans perceived this as problematic because the original aim of the institution of usufruct was alimentary, namely to provide for the living expenses of a surviving spouse during her or his lifetime. Under the regime of Augustus, this was solved by a *senatus consultum*, introducing an 'improper' form of usufruct namely the *quasi*-usufruct.[80] This form of usufruct is also recognised in France (FCC, art. 587), Germany (BGB, § 1067) and Belgium (BCC, art. 587). This kind of usufruct was also recognised by the Old Dutch Civil Code, but was abolished in the New Dutch Civil Code in 1992 (see section 6, below).

The *quasi*-usufruct regime, which is explicitly regulated by law, validates the reasoning underlying the modern approach to usufruct as explained in section 4, above. Here, again, the key is to re-define the obligation to restore the property in the light of the specific destination of the particular usufructuary assets.[81] If the destination of the asset is to be consumed, then the restoration cannot relate to the substance of the specific assets and the obligation to preserve the substance of the asset is thus channeled towards preserving it in a way that is compatible with its destination. If its destination is to consume the asset, consumption is allowed, and the obligation of restoration in kind is replaced by restoration of an equivalent. According to FCC/BCC, art. 587, the usufructuary shall restore either goods of the same quantity and quality or their value as appraised at the time of restoration.[82] The law is not clear regarding the precise extent of the restoration which is interpreted differently in Belgian[83] and French law.[84]

The ordinary rules of usufruct are also applicable to *quasi*-usufruct.[85] Goods that are immediately consumable are intended to make a swift

[80] D.7.5.5; D.7.5.7. [81] Verbeke, 'Modaliteiten', p. 171.
[82] Kluyskens, *Beginselen, Zakenrecht*, p. 182.
[83] Derine, Vanneste and Vandenberghe, *Zakenrecht*, p. 359.
[84] Veaux-Fournerie, 'Usufruit, caractères et sources'.
[85] Verbeke and Vanhove, 'Spelen met vruchtgebruik', p. 203.

exit from the nude owner's patrimony.[86] Even so, the destination indicated by the nature of the usufructuary object is not the only criterion. It was mentioned that the destination can also be indicated specifically by the donor/nude owner. Admittedly, in most cases, this corresponds to the natural destination of the property, but it need not always be the case. For example, money is in principle consumable. However, the ancient Roman coin in the collection of a numismatist is, according to the destination given by its owner, not consumable.[87] On the other hand, a Picasso painting is in principle not consumable. If this painting is, however, a mere investment and destined to be sold immediately to a high bidder, one can argue that it is a consumable asset.

Moreover, one may contractually agree on the consumable character of property.[88] Parties may, for instance, reach an explicit agreement that certain property is burdened with a *quasi*-usufruct, regardless of its inconsumable nature and destination.[89] Furthermore, this can also be inferred from the deed creating the usufruct.[90] The Belgian Minister of Justice is of the opinion that a conventional *quasi*-usufruct is valid. According to BCC, art. 579, usufruct is established by law or by a person's wish. BCC, art. 587 (*quasi*-usufruct) is not an exception to this rule.[91] Any property, even immovable property, can lose its natural character and degenerate, by agreement, into consumable property.[92]

Reserving a *quasi*-usufruct on the assets donated grants elaborate powers of control to the donor-usufructuary. Regarding fruits and income, the situation is no different from under the modern approach, as explained in section 4, above.

Since the donor-usufructuary is under no obligation to restore the asset itself, but merely an equivalent, he/she can behave like a *quasi*-owner during the usufruct period. The '*quasi*' element is explained by the fact that the donor-usufructuary is bound to manage the property in accordance with its destination or intended purpose, since he/she has

[86] Grimaldi, 'L'emploi', pp. 494–6. [87] Verbeke, 'Creatief met vruchtgebruik', p. 552.

[88] de Page, 'Le Quasi-usufruit', p. 157; Grimaldi, 'L'emploi', pp. 493–6; Verbeke, 'Quasi-vruchtgebruik', p. 50.

[89] Dekkers and Dirix, *Handboek*, p. 186; de Page, *Traité élémentaire*, p. 368; Nudelholc and Karadsheh, 'Réflexions', p. 409.

[90] Derine, Vanneste and Vandenberghe, *Zakenrecht*, p. 358.

[91] *Vragen en antwoorden*, Kamer, 2001–2. Answer 16 Oct. 2001 to question no. 356, 10983.

[92] Baudry-Lacantinerie, *Précis de droit civil*, pp. 789–90; Verbeke, 'Quasi-vruchtge bruik', p. 51.

an obligation to restore the usufructuary property.[93] The 'owner' element is also present since he/she can perform all acts of alienation and disposition without the consent of the nude owner, in so far as these acts are in accordance with the destination of the property. The destination is consumption, and consumption implies alienation.[94] Theoretically, the donor-usufructuary has no more powers than a normal usufructuary: all his/her actions must respect the destination of the assets. Realistically however, the donor-usufructuary has significant powers because the destination of the assets is consumption and he/she is only obliged to restore an equivalent.[95]

There has been some dispute with regard to the validity of a donation with reservation of a *quasi*-usufruct under French and Belgian law. Opponents take the view that such reservation is incompatible with the irrevocability of the donation (FCC/BCC, art. 894 and BCC/FCC, art. 946) and the consequent conflict with the principle '*donner et retenir ne vaut*'.[96] Another view is that in such a case there is no transfer of ownership in favour of the donee.[97] The majority opinion, however, correctly accepts its validity, pointing out that a reservation of *quasi*-usufruct does not bestow on the donor the freedom to revoke the donation and is thus in line with the irrevocability requirement of FCC/BCC, art. 946. The usufruct, and not the right of alienation and disposal, is reserved by the donor.[98] These rights are inherent in a *quasi*-usufruct but not in an absolute sense. He/she is still bound to restore the property at the end of the term of the usufruct. Moreover, FCC/BCC, art. 949 allows the reservation of any usufruct by the donor without making a difference between the various forms a usufruct can take.[99]

In conclusion, it is quite clear that the institution of *quasi*-usufruct is very attractive from an estate planning perspective. The control which the usufructuary can exercise comes very close to that of a *quasi*-owner.

[93] Grimaldi, 'L'emploi', pp. 494–6 and the references; Verbeke, 'Creatief met vruchtgebruik', p. 551. The owner is merely an ordinary creditor. He has no real claim against the usufructuary (Derine, Vanneste and Vandenberghe, *Zakenrecht*, p. 359).

[94] Baudry-Lacantinerie, *Précis de droit civil*, p. 790; Brault 'Un convention', p. 3; Verbeke, 'Schenking met voorbehoud vruchtgebruik', p. 265.

[95] Verbeke, 'Quasi-vruchtgebruik', p. 42.

[96] Chappert, 'La Donation', pp. 907–8; de Wulf, 'Schenking roerend goed', p. 164.

[97] Sagaert, 'Oude zakenrechtelijke figuren', p. 235.

[98] de Page, 'Les Donations', p. 140; Grimaldi, 'La Donation', p. 12; van Laere, 'De civiel- en fiscaalrechterlijke grenzen van schenking', p. 197.

[99] van Laere, 'De civiel- en fiscaalrechterlijke grenzen van schenking', p. 197.

In respect of income that can be gained, his/her position is approximately the same as according to the modern approach. Consequently, one may very well doubt whether there is any better alternative for the usufructuary. A brief journey to the Netherlands teaches us that, in fact, there is!

6. The twisted face

Dutch law endows the usufructuary with more extensive powers than any other jurisdiction. Some authors even argue that the new Dutch Civil Code (DCC) has denaturised the concept of usufruct, resulting in what we have called here the 'twisted' face of usufruct. On 1 January 1992, the new statutory provisions regarding usufruct entered into force: Title 8 of Book 3 of the new DCC. A fundamental, even revolutionary[100] change is that the requirement to keep the usufructuary assets intact (*salva rerum substantia*) disappeared from the statutory law on usufruct.

The Dutch usufruct offers an ideal position to the usufructuary regarding control over the usufructuary assets and the income that can be gained from these assets. Even the new default rules provide extensive powers with regard to consumption and disposal of usufructuary assets. These powers can even be increased by a contractual expansion of the position of the usufructuary.

6.1. *Default rules*

DCC, art. 3:207 stipulates that the usufructuary is entitled to use or consume usufructuary assets. Use and consumption are governed by the rules agreed upon at the constitution of the usufruct. In the absence of any such rules, the usufructuary must behave with due regard of the nature of the usufructuary assets and local customs regarding their use or consumption. The law offers no clear description of consumable property. In the official explanation of the new DCC, consumable property is described as property which is consumed by its mere use (by wear and tear).[101] Hence the nature of the goods is crucial in determining the consumable character of the property. In spite of the official explanation, a wider and more flexible meaning must be given to the term consumption. In general, consumption is regarded as the decay of goods through wear and tear by individual or multiple use.[102]

[100] Van Oven, 'Het Vruchtgebruik in het Ontwerp Nieuw BW', p. 361.

[101] van Zeben and Dupun, *Parlementaire geschiedenis*, p. 639.

[102] See in general Bos, 'Vruchtgebruik op aandelen'; van Gaalen, 'Vruchtgebruik', p. 238.

Upon extinction of the usufruct, the owner is entitled to the restoration of the usufructuary assets, at least in so far as the usufructuary or his legal successors are unable to prove that these assets have been consumed or have perished by accident (DCC, art. 3:215, § 1). Since a usufruct usually expires on the death of the usufructuary, the burden of proof is likely to fall on the legal successors of the usufructuary. Hence the usufructuary will have to provide the legal successors with evidence of consumption, unless the successors are the same persons as the owners.[103]

A significant innovation is that the usufructuary is entitled to use and consume the usufructuary assets without being obliged to restore either the assets or its equivalent upon extinction of the usufruct. This means that *quasi*-usufruct (where consumption is allowed subject to the obligation to restore an equivalent, see section 5, above) has been abolished under Dutch law. At this point Dutch law has made a complete break with the traditional institution of *quasi*-usufruct compared with French and Belgian law. Even in the case of the conventional *quasi*-usufruct, the French and Belgian usufructuary is obliged to restore an equivalent.

Furthermore, DCC, art. 3:212, § 1 stipulates that if the usufructuary assets are destined to be alienated the usufructuary is entitled to alienate the assets in accordance with their intended purpose. A classic example is trade stocks.[104] The law explicitly grants the usufructuary the power to dispose of these assets. In the absence of any statutory basis, the usufructuary is only permitted to dispose of the usufructuary assets with the consent of the nude owner or with authorisation of the Cantonal (district) Court (DCC, art. 3:212, § 3). The Cantonal Court may only authorise such a disposal if it serves the interests of both the nude owner and the usufructuary and if the interests of neither are prejudiced by the disposal. If the usufructuary legally disposed of the usufructuary assets in accordance with DCC, art. 3:212, the assets replacing the original assets still belong to the nude owner and are still burdened with a usufruct pursuant to the doctrine of real subrogation (DCC, art. 3:213).[105]

6.2. *Contractual expansion*

The already strong position of the usufructuary under the default rules can even be further strengthened contractually. Parties can agree to an

[103] van Gaalen, 'Vruchtgebruik', p. 166.
[104] Mijnssen, Van Velten and Bartels, *Asser, Eigendom*, p. 287.
[105] Berenschot, 'Enige aspecten van de plaats van vruchtgebruik', p. 178.

expansion of the usufructuary's powers of consumption and disposal (DCC, art. 3:212, § 2).[106]

Consequently, parties may include rules in the constitutive deed that an asset is consumable in spite of its obvious inconsumable nature (DCC, art. 3:207). Furthermore, DCC, art. 3:215 stipulates that the usufructuary can be empowered to *complete* or *partial* consumption of the usufructuary assets by virtue of a contractual provision. In the absence of any limitation, the usufructuary is in principle entitled to consume all of the usufructuary assets without any obligation of restoration whatsoever.

Expansion with regard to powers of disposal is also possible. The default rules state that alienation by the usufructuary without the consent of the nude owner is permitted only if this is consistent with the purpose or destiny of the usufructuary assets. Nevertheless, parties can agree that the usufructuary will be entitled to dispose of the usufructuary assets on his/her own regardless of the destination of the property (DCC, art. 3:215). An explicit agreement to allow the usufructuary to dispose of the assets releases the usufructuary of the obligation to invest the goods in the best interests of the nude owner imposed by DCC, art. 3:214, § 1.[107] Other modalities are also possible. The power of disposal can be subjected to the consent of one or more other persons, generally a third party such as an asset manager (DCC, art. 3:215, § 2). The objective in doing so may be to retain some control in the interest of the nude owner. If the usufruct is placed under administration,[108] the co-operation of the administrator is required for disposal and consumption of the assets (DCC, art. 3:215, § 2).

It is clear that the new Dutch concept of usufruct offers abundant possibilities in the sphere of estate planning. Not only can a donor retain an income by agreeing upon the consumable feature, but he/she can in addition reserve vast powers of disposal. The donor can make a contractual arrangement that the usufructuary can dispose of the usufructuary assets without the consent of the nude owner. Since there is no obligation of restoration of the assets whatsoever (neither in kind nor by equivalent), maximum control over the assets and income gained therefrom can be reserved.

106 van Gaalen, 'Vruchtgebruik', p. 154.

107 Lubbers, 'Vruchtgebruik', p. 134.

108 Civil Court, art. 4:153, para 1. Until the coming into force of the new Dutch Inheritance Law on 1 Jan. 2003, the statutory arrangement on administration of usufruct was found in Civil Court, art. 3:204.

6.3. *Limits*

The usufructuary must administer the usufructuary assets with the care of a prudent man (DCC, art. 3:207, § 3). This obligation plays a central role in the exercise of a usufruct[109] and can trigger liability on the part of the usufructuary during the existence of the usufruct,[110] or of his/her heirs upon extinction of the usufruct.

A difficult question is whether or not the usufructuary's obligation of proper care results in a limitation of the usufructuary's power to alienate and consume the assets, even if this power is not limited by the deed creating the usufruct. In our view, this issue reveals the paradox between the very essence of the right of usufruct, which is conservation of the capital, and the power to dispose of and consume the usufructuary assets.[111] It is arguable, under the traditional and even the modern concept of usufruct, where maintenance of the substance of the assets is fundamental, that some restraint in the usufructuary's exercise of his powers is justified. However, to take such a view is to apply rules from another framework that is not in place here. Indeed, the statutory freedom that Dutch law allows a usufructuary in the exercise of his/her rights is unlimited. Based on DCC, art. 3:215, § 1, he/she can be empowered *completely* to dispose of and consume the usufructuary assets without any obligation towards the owner. Hence the law offers no basis for restrictive interpretation of the power of the usufructuary to dispose and consume.

If the usufructuary does not comply with his/her obligations, including the obligation of proper care, the Cantonal (district) Court can, at his/her request, grant the nude owner the right to manage the assets or place the usufructuary assets under administration (DCC, art. 3:221, § 2). In view of the possible wide powers of the usufructuary, namely full rights of disposal and consumption of the usufructuary assets, the Cantonal (district) Court will probably be reluctant to find that the usufructuary has failed seriously to comply with his/her obligations. The scenario will be different if limitations on the powers of the usufructuary have been included in the constitutive deed set forward by, for example, the donor. This will of course be unlikely in the situation where the donor wants to retain maximum control of the assets.

[109] Mijnssen, Van Velten and Bartels, *Asser, Eigendom*, p. 275.
[110] Supreme Court of the Netherlands, 9 Jan. 1998, NJ (1999), p. 285.
[111] See also Mellema-Kranenburg, 'Twee buitenbeentjes', pp. 777–8.

The Dutch Civil Code provides expressly that if the usufructuary is granted the additional rights of disposal and consumption of the usufructuary assets, he/she may donate these assets in the form of small donations (DCC, art. 3:215, § 3). We do not believe it is possible for the donor to stipulate that he/she will be entitled to make larger donations or to dispose of these assets by last will. Such an entitlement would be contradictory to the inherent nature of usufruct.

7. Conclusion

From a tax and estate planning perspective, the Dutch usufruct offers the most attractive possibilities – from a civil law point of view – with regard to facilitating the aspiration of a donor who desires to donate assets and yet, through the reservation of a usufruct, retain an almost absolute power of control over the assets and the income gained from the assets. In fact, the usufructuary under Dutch law is not obliged to restore the property in whatever form, neither in kind nor by equivalent.

However, for many continental lawyers, the capacity on the part of a usufructuary fully to dispose of the usufructuary assets, enjoy all of the income and simply consume the capital, without any obligation to restore the assets to the nude owner, amounts to a complete negation of the essential features of a usufruct. The vast majority of authors are of the opinion that the reservation of a usufruct granting such entitlement to the usufructuary in a deed of donation is incompatible with the irrevocability principle inherent in the concept of a donation (BCC/FCC, art. 946).[112] Not surprisingly, this poses no problem whatsoever in the Netherlands since 2003 and in Germany, where donations containing revocability clauses have been legalised (BGB, § 346). In other jurisdictions, such as Belgium and France, donations between spouses are also revocable (BCC/FCC, art. 1096). Hence the Dutch type of

[112] Barbaix, *Het contractuele statuut van de schenking*, p. 533 and cf. de Wulf, 'Schenking van roerend goed', p. 164; Sagaert, 'Oude zakenrechtelijke figuren', p. 235; *contra* Verbeke, 'Creatief met vruchtgebruik', p. 568; Nijs, van Zantbeek and Verbeke, 'Schenken met behoud van bezit', pp. 25–6; Verbeke, 'Modaliteiten', p. 180; Verbeke and Vanhove, 'Spelen met vruchtgebruik', pp. 213–16; Verbeke, 'Bevoegdheid Vruchtgebruiker', p. 408. Barbaix, *Het contractuele statuut van de schenking*, pp. 533 ff. is of the opinion that partial powers of consumption (without the obligation of any kind of restitution) can be compatible with the irrevocability rule of the donation (cf. the response in Verbeke, 'Alstublieft en dank u wel!', pp. 185–8).

usufruct can in such cases in these jurisdictions be perfectly reconciled with the rules pertaining to donations.

One does not need to go that far, however, to appreciate the virtues and benefits of usufruct reservation clauses in estate and tax planning instruments. Both the *quasi*-usufruct (see § 4, above) and the modern interpretation of the ordinary usufruct (see § 3, above) offer considerable possibilities for the donor to reach a compromise between two objectives: on the one hand, to transfer assets to the next generation by means of donation, and on the other hand, to retain an acceptable measure of control over the assets and income gained from the assets by the reservation in the deed of donation of a usufruct over the assets, fortified by whatever clauses he/she desires to strengthen his/her position as usufructuary. This explains why the utilisation of the concept of usufruct is such a popular technique among estate planners in certain civil law jurisdictions.

PART II
Case studies

Case 1
Various instances of time-limited interests

A is the owner[1] *of a residential property/a farm. A wants to give B a right relating to the property which is limited in time in the sense that it is certain not to last for ever*[2] *and that it entitles B to live on the property or exploit the farm.*

Briefly indicate the various ways in which this can be done, mentioning in each case the main characteristics of the right (for example, time limits, termination) and how it is constituted between the parties (formalities).

Comparative observations

With the exception of England,[3] Scotland and Denmark,[4] which acknowledge only leases and licences as time-limited interests in land, the other jurisdictions recognise certain time-limited interests in land as either limited real rights or as giving rise to contractual claims with regard to the land. The main instances of time-limited interests in the first category are the personal servitudes of usufruct, right of use and right of habitation, hereditary building leases (*superficies*) and hereditary land leases

[1] Or the functional equivalent, for example, a holder in fee simple.

[2] Do not include time sharing or financial leasing if the economic aim is for the lessee to acquire ownership at the end.

[3] England recognises leases or tenancies as estates rather than as limited real rights in land. It had formerly recognised something similar to the continental usufruct in the form of a lease for life (See McClean, 'The Common Law Life Estate') but this institution was converted into a long term lease by the Law of Property Act 1925. The English and Scottish licence approximates in some sense the continental revocable permission (*precarium*) and a beneficiary under a trust of land may in certain circumstances be permitted to occupy the land held in trust. These institutions, however, only give rise to personal rights.

[4] Danish law also does not recognise various categories of limited real rights, but instead regulates such kinds of transactions contractually through the contract of lease.

(*emphyteusis*). By contrast, ordinary land leases, loans and precarious holding of land only give rise to contractual claims with regard to the land. In this category, some jurisdictions acknowledge that registered land leases give rise to limited real rights while others accord at least some proprietary effects to registered or even non-registered land leases.

For the validity of *leases*, most jurisdictions, except England and Poland, require the payment of rent. Poland recognises a rent-free agricultural lease where the tenant only has to pay taxes and other expenses related to the property. In some jurisdictions, rent could be paid *in natura* from the proceeds of the land. Most European jurisdictions distinguish between residential and agricultural leases and regulate them by separate provisions in their Civil Codes or in special statutes. Although writing is generally not required for the constitution of a lease, most jurisdictions reduce their leases to writing in order to facilitate proof or for tax purposes. In addition, most jurisdictions require execution in a notarial deed for the validity of long leases and registration for enforceability against third parties. The maximum duration of leases ranges from ten years for residential leases in Poland, twelve years for agricultural leases in the Netherlands, thirty years for long leases in, for instance, Portugal, which reduces leases for life and longer leases to thirty years, and Belgium, which allows long leases for ninety-nine years or for life. Most leases may be terminated on account of material breach or on sufficient notice being given to the tenant. The Polish Civil Code contains the interesting provision that on the death of a residential tenant the lease is transferred automatically to the tenant's spouse, cohabitee, children or persons to whom the tenant was obliged to pay alimony, provided they occupied the premises on a permanent basis.

Most civil law jurisdictions recognise the *personal servitudes* of usufruct, the right of use and the right of habitation and accept that the last two rights accord lesser rights to the holder and that they are inalienable owing to their intensely personal character. Other jurisdictions such as Germany subsume the rights of use and habitation under the category of lesser personal servitudes. While the majority of jurisdictions require registration for the enforceability of personal servitudes against third parties, it is interesting that quite a number of them require little formalities or registration for their validity. Unlike leases, which are concluded for commercial reasons, personal servitudes are aimed at providing a livelihood mostly to family members until death. Personal servitudes usually expire on the death of the holder or after a period of thirty years if the holder is a juristic person, but they can also be constituted for a fixed shorter term or indefinitely. In the last case, personal servitudes approximate leases and are constituted for less personal reasons. The Greek and Austrian Civil Codes even allow personal servitudes to pass to the heirs of the holder, subject to restrictions as to the order of succession.

Most jurisdictions, notably Austria, Belgium, Portugal, Spain and Poland, accept that the holder of a *usufruct* in principle has the right to use the land and to enjoy the fruits of the land and must return the land on termination of the usufruct without impairment of its substance.[5] It is disputed whether a usufruct as such or only the rights under a usufruct can be transferred. The Austrian Supreme Court and the majority of Austrian academic opinion, as well as South African and Polish law, support the position that only the rights under a usufruct and not the usufruct itself can be transferred. The Dutch and Belgium Civil Codes imply that the usufruct as such can be transferred but adds that such alienation does not affect the duration of the usufruct which is still linked to the life of the original usufructuary.

On the issue of sub-lease by the usufructuary, Austrian law deviates from the position that subordinate rights created by a usufructuary expire on the termination of the usufruct. Instead, it holds that subleases do not expire automatically but are transferred to the landowner who is subrogated for the usufructuary in the contract of lease. In Belgium, the landowner is also obliged to respect a lease with a fixed date for a period not exceeding nine years, except in case of fraud, and a lease concluded for a period exceeding nine years for the nine-year period already started on termination of the usufruct. In tandem with this rule, Austrian law obliges a usufructuary to take over lease contracts that the landowner had concluded before the usufruct was created.

Generally, the *right of use* allows use of the land but use of the fruits only to meet the daily needs of the holder and his/her family.[6] In Portugal, the family of the holder includes his/her spouse, their children, other relatives to whom the holder owes a duty of support, and domestic personnel, with the extent of the right depending on the holder's social and economic status. In Belgium, Portugal, Spain and Hungary, the parties are free to determine the content and extent of a right of use and the rules on usufruct are applicable in so far as they are compatible with the right

[5] This obligation is interpreted in Spain and Italy as an obligation to preserve the economic destiny of the property.

[6] See e.g. the reports of the Netherlands, Spain, Italy and Hungary.

of use. An important difference with usufruct is that the holder of a right of use is not entitled to alienate his/her rights to another. As an exception, South African law allows the holder of a right of use in respect of a house to rent out some rooms in the house on condition that he/she resides in the house as well. Because of its strictly personal character, a right of use cannot be created in favour of a juristic person.

The *right of habitation* entitles the holder to reside in a dwelling, or part of a dwelling, belonging to another together with his/her family, other dependants, and in Greece, the domestic personnel that his/her social position allows for. In Poland, only minor children are allowed to reside in the dwelling with the holder of the right but they may stay on once they have achieved majority. Normally, the right of habitation expires on the death of the holder, except under Austrian case law and the Polish Civil Code, which allow parties to agree that the right of habitation will pass to a spouse, parents or even the children of the holder.

If the content of the right of habitation is not specified in the will or constitutive agreement, the default position is that the right must satisfy the needs of the holder of the right and his/her family. One Austrian commentary states that the residential space over which a right of habitation can be created can include minor rooms or outside surface connected to the rooms, such as a backyard. Unlike the right of use, the right of habitation does not entitle the holder to the natural fruits of the land, although South African law does allow the holder to rent out rooms in the dwelling and to keep the proceeds as civil fruits.

As in the case of *usus*, the general provisions governing usufruct of immovables apply by analogy to habitation, in so far as they are compatible with the nature of habitation[7] and, likewise, the holder of a right of habitation is not allowed to transfer his/her rights.

Interestingly, Polish law allows the seller of land to reserve for himself/herself a right of habitation in the residence on the land in order to provide for his/her specific needs. It may oblige the purchaser of the land to take the seller into the house and provide him/her with accommodation, food and clothes, electricity and heating, to take care of him in times of illness and to pay the holder's eventual funeral costs. In addition, the purchaser may be saddled with a right of usufruct or of use or habitation or be required to pay an annuity or part of the produce of the land to the seller. Since the creation of the above right involves the transfer of land, the contract must take the form of a notarial deed

[7] See e.g. the reports of Greece, Belgium, Portugal, Spain and Italy.

which may, but need not, be registered and even if not registered would be enforceable against a *bona fide* acquirer of the land.

Most continental European jurisdictions, except Greece and Hungary, recognise a *hereditary building right* as a limited real right which allows the holder to erect buildings on the land of another in return for payment of a small rent, typically on a yearly basis.[8] In Austria, Germany, Belgium, Spain, Portugal, Italy and Poland, a building right can also be established in respect of existing buildings, which entitles the holder (mostly a developer) to enlarge, modernise or reconstruct existing buildings. In Belgium, Portugal, Spain and the Netherlands, a building right also entitles the holder to improve the land by planting trees and crops or to take over existing trees and plants and to continue to improve the agricultural condition of the land.

Unlike a personal servitude, the hereditary building right is transferable and transmissible to heirs. The main effect of this right in Austria, Germany, Belgium, Spain,[9] Italy and Poland, is that its holder becomes full owner of the structure (or plantation) for the duration of the right as opposed to the holder of a mere limited real right.[10] It therefore forms an exception to the general rule that the landowner owns all accessories, in particular structures, which are permanently attached to the land. He may use, enjoy or demolish the structures or plants, provided that he returns the land in the condition in which he received it.[11]

Originally, the hereditary building right was introduced in order to encourage people of modest income to build residential accommodation for themselves. People who could not afford to purchase the land were put in a position to become full owners of a structure built on their behalf on someone else's land against payment of a modest rent. Originally and also presently, building rights were and are also granted by the state or local authorities for the purpose of improving undeveloped land subject to specific obligations.[12] Nowadays, this institution is often used for complex arrangements in land development.[13]

[8] In Belgium, a hereditary building right can also be constituted gratuitously.

[9] Under Spanish law, the holder becomes only a 'temporary owner'.

[10] This is the view in South Africa and the minority view in Italy.

[11] Note that in Poland the building, once erected, must be maintained in a proper condition and even rebuilt if it has been damaged during the term.

[12] In Poland the grant of a hereditary building right is restricted to public authorities but academics favour its extension to private landowners and its replacement by the German *Erbaurecht*.

[13] See Cases 10–12 below.

In Austria, the building right may not be established for fewer than ten years, and in Germany and Poland for not fewer than thirty or forty years respectively. In Belgium, the duration of the right is restricted to fifty years, in Spain and Poland to ninety-nine years, in Austria to 100 years, while in Germany it can be granted for an indefinite period. Most jurisdictions require that the agreement to establish a building right must be reduced to writing, executed notarially and registered in the Land or Mortgage Register for enforceability against third parties. German law requires that a building right must always be ranked first in the Land Register.

The building right is terminated by destruction of the building or plants, merger of the property into the hands of the holder and, in the case of the right to plant, if the soil becomes infertile.[14] On termination of the right, the landowner automatically acquires ownership of the building or plants. The Austrian statute provides that, failing any other agreement in this respect, the landowner has to compensate the developer for a quarter of the value of the building. Under Belgian law, the holder of the right is entitled at its expiry to claim compensation for the actual value of the plants, structures or buildings he/she erected and of the improvement of the structures or plants he/she took over from the landowner at the inception of the right.

Only a few European legal systems, notably Belgium, France, Spain, Italy and the Netherlands, recognise a *hereditary land lease* as a special limited real right in addition to a hereditary building right (*superficies*). This old-fashioned real right stems from the Roman institution of *emphyteusis*. It is mostly granted in respect of agricultural land but in some countries such as the Netherlands, it is also established with regard to urban land owned by large cities and it is thus an important source of income for city councils.

In general, a hereditary land lease confers a greater right than a building right and permits all kinds of improvement besides improvement by building and planting in return for payment of an initial deposit and a small periodic, usually yearly, rent. In general, a hereditary land lease is alienable and transmissible as well as attachable by the creditors of the leaseholder. Spanish law goes so far as to accept a dual ownership, with the landowner retaining direct ownership (*dominium directum*) and the holder of the perpetual land lease gaining beneficial ownership (*dominium utile*) of the land and to liken it to co-ownership on

[14] For further modes, see the Portuguese report.

account of its free alienability. The default position in the Dutch Civil Code is that the holder of the perpetual land lease may exercise the same rights of enjoyment over the land as the owner.

Hereditary land leases are regulated by legislation in Belgium and France and by the provisions of the Spanish, Italian and Dutch Civil Codes. Hereditary land leases may be granted for between eighteen and ninety-nine years in France and between twenty-seven and ninety-nine years in Belgium. In Italy, the minimum duration of a hereditary land lease is twenty years, but, like in the Netherlands and Spain, it may be granted in perpetuity. A hereditary land lease is most frequently created by a state grant, by an agreement between the parties or by prescription. The jurisdictions generally require that the agreement to establish a building right must be reduced to writing, executed notarially and registered in the Land or Mortgage Register for enforceability against third parties.

On expiry of the hereditary land lease, the land, together with all improvements, returns to the owner. The holder will usually have the right to be compensated for the improvements – in Italy, only to a modest degree. In the Netherlands, the holder of the hereditary land lease is entitled on expiry of the lease to remove all improvements on the condition that he/she restores the land to its previous condition. If not, the landowner is normally obliged to take over the improvements upon paying the leaseholder their value.

Today, the hereditary land lease has been eclipsed by the hereditary building right. It is seldom used in practice and, in Italy, most existing hereditary land leases were created decades ago. The reason for this is partially because the landowner is not allowed to demand a business-related yearly rent from the leaseholder and is not able to increase the rent in the light of changed circumstances. In the Netherlands, the hereditary land lease may be combined with a hereditary building right.

Most jurisdictions recognise a *gratuitous loan for use of land* derived from the Roman institution of *commodatum*. Some jurisdictions still regard a loan of land as a 'real' contract requiring a transfer of possession of the land, while others regard it as consensual in nature. While all jurisdictions accept that a loan for use creates merely personal rights, they attach certain proprietary consequences to a loan by protecting the occupation of the borrower against trespass and disturbance.

The borrower is under an obligation to return the property to the lender when the term of the loan expires, after he/she has used it or after a reasonable time. A loan granted for an indefinite term is generally revocable, usually on reasonable notice or immediately, where the lender is in urgent and unforeseen need of the property, where the borrower uses the property in a manner contrary to the terms of the contract, causes the property to deteriorate or unlawfully transfers the property to another. The borrower must make proper use of the property and is liable for all loss caused by improper use or use of the property in breach of the terms of the contract. The lender remains entitled to the fruits of the property.

In the case of a *revocable loan of land*, derived from the Roman *precarium*, the borrower's position is very insecure since the permission (licence) may be revoked at any time. It is gratuitous, except in France and Belgium, where it requires a (modest in France) financial counterprestation. Most jurisdictions regard *precarium* as a special kind of gratuitous loan and regulate it by the same principles. In Portugal and Spain, it is usually granted among family members and the mere permission of the owner coupled with transfer is sufficient for its creation. The contract is revocable at will, except in South Africa, where the courts regard *precarium* as a more secure form of tenure and require reasonable notice and sometimes a just reason (*ňova causa*) for its revocation.

Gratuitous loans seldom occur in respect of land, except in the form of a revocable permission for family members or farm employees to occupy part of the land on a farm in South Africa. In Poland, a variant of a loan for use is used in order to make residential premises gratuitously available to persons in need. In such circumstances, the borrower is not obliged to pay rent, but is held responsible for the maintenance of the property.

Austria

A and B can enter into a *lease* contract (*Bestandvertrag*). Under Austrian law, a lease gives rise to a personal right to use the leased object (such as land). The tenant has to pay rent. If the right to use the object is granted at no charge, this is not a lease but a loan. A lease contract does not require a specific form and is effective as soon as the parties have agreed on the leased object and on the rent.

There are two types of lease: an ordinary lease or tenancy (*Miete*) and a fruit-bearing or income-producing (usufructuary) lease (*Pacht*). Both are governed by Civil Code, § 1090. Under an ordinary lease, the tenant acquires the right to use the leased object. By contrast, under a fruit-bearing (usufructuary) lease contract, the tenant is entitled not only to use the leased object, but also to enjoy its fruits.[15] Hence, the right to use a flat is granted by an ordinary contract of lease. However, if a plot of land and its buildings serving the cultivation of the land are leased largely for agricultural purposes, the underlying contract is an agricultural fruit-bearing (usufructuary) lease. Equally, if a plot of land with premises is leased largely for the management of a business, the underlying contract is a business usufructuary lease. If a contract has elements of both a tenancy and a usufructuary lease, the essential elements prevail.[16]

The difference between a tenancy and a usufructuary lease is important because the Law on Tenancy applies only to tenancies and not to usufructuary leases. The Law on Tenancy contains various obligational provisions for the benefit of the tenant, in particular regarding termination (Law on Tenancy s 29) and rent (Law on Tenancy s 16 and 26). In practice, difficulties arise in particular as to the differentiation between the business usufructuary lease, which is governed only by Civil Code, § 1090 and the tenancy of premises, which (at least partly) may fall under the Law on Tenancy. The classification of the contract depends on whether it only allows for the use of a building or also for the use of business equipment and utilities, machinery, stock, goodwill, business licences etc. If the contract imposes on the tenant the obligation to manage an enterprise, the legal relationship is deemed to be a usufructuary lease.[17]

According to the general rules of the Civil Code, lease contracts can be for a fixed or an indefinite period of time. A contract for a fixed period of time expires after the period has lapsed and may only be terminated earlier owing to material breach (Civil Code, § 1117). Lease contracts for an indefinite period can be terminated by complying with certain agreed periods of notice or by a material breach without such compliance (Code on Civil Procedure, § 560).[18] The Law on Tenancy contains obligational provisions regarding termination which deviate from the

15 Schauer, in Koziol and Welser, *Bürgerliches Recht*, vol. 1, p. 216; Würth, in Rummel, *Kommentar*, § 1091, para. 1.

16 Schauer, in Koziol and Welser, *Bürgerliches Recht*, vol. 1, p. 216.

17 3 Ob 274/02v; JBl (2003), p. 643; 7 Ob 87/04a; wobl (2005), p. 205; 4 Ob 258/05b; wobl (2006), p. 269 (Hausmann); Iro, *Kommentar*, § 1091, para. 2; Schauer, in Koziol and Welser, *Bürgerliches Recht*, vol. 1, pp. 216 ff.

18 ss. 1113 ff. *Allgemeinen bürgerlichen Gesetzbuch*; Schauer, in Koziol and Welser, *Bürgerliches Recht*, vol. 1, pp. 235 ff.

provisions of the Civil Code. If residential premises are leased for a definite period, the lease must be for a period of at least three years (Law on Tenancy, s. 29, para. 1, line 3b). Contracts for an indefinite period can only be terminated by the landlord if he/she has good reason to do so (Law on Tenancy, s. 30). When the tenant of a residential lease dies, the lease is transferred to certain relatives: the spouse or the partner of the tenant if this person has been living with the tenant in the same household for a certain period.

An agricultural lease is additionally governed by the Law on Agricultural Leases. This statute contains obligatory provisions as to rent (Law on Agricultural Leases, s. 4) and lays down so-called benchmark periods (Law on Agricultural Leases, s. 5). The benchmark period is fifteen years for the lease of an agricultural business dedicated above all to horticulture, vinery or pomiculture; ten years for the lease of any other agricultural business or a single plot of land used for horticulture, vinery or pomiculture; and five years for all other agricultural leases. If a contract is concluded for a period shorter than the benchmark period, the tenant may apply for an extension. The court must grant such an extension if the interests of the tenant outweigh the interests of the landlord (Law on Agricultural Leases, s. 6, para. 3). Such an extension is also possible if an agricultural lease is concluded for an indefinite term and the landlord terminates the contract before the expiry of the benchmark period.[19]

The right to use the leased object and the right to enjoy its fruits are rights *in personam*. Nevertheless, the tenant has certain remedies against third persons who interfere with his/her rights.[20] It is possible to register the lease in the Land Register in order to make it enforceable against third parties (Civil Code, § 1095).[21] In the past, the Austrian Supreme Court only allowed the registration of leases for a fixed period. The court argued that – in consideration of Civil Code, § 1120 – the registration of a lease contract for an indefinite period would be useless.[22] Today, the Supreme Court allows the registration of all lease contracts, which restricts the statutory right of the landlord to terminate the lease in any form.[23]

[19] 1 Ob 530/82; MietSlg 34/16. [20] For details, see Cases 2–4. [21] See Case 2.

[22] 7 Ob 88/72; SZ 45/47; 5 Ob 221/60; SZ 33/68; 5 Ob 500/59; SZ 32/124; Iro, *Kommentar*, § 1095, para. 1. For a critical analysis, see Schauer, 'Zur Verbücherung', p. 631. Regarding the protection under Civil Codes 1120, see Cases 2 and 3.

[23] 5 Ob 90/06f; EvBl (2007), p. 10 following Schauer, 'Zur Verbücherung', pp. 636 ff.

Typically, contracts for residential leases are based on standard form contracts, the aim of which is to deviate as far as legally possible from the rules which are to the advantage of the tenant.

A can grant B a *personal servitude* (*Personalservitut*) with regard to the land. The personal servitudes are usufruct, the right of use and the right of habitation (Civil Code, § 478). It is also possible to create irregular servitudes, for example, a right of way, for the benefit not of land but of a certain person (Civil Code, § 479).[24]

In principle, the consensual creation of servitudes requires an agreement and registration in the Land Register (Civil Code, § 481, para. 1). However, the Austrian Supreme Court and a part of the academic literature also recognise unregistered servitudes, provided that these servitudes are manifest,[25] namely evidenced by recognisable objects or facts.[26] In such cases, the manifest character of the servitude is a substitute for registration.[27] There is no clear answer to the question whether this substitution of the registration is possible not only in the case of real (praedial) servitudes but also in the case of personal servitudes. The Austrian Supreme Court had formerly argued that personal servitudes could never be manifest and therefore always had to be registered.[28] According to more recent decisions, the Supreme Court also accepts an unregistered right of habitation which is manifest.[29] This is the case, for example, if the access to the premises subject to this right is apparently blocked.[30]

Personal servitudes may be created for an indefinite period or for a definite period of time. They expire at the latest with the death of the holder, unless they are expressly extended to the heirs. If the agreement

[24] Koch, in KBB, § 479, para. 1.

[25] 8 Ob 2024/96; NZ (1996), p. 302; 1 Ob 587/95; JBl (1996), p. 458; 7 Ob 547/95; wobl (1996), p. 240 (critical comment by Schauer); 7 Ob 560/94; NZ (1995), p. 108; 8 Ob 622/91; Hofmann, in Rummel, *Kommentar*, § 481, para. 2; Koch, in KBB, § 481, para. 4; *contra* Schauer, 'Zur Verbücherung', p. 240; Kletecka, in Koziol and Welser, *Bürgerliches Recht*, vol. 1, p. 429; Rubin, 'Offenkundige', p. 545.

[26] Hofmann, in Rummel, *Kommentar*, § 481, para. 2; 7 Ob 560/94; NZ (1995), p. 108; 8 Ob 622/91; 1 Ob 1/84; NZ (1987), p. 22; 3 Ob 43/55; SZ 28/30.

[27] 8 Ob 2024/96; NZ (1996), p. 302; 7 Ob 547/95; wobl (1996), p. 240 (critical comment by Schauer).

[28] 8 Ob 622/91; 1 Ob 615/78; MietSlg 30.050; 3 Ob 43/55; SZ 28/30; *contra* 8 Ob 137/75; SZ 48/78.

[29] 1 Ob 14/97h; immolex 1997/143; 1 Ob 587/95; JBl (1996), p. 458; 7 Ob 547/95; wobl (1996), p. 240 (critical comment by Schauer). For a critical analysis, see also Rubin, 'Offenkundige', p. 545.

[30] 1 Ob 587/95; JBl (1996), p. 458.

does not specify the heirs, it is presumed that only the children will be entitled (Civil Code, § 529). Inheritance of personal servitudes is subject to the limits of Civil Code, § 612.[31] Accordingly, if the agreed heirs are not descendants of the holder, they must be alive when the agreement is made. Servitudes for a fixed term automatically expire at the end of the term (Civil Code, § 527). In principle, servitudes are highly personal and cannot be transferred to another person (Civil Code, § 485).[32]

A personal servitude created in favour of a juristic person expires with the dissolution of that person.[33]

The usufructuary has the right to use the land and to enjoy its fruits to the extent that it does not interfere with the substance of the land (Civil Code, § 509). He/she may also sub-let the land. On expiry of the usufruct, such a sub-lease does not end automatically, but is transferred to the landowner (Civil Code, § 1120).[34] The usufructuary has to take over a lease contract that the landowner had concluded before the usufruct was created.[35]

Whereas other servitudes cannot be transferred, special rules apply to the usufruct. According to some decisions of the Supreme Court, the usufruct as such is transferable, while according to other decisions and the majority view in academic literature, only the rights flowing from the usufruct may be transferred.

The *right of use* is similar to the usufruct. However, the usuary is allowed to enjoy the fruits only to the extent necessary for personal purposes (Civil Code, § 504).

The *right of habitation* is a proprietary right to use residential property (Civil Code, § 521). Depending on its concrete form, the right of habitation is governed either by the provisions regarding usufruct or by the provisions regarding the right of use.[36] The right of habitation can be created for the use of residential space including adjoining rooms and related outside surface.[37]

[31] Hofmann, in Rummel, *Kommentar*, § 529, para. 1. [32] For details see Case 9.

[33] Kiendl-Wendner, in Schwimann and Verschraegen, *Praxiskommentar*, vol. 2, § 529, para. 1.

[34] 4 Ob 3/29; JBl (1928), p. 392; Kletecka, in Koziol and Welser, *Bürgerliches Recht*, vol. 1, pp. 425 ff. As to s. 1120 Civil Code, see Case 2 and, as to its application to *ususfructus*, Case 10.

[35] 1 Ob 171/48; SZ 21/152; 8 Ob 678/90; wobl (1992), p. 113; Kletecka, in Koziol and Welser, *Bürgerliches Recht*, vol. 1. pp. 425 ff.

[36] 5 Ob 2121/96; NZ (1997), p. 130 (Hoyer); 5 Ob 83/97k; NZ (1998), p. 306 (Hoyer); 8 Ob 55/97i; wobl (1998), p. 311; Koch, in KBB, § 521, para. 1; Kletecka, in Koziol and Welser, *Bürgerliches Recht*, vol. 1. p. 427.

[37] Koch, in KBB, § 521, para. 2.

A can grant B a *building right* governed by the Law on Building Rights (*Baurechtsgesetz* as amended by BGBl 1990/258). The building right is the proprietary right to have a building on or under the surface of a plot of land which belongs to somebody else. It is alienable and transmissible (Law on Building Rights, s. 1). The purpose of this right is for the ownership of the land to remain with the owner while simultaneously granting a developer a proprietary right to erect buildings on the land without buying the land.[38] The building right can also be created in respect of an existing building.[39]

The building right is considered an immovable object (Law on Building Rights, s. 6, para. 1). The building is an accessory of the building right and is therefore an immovable object as well.[40] The owner of a building right has ownership of the building, but only a right of use with regard to the land (Law on Building Rights, s. 6, para. 2).

The building right cannot be created for fewer than ten or more than 100 years (Law on Building Rights, s. 3, para. 1). When the building right expires, the landowner acquires ownership of the building and, failing any other agreement in this respect, has to compensate the developer for a quarter of the value thereof (Law on Building Rights, s. 9).

The creation of a building right requires registration in the Land Register as a charge of the respective land (Law on Building Rights, s. 5, para. 1).

The granting of *rights of use* over *agricultural land* often requires approval by the state authorities.[41]

Land and parts of a land may also be the object of a *loan for use* (*Leihe*) or a *precarium* (*Prekarium*).[42] A loan for use agreement obliges the lender to permit the borrower to use the land at no charge (Civil Code, § 971). A loan agreement is a so-called 'real contract' and comes into existence only when the object is actually handed over to the borrower (Civil Code, § 971).[43] Rights of the lender are personal rights. Nevertheless, the borrower has at least possessory remedies against third persons who

[38] Kletecka, in Koziol and Welser, *Bürgerliches Recht*, vol. 1. p. 435.

[39] Kletecka, Rechberger and Zitta, *Bauten*, p. 31, para. 33; Kletecka, in Koziol and Welser, *Bürgerliches Recht*, vol. 1. p. 434.

[40] Kletecka, in Koziol and Welser, *Bürgerliches Recht*, vol. 1. p. 435.

[41] Hofmann, in Rummel, *Kommentar*, § 509, para. 1; Law on Transfer of Tirol (*Grundverkehrsgesetz*), s. 4.

[42] 6 Ob 604/86; EvBl (1987), p. 134; Koziol, in Koziol and Welser, *Bürgerliches Recht*, vol. 1, p. 203.

[43] Welser, in Koziol and Welser, *Bürgerliches Recht*, vol. 2, p. 205.

interfere with his/her right to use the object (Civil Code, § 974).[44] A loan for use can be for a fixed or an indefinite period. If not agreed otherwise, a reasonable termination period applies in the case of the latter.[45]

If the borrower is obliged to give the object back whenever the lender asks him to do so, the loan is deemed to be a *precarium*. Principally, a *precarium* is governed by the provisions regarding the loan (Civil Code, § 971). However, unlike the borrower under a 'normal' loan, the borrower under a *precarium* does not have any possessory remedies against third persons who interfere with his/her rights.[46]

With the exception of limited possessory protection, the lender is not protected against third parties. As such, this report will not deal further with loans.

Belgium

The owner, A, must decide whether to grant rights *in personam* or rights *in rem* to B. B will be referred to as the 'tenant' if rights *in personam* are granted, and as the 'holder' if rights *in rem* are granted.

Rights *in personam* are rights that only have effect between the parties. They do not confer an interest in the property itself. The rights *in personam* that could be granted to B in the case above are the residential lease, the agricultural lease, the loan for use and *precarium*. These rights *in personam* will be discussed briefly in this section. The residential and agricultural leases will be dealt with in this report only to the extent that they confer (some kind of) interest in the property itself.

Rights *in rem* usually offer more stability to their holders than rights *in personam*. They usually grant a right of use and exploitation with regard to the property and thus guarantee a source of income from the property for the holder over a long period of time. From a tax point of view, the constitution of a lease with regard to a building does not allow the owner/constructor to deduct the input VAT paid on the erection or purchase of the building from the rent, whereas the constitution of rights *in rem* may enable him to do so under certain conditions. Moreover, in certain circumstances, the acquisition of rights *in rem* might be considered as an alternative to a purchase. The rights *in rem* that could be granted to B in the case above are usufruct, use, the right

[44] *Ibid.* 203. [45] Binder, in Schwimann, *Praxiskommentar*, vol. 4, § 971, para. 14.
[46] Welser, in Koziol and Welser, *Bürgerliches Recht*, vol. 2, p. 203.

of habitation, the hereditary building lease (*superficies*) and the hereditary lease of land (*emphyteusis*).

In general, the aforementioned rights are constituted between parties without any formalities (unless indicated otherwise hereafter). Nevertheless, for evidentiary purposes, also between the parties, the Belgium Civil Code, art. 1341 in principle requires a deed prepared by a notary or a written contract if the value of the property exceeds EUR 375.[47]

A *residential lease* (*woninghuur, bail de résidence principal*) is defined as a lease of accommodation used by the tenant with the landlord's express or tacit agreement, as his/her principal residence, in return for payment of an agreed rent. The Law on Residential Lease of 20 February 1991 art. 1bis, as amended, suggests that a residential lease contract should be in writing and should contain specific clauses. A written document is, however, not required for the validity of the contract nor as proof for its existence (notwithstanding the application of the rule of Civil Code, art. 1341 mentioned above). However, any party can demand the reduction of the contract to writing and its completion or signing by the parties to the contract.

In principle, residential leases are concluded for a period of nine years. If the contract is reduced to writing, it is possible to conclude a residential lease for a period of between nine and ninety-nine years, and even for the life-time of the tenant, or for a shorter period of up to a maximum of three years. The tenant has a statutory right to terminate a nine-year (or longer) lease at any time subject to three months' notice. If the tenant terminates the lease during the first three years, the landlord can claim an indemnity.[48] The landlord may terminate the lease subject to six months' notice, at any time, if the premises are required for his/her own use or for the use of specified close relatives. He/she may also terminate the lease at the end of a three-year period, subject to six months' notice, if he/she intends to reconstruct or renovate the residential premises in a substantial manner. He/she is also entitled to terminate the lease at the end of a three-year period, subject to six months' notice, without such intention, subject to the payment of an indemnity of nine months' rent at the end of the first three-year period and of six months' rent at the end of the second three-year period.

[47] As opposed to proof between and against commercial parties which is free (Code of Commerce, art. 25).

[48] An indemnity of three, two or one month's rent, if the lease ends during the first, second or third year respectively (Law on Residential Leases, art. 3, s. 5).

If no party terminates the lease at the end of the lease period of nine years, the contract is prolonged automatically by another three-year period. A lease for a shorter period than three years cannot be terminated by either party prior to the end of the lease term. If no party terminates such a lease three months before the end of the term the lease is automatically converted into a nine-year lease coming into effect from the start of the short-term lease. A lifetime lease cannot be terminated by the landlord: it ends by operation of law upon the death of the tenant, or on termination by the tenant.

An *agricultural lease* (*landpacht, bail à ferme*) is a contract by which the landlord grants the tenant the right to exploit land mainly for agricultural purposes in return for payment of an agreed rent. Agricultural leases are governed by the Law on Agricultural Lease of 23 October 1969, as amended. This Law is clearly made to protect the farmer tenant. An agricultural lease must be concluded in writing (Law on Agricultural Lease, art. 3), not for validity, but merely for evidentiary purposes (*ad probationem*), at least for the landlord. Agricultural leases must be concluded for a minimum period of nine years (but not exceeding ninety-nine years) and also for the lifetime of the tenant. In the absence of a notice of termination, the lease is automatically extended for consecutive periods of nine years. If the tenant wants to terminate the lease, he/she must give a notice period of at least one year. The landlord may terminate the lease only in limited circumstances and subject to a notice period of between three months and four years.

A can grant B a right of *usufruct* (*vruchtgebruik, usufruit*) (Civil Code, arts. 578–624). Usufruct is a right *in rem* which allows the holder to use and enjoy property belonging to another for a limited period of time, provided that the substance of the property is preserved and that the holder exploits the property like a reasonable man. If it is granted to a private individual, it may not exceed his/her lifetime and will expire on death, even if death occurs before the expiry of the term for which the usufruct was granted. The duration of a usufruct constituted in favour of a legal person such as a company or a foundation may not exceed thirty years. Usufructs may be created by law, prescription, testament or will or by contract. If A grants a right of usufruct on agricultural land to B for a fixed term, the usufruct will be subject to the provisions of the Law on Agricultural Lease. Apart from the death of the usufructuary, the usufruct will also terminate on expiry of the term for which it has been granted, complete destruction of the property, merger (acquisition of the ownership of the property by the holder, acquisition of the nude property by the usufructuary or the acquisition of both rights by a third party), non-use for thirty years, renunciation of his/her rights by the holder, dissolution in case of mismanagement (Civil Code, art. 618), or cancellation of the title.

The *right of use* or *habitation* (*recht van gebruik of bewoning, droit d'usage ou d'habitation*) (Civil Code, arts. 625–35) is analogous to usufruct, with the addition of a few nuances. It is a right *in rem* to use and reside in immovable property. If constituted by agreement, parties can freely decide on the scope and content of the right of use and habitation. Contrary to the right of usufruct, the holder of the right of use and habitation may not transfer his/her right (Civil Code, arts. 631 and 634). The provisions relating to usufruct apply to the extent compatible to use and habitation. Comments related to usufruct further in this report equally apply to the right of use and habitation, unless otherwise indicated.

A can conclude a *hereditary land lease* (*emphyteusis, erfpacht, droit d'emphytéose*) with B, governed by the Law on *Emphyteusis* of 10 January 1824 and subject to the agreement between the owner and the tenant (leasehold tenant/*emphytéot*/*erfpachter*). A heritable land lease constitutes a right *in rem* in favour of the holder to use and exploit the property of the grantor in return for payment of an annual charge (a significant payment in advance may also be agreed upon). It is essentially a temporary right: it must be contracted for a period of not fewer than twenty-seven years and not more than ninety-nine years.

It can be created by prescription, contract or will. The holder may exercise all the rights of enjoyment and exploitation of land, provided that the value of the property is not reduced. It includes inter alia the right to rent out the property and to improve the land by cultivation thereof and by the construction of buildings. At the expiry of the land lease, the tenant will not be entitled to claim compensation for this cultivation or for the constructed buildings, unless otherwise agreed. Apart from the death of the holder, the leasehold ends at the end of term for which it has been granted, at complete destruction of the property, merger, non-use for thirty years, renunciation of his/her rights by the holder, dissolution or cancellation of title.

A can grant B a *hereditary building lease* (*opstalrecht, droit de superficie*) governed by the Law on *Superficies* of 10 January 1824 and subject to the agreement between the parties. It is a right *in rem* in favour of the holder and entitles the holder to own buildings, works or agricultural improvements effected by him/her on the land of another. It is time-limited with a maximum duration of fifty years, but it can be renewed indefinitely. The hereditary building lease can also be granted with regard to existing buildings on the land, provided the holder compensates the owner for the value of the buildings at the inception of the right.

While the grantor of the right remains the owner of the land, the holder is – for the duration of his/her right – the sole owner of everything erected or planted on the surface of the land. He/she is entitled to use, enjoy and even demolish these items, provided he/she returns the land in the condition in which he/she received it. When his/her right expires, the holder is entitled to claim compensation for the actual value of the plants, works or buildings he/she erected and the existing plants, works or buildings he/she acquired from the landowner at the inception of the lease. Apart from the death of the holder, the heritable building lease ends on expiry of the term for which it has been granted, complete destruction of the property, merger, non-use for thirty years, renunciation of his/her rights by the holder or cancellation of title. The possibility of dissolution is disputed.[49]

A *loan for use* (*bruiklening, commodat*) (Civil Code, arts. 1875–91) is a gratuitous contract by which the lender grants the temporary use of movable or immovable property to the borrower. The sole obligation of the borrower is to return the property to the lender after the borrower has used it as permitted under the contract or on expiry of the agreed term. In exceptional circumstances it is possible for the lender to reclaim the property if he/she needs it urgently and unexpectedly. The traditional view (although contested in recent doctrine) is that the loan for use is a real contract, meaning that the contract is only constituted validly between the parties by the actual delivery of the property.

Precarium (*bezetting ter bede, occupation précaire*) is a contract where the owner of immovable property allows another party to use and occupy that property temporarily in return for payment and at will. This means that the owner can terminate the contract at any time, subject to reasonable notice being given. Although the occupier may use and enjoy the property, his/her right is very precarious as it lasts only as long as it pleases the owner. This type of contract has been created by case law and practice for situations where it is not suitable to conclude an ordinary contract of lease, for instance, in situations where it is prudent to give only a temporary right before entering into a more

[49] Derine, Vanneste and Vandenberghe, *Zakenrecht*, B, no. 1034; Sagaert, Tilleman and Verbeke, *Vermogensrecht*, no. 1013.

permanent arrangement. An example is where the prospective precarist has entered into negotiations for the lease of another property in six months' time, but is awaiting the finalisation of the lease, or in a situation where the landowner has received a notice of expropriation which may only be implemented in another year's time or where the landowner plans to demolish the property within a year. For the contract to be a *precarium* and thus not subject to the protective rules applying to residential, commercial or agricultural leases, strict conditions apply. Among others, it must be the joint intention of the parties to create such a temporary contract.

Denmark

Different sets of rules are relevant depending on which kind of property the right concerns. It is also of great importance how the contract is categorised. The main focus will be on contracts of synallagmatic nature, that is, where the parties to the contract both have rights and obligations. Contracts on accommodation and support (*habitatio* and the right of usufruct) provided by the new owner of immovable property for its former owner, especially by a child for his/her parents, are normally considered to be synallagmatic and are as such covered by the provisions of the Law on Private Housing.[50] It cannot be ruled out, though, that some of these agreements are too atypical to be considered as falling under the auspices of the law. In that case, and in situations of contracts of gratuitous nature, no statutory law applies. Only the provisions of the contract and the interpretation thereof are of importance. Contracts of this kind will be treated as contracts regarding land, even though buildings are also involved, and the same rules will apply.

If B obtains the right to exploit *land*, the parties are free to regulate such right by almost any contractual terms. Contracts can be created for an indefinite period or be limited in time to a term agreed to by the parties. If the contract is for an indefinite period, each party can end the contract by giving notice of reasonable length,[51] unless otherwise agreed to by the parties. If the duration of the contract is fixed, it will expire on the agreed date. Contracts limited in time will normally be

50 See Krag Jespersen, *Lejeret*, vol. 1, pp. 61–3 and Western High Court decisions of 3 Dec. 1976 (UfR (1977), p. 343) and of 4 June 2003 (UfR (2003), p. 2171).

51 The rule of UNIDROIT Principles Art. 5.1.1 and Principles on European Contract Law Art. 6:109 apply.

considered irrevocable.[52] If the land in question has a title number in the Land Register, the time limit may not exceed thirty years[53] (ten years if the land in question is part of a portion of land without title number) (Law on Subdivision of Land,[54] s. 16 and Law on Farms, s. 28).[55] The Law on Farms, s. 27 prescribes similar restrictions when a farm is rented in its entirety. The length of such a contract must not exceed thirty years. There are no formal requirements for the formation of the contract.

In the case of a *lease of a building for residential purposes*, the contract will be regulated by the Law on Private Housing[56] and the Law on Farms, ss. 27 and 28. The owner (A) will normally retain permanent residence on the farm (Law on Farms, s. 8). The lease can be for an indefinite period, in which case the tenant can terminate the contract by giving three months' notice, unless the parties have agreed that the contract is irrevocable or have agreed on a shorter or longer period of notice (Law on Private Housing, s. 81). The landlord (A) can terminate the contract by notice in only a very limited number of situations regulated by the mandatory and exhaustive rules of the Law on Private Housing, s. 83. The Law on Farms, s. 28(3) gives the landlord the opportunity to terminate the contract with a six-month notice if he/she needs the buildings for a permanent residence on the farm. The lease can be for a fixed period (Law on Private Housing, s. 80) but this can be overruled if the landlord's reasons for fixing the period are not justifiable (Law on Private Housing, s. 80(3)). If this happens, the lease would be for an indefinite term. The parties to a fixed-term contract can include a clause in the contract that the lease may be terminated by notice of a certain length of time. If the contract does not concern a farm in its entirety, the contract must not exceed thirty years (Law on Farms, s. 28(1)). No formal requirements are to be met for the formation of the contract, but it must be in writing if one of the parties insists (Law on Private Housing, s. 4(1)).

In the case of a *lease of a building for non-residential purposes*, the Law on the Lease of Commercial Premises[57] applies in combination with the

[52] See Gomard, *Obligationsret*, p. 17. This is not an operative rule but an assumption.
[53] According to court practice, it will suffice if it is possible to end the contract with thirty years' notice: see Eastern High Court decision of 26 Mar. 1998 (UfR (1998), p. 1011).
[54] Consolidated Act no. 494 of 12 June 2003 and later amendments.
[55] Consolidated Act no. 1202 of 9 Oct. 2007.
[56] Consolidated Act no. 188 of 27 Feb. 2007 and later amendments available, in an unofficial translation, at www.english.ism.dk/MinistryOfSocialWelfare/legislation/social_affairs/rent/Sider/Start.aspx.
[57] Act no. 934 of 20 Dec. 1999 and later amendments.

Law on Farms, ss. 27 and 28. The rules on termination of contracts for an indefinite period are very similar to the rules concerning lease for residential purposes (Law on Commercial Premises, ss. 60–3). However, the tenant will sometimes be entitled to compensation where the landlord terminates the contract on notice (Law on Commercial Premises, s. 66), but this rule is not mandatory. If the contract is for a fixed period, a rule identical to the rule under the Law on Private Housing, s. 80 is to be found in the Law on Commercial Premises, s. 63. If the contract does not concern a farm in its entirety, the contract must not exceed thirty years (Law on Farms, s. 28(1)). As in the other cases, there are no formal rules on the formation of the contract. However, the contract must be executed in writing if any party so demands (Law on Farms, s. 5).

In *combined contracts*, where the contract between A and B concerns land and buildings, the statutes concerning the lease of buildings will apply only if the buildings are the most essential part of the contract. The Law on Private Housing will apply if access to a residence is considered to be the most important part of the agreement. If the right of using buildings for other purposes is the major part of the agreement, the provisions of the Law on Lease of Commercial Premises will regulate the contract in its entirety. If the use of land is the substantial part of the contract, the Law on Farms regulates the relationship between the parties.

England

Under the common law, one speaks of ownership not of the land itself but of an 'estate in land'. Ownership of an estate in land entitles one to exclusive possession over that land for a period of time. After the enactment of the Law of Property Act 1925, only two forms of estate may be owned:

(a) the fee simple, absolute in possession (a right to exclusive possession forever – in practical terms, ownership); or
(b) a term of years absolute (a right to exclusive possession for a period of time).[58]

The latter is a '*lease*' in the English sense. It is by far the most common way in which time-limited interests are created over land today. In order

[58] Law of Property Act 1925, s. 1(1)(a) and (b).

for it to be a valid lease, the 'term' (length) of the lease must be certain. This can be achieved in two ways: either the lease is given for a set period of time or until a fixed date, after which the lease comes to an end, or it is granted in some smaller increment (a week or a month is common in residential lettings), which will recur until brought to an end by one of the parties. The former is a so-called 'fixed term' and the latter a 'periodic' tenancy. It is trite law that the lease must also grant the right to exclusive possession of the land (this is sometimes called the 'hallmark of the lease'). It would seem not to be essential, however, that rent be payable.[59]

When discussing leases, the distinction made between law and equity in English real property law, though largely irrelevant in our modern age of registration, becomes unavoidable. To understand this distinction, it is necessary to distinguish between three possible cumulative formality hurdles or stages which one might encounter when creating a lease. Parties to a lease may:

(a) enter into a contract to agree to the grant of the lease, which must be in writing (Law of Property (Miscellaneous Provisions) Act 1989 (hereafter LP(MP)A) s 2);
(b) transfer (or 'grant') the lease; and
(c) ensure any necessary publicity requirements are fulfilled (as to which, see below).

It is not necessary to contract to grant a lease, though it might suit the parties commercially to enter into a separate agreement to lease. These agreements are frequently encountered in commercial leases, for instance, where obligations are imposed before the commencement of the lease or are outside the remit of the landlord and tenant relationship. Accordingly, stage one may be totally bypassed. If, however, the parties do enter into a written contract complying with the Law of Property (Miscellaneous Provisions) Act, such a contract will be specifically enforceable at equity, and an equitable lease will have been created.[60] Most parties will not, however, undertake stage one without moving on to stage two, so that equitable leases are not frequently encountered in practice.

At stage two, a lease can be granted in two ways. The basic position is that a lease must be granted by deed (Law of Property Act 1925, s. 52). It is possible in limited circumstances to grant leases orally (Law of

[59] Law of Property Act 1925, s. 205 (xxvii). [60] *Walsh* v. *Lonsdale* (1882) 21 ChD 9.

Property Act, ss. 52(2)(d) and 54(2)). Leases may be granted orally (by 'parol') if they are leases for a term not exceeding three years at best market rent, reasonably obtainable without taking a fine. In practice, and for obvious pragmatic reasons, short leases are usually accompanied by a written agreement to evidence the terms thereof.

At stage three, one must distinguish between registered and unregistered land. In England, there are at present two systems of publicity available. The older (and much less important) system of unregistered land depends on presenting title deeds ('stage two documents') to prove ownership. Furthermore, those interests that are legal in nature bind the world. Those that are equitable bind everyone except the *bona fide* purchaser for value of a legal estate without notice. Excepted from that general category of equitable interests are so-called 'land charges', which must be placed on the Land Charges Register. This is a special register of burdens as specified in the Land Charges Act 1972. Equitable leases, being based on contracts for the sale of land, fall within Class C (iv) land charges, as defined in section 2(4) of that Act, and are void against third-party purchasers, unless registered as Land Charges (s 4(6)). Leases which have complied with stage two are legal leases in unregistered land, and bind the world.

With registered land, matters are rather different. Since 1926 (the year the Land Registration Act 1925 came into force), England has had a system of registered title, whereby the Register could be consulted by the public to see who owned what estate, and what rights and burdens were attached to such land. That system has been updated. Over 95 per cent or so of land in England is registered. In light of this, registered land will be concentrated upon. The matter is now dealt with under the new Land Registration Act 2002 in the following manner:[61]

(a) Equitable leases can be protected by placing notice thereof on the registered title of the land in respect of which they are granted (see generally ss. 32 ff.). If they are not so protected, it would seem that they can still bind if, at the time of the purchase, the owner of the equitable lease is in actual occupation of the land (Schedule 3(2)). Failure to do so renders the right unenforceable in any circumstances.
(b) Leases which have complied with any relevant stage two formalities, but which do not exceed seven years in term length, will bind

[61] See also s. 93 of the Act for the rules relating to electronic conveyancing, once this becomes the norm.

purchasers of the registered land even if not entered onto the Register (Schedule 3(1)).

(c) Leases over seven years will have to be registered under their own title (s 4(1)(c)). Failure to register means that the leases have no effect at law (s 27(2)(b)). They will then only have effect at equity, and must be protected in the same way as those rights in (a).[62]

There are a number of methods by which a lease can come to an end.[63] The main ones are:

(a) effluxion of time under fixed term tenancies;
(b) giving a notice to quit under a periodic tenancy;
(c) exercise of a 'break clause', that is the right, conferred by contract, to end the lease;
(d) forfeiture of the lease;
(e) surrender of the lease by the tenant to the landlord (an act requiring mutuality between the parties);
(f) frustration under the lease – though this will only occur very rarely; and
(g) disclaimer of a lease in the case of bankruptcy or insolvency.

It is important to note that the two methods of terminating leases in (a) and (b) above are seldom effective to bring the relationship of landlord and tenant to an end. This is because most leases today are governed by one or other statutory code.[64] These statutory codes generally aim to protect the tenant (by conferring upon him 'security of tenure'), so that the lease cannot be terminated by notice at common law, but only by a statutory notice, generally specifying some reason (a statutory 'ground' or 'case')[65] why possession is being sought by the landlord. Absent such a reason, no claim for possession may be sought.

The other significant termination method, and the only other one which requires elaboration, is forfeiture.[66] A well-drafted lease will

[62] As to which, see Bignell and Harpum, *Registered Land*, paras. 3–11 ff.

[63] The full law relating to the termination of tenancies is too complex to deal with here. Those interested in the minutiae are referred to Lewison, *Woodfall's Law of Landlord and Tenant*, paras. 17–21 to 17–96.

[64] Modern private residential leases: Housing Act 1988 (creating the assured and the assured shorthold tenancy); older private residential leases: Rent Act 1977; public residential leases: Housing Act 1985; business tenancies: Part II of the Landlord and Tenant Act 1954 (as amended); agricultural tenancies: a mosaic of statutes, but the Agricultural Holdings Act 1986 and the Agricultural Tenancies Act 1995 are often encountered.

[65] These vary from statute to statute, but rent arrears, misconduct by the tenant or some pressing need by the landlord can frequently be encountered.

[66] See Land Registration Act, s. 146 (for breaches other than non-payment of rent).

contain a 'proviso for re-entry', stipulating that the landlord may re-enter the premises (thereby ending the lease) for certain breaches specified in the proviso (but not for those left out). The law then distinguishes between forfeiture for non-payment of rent on the one hand, and for other breaches on the other. If the breach complained of is that rent has not been paid, the landlord may retake possession, provided the rent has been formally demanded (or the lease has dispensed with that requirement) and the tenant has been in arrears for at least six months.[67] Forfeiture for non-payment of rent is governed by section 146 of the Law of Property Act 1925. The effect of this is that, prior to re-entering, the landlord must serve a notice to give the tenant a reasonable time to remedy any breaches of covenant in so far as they are remediable. Disrepair is a remedial breach. Sub-letting contrary to a covenant is irremediable (and the only breach which is).[68]

Other use rights which give the right to occupy or otherwise exploit land can be dealt with more briefly. First, there are licences. These are essentially permission for others to be on the land. They may be bare permissions, or may be permissions strengthened by contract and subject to contractual remedies (most notably specific enforcement in some circumstances). They are not properly considered rights in land, however, and are merely personal in nature.[69] Further, a beneficiary under a trust of land may be permitted to occupy the land held on trust in certain circumstances.[70] While the beneficial interest is commonly thought to be an equitable property right, the right to occupy is contingent on the decision of the trustees exercising their discretion to permit it to be occupied. That occupation may then be time-limited in some sense. This is not a mechanism found in practice. Finally, the House of Lords[71] recently found that it is possible to have a purely contractual lease which does not confer an estate in land, but which does confer some right to exclusive possession, probably (but this is not settled) against the landlord. While the case has been viewed critically in England, it has not been overruled, but nor has it, to the knowledge of this writer, been applied.

An English institution similar to civilian usufruct[72] was introduced by the Settled Land Act 1882. This statute gave significant powers to a

[67] See County Courts Act 1984, s. 139; Common Law Procedure Act 1852, s. 210.
[68] *Scala House* v. *Forbes* [1974] QB 575. [69] See *Ashburn Anstalt* v. *Arnold* [1989] ch. 1.
[70] See ss. 12 and 13 of the Law on Trusts of Land and Appointment of Trustees 1996.
[71] *Bruton* v. *London and Quadrant Housing Association* [2000] AC 406.
[72] The editors are indebted to Dr Xu Lu from the University of East Anglia for this part of the English report.

'tenant for life' (or 'life tenant'), including sale, leasing, mortgaging and otherwise dealing with the land.[73] This interest, known as a 'strict settlement', was capable of being a separate legal estate at the time, independent of the fee simple estate held by the persons entitled to the property after their death. This was probably the closest to a proper liferent (or civilian usufruct) that English law has ever offered.

Some significant changes were introduced by the Birkenhead legislation of 1925, most noticeably the Law of Property Act 1925 and the Settled Land Act 1925. A strict settlement ceased to be a legal estate thereon and would have to take effect in equity.[74] The life tenant would have the legal estate vested in him/her and act as the trustee of the property,[75] holding it in trust for the benefit of the person entitled to it in remainder (that is, after the death of the life tenant). The life tenant was entitled to enjoy the profit and income from the property, or even to sell the property as the legal owner and trustee. His/her only obligation was owed to the beneficiary in accounting for the payment of capital money received.[76] The capital money was then treated as if this was the land in terms of its enjoyment during the life of the life tenant and its distribution after his/her death.

This form of strict settlement can no longer be created after January 1 1997, when the Trusts of Land and Appointment of Trustees Act 1996 came into force.[77] Because the previous form was essentially analogous to a trust, it was then merged with the other type of trust, a 'trust for sale', that existed before the above-mentioned Act. Settlements created before 1997 continued to be governed by the 1925 Act. The expectation was obviously that this concept will die alongside the life tenants. Therefore, after 1997, only one form of trust involving land can be created, namely the 'trust of land'. Whether the trustee is a 'life tenant' or not in the mind of the settlor who created the trust, is irrelevant, or at least not given any differentiating treatment by law. 'Trustees of land' have in relation to land all the powers of an absolute owner.[78] The

[73] Harpum, Bridges and Dixon, *Megarry and Wade: Property*, para. 10-006.

[74] Law of Property Act 1925, s. 1(1) only recognised two legal estates, namely the 'fee simple absolute, in possession' (freehold) and the 'term of years absolute' (leasehold). S. 1(3) provided that all other interests in land could only take effect in equity.

[75] Harpum, Bridges and Dixon, *Megarry and Wade: Property*, para. A-055. There are, however, 'trustees of settlement', which are quite distinct from the position of the life tenant as a trustee: see Settled Land Act 1925, s. 30.

[76] Settled Land Act 1925, s. 18. [77] s. 2(1).

[78] Trusts of Land and Appointment of Trustees Act 1996, s. 6.

'intended life tenant' would also certainly be a beneficiary entitled to the income of the property or the use of the property during his/her lifetime, while the other beneficiaries are essentially entitled to the property after his/her death. All such interests can be freely assigned or transferred as can any other equitable ownership of land.

An alternative to strict settlement/trust of land has always been possible by using an artificially long lease with a condition for its termination. An example will be a lease of a house granted to A for seventy-five years on a rent of £1 per annum, subject to termination by serving a one-month notice by the landlord if A dies before the end of the lease.[79] However, there are noticeable differences in using this method. A will never be the legal owner of the property. Furthermore, however little the rent is, he/she will still need to pay (although rent-free leases are not impossible according to one authority). A life tenant is the legal owner and does not have to pay anyone. Even only as a trustee in a trust of land created after 1997, he/she may possibly sell the land and such a disposition may well be binding without the consent or knowledge of other beneficiaries under certain circumstances.[80] A tenant, however long and lucrative his/her lease agreement is, obviously cannot act on behalf of his/her landlord with regard to the freehold title to the property. However, strict settlement was losing popularity even before its prospective abolition by the Trusts of Land and Appointment of Trustees Act 1996.

France

A may grant B a *lease*, a contract by which the landlord undertakes to grant the tenant the undisturbed enjoyment of the property for a given period of time in return for the payment of rent. The lease is tacitly renewed at the date fixed by the parties (Civil Code, art. 1738) unless the landlord has given notice to quit (Civil Code, art. 1739). This notice can be accompanied by a proposal for renewal, which then constitutes a new offer to lease which the tenant can accept or refuse.

[79] An example of a lease similar in form is provided by s. 149(6) of the Law of Property Act 1925 where a lease granted for the life of a person would be converted into a fixed term lease of ninety years terminable on the death of the person. This provision was intended to deal with leases granted for indeterminable terms but at a rent or for a fine (premium) before the commencement of the 1925 Act.

[80] Such as through the mechanism of 'overreaching', as provided by ss. 2 and 27 of the Law of Property Act 1925.

In principle, the tenant only has a personal right against the landlord. This remains true for leases subject to particular rules, such as residential and agricultural leases. However, certain immovable leases (such as the hereditary lease of land (*emphyteusis*)) confer on the tenant a real right in the immovable property leased.

Residential leases are governed by a great variety of legislation. At present, the lease of premises for use as a principal residence or for such use combined with professional use is governed by the mandatory provisions of Law 1989–462 of 6 July 1989, as amended by various more recent enactments such as Law 2009-323 of 25 March 2009. The residence subject to the lease must be in an acceptably good order and suitable for use as a dwelling (art. 6). The contract must be drawn up in writing (art. 3) and must, in particular, state the date when the lease will take effect, and its duration. With certain exceptions (leases accessory to a profession, seasonal leases, leases of furnished premises or leases of vacation residences), the contract must be concluded for a period of at least three years if the landlord is a natural person, a non-commercial family partnership or a co-owner, and at least six years if the landlord is a juristic person (art. 10). The lease is renewed tacitly for the same term if the landlord has not given notice to quit in the manner and within the periods set by law or has not made an offer with respect to its renewal. An exception (art. 11) is the case where the landlord is a natural person who would be justified to be restored in the residence for professional or family reasons when a specific event occurs. In that case, the parties can conclude a contract for a term shorter than three years but which must be at least one year.

The regime set by the general Law on Agricultural Leases or *Statut du fermage* (art. L 411-1 and following on the Rural Code) contains mandatory provisions which apply, save in the cases exempted by law, whenever agricultural land is placed at a tenant's disposal by onerous title for agricultural exploitation. In order for the tenant to secure a proper investment, it is mandatory that the duration of the lease should be at least nine years (tacitly renewable except where eighteen months' notice to quit has been given on a legal ground). In principle, an *agricultural lease* must be concluded in writing, but an oral agricultural lease is also deemed valid for a period of nine years.

The legislator encourages long-term leases by the following particular rules:

(a) If the duration of the initial lease is at least eighteen years, it is renewable for nine-year periods (art. L 416-1 amended by *Ordonnance* 2006-870 of 13 July 2006).
(b) If the duration of the initial lease is at least twenty-five years (art. L 416-3 amended by Ordonnance 2006-870 of 13 July 2006), the parties may agree that the lease may be renewed tacitly at its expiry, with no limit as to its new duration. Each party will then be able to decide each year whether or not to terminate the lease, with effect at the end of the fourth year after the notice was given. In the absence of a stipulation as to tacit renewal, the lease expires at the end of the agreed term, without the landlord being bound to give a notice to quit.
(c) The length of a long-term lease can also be fixed so as to permit the tenant to reach retirement age (art. L 416-4). Such a lease is called a 'career lease' when it has a term which exceeds twenty-five years and shall expire at the end of the year in which the tenant reaches retirement age (art. L 416-5).

Where the lease is for more than twelve years, the contract must be drawn up by a notary since the law contains a mandatory provision that it must be registered in the Land Register (*Décret du 4 janvier 1955 sur la publicité foncière* art. 28). Since the enactment of the *Loi d'orientation agricole* 2006-11 of 5 January 2006, the tenant can create a *fonds agricole* (Rural Code, art. L 311-3) by filing a declaration with the competent Chamber of Agriculture. The majority of the first *fonds agricoles* were equestrian centres, defined as agricultural, since 2005 (Rural Code, art. L 311-1, para. 1).

The legislator, in line with economic reality, regulates 'multi-year grazing agreements' for areas designated as mountain zones (Rural Code, art. L 481-1) in accordance with a special legal framework which differs from the framework under the Law on Agricultural Leases (*Statut du fermage*). This enables owners of agricultural property to lease their property to *Société d'aménagement foncier et d'établissement rural* (*SAFER*) (a *quasi*-governmental non-profit company which organises the use of rural land). The legislator also provides for partners to put agricultural property at the disposal of a partnership through a contract which is not categorised as a lease (Rural Code, art. L 411-2).

Certain leases are classified as 'atypical' because they confer a real right upon the tenant, because the tenant does not have exclusive use of the property, or because the tenant shares the fruits and crops of the land with the landlord.

The *hereditary lease of land* (*emphyteusis*), (Rural Code, arts. L 451-1 ff.), is not subject to the *Statut de fermage* and typified by its marked agricultural character and a small rental payment (the *canon emphytéotique*), yet it has come into urban use, accompanied by a more substantial rental payment, without this affecting its categorisation. It not only confers peaceable enjoyment of the immovable on the hereditary tenant but confers a real right, termed *emphyteusis*, which entitles the tenant to improve the land and to build on the land (*droit de superficie*). Although it is a time-limited interest, it has a long duration of between eighteen and ninety-nine years. This lengthy term allows the hereditary tenant to develop the land through cultivation and the construction of buildings.

The *lease for construction*, introduced by the law of 16 December 1964 (Code for Construction and Habitation (CCH), arts. L 251-1 ff.) is a lease under which the principal undertaking of the tenant is to erect buildings and other constructions on the land and to keep them in good condition for the entire duration of the lease (CCH, art. L 251-1). The tenant enjoys a real right comparable to *emphyteusis* (CCH, art. L 251-3), a time-limited building lease or surface right. The duration of the lease must be between eighteen and ninety-nine years (CCH, art. L 251-1, para. 3) without a right on the part of the landlord to give notice to quit during this period. The essential difference between this lease and *emphyteusis* is that the tenant in a lease for construction of buildings requires the payment of market rent as an essential counter-performance. The lease for construction is in essence a reincarnation of the Roman *superficies*.

The *bail à domaine congéable* (*usus*) confers on the tenant, in return for the payment of rent, the *right of use and enjoyment* of the land as well as a building right (surface right) for the purpose of raising livestock and growing fruit trees and vineyards. It is subject to the *Statut du fermage*, but is seldom used.

The *bail à complant* (vineyard lease) permits the tenant to plant a vineyard on the land of another at his/her own expense and to use and exploit it for the entire lifetime of the vines. This contract resembles the one described above by virtue of the rights it confers on the tenant, yet it is not subject to the *Statut du fermage* and is similar to a crop-sharing arrangement obliging the tenant to share his/her crop (wine or raisins) with the landlord.

The *bail à métayage* or sharecropping lease (*Black's Law Dictionary*) (Rural Code, arts. L 417-1 ff.), differs from other rural leases in that the tenant undertakes to farm on the condition that he/she shares the products of the farm with the landlord in place of payment of rent.

A can grant B a *usufruct* of his/her property (Civil Code, arts. 578 ff.). A usufruct can be established by law (for example, in favour of the surviving spouse) or by an intentional grant on the part of the owner. A usufruct is rarely conferred by onerous title such as sale and is generally conferred gratuitously by donation or by will. Usufruct is necessarily a time-limited interest: it expires on the term agreed on or upon the death of the usufructuary, whichever occurs first (Civil Code, art. 617). The duration of a usufruct granted to a juristic person may not exceed thirty years (Civil Code, art. 619).

The usufructuary has a real right in the property: the right of ownership is divided between the usufructuary and the nude owner, with the latter destined to become full owner at the end of the usufruct. The usufructuary has the right to use and enjoy the property and to take its fruits (*usus* and *fructus*) in the same way as the owner of the property, but on condition that its substance be preserved. The usufruct over residential premises or a farm allows B, as usufructuary, to occupy the premises or exploit the farm himself, or to lease out the premises or farm and appropriate the rent as civil fruits. Since a usufruct in land is recognised as a real right, it must be executed in a notarial deed and registered in the Land Register (Decree of 1955, art. 28) for it to be enforceable against third parties. The donation of a usufruct, like all donations of rights in land, requires for its validity the preparation of a notarial deed (Civil Code, art. 931).

Rights of use and habitation are constituted in the same manner as usufruct (Civil Code, arts. 625 ff.). They also expire on the death of the holder. They are, however, less substantial than the right of usufruct: they only permit the holder to use the property or to reside on the premises with his/her family. The rights of use and habitation are subject to the same formalities as the usufruct of land.

Loan for use is the gratuitous (Civil Code, art. 1876) loan of property which can be used without damaging it (Civil Code, art. 1874). If rent is stipulated, the contract is not one of loan for use, but of lease. The lender hands over the property to the borrower for use, subject to the obligation to return it after such use (Civil Code, art. 1875). The loan for use of land does not give rise to a real right which may be registered in the Land Register. The borrower only has a personal right; the lender remains full owner (Civil Code, art. 1877). Civil Code, art. 1888 specifies that the lender may reclaim the property only on expiry of the agreed term or, failing this, only after it has served the use for which it was borrowed. Civil Code, art. 1889, however, provides that even before such time the court may compel the borrower to return the thing to the lender if the lender can prove that he has an urgent and unforeseen need of the property. Initially, the *Cour de cassation* interpreted these two provisions in the case of the loan of an apartment in the sense that return of the apartment is only merited if it has been established that the need of the borrower has ceased or that the lender has an urgent and unforeseen need to reclaim his/her property.[81] However, the *Cour de cassation* has since reversed its position. Reasoning that the borrower's obligation to return the thing borrowed, after having made use of it, is the essence of a loan for use (Civil Code, art. 1875), the *Cour* decided that in the absence of an agreed foreseeable term in the case of a 'thing of lasting use' (including an apartment), the lender is entitled to end a loan for use at any moment, by giving reasonable prior notice.[82]

By this contract, the parties agree that the occupant shall only have a right of *precarious enjoyment* in return for a modest financial counter-performance. The precariousness of the enjoyment is characterised by the fact that the contract can come to an end at any time, whether by will of the owner or by the occurrence of an event contemplated by the parties. It is of no use to stipulate a term, since this contract is subject to interruption at any moment, without serving notice or owing any indemnity, even if it has lasted for a good number of years. The case law ensures that the aim of an agreement for precarious occupation is not to circumvent the mandatory provisions of the law in a fraudulent manner. Hence the compensation to be paid by the *precarist* must be modest to avoid the contract being re-characterised as a lease. If the contract allows the *precarist* to reside on the property, the case law looks to the intention of the parties and requires a legitimate reason to justify the non-application of legislation pertaining to residential leases. As for agricultural leases, art. L 411–2 of the Rural Code specifies the instances in which one may agree to a precarious occupation of agricultural land.

Germany

A can grant B a residential lease with regard to the residential property (*Wohnraummiete*) and an agricultural lease (*Landpachtvertrag* Civil Code, § 585) in respect of the farm.

[81] Civ. 1, 3 Feb. 1993; D 1994 248; Civ. 3, 4 May 2000; Bull. civ. III no. 97.
[82] Civ. 1, 3 Feb. 2004; Bull. civ. I, no. 34; Civ. 3, 19 Jan. 2005; Bull. civ. III, no. 12.

The lease of residential property is governed by the provisions of the contract of *lease* (*Mietvertrag*, Civil Code, § 535). *Mietvertrag* is a contract whereby the landlord undertakes to provide the tenant with the use of movable or immovable property during the term of the lease in return for the payment of an agreed rent. While writing is not a strict legal requirement for the constitution of a valid lease, lease agreements of immovable property are typically reduced to writing. The vast majority of *residential leases* (*Wohnraummiete*) are based on standard form contracts prepared by various homeowners' associations. The aim of these contracts is to deviate as far as legally permissible from the detailed set of 'tenant-friendly' rules contained in the German Civil Code. The law places no limit on the duration of a lease. A residential lease that is not in writing will be deemed to have been entered into for an indefinite period of time (German Civil Code, § 550). In practice, most residential leases are entered into either for an indefinite period or a fixed period of between one and five years. Under German law, a lease is not capable of registration in the Land Register (*Grundbuch*)[83] as the right of lease is not recognised as a real right. We shall see below, however, that although not strictly a real right, the right of lease does have certain proprietary effects.

Where the property concerned comprises a farm, an *agricultural lease* can be granted (*Landpachtvertrag* Civil Code, § 585), which is a special type of lease (*Pacht* Civil Code, § 581). The conceptual difference between a normal lease (*Miete*) and *Pacht* is that *Pacht* entitles the tenant not only to use the leased property but also to enjoy the fruits. *Pacht* and *Landpacht* are each subject to a set of special rules supplementing or superceding the general rules on lease.

A can grant B a *usufruct* (*Nießbrauch*) over the property (Civil Code, § 1030). Usufruct is a highly personal limited real right which entitles the holder to use another's property and to enjoy its natural and civil fruits (for example, to receive the rent if the property is let out). Writing is not required for an agreement to create a usufruct. However, since a usufruct is recognised as a limited real right under German law, registration in the Land Register is a formal requirement for its creation (Civil Code, § 873). The recording officer at the Land Register (*Grundbuchamt*) will only register the usufruct if the landowner's consent to the registration (*Eintragungsbewilligung*) is certified by a notary (Land

[83] In this regard German law differs from Swiss law (cf. Swiss Law of Obligations, arts. 260 and 282) and from Austrian law (cf. Austrian Civil Code, § 1095).

Register Code (*Grundbuchordnung*), § 29). It is not, however, necessary for registration to have the agreement itself executed notarially. A usufruct cannot extend beyond the lifetime of the usufructuary (Civil Code, § 1061).

A can grant B a *limited personal servitude* (*beschränkte persönliche Dienstbarkeit*) over the property (Civil Code, § 1090). The limited personal servitude entitles the holder to use the property in a specified way as agreed to between the parties. The right of habitation (*Wohnungsrecht*), namely the right to use a building or a part of a building as a residence to the exclusion of the owner, is specifically dealt with in Civil Code, § 1093. If the owner and the holder of the limited real right are both entitled to use the building (for example, where the right-holder is the owner's spouse), only a limited personal servitude can be granted according to Civil Code, § 1090. Like a usufruct, a limited personal servitude or a right of habitation cannot extend beyond the lifetime of its holder (Civil Code, §§ 1090(2) and 1061). Creation of these rights follows the same rules as those for the creation of a usufruct. In practice, *Wohnungsrecht* as well as *Nießbrauch* are often established in the context of *inter vivos* transactions between elderly people and their children in order to avoid or reduce inheritance tax. Under such an arrangement, the parents would convey their property to their children (transfer of ownership) and would in return be granted a usufruct or a right of habitation over the property.

A can grant B a permanent right of *habitation* (*Dauerwohnrecht*) in accordance with, § 31(1) of the Law on Apartment Ownership (*Wohnungseigentumsgesetz*) of 1951.[84] The main difference between this right and a limited personal servitude is that while the latter is a strictly personal limited real right, this right is transferable and transmissible to heirs (inheritable). Unlike the creation of a limited personal servitude, the creation of a permanent right of habitation requires the inclusion of certain mandatory provisions to regulate certain aspects of the right (Law on Apartment Ownership, § 32(3)). Again, registration in the Land Register (*Grundbuch*) is a formal requirement for the creation of the right.

[84] In addition to the permanent right of habitation (*Dauerwohnrecht*), the Law on Apartment Ownership (*Wohnungseigentumsgesetz*) also provides for a permanent right of exploitation (*Dauernutzungsrecht*), which affords a right to exploit a building for non-residential purposes (Law on Apartment Ownership, § 31(2)).

A can grant B a *loan for use* (*Leihe*) of the property (Civil Code, § 598). Unlike lease, a loan for use is gratuitous. It is created solely by an agreement between the parties with neither handing over of the property nor writing required. Loan for use merely creates contractual rights and as such cannot be registered in the Land Register (*Grundbuch*). Since it is almost never effective vis-à-vis third parties and is seldom used in relation to land, it will not be dealt with in this report.

A can grant B a *hereditary building right* (*Erbbaurecht*). A hereditary building right is a real right regulated by special subordinate legislation, namely the Regulations on Hereditary Building Rights (*Erbbaurechtverordnung*) of 1919. It gives the holder the transferable and heritable right to build or develop the land above or below the surface. In return, the landowner usually receives rent (*Erbbauzins*) for the duration of the right. The right may also be created in relation to existing structures on the land. The main effect of the right is that its holder becomes full owner of a structure built on someone else's land for the duration of the right. It therefore forms an exception to the general rule that the landowner owns all accessories, in particular structures, which are permanently attached to the land (Civil Code, § 94). Originally, *Erbbaurecht* was introduced in order to encourage people of modest income to build residential accommodation for themselves. People who could not afford to purchase the land were then in a position to become full owners of a structure built on their behalf on someone else's land. Today, this right is often used for complex arrangements in land development.[85]

By virtue of provisions on the sale of land, the agreement to create a hereditary building right must be executed notarially (Civil Code, § 311(1) and Regulations on Hereditary Building Rights, § 11(2)) and, as a recognised real right, it must be registered in the Land Register (*Grundbuch*) to be valid (Civil Code, § 873 and Regulations on Hereditary Building Rights, § 11(1)). The landowner's consent to the registration of the right (*Eintragungsbewilligung*), as in the case of usufruct, must be certified by a notary (Land Register Code, § 29). A building right must always be ranked first in the Land Register (Regulations on Hereditary Building Rights, § 10). Although there are no limitations as to the minimum duration of the right, a building right is typically created for a term of at least thirty years (very often for ninety-nine years). However, it can also be created for an indefinite term. When the hereditary building right expires, ownership of the structures passes

[85] See Cases 10–12.

automatically to the owner of the land. The holder of the hereditary building right is entitled to compensation.

Greece

A can grant B a *lease* of the property (Civil Code, arts. 574 ff.). Greek law draws a distinction between *ordinary leases* and *leases of agricultural land* or other fruit-bearing property. Unless otherwise regulated, the provisions on ordinary leases apply *mutatis mutandis* to agricultural leases (Civil Code, art. 620). As stipulated in the Law on Residential Leases (1703/1987 art. 1, § 3), the lease of residential property is regulated by the terms of the contract and the ordinary provisions on the lease of property (Civil Code, arts. 574–618), unless otherwise provided in the Law on Residential Leases. An ordinary lease is a contract by which the landlord undertakes to provide the tenant with the use of a property against payment of the agreed rent. A lease concluded for a fixed term terminates upon the expiration of such term without any formality. If the property is leased as a primary residence, the term of the lease cannot be fewer than three years. An agreement shortening the said term can be entered into only after at least six months have elapsed from the beginning of the contract and the agreement must be notarially executed (Law on Residential Leases 1703/1987 art. 2, § 1, as replaced by Law 2235/1994 art. 1, § 5). A lease for an indefinite period of time requires notice on the part of either of the parties to bring it to an end (Civil Code, art. 608). A lease concluded for a period of more than thirty years or for the lifetime of the landlord or the tenant is also terminable by notice of either party after the lapse of thirty years (Civil Code, art. 610). Where a residence is leased as a family home with the knowledge of the landlord, the landlord is not allowed to terminate the lease without notifying the spouse of the tenant on the same terms as required for the tenant (Civil Code, art. 612A).

Writing is not strictly required for the constitution of the lease.[86] However, a lease of immovable property for a period of more than nine years must be notarially executed and transcribed in the Mortgage Register for the lease to be effective against third parties (Civil Code, arts. 618 and 1208).[87] The vast majority of residential leases are based on standard form contracts prepared by homeowners'

[86] Filios, *Obligations*, p. 197; AP 1331/1976; NoV (1977), p. 931.
[87] Filios, *Obligations*, pp. 271–2.

associations. The aim of these contracts is to deviate as far as legally permissible from the rules of the Civil Code favouring tenants. Lease contracts are also drafted in writing to facilitate proof and for tax purposes since Greek tax legislation requires the presentation and deposit of a copy of the lease contract to the relevant tax authorities.

The Greek Civil Code distinguishes between two kinds of agricultural leases depending on whether the agreed rent is payable in money (Civil Code, arts. 619–40) or *in natura*, which is a share in the produce of the farm (Civil Code, arts. 641–7). In the first instance, the lease must be for a minimum of four years (Civil Code, arts. 619 ff.). If the lease is concluded for a shorter term, it will nevertheless remain valid for four years (Civil Code, art. 634). In the second instance, the crop-sharing contract allows the tenant to exploit the land against payment of a share of the produce. If not specified in the contract, the share is determined in accordance with local custom (Civil Code, art. 641). If such a lease has been concluded for the lifetime of the tenant-farmer or for a term exceeding ten years, the tenant-farmer shall have the right, after the lapse of ten years, to terminate the lease at the end of the harvest period after giving one year's notice. Any agreement to the contrary is not valid (Civil Code, art. 646).

A can grant B a *usufruct* (*Επικαρπία*, *Epikarpia*) over the property/farm (Civil Code, arts. 1142 ff.). Usufruct is a personal servitude which allows the holder to use and enjoy the fruits of the property of another without impairing the substance thereof. The contract creating a usufruct over immovable property must be executed in a notarial deed and must be transcribed in the conveyance records (as opposed to the mortgage records) in the Land Register (Civil Code, arts. 1143, 1033 and 1192).[88] The usufruct is extinguished with the death of the usufructuary or after a shorter term if so agreed. The usufruct constituted for the benefit of a legal entity is extinguished when that entity is dissolved (Civil Code, art. 1167).

A can grant B the personal servitude of *habitation* (*Οίκηση*, *Oikissi*) whereby the holder obtains the real and exclusive right to reside in a building belonging to another or to use a part thereof as a residence (Civil Code, arts. 1183 ff.) together with his/her family and the domestic personnel which corresponds to his/her social position (Civil Code, art. 1184). The right of habitation expires upon the death of the beneficiary (Civil Code, art. 1185). The general provisions governing the usufruct of

[88] The Greek legal system provides for the publicity of real rights on immovables. Thus conveyance records, mortgage records, books of claims and attachments are all kept, in the Conveyance and Mortgage Registers (art. 1 of Legislative Decree 4201/1961).

immovables apply by analogy to habitation, in so far as they are compatible with the nature of habitation (Civil Code, art. 1187).

The usufruct and the right of habitation are often established in the context of *inter vivos* transactions between elderly people and their children in order to avoid or reduce inheritance tax. Under such an arrangement, the parents would convey their property to their children and would in return be granted a usufruct or a right of habitation over the property.

A can grant B a *limited personal servitude* with regard to a residence or a farm. Such servitude would grant the holder the right to use the property in a certain way (Civil Code, art. 1188). As the content of the servitude can also be the content of a *praedial* servitude (Civil Code, art. 1188, para. 2), A can, for instance, grant B the right to use a certain road on the farm, to water and to let his/her cattle graze, or to cut wood on his/her farm (Civil Code, art. 1188, para. 2 in combination with Civil Code, art. 1120). In case of doubt, the extent of the limited personal servitude will be determined with regard to the personal needs of the holder (Civil Code, art. 1189).[89]

With the exception of L 3741/1929, which remains in force after the introduction of the Civil Code and which recognises exclusive ownership in an apartment or a floor, and co-ownership in all common parts of a block of flats, and LD 1024/1971, which recognises exclusive ownership in one or more individual buildings (or part thereof) built on common property, and co-ownership in all common parts, there is no mechanism in Greek Law similar to *superficies* because of the general rule that the landowner owns all component parts of the land, including particular structures and buildings that are permanently attached to the land (Civil Code, arts. 953 and 954).[90]

[89] The holder may be considered to be entitled to construct a building on the land encumbered with a usufruct, provided that the present economic purpose of the property is preserved (Civil Code, art. 1148). In such a case the ownership of the building is regulated by Civil Code, art. 955, § 1, sent. 2 (read with Civil Code, art. 953 *e contrario*), which provides that buildings and other structures erected on the ground by the holder of a real right are susceptible to real rights separate from those on the land (Karasis, in Georgiades and Stathopoulos, *GCC, Collective Analysis*, art. 1148, no. 10 (86); Dimakou, in Georgiades and Stathopoulos, *GCC, Collective Analysis*, art. 955, nos. 26 ff. (65–6)).

[90] The only exception to this rule is the one introduced by Civil Code, art. 955, which expressly provides that things attached to the ground for temporary purposes, though firmly fixed, as well as buildings constructed by a holder of a real right (e.g., a usufructuary), do not become component parts insusceptible of separate real rights.

A can grant B a *loan for use* (*Χρησιδάνειο*, *Chrissidaneio*) of the property (Civil Code, arts. 810 ff.). Loan for use is a gratuitous contract whereby a person hands over property to another for his/her use, subject to an obligation on the part of the holder to return the property when the contract expires. Writing is not required,[91] but delivery of the property is essential for the completion of a loan for use. A loan for use may be for a definite term. However, if no term has been fixed, the borrower must return the property after having used it, or when the time period in which he/she could have made use of the property has passed (Civil Code, art. 816). The position of the holder is very precarious as the lender may, where the lender himself/herself is in urgent and unforeseen need of the property, where the holder uses the property in a manner contrary to the contractual conditions, where the holder causes the property to deteriorate, or where the holder has unlawfully given the use of the property to another, reclaim the property even before it is due (Civil Code, art. 817).

Hungary

Hungarian law recognises time-limited rights in land that are *in rem* and *in personam*. The time-limited rights *in rem* are usufruct (*haszonélvezet*) and the right of use (*használat*), which are regulated by the Hungarian Civil Code (Civil Code, §§ 157–65). The time-limited rights *in personam* are leases in general and loans for use (*haszonkölcsön*). Leases include residential leases (*lakásbérlet*), which are partly governed by special legislation (Law on the Lease of Flats and Non-residential Premises and on Certain Provisions Relating to their Alienation, hereafter Law on Residential Lease) and income-producing leases (leases for profit, *haszonbérlet*), which in turn include leases of agricultural property (*termőföld haszonbérlete*), which are also governed by special legislation (Law on Lease of Agricultural Land).

The Hungarian Civil Code (Civil Code, §§ 423–33) contains provisions concerning the *lease* of residential and non-residential premises (*lakásbérlet*) in general, which is further mainly regulated in special legislation (Civil Code, § 434; Law on Residential Lease). It also contains provisions concerning the income-producing lease (lease for profit) (Civil Code,

[91] Filios, *Obligations*, p. 358; AP 672/2008; EllDni (2006), p. 1096; AP 463/2004; EllDni (2004), p. 1686; AP 170/2003; EllDni (2003), p. 137; Athens Court of Appeal, 10753/1991, no. V 1992, 574.

§§ 452–61), the *differentia specifica* of which relates to income-producing property, including agricultural land, which in turn is governed by a special law (Law on Lease of Agricultural Land).

Under an ordinary contract of lease, the landlord is obliged to transfer the use of the property to the tenant on a temporary basis in return for the payment of rent. The landlord warrants that the object of the lease will be suitable for the use stipulated in the contract for the period stipulated therein, and that no third person has rights related to the property that could disturb or exclude the tenant's use (Civil Code, §§ 423–4).

The tenant must use the property in a proper manner and in accordance with the provisions of the contract and is liable for loss caused by improper use (Civil Code, § 425(1)). The tenant usually must pay a deposit in advance and the rent on a regular basis. If the tenant fails to pay the rent, the landlord may terminate the contract with immediate effect, provided there was a written demand for the payment of rent which contains a warning in regard to the consequences of the failure to pay and which affords the tenant an appropriate period of grace. Rent cannot, however, be claimed for the period during which the tenant could not use the property due to a cause beyond his/her control.

The lease terminates upon expiry of the term stipulated, upon the emergence of circumstances provided for in the contract or if the leased property is destroyed (Civil Code, § 430). A lease for a fixed term cannot be terminated early unless there is a material breach of contract by the tenant.[92] The lease for an indefinite period of time[93] can be terminated with fifteen days' notice. However, in the case of a residential lease, the landlord cannot terminate the contract with less than three months' notice,[94] while the tenant may terminate the contract with fifteen days' notice at the end of the month (Law on Residential Lease, § 26). The law accords greater protection to the tenant of residential property owned by the state and regional government bodies.[95]

[92] The landlord can terminate the contract with immediate effect where the tenant uses the property in an improper manner or contrary to the stipulations of the contract or if the tenant does not pay the rent despite a request by the owner with the attendant grace period (Civil Code, §§ 425(2)(c)) and 428(2)).

[93] A lease for a fixed term converts into a lease for an indefinite time if after the expiry of the fixed term the tenant keeps on using the object of the lease without objection by the owner within fifteen days (Civil Code, § 431(2)).

[94] Law on Residential Lease, § 26(5).

[95] Until privatising the majority of these flats, it was a well-settled practice to 'sell' these 'rights of lease' as if they were rights in *rem* as the tenants were afforded protection

After the termination of the lease, the tenant must return the property to the landlord. In the case of land, the tenant is not allowed to retain possession of the property for claims against the landlord arising from the lease. In case of unlawful retention, the tenant is liable for all loss resulting from the retention. The tenant can remove, at his/her own cost and without impairing the property, improvements erected on the property (Civil Code, § 432(2)–(4)).

The leases of income-producing property and agricultural property (farmland) are treated as special types of leases. Under an income-producing lease, the tenant is entitled to use the property and collect its fruits for a period of time, in return for payment of rent which may be in cash or in kind. The general rules on lease apply to issues not governed by the provisions of the Civil Code on income-producing leases. Special legislation, which contains additional rules and provisions that derogate from the general rules concerning lease, applies to a lease of agricultural land (Law on Lease of Agricultural Land). There are, in principle, no formal requirements for the constitution of an income-producing lease (lease for profit). However, a lease of agricultural land must be reduced to writing.

The tenant can only use the property and collect its fruits according to the rules of normal management of the property. The tenant of agricultural property must cultivate the property in a proper manner and take care to maintain its productivity.

The rent is to be paid periodically or at the end of the term of the lease. If, in a given year, the property yields less than two-thirds of the average harvest, the tenant can claim an equitable reduction or waiver of the rent. The landlord must be notified of the claim prior to the gathering of the harvest. Reduction of the rent or its waiver cannot be claimed for previous years. The landlord has a lien on the fruits of the property and on the tenant's assets brought onto the property for outstanding rent.

An income-producing lease established for a fixed term can only be terminated in extraordinary circumstances that justify termination

resembling the status of an owner. If the owner of the residential property is the state or local government, the landlord can only terminate the contract on the basis of the grounds specified by the Law on Residential Lease where (a) the tenant does not pay the rent despite the grace period granted by the landlord, (b) he/she does not perform any other significant obligations undertaken in the contract, (c) the tenant or his/her cohabitant does not obey the norms of peaceful coexistence or they behave disgracefully, (d) the tenant or his/her cohabitant impairs or use improperly the common premises, or (e) the landlord offers a substitute flat, in exchange for the one concerned (Law on Residential Lease, §§ 24(1))and 26(6)). Special rules apply to leases of flats owned by local governments (Law on Residential Lease, § 26(7)).

with immediate effect. A general income-producing lease (lease for profit) established for an indefinite period can be terminated with one month's notice, whereas an income-producing lease of agricultural property can be terminated only with six months' notice and only at the end of the harvest period. In extraordinary circumstances the lease for profit can be terminated with immediate effect.[96]

Usufruct is a limited right *in rem*, in the sense that it draws on rights from the entire spectrum of property rights. The usufructuary is entitled to possess, use and collect the fruits of the property which is owned by another person. The rules of usufruct are to be applied *mutatis mutandis* to the usufruct of intangible property (for example, intellectual property, rights and receivables) (Civil Code, § 164(1)). During the existence of the usufruct, the nude owner can use the property and collect its fruits only to the extent that the holder of the usufruct does not exercise these rights (Civil Code, § 157(2)). Transfer of title to the property to a new owner does not affect the existence of the usufruct.[97]

Usufruct can be established for a fixed term but cannot last longer than the lifetime of the usufructuary (Civil Code, § 157(4)). Usufruct may be established by law, court order, administrative decision or contract, but will only be constituted validly upon registration in the Land Register. In the absence of registration, the usufruct can be enforced against the acquirer of the property only if he/she acted in bad faith or acquired the property without consideration (Civil Code, § 158).

Writing is not required for the constitution of a usufruct or a right of use over property. Rights, facts and data can, in principle, however, be entered into the Land Register, but only if they can be proved by a public

[96] The lease can be terminated with immediate effect if (a) the tenant impairs the property despite the warning of the owner or the property is gravely endangered, (b) the tenant does not cultivate the land concerned despite the warning of the owner or manages the property in a way that seriously endangers the efficiency of the production and productivity of the land, the livestock or the equipment, (c) the tenant does not pay the rent or the taxes within the period prescribed despite a request by the owner. If the tenant does not acknowledge the termination with immediate effect within three days the owner has recourse to the courts for a period of eight days. Where the owner fails to approach the court the termination with immediate effect expires. The claim for termination must be in writing (Civil Code, § 457). The heirs of the tenant can terminate the contract even if the deceased died less than six months before the end of the harvesting period but only thirty days after the deceased estate has been finalised (Civil Code, § 458). In case of an income-producing lease of agricultural property, the land is to be returned in a condition in which production can be continued immediately (Civil Code, § 460).

[97] Lenkovics, *A dologi*, p. 233.

deed, for example, a private deed countersigned by an attorney, or one approved by a final administrative or court decision (Law on the Land Register, § 8).[98] In theory, this provision concerning the Land Register does not affect the rule that a contract for establishing a usufruct or a right to use does not have to be in writing, since an oral contract can be still registered if it is supported by a deed specified in law. Accordingly, one of the parties to an oral contract may seek a declaratory judgment that the contract came into existence and this judgment can serve as a basis for entering the usufruct or the right of use in the Land Register. Notwithstanding this theoretical possibility, such oral contracts are unknown in practice, since they trigger a very burdensome procedure with a high level of risk in terms of proof.

The usufructuary is obliged to adhere to standards of ordinary management of the property (Civil Code, § 159(1)). He/she is obliged to inform the owner of any threatening danger or actual loss, including the case where a third person interferes with the exercise of his/her rights. Furthermore, the usufructuary is obliged to tolerate any measures taken by the owner to repair or to prevent damage to the property (Civil Code, § 159(3)).

Upon termination of the usufruct, the usufructuary has to return possession of the property to the owner. He/she is liable for any damage to the property unless he/she can prove that he/she managed the property as a reasonable person would. The usufructuary is not obliged to indemnify the owner for the decrease in the value of the property due to normal use. The usufructuary can dispose of assets susceptible of deterioration, equipment and livestock in accordance with the standards of ordinary management. However, he/she has to replace them when the usufruct terminates, and if this is not possible, he/she is obliged to reimburse the owner for their value.

The owner is entitled to control the way in which the usufructuary exercises his/her rights. The owner may demand security after unsuccessfully warning the usufrutary not to act in a particular way, if he/she discovers that the usufructuary is not using the property in a proper manner, impairs the substance of the property or endangers its return after the termination of the usufruct. If the usufructuary does not provide security, the owner can request the court to suspend the exercise of the usufruct

[98] 1997 *évi CXLI törvény az ingatlan-nyilvántartásról*, § 8 (Law no. CXLI of 1997 on the Land Register); Lenkovics, *A dologi*, p. 158.

until security is provided. The owner is also entitled to these rights against the successor-in-title to the usufructuary (Civil Code, § 161).

On the basis of the right of use, the usuary is entitled to use and collect the fruits of the property, but only in order to meet his/her needs and the needs of family members living with him/her. The right of use is highly personal and as such cannot be transferred to third parties. In all other respects, the rules of usufruct apply (Civil Code, § 165).

Loan for use is a gratuitous contract where the borrower is allowed to use the property for no consideration (Civil Code, §§ 583–5). The lender is obliged to transfer the use of the property temporarily and gratuitously and the borrower is obliged to return the property upon expiry of the loan for use. The lender can refuse to perform the contract if his/her own circumstances or the circumstances of the borrower change to the extent that he/she cannot be expected to perform the contract or if he/she is entitled to terminate the contract with immediate effect. The borrower must use the property properly and is liable for loss resulting from improper use or caused by use of the property in breach of the contract. The lender is entitled to the fruits of the property.[99]

The loan for use ceases to exist when the stipulated period expires or it is no longer necessary for the stipulated purpose, upon termination of the contract and the return of the property, upon the death of the borrower, or upon termination with immediate effect. If the loan for use is for an indefinite period, it may be terminated with fifteen days' notice. The lender's heirs can exercise the right of termination even if this would not otherwise be possible. The borrower can tender return of the property at any time and the lender cannot refuse to take back the property without reasonable justification.

The loan for use can be terminated with immediate effect if its purpose becomes impossible, if the borrower impairs the property, uses it improperly, abandons its use to a third person without the permission of the lender, where there is a danger that the borrower will not return the property in a sound condition, if the relationship between the parties breaks down due to the conduct of the borrower or if the lender needs the property for a reason not known to him at the time the contract was concluded.

[99] Nevertheless, ownership of the fruits is acquired only upon taking possession (Civil Code, § 125(1)).

Italy

A can grant B a *lease* (*locazione*) of the property (Civil Code, arts. 1571 ff.). Under a contract of lease, the landlord undertakes to provide the tenant with the enjoyment of property for a certain period of time in return for the payment of rent. If the lease has a term of more than nine years, it must be constituted in writing (Civil Code, art. 1350, no. 8). Where the object of a lease comprises the enjoyment of income-producing property, it is called a *hire* (*affitto*) (Civil Code, art. 1615) and is subject to slightly different rules. Generally, a lease cannot be granted for more than thirty years (Civil Code, art. 1573), but a lease of residential premises can be granted for the entire life of the lessee, and for two consecutive years after his/her death (Civil Code, art. 1607).

A can grant B a *usufruct* (*usufrutto*) over the property (Civil Code, arts. 978 ff.). Usufruct is a real right of use and enjoyment of property, subject to the obligation of preserving its economic destination. The duration of usufruct cannot exceed the life of the usufructuary. Writing is required for a contract constituting a usufruct (Civil Code, art. 1350, no. 2).

A can grant B a *right of use* (*uso*) or a *right of habitation* (*abitazione*) (Civil Code, arts. 1021 ff.). These real rights are similar to usufruct, but more limited in scope: the right of use (*uso*) entitles the usuary to use the property and, if it produces fruits, to collect the fruits to the extent necessary for his/her and his/her family's needs; the right of habitation (*abitazione*) entitles the holder to reside in the house. Writing is required for a contract constituting these rights (Civil Code, art. 1350, no. 4). Civil Code, art. 1026 stipulates that the provisions relating to usufruct apply, to the extent that they are compatible, to use and habitation. Unless otherwise indicated, all comments on usufruct are equally applicable to use and habitation.

A can grant B a *loan for use* (*comodato*) (Civil Code, arts. 1803 ff.). A loan for use is a gratuitous contract whereby the lender transfers property to the borrower for his/her use under the obligation to return it to the lender. Writing is not required, but handing over of the property is essential for the completion of the contract of *comodato*. If no term is specified, the borrower must return the property after he has used it for the purpose envisaged in the contract. In addition, the lender may reclaim the property before the due term where he/she finds him/herself in an urgent and unforeseen need of the property.

In the case of a farm, A can also grant B a *hereditary land lease* (*emphyteusis, enfiteusi*) (Civil Code, arts. 957 ff.), which is a long-term real right to use and enjoy the land as if it were owned outright in return for payment of rent. The essence of the right is an undertaking of the holder to improve the land. *Enfiteusi* cannot be granted for less than twenty years; it can be granted in perpetuity. *Enfiteusi* is seldom used in practice and most existing *enfiteusi* were created decades ago. This can be partially explained by the fact that the legislation is highly unfavourable to the owner (Law No. 607 of 22 July1966, Law No. 118 of 18 December 1970, Law No. 270 of 14 June 1974). It limits the rent that can be imposed and allows the *enfiteuta* to redeem the land by paying a modest sum. Since it is very seldom used, *enfiteusi* will not be dealt with further.

Another possibility may be a *hereditary building right* (*superficie*) (Civil Code, arts. 952 ff.) which allows the holder to erect and maintain a building above the soil of another and to acquire ownership of the structure. He/she can also transfer ownership of an existing building separately from ownership of the soil. The owner of residential property can transfer the *proprietà superficiaria* (ownership of the building but not of the soil) for a fixed term. On the expiration of the term, the owner of the soil also becomes the owner of the building. *Superficies* will be dealt with in Cases 10–12, which deal with its more typical use.

The Netherlands

Under a contract of *lease*, the landlord agrees to provide the use of movable or immovable property to the tenant in exchange for a counter-performance (Civil Code, art. 7:201). There are no formal requirements. Although the contract does not have to be in writing[100] and registration in the Land Register is not only not required, but even impossible, a lease is nonetheless enforceable against third parties.

The Law on Agricultural Lease (*Pachtwet*) defines an *agricultural lease* as any contract in any form, regardless of its heading, according to which one party commits itself to provide to the other party a farm or a piece of land in exchange for a counter-performance (Law on Agricultural Lease, art. 1 d). In the near future, the special Law on Agricultural Lease (*Pachwet*) will become part of the Civil Code. The definition of agricultural lease will be found in Civil Code, art. 7:311.

No formalities are required in order validly to enter into an agricultural lease.[101] This prevents the landlord from circumventing the

[100] Asser and Abas, 'Bijzondere Overeenkomsten', p. 11.
[101] Asser and Snijders, 'Pacht', pp. 23 ff.

protection provided to the tenant through non-compliance with formalities or by classifying the contract as something other than an agricultural lease.[102]

Pursuant to art. 12 of the Law on Agricultural Lease, an agricultural lease lasts for a fixed period of time – in the case of a farm, for twelve years (Law on Agricultural Lease, art. 12 I, in future, Civil Code, art. 7:325). It is possible to enter into a contract for a longer fixed period of time (Law on Agricultural Lease, art. 12 II), but a lease for a shorter term may only be concluded with the permission of the Agricultural Lease Department (*Grondkamer*) (Law on Agricultural Lease, art. 12 III). Such permission is only granted in specific circumstances and provided the public agricultural interest is not harmed. A contract for an indefinite term is void and will be converted into a contract of the statutory term, which, in the case of a farm, is twelve years.[103]

Apart from the right of *usufruct* (*vruchtgebruik*) (Civil Code, art. 3:201), there is also a specific type of the right of usufruct, namely the *right of use and habitation* (*het recht van gebruik en bewoning*) (Civil Code, art. 3:226).

The right of *usufruct* entitles the usufructuary to use the land of another and to enjoy its fruits (Civil Code, art. 3:201). This limited real right is very similar to the right of *emphyteusis*. The difference is that the latter can only be created with respect to immovable property whereas usufruct can be created with respect to movables, immovables and rights (Civil Code, art. 3:201 and 3:1). Usufruct expires on the death of the usufructuary (Civil Code, art. 3:203).

Apart from by will or by operation of law, usufruct comes into existence by agreement *inter vivos* or by prescription (Civil Code, art. 3:202). In order to create the right of usufruct, the following requirements must be met (Civil Code, arts. 3:98, 3:84 and 3:89). First, the creator of the right of usufruct must be entitled to do so (*beschikkingsbevoegdheid*). Secondly, there must be a valid legal reason justifying the creation of a right of usufruct (*geldige titel*) and, finally, a notarial deed indicating an intention to create the right of usufruct must be drawn up between the parties. This notarial deed must be registered in the Land Register.

A right of usufruct can also come into existence by means of prescription. The period of prescription is ten years where it concerns a *bona fide* usufructuary who had continuous possession of the right of usufruct (Civil Code, art. 3:99). However, where it concerns a *mala fide*

[102] Rodrigues Lopes, *Pacht*, pp. 28 ff.

[103] Asser and Snijders, 'Pacht', p. 72.

usufructuary, the *actio* will prescribe after a period of twenty years and the possessor will become the person entitled to the right of usufruct (Civil Code, art. 3:105).

The statutory provision (Civil Code, art. 5:101) describes the *hereditary building lease* (*superficies, opstal*) as a limited real right to erect and own buildings, works and plants on a parcel of land which belongs to someone else. In order to create a right of *superficies*, the same requirements as for the establishment of a usufruct must be met (Civil Code, arts. 3:98, 3:84 and 3:89). A right of *superficies* can also come into existence by means of prescription if the same requirements as for the acquisition of a usufruct by prescription are complied with (Civil Code, arts. 3:99 and 3:105).

The *hereditary land lease* (*emphyteusis, erfpacht*) entitles a person to develop the land of another by the erection of buildings or the planting of plants (Civil Code, art. 5:85). In order to create a right of *emphyteusis*, the same requirements as for the establishment of a usufruct or a hereditary building right (*superficies*) must be met (Civil Code, arts. 3:98, 3:84 and 3:89). A right of *emphyteusis* can also come into existence by means of prescription if the same requirements as for the acquisition of a usufruct or a hereditary building right (*superficies*) by prescription are complied with (Civil Code, arts. 3:99 and 3:105).

Poland

The first possibility is to create an ordinary *lease* by means of a contract in which the landlord assumes the obligation to give the tenant the use of the property for a fixed term or for an indefinite period of time and the tenant assumes the obligation to pay the landlord the agreed rent (Civil Code, art. 659, § 1).[104] The ordinary lease does not entitle the tenant to the fruits of the leased property and is in practice not applied to the lease of agricultural property (see the income-producing lease, discussed later). The lease of land or premises for a period exceeding one year must be reduced to writing. If this formal requirement is not observed, the lease is converted into a lease for an indefinite term (Civil Code, art. 660). In practice, many leases are made orally and not submitted to the tax authority in order to evade the tax on legal transactions. If the state should decide to tax lease contracts, the tax

[104] Act of 23 Apr. 1964, Dz.U.64, no. 16, item 93, with subsequent amendments.

authorities will require it in written form, regardless of the requirements posed by civil law.

The maximum term for a lease is ten years. Such a lease may only be terminated by the parties if the contract specifies the reasons for and the ways in which the lease may be terminated (Civil Code, art. 673, § 3). If the parties contract for a term of more than ten years, the contract is deemed to have been made for an indefinite period of time after the lapse of ten years (Civil Code, art. 661), which in essence means that each party may give notice and terminate the lease after that. Notice periods may be agreed on by the parties. If none was set, the Civil Code supplies specific statutory notice periods (Civil Code, art. 673, § 2).

The above are general rules on leases and apply to residential leases unless special statutes (*legi speciali*) state otherwise. The Law on Protection of Tenants, the Law on Residential Stock of Local Governments and the Amendment of the Civil Code Act 2001[105] generally apply to residential leases and to all instances where residential premises are used (excluding the lease of hotel rooms and other accommodation for tourist or recreational use). The most important difference between these specific laws and the general rules on lease concerns the possibility of terminating a residential lease in accordance with specific notice periods. The specific rules state that if a tenant who pays rent is not in breach of the contract, the landlord may terminate a lease for an indefinite period with either six months' notice if the tenant is entitled to use other premises or the landlord supplies him/her with alternative accommodation, or three years' notice if the tenant is not entitled to use another premises or the landlord does not supply him/her with alternative accommodation, and if the landlord intends to live on the premises himself/herself (Civil Code, art. 11).

If the lease concerns land (or a part thereof) for which a Register is available (which is usually the case), it may be registered in that Land Register. Article 16, § 1 of the Law on Land Register and Mortgages 1982 (LRM),[106] provides that personal rights and claims may be registered. Such registration causes that right (or claim) to be effective against rights acquired subsequent to registration through legal transactions, but not against a way of necessity or encroachments of buildings or structures on neighbouring land (LRM, art. 17). This provision is particularly important to tenants: if the landlord sells the leased property, the

[105] Law of 21 June 2001, Dz.U.05, no. 31, item 266, text with amendments.
[106] Law of 6 July 1982, Dz.U.01, no. 124, item 1361, with subsequent amendments.

purchaser takes the place of the landlord, but with the ability to terminate the lease by serving notice in accordance with the statutory notice periods. If, however, the lease was for a fixed term and reduced to writing and the lessee has entered into possession of the property, the purchaser may not terminate the lease (Civil Code, art. 678).

If the tenant of a residential premises dies, his/her place is taken by his/her spouse, his/her children and the children of the spouse, a cohabitee of the lessee and persons to whom the lessee was obliged to pay alimony. The above become tenants only if they permanently occupied the premises with the tenant until his/her death. They may terminate the lease by serving notice within the statutory notice periods, even if the lease was created for a fixed term (Civil Code, art. 691).

The Civil Code also provides for an *income-producing lease* (*fruendi lease*) on fruit-bearing or income-producing property, which, compared to the ordinary lease, has an additional element entitling the tenant not only to use the leased property but also to collect and utilise the fruits it produces (Civil Code, art. 693, § 1). The income-producing lease applies to movables and immovables which bring forth fruits as well as to rights which generate 'fruits' (profits). Apart from a number of special provisions which only apply to income-producing leases (Civil Code, arts. 693–709), the general provisions on ordinary leases apply *mutatis mutandis* to income-producing leases (Civil Code, art. 694).

The maximum term for an income-producing lease is thirty years. If the term of the lease is for more than thirty years the contract, following the lapse of the thirty year period, is deemed to have been made for an indefinite term (Civil Code, art. 695), which in essence means that each party is entitled to terminate the lease simply by giving notice. The statutory notice period for terminating an income-producing lease of agricultural land is one year before the end of the lease and in all other cases six months before the lapse of the lease year. The parties may agree on other notice periods.

It is also worth noting that Civil Code, art. 708 provides for the creation of *a right similar to an income-producing lease*. This innominate right relates to agricultural land and is rent free, but the person entitled is obliged to pay taxes and other expenses connected with the ownership or possession of land. This right is regulated by the rules on both income-producing leases and loans for use. The provisions of the Land Register and Mortgages Act on registration mentioned above apply here as well. Both types of leases and the innominate right described in Civil Code, art. 708 are personal rights based on contract but upon registration, their effectiveness is similar to that of real rights. LRM, art. 31, § 1 requires that an entry in the Register must be made on the basis of a written document with signatures certified by a notary, unless special provisions require a more stringent form (which is not the case for leases and art. 708).

A can grant B a *usufruct* of the property in question (Civil Code, art. 252) by virtue of which an encumbrance is created on the property of another which entitles the usufructuary to use the property and to reap its fruits. Note that under Polish law a usufruct is a separate limited real right and not a kind of personal servitude such as, for instance, the right of habitation. Note further that it is mainly created through a contract concluded between the parties. A usufruct may relate to movables, immovables and rights capable of being transferred which produce fruits or income. It may be established gratuitously or for value and for a fixed or an indefinite term.

The content of the right resembles the *fruendi* lease, but the latter always gives rise to a personal right and is always for value (rent). Also, as a rule, it is possible to transfer the *fruendi* lease, whereas usufruct as such is non-transferable and intransmissible. The usufructuary is, however, entitled to allow another person to exercise the right on the basis of, for example, a lease or loan for use. The usufruct terminates at the death of a natural person or dissolution of a legal person. Therefore, unlike the *fruendi lease*, which is aimed at satisfying commercial or economic needs, the purpose of usufruct is to satisfy the needs of a more personal type such as providing financial support to a family member. It is usually created with respect to land, particularly agricultural land.

To create a usufruct, the owner is required to state his/her intention in the form of a notarial deed. However, the usufructuary's acceptance of the usufruct does not require any particular form (Civil Code, art. 245, § 2). Both parties usually appear before a notary and the whole contract takes the form of a notarial deed. Usufruct may, but does not have to be, registered. If it is, it will be effective against future purchasers of land, who will not be able to argue that they were in good faith and were not aware of the existence of the usufruct.

A can grant B a *personal servitude* (Civil Code, art. 296). A personal servitude, for instance, the right of habitation, relates to immovables only and entitles the holder to use the property in a specified way agreed to by the parties. It burdens the immovable property in question and is a limited real right. It may be created gratuitously or for value, and for a fixed or indefinite term. The content of a servitude is not as wide as that of a usufruct. The holder of a personal servitude may perform only specified actions with regard to the immovable property, for instance, use it or inhabit a dwelling on the land. He/she may not use and reap the fruits of the property like the holder of a usufruct. Thus Polish personal servitudes resemble the institutions of use and habitation encountered in other jurisdictions.

A personal servitude is created in the same manner as a usufruct (Civil Code, art. 245, § 2) to fulfil the personal needs of a given person. Therefore, it is not transferable and may not be exercised by anyone other than the holder himself/herself (Civil Code, art. 300). A personal servitude cannot persist beyond the death of the holder (Civil Code, art. 299). A special type of a personal servitude is the servitude of habitation regulated in Civil Code, art. 301. Without any express definition in the Civil Code, one must assume that it entitles the holder to inhabit a dwelling together with his/her spouse, minor children, other dependants and domestic servants (Civil Code, art. 301, § 1). Children who resided with him/her as minors may remain in the dwelling after reaching adulthood. It is interesting to note that Civil Code, art. 301, § 2 stipulates that the parties may agree that upon the death of the holder the servitude of habitation will pass to his/her children, parents and spouse. Just like usufruct, the right of habitation may, but need not be, registered with the same effects if registered.

A very interesting contractual right[107] that A may grant B is a *lifetime habitation*. This right is created through a contract of sale by virtue of which the seller (B) transfers the ownership of immovable property (land) to another person (A) and in return the latter undertakes to take the seller (B) into his/her home and provide him with food, clothes, accommodation, energy and heating, care in times of illness and to organise and pay for his/her funeral. Additionally, the person who acquires the land may be obliged by a provision in the contract to create a usufruct or a right of habitation or provide money or things designated in kind (Civil Code, art. 908). Since the above-mentioned contract contains the obligation to transfer land, it must be executed in a notarial deed (Civil Code, art. 158).

[107] A lifetime habitation is a mere contractual right, which in effect encumbers immovable property in the same way as a limited real right. However, since a *numerus clausus* of real rights are recognised in Poland, a lifetime habitation cannot be classified as a limited real right.

The right under a lifetime habitation is strictly personal and therefore not transferable or transmissible on death. Since it burdens land, the provisions on limited real rights are to be applied analogously (Civil Code, art. 910). Like many of the limited real rights it may be, but does not have to be, registered. Although it is created simultaneously with the transfer of land, the notary is not obliged to file for the registration of a lifetime habitation. In practice, many notaries would offer the client their services in filing for registration of a lifetime habitation or at least inform them of such a possibility. However, even without registration, it will be effective against a purchaser of the immovable who was in good faith (LRM, art. 7.2).

The state or a local authority can grant B a *perpetual usufruct* (an adapted *superficies*) with regard to its land. This right is regulated in Civil Code, arts. 232–43 and also in various provisions of the Law on Management of Real Property 1997 (LRM).[108]

A perpetual usufruct of land is a real right to exploit the land of another, usually through the erection of buildings in return for the payment of a yearly rent. The scope of the right is limited by statutory provisions, rules of socio-economic justice and by contractual provisions, which usually confine the enjoyment of land to specified purposes or contain other constraints agreed to by the parties. Perpetual usufruct is, unlike personal servitudes, alienable and transmissible. It may be sold, mortgaged or transmitted to heirs.

If the scope of the perpetual usufruct allows for the erection of buildings on the land of another, the holder of the right will become the owner of the buildings that he/she erected for the duration of the perpetual usufruct. Such ownership is, however, linked to the perpetual usufruct of the land which means that the buildings may only be transferred together with the perpetual usufruct and vice versa.

The dual ownership of the land and the buildings on the land can be explained historically. Perpetual rights to land were originally created in order to allow the State to make urban land available to citizens for residential development. The State did not, however, wish to transfer ownership of land into private hands, as this was contrary to socialist ideology. On the other hand, citizens needed some security of title to persuade them to invest their own money in building a house. Perpetual usufruct was a compromise which allowed the State to retain ownership

[108] Act of 21 Aug. 1997, text with amendments, Dz.U.00, no. 46, item 543, with subsequent amendments.

of the land, while simultaneously granting ownership of completed buildings to the perpetual usufruct holders. The combination of ownership of the building with a perpetual usufruct is in practice regarded as sufficient security of title to encourage housing developments.

Perpetual usufruct may be attached in execution for the non-payment of debts. Perpetual usufruct may be created for a maximum term of ninety-nine years and a minimum term of forty years. The usufruct holder is entitled to ask that his/her right be prolonged for another term. The owner may only decline due to an important social interest (for example, a pending public purpose investment requiring expropriation). After expiry of the right, the building and other improvements revert to the owner, namely the State or local authority, leaving the perpetual usufructuary with a claim for compensation for the value of the buildings and other improvements constructed by him/her. Perpetual usufruct is popular among developers for gaining access to land which belongs to the State or other public authority. This land is frequently attractively located, but not designated for sale. The perpetual usufruct is created by a notarially executed contract and comes into existence on registration in the Land Register.

A can grant B a *loan for use* of the property (Civil Code, art. 710). This right is created through a contract in which the lender allows the borrower the gratuitous use of property for a certain purpose for a fixed or an indefinite term. If the contract was concluded for an indefinite term, the loan will come to an end once the borrower has made use of the property for the purpose for which it was lent or when the time during which he could have made such use, elapses (Civil Code, art. 715). Unlike a lease, a loan for use is gratuitous and requires transfer for its validity. A loan for use creates personal rights but, just as is the case with a lease, it may be registered (LRM, arts. 16, 17 and 31). This means that a registered loan for use will be effective against third parties who acquire rights to land subsequent to the registration of a loan for use. In practice, a loan for use is commonly employed for the loan of residential premises. It is possible to create a variation of this right by requiring the borrower to cover maintenance and management expenses connected with the premises instead of paying rent.

Portugal

A can grant B a *lease* (*locatio*) of the property governed by the provisions of the Portuguese Civil Code (Civil Code, arts. 1022–63) (see the chapter in *Special Contracts under the Law of Obligations* in this series). A lease is a contract whereby one party (landlord) grants another party (tenant) the use of property for a certain period of time in return for payment of rent. The essential terms of a contract of lease are the identification of the parties and the property to be leased and the payment of rent. A distinction is made between leases of movables and leases of immovables. Leases of urban immovables (*arrendamento*) are governed by the Portuguese Civil Code (Civil Code, arts. 1064–113).[109] Agricultural and forestry leases are now regulated by Decree-Law 294 of 13 October 2009, which replaced the old regime of agricultural[110] and forestry [111] leases.

The contract of lease must be in writing if it is to last more than six months (Civil Code, art. 1069). Registration in the Land Register is required to make leases of residential, commercial, industrial or professional premises lasting more than six years enforceable against third parties. Leases of other premises lasting less than six years need not be registered to be enforceable against third parties.

A contract of lease of agricultural property is usually reduced to writing and a copy thereof must be delivered to the Tax Office and the Regional Department of the Ministry of Agriculture within thirty days after conclusion of the lease (Decree-Law 294/2009, art. 3). Agricultural leases need not be registered and no administrative fees are payable (Decree-Law 294/2009, art. 6).

Portuguese law, in general, does not allow leases for a term of more than thirty years. A clause purporting to allow a 'lease for life' or a lease exceeding thirty years would be void but would not invalidate the entire contract. The term of the contract would simply be reduced to the thirty-year limit (Civil Code, art. 1025). An exception is made in the case of forestry leases, which may be concluded for a term of between seven and seventy years (Decree-Law 294/2009, art. 9(1)). Agricultural leases must be concluded for a term of at least seven years (Decree-Law 294/2009, art. 9(1)) and is renewed automatically if none of the parties gives notice of termination (Decree-Law 294/2009, art. 9(3)).

A lease of urban dwellings can be time-limited (*contratos com prazo certo*). However, it cannot last less than five years or more than thirty years (Civil Code, art. 1095). Only if the contract is for transitory purposes, such as tourism or education, no minimum duration is required. At the end of the fixed period, non-transitory leases are automatically

[109] Replacing Law 6/2006 of 27.02 (NRAU). [110] Replacing Decree Law 385/88 of 25.10.
[111] Replacing Decree Law 394/88 of 8.11.

renewed (for successive three-year periods) if neither of the parties gives notice of termination (Civil Code, art. 1096).

If parties do not fix a time-limit for the contract, it is considered to be of indefinite duration (*contrato de duração indeterminada*). The parties concluding commercial, industrial or professional leases can freely agree on the duration of the lease and, if not fixed, the duration is set at ten years (Civil Code, art. 1110(2)).

A lease will terminate on expiry of a fixed term (*caducidade*),[112] by mutual agreement (*revogação*) or by notice based on a specific cause prescribed by law. To prevent the automatic renewal of fixed term leases, the landlord must notify the tenant and the tenant the landlord at least one year or 120 days respectively, before the end of the term.

A distinction is made between an 'ordinary' (*resolução*) and a 'specific' notice (*denúncia*). An 'ordinary' notice is appropriate where the material breach of a contractual term destroys the relationship between the parties to such an extent that it is not just and reasonable to expect the other party to continue the relationship (Civil Code, art. 1083). 'Specific' notice is required in cases where the landlord has an objective and legitimate interest in the termination of the lease contract (for example, where the landlord needs the premises for his/her own use or for that of his/her family or where he/she wants to rebuild or restructure the premises). Specific notice (*ad nutum*) is only possible in leases concluded for an indefinite term. Specific notice by the landlord will become effective five years later (which is the minimum duration for an indefinite term lease). The tenant may give specific notice by advance notice of at least 120 days before termination.

Portuguese academic opinion is divided on the question of whether a tenant acquires a real or property right on entering into possession of the leased premises or land. The minority view is that he/she does acquire a property right enforceable against the world.[113] The majority view is, however, that he/she acquires only a relative contractual (personal) right.[114] The latter view, supported by case law, led to the conclusion that since the lease creates purely contractual rights, the landlord need not be the owner of the leased property and that persons with the right to administer the property are capable of establishing leases

[112] Garcia, *Arrendamento Urbano*, pp. 206 ff.

[113] Oliveira Ascensão, *Direito Civil*, p. 519; Menezes Cordeiro, *Direitos Reais*, p. 689; Pinto Futardo, *Direitos Reais*, p. 161.

[114] Mesquita, *Obrigações Reais*, pp. 131 ff.; Coelho, *Arrendamento*, pp. 205 ff.; Pires de Lima and Autunes Varela, *Código Civil Anotado*, vol. 3; Pinto Furtado, *Manual*, p. 64.

with regard to that property.[115] Despite the non-proprietary nature of the right of the tenant, the latter's right is strongly protected by the law. Civil Code, art. 1037 accords a tenant the same protection as a possessor by extending the remedies for disturbance or deprivation of possession to the tenant.[116]

A may grant B a right of *usufruct* (*direito de usufruto*) over the property. Usufruct is a real right that entitles the usufructuary to use the property and to take its fruits without impairing its form or substance (Civil Code, art. 1439).[117] A usufruct can be created by contract, by last will, by adverse possession (*usucapio*) or by legal provision (Civil Code, art. 1440). The usufruct cannot exceed the lifetime of the usufructuary or endure for more than thirty years if the usufructuary is a company, an association or a charity (Civil Code, art. 1443). A usufruct automatically expires on the death of the usufructuary, on expiry of its term, or where the usufructuary acquires ownership of the property in question. Renunciation by the usufructuary (Civil Code, art. 1476), non-use of the property for a period of twenty years or complete destruction of the property will also bring the right to an end. For a usufruct to be enforceable against third parties, it must be embodied in a written deed (*escritura pública*) executed by a notary, or in a private document certified by a notary (*documento particular autenticado*),[118] and registered against the title deeds of the servient property.

All the provisions mentioned above are mandatory.

A can grant B the real *right of use and habitation* (*direito de uso e habitação*) over the property. The right of habitation concerns the use of a dwelling (Civil Code, art. 1841 no. 2). The right of use entitles the usuary to use the property and to take its fruits but only to satisfy personal and family needs (Civil Code, art. 1484 no. 1) determined by reference to the holder's social and economic status (*condicão social*) (Civil Code, art. 1486). The family of the holder of the right includes his/her partner, unmarried children, other relatives to whom the usuary owes maintenance and employees living with him/her (Civil Code, art. 1487).

The right of use and habitation can be created by contract, by last will or by legal provision. Unlike usufruct, however, it cannot be acquired by

[115] The lease will nevertheless expire along with the principal right (Civil Code, art. 1051).

[116] Mesquita, *Obrigações Reais*, pp. 148 ff.

[117] Unless otherwise indicated, all the provisions refer to the Portuguese Civil Code, approved by Decree 47344 of 25.11.66 and came into force on 01.06.67.

[118] Art. 22 of Decree-Law 116/2008 of 24 July.

adverse possession (Civil Code, art. 1485). The rules on the termination of a usufruct apply equally to the right of use and habitation (Civil Code, art. 1485).

For a right of use and habitation to be enforceable against third parties, it must be embodied in a written deed executed by a notary, or in a private document certified by a notary (*documento particular autenticado*),[119] and registered against the title deeds of the servient property.

The rules mentioned above are also mandatory.

A can grant B a *hereditary building lease* (*direito de superfície*). The right of *superficies* entitles the holder to erect a building or to plant crops and trees (in the case of a farm) (*construir uma obra ou fazer plantações*) on another's property, perpetually or for a certain period of time. This also comprises the right to retain and use (*manter*) existing buildings, crops or trees on the land (Civil Code, art. 1524). The right of *superficies* can be created by contract, last will or adverse possession as well as by alienation of a building or trees on the property separately from the soil (Civil Code, art. 1528). When created by the State or other public authority, the holder of the right may be subjected to specific obligations (Civil Code, art. 1527).[120] There is no legal limit on the duration of a right of *superficies*. The right of *superficies* expires if the holder does not complete the building or the planting before the time limit set by the parties or before the legal limit of ten years. Termination will also occur where the building or trees are destroyed without being restored, on expiry of a fixed term, on the holder acquiring ownership of the property, when the soil no longer yields fruits (becomes infertile), or if a public authority expropriates the property (Civil Code, art. 1536).

For a right of *superficies* to be enforceable against third parties, it must be embodied in a written deed executed by a notary, or in a private document certified by a notary (*documento particular autenticado*),[121] and registered against the title deeds of the servient property.

[119] *Ibid.*

[120] Decisions of the Supreme Court of Justice of 29.10.1999 [Process 98B682] (a right of *superficies* was granted by the City Council to develop an industrial area); of 4.10.1995 [Process 087611] (a right of *superficies* was created, in favour of an association aiming to help handicapped children); Decisions of the Administrative Supreme Court of 31.10.2001 [Process 046777] (the City Council created a *superficies* right, in favour of a housing co-operative); and of 5.7.1994 [Process 033571] (the City Council created a right of *superficies* entitling the holder to build a kindergarten), all available at www.dgsi.pt.

[121] Art. 22 of Decree-Law 116/2008 of 24 July.

A can grant B a *loan for use* (*commodatum*). The *commodatum* is a gratuitous contract by which one party lends property to another, subject to the obligation to return the property after use (Civil Code, arts. 1129–41). Writing is not required, but handing over the property is essential for the completion of the contract of *commodatum* (*real quod constitutionem*).

A loan for use may be concluded for a fixed term or for a certain purpose. In the case of non-completion, the property may be reclaimed only on the basis of an objective and just ground such as an urgent and unforeseen need for the property. However, where the property is lent for an indefinite term, the contract is terminable at the will of the lender (Civil Code, art. 1137 no. 2). Portuguese law does not draw a distinction between a *precarist* whose holding of the property is revocable at the will of the lender and an ordinary borrower for use. Both contracts are governed by the same provisions.

Loans of urban premises or rural land are, except among relatives, not common in Portugal.

Scotland

There are three ways in which this can be achieved. The first is where A grants B a lease of the property. The second is for A and B to enter into some contract which confers a less complete right upon B than a lease does. Typically this is known as a 'licence'. The third possibility is for A to grant B a liferent of the property.

A *lease* is a contract by which one person (the landlord) grants and another (the tenant) accepts the possession of property for a period of time in return for payment of a periodical payment (rent).[122] There is a general law of leases (mostly, but not exclusively, common law) which applies to all leases. This is supplemented by various statutory 'special regimes', which apply to leases of certain types of property and give effect to policy considerations particular to that type of property. Both residential and agricultural property is subject to such special regimes and they will thus be considered in this report.

There are four 'cardinal' elements to a contract of lease: the parties, heritable (immovable) property, rent, and duration (or 'term').[123] The

[122] For various modern attempts at a definition, see Rankine, *Leases*, p. 1; Paton and Cameron, *Landlord and Tenant*, p. 5; McAllister, *Leases*, p. 1.

[123] Paton and Cameron, *Landlord and Tenant*, p. 5; *Gray* v. *Edinburgh University* 1962 SC 157 (IH) 162.

rent need not be monetary and can be nominal (a 'peppercorn rent') but there must be a periodical payment and not only a one-off payment at the beginning of the contract (a 'grassum').[124] There can be both a rent and a grassum. The term of a lease need not be definite: it can be granted for an indefinite period or until the occurrence of an event.[125] A lease executed on or after 9 June 2000 has a maximum duration of 175 years.[126] Although the point is not entirely free from doubt, the right must most likely be to the exclusive possession of the land in order to amount to a lease. A contract which confers only certain uses of the land will not qualify.[127]

The exact content of the right differs depending upon which type of property is leased. In general, the landlord must place the tenant in possession of the property[128] and maintain him/her in possession, do nothing and, in so far as he/she is concerned, allow nothing to be done to oust the tenant from possession.[129] In return, the tenant is bound to enter into possession of the property on the date of entry and remain in possession during the lease.[130] The tenant is bound to take reasonable care of the property[131] and to pay the rent.[132]

In order to terminate the lease, even on its contractual termination date (the 'ish'), either the landlord or the tenant must serve a notice to quit, indicating that he/she wishes the lease to end on the termination date. Otherwise it is automatically extended by tacit relocation on the same terms and conditions as before, except to the extent that these terms and conditions are inconsistent with a lease for year to year.[133] If the original lease duration was for less than one year, the extension will

[124] Rankine, *Leases*, p. 114; *Mann* v. *Houston* 1957 SLT 89 (IH) 92.

[125] Rankine, *Leases*, p. 115; Paton and Cameron, *Landlord and Tenant*, p. 7.

[126] Abolition of Feudal Tenure (Scotland) Act 2000, s. 67.

[127] Paton and Cameron, *Landlord and Tenant*, p. 14. Rankine's definition was broader (*Leases*, p. 1), but various cases in the 1930s adopted the narrower approach that a tenant must have an exclusive right to the land: see *John Menzies and Co.* v. *Glasgow Assessor* 1937 SC 288 (IH) 295 297 and *Austin Reed Ltd.* v. *Glasgow Assessor* 1937 SC 317 (IH) 323–4. The original broader approach enjoyed an apparent revival, in *Brador Properties Ltd.* v. *British Telecommunications plc* 1992 SC 12 (IH) 19 but that has not resulted in a change in approach in subsequent texts: see McAllister, *Leases*, para. 2.40; Coulsfield and MacQueen *Gloag and Henderson*, para. 36.01 and Gordon and Wortley, *Land Law*, para. 18–06.

[128] Rankine, *Leases*, p. 200; Paton and Cameron, *Landlord and Tenant*, p. 127.

[129] Rankine, *Leases*, p. 213; Paton and Cameron, *Landlord and Tenant*, p. 128.

[130] Rankine, *Leases*, p. 233; Paton and Cameron, *Landlord and Tenant*, pp. 135–6.

[131] Paton and Cameron, *Landlord and Tenant*, pp. 138–9. [132] *Ibid.* 139–41.

[133] *Neilson* v. *Mossend Iron Co.* (1886) 13 R (HL) 50 54; *Commercial Union Assurance Co.* v. *Watt and Cumine* 1964 SC 84 (IH) 88.

be for the same period; if originally for one year or more, the lease will automatically be extended for one year.[134] Common law and statute law combine to provide a complex amalgam of periods for serving notice to quit.[135] A lease may also be prematurely brought to an end in certain circumstances: the parties may have agreed that one or both may terminate the lease (a 'break clause') or the landlord may 'irritate' the lease in response to breach by the tenant.

Leases of both residential and agricultural property are subject to special statutory regimes, the most important feature of which is the impact on the landlord's ability to remove the tenant at the expiry of the lease. A lease of a private dwellinghouse must not exceed twenty years.[136] The Housing (Scotland) Act 1988 created the 'assured tenancy' and 'short assured tenancy'. Wherever a house is let as a separate dwelling to one or more individuals, one or all of whom will occupy the house as their only or principal home, it is an assured tenancy unless it falls into the list of excluded types of let, which includes, for example, holiday lets and lettings by certain educational bodies to students.[137] The tenant has security of tenure, allowing him/her to remain on the property after the period of the contract of lease has come to an end.[138] The 'contractual tenancy' is followed by a 'statutory tenancy'. An assured tenant can only be removed from the premises by court order, which will only be granted if one of various statutory grounds is made out.[139] Obviously, landlords are keen to avoid granting security of tenure. This can be done by creating a 'short assured tenancy'. Prior to the tenancy commencing, the landlord must serve on the tenant a notice, in the specified form, stating that the tenancy is to be a short assured tenancy.[140] (Such tenancy must be for six months or longer.) The landlord then has an absolute right to regain possession of the subjects at the end of the contractual term, provided that tacit relocation is not operating.[141] The landlord is to draw up a formal document detailing the terms of any assured tenancy and provide a copy to the tenant.[142] Should he/she fail to do so, the court may draw up such a document. Short assured tenancies are by far the most common form of private residential let. A separate regime covers social housing and is not considered here.

[134] Paton and Cameron, *Landlord and Tenant*, p. 221. See generally Halliday, 'Tacit Relocation', p. 201.
[135] Detailed at McAllister, *Leases*, paras. 9.22–9.29.
[136] Land Tenure Reform (Scotland) Act 1974 ss. 8 and 9 (henceforth LTR(S)A 74).
[137] Housing (Scotland) Act 1988, s. 12 and Schedule 4 (henceforth H(S)A 88). [138] s. 16.
[139] s. 16(2), s. 18 and Schedule 5. [140] s. 32. [141] s. 33. [142] s. 30.

Leases of agricultural property are also subject to a statutory regime, the mainstay of which is the legislation relating to agricultural holdings. Again the tenant, in certain circumstances, has security of tenure beyond the agreed contractual term. Four other key aspects are that:

(a) the tenant is, on removal from the property, entitled to be compensated for improvements which he/she carried out to the property;[143]
(b) disputes are to be resolved by means of a special court (the Scottish Land Court);[144]
(c) in some circumstances, the tenant has a pre-emptive right to buy the agricultural holding in the event that the landlord puts it up for sale;[145] and
(d) there are particular rules about succession to tenancies.[146]

An agricultural holding is a lease of agricultural land, defined as 'land used for agriculture for the purposes of a trade or business'.[147] Agriculture itself is expansively defined.[148] Following recent reforms, there are now various types of agricultural holdings. One is a 'grazing let', where agricultural land is let for the purpose of it being used only for grazing or mowing during some specified period of the year.[149] A 'short limited duration tenancy' (SLDT) is a lease of agricultural land for not more than five years which may be terminated by agreement.[150] A limited duration tenancy (LDT) is a lease of agricultural land for not less than fifteen years.[151] (A lease for any period between five and fifteen years takes effect as a lease for fifteen years.) A tenant of a LDT does not have security of tenure (in the sense that there is no rule that he/she cannot be removed unless the landlord establishes one of various specified grounds), but the normal rules of tacit relocation are modified: if certain prescribed steps are not taken to bring the tenancy to an end at its termination date, it will continue on a 'cycle of continuations' until these steps are taken. Initially, there are two 'short continuations' of three years, followed by a fifteen-year continuation, which cycle will be repeated indefinitely until the lease is terminated.[152]

143 Agricultural Holdings (Scotland) Act 1991 Pt. IV (henceforth AH(S)A 91); Agricultural Holdings (Scotland) Act 2003 Pt. 4 ch. 1 (henceforth AH(S)A 03).
144 AH(S)A 91 Pt. VII; AH(S)A 03 Pt. 7. 145 AH(S)A 03 Pt. 2.
146 AH(S)A 91, s. 11; AH(S)A 03 ss. 20 and 21. 147 AH(S)A 03, s. 93; AH(S)A 91, s. 1(2).
148 AH(S)A 91, s. 85(1).
149 AH(S)A 03, s. 3. Such a lease may not be for more than 364 days.
150 AH(S)A 03, s. 6(2). 151 AH(S)A 03, s. 5. 152 AH(S)A 03, s. 8.

Then there is the possibility of a '1991 Act Tenancy'.[153] A lease of an agricultural holding will only be a 1991 Act Tenancy if the lease is in writing and expressly states that the 1991 Act is to apply to it.[154] Such a tenant enjoys full security of tenure. After the contractual period of the lease has come to an end, the lease will continue from year to year by tacit relocation until a notice to quit is served by the landlord. In most cases, the tenant may respond with a 'counter-notice' and the notice to quit will have no effect unless the Land Court consents to its operation. It may only do so on certain limited grounds, such as that the carrying out of the purpose for which the landlord proposes to terminate the tenancy is desirable in the interest of good management of the estate or that greater hardship would be caused by withholding consent to the notice than by granting it.[155] In respect of each type of agricultural holding, there should be a written lease detailing specified matters.[156] If there is no such written document, the terms can ultimately be determined by the Land Court.

There are also more specialised statutory regimes which apply to agricultural leases of crofts and small landholdings,[157] which provide security of tenure. Although these apply to a substantial proportion of agricultural land in Scotland, they are, however, not of general application and it is far more difficult for such a tenancy to be created anew. The origins of crofting tenure lie in the response to the Highland Clearances, when tenants in the Scottish Highlands were evicted from property during the eighteenth and nineteenth centuries in order to leave the land free for other, 'more-profitable', uses.[158] Primarily, the crofting legislation applies to existing holdings. Since 2007, it has once again been possible to create new crofts.[159] This requires the approval of the Crofters Commission and it can only be done in certain areas.[160] This report will focus upon agricultural holdings legislation.

153 So named because the rules for these types of tenancy are found in AH(S)A 91.

154 AH(S)A 03, s. 1(2).

155 AH(S)A 91 Pt. III, in particular, ss. 21–4. For an overview of the procedure, see Dervaird and Usher, 'Agriculture'.

156 AH(S)A 91, s. 4; AH(S)A 03, s. 13.

157 Gloag and Henderson, *Law of Scotland*, paras. 36–49 to 36–53.

158 Flyn and Graham, 'Crofting', para. 1.

159 Crofters (Scotland) Act 1993, s. 3 A(1), inserted by Crofting Reform (Scotland) Act 2007, s. 16.

160 Primarily in one of the seven crofting counties in the Highlands and Islands, but now also in other areas designated by the Scottish Ministers: Crofting (Designation of Areas) (Scotland) Order 2010/29. For details, see Flyn and Graham, 'Crofting'.

The law distinguishes between long and short leases, and urban and rural leases. The first is relevant to how the lease may be made to bind successors to the landlord and so is detailed in the response to Case 2. The urban/rural divide is of relevance to the repairing obligations and to how the tenant may deal with his/her right. It is outlined in the response to Case 5.

A contract between A and B to allow B to occupy A's property which does not amount to a lease, amounts to a *licence*. Sometimes it is referred to as a 'right of occupation'. This is an amorphous concept, probably developed under English influence. Parties will attempt to create a licence typically in order to avoid the application of one of the statutory regimes mentioned above or the tax consequences of the agreement being a lease, and because granting a lease is not permitted in the circumstances. The courts are astute to preventing licences from being used for this purpose.[161] If what the parties have agreed to amounts to a lease, the fact that they have labelled it a 'licence', will not prevent the court from holding that it amounts to a lease. A contract may be held to be a licence because it does not grant a right to use the land itself, but only to use a particular part of it or to put a particular part of it to some use.[162] It may lack one of the other cardinal requirements for a lease (for example, rent). Tacit relocation does not apply to a licence. What other legal systems might categorise as a loan of land (that is, an agreement that B may use A's land for no consideration), will be treated as a licence.

A may also grant B a *liferent* which entitles B to enjoy the use and benefit of the land, without encroaching on its substance, either for B's lifetime or for some other (shorter) period.[163] B is the 'liferenter' and A the 'fiar'. The law distinguishes between 'proper' and 'improper' liferents.[164] Only in a proper liferent does B obtain a real right (on which, see Case 2). Initially, following Roman terminology, the proper liferent was viewed as a 'personal servitude', but that terminology is not common now.[165] Scots law did not receive the other personal servitudes, *usus* and *habitatio*, recognised by Roman law.[166] For some time it was said that the fiar and liferenter had two separate but co-existent estates, each burdening the other, but the

[161] *Brador Properties Ltd.* v. *British Telecommunications plc* 1992 SC 12 (IH) 20.
[162] Paton and Cameron, *Landlord and Tenant*, p. 12.
[163] Gordon and Wortley, *Land Law*, para. 17-01; Erskine, *Institute*, II. ix. 39.
[164] Gordon and Wortley, *Land Law*, para. 17-02; Styles, 'Liferent', paras. 1608–9.
[165] Stair, *Institutions*, II. vi. 1; Erskine, *Institute*, II. ix. 39.
[166] Erskine, *Institute*, II. ix. 39. A right of occupancy may of course be created by means of a trust: *Milne's Tr.* v. *Milne* 1920 SC 456 (IH) 460.

prevalent view today is that the liferent is a subordinate real right, burdening the fiar's ownership.[167] The right is created by A executing and delivering a deed granting B the right and B then registering that deed in the appropriate Land Register.[168] Proper liferents are now relatively rare. Indeed, Paisley[169] has described them as 'virtually unknown'.

The '*improper liferent*' is now far more common. Here the liferenter's entitlement (and, indeed, the fiar's), is effected by means of a trust. Title to the property is held by trustees. They hold as fiduciaries, bound to administer the trust fund to fulfil the purposes of the trust. They hold for the liferenter and fiar as beneficiaries, and will transfer ownership of the property to the fiar when the liferent comes to an end. The trustees are subject to all of the duties of trust law,[170] which are beyond the scope of this project. A beneficiary only has a personal right against the trustees, although the beneficiary is protected against the trustee's insolvency.[171] One of the reasons for the popularity of the 'improper liferent' is the flexibility to create custom designed rights.[172] An improper liferent obviously does not adhere to the model of A owning the property and granting B a subordinate real right, which this project aims to analyse. Instead, B has the same character of right as any other beneficiary under a trust. For this reason, it is not considered in detail in this report, although some points of interest are noted.

If granted in respect of a private dwellinghouse and for payment, the right must be longer than twenty years.[173] The liferent must terminate upon B's death. The grant can also provide for earlier termination on the expiry of a fixed term or upon the occurrence of some specified event, such as B's marriage.[174]

[167] Styles, 'Liferent', para. 1608.

[168] Abolition of Feudal Tenure (Scotland) Act 2000, s. 65. The right exists from the delivery of the deed but is not made real until registration. There are currently two systems of land registration in operation: the Register of Sasines (a deeds register) and the Land Register (a register of title). Registration, in the (newer) Land Register is prompted only by certain trigger events and the granting of a liferent is not one. A liferent is to be registered in the Register in which the land itself is registered: Land Registration (Scotland) Act 1979, s. 2 (henceforth LR(S)A 79).

[169] Paisley, 'Real Rights', p. 290.

[170] On the law of trusts generally, see Wilson, *Trusts*; Chalmers, *Trusts*; Gordon and Wortley, *Land Law*, ch. 16.

[171] Property held in trust is not available to the trustee's personal creditors: *Burnett's Tr.* v. *Grainger* 2004 SC (HL) 19.

[172] Paisley, 'Real Rights', p. 290. [173] LTR(S)A 74, s. 8.

[174] *Chaplin's Trs.* v. *Haile* (1890) 18 R 27 (IH) 31. *McLeod's Trs.* v. *McLeod* 1916 SC 604 (IH) 610 is

Each of the three rights mentioned must be in writing in order to be validly *constituted* (unless it is a lease or licence with a duration of one year or less).[175] A document signed by the granter/s is required.[176] This signed document must be registered for a liferent or a long lease to be made real. According to one view, a lease or a licence is not invalid even though it has not been executed in compliance with the rules, provided that one party (A) has relied on the contract, the other (B) knew of that reliance or had acquiesced in it and the first party (A) has as a result of his/her reliance been affected to a material extent and would be adversely affected to a material extent if the second party (B) were able to withdraw from the contract. It was recently held that this view does not apply to a lease.[177] Given the drafting of the relevant statute, this may be correct, although it would be a considerable, and seemingly unintentional, change from the previous law.

South Africa

A can grant B a *lease* of the property agreed between the landlord and the tenant regarding the object of the lease, its duration, the rent to be paid and the fact that the tenant is to receive the temporary use of the property. Unless otherwise agreed, default provisions based on the intended use of the property govern the lease.[178] Although writing is not a requirement,[179] the parties may require reduction to writing for the validity of or as proof of the conclusion of the lease.[180] The lease creates merely contractual rights. To acquire real (property) rights, the tenant must occupy the property in the case of a short lease (less than ten years) or have a notarial long lease (ten years or more) notarially executed and registered in the Land Register.[181] A lease may be concluded for a definite term or the duration may be at the will of the landlord or tenant. If there is no agreement as to duration, it is treated as a periodic lease, the term being that under which the rent is payable.

an example of a liferent to endure so long as the liferentrix remained unmarried. Other grounds for termination are renunciation, negative prescription and confusion.

175 Requirements of Writing (Scotland) Act 1995, s. 1 (henceforth ROW(S)A 95). This is, in addition to individual statutory requirements.

176 ROW(S)A 95, ss. 2 and 7.

177 *The Advice Centre for Mortgages* v. *McNicoll* [2006] CSOH 58, 2006 SLT 591, paras. 19–23, criticised at 2006 SLT *(News)* 254.

178 See Cooper, *Landlord and Tenant*, pp. 3–4.

179 General Law Amendment Act 50 of 1956, s. 1(1); Formalities, in Respect of Leases of Land Act 18 of 1969, s. 1(1).

180 See Cooper, *Landlord and Tenant*, pp. 75–6.

181 Deeds Registries Act 47 of 1937, s. 3(1)(p) and 77(1); Cooper, *Landlord and Tenant*, p. 276.

The Rental Housing Act 50 of 1999, dealing with residential leases, restates to a limited extent some of the common law rights and obligations of the landlord and tenant.[182]

A can grant B a personal servitude of *usufruct* over the property. Usufruct is an intensely personal, limited (subordinate) real right which entitles a person to use and enjoy another's property and to take its fruits without impairing the substance.[183] A usufruct cannot exceed the lifetime of the usufructuary.[184] A usufruct is created by last will or *inter vivos* by an agreement between the parties. The intention of the parties must be to create a usufruct and not merely contractual rights.[185] Writing is not required for an agreement to create a usufruct. To create a real (property) right, however, a notarial deed will have to be executed and registered against the title deeds of the servient property.[186]

It is possible for A to grant B the lesser personal servitudes of *use* (*usus*) or *habitation* (*habitatio*) over the property. The usuary of a farm may use the property and collect fruits for domestic use. The usuary of a residential property may occupy it with his/her family and let out part of the house provided he remains in occupation.[187] The *habitator* may occupy the house or let it out. Like a usufruct, use or a right of habitation cannot extend beyond the lifetime of its holders. The contract to create such rights need not be in writing, but will have to be notarially executed and registered to have proprietary effect.[188]

A can grant B a *revocable grant* (*precarium*) which would entitle B to remain on A's property gratuitously until the permission is revoked.[189] No formalities are required for the creation of this interest. South African courts regard *precarium* as a form of tenure and require reasonable notice and sometimes a just reason for its revocation.[190] Whilst disturbance of a *precarist's* factual occupation gives rise to a possessory remedy, *precarium* is not recognised as a real right capable of registration.

182 See in general Du Bois, *Wille's Principles*, p. 910.

183 Voet, *Commentarius*, 7.1.3.

184 *Bhamjee* v. *Mergold Beleggings (Edms) Bpk* 1983 4 SA 555 (T); Deeds Registries Act 47 of 1937, s. 66.

185 *Coetzee* v. *Malan* 1979 1 SA 377 (O).

186 Deeds Registries Act 47 of 1937, ss. 65 and 67; Nel, *Jones: Conveyancing*, pp. 214–15.

187 Voet, *Commentarius*, 7.8.1–2; *Kain* v. *Khan* 1986 4 SA 251 (C) 256.

188 Deeds Registries Act 47 of 1937, ss. 65 and 67; Nel, *Jones: Conveyancing*, pp. 214–15; van der Merwe, 'Servitudes', para. 446.

189 Cooper, *Landlord and Tenant*, pp. 7–8.

190 *Lechoana* v. *Cloete* 1925 AD 536.

A can grant B a *loan for use* (*commodatum*) of the property.[191] Unlike lease, it is gratuitous and, unlike *precarium*, it lasts for a specified time or purpose and is not terminable at will. Neither handing over of the property nor writing is required for its creation. Although disturbance of factual control entitles the borrower to a possessory remedy, loan for use is not a recognised real right and cannot be registered to give it proprietary effect.

A can grant B a *hereditary land lease* (*emphyteusis, erfpag*) or perpetual quitrent, its English law equivalent adopted in South Africa. This form of tenure, mostly employed for property development on land owned by the state or public authorities, is now seldom used in practice and most existing quitrent had been created decades ago. The quitrent payable to the state was abolished and legislation provides for existing hereditary land leases (perpetual quitrent) to be converted to full ownership.[192]

A can grant B a *hereditary building lease* (*superficies*) or its English counterpart, the ninety-nine-year leasehold, also adopted in South Africa. Here again, the ninety-nine-year leasehold has swamped the Roman-Dutch *superficies*, and legislative provision makes conversion into ownership possible. This is also true of the statutory ninety-nine-year leasehold introduced in 1978 to grant people in Black urban areas greater security of tenure.[193]

A final English form of land tenure transplanted into South African law was *leasehold*, which could take the form of a perpetual lease, a ninety-nine year lease or a lease for an indefinite period coupled with a right of renewal. This institution was mainly used where the State did not want to grant state land as freehold, but rather as a lesser tenure. The tendency to equate leaseholders with owners, led to the statutory conversion of certain leaseholds to ownership. Thereafter leaseholds trickled down to a few isolated cases.[194] I have come across seaside cottages and timeshares being sold as thirty-year leaseholds, with the rights of the holders expiring after thirty years and the public authority or developing agency being entitled to sell or lease out the cottages or time shares anew.

[191] Voet, *Commentarius*, 13.6.1; *Adamson* v. *Boshoff* 1975 3 SA 221 (C) 225.

[192] See Van der Merwe, De Waal and Carey Miller, 'Property and Trust Law', ss. 858–9.

[193] See further Van der Merwe, '*Numerus clausus*', p. 802.

[194] See in general Van der Merwe, De Waal and Carey Miller, 'Property and Trust Law', s. 860.

Spain

A can grant B a *lease* (*arrendamiento*) of the property. The lease is a contract by which the landlord undertakes to provide the tenant with the enjoyment of movable or immovable property for a certain term in return for rent. It is created as soon as the parties agree on the object of the lease and the rent to be paid. In addition to general provisions in the Spanish Civil Code, leases of urban and agricultural property are primarily governed by the Law on Urban Lease (*Ley de Arrendamientos Urbanos*) of 24 November 1994 and the Law on Rural Lease (*Ley de Arrendamientos Rústicos*) of 26 November 2003 respectively, amended by the Act of 30 November 2005. The Law on Urban Lease draws a distinction between urban premises leased for residential purposes (*arrendamiento de vivienda*) and urban premises leased for other purposes (*arrendamiento para uso distinto del de vivienda*). The latter category includes not only periodic (seasonal) leases (*arrendamiento de temporada*) but also leases of premises for industrial, commercial, handicraft, professional, recreational, welfare, cultural and educational activities (Law on Urban Lease, art. 3.2).[195] Urban leases for residential purposes are regulated primarily by the mandatory provisions of Titles I and IV of the Law on Urban Lease and, in the case of specified leases, by Title II of the Act. Failing this, recourse may be had to contractual arrangements between the parties and ultimately to the provisions of the Civil Code. Urban leases for non-residential purposes are regulated primarily by contractual arrangement and, failing that, by Title III of the Law on Urban Lease and, as a last resort, by the Civil Code (Law on Urban Lease, art. 4). The Law on Rural Lease defines a rural lease as a lease of land for agricultural, cattle-raising or forest exploitation (art. 1). Rural leases must be concluded for a minimum period of three years. If not, they are considered null and void (Law on Rural Lease, art. 12).[196]

Although writing is not required for the constitution of an urban lease (Civil Code, art. 1278), it is a requirement for a rural lease (Law on Rural Lease, art. 11.1). Nevertheless, in order to be effective vis-à-vis third parties, a lease contract must be reduced to writing and notarially executed (Civil Code, arts. 1280–3 and 1549).[197] The lease itself merely

[195] Leases of immovables which are excluded by this Law are listed in art. 5.

[196] Note that art. 12 of the Law excludes leases for less than this period. A proposed amendment to the Law on Rural Lease stipulates a minimum period of five years.

[197] The contract can only be registered in the Land Register if it is notarially executed, as stipulated, in the Law on Hypothecs, arts. 2–5 with reference to art. 3 of the same Law.

creates contractual rights between the parties. It entitles the tenant to claim occupation (or delivery) of the property and obliges him to pay the agreed rent. Registration of the lease does not change the personal right into a real right but renders the lease enforceable against third parties. The fact that the tenant entered into possession, entitles him/her to institute an interdict if his/her possession is disturbed.

A can grant B a *usufruct* (*usufructo*) over the property which entitles the holder to use and enjoy the property of another subject to the obligation to preserve its form and substance (Civil Code, art. 467).[198] Since the 1960s, this obligation has been interpreted as an obligation to preserve the economic destiny of property subject to the usufruct.[199] A usufruct normally expires on the death of the holder (B), but can also be terminated in other ways, for example, where the object of the usufruct is destroyed (Civil Code, art. 513). If the usufructuary is a juristic person (a company or an association), Civil Code, art. 515 Civil Code limits the duration of the usufruct to thirty years.[200] Neither writing nor any other formalities are required for a contract to create a usufruct,[201] except in the case of an *inter vivos* contract without consideration which must be reduced to writing and notarially executed[202] owing to the fact that the rules on donations (Civil Code, art. 633) require such a public document.[203] A usufruct may also be created by will, operation of law (for example, the usufruct of the surviving spouse on the assets of a deceased spouse) or prescription (*usucapio*). Since, generally, with the exception of mortgages, registration is not required for the constitution of real rights, it is not necessary for the constitution of a usufruct. However, the Law on Hypothec (Mortgage), art. 13 provides that all

[198] Note that some Autonomous Communities, in Spain (such as Galicia, the Basque Country, Navarra, Catalonia, Aragón and the Balearic Islands) have the right to enact their own civil legislation. Thus Laws 408–22 of Fuero Nuevo of Navarra and the Civil Code of Catalonia (Book V, Title VI, Ch. I, arts. 561-1 to 561-37) contain fairly detailed provisions on usufruct.

[199] Lacruz Berdejo, *Elementos*, vol. III-2, p. 25.

[200] See also Law 421 of Fuero Nuevo of Navarra. Law 411 provides that if the holder is a corporation, the ususfruct expires after a period of 100 years, unless a lesser period was stipulated or agreed upon.

[201] If it is not notarially executed, the real right of usufruct cannot be registered in the Land Register (Law on Hypothecs, art. 3 with reference to art. 2.2 of the same Law).

[202] Lacruz Berdejo, *Elementos*, vol III-2, p. 11.

[203] The Spanish Civil Code does not favour donations because it empowers certain persons. To make sure that donations are actually intended, it requires the contract of donation to be notarially executed.

limited real rights (for example, usufruct) may be registered and if registered, shall be enforceable against the world at large.

A can grant B a *right of use* (*derecho de uso*) over the property (Civil Code, art. 523-9). In principle, this right restricts the holder to the use of the property (*uti*) and enjoymentof its fruits to the extent necessary to meet the daily needs of the holder and his/her family (*ad usum quotidianum* Civil Code, art. 524).[204] The right of use also expires on the death of the holder and the other causes mentioned under usufruct. Writing is not required for the constitution of a right of use but, as in the case of usufruct, a right of use created *inter vivos* for no consideration, has to be in writing and notarially executed (Law on Hypothec (Mortgage), art. 3 with reference to art 2.2).

A can grant B a *right of habitation* (*derecho de habitación*) over the property, which entitles the holder to reside in those rooms of a house that are required to meet his/her needs and those of his/her family (Civil Code, art. 524, para. 2).[205] In Spain, a right of habitation is often granted by the court to a divorced spouse entitling him/her to remain in the family home with the children. The right is created and terminated in the same way as a usufruct. Writing is not required for its constitution but if the right is to be registered it must be reduced to writing and notarially executed (Law on Hypothec (Mortgage), art. 3 with reference to art. 2.2).[206] The rules relating to usufruct apply, to the extent that they are compatible, to use and habitation (Civil Code, art. 528).

A very old-fashioned type of time-limited interest occurs when A grants B a *hereditary land lease* (*emphyteusis, enfiteusis*) over immovable property such as a farm (Civil Code, arts. 1605 and 1628), usually in perpetuity. By granting the *emphyteusis*, A, the owner of the land, retains the 'direct ownership' (*dominio directo*) of the land while B obtains the beneficial ownership (*dominio útil*) in return for the payment of rent in the form of money or a share in the produce of the land. Since the holder is allowed to transfer his/her right to another, this institution is sometimes likened to a form of co-ownership whereby co-owners are allowed freely to dispose of their shares in the property. Constitution of this long-term right of indefinite duration requires writing and notarial

[204] See also Law 423-426 of Fuero Nuevo of Navarra and Civil Code of Catalonia (Book V, Title VI, Ch. II).

[205] See also Law 423-426 of Fuero Nuevo of Navarra and Civil Code of Catalonia (Book V, Title VI, Ch. II).

[206] Law on Hypothecs, art. 13 provides that all limited real rights may be registered.

execution in a public deed (Civil Code, art. 1628).[207] The *emphyteusis* is seldom used in practice, presumably on account of its perpetual duration. For this reason, it will not be further dealt with in this report.

A can grant B a *hereditary building lease* (*superficies, derecho de superficie*). This right entitles the holder to build a structure or to plant on land belonging to someone else. The holder is considered to benefit from some kind of 'temporary ownership' over the structure or produce of what he has planted. The Civil Code does not contain any provisions on *superficies*, which is governed (with regard to the right to build) by arts. 40 and 41 of the Spanish Law on Land 2008, the laws of the Fuero Nuevo of Navarra and the Civil Code of Catalonia (Book V).[208] The last not only regulates the right to build but also the right to plant (Catalonia Civil Code, art. 564-1). The agreement to create a right of *superficies* must be reduced to writing, notarially executed[209] and registered in the Land Register (Spanish Law on Land, art. 40.2). The public deed must specify the duration of the right of *superficies*, which must not be longer than ninety-nine years (Spanish Law on Land, art. 40.2).[210] The right of *superficies* can only be granted by the owner of the land (public authority or private person) (Spanish Law on Land, art. 40.2, para. 2). By contrast, Catalonia Civil Code, art. 564-3.1 allows not only owners but also holders of rights *in rem* to grant a right of *superficies*.

A can grant B a *loan for use* (*commodatum, comodato*) (Civil Code, art. 1741-52 and Laws 539 to 541 of the Fuero Nuevo of Navarra) whereby the lender hands over property to another person for his/her gratuitous use, subject to an obligation to return the property. Unlike a lease, the borrower does not have to pay rent. Despite a number of contrary decisions of the Spanish Supreme Court (*Tribunal Supremo*), which regard a contract of loan as a real contract, the majority view[211] is that it should be regarded as a consensual contract which does not require the handing

[207] The hereditary land lease (*emphyteusis*, *enfiteusis*) can be registered, in the Land Register (Law on Hypothecs, art. 2.2).

[208] Law 430-432 of Fuero Nuevo of Navarra; Civil Code of Catalonia (Book V, Title VI, Ch. IV, arts. 564-1 to 564-6).

[209] Writing is not required, in Navarra, but Catalonia Civil Code, art. 564-3.2 requires writing and notarial execution where the holder is given a right to build or to plant on the owner's land.

[210] The Navarra legislation does not set a term, whereas the Catalonia Civil Code sets a maximum term of ninety-nine years (Catalonia Civil Code, art. 564-3.2.a).

[211] E.g. Jordano Barea, *La categoría*, pp. 53–7. Modern authors disagree since they are of opinion that the parties are bound by the contract. See de Ángel Yágüez, 'Comment', pp. 1600–2; Lacruz Berdejo, *Elementos*, vol. 2, pp. 170–1.

over of the property, but merely consensus between the parties. Writing is also not required for a valid contract of loan. The contract may be for a fixed term. If the term is not fixed, the borrower is obliged to return the property after he/she has used it for the purpose for which it was borrowed.[212] In cases of urgent and unforeseen need, the lender can reclaim the property before its return is due (Civil Code, art. 1749). Where no term is fixed or where the property is not lent out for a specific purpose, the loan is considered revocable and the lender can claim for the return of the property at will (Civil Code, art. 1750). Some commentators regard such revocable loan for use as a form of *precarium*.[213]

A can grant B a *precarium* (*precario*), which entitles B to remain on A's property gratuitously until the permission is revoked. This institution differs from lease in that the *precario tenens* (*precarista*) pays no rent for the use of property. It is usually granted among members of a family and the mere will of the owner is sufficient for its creation. No formalities are required for a *precarium*, which may be granted expressly or tacitly. Spanish law generally regards *precarium* as a variety of a loan for use.[214]

212 This is the only way in which a contract established under Law 539 of Fuero Nuevo can be terminated.

213 See de Ángel Yágüez, 'Comment', p. 1619; Lacruz Berdejo, *Elementos*, vol. 2, p. 175.

214 de Ángel Yágüez, 'Comment', pp. 1618–20; Lacruz Berdejo, *Elementos*, vol. 2, p. 175.

Case 2
What happens if land subject to a time-limited interest is conveyed to a third party?

Some time after the creation of the time-limited right concerned, A conveys the property to a third party C.

Will the right of B remain enforceable against C if the latter acquires the property for value/no consideration?

If so, briefly indicate to what extent actual or constructive knowledge, publicity or registration affects the position of C.

Mention also if other criteria are relevant, for example, a certain period of occupancy.

Comparative observations

Some jurisdictions recognise registered *land leases* as limited real rights, while others such as Germany, Austria, Belgium and Poland hold that land leases merely create personal rights, but with proprietary effect when possession is transferred or the lease is registered. Consequently, if B concluded a long lease[1] and has obtained possession of the land[2] or the lease was registered before the conveyance of the property to C, B can enforce the lease against C.[3]

In most jurisdictions, registered leases are generally enforceable, irrespective of whether C acquires the land for value or not and irrespective of C's actual or constructive knowledge of the existence of the lease. In South Africa, C will be bound by B's unregistered long lease

[1] Long leases are those of ten years or more in South Africa, nine years or more in Greece, Belgium and Italy and six years or more in Portugal. Note that registered short leases are also enforceable in Spain.

[2] In Italy and South Africa, an unregistered long lease would nevertheless be enforceable against C for nine or ten years respectively, provided the lessee remains in possession.

[3] In Belgium, agricultural leases for more than nine years need not be transcribed in the Mortgage Register for enforceability against third parties.

where C is either a universal successor or acquired the property gratuitously (*titulo luctrativo*). If C is a particular successor he/she will only be bound if he/she had actual knowledge of the lease on transfer of the property.

In jurisdictions which do not allow leases to be registered, enforceability of the lease against C is apparently based on acceptance of the maxim 'sale does not supersede hire' or 'hire trumps sale', coupled with possession of the property or certain formal requirements like a deed of lease bearing a certified date.[4] Under Danish law, ordinary leases of land, irrespective of their duration, are protected against third parties such as C even if they are not registered and without any period of previous occupancy. However, extraordinary contractual terms will be enforceable against C only if they are registered, if C had previous knowledge of their existence or if C acquires the land or premises for no consideration. If the lease trumps the sale, most jurisdictions allow the third party (C) an action against A for non-disclosure if the lease was not evident.

Interestingly, Spanish law inverts the above maxim to read *emptio tollit locationem* or *venta quita renta* and accepts in principle that sale supersedes lease, unless the parties agree otherwise or the lease is registered and C therefore has knowledge of the lease. Even so, the Laws on Residential and Agricultural Leases entitle the tenant of an unregistered lease to remain on the property for a minimum period of three and five years respectively. If C acquires the property in good faith and for value (and the lease is not registered), C will only have to respect the lease for the next five years, irrespective of the period stipulated in the lease. In all other cases where the agreed duration of the lease between A and B exceeds five years, B will be able to remain on the property until the expiry of the lease.

If the deed of lease does not have a certified date, Greek law allows C to terminate the lease and evict the tenant on a month's notice if the lease is for a term of a year or less and on two months' notice if the term exceeds a year. However, if the property is leased as a primary residence, the new owner may terminate the lease only after three years have elapsed from the start of the lease. To terminate an agricultural lease

[4] Under Belgian law, for example, a lease is enforceable against C if it bears a certified date or if the tenant has occupied residential premises for at least six months. Under Portuguese law, short residential leases for a term of fewer than six years and agricultural and forestry leases which have been reduced to writing are enforceable against C on the basis of the above maxim.

executed in a deed without a certified date, the required period of notice is six months, which shall be effective at the end of the harvest period. If the new owner terminates the lease in this way, the tenant has a claim for compensation against the landlord (A) for breach of contract. In Poland, C may only terminate a residential lease which does not comply with the requirements if the premises have not yet been occupied.

In most jurisdictions, for instance, Germany, Austria, Greece, South Africa and Hungary, the concept of subrogation is employed to transfer[5] the rights and obligations of the landlord (A) automatically to C, who thus steps into the shoes of the former landlord.[6] Rents paid in advance to A, assignments of future rents by A, as well as attachments of rent effected by A's creditors, are not effective vis-à-vis the new owner (C) in respect of rents due more than three months after B was notified of the transfer.

In contrast to leases, most jurisdictions accept that *personal servitudes* are limited real rights enforceable against the world if they are registered in the Land Register or transcribed in the Mortgage Register. Thus, if a personal servitude such as usufruct is registered in the name of B, his/her rights will prevail against C. This result is based on the publicity inherent in registration and follows irrespective of whether the acquisition has been for value or not and irrespective of C's actual or constructive knowledge.[7]

If C acquired the land for value and in good faith, he/she will not be bound by an unregistered personal servitude. If he/she had actual knowledge of the servitude, he/she will be bound and may be forced to co-operate in the registration of the servitude.[8] In Poland, C will not be considered to be in good faith if the Register contains a notification of a pending entry or if the personal servitude concerned is a lifetime habitation right.

If, for whatever reason, the registration of B's right is cancelled by mistake, B will only be protected in German law if C acquired the property with actual and not mere constructive knowledge of B's personal servitude. If the acquisition by C was for value, B has a claim for unjustified enrichment against A; if it was gratuitous, B can claim reregistration of his/her real right.

[5] Subject to any contrary agreement in the lease.

[6] In Austria, this applies only if the lessee is already in possession. Uncommon ancillary contractual provisions which limit the lessor's right of termination do not bind C. Full transfer is only possible if the lease is registered.

[7] Hungarian law expressly states that C will be considered to have had constructive knowledge of a registered personal servitude.

[8] See e.g. the Austrian, Belgian, South African and Polish reports.

All the jurisdictions treat *other limited real rights* recognised by their systems the same as personal servitudes. If these rights are registered in the Land Register or transcribed in the Mortgage Register, they will prevail against a later owner of the land (C). This is for instance the case with a hereditary building right (*Erbbaurecht*) in Germany, France, Belgium, Portugal and Spain[9] and the hereditary land lease (*emphyteusis*) in France and Belgium. In Austria, the holder of a building right is deemed to acquire ownership, which is enforceable against C, on construction of the building. In Italy, a hereditary building right (*superficie*) is only enforceable against C if there is a stipulation to this effect in the agreement between A and C.

In France, a *loan for use* can be enforced against C if the date of the loan was certified before C's acquisition or if C knew that the loan existed when he acquired the land. The *precarious* occupant will not, however, be able to enforce his/her rights against C.

Austria

The effect on the *lease* by the conveyance to C depends on the following three circumstances: (a) whether the tenant has already been given possession of the property before it was sold; (b) whether the lease falls under the Law on Lease; and (c) whether the lease is registered with the Land Register.

> (a) The tenant only has personal rights against the landlord and such rights, in principle, do not have any effect on third persons. However, if the tenant has already been given possession of the property, the contract of lease is transferred to the transferee (C) and the latter substitutes the transferor (A) as landlord (Civil Code, art. 1120).[10] However, contractual provisions on termination which are to the disadvantage of the landlord are not binding on the transferee. Hence, the new landlord is entitled to terminate the contract in accordance with the statutory provisions of the Civil Code, irrespective of contrary contractual provisions.[11] He/she must, however, assert this right to terminate the contract within a reasonable period, otherwise the

[9] Under the Spanish Land Law of 2008 a hereditary building right (*superficies*) is only established once it had been registered.

[10] 1 Ob 300/01a; NZ (2003), p. 17; 7 Ob 53/01x; wobl (2002), p. 89; Iro, *Kommentar*, § 1120, paras. 1 and 5.

[11] 1 Ob 248/03g; 1 Ob 344/99s; JBl (2000), p. 793; Iro, *Kommentar*, § 1120, para. 6.

contractual provisions on termination (if there are any) will become binding on him/her as well.[12]

(b) If the lease falls under the Law on Lease, the transferee takes over all rights and duties of the landlord under the lease agreement, including provisions on termination (Law on Lease, s. 2, para. 1, sent. 4). There is thus no specific right to terminate as under Civil Code, s. 1120. Only uncommon ancillary clauses are not binding on the transferee, provided that he/she neither knew nor ought to have known about them (Law on Lease, s. 2, para. 1, sent. 5).[13]

(c) If the lease is registered in the Land Register, the transferee takes over all rights and duties arising from the lease, irrespective of whether the contract falls under the Law on Lease or not. The right to terminate the contract under Civil Code, s. 1120 does not apply in this case.[14]

The holder of a *personal servitude* has a real right which is protected against third persons and also against the transferee of the land.[15] Generally, the legal protection of rights arising from servitudes requires the registration of the servitude in the Land Register. However, the Austrian Supreme Court and the majority of academic writers also protect the holder of an unregistered servitude, provided that the servitude meets certain requirements of publicity.[16]

However, even if a non-registered servitude comes into existence, it can never be enforced against a third person who in good faith acquires the land free from encumbrances against payment[17] and without the acquirer knowing or having ought to have known that a servitude exists.[18] Such acquisition in good faith is not possible if the servitude is registered, because the Land Register does not allow people to rely on facts which conflict with the registration in the Land Register.[19]

A *hereditary building right* is a right *in rem*. As mentioned above, the holder of such a right has ownership of the building. Hence, the building cannot be sold by the landowner. As to the land, the holder of the building right has a proprietary right of use which he can also enforce against third persons.

[12] Iro, *Kommentar*, § 1120, para. 6.

[13] 9 Ob 160/02y; wobl (2003), p. 291; Iro, *Kommentar*, § 1120, para. 8.

[14] 3 Ob 191/98d; Iro, *Kommentar*, § 1120, para. 6.

[15] 7 Ob 547/95; wobl (1996), p. 240 (critical comment by Schauer).

[16] See Case 1.

[17] 6 Ob 737/87; JBl (1990), p. 314; Kletecka, in Koziol and Welser, *Bürgerliches Recht*, vol. 1, p. 364.

[18] 1 Ob 587/95; JBl (1996), p. 458; 5 Ob 563/93; SZ 66/152; 1 Ob 566/89; SZ 62/62; 1 Ob 1/84; NZ (1987), p. 22.

[19] Kletecka, in Koziol and Welser, *Bürgerliches Recht*, vol. 1, p. 364.

Belgium

A right *in personam* (such as a *lease*, *loan for use* or *precarium*) is generally not enforceable against third parties. However, an agricultural lease concluded between A and B will be enforceable against C, even without registration or publicity (Law on Agricultural Lease, art. 55). A residential lease will also be enforceable against C where A and B have concluded the lease with a certified date before the acquisition of ownership by C, or where the residential tenant has occupied the property for a period of at least six months. In the latter case, however, C can under strict conditions and on limited grounds terminate the lease with B (Law on Residential Lease, art. 9). The date is certified in a notarial deed and in the case of a private agreement through registration of the document,[20] death of (one of) the signatories of the contract or when the principal elements of the document have been mentioned in an authentic deed such as a deed prepared by a notary (Civil Code, art. 1328). The fact that the property has been acquired for value or without consideration is not relevant in this regard.

A lease concluded for a period exceeding nine years or an acknowledgement that rent was paid for at least three years in advance must be executed in a notarial deed and recorded with the Mortgage Register in order to render it enforceable against third parties (Law on Mortgage, art. 1). This does not apply in the case of an agricultural lease concluded for a period exceeding nine years (Law on Agricultural Lease, art. 55). A residential lease concluded for more than nine years, yet not recorded in the Mortgage Register, but with a certified date or a minimum occupation period of six months, is enforceable against C only for the period of nine years that has started at the moment of C's acquisition.

The *usufruct*, the *hereditary land lease* (*emphyteusis*) and the *hereditary building lease* (*superficies*), if created by contract, must be notarially executed and recorded in the Mortgage Register in order to be enforceable against third parties (Law on Mortgage, art. 1). When the publication formalities are fulfilled, rights *in rem* are enforceable against, and must be recognised by, third parties. Before recording, B's rights will not be enforceable against third parties who contracted in good faith (without actual notice). The fact that the property has been acquired for value or without consideration, does not affect the outcome.

[20] Registration, to be distinguished from the recording, in the Mortgage Register, is in essence a fiscal requirement. A lease contract must be presented to the Officer of Registration of Taxes, who levies this registration tax. Since 2007, the registration of residential leases is still mandatory, but has become tax free.

Denmark

The answer will be divided into three parts, depending on whether the use of land, the use of buildings for residential purposes or the use of buildings for other purposes, is the essential part of the contract.

If the *land* is sold to a new owner, B is protected as long as his/her rights can be said to be ordinary or usual.[21] This follows from the Law on Registration of Property, s. 3,[22] which states that these rights are protected against anyone without registration. No fixed period of previous occupancy is required. If B acquires extraordinary rights, the transfer to C will, if C is in good faith, extinguish such rights (Law on Registration of Property, s. 1) but not if C acquires the property without consideration. Moreover, B's extraordinary rights will stand if registered in the Land Register before transfer of the property to C.

If *buildings are leased for housing purposes*, a rule very similar to the Law on Registration of Property, s. 3 is found in the Law on Private Housing, s. 7. This section provides that tenants' rights have validity without registration and that the provision cannot be deviated from to the detriment of the tenant. The rights of B must therefore be respected by C without B having to prove a fixed period of previous occupancy. If the tenant B is given extraordinary rights, they must be registered in order to be enforced against a new owner of the property. If not registered, they will be extinguished if C acquires the property in good faith (Law on Registration of Property, s. 1) but not if C acquires the property without consideration.

If *buildings are leased for other purposes than housing*, the Law on the Lease of Commercial Premises, s. 6 contains a rule that is exactly the same as the rule found in the Law on Private Housing, s. 7. Identical rules therefore apply to the rent of premises rented for other purposes than housing.

England

Consideration is necessarily confined to the *lease* here. The reader is referred to Case 1. Depending on the nature of the interest which is

[21] The rights will normally be considered ordinary if they concern part of the land, are limited in time to a maximum of one year, or, in case the contract is unlimited, in time it can be cancelled by a maximum notice period of six months. See Mortensen, *Tinglysning*, p. 103.

[22] Consolidated Act No. 158 of 9 Mar. 2006 and later amendments.

being asserted against C, and depending on whether one is dealing with registered or unregistered land, different *publicity requirements* apply. Without compliance with those publicity requirements, that right cannot be enforced against third parties. There is no room for notice or knowledge of the interest by other means as a way of burdening the land with the lease.

France

Where a landlord sells the property subject to a *lease*, the purchaser may not evict the agricultural tenant, crop-sharer or tenant who concluded a lease in authentic form or with a certified date (Civil Code, art. 1743). The parties to a non-agricultural lease can reserve the right to evict the tenant (Civil Code, art. 1743). However, since mandatory legislation on commercial and residential leases forbids such clauses, they are the exception in practice.

The purchaser is only bound if the lease is concluded prior to the sale. To prevent back-dating of the lease, the lease must be in authentic form or have a certified date (Civil Code, art. 1743). A lease signed privately has a certified date from the date of registration, or from the date of the death of one of the signatories or from the date that the contract was reduced to an authentic form (Civil Code, art. 1328). Case law does not, however, regard this requirement as mandatory. The courts have stated that the purchaser is allowed tacitly to renounce his/her right to use absence of a certified date as a defence[23] and has laid down that the absence of a certified date can only be raised by a good faith acquirer.[24] Consequently, a purchaser is bound to respect the lease where he/she has acquired the leased land (whether for value or not) with knowledge of the existence of the lease.

In the case of a lease (such as an agricultural lease for longer than twelve years), which must be registered by public notice in the Land Register under the Decree of 1955 (*Décret de 1955*), a purchaser who registers his/her right of ownership after the lease was registered must respect such lease, even if he/she had no knowledge of its existence. Yet, where the purchaser had knowledge of the existence of the lease, he/she is bound to respect it even if it had not been registered. Non-registration would prevent the lease from being enforceable against the purchaser

[23] Cass. Soc., 15 July 1953; D 1953 729. [24] Civ. 3, 12 Mar. 1969; Bull. civ. III, no. 217.

only after a period of twelve years had expired.[25] With respect to agricultural leases, art. L 411–69 of the Rural Code provides that the public official entrusted with the sale must inform the purchaser that he/she will have to indemnify the tenant for improvements on the leased property on termination of the lease.

Since A has burdened the property with a *usufruct* in favour of B, he/she can only transfer the nude ownership of the land to the purchaser C. B's usufruct is recognised as a real right, the creation of which is subject to the provisions on registration of rights in land. It can therefore be enforced against C as soon as the formal requirements of these provisions have been complied with. Civil Code, art. 621, para. 2 provides that if property subject to usufruct is sold without the consent of the usufructuary, the usufructuary continues to enjoy the usufruct, unless he/she has expressly waived it. Even the court may not, on request of a nude owner, order the sale of full ownership of land subject to a usufruct against the wishes of the usufructuary (Civil Code, art. 815–5, para. 2). The same applies in the case where land subject to a right of habitation is transferred to C.

By analogy, the same reasoning as for usufruct applies to land burdened with *other real rights* such as a *hereditary building right* (*emphyteusis*), a *hereditary building lease* and a *lease for construction*. A cannot transfer the full ownership of the land already burdened with these rights to C and C must respect the holders of these rights.

By analogy to a lease which, like *a loan for use*, only gives rise to a personal right, one can reason that the borrower (B) will only be able to enforce his/her right against the purchaser C if the date of the loan was certified prior to the sale to C or if C knew that the loan existed when he/she acquired the property. In practice, a loan for use, often granted among family or friends, is rarely reduced to writing. Therefore, in the absence of a privately signed loan agreement, the loan for use can only be enforced against the purchaser where it can be proved that the latter had knowledge of the existence of the loan. Furthermore, case law (cited above) allows the lender to claim his/her property at any time on reasonable notice and to sell it free from any right of occupation.

The precarious position of the *precarist* (B) allows the owner to claim his/her property back at will and in particular to sell it free from any right of occupation. A *precarist* cannot enforce his/her right against a third party purchaser (C).

[25] Civ. 3, 7 Mar. 2007; D 2007; AJ 942.

Germany

B's *lease* would be protected against C if he/she has obtained possession of the property prior to the transfer of ownership to C. If the landlord transfers a leased property to a third party, the latter automatically assumes the rights and obligations of the landlord arising from the lease (Civil Code, § 566(1)). This protection is based on the rule that 'hire trumps sale'. B is protected even if C had no knowledge of the lease and irrespective of whether he/she acquired the property for value or without consideration. Since it is not possible to register lease agreements in the Land Register, there will be no publicity as to the existence of the lease. Of course, C would be entitled to compensation if A had not disclosed the existence of the lease to C.

The rule 'hire trumps sale' is also applicable in the case of an agricultural lease of land (*Landpachtvertrag*) (Civil Code, § 593b).

Rights capable of registration such as a duly registered *usufruct* (*Nießbrauch*), *right of habitation* (*Wohnungsrecht*), *permanent right of habitation* (*Dauerwohnungsrecht*) or a *permanent building right* (*Erbbaurecht*) will be enforceable against C, irrespective of C's knowledge or whether C acquired the property for value or not.

If, for whatever reason, the registration of B's right in the *Grundbuch* is cancelled by mistake, B will only be protected if C acquired the property with actual knowledge that it is subject to B's right (Civil Code, § 892(1)). Constructive knowledge will not exclude a *bona fide* acquisition by C. If B's right is cancelled by mistake in the Land Register (*Grundbuch*) without C having actual knowledge of its creation (*bona fide acquisition*), a further distinction must be made between an acquisition for value and an acquisition for no consideration. If C acquired the property for value, B is limited to claims for unjust enrichment against A (Civil Code 816(1), sent. 1). If, however, C acquired the property for no consideration, B can claim that C allows his/her (B's) real right to be registered again (Civil Code, § 816(1), sent 2).[26]

Greece

Greek law distinguishes between a *lease* on immovable property evidenced by a document with a certified date and a lease without such a date. If the lease is contained in a deed with a certified date, the transfer

[26] Bundesgerichtshof BGHZ 81, 395.

of the property by the landlord (A) to a third party (C) would have the effect that the new owner (C) would be subrogated to the rights and obligations of the former owner A (Civil Code, art. 614). This would mean *inter alia* that the new owner, subject to any agreement to the contrary contained in the lease,[27] must allow the tenant to exploit the property until the expiry of the lease. If the contract is not executed in the above manner, or contains a stipulation that, upon alienation of the property, the new owner shall have the right to evict the tenant, the new owner is entitled to terminate the lease on a month's notice if the term of the lease is for a year or less than a year, or on two months' notice if it exceeds a year (Civil Code, art. 615), unless the property was leased as a primary residence, where the contract may only be terminated after three years have elapsed from the start of the lease (Law 1703/1987, art. 2, § 1, as replaced by Law 2235/1994, art. 1, § 5). In this situation, the tenant will have a claim for compensation on account of the landlord's breach of contract. Rent paid in advance to A, assignments of future rents by A, as well as attachments of rents effected by A's creditors, shall not be effective vis-à-vis the new owner C in respect of rent for more than three months, computed as from the date the new owner C notified the tenant B of the transfer of the property to himself/herself (Civil Code, art. 616).

Greek law prescribes that leases for a term exceeding nine years must be transcribed in the conveyance records of the Land Register in the district where the property is situated (Civil Code, art. 1208). If notarially executed and transcribed, such a lease will be effective against the new owner to whom the property has been transferred (Civil Code, art. 618).

We have seen that a *lease of agricultural land* (including a crop-sharing lease) is governed by the same provisions as an ordinary lease, unless regulated differently in specific provisions of the Civil Code (Civil Code, arts. 620 and 641, § 2). In this respect the provisions on an agricultural lease (Civil Code, art. 637) require that in the case of a lease not contained in a deed bearing a fixed date the new owner (C) must give at least six months' advance notice should he/she wish to evict the lessee (B). Such notice shall only take effect after the leased land has been harvested.

Since *usufruct* is one of the recognised real rights in Greek law (Civil Code, art. 973), B's right is absolute and can be invoked against everybody (*erga omnes*) subject to the proviso that the usufruct must be executed in a notarial deed and transcribed in the Land Register before registration of the transfer of the land to C (Civil Code, arts. 1143, 1033 and 1192(2)). Lack

[27] Antapasis, in Georgiades and Stathopoulos, *GCC, Collective Analysis*, art. 614 no 29 (364).

of transcription results in the non-constitution of the usufruct (Civil Code, art. 1198). The same rules apply in the case of the personal servitude of *habitation* (Civil Code, art. 1187. See also the answer to Case 1 above).

In the case of a *loan for use*, B's right will not be enforceable against C. The borrower for use only acquires the personal right to use the property (Civil Code, art. 810). [28] The contract of loan for use gives rise to a relative right which can only be enforced *inter partes* (principle of relativity of obligations (Civil Code, art. 287)). Consequently, the new owner of the property (C) will have the right to demand from B acknowledgement of his/her ownership and the return of the property to him/her (C) (Civil Code, art. 1094). B is not entitled to refuse restitution of the property (Civil Code, art. 1095). However, since B will no longer have the use of the property, he/she will have a contractual claim for damages against A for subsequent impossibility of performance.

Hungary

It is a common rule for all types of *leases* (ordinary, residential, income producing or income producing in respect of agricultural property) that where the title of the property is transferred, the new owner in principle acquires the property encumbered with the lease, even if the purchaser acted in good faith and had no actual or constructive knowledge of the existence of the lease. In the case of a lease for a fixed term, the acquirer cannot terminate the contract unless the tenant deceived him/her as to the existence or the substantive content of the main conditions of the lease (Civil Code, § 432(2)). It must be stressed that the initial landlord cannot terminate a lease for a definite term either.[29] In this case no actual or constructive knowledge is required on the part of the purchaser, nor is any public notice mechanism provided for since lease contracts cannot be entered in the Land Register, with the exception of the lease of agricultural property, which can be registered specially for

[28] See Case 1.

[29] Where the identity of the landlord changes, the transfer of the claim for rent is governed by the rules of assignation. Through the assignation the assignee steps into the shoes of the assignor. The obligor can enforce against the assignee all claims that existed following intimation of the assignation (Civil Code, § 432(3) and, §§ 328–9). If the tenant paid rent, in advance, the landlord cannot claim rent for the period covered unless he/she was not or should not have been aware of the advance payment when concluding the contract (Civil Code, § 432(4)).

other purposes (Law on Agricultural Property, § 25/A-25/D). The exercise of possession by the tenant can be seen as a form of public notice. However, the above rule does not require that the tenant actually take possession of the property and consequently it does not follow that the latter's taking possession of the property must precede that of the purchaser.

Both *usufruct* and the *right of use* are rights *in rem* and accordingly have effect *erga omnes*. Rights *in rem* over immovable property will survive the transfer of title to the property if their registration precedes the registration of the transfer of title.[30] C's knowledge of the pre-existing usufruct or right of use is irrelevant as the doctrine of constructive notice finds application where rights are registered over immovable property. In this regard it is irrelevant whether or not the purchaser acquired the property for value or for no consideration.

As regards the *loan for use*, there is no provision which conflicts with the privity of contract and the relative structure of contractual legal relationships.

Italy

The right of the tenant (B) remains completely enforceable if the *lease* was registered in the Land Register before registration of the transfer to C (Civil Code, arts. 1599 and 2644). Alternatively, the tenant will only be protected for a period of nine years from the conclusion of the contract if the lease was not registered (Civil Code, art. 1599). Only leases granted for more than nine years therefore require registration in order to be enforceable (Civil Code, art. 2643 n. 8).

If B was granted a *usufruct*, *use*, *habitation* or a *hereditary building right*, his/her right remains enforceable if the legal act constituting the limited right or transfer of ownership in the building (in the case of a hereditary building right) was registered before registration of the transfer to C (Civil Code, art. 2644).

The right of the *borrower* is not enforceable against C[31] (unless there is a stipulation to this effect in the agreement between A and C).

30 Note that the validity of a usufruct and a right of use requires either registration or acquiring possession.

31 See e.g. Cass. civ. 15/05/1991 n. 5454.

The Netherlands

In the case of a *residential lease*, the transfer of ownership of the leased object will not end the lease. The new owner assumes all rights and duties of the former owner, even in the case of a forced sale (on execution) (Civil Code, art. 7:226), and thus automatically becomes the new landlord. The same applies to an *agricultural lease* under (Law on Agricultural lease (Pachtwet), art. 34; in future: Civil Code, art. 7:361).

The answer to Case 1 described the requirements to be met in order validly to create a right of *usufruct*, *hereditary building lease* (*superficies*) or *hereditary land lease* (*emphyteusis*). One of the requirements is registration of the notarial deed in the Land Register (Civil Code, arts. 3:98, 3:84 and 3:89). The underlying idea is that registration provides publicity to real rights.[32] In other words, there is a possibility for C to become aware of the limited real rights that encumber the land. C should have checked the Register and should have known about B's limited real right (Civil Code, arts. 3:23 and 3:24). If B's interest has been registered prior to C's interest, C must accept that B is entitled to a limited real right of *superficies*, *emphyteusis* or usufruct, regardless of whether C obtained the property for value or for no consideration.

A feature of a limited real right is that it can be enforced against any third party. This characteristic is not explicitly laid down in the Civil Code, but follows from the fact that limited real rights, in this case the rights of *superficies*, usufruct and *empheutysis*, have absolute effect against third parties. The enforcement of a (limited) real right against any third party is discussed in detail in the literature.[33]

If the right of *superficies*, *emphyteusis* or usufruct has come into existence by prescription, it can be registered (Civil Code, art. 3:17, sub. 1) in the Land Register. However, there is no duty to do so. But in case of prescription, B's interest works against third parties and thus against the subsequent owner of the land (C) even though B's interest had not been registered. Third-party protection against unregistered interests (BW, art. 3:24) therefor does not apply where the unregistered interest has been created as a result of prescription (BW, art. 3:24, para. 2e).[34]

[32] Pitlo, 'Goederenrecht', no. 21, p. 53.

[33] Asser, Mijnssen and de Haan, 'Algemeen Goederenrecht', no. 28; Pitlo, 'Goederenrecht', no. 24; Snijders and Rank-Berenschot, *Goederenrecht*, nos. 65–7. For usufruct, see Kleijn, *Vruchtgebruik*, no. 1.

[34] Pitlo, 'Goederenrecht', no. 75.

Poland

As has been noted before, B will be protected against C if the *lease* is created for a fixed term, reduced to writing with a certified date (where the date has been confirmed by a notary or a public body by, for example, endorsement with a seal or stamp) and the property has been physically transferred to the tenant. In such circumstances, the purchaser may not terminate the lease (Civil Code, art. 678) and must endure the tenant on the property. In this case it does not matter whether the transfer is for consideration or not and whether or not the acquirer (C) has knowledge of the lease. If the lease agreement does not meet the criteria mentioned above, C may terminate the lease by giving notice complying with the statutory notice periods. Article 678 does not apply to leases of residential premises (Civil Code, art. 692). In such cases, C may only terminate the lease by giving notice if the premises have not yet been occupied by the tenant. This right can, however, not be exercised by C if the residential lease has been registered in the Land Register.

Civil Code, art. 694 provides that the general provisions on leases must be applied to special types of leases which have not been regulated in an exhaustive manner. Consequently, Civil Code, art. 678 may be applied to an income-producing (*fruendi*) lease. This means that C may terminate the income-producing lease by giving notice in accordance with the statutory notice periods. However, if the contract is concluded for a fixed term, reduced to writing with a certified date, and the property has been transferred to the tenant, C must respect the income-producing lease. Consequently, Civil Code, art. 678 provides some protection to tenants of ordinary and income-producing leases in case of a sale, but the fact that most lease contracts are concluded in a regular written form is insufficient in practice to prevent the purchaser from giving notice and terminating the lease.

Tenants, therefore, make use of a better instrument to protect their interests, namely entry of the lease into the Land Register. Registration causes a right which is contractual in nature to become effective *erga omnes* and thus against purchasers of the land after the entry was made. If no such entry has been made, the tenant may only resort to Civil Code, art. 678, which in practice will provide inadequate protection owing to the form in which most leases or income-producing leases are concluded in practice.

In principle, a *lease* thus gives rise to a mere contractual or personal right, which is only enforceable *inter partes*. However, the legislator extended the enforcement of a lease in two instances by making a lease executed in the form prescribed by Civil Code, art. 678 and a lease registered in the Land Register, enforceable against the *bona fide* purchaser of the land.

In the case of *usufruct*, the situation is different as it is a real right, effective *erga omnes*. As a rule, C will not be able to terminate the usufruct if the usufruct is registered or if the Land Register contains a notification of a pending entry of a usufruct (Law on Land Register and Mortgages, art. 8). If, however, the right of B has not been registered, his/her right will terminate upon conveyance to C if the cause of the conveyance is a legal transaction (and not, for example, inheritance or expropriation), is made for value (LRM, art. 5) and C is not in bad faith. C will be in bad faith if he/she knew or easily could have found out that the Land Register does not reflect the legal status of the land (LRM, art. 6). LRM, arts. 5 and 6 will not protect C if the Land Register contains a notification of a pending entry (LRM, art. 8). Therefore, as a rule, usufruct will be effective against C, unless C claims that he/she relied on the fact that the usufruct is not registered in the Land Register and the transaction is for value and not gratuitous.

Lifetime habitation is always protected, even against purchases for value and in good faith, regardless of whether it is entered in the Land Register or not. Moreover, if this right is created together with the right of usufruct (that is, the person entitled to lifetime habitation also becomes the usufructuary of land he/she has sold to B), the usufruct will be viewed as an inherent part of lifetime habitation (Civil Code, art. 908, § 2) and will therefore not be extinguished upon transfer of property. However, if B transfers property to C, the holder of the lifetime habitation may demand that his/her right be converted into an allowance (annuity or pension) equal in value to the value of lifetime habitation (Civil Code, art. 914). The reason for this is that the person entitled to the lifetime habitation may not want to live with the purchaser of the immovable, oftentimes a complete stranger. The holder of the lifetime habitation may therefore choose to convert his/her right into an allowance and organise his/her living needs in an alternative manner (for example, by renting somewhere or by moving into a care facility). Lifetime habitation is capable of registration and, although it is in essence a contract, the legislator affords it extended protection, making it even stronger than a traditional real right.

Hereditary lease of land (hereditary usufruct or *empthyteusis*) may only be created on land owned by the State or local government. The Management of Real Property Act 1997 permits the State or local government to transfer land between them and obliges them to notify the holder of the hereditary land lease (hereditary usufruct) of the transaction (MRP, art. 32, § 3). Apart from this, the State or local government is not permitted to sell land encumbered with a hereditary land lease (hereditary usufruct) to anyone other than the holder (MRP, art. 32, § 1). The transfer of the land to C would therefore be void. Since registration is required for the validity of a hereditary land lease, no legal consequences are attached to unregistered hereditary land leases.

Portugal

The position of a *tenant* is governed by the maxim *emptio non tollit locatum* contained in Civil Code, art. 1057, which provides that sale does not supersede lease. Consequently, any person acquiring the rights of the landlord will succeed to the rights and obligations of his/her predecessor and would thus have to allow the tenant, without prejudice to the registration provisions, to continue his/her lease for the remaining period. Although the maxim specifically refers to sales, it covers all kinds of alienations including legacies, donations or the constitution of a usufruct.

As mentioned in Case I, residential leases for a term of less than six years, agricultural leases and forestry leases must be reduced to writing but do not require registration for its validity. Therefore, if concluded in written form before the conveyance of the property to C, these contracts will be enforceable against C.

Both residential leases for a term of more than six years and leases of premises for commercial, industrial or professional purposes, require registration prior to the conveyance to C for their enforceability. Any other factors, such as knowledge or occupancy, are irrelevant.

Under the Law on Real Property Registration (art. 5),[35] only a duly registered real right is enforceable against third parties. The *personal*

[35] The function of registration in Portugal is to provide publicity of the legal title of the property for enforceability (*oponobilidade*) against third parties (Law on Registration, art. 5). If the owner sells the same property to two different purchasers, whoever registers first becomes the new owner. Preference among the successive buyers depends on the order of entry of their respective titles in the Land Register. Under the Portuguese legal system registration is not required for the creation or transfer of a real right, except for the creation of mortgages on land. Ownership and limited real rights on land are validly acquired without registration in the Land Register. Unregistered contracts and other transactions involving land are enforceable *inter partes* between the parties and their heirs (Law on Registration, art. 4). The role of land registration here is to solve a conflict between a successor-in-title and another person who has an incompatible or conflicting

servitudes of usufruct, use and habitation as well as the institution of *heritable building lease* (*superficies*) are recognised as real rights in Portuguese law. Hence, if A conveys the property to C, the right of B, if duly registered, remains enforceable against C, irrespective of whether he/she acquired the property for value or not. An unregistered personal servitude or heritable building lease, although valid and enforceable *inter partes*, cannot be enforced against C.

Scotland

Only a *lease* and *proper liferent* give B a real right protected against transfer of ownership of the subjects by A.

At common law, a *lease* is a contract. The tenant (B) is simply the personal creditor of the landlord (A).[36] If A transfers to C, B has a contractual claim against A,[37] but none against C. Since the coming into force of the Leases Act 1449, tenants have been protected against transfer by the landlord. The precise effect of that Act is disputed: some take the view that the tenant's right is only *akin* to a real right, others that it is a fully fledged real right.[38] There has not been the debate on this point in Scots law that there has been in other systems and the point has not been resolved.[39] Certainly, when a lease is registered, the tenant obtains a real right, for the statute says so.[40] For ease, this scenario refers to the tenant having a 'real right', acknowledging that it may not be strictly accurate.

The law distinguishes between 'short' and 'long' leases. A short lease becomes real by possession and a long lease only by registration. A long lease is a probative lease with a duration exceeding twenty years (or which contains provisions which allow the tenant to extend the duration of the lease to more than twenty years).[41] All other leases are short

claim with regard to the same property with preference given to the successor who registers his/her interest first. Registration in the Land Register raises a presumption of title. Conversely, if there is no registration, the presumption is that there is no right or that the right has been cancelled and does no longer exist (Law on Registration, art. 7).

36 Stair, *Institutions*, I. xv. 4; Rankine, *Leases*, p. 132; Paton and Cameron, *Landlord and Tenant*, p. 103.

37 Bankton, *Institute*, I. xx. 1–2; Erskine, *Institute*, III. iii. 15; Bell, *Commentaries*, I. 64; Bell, *Leases*, p. 88.

38 See, generally, Guy, 'Registration of Leases', p. 234.

39 Hugo and Simpson, 'Lease', pp. 306–8.

40 LR(S)A 79, s. 3(3).

41 LR(S)A 79, s. 28(1). So the position is not, as contended by e.g. Gloag and Henderson, *Law of Scotland*, para. 36.04, that leases which exceed twenty years are long leases. The lease must also be probative. The existing terminology is therefore inaccurate: a 'short'

leases. The tenant of a short lease acquires a real right if he/she meets the requirements of the Leases Act 1449, viz.:[42]

(a) if the lease is for more than one year, it must be in formal writing;
(b) the lease must have an ish;
(c) the subjects of the lease must be land;
(d) the tenant must possess the property by virtue of the lease;
(e) there must be a rent which is not merely elusory; and
(f) the grantor of the lease must have title to grant it.

In some respects, these requirements are narrower than those for a contract of lease to be constituted. Whereas there can be a valid contract of lease which does not have a definite duration in order to be protected by the 1449 Act, the ish of the lease must be definite.[43] The lease must be of land, that is to say, of 'heritable subjects', which are 'capable of such open and continuous possession as may naturally suggest to a singular successor the existence of a lease'.[44] The Act applies to urban and rural property. The tenant must have entered possession of the property on or after the date of entry in order for the Act to apply. Possession prior to the date of entry will not suffice.[45] Possession can either be natural (where the tenant himself/herself possesses the subjects) or civil (where the tenant possesses by another, namely a sub-tenant).

If the lease is a long lease, it can only be made real by registration in the Land Register.[46] The possibility of registering a long lease was first introduced in 1857, when it was optional. The benefit of registration was that it enabled the tenant to grant security over the lease. Now it is mandatory in order to obtain a real right in respect of a long lease. It has been held that if a long lease has not been registered, the tenant has no claim in damages against the landlord if he subsequently transfers ownership of the property and the tenant's possession is interfered with.[47]

The date which determines whether B's right binds C is the date when C registers title to the land. In order for C to be bound there must either

lease could, in fact, be very long. 'Registrable' and 'non-registrable' would be better suited to the task.

42 See, on interpretations of these requirements, Rankine, *Leases*, pp. 134–47; Paton and Cameron, *Landlord and Tenant*, pp. 104–14; McAllister, *Leases*, paras. 2.24–2.29.

43 *Carruthers* v. *Irvine* (1717) Mor. 15 195.

44 *Campbell* v. *Mackinnon* (1867) 5 M 636 (IH) 651.

45 Paton, *Hume*, vol. 4, p. 81; Erskine, *Institute*, II. vi. 25. Nor will acts preparatory to taking possession: *Millar* v. *McRobbie* 1949 SC 1 (IH) 7–8.

46 LR(S)A 79, s. 3(3). See generally Scottish Law Commission, *Report on Land Registration*, Part 9.

47 *Palmer's Tr.* v. *Brown* 1989 SLT 128 (OH) 131F.

be possession (in a short lease) or registration (in the case of a long lease) by that date. No distinction is drawn between a successor who acquires for value or gratuitously: both are bound by the lease. Nor does it matter whether C was aware of the lease. Possession or registration provides sufficient publicity to alert C to the lease. There is academic support for holding that knowledge of B's right or a gratuitous transfer would make a difference if, when C acquired, B had not yet taken the required steps to make his/her right real. Scots law recognises a rule (known as the 'offside goals' rule) in respect of competitions of title in which a right which has not yet been made real can affect a singular successor if he/she knew of the right before he/she completed his/her own title.[48] So, if A grants a disposition (a deed of transfer) of land to B on day one and then fraudulently also to C on day three, and C registers its disposition on day five, C's title will be voidable if C knew[49] of the prior grant to B or acquired gratuitously or for a manifestly inadequate consideration.[50] Existing case law, such as it is, holds that rule not to apply to leases.[51] If A grants a lease to B on day one and a disposition to C on day three, and C registers the disposition before B either takes possession or registers the lease, B's right does not bind C even if he/she is aware of it. That position has been criticised[52] and the majority of academic opinion supports changing the law to provide B with a claim in those circumstances.

The effect of B's right being real is that when C acquires title, C steps into A's shoes in the contract of lease. The contract runs with the land. C 'comes into the place of his/her predecessor (A) in all leases existing at the date of his/her purchase, and is entitled to all the future rents and other benefits of such leases, and liable in all the obligations prestable against the landlord subsequent to the date of his/her entry'.[53] However, it is not every term of a lease which will run with the land. The law distinguishes between 'real' and 'personal'

[48] Reid et al., *Property*, paras. 695–700; Wortley, 'Double Sales', p. 29; *Rodger (Builders) Ltd.* v. *Fawdry* 1950 SC 483 (IH) 499–501.

[49] The point in time at which knowledge is assessed is important but not yet finally resolved: cf. *Alex Brewster and Sons* v. *Caughey* 2002 GWD 15-506; Anderson, '"Offside Goals"', pp. 290–1.

[50] *The Advice Centre for Mortgages* v. *McNicoll* [2006] CSOH 58, 2006 SLT 591, para. 45.

[51] *Johnston* v. *Monzie* (1760) 5 Brown's Supplement 877; *Birbeck* v. *Ross* (1865) 4 M 272 (OH) 276–7; *Jacobs* v. *Anderson* (1898) 6 SLT 234 (OH); Reid et al., *Property*, para. 697. Cf. previously *Richard* v. *Lindsay* (1725) Mor. 15 217.

[52] Reid et al., *Property*, para. 697; Brand, Steven and Wortley, *Conveyancing Manual*, para. 32. 60.

[53] *Barr* v. *Cochrane* (1878) 5 R 877 (IH) 883.

conditions: only real conditions form part of the contract of lease which runs with the land.[54] Personal conditions bind and benefit only the original landlord (A). The issue has arisen mostly in respect of leases of commercial premises where it has been held that an option in favour of the tenant to purchase the leased property does not bind a successor landlord.[55] Stated abstractly, the distinction is between terms of the original parties' agreement which are 'referable to their relationship as landlord and tenant' (which are real conditions and do transmit to C) and those which are extrinsic to that relationship (which are personal conditions and do not transmit).[56]

Once constituted as a real right by registration, B's *liferent* is enforceable against the world. It therefore remains enforceable against C. Although there appears to be no decision on the point, it is thought that the 'offside goals' rule would apply to protect B's position prior to registration. If, therefore, after the grant of a proper liferent to B, A, in breach of that grant, subsequently grants a disposition to C and C registers before B, C will be bound by B's right if C knew of B's right or acquired gratuitously or for a manifestly inadequate consideration.

South Africa

In the case of a *lease*, the tenant (B) will be protected against C if he/she has converted his/her contractual right into a real right by obtaining possession of the property (short lease) or by registration of a long lease over ten years.[57] Under an unregistered long lease, a tenant in possession is protected for a period of up to ten years.[58] This protection is based on the reception of the Germanic and later Roman-Dutch rule *huur gaat voor koop* (hire trumps sale) into modern South African law.[59] This rule covers not only sale but all kinds of alienations such as legacies, donations and the constitution of a usufruct. In terms of the rule, B's lease, which was established first, would prevail over the

[54] Paton and Cameron, *Landlord and Tenant*, pp. 95–7; McAllister, *Leases*, paras. 2.31–2.38. This area is considered in Webster, 'Relationship of Tenant and Successor Landlord', chs. 3–7.

[55] *The Advice Centre for Mortgages* v. *McNicoll* [2006] CSOH 58, 2006 SLT 591, para. 39.

[56] *Montgomerie* v. *Carrick* (1848) 10 D 1387 (IH) 1396.

[57] *Canavan and Rivas* v. *New Transvaal Gold Farms* 1904 TS 136.

[58] Cooper, *Landlord and Tenant*, pp. 275, 280, 310; Kerr, *Lease*, para. 191.

[59] See Cooper, *Landlord and Tenant*, p. 275 n. 16 citing twenty-six decisions of the High Court of South Africa and seven of the Supreme Court of Appeal, in support.

real right (ownership) acquired by C by virtue of the *prior in tempore* principle. This is the position even though C had no knowledge of the lease[60] and even though he acquired the property for value.

However, even if B's contractual right has not been converted into a real right by registration or occupation, A's successor C could still be bound by the lease contract. In this situation we must look at whether C is a universal or particular successor and whether he/she had knowledge of the lease or not. Based on a misinterpretation of a passage of the Roman-Dutch writer Voet,[61] South African courts have placed a successor by lucrative title (*titulo lucrativo*) (without any consideration) in the same category as a universal successor who inherits both the rights and obligations of an estate. The courts held that both these kinds of successors are bound by the contract of lease between the landlord (A) and the tenant (B).[62] But a universal succcessor is bound because he/she succeeds to both rights and obligations and not because he/she received something for nothing. Therefore, on this reasoning, the acquirer without value (*titulo lucrativo*) will not be bound by the lease by reason of his/her lucrative title only.[63]

A particular successor is, however, bound to the extent of his/her knowledge by the contractual obligations of the lease if he/she (C) had actual knowledge thereof at the time of transfer.[64]

A duly registered *usufruct* creates a real right in the property enforceable against the whole world and thus against C, irrespective of C's knowledge or whether he acquired the property for value or not. Without registration, the usufructuary (B) only has a personal right to have the usufruct registered and C will only be bound by the usufruct if he/she acquires the property with actual knowledge of the unregistered usufruct.[65] In such an instance, C will be required to assist in having the usufruct registered.[66] The legal position will be the same if C acquired the property by lucrative title.[67]

60 See Cooper, *Landlord and Tenant*, p. 284 n 82; *Frye's Pty Ltd.* v. *Ries* 1957 3 SA 575 (A) 582.
61 Voet, *Commentarius*, 19.2.1. 62 *Kessoopersadh* v. *Essop* 1970 1 SA 265 (A) 273 285.
63 Voet, *Commentarius*, 19.2.17; De Wet and Van Wyk, *Kontraktereg*, p. 375; Cooper, *Landlord and Tenant*, pp. 283–4.
64 See Formalities in Respect of Leases of Land Act 18 of 1969, s. 1(2)(b); Cooper, *Landlord and Tenant*, pp. 284–8, 309–11.
65 Van der Merwe, 'Servitudes', para. 457.
66 See *Erasmus* v. *Du Toit* 1910 TPD 1037 qualified in *Frankel Pollak Vinderine Inc* v. *Stanton* 2000 1 SA 425 (W).
67 *Oliver* v. *Matzner and Matzner* 1942 TPD 324 330.

The same principles apply *mutatis mutandis* to the personal servitudes of *use* and *habitation*.

Spain

When the contract of *lease* is not governed by the Laws on Rural or Urban Lease, the Civil Code (art. 1571) provides that B's right will be extinguished on conveyance of the property to C. This follows the ancient Roman law rule that sale supersedes hire: *emptio tollit locatio* or *venta quita renta*. This will be the position unless the parties to the contract of sale (A and C) have agreed otherwise,[68] or the Law on Hypothecs (LoH) provides otherwise.[69] The Laws on Urban and Rural Lease changed this position. Under a contract of lease of both rural and residential property, the tenant (B) will be able to enforce his/her right against C after the property is conveyed to B. This seems to be the case even if C acquires the property *bona fide* and for value in terms of the LoH, art. 34 (Law on Rural Lease, art. 22)[70] and Law on Urban Lease, art. 14, para. 1) and even if the lease was not registered.[71] Under a rural lease, C will have to allow B to remain on the property for the minimum period (three years) or for any extension thereof.[72] By contrast, in a lease of residential property, the right will always remain enforceable for at least the first five years of the contract[73] (Law on Urban Lease, art. 14, para. 1). Where C is protected by LoH, art. 34,[74] he/she will have to respect the contract only for the rest of the remaining five-year period, irrespective of the fixed term of the lease (Law on Urban Lease, art. 14,

[68] Lucas Fernández, 'Comment on article 1571', p. 1139.

[69] It is understood that this occurs when the lease contract was registered in the Land Register (Lucas Fernández, 'Comment on articles 1571 and 1572', pp. 1353–4). In such a case C cannot argue that he did not know that the lease contract existed.

[70] Law on Hypothecs (LoH), art. 34 protects the purchaser in good faith who has acquired the property for value from a person who had apparent authority to convey ownership in immovable property in the Land Register. This article protects a bona fide purchaser who acquires for value and from a person who apparently has the capacity to convey the ownership over the immovable in the Land Register. This means that B will be protected even when the lease contract was not registered. See Vattier Fuenzalida, 'Comment', pp. 250–1.

[71] Fínez Ratón, 'Comment', p. 204.

[72] Vattier Fuenzalida, 'Comment', p. 254.

[73] Note that the contract can last as long as the parties decide, but, if the agreed term is under five years, the contract will be compulsorily extended (*prorrogado*) year by year for a minimum of five years (Law on Urban Lease, art. 9).

[74] C must have acted in good faith and must have acquired for value from a registered owner without the lease being registered in the Land Register (Fínez Ratón, 'Comment', p. 205).

para. 2).[75] In all other instances (that is, when the purchaser C is not protected by LoH, art. 34), where the fixed term of the lease between A and B exceeds five years, the lease will be enforceable until expiry of such term (Law on Urban Lease, art. 9). Where the parties (A and B) have agreed that conveyance of the property shall extinguish the contract, the purchaser C will be bound by the lease only until the first five years have expired (Law on Urban Lease, art. 14, para. 3).

In the case of *usufruct*, *right of use* and *right of habitation*, B's right remains enforceable against C[76] if the limited real right is registered in the Land Register before the property is conveyed to C (LoH, art. 13).[77] This is the position irrespective of C's knowledge or whether he/she acquired the property for value or not. Regional laws contain no special provisions on this issue.

Since a *loan for use* creates mere personal rights between the parties, the right of the borrower (B) cannot be enforceable against C unless this is specifically provided for in the contract between A and C.[78] The Fuero Nuevo contains no special rules on this issue.

Precarium is never enforceable by B against the new owner (C), as it is a gratuitous concession granted by the owner (A), which remains revocable at his/her will. The conveyance of property to C can be construed as an implied revocation of the permission given to B to use A's property.

As already mentioned, all limited real rights may be registered and if registered shall be enforceable against the world at large (LoH, art. 13). Since a *hereditary building lease* (*superficies*) is recognised as a limited real right, it becomes enforceable vis-à-vis C as soon as it is registered. Under Spanish Land Law (SLL) of 2008, art. 40.2, registration is needed for the constitution of the right of *superficies*. At the same time, non-registered real rights are not enforceable against third parties (LoH, art. 32). Once

[75] In this case, A will have to indemnify B with one month's rent for each of the remaining years over the five years' term.

[76] But this occurs just until the expiration of the term for which the real right was created. Civil Code, art. 489 allows A, the nude owner (*nudo propietario*), to transfer his/her right of ownership. Civil Code, art. 513 lists the ways of termination of usufruct: conveyance of the property is not included among them. Civil Code, art. 529 provides that the rights of use and habitation expire in the same ways as usufruct.

[77] Lacruz Berdejo, *Elementos*, vol. 3, p. 196.

[78] Although the Civil Code contains no special provision on conveyancing of the property temporarily given to B, Civil Code, art. 1742 provides that in the case of A's death the latter's rights and duties are transmitted to his/her heirs who will have to respect B's position, except 'when the loan was agreed by taking into account the personal qualities of B' (when it is a contract *intuitus personae*). In this case, the heirs of B have no right to continue with the use of the property.

registered, the hereditary building lease will consequently be effective against C, irrespective of his/her knowledge or whether he/she acquired the property for value or not. Catalonia's Civil Code, art. 564–3.3 provides that registration is not required for the constitution of a hereditary building lease (*superficies*). Registration of the constitution or modification of the right or knowledge of the right on their part is required for the enforceability of the right against third parties.

Case 3
What happens if land subject to a time-limited interest is attached in execution of a debt or the landowner becomes insolvent? Does a previously registered mortgage rank above a subsequently constituted time-limited interest?

Some time after the creation of the time-limited right concerned:

- *creditors of A attach the property;*
- *A becomes insolvent/bankrupt.*

Is the time-limited right of B included in the attachment or insolvency/bankruptcy assets?

If A has created a prior mortgage on the property, will the time-limited right be enforceable against the mortgage creditor?

Comparative observations

Most jurisdictions accept that a *lease* which has been created as a property right prior to the *attachment* of the assets of A, followed by a forced sale, will prevail against a purchaser in a forced sale.[1] As in Case 2, the rights of the lessee will be subrogated to the rights of the purchaser in the forced sale,[2] sometimes subject to certain conditions.[3] The requirements for a lease to be converted to a property right are the same as under Case 2.

[1] See e.g. the Greek, French and Belgian reports for the termination of a lease concluded after attachment of the property.

[2] In Germany the purchaser in a forced sale may serve a notice of termination on B without having to show a justified interest.

[3] See e.g. the German, Austrian, Greek, French, Portuguese, Scottish, South African and Polish reports. Portuguese doctrine treats the priority of the lease in attachment proceedings as an application of the doctrine of subrogation rather than the *prior in tempore* principle. Hungarian law requires that the purchaser must notify the tenant that rent must henceforth be paid to him/her.

Although Spanish law does not accept the Roman law maxim *emptio non tollit locationem*, a lease registered in the Land Register will prevail on attachment and, in the field of urban leases in particular, there has been a tendency to afford greater protection to tenants on attachment of the property. In Italy, leases registered prior to the attachment will prevail as well as unregistered long leases for longer than nine years for the first nine years of the lease. If the date of shorter leases is not certified, but the lessees entered into possession before attachment, the purchaser has to honour the lease for specified periods, which vary according to the nature of the lease. In England, if creditors of A seek a charging order against A's property to secure payment of a judgment debt, the order is limited to A's reversionary interest in the land subject to the lease and the lease of B, which is a separate estate, is not included in the procedure. In Denmark, B's rights in terms of an ordinary lease will be protected both in case of attachment of A's property by his/her creditors and in the event of A's insolvency. Extraordinary lease provisions will also be protected if they were registered before the attachment of A's property or A's bankruptcy.[4]

In most jurisdictions, for instance, Germany, Austria, Belgium, Spain, Portugal and South Africa, a prior *lease* will also prevail in a *sale in insolvency* and the purchaser will also be subrogated for the lessor A.[5] Similarly, in England, the reversion of the lease vests in the trustee on bankruptcy of the landlord and the trustee is subject to all the liabilities which bind the bankrupt landlord. However, the lease of B, being a separate estate, is not included in this procedure.

The court may, in certain circumstances, revoke a lease concluded in Greece and Belgium during the so-called 'suspect' period, that is, between the date A defaulted on his/her payments and the date of the official declaration of the bankruptcy by the court. The instances are where the rent is disproportionately lower than the market rent and where the tenant knew that the landlord was insolvent or that the lease was concluded fraudulently for the purpose of defrauding A's creditors.[6]

In exceptional cases, the administrator in insolvency is entitled to terminate a residential or agricultural lease to facilitate the proper

[4] If not registered, these rights will be extinguished even if the creditors were in bad faith.

[5] See e.g. the German, Austrian, Belgian, Spanish, Portuguese and South African reports.

[6] See the Greek and Belgian reports.

management of the bankrupt estate. Similarly, in Spain, either the insolvent landlord or the administrator in insolvency may request the court to terminate the lease on the ground that it is in the best interests of insolvency proceedings or that the lease impedes the sale of the assets. The court may then award damages to the tenant for the loss of the lease.[7] In all cases of termination, reasonable notice must be given to the tenant.[8]

Most jurisdictions accept that a *mortgage registered prior* to the conclusion of the lease ranks higher than the lease, with the result that the land need not be sold subject to the lease.[9] If the tenant acted *bona fide*, some jurisdictions accept that a lease registered after the mortgage will still be enforceable for nine years in Belgium and Italy and a residential lease for five years in Spain against the purchaser in a forced sale. Only Hungarian law seems to accept that a lease registered after the mortgage can still be enforced against the purchaser in a forced sale.

In South Africa, the owner of mortgaged property may conclude a short lease or register a long lease without the consent of the mortgage creditor, provided that this is not precluded by the mortgage agreement. If the mortgage is enforced, the property must first be offered for sale subject to the lease. Only if the highest bid is insufficient to discharge the mortgage debt, may it be sold free of the lease which would extinguish the lease. The lessee will have a contractual claim against A for loss suffered but this will rank as a concurrent (unsecured) claim against A's insolvent estate. In Denmark, if the rights of the tenant are protected under the Private Housing Act or the Commercial Premises Rent Act, they can be enforced even against a previously registered mortgage.

In most jurisdictions, the fact that a *personal servitude* has been registered in the Land Register or transcribed in the Mortgage Register[10] is sufficient to render it enforceable against a purchaser in a forced sale after *attachment proceedings*.[11] In Hungarian law this also applies to

[7] See the Spanish and Polish reports.

[8] See the Portuguese, Danish and Polish reports. This was decided authoritatively by the Portuguese Supreme Court.

[9] See the German, Austrian, Greek and Polish reports.

[10] In addition, the Spanish Code of Civil Procedure allows occupiers with sufficient title to remain in possession without requiring their titles to be registered.

[11] See the German, Austrian, Greek, French, Belgian, Dutch, Portuguese, Spanish, Italian, South African, Hungarian and Polish reports. In Belgium this is subject to the exceptions described in the report under lease.

personal servitudes which are created automatically by operation of law and in Poland to a usufruct or lifetime habitation which has been called to the bailiff's attention at least three days prior to the forced sale.

In most jurisdictions, the fact that a personal servitude has been registered also suffices to afford it priority on in-gathering of the assets and sale of the property in *insolvency proceedings*.[12] The purchaser in a forced sale acquires the property subject to B's right. In Greece and Belgium, the position is different in the case of personal servitudes registered during the so-called 'suspect period' as described under lease. Under Spanish and Austrian insolvency law, dispositions that adversely affect creditors (for example, if not granted for consideration) can be set aside if they are granted within the two years preceding the declaration of insolvency. In Poland, a usufruct, lifetime habitation or hereditary land lease (*emphyteusis*) previously granted, will not expire on A's insolvency if it is registered or the bankruptcy court is notified within the specified time limits.

In most continental jurisdictions, registered real rights rank in order of their registration according to the principle *prior in tempore potior in iure*. Thus, a *prior registered mortgage* will rank above a subsequently registered personal servitude. If the land is sold free of the servitude and the proceeds of the forced sale is sufficient to satisfy the mortgage debt, Dutch law gives the holder of the personal servitude a preferential claim for the value of the servitude on the surplus of the sale and all the other assets of the landowner (A).

The German and South African reports show that a ranking agreement reached with the mortgage creditor can result in the land being sold subject to the personal servitude in a forced sale. This is the case where the mortgage creditor gives his/her written consent that the personal servitude is freed from the prior mortgage.

In Greece, France and Austria, the holders of personal servitudes are entitled to offer to satisfy the mortgage creditor's claim by set-off or by public deposit of the amount owed. In exchange for payment, they are subrogated to the mortgage creditor's rights. In Spain, the Spanish Code of Civil Procedure compels the Land Registrar to inform the holders of registered personal servitudes of the impending calling up of the prior mortgage. These holders are then given the option to pay the full outstanding debt secured by the mortgage in return for retaining their rights and being subrogated to the position of the mortgage creditor.

[12] See the German, Austrian, Dutch, South African and Hungarian reports.

This means that the equity in the land (the difference between the value of the land free from the personal servitude and the land subject to the servitude) acts as security for the claim taken over by them. If they do not exercise this option, the fact that their rights were registered after the mortgage means that they will not prevail in a forced sale or in insolvency and their real rights will be cancelled, allowing the purchaser to acquire the property unburdened.

With regard to *other limited real rights*, the German report shows that a *hereditary building right* (*superficies*) must always be ranked first in order to be validly created. Subsequent ranking agreements with regard to this right are excluded. It will therefore always survive attachment proceedings by A's creditors and will not form part of the landowner's (A's) assets in insolvency proceedings. The German Insolvency Code provides the holder of a hereditary building right (*superficies*) with a right of vindication against the insolvent estate to protect his/her right in the property from becoming part of the assets of A's insolvent estate. In the rest of the jurisdictions,[13] hereditary building rights (*superficies*) and hereditary land leases (*emphyteusis*) are treated the same as personal servitudes in the case of the attachment of A's assets and on the insolvency of A.

The one exception is Poland. If land subject to a hereditary land lease (*emphyteusis*) is sold in execution, the lease will expire and the holder will be entitled to claim an amount equivalent to the value of the hereditary lease from the proceeds of the sale. In practice, the creditors of local authorities will, however, look for assets other than land encumbered with a hereditary land lease to attach that can be sold off more swiftly and at a lower cost. Theoretically, land belonging to a local authority and burdened with a hereditary land lease in Poland could be gathered in by the trustee in insolvency and sold in a public sale. It is, however, a very contentious issue whether local authorities can be liquidated and it never occurs in practice.

The rule that a hereditary building right in Germany must always be ranked first means that it will prevail against a *prior mortgage*. In the other jurisdictions, the position will be more or less the same as in the discussion under personal servitudes.

In Spain, A's creditors can attach property subject to a *loan for use* and such property forms part of A's insolvent estate. If, however, the property is sold in execution, the Code of Civil Procedure grants the court a

[13] See e.g. the Austrian, Belgian, Spanish, Italian and Dutch reports.

discretion to make an order that the holder has 'sufficient title' to remain in possession of the property. In the case of insolvency, the insolvent or the insolvency administrator may apply for the termination of the loan if it will serve the interests of the insolvency proceedings. In Italy and Belgium, the right of a holder for use (*comodatario*) is not protected against creditors.

Austria

On application of the judgment creditor, the competent court may satisfy the judgment by liquidating the land either by forced administration (Law on Execution, § 97) or by forced auction (Law on Execution, § 133). Hence, the judgment creditor will be satisfied either by the income of the property (such as the rent for a lease) or by the purchase price.

The placing of the land under *forced administration* does not have any effect on existing *lease* contracts (Law on Execution, § 111, para. 1). Civil Code, § 1120 does not apply in this case.[14] However, the tenant is directed to pay the rent to the administrator and not to the owner (Law on Execution, § 110) so that the money can be used to satisfy the judgment creditor (Law on Execution, § 109).

If the property is sold in execution, the question arises whether the right of the tenant may be enforced against the successful bidder. Similarly to the contractual sale of land, the answer to this question depends on whether: (a) the tenant has already been given possession, (b) the lease falls under the Law on Tenancy, and (c) the lease is registered in the Land Register.

(a) If the tenant has already been given possession of the property, Civil Code, § 1121, sent. 2 provides that the contract is transferred to the successful bidder who substitutes the previous landlord. He/she takes over the whole lease contract, including any accessory clauses, except for provisions on termination which are to his/her disadvantage.[15]

(b) If the lease contract falls under the Law on Tenancy, the successful bidder has no specific right of termination under Civil Code, art. 1120 (Law on Tenancy, § 2, para. 1, sents. 4 and 5). The whole contract is transferred with the exception of uncommon accessory clauses of which the successful bidder neither knew nor ought to have known.[16]

[14] Angst, *Kommentar*, § 111, para. 2.

[15] 1 Ob 344/99s; JBl (2000), p. 793; Iro, *Kommentar*, § 1121, para. 2.

[16] 8 Ob 122/00z; OGH 22.12.1998, 5 Ob 117/98m; immolex 1999/70.

These two rules will also apply if the creditor has a prior mortgage.[17] In order to avoid devaluation of the mortgaged property by the creation of leases, the mortgage creditor can claim non-conclusion of new or cancellation of existing lease contracts. However, the lease can only be cancelled against the tenant if the tenant acted negligently (Civil Code, § 458).[18]

(c) If the lease is registered in the Land Register, it is treated like a servitude (Civil Code, § 1121 and Law on Execution, § 150, para. 3). The successful bidder has to take over the contract and does not have a right to terminate in accordance with CC§ 1121, sent. 2. If the creditor is a mortgage creditor, the ranking in the Land Register (which depends on priority) is decisive, as it is for servitudes.

If the landlord becomes *insolvent*, the lease contract continues. There is no specific right of termination in this case. If the object of the lease is sold in the course of insolvency proceedings, the provisions regarding sales in execution apply.[19] The rights of mortgage creditors are enforced in accordance with the provisions of the Law on Execution. The same rules as described above apply.[20]

The forced administration does not have any effect on *personal servitudes*. In a sale in execution, the successful bidder acquires the land subject to the servitude. In the case of a prior mortgage, the mortgage will rank higher than the servitude (Law on Execution, § 150). The successful bidder will only acquire the land subject to the servitude if the proceeds of the sale subject to the servitude are sufficient to satisfy the mortgage creditor.[21]

By an analogous application of Civil Code, § 462 and Law on Execution, § 200, no. 2, the holder of a lower ranking servitude is entitled to acquire the better rank of the mortgage creditor by satisfying his/her claims. Thereby he/she can make sure that the successful bidder acquires the land subject to the servitude. When he/she redeems the mortgage, he/she acquires the claim together with the mortgage concerned.[22]

[17] See e.g. Austrian Supreme Court 18.9.1986, 5 Ob 576/86; SZ 59/155.

[18] 6 Ob 107/98y; MietSlg 50.029; 6 Ob 136/98p; EvBl (1998), p. 184; 8 Ob 254/99g; immolex 2000/145; Kletecka, in Koziol and Welser, *Bürgerliches Recht*, vol. 1, p. 391; Hofmann, in Rummel, *Kommentar*, vol. 1, § 458, para. 6.

[19] Oberhammer, in Konecny and Schubert, *Insolvenzgesetze*, § 24, para. 1.

[20] Schulyok, in Konecny and Schubert, *Insolvenzgesetze*, § 48, paras. 168 ff.

[21] 3 Ob 102/84; JBl (1986), p. 124 (comment by Hoyer).

[22] JBl (1986), p. 124 (comment by Hoyer); Hofmann, in Rummel, *Kommentar*, vol. 1, § 462, para. 3; Angst, *Kommentar*, § 200, para. 4.

The same rules apply if the land concerned is sold in the course of insolvency proceedings.[23]

The *hereditary building right* is governed by the same rules as those applicable to personal servitudes (Law on Building Rights, § 11). Note that Austrian insolvency law allows certain contracts and dispositions to be set aside upon application of the creditor if they were wilfully made to the detriment of the creditor, provided that the other party to the respective disposition/contract acted at least negligently (Law on Insolvency, §§ 27 ff.).

Belgium

The time limited rights *in rem* of B (usufruct, hereditary land lease (*emphyteusis*), or hereditary building lease (*superficies*)) cannot be attached by the creditors of A or included in the insolvency/bankruptcy assets of A provided that, in the case of attachment the time-limited rights have been recorded in the Mortgage Register prior to the attachment (transcription of the attachment documents), and in the case of insolvency/bankruptcy the time-limited rights have been recorded in the Mortgage Register before the bankruptcy is declared.

In general, rights *in personam*, such as a *loan for use* and *precarium*, are included in the attachment or insolvency/bankruptcy assets. An agricultural lease is, however, excluded (Law on Agricultural Leases, art. 55).[24] A residential lease with a certified date prior to the attachment or bankruptcy is also excluded (Code of Civil Procedure, art. 1575). Although contested, it is usually accepted that this also holds for a residential lease without a certified date but with a minimum period of six months' occupation by the tenant.[25] Exceptionally, however, the curator/administrator can terminate a residential or agricultural lease if this is necessary for the effective management of the estate under bankruptcy (Law on Bankruptcy of 8 August 1997, art. 46).[26]

If B concluded the contract creating a time-limited right in the so-called suspect period (namely, from the moment as determined by the court that A stopped paying his/her debts), and B knew that A was insolvent, the administrator in insolvency may decide that the

[23] See e.g. 2 Ob 212/98k; NZ (2000), p. 138.

[24] See e.g. Supreme Court of 28 Nov. 2008, ARC 07.0358.N, available at www.cass.be.

[25] See e.g. Dambre and Hubeau, *Woninghuur*, nos. 1232 ff.

[26] Supreme Court of 10 Apr. 2008, C.05.0527.N, available at www.cass.be.

time-limited right is not excluded from the insolvency assets of A (Law on Bankruptcy, art. 18). The time-limited right is automatically included if it was granted gratuitously during the suspect period (art. 17). The position is the same if the time-limited right is deemed to have been concluded in order to defraud A's creditor (art. 20).

If A created a *mortgage prior* to the time-limited right, the mortgage creditor is in general entitled to demand immediate payment from the debtor if his/her security is diminished (Civil Code, art. 1188 and Law on Mortgage, art. 79). If the mortgage creditor has made his/her right public by recording the mortgage in the Mortgage Register, then the right cannot be frustrated by a later time-limited real right, since such right will not rank higher than the prior mortgage. The later time-limited right is therefore not enforceable against the mortgage creditor. If, however, the prior contract to mortgage was not recorded in the Mortgage Register prior to the recording or transcription of the time-limited right, the mortgage creditor can claim the debt from A, but may not enforce the mortgage against B, except if he/she can prove that B was not in good faith and had actual notice of the mortgage at the time of the acquisition of his/her time-limited real right. Moreover, if the time-limited right was granted with a fraudulant intention, the mortgage creditor can use the *actio Pauliana* to render the time-limited right unenforceable (Civil Code, art. 1167).

The mortgage creditor must respect a residential or agricultural lease concluded by A in good faith. Where the lease is concluded for more than nine years, then only the nine-year period already started must be respected (Law on Mortgage, art. 45 *in fine*). This is so even if the mortgage was registered prior to the lease.

Denmark

As a starting point, the rights of B are included, but a *creditor* as well as the *administrator in bankruptcy* must respect B's rights to land and buildings in exactly the same way as A must respect them (Law on Registration of Property, s. 1). The protective provisions of the Law on Registration of Property, s. 3, the Law on Private Housing, s. 7 and the Law on Commercial Premises Rent, s. 6 also ensure B's rights against A's creditors and A's estate in bankruptcy.

There are two exceptions to this. First, extraordinary rights under a contract of lease can be extinguished, but only if the creditor or the estate in bankruptcy registers the right before B. Under these circumstances creditors may extinguish the rights even if in bad faith (Law on

Registration of Property, s. 1(2)). Secondly, the estate in bankruptcy may adopt all synallagmatic contracts made by A, or by customary or reasonable notice, terminate long-term contracts whether irrevocable or not (Law on Bankruptcy, s. 61).[27] If B is protected against termination under the Law on Private Housing or under the Law on Commercial Premises Rent, this protection cannot be set aside.

Any *prior mortgage* must respect the rights of B, even if granted later, due to the provisions mentioned in Case 2. If B is granted extraordinary rights, these will only stand if B in good faith registered his/her right before the mortgage deed was registered in the Land Register.

England

The basic position in respect of the bankruptcy of the landlord is that the reversion of the *lease* vests in the trustee in bankruptcy, and is subject to all the liabilities which bind the bankrupt.[28] The rights of B, being a separate estate, are not included in these procedures. Further, it is also possible for creditors to seek a charging order against the reversion on the basis of a judgment debt. Again, however, this is limited to the reversion – the rights of B are entirely separate and not included in the procedure.

As to the *right to lease mortgaged property*, it is acknowledged by statute[29] that both mortgagor and mortgagee have the right, subject to contrary agreement, to lease the property which has been mortgaged. If, contrary to such an agreement, the property is leased, the lease will be void as between tenant and mortgagee, but valid as between tenant and landlord/mortgagor.[30]

France

Under Civil Code, art. 2284 and 2285 (Ord. no. 2006–346 of 23 March 2006) (ex arts. 2092 and 2093 Civil Code), the creditors of A may *attach* to sell the movable and immovable property owned by A to satisfy their debts from the proceeds of the sale. Civil Code, art. 2193 (Ord. no. 2006–461 of 21 April 2006) provides that, in the absence of specific legislative provisions, attachment and sale in execution of immovable property can extend to all real rights that pertain to the property,

[27] Consolidated Act No. 1259 of 23 Oct. 2007 and later amendments.

[28] See Berry, Bailey and Shaw Miller, *Personal Insolvency*, para. 25.3; Insolvency Act 1986, ss. 283, 306 and 436.

[29] See Law of Property Act 1925, s. 99.

[30] *Rust* v. *Goodale* [1957] ch. 33.

including their accessories deemed immovable. The attachment of an immovable includes its fruits other than those covered by a previous attachment (Civil Code, art. 2194, Ord. 21/04/2006). Thus a distinction is made according to whether B's time-limited right with regard to A's property is a personal or a real right.

If B has a *personal right* with regard to the land which is prior in time to the attachment, for example, where B is a *tenant*, A's creditors can attach and sell the land in execution only subject to the lease. In fact, the creditor who attaches the property, as well as the new purchaser, will find that the lease is enforceable against them (Civil Code, art. 2199, Ord. 21/04/2006). Whatever their length, leases concluded by the landowner/debtor (A) after the attachment, however, cannot be enforced against the creditor or against the new purchaser who attaches the property. Proof that the lease was prior in time may be supplied by any means.

The provisions on attachment do not cover other contracts such as a *loan for use* and a *precarious loan*, which are rarely used in practice. By analogy, the answer to Case 2 will also apply in this case.

Where B has a *real right* such as a *usufruct* on the property prior in time to the attachment, A's creditors only have rights with respect to the nude ownership of the property (namely the entitlements of ownership which A retained). The landowner/debtor (A) is not entitled to alienate or burden his/her property with other real rights after attachment as attachment renders the property unavailable and limits the debtor's rights of enjoyment and administration (Civil Code, art. 2198, Ord. 21/04/2006). The attachment of land can, however, be enforced against third parties from the time of its publication in the Land Register (Civil Code, art. 2200, Ord. 21/04/2006). Real rights which were not registered prior to the registration of the attachment cannot be enforced against the creditor or the purchaser at the sale in execution (whether under judicial authority, by private agreement or by auction). Thus B's real right can be enforced against A's creditors if it was registered in the Land Register prior to the attachment.

The above also applies in the case of the insolvency of A.

If A has created a *prior mortgage* (*hypothèque*)[31] over the property, B as a usufructuary will not be able to enforce the usufruct against the

[31] Please note that for this answer the word 'mortgage' has been used although there is an essential difference between the traditional mortgage and the French *hypothèque*: the latter is not a transfer of the legal title to the mortgagee, defeasible on payment of the debt, but only a real right in the property owned by another, securing a debt. Thus it has similar features as the charge by way of legal mortgage.

mortgage creditor. B will, however, be entitled to pay A's debt secured by the mortgage in order to prevent the attachment and sale of the property, in which case he/she will then have a right of recourse against the nude owner (Civil Code, art. 611). It may also be noted that the purchaser of a real right (whether time-limited or not) who is not entitled to enforce this right against a creditor who attaches the property to which the right pertains because the right was not registered or only registered after the attachment, can nevertheless prevent the attachment by depositing a sum sufficient to discharge the principal debt, interest, and costs incurred due to the attachment creditor and to the registered mortgage (*hypothèque*) creditor (Civil Code, art. 2200, para. 2, Ord. 21/04/2006). Where A had previously granted a mortgage (*hypothèque*) in favour of a creditor and this security in the immovable had been registered prior to the granting of a time-limited right to B, B cannot enforce his/her right against the mortgage creditor.

Germany

A's property may only be attached and sold in execution by his/her execution creditors subject to B's *lease* (*Gesetz über die Zwangsversteigerung und die Zwangsverwaltung* (Law on Forced Sale and Forced Administration), § 57). However, the person acquiring the property in the forced sale is entitled to give notice of termination to B without having to show a justified interest (Law on Forced Sale, § 57a). Certain limitations are applicable in the case of the forced sale of property subject to a residential lease (cf. Civil Code, § 573).

The same considerations apply in insolvency proceedings against A (*Insolvenzordnung* (Insolvency Code) § 111).

In the case of *personal servitudes*, the ranking (*Rang*) of B's right as registered in the Land Register is the key in attachment proceedings against A. The ranking or order of precedence among several competing rights is determined by the sequence of entries in the Land Register unless all holders of rights concerned agree otherwise (Civil Code, § 879).

If B's right has been registered prior to the creditor's right, or if the creditor has initiated the attachment proceedings merely on the basis of a personal right, the acquirer of the property put on forced sale (*Zwangsversteigerung*) acquires the property burdened with B's right. If, however, the creditor has a prior mortgage, B loses his/her right (Law on Forced Sale, § 52(1) and, § 91(1)). B is limited to a claim for compensation to be satisfied out of the remaining proceeds of the forced sale (Law on Forced Sale, § 92(2) and, § 121).[32]

The agreement creating a permanent right of habitation (*Dauerwohnrecht*) may stipulate that the right-holder will retain his/her right even in a forced sale initiated by a creditor with a prior registered mortgage. It must be noted, however, that such a provision will require the consent of the mortgage creditor (Law on Apartment Ownership, § 39).

In insolvency proceedings against the landowner (A), B has a remedy (right of vindication) by which he can isolate his/her right from the insolvency assets according to Insolvency Code, § 47 (*rei vindicatio* in insolvency). B's right is not included in the insolvency assets if he makes use of the remedy.

Since a *hereditary building right* must always be ranked first to be validly created and subsequent changes of this ranking will be excluded (Regulations on Hereditary Building Rights, § 10), it will always survive attachment proceedings against the owner of the property (Regulations on Hereditary Building Rights, § 25).

In insolvency proceedings against the landowner (A), the Insolvency Code (§ 47) provides B with a right of vindication against the insolvent estate to protect his/her right in the property. By using this remedy, the holder can ensure that his/her right is not included in the insolvency assets of A.

Greece

The Greek Code of Civil Procedure (CCP, art. 1009) provides that if property subject to a *lease* is sold at a *forced sale*, Civil Code, arts. 614 and 616 are applicable by analogy. This means that if A's creditors attach the property only a lease which can be evidenced by a deed bearing a certified date or, in the case of a lease for more than nine years, a lease which is notarially executed and transcribed in the conveyance records of the Land Register can prevail (Civil Code, art. 618).[33] It has been pointed out[34] that the said CCP, art. 1009 must be interpreted in correlation

[32] See Petzold, *Münchener Kommentar*, § 1030, no. 34 (usufruct). See also *ibid.* no. 33 regarding the usufructuary's right to prevent a forced administration (*Zwangsverwaltung*) of the property.

[33] See Case 2.

[34] Nikolopoulos, in Kerameus, Kondylis and Nikas, *Code of Civil Procedure*, vol. 1, p. 1009, no. 5; Yessiou-Faltsi, *Forced Execution*, p. 127.

with CCP, art. 997, para. 1. Accordingly, it applies to leases that have been entered into before the attachment.

The consequences of a lease executed after attachment are stated in CCP, art. 997, para. 1, as amended by Law 2298/1995, art. 4, para. 22. CCP, art. 997, para. 1 sents. 2 and 3 provides that if the property is leased after its attachment the bidder can terminate the lease within three months from the transcription of the summary of the adjudication report. In such a case, the lease ends after six months and the execution provided in CCP, art. 1005, para. 2 follows. The right of the bidder to terminate a lease which cannot be evidenced by a deed bearing a certified date (Civil Code, art. 615 in combination with CCP, art. 1009) is not affected (CCP, art. 997, para. 1, sent. 4).

On A's *bankruptcy* some time after the creation of the lease, the *lease*, as a rule, being a contract that has a continuous character, continues to be valid, unless otherwise stipulated in the law or the contract (Law on Bankruptcy 3588/2007, *Πτωχευτικός Κώδικας*, art. 31). Consequently, the property must be sold subject to the lease in a forced sale. It must be checked, however, if the lease was concluded during the so-called 'suspect' period, that is, between the date when the debtor stopped making any payments and the official declaration of the bankruptcy by the court (Law on Bankruptcy, art. 41).[35] A lease concluded during the 'suspect' period is obligatorily revoked by the court if the rent is disproportionately low (Law on Bankruptcy, art. 42) or if the tenant knew on conclusion of the lease that the landlord had stopped all payments to creditors and that the lease was detrimental to them (Law on Bankruptcy, art. 43). A court decision is needed for the revocation (Law on Bankruptcy, art. 48). If the lease is concluded after the declaration of insolvency, it would be inoperative, as are all acts of administration of the insolvent's property made without the approval of the insolvency administrator (Law on Bankruptcy, art. 17, § 1).

Where property subject to a registered *personal servitude* of usufruct or habitation is *attached*, the personal servitude will prevail in a forced sale if it was created before the attachment and eventual forced sale of the property. This means that the property will be sold subject to the usufruct or right of habitation. The position will presumably be the same in the case of A's insolvency unless the usufruct or habitation has been registered during the 'suspect' period.

[35] The term 'suspect period' follows the French term '*période suspecte*', suggesting the influence of French models on Greek commercial law.

A usufruct or right of habitation transcribed after the *inscription of a mortgage* cannot be enforced against the mortgage creditor. This is an application of the *prior in tempore* principle that governs conflicting real rights. The usufruct or right of habitation is consequently extinguished by the forced sale of the property.[36] However, the Greek Civil Code (Civil Code, art. 319) offers some relief to holders of servitudes who run the risk of forfeiting their rights when the property is sold in execution. They are namely entitled to offer to satisfy the creditor's claim by set off or by public deposit.[37] The holder of the real right will be subrogated to the rights of the creditor to the extent that the latter has been satisfied.

Hungary

If creditors of A *attach the property*, both rights *in rem* and lease contracts, including an income-producing lease on land, in principle remain enforceable against the creditors.

Immovable property is to be sold in execution resulting in immediate possession with the date of entry (in the Land Register) to follow immediately after the sale. Immovable property must, however, also be sold subject to a *lease* concluded before the institution of the execution procedure. This is the case in all situations except where the debtor and the mortgage creditor agreed to sell the property with immediate possession and the lease contract was concluded in spite of this agreement (Law on Court Enforcement, § 141(1),(2) and (3)(a)). The buyer at the sale in execution is entitled to rent due following his/her purchase, provided that the buyer notified the tenant in advance. If the buyer at the sale in execution fails to notify the tenant or notifies him/her retrospectively, the former is liable for the resulting loss (Law on Court Enforcement, § 154).

Attached immovable property is sold by auction through court enforcement procedures. If a party purchases immovable property in this way, his/her title to the property will be burdened by a *usufruct* and a *right of use* if these rights have been registered in the Land Register. Nevertheless, if these rights are based on law and not on contract or

[36] Georgiades, *Property*, vol. 2, p. 55.

[37] Stathopoulos, *Obligations*, § 17, no. 39, n. 53 (957).

court or administrative decisions, they will prevail even where they are not registered.[38]

In the case of A's *insolvency or bankruptcy*, rights *in rem* such as *usufruct*, use and *residential lease* contracts concluded with natural persons will not be included in the insolvency or bankruptcy assets. In all other instances the time-limited rights of B are included in the insolvency or bankruptcy assets. In the event that the time-limited right is based on a right *in rem*, the administrator in insolvency will not gain access to it. The property can only be disposed of still encumbered by the right *in rem*. As regards the different contracts of lease, including an income-producing lease, the administrator can exercise only the rights that the initial insolvent landlord was entitled to. The administrator can normally terminate or cancel the contracts of the insolvent debtor with immediate effect. This is, however, not possible in relation to residential lease contracts concluded with natural persons, save where the object of the lease is an official residence or a garage (Law on Reorganisation, Bankruptcy and Winding-up Procedures, § 47(3)).

If A has created a *prior mortgage* on the property, the subsequent time-limited right cannot be enforced against the mortgage creditor. The latter's right to satisfy his/her claim is not affected by the rights relating to the property that were acquired following the establishment of the mortgage (Civil Code, § 256(1)). The buyer at the sale in execution acquires the property unencumbered by the subsequent *usufruct* or *right of use* (Law on Court Enforcement, § 137). However, a *lease* may remain enforceable against the buyer at the sale in execution if it is occupied by a tenant on the basis of a lease contract concluded before institution of the court enforcement procedure,[39] save where the debtor and the mortgage creditor agreed that the sale of the property would be with immediate possession and the lease contract was concluded despite this agreement (Law on Court Enforcement, § 141 (1), (2) and (3)(a)).

38 Notwithstanding the preceding provision, the usufruct and the right to use do not restrict the ownership of the auction purchaser, irrespective of whether it is registered or not, if the usufructuary is responsible for satisfying the claim of the person initiating the enforcement procedure or if the usufruct was created by contract after establishing the mortgage (Law on Court Enforcement, § 137 and § 141(3)(b)).

39 The residential lease can be terminated with three months' notice.

Italy

Where there is *attachment* of A's property followed by a sale in execution (forced sale), a *lease* consented to by A is enforceable against the purchaser if it was created with a certified date[40] prior to the attachment. A lease of land in excess of nine years, which has not been registered prior to the attachment, can only be enforced against the purchaser for nine years from the commencement of the lease. In any case, the purchaser is not bound to honour the lease when the stipulated rent is less than one-third of a fair rental or the rental stipulated in previous leases. If the lease does not have a certified date but occupancy by the tenant occurred prior to the attachment of the property leased, the purchaser in a forced sale is only bound to honour the lease for a period corresponding to the term stipulated for leases for indefinite terms, which depends on the nature of the property (Civil Code, art. 2923).

In the case of *bankruptcy* of the landlord, the lease is not automatically terminated. If the lease is going to outlast the bankruptcy by more than four years, the liquidator can notify, within one year from the filing of bankruptcy, his/her intention to terminate the lease after four years (art. 80, Regio decreto, 16 Mar. 1942 n. 267).

In the case of a *prior registered mortgage*, the situation concerning leases is not clear. According to the prevailing opinion, a lease is enforceable against the purchaser if the lease was created with a certified date prior to the attachment by the mortgagor (even if it was only registered after registration of the mortgage).[41] According to a minority opinion, a lease is only enforceable against the purchaser if the lease was created with a certified date prior to registration of the mortgage.[42] A lease of immovables in excess of nine years, which has not been registered prior to the attachment by the mortgagor (or prior to registration of the mortgage), can only be enforced against the mortgage creditor for the nine-year period from the commencement of the lease. In any case, the purchaser is not bound to honour the lease when the

[40] Civil Code, art. 2704 stipulates that the date of a private written contract is fixed (certified) from the date on which the contract was registered, or from the date of death, or supervening physical incapacity to sign of the person who signed it, or from the date on which other circumstances occur which establish with equal certainty that a written contract was drawn up previously.

[41] See Gorla and Zanelli, 'Del pegno', p. 254; Chianale, 'L'Ipoteca', pp. 353–4.

[42] See Rubino, 'L'ipoteca', p. 375.

stipulated rent is less than one-third of a fair rental or the rental stipulated in previous leases (Civil Code, art. 2923).

The interests of a holder of a *usufruct, use, habitation* or *hereditary building right* (*superficie*), are protected if they have been registered before attachment by creditors. A creation of a usufruct, use, habitation or transfer of the building, which has been registered after the attachment, has no prejudicial effect on A's creditors, even where it was created (without registration) prior to the attachment (Civil Code, art. 2914). The same principles apply in case of bankruptcy.

If the constitution of a *usufruct, use* or *habitation* is registered after a *prior registered mortgage*, it cannot be enforced against the mortgage creditor who can cause the property to be sold free of the limited real right. Such a right is extinguished by the foreclosure and sale of the property. The holder will only be able to claim the value of his/her respective right if there is a surplus after the claim of the prior mortgage creditor has been satisfied (Civil Code, art. 2812). If the mortgage is registered after the registration of the usufruct or other real rights, the land must be sold subject to these real rights.

If B's *hereditary building lease* (*superficie*) is registered after the registration of the mortgage, he/she has the option (Civil Code, arts. 2812 and 2858 ff.) to release the property, to pay off the mortgage creditor, or to free the property from the mortgage, pursuant to the procedure designed for any third person transferee who has registered the instrument effecting the transfer after the registration of the mortgage (Civil Code, arts. 2889 ff.). If none of these options is exercised, the mortgage may be foreclosed against B.

The right of the *comodatario* is never protected against attachment by A's creditors.

The Netherlands

Leases are protected in the case of *attachment* by the landlord's creditor and in the case of the landlord's *insolvency*. Upon a forced sale (by a creditor or the receiver in bankruptcy), the buyer takes subject to the lease in the same way as in a normal sale (Civil Code, art. 7:226). The same provisions apply to agricultural leases (Law on Agricultural Leases (*Pachtwet*), art. 34, in future Civil Code, art. 7:361).

In principle, a mortgagee is bound by any *lease contract* whether the contract is concluded prior to or after the registration of the mortgage. The reason is that leases work against third parties. In practice, however, almost all mortgagees stipulate a so-called lease prohibition in their mortgage terms (Civil Code, art. 3:264). According to Civil Code, art. 3:264, this means that after the creation of the mortgage, the owner is either unable to enter into a new contract of lease or he/she is restricted in his/her ability to do so. The prohibition also works against third parties such as the tenant. If a new lease is made contrary to the lease prohibition, the tenant has to leave the premises after execution, although there are some protective measures to protect the tenant's interests. This rule also applies to agricultural leases, though under different conditions.

The effect of a limited real right is that it can be enforced against any third party. Regardless of whether it is a right of *usufruct*, a *hereditary building lease* (*superficies*), or a hereditary land lease (*emphyteusis*), B is protected against creditors and he can continue enjoying his/her right as if no bankruptcy proceedings have taken place.[43]

In the case of *bankruptcy proceedings*, the creditors can do nothing. Only the receiver in bankruptcy can act on behalf of the creditors (Law on Bankruptcy (*Faillissementswet*), art. 25). If the property is sold by the receiver in bankruptcy, the new owner will obtain the property encumbered with a limited real right. This is a consequence of the *droit de suite* of a real right, which is discussed in detail in legal literature.[44]

If A has created a *prior mortgage* over the property, it does not matter whether A has become insolvent, since the mortgage creditor can enforce his/her right of mortgage as if there is no bankruptcy. If the mortgagor does not perform his/her obligations, the mortgagee may call up the mortgages and sell the property on which the mortgage is registered (Civil Code, art. 3:268).

If a *prior mortgage* has been registered before the *usufruct*, *hereditary building lease* (*superficies*), or *hereditary land lease* (*emphyteusis*) is registered, these limited real rights will not be enforceable against the mortgage creditor owing to the fact that the right of the mortgage creditor is stronger because it was first in time (Civil Code, art. 3:21). In this case, it implies that the mortgage creditor can enforce his/her right against B (Civil Code, art. 3:273). B does, however, have a claim for damages due to the loss of his/her right, which has a very high ranking (Civil Code, art.

[43] Pitlo, 'Goederenrecht', no. 24.

[44] Asser, Mijnssen and de Haan, 'Algemeen Goederenrecht', no. 28; Pitlo, 'Goederenrecht', no. 24; Snijders and Rank-Berenschot, *Goederenrecht*, no 67. As to the right of usufruct, see Kleijn, *Vruchtgebruik*, no. 1.

3:282). Although B loses his/her interest, his/her claim for damages will be paid out of the surplus value of the property sold in execution. First, the cost of the execution will be paid from the proceeds of the forced sale. Thereafter, the claim of the mortgage creditor follows and only thereafter will B's claim be satisfied out of the surplus, if any. If B's claim cannot fully be paid out of the surplus, he/she will have an unsecured claim in bankruptcy for the remainder, as B's preference is limited to the surplus.

If a right of usufruct, *superficies*, or *emphyteusis* has been registered prior to the registration of the mortgage, the mortgage creditor does not have priority and his/her right will rank lower than the rights of the limited right holders (Civil Code, art. 3:21). This is because the mortgage creditor could have checked the Land Register to see whether any rights had been registered against the property.

Poland

The attachment of A's property may only take place within execution proceedings and is performed by the bailiff. The effect of the attachment is that A's property is sold in a forced sale (execution). As a general rule, all rights encumbering the immovable expire once the sale in execution of immovable property is completed. The holders of the rights are entitled to satisfy their claims from the proceeds of the sale (Polish Code of Civil Procedure (CCP), art. 1000, §1).[45]

Upon completion of the sale in execution of property subject to a *lease including an income producing lease* (*fruendi* lease), the purchaser is subrogated to the rights of the landlord (CCP, art. 1002). This is an exception to the general rule expressed in CCP, art. 1000. The rights under these contracts are not extinguished. Instead, Civil Code, arts. 678 and 694 provide that the purchaser in a sale in execution acquires the property subject to B's lease.

As an exception to the general rule, *usufruct*, *personal servitudes* and *lifetime habitation* will not expire if they had been registered or if the bailiff had been notified of their existence at least three days prior to the sale in execution. This is subject to the condition that these rights have priority over existing mortgages, if any, and that the proceeds from the sale are sufficient to cover the value of these rights (CCP, art. 1000, § 3).

[45] Act of 17 Nov. 1964, Dz.U.64, no. 43, item 269, with subsequent amendments.

Consequently, in a number of instances, B's right will not expire, and the purchaser will acquire an encumbered immovable.

In theory, there may be a situation where land belonging to the local authority and being encumbered with a *hereditary land lease* (hereditary usufruct, *emphyteusis*) is attached and sold in execution proceedings by the creditors of the local authority. In that case, the hereditary land lease will expire and the holder will have a claim to recover the value of the right from the proceeds of the sale. In practice, the creditors will usually find other assets which are quicker to sell under a more cost-effective execution proceedings.

The holders of the rights which do not expire on a sale in execution are therefore entitled to satisfy their claims from the proceeds of the sale. This is done in the order prescribed in CCP, art. 1025 which lists nine categories. The seventh category comprises, inter alia, *mortgages*, pledges, rights with statutory priority and rights noted in an inventory of the land prepared by the bailiff before commencement of attachment proceedings.

In the case of *insolvency (bankruptcy)*, the Law on Bankruptcy and Reorganisation 2003 (hereafter LOB) applies.[46] A's assets would be sold by the insolvency administrator. CCP, art. 313, § 2 provides that the sale of an immovable by the administrator causes the expiry of all rights burdening that immovable. In return, the holders of personal or limited real rights are entitled to recover the value of the expired rights from the sum received upon the sale of the immovable.

Contrary to the general rule, a *lease* does not expire on account of bankruptcy proceedings (LOB, art. 108; Civil Code, arts. 678 and 694 as mentioned in Case 1). However, the Bankruptcy Court may terminate any lease with three months' notice if its existence hinders the sale of the assets or if the rent agreed on is lower than the market rent for similar premises (LOB, art. 109).

According to the general rule stipulated above, a *personal servitude* will expire upon the sale in insolvency of the land, but the holder is entitled to receive monetary compensation for the value of the expired right. This applies not only to a registered personal servitude, but also to an unregistered personal servitude if brought to the attention of the Bankruptcy Court within the specified period (which ranges between one and three months). The period is contained in the notification of bankruptcy (LOB, art. 51, §1.5).

[46] Act of 28 Feb. 2003, Dz.U.03, no. 60, item 535.

As an exception to the general rule, *usufruct* and *lifetime habitation* do not expire as a result of bankruptcy proceedings (CCP, art. 313, § 3) if they have priority over mortgages registered against the property or if the value of the immovable property is sufficient to cover the value of the usufruct and the lifetime habitation.

The above rules also apply if land subject to a *hereditary land lease* (hereditary usufruct) is sold during bankruptcy proceedings. However, limited real rights on the land created before it was burdened with a hereditary land lease do not expire (CCP, art. 1011). In theory, land belonging to a local authority may be sold upon the insolvency of that local authority. It is, however, a contentious issue whether local authorities can be declared bankrupt in Poland.

If A has created a *prior mortgage* over the property, the mortgage creditor has the right to satisfy his/her claim from the proceeds of a sale in execution or on bankruptcy (LOB, art. 336). Any surplus will be included in the sum divisible among the concurrent creditors. The mortgage creditor will therefore recover his/her money before any other creditors are entitled to the proceeds of the sale. From the above comments it is clear that in the case of a prior mortgage the mortgage creditor would have priority over the holders of rights established subsequently.

The question of priority here is solved according to the general rules of priority (CCP, art. 1026, § 1; Civil Code, art. 249 and the Law on Land Register and Mortgages, arts. 11 and 12). The order of priority of these rights follows general rules: unregistered rights enjoy priority according to the date of their establishment; registered rights have priority over non-registered rights and in the case of more than one registered right over the same property, priority is determined on the basis of the moment when a request for an entry in the Register was made (Civil Code, art. 249; Law on Land Register and Mortgages, arts. 11 and 12).

Portugal

Property subject to a *lease* in favour of B may be *attached and sold in execution* by the executing creditors of A. The lease is, however, not included in the attachment assets. If the lease contract was concluded before the attachment of the property, the general rule according to Civil Code, art. 1057 is that the purchaser will acquire all the rights and obligations of A with regard to the property. Thus, if the property is encumbered with a valid (registered or unregistered) lease, the purchaser will be bound to recognise it and to allow the tenant to exercise the lease for the remainder thereof. Consequently, the tenant's right prevails over the right of the purchaser, unless the lease was concluded *after* the executing creditor attached the property (Civil Code, art. 819). The same rules apply in the case of the insolvency of A.

Property burdened with a *personal servitude* in favour of B does not prevent the property from being attached (*penhorados*) and sold in execution by the executing creditors of A. If the personal servitude is embodied in a written deed, executed or certified by a notary and registered against the title deeds of the servient property, it is enforceable against third parties, according to its rank or priority.[47] If A grants a usufruct to B and two years later his/her creditors attach the servient property, the sale on execution only encompasses the nude property. The acquirer in execution will acquire a burdened property.

Prior registration of B's right provides publicity and enforceability against third parties. The sale in execution must therefore be conducted subject to the personal servitude in favour of B. Civil Code, art. 824, no. 2 states that if the property is sold in execution, a real *right of use* registered before the constitution of the mortgage or attachment of the property remains valid (Civil Code, art. 824, no. 2).[48] The personal servitude is thus not included in the attachment assets.

If the property is attached and sold without mention of it being burdened with a personal servitude, the holder of the servitude may challenge the title of the purchaser in court. The purchaser cannot rely on the fact that he/she purchased the property *bona fide*, but is allowed to rely on general defences based on mistake or fraud. It is important to note that the personal servitude must have been registered before the execution proceeding commenced (Law on Registration, art. 2(1)(a)). If the personal servitude is registered after registration of the attachment, it will not be enforceable against third parties such as creditors in execution (Civil Code, art. 819).

The *insolvency assets* only include property of the insolvent (Law on Insolvency, art. 46).[49] The *personal servitude* is not considered an asset of the insolvent; rather, it is enforceable against the administrator in insolvency.

[47] The right registered first prevails over later registered rights over the same property according to the date of registration (Law on Registration, art. 6).

[48] See Court of Appeal Porto of 12.04.1998 [Process 9721249], available at www.dgsi.pt.

[49] Code of Insolvency and Reorginisation of Enterprises, approved by Decree Law 53/2004 of 18.03, as amended by Decree Law 200/2004 of 18.08, 76-A/2006 of 29.03, 282/2007 of 07.08 and 185/2009 of 12.08.

If A, having burdened the land with a duly constituted and registered personal servitude in favor of B, becomes insolvent, the right of B is protected. Prior registration of B's right provides publicity and enforceability also against creditors in insolvency. If the personal servitude was created without any consideration, and A's creditors suspect that it was done to prejudice the insolvency assets, they can use the *actio Pauliana* (Civil Code, art. 610) to remedy the situation. It should be noted, however, that this action is available to all creditors and not only to creditors involved in an insolvency process.

If the owner has created a mortgage over the property and then becomes insolvent, the mortgage creditor has a 'secured credit' (Law on Insolvency, art. 47(4)(a)). According to the Law on Insolvency, art. 174, the mortgage creditor is paid after his/her claim and priority ranking have been confirmed by a court decision (art. 173).

The question whether a *lease* is enforceable against a mortgage creditor who has registered a *prior mortgage* on the property, has led to a strong debate in Portuguese case law and academic literature. Portuguese law does not prohibit the owner of mortgaged property to conclude an enforceable lease over the property. If A registers a mortgage in favour of C and then duly concludes a lease with B, it is contested whether the lease in favour of B will be enforceable against the mortgage creditor.[50] Civil Code, art. 824, no. 2 states that on a sale in execution of the property, real rights of use (*direitos reais de gozo*) over the property will remain valid if they were registered *before* the registration of the mortgage or the attachment of the property. Consequently, it is clear that a right of usufruct registered after the registration of the mortgage will expire. However, since a lease is not one of the recognised real rights in Portuguese law, it does not necessarily follow that a lease concluded after the registration of a mortgage will likewise expire.[51] However, doctrine and case law have disputed this conclusion by finding that Civil Code, art. 824, no. 2, which states that rights expire after a sale in execution, also refers to leases. The Supreme Court of Justice[52] concluded that the fact that the lease is not a real right does not prevent its

[50] This question is very important owing to the fact that a lease is commonly considered as a strongly protected right which can only be terminated in very limited circumstances. The granting of a lease over property may greatly decrease the value of the property.

[51] Mesquita, *Obrigações Reais*, p. 140; Remédio Marques, *Curso*, pp. 408 ff.; Vieira, 'Arrendamento de Imóvel', vol. 4, p. 437.

[52] Decisions of the Supreme Court of Justice of 15.02.2005 [Process 04A4786]; of 05.02.2009 [Process 08B4081], available at www.dgsi.pt.

analogous inclusion in Civil Code, art. 824, no. 2. To sum up, the tenant's rights will not prevail over the right of the mortgage creditor, except where the lease was concluded *prior* to the registration of the mortgage.

Under Portuguese law, property rights are ranked according to the maxim *prior in tempore, potior in iure*. Since the ranking of B's right depends on prior registration, the fact that the *personal servitude* was registered after the registration of a mortgage on the property means that the personal servitude of B will not prevail against the *prior mortgage*. Note that mortgages constitute one of the few cases in Portuguese law where registration is necessary for the validity (as opposed to the enforceability) of a real right.[53] If registered, Civil Code, art. 686 grants the mortgage creditor a priority right with regard to the proceeds of the sale, subject to special privileges that rank above the mortgage or real rights registered before the mortgage.[54] There is no rule against the constitution of a personal servitude or a second mortgage on property which is already burdened with a mortgage. If a conflict arises, however, the first mortgage creditor has priority with regard to the proceeds of the sale (of all property and not only of the nude property). Further, in such a situation, the personal servitude would expire (Civil Code, art. 824: if the property is sold in execution, only real rights of use registered before the constitution of a mortgage or attachment of the property remain valid). The holder will then have a right to compensation for termination of his/her right, but his/her claim will rank lower than the claim of the mortgage creditor. Normally, the price obtained in a sale in execution would not be enough to pay this compensation.

If A created two mortgages (in favour of B and C), instead of a mortgage and a personal servitude, the situation will be different. The court will order the selling of the property free from the mortgages and grant the creditors a share of the proceeds resulting from the sale, according to their priority ranking.

Scotland

Competition between real rights is regulated by the maxim *prior tempore, potior iure*: prior in date, preferable in right.[55] In the event of A's

[53] In general, registration has declarative value: it renders the registered rights enforceable against third parties.

[54] This only applies to real rights registered after the registration of the mortgage.

[55] Reid et al., *Property*, paras. 684–7. This is now subject to the rules of land registration

creditors attaching the property or A becoming insolvent, B's time-limited right is not included in the attachment or insolvency assets (for it is an asset in B's estate and not in A's). Provided that B's right has been constituted as a real right, it binds attaching creditors and survives A's insolvency.

'Diligence' is the name given by Scots law to the procedure for enforcing debts against a debtor's assets. The relevant diligence to attach land is adjudication, although it is not often used.[56] The creditor must obtain a decree of adjudication from the Court of Session. That has the effect of a heritable security (mortgage) in favour of the adjudging creditor. The decree must be registered in the appropriate Land Register. If the debt remains unsatisfied at the end of a ten-year period (the 'legal'), the creditor can acquire ownership of the land. In the meantime, by a further court action (of maills and duties), the creditor *can draw the rents from any tenants* or, if there is none and the debtor is in personal occupation, eject the debtor and let out the subjects.[57] The decree of adjudication carries with it the rent due at the ensuing term and all subsequent terms, but not arrears due prior to the date of the decree.[58] The Scottish Parliament has enacted legislation to replace adjudication with a new diligence known as 'land attachment', which will make it easier for a debtor's land to be sold by creditors.[59] However, the relevant provisions have not yet been brought into force and it is not clear that they will be.

The precise behaviour of B's *lease* in the event of A's insolvency is complex. Assuming that A is an individual, the relevant insolvency regime is sequestration and the insolvency official the 'trustee in sequestration'. Although the lease survives A's insolvency and B is able to remain on the property,[60] the extent to which the trustee in sequestration is liable to implement A's obligations depends on how the

where, by reason of the positive effect of the Land Register, a later registration defeats an earlier one, subject to the possibility of the Register being rectified because it does not accurately reflect what should be the position applying the 'ordinary rules' of property law. The Scottish Law Commission proposes to abolish this 'bijural' aspect of registration in the Land Register: Scottish Law Commission, *Report on Land Registration*, para. 3.11.

[56] See Gretton and Maher, 'Diligence', pp. 189–215 for an overview.

[57] *Ibid.* para. 202. [58] Stewart, *Treatise Diligence*, p. 621.

[59] Bankruptcy and Diligence (Scotland) Act 2007, Part 4.

[60] Unless, owing to the circumstances in which it was concluded, the lease is reducible as an unfair preference or a gratuitous alienation in B's favour.

insolvent estate is administered. The trustee is liable to implement the conditions of the lease at least to the extent of rents received by him/her.[61] But he/she may simply sell the property without adopting the lease, in which case it is said that he/she incurs no liability for any special obligations (such as repairs) incumbent on A. In respect of those claims, B must rank as a personal (that is, unsecured) creditor on A's estate.[62]

Security over land in Scots law is constituted by a standard security.[63] One of the conditions of such a security is that the debtor may not let the property without the creditor's consent.[64] Any lease granted without the creditor's consent is voidable at the instance of the creditor,[65] that is to say it is valid but may be reduced by the creditor. Once reduced, the creditor may remove the tenant. In the case of an assured or short assured tenancy, particular statutory procedures must be followed, but the tenant can still be removed.[66] Pending the removal of the tenant, the creditor is entitled to receive the rent.[67]

An adjudging creditor[68] and a trustee in sequestration[69] both take subject to previously constituted real rights and so are bound by B's *liferent*. It is not included in the insolvent estate, for it is an asset in B's estate and not in A's.

South Africa

The property of A, subject to the *lease* in favour of B, may be *attached* and sold in execution by A's creditors, but always subject to the lease, unless B has agreed otherwise.[70] The time-limited right of B is not therefore included in the assets which can be attached on A's bankruptcy/insolvency.

The *insolvency* of the landlord (A) does not terminate the *lease* and the lease is not included in the insolvency assets of A.[71] The administrator

61 *Harvie* v. *Haldane* (1833) 11, S872 (IH).

62 Rankine, *Leases*, pp. 52–3; Paton and Cameron, *Landlord and Tenant*, pp. 192–3; *Harvie* v. *Haldane* (1833) 11, S872 (IH); *Harkness* v. *Rattray* (1878) 16 SLR 117 (IH).

63 Conveyancing and Feudal Reform (Scotland) Act 1970, Part 2, especially s. 9 (henceforth CFR(S)A 70).

64 CFR(S)A 70 Schedule 3, Standard Condition 6.

65 *Trade Development Bank* v. *Warriner and Mason (Scotland) Ltd.* 1980 SC 74 (IH).

66 *Tamroui* v. *Clydesdale Bank plc* 1997 SLT (Sh Ct) 20.

67 CFR(S)A 70 Schedule 3, Standard Conditon 10(3).

68 Gretton and Maher, 'Diligence', para. 209.

69 Bankruptcy (Scotland) Act 1985, s. 31(1)(b).

70 High Court Rules r. 45(10); *Schoeman* v. *Aberdeen Trading Co. (Pty) Ltd.* 1955 1 SA 100 (C).

71 *Norex Industrial Properties* v. *Monarch SA Insurance Co.* 1987 1 SA 827 (A) 837J; Smith, *Insolvency*, para. 175; Cooper, *Landlord and Tenant*, p. 323.

in insolvency is obliged to sell the property subject to the lease and the tenant's real right prevails over the right of a purchaser in a forced sale.[72]

The owner (A) of mortgaged property may, unless precluded by the mortgage agreement, conclude a *lease* of the mortgaged property and register a long lease without the mortgage creditor's consent as long as it does not prejudice the mortgage creditor's security.[73] If the *prior mortgage* is enforced, the property must first be sold subject to the lease.[74] Only if the highest bid is insufficient to discharge the mortgage debt, may it be sold free of the lease.[75] The effect of such a sale is that the lease is extinguished.[76] The tenant (B) has a claim for breach of contract against A for loss suffered.[77] This claim will rank as a concurrent claim on the insolvency of A.

Likewise the property of A, subject to a *personal servitude* in favour of B, may be *attached* and sold in execution. However, the sale in execution will be subject to the usufruct of B.[78] The time-limited usufruct of B is therefore not included in the execution assets of A.

In principle, the *insolvency* of the nude owner (A) does not terminate the *personal servitude* (usufruct, use or habitation) registered against the property. In a sale by the insolvency administrator, B is protected in that the property can only be sold and acquired by the purchaser subject to the personal servitude. Note, however, that if the nude ownership ripens during insolvency (for example, if the usufructuary dies), full ownership will immediately vest in the owner (A) and will thus become part of his/her insolvency assets.[79]

Under the Deeds Registries Act, a personal servitude can only be constituted over property already burdened with a *prior mortgage* with the written consent of the mortgage creditor. This consent must be to the effect that the personal servitude may be registered free from the bond.[80] Consequently, unlike lease, a situation can never arise where on

[72] *Shell Rhodesia* v. *Eliasov* 1979 3 SA 915 (R) 917. A stipulation in a lease that it will terminate or be varied upon the sequestration of the landlord's estate is null and void: Insolvency Act 24 of 1936, s. 37(5).

[73] Cooper, *Landlord and Tenant*, p. 24; *ABSA Bank* v. *Sweet* 1993 1 SA 318 (C).

[74] See Cooper, *Landlord and Tenant*, pp. 24, 304 and 323.

[75] Cooper, *Landlord and Tenant*, p. 25; *Timm* v. *Kay* 1954 4 SA 585 (T) 586.

[76] See decisions quoted in Cooper, *Landlord and Tenant*, p. 323 n. 75.

[77] De Wet and Van Wyk, *Kontraktereg*, p. 461.

[78] High Court Rules r. 45(10); *Schoeman* v. *Aberdeen Trading Co. (Pty) Ltd.* 1955 1 SA 100 (C).

[79] *Wasseman* v. *Sackstein* 1980 2 SA 536 (O). See Smith, *Insolvency*, para. 159.

[80] Deeds Registries Act 47 of 1937, s. 65(3). See Nel, *Jones: Conveyancing*, p. 211.

mortgage foreclosure the land has to be sold free of the personal servitude if the proceeds of the sale are insufficient to discharge the claim of the mortgage creditor. The effect of such consent in fact represents a ranking agreement, ranking the personal servitude above the mortgage. This means that the land must always be sold subject to the servitude in a sale in execution.

Spain

The Spanish Civil Code (art. 1571) accepted the Roman maxim *emptio tollit locationem* (sale breaks hire). The general principle is that the tenant acquires only personal rights under the contract of *lease* which will not be enforceable on *attachment* or sale of the property in execution and will form part of the insolvent estate of A unless the lease has been registered in the Land Register.[81] Nevertheless, some Spanish decisions, mostly in the field of urban leases (which can by analogy apply to rural leases) seem to lend support to a broader protection of the tenant, based on the principle that his/her possession should be protected as far as possible.[82] The generally accepted view therefore is that although B's lease will be subject to attachment and will form part of A's insolvent assets, both in the case of attachment and insolvency, B's possession of the land will still be granted protection irrespective of registration. If A loses ownership of the property on account of a forced sale, B can retain his/her possession of the property for the first five years of the lease. If the term of the lease is fixed at more than five years, the lessee will only be able to enforce the lease on attachment and on insolvency of A for the whole term if the lease was registered prior to the attachment or insolvency (Law on Urban Leases, art. 13.1, para. 2).

The wide protection granted to residential tenants reflects the intention of the Spanish legislator to stimulate the weak residential lease industry in a country where people prefer to purchase rather than to lease residential premises.[83]

[81] Díez-Picazo, *Fundamentos*, vol. 3, p. 347.

[82] Authors that have written about the new Law on Rural Lease do not deal with this topic, although they consider that art. 22 refers to the transfer of the rural property in a very broad sense (Vattier Fuenzalida, 'Comment', pp. 250–1). If the lease contract was concluded before the attachment, it is certain that the acquirer will be bound by the lease until the minimum term (three to five years) expires. It is currently uncertain what the position is if the lease contract was concluded afterwards.

[83] See the Preamble of the Law on Urban Leases Part I, paras. 7 and 8.

Consequently, if a house or an apartment subject to an urban lease is attached and sold in execution, B will be entitled to remain in possession until the lease expires. The only exception is where the purchaser in execution is protected by the Law on Hypothecs, art. 34 (Law on Urban Leases, art. 14). The purchaser will, for instance, be protected where the lease has never been registered in the Land Register. If B *bona fide* registers the lease after the attachment, the lease will only expire after the lapse of the first five years (Law on Urban Leases, art. 13.1, paras. 1 and 2).[84]

Property burdened with a *usufruct, a right of use* or *habitation* can be attached. Since they are recognised as limited real rights in Spanish law, they will obtain the characteristics of real rights when registered (Law on Hypothecs, art. 13). They are therefore enforceable against the purchaser in a forced sale, leaving the holder (B) in the position to exploit the property until his/her right is extinguished. In addition, the Code of Civil Procedure (CCP), art. 704.2 allows occupiers with 'sufficient' title to remain in possession of the property without requiring that their title be registered.[85]

The Spanish Law on Insolvency (art. 61) regulates B's position in the case of A's *insolvency*.[86] It states that contracts entered into by the insolvent before his/her insolvency are not affected by the insolvency (*concurso*). Thus, in principle, contracts of *lease*, irrespective of kind, will remain in force until its expiry. Nevertheless, the Law on Insolvency gives either the insolvency administrator or the insolvent (A) the option to apply for the termination of the contract if it can benefit the insolvency proceedings (Law on Insolvency, art. 61.2, para. 2). The competent court has the discretion to award damages to B if it finds that the termination of the lease is in the best interest of the parties.

The insolvency of an owner whose property is burdened with a registered *usufruct, use* or *habitation* will not affect the real rights of the holder of these rights (B). This is, however, subject to the Law on Insolvency, art. 71 which provides that dispositions that adversely affect creditors can be set aside (*rescindibles*) if they were carried out within two years before the declaration of insolvency.

A *hereditary building lease* (*superficies*) is a real right that requires registration for its constitution (Spanish Land Act 2008, art. 40.2). The land

[84] Rojo Ajuria, 'Comment', pp. 190–1.

[85] It is the court which will decide if the occupier has sufficient title.

[86] *Ley concursal* (Law on Insolvency) of 9 July 2003.

which is burdened with a building lease can be attached and it can also form part of the insolvency assets. In the case of a forced sale, the holder will retain his/her right in respect of the building if the building lease was entered in the Land Register before the land was attached or insolvency declared. The purchaser will thus obtain the land subject to the building lease.

In principle, A's creditors can attach property subject to a *loan for use* and this property will form part of A's assets in insolvency. If there is a forced judicial sale of the property, the court will have to decide whether the borrower (B) has 'sufficient title' to be maintained in his/her possession of the property (CCP, art. 704.2). In a case of insolvency, the Law on Insolvency, art. 61.2 is applicable, as discussed under contracts of lease.

If a *prior mortgage* is constituted and registered in the Land Register before a *residential lease* is entered into, the lease will be effective against a purchaser in a forced sale for the first five years only (Law on Urban Leases, art. 13.1),[87] after which the contract will expire.[88] Decisions of the Supreme and Constitutional Courts require good faith on the part of the tenant.[89] This is an indication of the greater protection offered to the residential tenant in that attachment of the prior mortgaged property does not result in the termination of the lease if it is not proved that the landlord and tenant acted in bad faith.[90] When the lease contract is entered into and registered before the mortgage is registered in the Land Register, it will continue to be effective for the entire term agreed upon (Law on Urban Leases, art. 13.1, para. 2).[91]

If A has registered a *prior mortgage* over the property before a *right of usufruct, use* or *habitation* was registered in the Land Register, the position will be governed by CCP, art. 659 (see also CCP, art. 689.2). CCP, art. 659 stipulates that the holder of such a real right is entitled to be informed by

[87] Before the new Law on Urban Leases was enacted, the Spanish Supreme Court and even the Constitutional Court had already considered some cases where leases were concluded after the mortgage had been created. It was held that the attachment in execution of the property did not terminate the lease (e.g. Spanish Supreme Court Rulings, 23 Feb. 1991, 6 May 1991, 9 May 1996; Constitutional Court Rulings 6/1992, 13 Jan., 21/1995, 24 Jan.).

[88] Rojo Ajuria, 'Comment', pp. 194 ff.; Marín López, 'Comment', p. 104.

[89] See Supreme Court Rulings, 23 Dec. 1988, 17 Nov. 1989, 14 June 1997; Constitutional Court judicial decree (auto) 309/1994, 14 Nov.

[90] This will constitute a cause for extinction of the lease not mentioned in the Law on Urban Leases.

[91] Rojo Ajuria, 'Comment', p. 195.

the Registrar of the foreclosure on the mortgage and the intended sale of the mortgaged property. The holder is given the option to pay the full amount secured by the mortgage in return for retaining his/her right and being subrogated to the position of the mortgage creditor. This means that the equity remaining in the property will act as security for the debt. If the holder does not exercise this option, the fact that his/her right was registered after the mortgage means that he/she will not prevail in a forced sale in insolvency.[92] The registration of the right will be cancelled (CCP, art. 692.3 read together with CCP 674.2, para. 2) and the purchaser in the forced sale will receive the property free of any charge.

If A had registered a *prior mortgage* over the property before a *hereditary building lease* (*superficies*) was registered, the holder must be informed of an impending forced sale and has the choice to be subrogated on payment of the outstanding debt to the position of the mortgage creditor (CCP, art. 659 read with art. 689). If the holder does not exercise this option, his/her right would be cancelled after the sale since it was created after the mortgage was registered (CCP, art. 674 and 692.3). Note, however, that the Law on Hypothecs (art. 110) provides that constructions erected on the land after the mortgage was registered do not form part of the object of security. Although the hereditary building right (*superficies*) will not, therefore, by virtue of its registration after the mortgage, afford the holder any preference, his/her improvement of the land will entitle him/her to an action for unjustified enrichment against the mortgage creditor and the eventual purchaser of the land.

If a mortgage is created before B's *loan for use*, the court, in a forced sale on foreclosure of the mortgage, will again have to decide whether B has 'sufficient title' to remain in possession (CCP, art. 661). It is very doubtful that the court will decide that a borrower, who only has a personal right and obtains the use of the property for free, has 'sufficient title' to remain in possession.

[92] A case of a prior mortgage on the property was decided by the Constitutional Court (69/1995 of 9 May). The facts were the following: A's right of usufruct was created on 10 Nov. 1981 but it was not registered until 30 Nov. 1989. After the right was created but before it was registered A created and registered a mortgage (the registration took place on 15 September 1989) over the immovable property burdened by the usufruct. The Constitutional Court held that the right of usufruct, irrespective of the date it was created, was not enforceable against the purchaser of the immovable property in the execution procedure if the usufruct was registered after the mortgage had been registered in the Land Register.

Case 4 What happens if the holder of a time-limited interest is dispossessed?

Some time after the creation of the time-limited right concerned, C dispossesses B. Can B act directly against C for return of the property? Can B act directly against D who acquired the property from C?

Does it make a difference if the dispossession is effected by force or by fraud?

Comparative observations

The European jurisdictions divide the remedies available to the holder (B) of the time-limited interest against the dispossessor (C) into possessory remedies that must be instituted within a year, or within thirty days in Austria, unless extraordinary circumstances are present, and vindicatory remedies that are not subject to a time limit. In some jurisdictions, such as Portugal and South Africa, the dispossessed party is also entitled to a self-help remedy (called contra-spoliation in South Africa) where he/she has to act swiftly to regain possession before the situation has stabilised.

Most jurisdictions allow the dispossessed party to have the *status quo ante* restored if it can be proved that he/she was in peaceful possession of the land and was unlawfully dispossessed. Since *possessory remedies* are aimed at the protection of actual possession, questions as to ownership and the right to possess are not considered in such proceedings. Statutory defences and the dispossessed party's consent are factors which could render the dispossession lawful.

Most jurisdictions distinguish between possessors and mere holders (*detentors*) and only allow possessors to use the remedy. Many of these jurisdictions, however, extend the application of possessory remedies either by elevating certain traditional holders (*detentores*) to the status of possessors or by extending the remedy against dispossession to include such persons. Thus possessory remedies have been extended to tenants in occupation,[1] borrowers for use,[2] and holders of personal servitudes[3] and hereditary land leases.[4] In these cases the remedy can even be used against the landlord, lender or owner of the property.

Italian law and Portuguese law recognise a person as a possessor if he has *de facto* control over an object that is manifested by an activity corresponding to the exercise of ownership or another real right over the property. Thus the holder of a hereditary building right (*superficiarius*), who is regarded as the owner of the building, and the holder of a personal servitude, who exercises control in terms of a real right, qualify as possessors. In these jurisdictions, lessees and borrowers for use are, however, regarded as mere holders (*detentores*) and are therefore not entitled to a possessory remedy.

A few jurisdictions, such as Spain, Hungary and Poland, have discarded the traditional distinction between possessors and *detentores* and allow every person in physical control or peaceful possession of the land to institute an action (formerly an interdict) against the dispossessor for the recovery of possession. Thus the lessee, borrower for use, holder of a personal servitude or of a hereditary building right (*superficies*) are entitled to a possessory remedy. In English law, a claim for possession may be brought against a trespasser by any person who has a right to possession. This includes a tenant who has the immediate right to possess as opposed to the landlord whose right to possession is postponed until the end of the lease. A tenant can therefore bring an action for the recovery of possession unless his/her claim has been extinguished by a squatter having had adverse possession of the property for a period of twelve years. Danish law recognises some kind of possessory remedy (assisted by a bailiff) where a holder under a contract is dispossessed by C.

Although lessees in France are entitled to a possessory remedy, they are encouraged to proceed against the landlord who is contractually bound to place (and keep) the tenant in possession, except where the dispossession is caused by superior force. Legislation encourages the lessee to inform the lessor of the interference and allows the lessee a reduction in rent on account of the dispossession.

[1] E.g. under German, Austrian, French and South African law. Austrian law regards a lessee as the possessor of a right which offers the same protection as to a possessor of a corporeal object.

[2] E.g. under Greek law.

[3] E.g. in Greece and the Netherlands because their *quasi*-possession has been despoiled.

[4] E.g. under Dutch law.

In most jurisdictions,[5] the dispossession by C need not be by *force* or *fraud*, but it must be unlawful.[6] Summary restitution will be ordered without an investigation of the merits of the case. Other jurisdictions treat dispossessions by force or fraud differently. Under Greek law, dispossession by fraud does not give rise to a possessory remedy but can ground an action for rescission or a delictual action for damages. Portuguese law does not allow any defence against dispossession by force or fraud. The Italian Civil Code requires a violent taking, but case law has watered this down to a requirement of mere dispossession against the express or implied will of the holder. Similarly, South African law has watered down its earlier requirement of violent dispossession to unlawful deprivation of possession. Furthermore, Italian law has extended the possessory remedy to mere holders who are deprived violently or secretly of their possession. Under Belgian law, the strict requirement of possession for a year need not be complied with if a usufructuary, tenant or borrower for use is dispossessed by force or fraud.

In addition to possessory remedies, some systems allow a *quasi-vindicatory remedy* to all holders of property with a better right to possession than the person in actual possession.[7] Under Austrian law, this remedy is available to possessors who are in good faith able to prove title to the property and that the possession did not result from interference with the defendant's rights. Greek, Austrian and French law extend the remedies for the protection of ownership (*actio publiciana*, *vindicatio usufructus* and *actio confessoria*) to the holder of a personal servitude, while Belgian, Dutch, Italian and Polish law also analogously extend them to the holders of a hereditary building lease (*superficies*)[8] and a hereditary land lease (*emphyteusis*) on account of their real rights in the property. This allows B to institute a vindicatory action against either C or D (whoever is in possession) for the return of the property. Portuguese law entitles the holders of registered real rights to petition the court for a declaratory or mandatory order for the return of the property, as well as an injunction to stop future interference against all dispossessors except the landowner. The French Civil Code requires the

[5] See e.g the German, Austrian, Spanish, Hungarian, Polish, Danish and South African reports.

[6] This means without consent or by virtue of a legal or statutory right.

[7] See e.g. the Danish report.

[8] The Italian law allows a proper vindication because the holder becomes the owner of the building.

holder of the real right to notify the nude owner of the dispossession. The owner will be able to claim damages resulting from failure to notify him/her.

Some jurisdictions allow *recovery from the third person* (D) who acquired the property from the dispossessor (C) if it can be shown that D had participated, to an extent, in the unlawful dispossession.[9] Italian case law has interpreted this to mean that an action can be brought against the 'moral author' as opposed to the 'material author' of the dispossession, thus allowing the action to be brought against the person who has planned, instigated or ratified the dispossession. This is to some extent echoed by Polish law, which allows a possessory action against D only if the dispossession occurred on behalf of D. South African academic opinion will only allow a possessory action if D actively participated in the dispossession of B. This view is also supported by legal doctrine and case law in Austria, which require a personal interference by D in B's possession but regrettably personal interference is interpreted very widely as knowledge on the part of D that C dispossessed the land unlawfully.

Spanish case law does not allow recovery from D, especially if acquired *bona fide*, while some Spanish academics will allow a possessory action against any person in possession who has not yet acquired ownership of the dispossessed property. Polish law allows a possessory action against D only if the dispossession occurred on behalf of D.

Since a *quasi*-vindicatory remedy is not restricted to the dispossessor but to any person in possession of the despoiled property, the same rules as set out above in the case of C apply to D who acquired possession of the property.

Austria

A *tenant* who entered into possession of the land can sue anybody who interferes with his/her use of the land (Civil Code, § 339). A tenant is deemed to have a right to possess (*Rechtsbesitzer*) and to receive the same protection as a possessor of property (*Sachbesitzer*).[10] This provision protects possession irrespective of whether the protected person is the owner or has a right to possess.[11] The claimant only has to prove his/her

[9] See the German, Greek, Italian and South African reports.

[10] Kletecka, in Koziol and Welser, *Bürgerliches Recht*, vol. 1, pp. 258 ff.

[11] Iro, *Sachenrecht*, para. 15/55; Spielbüchler, in Rummel, *Kommentar*, § 339, para. 1.

actual possession and interference with such possession.[12] Civil Code, § 339 allows for declaratory actions, injunctions to refrain from further infringements and actions to claim for the restoration of possession. As Civil Code, § 339 only aims at protecting actual possession, the court considers neither ownership of the claimant nor his/her right to possession in these proceedings.[13]

The term 'interference' includes both minor disturbance and total dispossession or eviction.[14] Use of force is not a requirement.[15] An *action against D* requires that D can be classified as the person who personally interfered with B's possession.[16] Furthermore, according to some academic writers, D is deemed to be an interferer if he/she acquires the land from C in the knowledge that C acquired it by unlawful dispossession.[17]

It is not necessary that the person who interferes knows that he/she has no right to interfere. A claim according to Civil Code, art. 339 may therefore be allowed even if the interferer acts in good faith.[18] A claim will not, however, be allowed against someone who has a right to interfere by virtue of statutory provisions or an official enactment[19] or against someone who has good reason to believe that the possessor consented to the interference.[20]

A claim based on Civil Code, § 339 must be brought within thirty days. This period starts when B becomes aware of the interference and the person who interferes (CCP, s. 454, para. 1).

A tenant can also bring an *actio publiciana* under Civil Code, § 372.[21] Whereas the remedies under Civil Code, § 339 flow from actual possession, those under Civil Code, § 372 are based on the right to possess. Protection under Civil Code, § 372 requires so-called 'qualified possession'. This means that the possessor is in good faith and that he has a title to possess and 'proper possession'. 'Proper possession' means that

[12] Iro, *Sachenrecht*, para. 2/57.

[13] Kletecka, in Koziol and Welser, *Bürgerliches Recht*, vol. 1, p. 276; Iro, *Sachenrecht*, para. 2/64.

[14] Spielbüchler, in Rummel, *Kommentar*, § 339, para. 2.

[15] See the examples of Spielbüchler, *ibid.*

[16] 1 Ob 19/88; JBl (1989), p. 453; Spielbüchler, in Rummel, *Kommentar*, § 339, paras. 7 ff.

[17] Iro, *Sachenrecht*, para. 2/61; 1 Ob 19/88; SZ 61/188; JBl (1989), p. 453.

[18] Spielbüchler, in Rummel, *Kommentar*, § 339, para. 3; Iro, *Sachenrecht*, para. 2/60.

[19] Spielbüchler, in Rummel, *Kommentar*, § 339, para. 6.

[20] *Ibid.* § 339, para. 5.

[21] 1 Ob 26/46; SZ 21/1; 1 Ob 607/49; SZ 22/207; 1 Ob 515/77; SZ 50/10 with further references (all refer to tenancy); 2 Ob 570/77; JBl (1979), p. 425 (usufructuary lease); 8 Ob 687/89; JBl (1991), p. 787 (usufructuary lease); Eccher, *Kommentar*, § 372, para. 3; Spielbüchler, in Rummel, *Kommentar*, § 372, para. 5.

his/her possession is not in itself the result of an interference with the rights of the defendant. The idea behind Civil Code, § 372 is that a person with qualified possession is normally also the owner of the property concerned. In other words, the qualified possessor is protected because ownership is presumed. From this it follows that Civil Code, § 372 does not provide protection against somebody with a stronger title.[22] For example, it does not protect a tenant against the owner of the land.[23] It further does not protect one tenant against another tenant whose rights arise from a contract concluded with the landlord in good faith.[24]

The qualified possessor is protected against minor and major interference, against dispossession or eviction and, by analogy to Civil Code, § 364, para. 2, against emissions.[25] With an action brought under Civil Code, § 372, the tenant can claim restoration of possession and an order to refrain from further infringements.[26]

As in the case of a tenant, the possession of a *holder of a servitude* is protected by Civil Code, § 339. The principles discussed above apply to servitudes as well. Apart from possessory protection, the holder of a servitude also has proprietary remedies under Civil Code, § 523, which provide that the holder of a servitude can bring an action against both the owner of the servient land and any third person who interferes with his/her enjoyment of the land[27] or deny the existence of his/her servitude.[28] He/she can claim for a declaratory order,[29] an injunction to restrain from interference,[30] an order to abolish obstacles[31] or an order to acquiesce in the holder using the land in accordance with the servitude.[32]

These actions can also be brought under Civil Code, § 372 under which the claimant only has to prove legal title and proper possession.

[22] See e.g. 8 Ob 687/89; JBl (1991), p. 787.

[23] 7 Ob 623/88; MietSlg 40.025; Spielbüchler, in Rummel, *Kommentar*, § 339, paras. 3 and 5.

[24] Spielbüchler, in Rummel, *Kommentar*, § 339, para. 5; 7 Ob 654/89; JBl (1990), p. 447 (full panel, *verstärkter Senat*); 8 Ob 687/89; JBl (1991), p. 787; 4 Ob 350/98v; wobl (1999), p. 215.

[25] 7 Ob 654/89; JBl (1990), p. 447 (full panel, *verstärkter Senat*).

[26] 1 Ob 515/77; SZ 50/10 with further references; Spielbüchler, in Rummel, *Kommentar*, § 339, para. 5; 1 Ob 607/49; SZ 22/207; 1 Ob 26/46; SZ 21/1.

[27] 6 Ob 33/66; SZ 39/21; 6 Ob 541/81; MietSlg 33.050; 8 Ob 170/68; SZ 41/68; Hofmann, in Rummel, *Kommentar*, § 523, para. 6.

[28] Hofmann, in Rummel, *Kommentar*, § 523, para. 6.

[29] 6 Ob 33/66; SZ 39/21; OGH 11. 3. 1931, 3 Ob 93/31; SZ 13/54.

[30] 6 Ob 33/66; SZ 39/21; 6 Ob 541/81; MietSlg 33.050; 1 Ob 751/83; JBl (1984), p. 608.

[31] 8 Ob 170/68; SZ 41/68; 1 Ob 751/83; JBl (1984), p. 608; 1 Ob 622/95; NZ (1997), p. 213.

[32] 6 Ob 541/81; MietSlg 33.050.

The claimant furthermore has to be in good faith, but because of the legal presumption in Civil Code, § 328 it need not be proved.[33] The claim will be allowed against anyone who does not have a better title to possess, for example, if he/she is not in good faith or does not have a right to possess.[34] Civil Code, § 372, however, does not provide for any protection against the landowner.[35]

The *building right* is a real or proprietary right and as such protected against everybody.[36] It includes ownership as to the building and usufruct or a right of usage as to the land (Law on Building Rights, s. 6, para. 2).[37] Hence the holder of a building right is protected as an owner regarding the building and as the holder of a servitude regarding the land.

Belgium

To the extent that *usufruct*, *hereditary lease of land* (*emphyteusis*) and the *hereditary building right* (*superficies*) are duly recorded with the Mortgage Register, they are all rights *in rem* and not merely contractual rights against A. Therefore, B can indeed act directly against C for the return of the property. This action is based on the right of pursuit (*quasi*-vindicatory right) that the holders of limited real rights have against all persons in possession of their property.

Since the *quasi*-vindicatory right is general, the rights of B are not altered by the fact that the dispossession has been effected by force or fraud. However, where the dispossession of B was caused by C's fraud, B can enforce his/her rights against C even when his/her right of usufruct, *emphyteusis* or *superficies* has not been recorded in the Mortgage Register. C's conduct is regarded as fraudulent where he/she dispossessed B with actual prior knowledge of B's time-limited right. The rationale for this rule is that the formality of publicity by recording or registration in the Land Register is only needed to protect persons against third parties

33 2 Ob 25/50; SZ 23/225 (right of way); 3 Ob 545/50; SZ 23/287 (*ususfructus*); 6 Ob 111/63; SZ 36/82 (right of fishing); 2 Ob 229/73; SZ 47/29 (right of water); OGH 15.1.1986, 1 Ob 20/85; NZ (1986), p. 188; Spielbüchler, in Rummel, *Kommentar*, § 372, para. 1; Hofmann, in Rummel, *Kommentar*, § 523, para. 3.

34 Kletecka, in Koziol and Welser, *Bürgerliches Recht*, vol. 1, pp. 430 ff.

35 Spielbüchler, in Rummel, *Kommentar*, § 339, para. 5.

36 Spruzina, in Schwimann, *Praxiskommentar* III, § 1 BauRG, para. 12.

37 *Ibid*. III, § 6 BauRG, paras. 11 ff.

acting in good faith (and therefore not against third parties acting in bad faith who have actual notice of a prior real right).

Apart from the *quasi*-vindicatory action, the holder of the time-limited right *in rem* may have a direct claim against C based on his/her possession of the property (*bezitsvordering, action possessoire*). The Belgian Code of Civil Procedure, art. 1370 requires that (a) the claim based on possession must relate to immovable property which can be acquired by prescription; (b) the claimant must have been in possession of the property for at least one year; (c) the possession must be in compliance with the conditions for acquiring prescription (Civil Code, arts. 2228–35); and (d) the dispossession must have occurred less than one year before the claim was instituted. If the dispossession was effected by force[38] or fraud, it is not necessary to comply with the second and third requirements.

Similarly, B as the holder of a duly recorded real right will be able to act directly against D in accordance with the right of pursuit accorded to holders of real rights (*quasi*-vindicatory right). This also holds for his/her possessory action.

In general, the holder of a *mere personal right* does not have a *quasi*-vindicatory right and neither does he/she have a possessory action, unless the dispossession was effected by force or fraud, in which case he/she can act against C as well as D. Eventually B can sue C and/or D based on *quasi*-contract in the absence of a contract between B and C or D. In case of a lease (not loan for use), B will be entitled to hold the owner of the property (A) (contractually) liable for the disturbance caused by the third party (C) to the extent that C relies on a legal right for his/her disturbance and his/her disturbance does not amount to a mere factual disturbance of the property (Civil Code, art. 1726).

Denmark

Such dispossession is legal only if B has caused a fundamental breach[39] of contract and in this case B is of course not allowed any legal action unless C has taken the law into his/her own hands. If the dispossession is

[38] Force is anything that could give a reasonable person a reason to fear that he/she or his/her estate may suffer a substantial and immediate risk, evil or agressive act.

[39] Fundamental breach in Danish Law is in practice identical to UNIDROIT Principles, art. 7.3.1 and the Principles on European Contract Law (PECL), art. 8:103.

created illegally by C, B can regain possession with the help of the bailiff, and/or claim damages.

I assume that D has acquired the property in good faith. If B can prove his/her right to use the land and/or buildings, this right will be protected against D in terms of the provisions of the Law on Registration of Property, s. 3, the Law on Private Housing, s. 7 or the Law on Commercial Premises Rent, s. 6. Any extraordinary rights may be extinguished by D if not registered prior to D's right (deed or mortgage deed).

The use of any kind of *force* or *fraud* makes no difference to the answers above in relation to C if he/she is the one who has used force or committed fraud. Dispossession is not binding (Law on Contracts, ss. 28–30).[40] If somebody else wrongfully caused B to declare that his/her right had ceased, this declaration may be set up against a *bona fide* promisee (D), if the person in question obtained the declaration by actual or threatened imminent force (Law on Contracts, s. 28). Other kinds of violence or fraud may only be set up against a promisee (D) in bad faith (Law on Contracts, ss. 29 and 30).

England

The right of a tenant (like any other person who has the right to possess by virtue of an estate in land) is limited by a doctrine called adverse possession. This is a common law equivalent of *usucapio*, with the important gloss that it requires absolutely no good faith whatsoever. The doctrine merely states that a possessory action can be brought against a trespasser if his/her conduct was so expansive as to amount to exclusive possession as a matter of fact, and if that behaviour was without any lawful authority whatsoever. In those circumstances, the Limitation Act 1980, s. 15 precluded the person entitled to a possession claim (commonly the 'paper owner') from bringing that claim after twelve years. This meant that the squatter (as trespassers in adverse possession are known) was left with a possessory title and became owner, whereas the paper owner's title was extinguished. The paper owner was, however, entitled to bring possession claims within the twelve-year period.

This doctrine was felt to fit extremely poorly with land registration, and has therefore been recently modified in respect of *registered land only*, subject to limited exceptions, by Schedule 6 of the Land

[40] Consolidated Act No. 781 of 26 Aug. 1996.

Registration Act 2002 (LRA).[41] From now, adverse possession will not extinguish a paper owner's title – instead, after ten years' adverse possession, the squatter must now apply to be registered (LRA Schedule 6). On such application, the owner and other affected parties are notified. They will then have time to object. If they do not object within that time, registration proceeds. If they do object, the squatter may bring limited defences (LRA Schedule 6(5)). Successful applications in respect of land subject to leases mean that the squatter takes over the lease.[42]

France

French law distinguishes between the possessor (who possesses on his/her own behalf as an owner) and a *détenteur précaire* or mere holder or detentor (who holds the property by virtue of a title, such as a lease, which justifies his/her detention while establishing that he/she is not the owner). Thus, the *tenant*, the agricultural tenant, the *borrower* under a loan for use, the *usufructuary* and the holder of a *hereditary land lease* (*emphyteusis*) are detentors. The situation of the usufructuary, the holder of a right of habitation, the holder of a hereditary land lease of land (*emphyteusis*) and the holder of a hereditary building right (*superficies*) who have real rights in the property is more complex in practice. The usufructuary and the other holders are regarded as possessors in so far as they exercise the usufruct, hereditary lease or building right in their capacity as usufructuary or holder, but as mere holders or detentors with regard to the exercise of the right of ownership which remains vested in the nude owner of the property who exercises his/her possession through the medium of the usufructuary. Thus, the holder of a hereditary land lease (*emphyteusis*) exercises his/her right with regard to the property as a possessor, yet he holds the property as detentor on behalf of the owner.

The Civil Code, based on the idea that the possessor is generally the owner and that, even where this is not the case, the possessor is more worthy of protection than the third party who seeks to disturb

[41] The law has recently been restated by the House of Lords, in *Pye (Oxford) Ltd.* v. *Graham* [2003] 1 AC 419.

[42] For an explanation of the old law, see Harpum, *Megarry and Wade: Property*, paras. 21–061 to 21–068.

a peaceful state of affairs, protects persons in possession of the property, without regard to the basis of the right, by three possessory actions:

> (a) The oldest action is the action for restoration of possession (*action en réintégration*) which, since the Decree of 12 May 1981, allows a possessor to regain possession if he/she was dispossessed by an intentional violent act or by a *voie de fait*, a forceful act which is clearly unlawful.
> (b) The *action en complainte* protects possessors whose possession has lasted at least a year.
> (c) The *dénonciation de nouvel œuvre* is intended to terminate a disturbance of possession by a new construction undertaken by a neighbour.

Traditionally, the possessory actions were open only to possessors, and not mere holders or detentors. Thus, where a third party disturbed their detention, a tenant or an agricultural tenant had to turn to the landlord who, as possessor, was the person entitled to have the possession restored. Case law permitted a detentor to bring the action for restoration of possession only in the case of forceful dispossession. Since the reform of 1975, however, detentors have been granted all the possessory actions available against all third party dispossessors other than the person from whom they derived their rights (Civil Code, arts. 2278 and 2279 (ex Civil Code, arts. 2282 and 2283; Law no. 2008-561 of 17 June 2008). Possessory actions are therefore available to B whether he/she is a possessor or a detentor and whether his/her possession or detention is based on a real right in the property (for example, a usufruct) or only on a personal right against the owner who granted him the use and enjoyment of the property (for example, a lease). In principle, these possessory actions are available only to those who possessed or held the property peacefully for at least a year. An action for repossession may, however, be brought against a dispossessor by force even if the victim possessed or held the property for less than a year (CCP, art. 1264).

Since the law extends the protection of possession to mere detentors (Civil Code, arts. 2278 and 2279; Law of 17 June 2008), a dispossessed *tenant* can institute an action for restoration of possession against a third party in addition to his/her recourse against the landlord to have his/her possession restored. In practice, the tenant will rather opt for an action against the landlord who is bound to restore his/her possession and to allow him/her peaceful enjoyment of the property for the duration of the lease (Civil Code, art. 1719 amended by Law no. 2009-323 of

25 March 2009). The landlord is regarded as defaulting in this obligation if another tenant is present on the leased property[43] or if a previous tenant delays vacating the property.[44] The landlord will be freed from his/her obligation to restore possession if the dispossession by the third party constitutes a *force majeure*, namely an outside, unpredictable act which the landlord is incapable of resisting. In this regard it has been held that the landlord will remain responsible for the restoration of possession where a previous agricultural tenant unlawfully remained in possession of the property because his/her dispossession did not constitute superior force.[45] Indeed, Civil Code, art. 1725 in effect provides that the landlord is not bound to protect the tenant against dispossession by force by third parties who do not, in addition, claim any right in the leased property. In such a case, the tenant has to proceed against third parties in his/her own name.

If the dispossession is caused by a person who claims to have a right in the leased property, the legislator encourages the tenant not to proceed with a possessory action against the dispossessor since it is essential that the landlord, as possessor of the property, be informed of the dispossession. Where the tenant or the agricultural tenant has been disturbed in their enjoyment of the property as a result of an action in respect of the ownership of the land, they have a right to a proportional reduction of the rent, provided that the landlord was notified of the disturbance and the impediment (Civil Code, art. 1726). Where a dispossessor claims by force to have some right with regard to the leased property or where the tenant is himself/herself summoned to court to surrender all or part of the property or to allow the exercise of a servitude, the tenant must summon the landlord to court and designate the landlord as defendant in the action if he/she wishes to be excluded from the proceedings (Civil Code, art. 1727). Moreover, the tenant of agricultural property is required to inform the landlord of all encroachments on the property under penalty of having to compensate the landlord for all expenses and damages caused by the encroachment (Civil Code, art. 1768 and Rural Code, art. L411-26 amended by Ordonnance no. 2006-870 of 13 July 2006).

Since the occupation of a *holder by revocable permission* (*precarium*) is not a lease, the provisions on leases do not apply, not even to supplement the will of the parties. Hence A, the owner, is not bound to ensure

[43] Civ. 3, 16 Jan. 1980; Bull. civ. III, no. 13. [44] Civ. 3, 19 May 2004; Bull. civ. III, no. 99.
[45] Civ. 3, 28 Sept. 2005; Bull. civ. III, no. 175.

peaceful enjoyment to the occupant and is thus not bound to protect him/her against unlawful dispossession of the property.

Unlike a landlord, the nude owner (A) is not bound to warrant peaceful enjoyment to a usufructuary (B) who is dispossessed by a third party (C). The *usufructuary* has a real right and can avail himself/herself against any person and in particular against a third party who claims to be owner or who has entered into possession of the property, whether or not the third party is in good faith. To defend his/her right against the dispossessor (C), the usufructuary has, in addition to the *possessory actions* mentioned above, a specific *proprietary action*, namely the action to vindicate a usufruct (*l'action confessoire d'usufruit*). Possessory protection and *droitural* protection (protection of real rights) do not exclude each other (CCP, art. 1265). Hence *res judicata* in respect of possessory actions does not affect a substantive action based on a real right in the property. The fact that the usufructuary can act directly against the dispossessor does not, however, exempt the usufructuary from informing the nude owner of the disturbance or encroachment. If the nude owner is not informed, the usufructuary will be bound to compensate the nude owner for any damages suffered as if the usufructuary has committed the wrongful acts of encroachment or destructive act (Civil Code, art. 614).

Germany

German law regards a *tenant in occupation* as a possessor (*Besitzer*) and not as a mere detentor (*Besitzdiener*). Therefore B can bring a possessory action against C for unlawful deprivation of possession (*Besitzentziehung*) to have his/her possession restored within a year from being dispossessed (Civil Code, §§ 861 and 864). The remedy requires factual possession by the tenant coupled with unlawful self help (*verbotene Eigenmacht*) on the part of the dispossessor. Unlawful self help is defined as depriving someone of his/her possession against his/her will (Civil Code, § 858(1)). Force or stealth is not required. Where D has acquired possession of the property from C, B can only act directly against D if B can show that D had actual knowledge of C's unlawful dispossession (Civil Code, § 858(2)).

Apart from the possessory remedy considered above, the holder of a *personal servitude* or a *hereditary building right* (*Erbbaurecht*) has a vindicatory remedy. The owner's remedy to vindicate his/her property (Civil Code, § 985) is expressly extended to the holders of a *usufruct* (*Nießbrauch*)

(Civil Code, § 1065), a *permanent right of habitation* (*Dauerwohnrecht*) (Law on Apartment Ownership, § 34(2)) and a *hereditary building right* (*Erbbaurecht*) (Regulations on Hereditary Building Rights, § 11(1)). Although no express provision has been made in relation to the *personal servitude of habitation* (*Wohnungsrecht*), it is generally accepted that the holder also has the same remedy.[46]

It follows from the above that B only has to prove his/her real right and that C (or D) is in possession of the property to succeed with this remedy to have his/her possession restored.

Greece

Under Greek law, a person who holds property for another (*κατοχή*, *katohi*) in the capacity of a *tenant*, depositary or some other similar relationship (for example, a *borrower* under a loan for use) is afforded the same protection as a possessor against eviction or disturbance of his/her control over the property by third parties (Civil Code, art. 997).[47] Consequently, if B, as tenant, has been unlawfully dispossessed by C, B would be entitled to claim reinstatement of his/her possession from C (Civil Code, art. 987). If the requirements for a delictual action are fulfilled, a claim for damages may also follow.[48] If D, at the time of acquiring the property, knew that C had unlawfully evicted B, B will also be entitled to enforce his/her claim for reinstatement of possession against D (Civil Code, art. 984, § 2).

The holders of the *personal servitudes* of *usufruct* and *habitation* are considered *quasi*-possessors of the property if they exercise their rights with the intention of acting as lawful beneficiaries (Civil Code, art. 975). Since *quasi*-possessors can also claim protection of their possession (Civil Code, art. 996), B as the holder of a usufruct or a right of habitation will also be able to claim reinstatement from C and, if appropriate, compensation for damage caused by C's fault (Civil Code, art. 987 read with art. 984). Again, the position as regards D depends on D's knowledge at the time he/she acquires the property (Civil Code, art. 984, § 2 read with art. 996).

In addition, the holders of a *usufruct* and a *right of habitation* will have a remedy against C and D by virtue of the fact that they obtained real rights in the property. Civil Code, art. 1173 expressly provides that the

[46] Mayer, von Staudingers, *Kommentar*, § 1093, no. 38.
[47] Georgiades, *Property*, vol. 1, pp. 245 ff. [48] *Ibid*. 230–1.

provisions governing the protection of ownership are applicable by way of analogy if the right of a usufructuary is infringed. B will therefore have the right to demand that the new possessor acknowledges his/her real right and return the property (Civil Code, art. 1173 read with art. 1094). The holder of a right of habitation would be entitled to use the same remedy (Civil Code, art. 1187 read with arts. 1173 and 1094).

It is not a requirement under Greek law that the dispossession must have been by force.[49] All that is required is that the dispossession is unlawful and against the will of the holder (B) (Civil Code, art. 984, § 1). These are regarded as two separate requirements. The dispossession is considered unlawful if the dispossession occurs without a right, for instance, a right granted under a statute and if it occurred against the possessor's will (Civil Code, art. 984 and 987). If the possessor consents to the dispossession or if the dispossessor entices the possessor to give up possession by fraud, dispossession is still considered to be effected in accordance with the will of the possessor and the dispossessed will not be entitled to the remedy under Civil Code, art. 987. It has to be noted that, although Civil Code, art. 987 mentions only unlawfulness as a requirement, it is accepted in case law[50] and doctrine[51] that the conduct required is an act against possession as described in Civil Code, art. 984, namely an unlawful act taking place against the possessor's will. Nevertheless, the possessor who has been fraudulently enticed to give up his/her property is not denied protection by the law. Although the possessor is not entitled to the possessory remedy under, art. 984, he/she is still entitled to demand rescission of the contract under which he/she was fraudulently induced to give up possession (Civil Code, art. 147) and to compensation under the general tort provisions (Civil Code, art. 914 read with Civil Code, art. 149).

Hungary

B can act against both C and D, irrespective of the legal basis of his/her time-limited right (whether it be usufruct, right to use, lease, lease for profit or loan for use). In this regard it makes no difference whether the dispossession was effected by force or by fraud.

49 Balis, *Property*, pp. 44, 53.
50 Athens Court of Appeal 2747/1981 Harmenopoulos (Arm) 1982, 191.
51 Balis, *Property*, p. 53; Georgiades, *Property*, vol. 1, p. 207.

There is a generally recognised right of protection of possession. If somebody is dispossessed or if the possession of the property is disturbed, then he/she is entitled to protection of possession. The possessor is entitled to that protection against all parties, except an individual from whom he/she acquired the possession of the property through unlawful self-help. The possessor is afforded protection of possession against the author of his/her title to possess (for example, a landlord or lender) as provided by his/her legal title (Civil Code, § 188).

Italy

In Italian law, possession is defined as power over a thing that is manifested by an activity corresponding to the exercise of ownership or another real right (Civil Code, art. 1140). Where the activity is not exercised in terms of a real right, the holder is classified as a mere *detentor*. Since a *loan for use* (*comodato*) and *lease* (*locazione*) are regarded as mere contracts,[52] they do not create real rights and so the borrower and the tenant are considered to be merely *detentores*.

Under Civil Code, art. 1168 a person who has been violently or clandestinely deprived of possession can, within a year of the deprivation, sue the dispossessor for recovery of possession (*azione di reintegrazione*). This remedy is also available to a mere *detentor* who does not hold the object merely as a servant or friend of someone else. Thus, although they do not exercise control over the object in terms of a real right, both the *tenant*[53] and the *borrower*[54] can nevertheless institute an action for the restoration of possession. Since the holders of a *usufruct*, *use* or *right of habitation* exercise control in terms of a real right, they qualify as possessors and are entitled to recover possession in case of spoliation. The same is true for the holder of a *hereditary building lease* (*proprietario superficiario*), who is commonly regarded as the owner of the building.

Civil Code, art. 1168 requires a violent taking. Italian case law, however, qualifies as violent every dispossession carried out against the will (even the implicit will) of the possessor.[55] In light of this interpretation, practically every dispossession can be considered violent and thus every

[52] It is uncontroversial that the *comodatario* only has a personal right. The matter is more controversial for lease, but the prevailing opinion still denies that the lessee has a real right.
[53] See Cass. civ. 20/05/1963 n. 1306; Cass. civ. 05/03/1968 n. 710.
[54] See Cass. civ. 11/08/1986 n. 5008; Cass. civ. 30/06/1987 n. 5746.
[55] See Cass. civ. 23/02/1981 n. 1101; Cass. civ. 13/02/1999 n. 1204.

possessor will have a possessory remedy to have his/her possession restored.

Regarding D, return of possession under Civil Code, art. 1169 can be demanded from anyone who acquires possession of the object *inter vivos* or by legacy with knowledge of the dispossession. Italian case law, on the other hand, allows the action to be brought against the 'moral author' as well as the 'material author' of the dispossession. In this context, the 'moral author' has been interpreted as not just the person who has planned or instigated the dispossession, but every person who ratifies the dispossession or takes advantage of it.[56] The court will thus normally allow the action to be brought against D.

In addition to his/her possessory right to regain the property, the holder of a *usufruct* (*usufrutto*), *use* (*uso*) or *habitation* (*abitazione*) also has the right to follow the property into the hands of any possessor (*actio confessoria*). There is no time limit for the exercise of the action itself, although it must be noted that usufruct, use and habitation are extinguished by prescription through a period of non-use lasting twenty years (Civil Code, art. 1014). The holder of the *hereditary building lease* (*proprietario superficiario*), who is commonly regarded as an owner, can recover the thing from any person who possesses or has custody of it by vindication (*azione di rivendicazione*) (Civil Code, art. 948), which is not subject to prescription.

The Netherlands

Dutch law distinguishes between possessors as persons who exercise physical control for themselves and detentors who exercise physical control on behalf of someone else. If the person holds property for himself, he is considered the direct possessor. If the person holds the property though the exercise of physical control by another, he is regarded as an indirect possessor and the person holding on his/her behalf is classified as a detentor. According to this distinction, the *tenant*, the holder of a *personal servitude* (for example, usufruct) and the holder of a *hereditary building lease* (*opstalhouer*) or a *hereditary land lease* (*erfpachter*) are regarded as detentors (Civil Code, arts. 3:107, 3:108) rather than possessors (Civil Code, art. 3:107 I).

Civil Code, art. 3:125 provides that someone who acquires possession of property can institute the same remedies against a dispossessor or

[56] See Sacco and Caterina, 'Il possesso', p. 414.

disturber of his/her possession as the person entitled to the property. However, Civil Code, art. 3:125 only concerns possessory actions. As Dutch law distinguishes between possession and detention, the detentor cannot use a possessory action. This is remedied by law by giving detentors an action in tort for damages, in addition to a claim for restoration to their former condition (Civil Code, art. 3:125 III).

Civil Code, art. 3:125 must be distinguished from revindication, which is given on the basis of ownership and not on the basis of possession. What is often overlooked is the fact that holders of limited real rights can also use the *rei vindicatio* to protect their interests and to claim back the property from dispossessors.[57] This seems to follow from Civil Code, art. 3:218 (usufructuary)[58] and, art. 5:95 (holder of a hereditary land lease),[59] which simply state that, apart from the owner, the holder of the limited real right may also start proceedings against any person who violates his/her rights.

The time-limited holder of a real right thus has an action in tort as well as a *quasi* vindicatory action against the person who dispossessed him/her. In Dutch law it does not matter whether the dispossession was effected by force or by stealth.

Poland

If B has a *usufruct*, *personal servitude*, *lifetime habitation* or *perpetual usufruct* on the land, then, according to Civil Code, arts. 237 and 251 respectively, provisions on protecting ownership are to be applied accordingly. Therefore B may use both the *rei vindicatio* and the *actio negatoria* to request that his/her possession of the property be restored or to demand that any other activity which violates his/her right be stopped (Civil Code, art. 222). The *rei vindicatio* may be instituted against anyone who detains the property and thus also against D, unless the latter has a right effective against B (for example, where B, who is entitled through usufruct, leased the property to D). The *actio negatoria* may be directed against anyone who violates a given right in a way other than by detaining the property.

Note that according to Civil Code, art. 690 the tenant of premises (whether business or residential) may protect his/her right by making use of the provisions applicable to the protection of ownership.

[57] See Asser, Mijnssen, van Dam and van Velten, 'Zakelijke Rechten', no. 115.
[58] Kleijn, *Vruchtgebruik*, no. 1. [59] de Vries, 'Erfpacht en opstal', p. 84.

In addition, according to provisions of the Civil Code on possession, B (whether as usufructuary or as holder of a personal servitude, a lifetime habitation or a perpetual usufruct) will be treated as a possessor and will therefore have access to the following remedies:

> (a) B can restore his/her possession by using self help: if B was present when the dispossession was attempted, he/she may even use force against the dispossessor (Civil Code, art. 343, §1);
> (b) B can restore his/her possession by acting personally without undue delay after dispossession occurred, as long as he/she does not use force against the dispossessor (Civil Code, art. 343, §2); or
> (c) if the above do not apply to the facts of the case, B can bring a possessory claim to restore his/her possession.

B does not have to be in good faith or even have a legal title to possess the thing. The court will only determine which person was in peaceful possession of the property and restore possession to that person. The possessory claim prescribes after one year. The action can be brought against C or D if dispossession occurred in D's favour (Civil Code, art. 344). D does not have to take part, but C must dispossess B in order for D to become the possessor.

In possessory claims it is immaterial whether dispossession occurred by force. If dispossession occurred by fraud, then one would have to consider provisions on mistake and the possibility of B rescinding the contract in writing within one year of finding out about the mistake. This will invalidate any legal transaction which brought about his/her dispossession (Civil Code, art. 88).

Portugal

In all the above situations, B's right is protected against both C and D.

Under Portuguese law, the kind of control that a *tenant* or *borrower for use* acquires over the property under a contract of lease or loan for use, amounts to mere detention and not to possession of the property. Nevertheless, Portuguese law extends possessory protection to some detentors, *inter alia* the tenant and the borrower for use. The tenant has the same protection as the possessor when he/she is deprived of or disturbed in the exercise of his/her rights (Civil Code, art. 1037). This remedy may be sought even against the landlord, if the latter disturbs the control of the tenant or prevents him from exercising his/her right. Similarly, the borrower is entitled to use the possessory remedies to have his/her possession restored (Civil Code, art. 1133 no. 2). These remedies can even be used against the lender who obstructs or restricts the use of the property. It must be noted, however, that as a general principle the lender does not have a duty to protect the borrower against attacks from third parties (Civil Code, art. 1133 no. 1). This means that under Portuguese law the tenant and the borrower enjoy the same protection of possession as the holders of real rights, owing to their physical control over the property.

Since a duly registered *personal servitude* is recognised as a real right under Portuguese law, B has a right of pursuit of the property against any person (C or D) in unlawful possession of the property. If B can prove that he has a real right over the property and that C or D is in possession of the property, B can petition the court for a declaration of his/her rights and a mandatory order against C or D for the return of the property (Civil Code, art. 1311 read with art. 1315).[60] The exercise of this remedy is not subject to a time limit (Civil Code, art. 1313).

Apart from this *quasi*-vindicatory remedy, B can also rely on the remedies for the protection of possession. Possession (*posse*) is the *de facto* control over an object that is manifested by an activity corresponding to the exercise of ownership or another real right of use over the property (Civil Code, art. 1252). Since the holder of a personal servitude acquires a real right over the property, his/her factual control is recognised as *quasi*-possession, and not merely as detention (*detenção*) of the property. Therefore he is entitled to institute a claim for the recovery of lost possession (*acção para a restituição da posse*, corresponding to the Roman *interdictum recuperandae possessionis*). B will therefore have a claim for restitution of his/her possession on account of wrongful deprivation of the factual control over the property (Civil Code, art. 1277). Restitution will be ordered without a consideration of the merits of the case, for example, an investigation concerning the right of ownership (Civil Code, art. 1278). The deprivation need not be by force or fraud – any unlawful deprivation would suffice. Nevertheless, if the dispossession was effected by the use of violence against the property or the person[61] of the former possessor, the court may order summary

[60] Decision of the Supreme Court of Justice of 04.10.84 [Process 071598], available at www.dgsi.pt.

[61] See Decision of the Supreme Court of Justice of 25.11.98 [Process 98B410], available at www.dgsi.pt. The Supreme Court of Justice of 25.06.98 concluded that the breaking of a door in order to gain possession of a building amounts to violence against property.

restitution without giving the dispossessor an opportunity to defend himself/herself (Civil Code, art. 1279).

In the most urgent cases, the holder of a real right who is deprived of his/her possession can use self-help to restore the status quo (Civil Code, art. 316 read with arts. 314 and 1315).

The claim for restitution can be pursued not only against the dispossessor and his/her heirs but also against any third person who acquired possession of the property with knowledge of the unlawful dispossession (Civil Code, art. 1281, no. 2). Consequently, B has a possessory remedy against both C and D to have his/her possession restored. B can sue the dispossessor within a year of the deprivation or in the case of clandestine deprivation within a year after it came to his/her knowledge. In appropriate circumstances, B is entitled to institute a claim for damages (Civil Code, art. 1284).

Scotland

As a *tenant* or as a *proper liferenter*, B may act directly against C to recover the property. There are two bases on which B may do so.[62] The first is by asserting his/her right in the property which gives B a right to possession. Like ownership, both lease and liferent are real rights which confer upon their holder a right to possession of the property which is good against the world.[63] There are rules about the extent to which B must prove his/her title to the property. This depends on the defence advanced by C.[64] As this claim is based on B's right to possession, it can be advanced against both C and D, regardless of the circumstances in which they acquired possession.[65]

The second alternative is for B to rely upon *spuilzie* – the delict of vitiously dispossessing another.[66] In respect of heritable property, *spuilzie* is more specifically known as ejection. Although at one time actions of *spuilzie* were very frequent, they are now virtually unheard of due to greater civil order and the increasing ease with which title to land may

[62] See generally in respect of actions protecting the possession of land, Reid et al., *Property*, paras. 138–47, 151–7 and 161–6.

[63] *Ibid*. para. 141. [64] *Ibid*. paras. 142–7.

[65] Subject to it potentially being defeated by registration in the Land Register if, for some reason, the liferent were omitted from C's or D's title sheet. In those circumstances, B's remedy will be for rectification of the Register, or, if that is not available, indemnity from the Keeper of the Registers: LR(S)A 79, s. 9 and 12.

[66] Reid et al., *Property*, paras. 161–6.

be proven, which makes it easier to rely on one's right to land as the basis for one's claim. There is some discussion about whether *spuilzie*/ejection is a purely possessory remedy or whether B has to show some kind of right to the property in order to be able to bring such an action.[67] Professor Reid's[68] view is that it is a purely possessory remedy. Holders of subordinate rights can have possession. A tenant certainly has possession[69] and logically so too does a liferenter. Both could therefore rely upon this second type of claim. There is no requirement that the dispossession must have been by force or fraud, but it must have been without B's consent and without judicial warrant.[70] In respect of heritable property, *spuilzie* is not a *vitium reale* (a real vice)[71] and so B cannot use this remedy to recover possession from D.

In both types of claim to recover possession, in addition to claiming the return of the property, B is entitled to recover violent profits from D. This is an accounting in respect of the amount which the property might have yielded by the utmost diligence during the period in which possession was wrongfully withheld.[72] In urban subjects, these are customarily double the rent.[73]

South Africa

South African law regards a *tenant* as a possessor and not as a mere detentor. Consequently, B can institute a possessory remedy (*mandament of spolie*) against any person who has unlawfully deprived him/her of his/her possession.[74] This remedy is based solely on factual possession by the tenant and is available in all cases of unlawful deprivation and not only if the dispossession is the result of force or fraud.[75]

In addition, the tenant's real (property) right gives him/her a right of pursuit against anyone in possession.[76] South African courts recognise this in the case of a short lease. However, in the case of a registered long lease, the courts have confused the South African vindicatory remedy with the tort of trespass of the English law, which deals with the

[67] *Ibid.* para. 162. [68] *Ibid.* para. 125; Gordon and Wortley, *Land Law*, para. 14–05.
[69] Reid et al., *Property*, para. 125; Gordon and Wortley, *Land Law*, para. 14–05.
[70] Reid et al., *Property*, para. 164. [71] Stair, *Institutions*, II. xxx. 3.
[72] Reid et al., *Property*, paras. 167 and 169; Gordon and Wortley, *Land Law*, para. 14–29.
[73] *Jute Industries Ltd.* v. *Wilson and Graham Ltd.* (1955) 71 Sh Ct Rep 158 159.
[74] *Nino Bonino* v. *De Lange* 1906 TS 120.
[75] Van der Merwe, De Waal and Carey Miller, 'Property and Trust', s. 167.
[76] Cooper, *Landlord and Tenant*, p. 277 and authorities cited in n. 27.

wrongful disturbance of another's possession and makes the tenant's real action dependent on possession.[77] Thus B as the holder of a registered long lease may only eject D if he/she (B) has entered into possession. If not, the registered owner (landlord A) would be the proper person to sue for the ejection of the trespasser.[78] However, the better view is that the tenant of a long lease acquires a real right by registration without occupation which is *ex hypothesi* enforceable against any possessor, including D. B only has to prove his/her real right and that D is in possession of the property. In fact, both the registered owner (A) and the registered tenant (B) have a right to eject D.[79]

Holders of *personal servitudes* in occupation are regarded as possessors. Therefore B will have a *mandament of spolie* against C for restoration of possession on account of wrongful deprivation of the peaceful exercise of the servitude without having to prove his/her right to the servitude.[80] Where the dispossessor (C) has transferred the property to D, case law requires knowledge on the part of D before a possessory action (*mandament*) can be brought against him/her for speedy recovery of the property. Academic opinion is against such extension of the remedy and requires some kind of co-operation in the spoliation before the action can be brought against D.

The rationale for the possessory remedy is to prevent self-help and it is therefore available to all possessors deprived unlawfully of their factual control of the property. It is therefore also available to the *precarist* (under a *precarium*) and the *borrower for use* (under a *commodatum*).[81] South African law has thus by analogy extended the possessory remedy to all holders except persons who hold as servants or *quasi*-servants on behalf of another.

In principle, B as holder of a *personal servitude* acquires a real right in the property and consequently he/she may recover the property from any possessor (D). In modern South African law the Roman-Dutch proprietary remedy (*actio confessoria*) was unfortunately confused with the remedy of interdict (injunction) of the English law. The holder of a personal servitude must therefore approach the court for a declaration of his/her rights and request a mandatory interdict against D to restore the *status*

77 See Turpin, 'Right of Ejectment', pp. 145, 147.
78 *Bodasingh's Estate* v. *Suleman* 1960 1 SA 288 (N) 291C-D.
79 Cooper, *Landlord and Tenant*, pp. 277–80.
80 *Bon Quelle (Edms) Bpk* v. *Munisipalitiet van Otavi* 1989 1 SA 508 (A).
81 Van der Merwe, De Waal and Carey Miller, 'Property and Trust', s. 160.

quo ante.[82] This remedy does not extend to the *precarist* and the borrower for use because they only have personal rights with regard to the land.

Spain

All the aforementioned holders (tenant, usufructuary, usuary, *habitator* and borrower) obtain possession of the property. The only exception is the holder of a *superficies*, who, in addition to obtaining possession of the property, also becomes a time-limited owner of the building or the produce of things planted or sown on the soil. If any of these holders (including the *superficiary*) is disturbed in their possession by a third person (C), they can approach the court for an action to restore their possession. This action was formerly called an interdict (*interdicto*), but is currently described as 'the action to protect the possession of a thing or a right against those who dispossess or disturb (B's) possession' (Code of Civil Procedure, art. 250.1–4). Spanish law does not appear to make a distinction between possessors and detentors and allows any person in physical control of the property to bring the action, irrespective of his/her title.[83] The action must, however, be instituted within one year from the date of the dispossession or disturbance (Civil Code, art. 1968.1).

There are two opposing views on the question of whether B can act directly against D who acquired possession of the property from C. One group of authors, supported by most of the court decisions, will not allow B to proceed against D, especially if D acted *bona fide*.[84] On the other hand, another group reckons that the protection given to the possessor can be exercised – in the first year after the dispossession – against anyone who possesses but has not yet acquired ownership of the property,[85] irrespective of his/her *bona* or *mala fides*.

In Spanish law it is immaterial whether the dispossession occurred by force, fraud or in any other way. The only matter that can affect the situation is where D has acquired possession of the property in bad faith (*mala fide*) from the dispossessor C. In such a case B can proceed against D. This is also the position where C or D has committed a crime.

[82] *Ibid*. s. 736.

[83] Lacruz Berdejo, *Elementos*, vol. 3.1, p. 43. Díez-Picazo, *Fundamentos*, vol. 3, p. 645 expressly mentions the usufructuary, the tenant and the holders of a *superficies* and a loan for use.

[84] de los Mozos, *Tutela interdictal*; Martin Pérez, 'Comment'.

[85] Lacruz Berdejo, *Elementos*, vol. 3.1, p. 44; Garcia Valdecasas, 'La posesión incorporal', p. 336.

In such a case, the Criminal Court will order the dispossessor to restore possession.

The usufructuary, the holder of a right of use or habitation, and a hereditary building lease (*superficiarius*), as holders of limited real rights, can also make use of the *actio confesoria*. This is an action addressed to obtain a judicial declaration of the time-limited holder's right which is used when someone (C) disputes the holder's limited right.

Case 5
Duty of the holder of a time-limited interest to repair, replace and renew[1]

The tenant (B) has a time-limited right in a house/a farm of which A is the landlord (owner). Which of the two parties (A or B), if any, has the duty to repair, replace or renew where:

- *the central heating system becomes defective;*
- *the central heating system becomes obsolescent (without being defective);*
- *the roof is damaged in a storm;*
- *the fences on the farm become dilapidated;*
- *the paint on the building flakes off?*

Will it make a difference if one of the parties caused the damage?

Suppose the party responsible for repainting the building omits to do anything and owing to his/her omission the wall is seriously damaged. Who, if anyone, is now responsible for repairing the damage?

If possible, please mention the principles and/or the theoretical distinctions applicable to repairs, and then apply them to the individual cases.

Please indicate default and mandatory rules. Also indicate manifest and frequent contractual provisions deviating from default rules.

Comparative observations

The *default rule* in most of the jurisdictions is that the *landlord* is responsible for major (extraordinary) repairs and for smaller repairs needed to render the property fit for its purpose,[2] while the *tenant* is responsible

[1] The aim of Cases 5–9 is to examine the content of the time-limited rights which have proprietary consequences. Each type of time-limited right is considered separately and in each case it is indicated whether the applicable rule is mandatory or not.

[2] The purpose is determined by the terms of the contract and the surrounding circumstances, including the previous and known intended use of the land. In Austria, for example, the condition of a residential property must not pose a risk to the residents' health.

for minor (ordinary) repairs which fall outside this category.[3] Major repairs under the Portuguese Law on Urban Leases include works of which the cost will exceed two-thirds of the net annual income of the building, and improvements ordered by public authorities. The relevant Polish legislation provides that the landlord must ensure that installations for the provision of gas, water, heating, sewerage, electric current and lifts (elevators) function properly; maintain the common parts of the building in a functioning and clean state; and repair damage caused by *vis maior*. In South Africa and Belgium, the landlord is responsible for major structural repairs and all smaller repairs occasioned by the age or inferior quality of the materials involved. Defects caused by normal wear and tear fall outside this category and in South Africa they are presumed to have been caused by the tenant or his/her employees. The tenant is therefore responsible for these 'tenant's repairs', such as the repair of defective doors, windows, shutters, hinges and locks that are presumed to have been in a good condition[4] when the tenant entered into occupation.[5]

In England, except for some statutory regulation, it is left to the parties to regulate their repair obligations expressly in the lease itself. The Landlord and Tenant Act implies certain terms in favour of the tenant in respect of short leases of dwelling houses. The terms require the landlord to keep the following in repair: the structure and exterior of the dwelling house (including drains, gutters and external pipes); the water, gas and electricity service installations including basins, sinks, baths and sanitary conveniences but not other fixtures, fittings and appliances; and installations for heating spaces and water. The terms are mandatory but can be dispensed with by leave of the County Court. In agricultural tenancies, the model repair clauses in the Agricultural Holdings Act, among others, divide the repair of 'fixed equipment' between landlord and tenant. These clauses can be contracted out under threat of being subjected to arbitration.

[3] In Denmark, the default rule under the Law on Private Housing is that the landlord is responsible for keeping the premises in good repair and he/she has a duty to repair, replace and renew all items that fall into disrepair from whatever cause. The only duty of the tenant is to maintain and, where required, replace the lock and keys of the building.

[4] In the absence of a document attached to the lease detailing the condition of the property, Portuguese law presumes that the property was in good condition on transfer to the tenant.

[5] See also the default rule under the Hungarian and Spanish Laws on Residential Leases.

Most jurisdictions[6] will rule that the *defective heating system*, the *dilapidated fences* and the *flaking paint* will render the property unfit for the purpose for which it is let and will therefore hold the landlord responsible for repairing these defects if they were caused by age or inferior materials. In contrast, the German, Italian and Polish law pertaining to agricultural (or income-producing) leases will characterise the dilapidated fences, flaking paint and minor defects in the heating system as defects arising from normal wear and tear, the repair of which will be the responsibility of the tenant.

In most jurisdictions,[7] the landlord will be responsible for the repair of the *roof* in order to ensure that the premises is fit for the purpose for which it is used even though the defect was caused by *vis maior*.[8] In England, the landlord will be responsible for the repair of the roof if tiles were blown off by the wind, but not if the building was demolished completely by the storm. If the property is partially destroyed in Belgium, the owner is not obliged to rebuild.[9]

Most jurisdictions[10] will classify the replacement of an *obsolescent heating system* with a modern system not as a 'repair' but as an 'improvement'[11] for which the landlord is not responsible. Some jurisdictions, however, equate obsolescence with non-repair,[12] and classify it as a conservation measure[13] or include renewals under repairs and hold the landlord responsible, especially if the replacement improves the general condition of the residence and the costs do not exceed the rental income or public subsidy gained from the lease.[14] German law requires replacement by the landlord if the tenant can prove that his/her health is affected by the obsolescent system.

[6] E.g. Germany, Austria, Greece, Portugal, Spain, Denmark and South Africa under their default or mandatory rules (e.g. Belgium and Portugal under the Law on Urban Leases and England under special legislation).

[7] E.g. Austria, Greece, Spain, Italy, Belgium, Portugal, Denmark, South Africa and Poland (in the case of residential leases). In Portugal, the landlord will only be held responsible if repair of the roof is ordered by a public authority.

[8] The South African rationale is that the landlord is responsible for procuring insurance and paying the insurance premiums.

[9] See also the Scottish report.

[10] E.g. Germany, Greece, Portugal, Spain, Belgium, Scotland and Poland.

[11] Replacement is classified as a useful expense recoverable from the landlord based on actual or implied agency.

[12] See the English report. [13] See the Portuguese report.

[14] See the Austrian and South African reports, especially the latter on the replacement of guttering.

Most jurisdictions[15] accept that the *default rules* are not mandatory and that parties can deviate from them either expressly or impliedly in the contract of lease or in a separate contract. The tendency is to shift as many repair obligations as possible onto the tenant. In Germany, there is extensive case law on the extent to which parties may deviate from default rules. German courts take a conservative view and only allow the lessee of residential property to assume responsibility for minor repairs such as painting the walls of an apartment but not for major structural repairs. South African, Belgian and Danish law also construe all deviations strictly in order to saddle the tenant with as few repairing obligations as possible. In Danish law it is quite common to allow residential tenants to take on the duty of whitewashing the exterior and painting and papering the interior. In the case of a lease of a single-family house it is customary for the tenant to assume the duty to repair the outbuildings and garden. Portuguese law adopts a more liberal approach, especially in urban leases of commercial, industrial and professional property. Parties are allowed to agree in a written deed that ordinary and even extraordinary works of repair and improvements to the property will be the tenant's responsibility. The Polish legislation on agricultural leases makes provision for different default rules shifting some of the repair obligations to the tenant, who is then responsible for all repairs necessary to maintain the property in its former condition.[16]

In most jurisdictions,[17] the landlord will not be responsible for repairing defects or damage *caused by the tenant*, members of his/her family, guests or other persons for whom the tenant is responsible. The tenant must therefore observe the diligence of a reasonable man in using the property for the purpose specified in the contract or implied from the circumstances. This may require positive steps. A vineyard must, for example, be worked and manured in a timely fashion and cultivated carefully according to the standards of a prudent winegrower. A hotel must be exploited in a manner that attracts customers. If not regulated by the repairing covenant, the tenant in England must use the property in a tenant-like manner, must compensate the landlord for any defects or damage caused by his/her negligence and must return the property intact at the end of the tenancy. In Greece, the tenant will moreover be

[15] E.g. Germany, Greece, Portugal, Spain, South Africa, Denmark, Hungary and Poland. But cf. Scotland.

[16] See the Polish report.

[17] E.g. Germany, Austria, Greece, Spain, Italy, Belgium, South Africa and Denmark.

personally barred from claiming the cost of the repair of defects which were known to him/her at the time of the conclusion of the contract or which he was unaware of owing to gross negligence on his/her part. The same applies in respect of any claim by the tenant that the property lacks certain qualities that have been stipulated in the contract. In Denmark, damage caused by the negligence of one of the parties gives rise to delictual liability. If the cost of future repairs is saved, this may be deducted from the compensation awarded.

In most jurisdictions there is a duty on the tenant to inform the landlord if (urgent) repairs are needed and to allow the landlord to carry out the repairs in order to prevent further loss.[18] However, each party remains responsible for *loss caused by his/her negligent acts or omissions* and is responsible for all damage that flows from non-repair.[19] Thus, if a wall is seriously damaged on account of not being repainted on time, the landlord will bear the cost of its restoration if he/she was aware of the defective condition or should have been aware on account of his/her trade.[20] In Spain, the residential tenant may undertake the repairs and reclaim the costs from the landlord, whereas the agricultural tenant can compel the landlord to comply with his/her obligation by an order of court, an action for breach of contract, a request for reduction in rent or execution of the repairs, followed by a claim for reimbursement. In England, the loss caused by a failure to repaint can be characterised as permissive waste for which the tenant is responsible.

Most jurisdictions[21] adopt the rule that the *usufructuary* is responsible for ordinary repairs necessitated by his/her exploitation of the property in accordance with its economic purpose, whereas the nude owner is responsible for extraordinary repairs.[22] In general, this amounts to periodic repairs of moderate cost not exceeding the total rental income of the land (Austria and Spain) or two-thirds of the rental income (Portugal and Italy). The most important criterion for distinguishing ordinary and extraordinary repairs is whether the repairs are necessitated by normal wear and tear. The prevailing opinion in Italy is, however, that unless

[18] See e.g. the Greek, Belgian, Spanish, Portuguese, Italian, South African and Hungarian reports. The tenant will have to bear the loss resulting from non-timeous notification (in South Africa on the principle of *volenti non fit iniuria*).

[19] See e.g. the German, Austrian, Greek and Belgian reports.

[20] See the South African report.

[21] E.g. Germany, Greece, France, Portugal, Spain, Belgium, Italy, the Netherlands, South Africa, Hungary and Poland.

[22] The French, Belgian and Italian Civil Codes contain lists of major repairs.

serious damage might result from non-compliance with this obligation, the owner cannot force the usufructuary to carry out these repairs.[23] This is subject to the rule that the holder is obliged to return the property on expiry of the usufruct with the preservation of its substance, that is, in a state of good repair.[24]

If the nude owner delays in carrying out extraordinary repairs without justifiable reason, the usufructuary may carry out the repairs and his/her estate may claim the cost minus the cost of any deterioration from the nude owner at the expiry of the usufruct.[25] The usufructuary is under an obligation to warn the nude owner of the need to carry out urgent repairs.[26] An omission in this regard is usually traced back to bad management of the property and any resulting losses may be claimed from the usufructuary.

Most jurisdictions[27] will classify the repairs needed to restore the *defective heating system*, the *dilapidated fence* and the *flaking paint* as ordinary expenses which must be borne by the usufructuary. In Austria, this is subject to the condition that the costs do not exceed the amount which the usufructuary gains from the property. However, if any of the repairs involve major expense, for example, if the entire heating system or the entire fence has to be replaced, the repairs will be classified as extraordinary and the nude owner's responsibility.[28] In France, the nude owner will be responsible for replacing the fences, but not for limited and specific repairs to the fences.

Most jurisdictions will consider *minor* repairs to the *roof* necessitated by a storm (the replacement of a few tiles), as ordinary repairs for which the usufructuary is responsible. Major repairs needed for the conservation of the property will be classified as extraordinary, unusual or unforeseen, and the responsibility of the nude owner.[29] Interestingly, under Spanish law, any repairs necessitated by a storm will exceed the limits of ordinary repairs and will thus be the responsibility of the nude

[23] If the nude owner carries out the repairs, he/she is entitled to legal interest on the amount expended for the duration of the usufruct.

[24] The German and Polish rationale for the restriction to ordinary repairs is that the usufructuary is only entitled to the ordinary proceeds of the property and is not allowed to transform the property or to change its substance.

[25] See e.g. the reports of Portugal, Spain, Italy, the Netherlands and Hungary.

[26] See e.g. the Portuguese report.

[27] E.g. Germany, Austria, Greece, Portugal, Spain, Italy, Belgium, the Netherlands, South Africa, Hungary and Poland.

[28] See the German, Dutch and South African reports.

[29] See e.g. the German, Greek, French, Belgian, Portuguese, Italian, South African, Hungarian and Polish reports.

owner.[30] The Belgian Civil Code provides that if the storm is classified as an unforeseen event (*casus fortuitus*), neither the nude owner nor the usufructuary is under an obligation to rebuild what was destroyed by the storm. If the nude owner decides to replace the roof, he/she will bear the cost of replacement,[31] and if the usufructuary replaces the roof, he/she will bear the cost of replacement, but subject to recourse against the owner for any surplus value on termination of the usufruct. If the usufructuary carries out major repairs to the roof, the cost will be regarded as a necessary expense which can be claimed from the nude owner on expiry of the usufruct.

The replacement of an *obsolescent heating system* by a more modern system can be classified either as maintenance (repair) or as an improvement of the property. If regarded as repair, most jurisdictions[32] will classify the replacement as an extraordinary repair which the nude owner is obliged to execute. If classified as an improvement of the property, neither of the parties will be under an obligation to replace it.[33] If the usufructuary does replace the system, it will be classified as a useful improvement which can be removed without damage during the subsistence of the usufruct[34] or for which the usufructuary can claim reimbursement on the expiry of the usufruct (Portugal and Hungary),[35] probably under the doctrine of *negotiorum gestio*.[36]

Since usufructs are commonly created in wills, most of the jurisdictions could not provide an answer to the question whether or not the parties may *deviate from default rules*. It is, however, an important question since it is becoming more and more common to create usufructs *inter vivos*, for example, in Germany, where contractual provisions deviating from the default rules are frequently used in practice for tax reasons. The parties may stipulate that the usufructuary must bear all costs, including those of extraordinary repairs, or, conversely, that the nude owner must bear the expenses of the ordinary maintenance of the property. Agreements on repairs and expenses are binding on everyone who acquires the property or the limited right, provided it is registered in the Land Register (*Grundbuch*). In Belgium, the parties often agree that the usufructuary will be responsible for extraordinary repairs.

30 See the Spanish Civil Code, art. 500. 31 See the Belgian report.
32 E.g. Germany, Greece, Portugal, Spain, Belgium, Hungary and Poland.
33 See the Greek, Portuguese and Italian reports. 34 See the Spanish report.
35 See the Portuguese and Hungarian reports.
36 See the Greek and South African reports.

Any *negligent damage to the property* will usually be caused by the usufructuary. Since the usufructuary must preserve the substance of the property, damage negligently caused to the property by careless administration[37] will make him/her liable to the nude owner[38] for the cost of repairs,[39] or liable in delict for economic loss suffered by the nude owner.

Some jurisdictions[40] will classify painting of the wall as an ordinary repair and thus the responsibility of the usufructuary. If *serious damage is caused on account of negligent non-timeous repainting of the wall*, the usufructuary will be liable to the owner for all consequential loss suffered as a result of the neglect. If the repair is classified as extraordinary, the usufructuary will be obliged to notify the owner without delay of the deterioration of the building or of the preventative measures that can be taken to avoid unforeseen further damage. If the owner refuses to act or delays in carrying out the repairs, he/she will be liable for resulting consequential loss. However, in such a case the usufructuary will be allowed to execute the repairs and claim the costs from the nude owner, probably before expiry of the usufruct.

In most jurisdictions,[41] the rules applicable to usufruct also apply to the *other personal servitudes*, if compatible. Interestingly, Austrian law also obliges the nude owner to carry out ordinary repairs of residential premises which are subject to a right of use. Portuguese law, again, proportions the responsibility of the user and *habitator* for ordinary repairs, administrative expenses and taxes levied on the property if the holder of the right of use is only allowed to take part of the fruits or if the *habitator* only occupies part of the house. Under German law it is disputed whether a provision in an agreement establishing a right of use which changes the default rule to saddle the holder of the right of use with extraordinary repairs is valid.[42]

In terms of the Regulations under the German Law on Hereditary Building Rights, the maintenance obligations of the parties are determined by the constitutive agreement under which the *hereditary building right* is established. Unless the parties have agreed otherwise, neither the landowner nor the holder is under an obligation to maintain the structure in a reasonable state of repair. In practice, the constitutive

[37] See the Portuguese report. [38] In *quasi* contract, according to the German report.

[39] See the German, Greek, Portuguese, Belgian, South African and Polish reports.

[40] E.g. Germany, Greece and Portugal. [41] E.g. Belgium, Italy and South Africa.

[42] See the Austrian, Portuguese and German reports.

agreement often provides that the holder is under an obligation to maintain the structure and to bear all costs relating to ordinary and extraordinary repairs.

In the remaining jurisdictions, the repair obligation depends on whether the *hereditary building right* pertains to an existing building or to the erection of a new building. In the former case, the obligation of the holder is the same as that of the holder of a hereditary land lease under Belgian law.[43] Some Italian scholars are of the opinion that the *superficiarius* is in the position of an owner and therefore under no obligation to keep the building in a good state of repair or to expect the owner of the soil to repair the building. Other scholars maintain that at least some of the rules applicable to usufruct should also apply to the holder of a hereditary building right. Where the hereditary building right pertains to the erection of a new building, some jurisdictions[44] do not place any repair obligation on the holder and advise parties to regulate their maintenance and repair obligations in the constitutive agreement. In other jurisdictions,[45] the holder is held to be responsible for all repairs unless otherwise regulated in the constitutive agreement. The reason advanced is that the holder is considered the (temporary) owner of the new structure. Under Italian law, the holder may even demolish the structure. Under Polish law, this obligation is mandatory and not susceptible of alteration in the constitutive agreement.

The jurisdictions that recognise *hereditary land leases*[46] distinguish between ordinary (minor) and extraordinary (major) repairs and hold the holder of the hereditary land lease responsible for ordinary repairs and the landowner for extraordinary repairs, following the rules applicable to usufruct. The holder must notify the owner if extraordinary repairs are necessary and allow him/her to execute the repairs. Interestingly, the landowner is not legally obliged to carry out the repairs and if he/she does not do so the holder is not entitled to claim any damages. Holders are not responsible for major repairs unless they were the result of their dereliction of duty. In practice, a holder may often agree to be responsible for major repairs and in the Netherlands public authorities usually impose conditions of repair on the holders of hereditary land leases.

[43] See the Belgian report. [44] See e.g. the Belgian report.
[45] See e.g. the Austrian, French, Dutch, Italian, Spanish and Polish reports.
[46] See the Belgian and Dutch reports.

In France and Hungary, the duty to repair is on the *borrower for use* who is entitled to reclaim his/her expenses on expiry of the loan from the lender (in Hungary, on the basis of *negotiorum gestio*). The borrower will therefore have a duty to repair the heating system and repaint the flaking walls.[47] Neither party, however, is saddled with a duty to repair the dilapidated fences or the leaky roof.[48]

Austria

For *lease contracts*, the answer depends on whether and to what extent the contract falls under the Law on Tenancy. Which version of the Law on Tenancy applies depends on when the contract concerned was concluded. The following answers refer to the provisions currently in force and not to older provisions which may apply to older contracts.

The general principle under Civil Code, art. 1096 is that the landlord must surrender the leased property to the tenant in a condition suitable for the contractually agreed use and maintain it in this condition for the term of the lease.[49] Under an agricultural lease, the tenant is responsible for ordinary maintenance and repair of the leased buildings to the extent to which he/she can do so by using materials, such as wood,[50] from the leased property itself (Civil Code, § 1096, para. 2, which is not mandatory).[51]

If the landlord does not fulfil his/her maintenance duties, the tenant is exempt from paying (at least part of) the rent for the period during which the property is not suitable for the agreed use.[52] With regard to the lease of immovable property, a contrary agreement regarding rent reduction to the disadvantage of the tenant is not binding (Civil Code, § 1096, para. 1). Apart from rent reduction, the tenant can claim for specific performance of the maintenance duties under the lease or withdraw from the contract. If the landlord acted negligently, the tenant can also claim compensation for damages.[53] However, if the

[47] See the French and Hungarian reports.

[48] The French report offers a detailed discussion of the obligations of the borrower and the precarist.

[49] Würth, in Rummel, *Kommentar*, I, § 1096, para. 4.

[50] Iro, *Sachenrecht*, § 1096, para. 12.

[51] 4 Ob 591/89; wobl (1991), p. 2; 3 Ob 267/51; SZ 24/163; Würth, in Rummel, *Kommentar*, I, § 1096, para. 1.

[52] Würth, in Rummel, *Kommentar*, I, § 1096, paras. 10 ff.

[53] *Ibid.* I, § 1096, paras. 2 and 12.

impairment of serviceability was caused by the negligence of the tenant himself/herself, he/she will not be entitled to a reduction of rent[54] and, under Civil Code, § 1111, the tenant may be held liable for damages.

If a defect which requires repairs comes to light, the tenant must inform the landlord in order to avoid liability for consequential damages. The tenant may remedy the defect and demand reimbursement of the necessary expenses in accordance with the provisions governing *negotiorium gestio*. The tenant has to claim such reimbursement within six months after he/she has returned the leased property (Civil Code, § 1097).

Specific rules apply if the leased object is rendered unusable by events of *force majeure*, such as fire, flooding or storms. The landlord will not be obliged to reconstitute a condition suitable for the contractually agreed use, but neither will the tenant be obliged to pay the rent (Civil Code, § 1104). Furthermore, the tenant will be entitled to cancel the contract of lease.[55]

Specific rules apply if the contract falls *under the Law on Tenancy*.[56] According to, § 3, the landlord must maintain the leased property in a condition which corresponds to the customary standards of the area concerned. Furthermore, he/she must ensure that the leased object does not pose a risk to the residents' health. The parties are not allowed to deviate from these rules to the disadvantage of the tenant.[57]

The landlord must maintain the house and the parts and facilities which are used collectively by the residents (Law on Tenancy, § 3, para. 2 nos. 1 and 3) such as central heating systems and lifts (elevators). Other rules apply to the individual objects of the lease. The landlord must maintain them only to the extent that the defects can cause serious damage to the house or to the health of the inhabitants (§ 3, para. 2, no. 2). The tenant, on the other hand, must maintain the facilities such as the heating system or sanitary facilities in such a way that they do not cause damage either to the landlord or to other residents (§ 8).

If the tenant incurs expenses to effect improvements that will last even after termination of the contract of lease (for example, installation

[54] *Ibid.* I, § 1096, para. 11. [55] *Ibid.* I, § 1096, para. 2.

[56] In principle, provisions of the Law on Tenancy are obligatory (4 Ob 591/89; wobl (1991), p. 2). Hence, any rules relating to the Law on Tenancy described in the following paragraphs can be deemed to be mandatory unless they are explicitly defined as non-mandatory.

[57] 4 Ob 591/89; wobl (1991), p. 2; 10 Ob 510/87; JBl (1988), p. 522; Prader, *MRG*, § 3, n. 2; Prader and Kuprian, 'Erhaltungspflichten', p. 271.

of an intercommunication system or measures to reduce energy consumption), he/she can demand reimbursement of these expenses (§ 10). This claim cannot be waived in advance (§ 10, para. 7). The landlord has to undertake useful improvements such as the rearrangement of conduits or the heating system, provided they are functional for the general condition of the house and he/she can cover the costs with rental income and public subvention (§ 4, para. 2 no 1). In case of damages caused by *force majeure* (fire, water, weather), the landlord is obliged to restore the suitability of the property for lease to the extent to which the costs are covered by insurance (§ 7).[58]

According to these principles, the answers to the examples are as follows. Under both the Civil Code and the Law on Tenancy, the landlord must carry out the necessary repairs if the *central heating system* becomes defective.[59] The Civil Code and the Law on Tenancy differ where the central heating system only *becomes obsolescent*. According to the Civil Code, the landlord is not obliged to renew the system, but according to the Law on Tenancy, he/she has to renew it, provided the renewal benefits the general condition of the house and the costs can be covered by rental income and public subvention (Law on Tenancy, § 4, para. 2, no. 1).

If the *roof* is damaged by a storm, the landlord must repair it under the Law on Tenancy but not under the Civil Code.[60] However, the Civil Code allows the tenant to withdraw from the contract or to refuse to pay the rent.

If the *fences* of the farm become dilapidated, the landlord is obliged to repair them if such defect renders the farm unsuitable for its contractually agreed use. However, if they can be repaired with material from the farm (wood etc.), the tenant is obliged to repair it (Civil Code, § 1096, para. 2).

Repainting is necessary to maintain the contractually agreed use if, without repainting, the brickwork would be damaged. In this case, the landlord is obliged to undertake repairs both under the Civil Code and the Law on Tenancy because damages of the brickwork would render the building unserviceable for the contractually agreed use. In this case, the omission to repaint the building renders the landlord liable for any consequential damages.

[58] This provision is obligatory as well; see Würth, in Rummel, *Kommentar*, I, § 1104, para. 1.

[59] Binder, in Schwimann, *Praxiskommentar*, V, § 1096, para. 44.

[60] *Ibid*. V, § 1096, para. 52.

If the defect was caused by the negligence of the tenant, he/she is liable for any damage caused and not entitled to claim rent reduction.

The general principle is that the *usufructuary* must maintain the servient land and carry out repairs and replacements provided that he/she can cover the cost of these measures with the fruits and the income gained from the land (Civil Code, § 513). In so far as the income is not sufficient to cover maintenance expenses, the landowner is obliged to bear the extra burden.[61] The same provision stipulates that the usufructuary is liable for damages which he/she caused negligently, but not for defects brought about by using the land in conformity with the contract. The obligations of the usufructuary provided for in Civil Code, § 513 have not yet been explored in detail. According to legal doctrine, they generally correspond to those of the tenant of an income-producing (usufructuary) lease under Civil Code, § 1096, para. 2, and in order to interpret Civil Code, § 513 the corresponding provision of the German Civil Code (§ 1041) can be referred to.[62]

A different rule applies to the *right of use*. Under Civil Code, § 508, the owner is obliged to maintain the servient land in good condition and to perform all ordinary and extraordinary repairs as long as the cost of the repairs does not exceed the benefits which the owner draws from the property. Hence, in principle, the owner must maintain the land, buildings and equipment in a condition which renders them suitable for their agreed use.[63]

Regarding the examples mentioned in the question, it follows that (unless contractually agreed otherwise), as the holder of a usufruct, B has to repair the *heating system* and the *fences* as well as *repaint the wall*, provided that the respective costs are covered by what he gains from the property. However, if the *heating system* still works and is only *obsolescent*, neither A nor B is obliged to install a new one. As to the *roof*, the rule drawn from Civil Code, § 508, sent. 2 and by analogy to Civil Code, § 1104 is that the owner is not obliged to repair damages caused by *force majeure* such as fire, war, plagues and flooding. Hence, neither A nor B is obliged to repair the roof if it is damaged by a storm.

Different rules apply if B has a *right of use*. In this case, A (as nude owner or grantor of the right) is obliged to perform all ordinary and extraordinary maintenance work provided that the costs for this work

[61] 4 Ob 506/89; JBl (1989), p. 442. [62] Welser, 'Erhaltungspflicht', p. 145.

[63] Hofmann, in Rummel, *Kommentar*, I, § 508, para. 2; Kiendl-Wendner, in Schwimann and Verschraegen, *Praxiskommentar*, II, § 508, para. 1.

do not exceed the benefits to which he is entitled. Hence, A should be obliged to repair the heating system and the fence as well as repaint the wall. However, by analogy to Civil Code, § 1104, he/she will not be obliged to repair the roof when it is damaged by *force majeure*. Neither is A obliged to renew a heating system which is obsolescent but still in working order.

If B has a *hereditary building right* in respect of the land, he/she is considered to be the owner of the building. Therefore, A does not have any maintenance obligations in respect of the building. As to the land, B has, depending on the contract concerned, a usufruct or a right of use. In this regard the same rules as for servitudes apply.

Belgium

In a *residential* or an *agricultural lease*, the tenant is responsible for tenant repairs and the landlord for all other repairs (Civil Code, arts. 1720 and 1754). In general, tenant repairs amount to daily maintenance and repairs of minor damage, often caused by the tenant. Civil Code, art. 1754 provides a non-exhaustive list of examples. In practice, what will count as tenant repairs is governed by local customs.[64] The tenant will not be responsible for tenant repairs caused exclusively by ordinary wear and tear or *force majeure* (Civil Code, art. 1755). Landlord repairs are all repairs and works needed to maintain the property in such a condition that it may be used for the purpose for which it is let, with the exception of those repairs which are considered tenant repairs. Consequently, the landlord is not only responsible for extraordinary repairs (as the owner in a usufruct) and urgent repairs, but also for repairs caused by *force majeure*, defects, use and ordinary wear and tear. However, if these repairs are caused by failure on the part of the tenant to repair, the latter would be responsible for such omission.

These rules are mandatory (Law on Residential Leases, art. 2, § 2 as modified by the Act of 25 April 2007;[65] Law on Agricultural Leases, art. 56; except for Civil Code, art. 1754 containing examples of tenant repairs). Contractual provisions deviating from these rules are forbidden.

[64] For a detailed list, see e.g. Nyckees, art. 1754–1756 CC.

[65] Under the Law on Rural Lease the Government must define what specific repairs are for the owner but presently there is no Royal Decree, in this regard.

In the issues regarding the *central heating system*, *roof*, *dilapidated fences* and *repainting* of the building, the landlord will be responsible. Concerning the damage of the roof by a *storm*, it is important to note that the tenant can in no event be held liable for damage caused by *casus fortuitus*. If the property is partially destroyed, the landlord cannot be forced to rebuild (Civil Code, art. 1722). The landlord will be responsible for replacement or renewal of the *obsolescent central heating system*. However, in so far as the system is in working order and in a good condition, the landlord is not obliged to replace it. If the landlord replaces it voluntarily under a residential or agricultural lease, he/she will have to bear the costs, but can, subject to strict conditions, claim an increase of the rent due.[66]

The *usufructuary* (B) is responsible for ordinary maintenance of the property while the nude owner is responsible for extraordinary repairs (Civil Code, art. 605). Civil Code, art. 606 limits extraordinary repairs to the following: the repair of structural walls and façades and the renewal of beams, roofs, bearing walls, the entire roof of a building and the renewal of dykes. These are usually reconstruction and renewal works necessary for the general stability and preservation of the property as such. Repairs other than extraordinary repairs are considered to be normal maintenance. However, if such extraordinary repairs are necessitated by failure on the part of the usufructuary to perform normal maintenance, the latter will be responsible for such repairs (Civil Code, art. 605).

Parties may, and often do, contractually agree that the *time-limited right holder* shall also be liable for extraordinary repairs. It must be noted that the distinction in the Belgian Civil Code refers to houses and requires some interpretation when applied to other buildings.

The application of these rules will lead to the following results on the concrete issues presented here. The repair of the *central heating system* falls under ordinary repairs and it is thus the duty of the holder to execute the repairs. If the central heating system *becomes obsolescent* (without being defective), the Belgian Supreme Court[67] has held that the renewal or replacement of the central heating system of a theatre is an extraordinary repair for which the nude owner is responsible. If this can by analogy be applied to a house burdened with a usufruct, the nude owner will be responsible for the replacement. However, if the system is

[66] See for residential lease, Carette, 'Financiële aspecten', nos. 449 ff.
[67] Supreme Court of 3 Feb. 1927, Pas. 1927 I 143.

still functioning adequately, and a renewal or replacement is not necessary to heat the house, it is extremely doubtful whether the owner can be forced to do this.

In general, if the damage to the *roof* relates to the entire roof or a substantial part thereof, the cost of repair would have to be borne by the owner; if the damage only relates to a minor part of the roof, the usufructuary will be responsible for the repairs. However, the damage of the roof during a storm could be classified as a case of *casus fortuitus* (*toeval*). Neither the owner nor the holder is obliged to rebuild what is destroyed by *casus fortuitus* (Civil Code, art. 607). If that is the case, none of them will be obliged to replace the roof. If the roof is badly damaged and the owner decides to replace the roof, he/she will have to bear the cost of replacement.[68] If, on the other hand, the usufructuary replaces the roof, he/she bears the costs, but will have recourse against the owner for the increased value of the property on termination of the usufruct.

The repair of *dilapidated fences* is normally considered an ordinary repair to be borne by the usufructuary. Although Civil Code, art. 606 places the cost of the replacement of dykes on the nude owner, it is doubtful whether this may be extended by analogy to the repair of dilapidated fences. The *repainting* of the building when the paint flakes off is an ordinary repair for which the usufructuary is responsible.

The *party who caused the damage* will in principle be responsible to compensate for it. In the case where the usufructuary omits to repaint the building and the wall is seriously damaged as a result of this omission, he/she will be responsible for the repairs even if they can be classified as extraordinary repairs normally borne by the nude owner (Civil Code, art. 605).

In a *hereditary land lease* (*emphyteusis*), the landlord has no duty to repair (not even extraordinary repairs) unless otherwise agreed (Law on Emphyteutic Leases, art. 5).[69] Analogous to the rules that apply to usufruct, the holder of the hereditary land lease (B) must take care of all ordinary maintenance and repairs (art. 5).[70] The owner is contractually responsible for extraordinary repairs, but if such repairs are the consequence of a failure to perform normal maintenance repairs by the holder, the latter will be liable. In practice, parties often agree that

68 de Page and Dekkers, *Traité élémentaire*, no. 349.

69 Derine et al. 'Zakenrecht', no. 1007.

70 Thus, a dispute may arise about extraordinary repairs, in the absence of a contractual agreement.

the holder of a hereditary land lease shall also in such circumstances be liable for extraordinary repairs.

All issues regarding the defective or obsolescent *central heating system*, the damage to the *roof by a storm*, the repair of the *dilapidated fences* and the *repainting of the building*, will by analogy be solved in the same way as in the case of *usufruct* as set out above, except that the owner has no duty to repair, unless agreed otherwise.

Since the Law on Building Lease contains no rules regarding repair, it is generally accepted that the rules applicable to hereditary land lease as set out above apply *mutatis mutandis* to a *hereditary building right* (*superficies*).[71] However, since the holder is treated as the owner of the construction, he/she will not be under an obligation to maintain or repair the building. It is different of course when the hereditary building lease pertains to the use of an existing building: in that case, the rules on hereditary leases of land apply by analogy.

In the absence of legislative rules, it is important to regulate the parties' duties regarding repair and maintenance in the contract. Here too the issues regarding the defective or obsolescent central heating system, the damage to the roof by a storm, the repair of the dilapidated fences and the repainting of the building will by analogy be solved in the same way as in the case of usufruct as set out above.

Denmark

In a *lease of buildings for housing purposes*, the default rule is that the landlord is responsible for keeping the premises in proper repair (Law on Private Housing, s. 19). During the tenancy, the tenant must maintain and, where required, replace locks and keys (s. 20). These rules are not mandatory and may be deviated from (s. 24). It is a common contractual practice for tenants to take on the duty to maintain the flat by whitewashing, painting or papering. Because the rules are not mandatory, tenants may undertake additional duties specified in the lease. If the rented dwelling is a single-family house, it is common for the tenant to take on a duty to maintain (but not to replace or renew) other parts of the building and its surroundings, for example, the garden.

The *default rule* concerning the examples in Case 5 is that the landlord (A) has the duty to repair, replace or renew everything. Contractual provisions will often lead to the tenant being responsible if the *paint*

[71] Derine, van Neste and Vandenberghe, *Zakenrecht*, no. 1027.

flakes off inside, but not outside, the rented premises. If the time-limited contract concerns a single-family house, the tenant may have the duty to paint the outside as well and perhaps to repair the *fences* and the *heating system*. Only in very rare circumstances will the tenant have taken on any other of the duties mentioned.

If any one of the parties (A or B) has caused damage, either intentionally or through negligence, that party can be held liable in delict. The party at fault must pay damages regardless of who has the duty to repair. The measure of damages is based on a principle of restitution, which means that the injured party's loss is to be compensated in full, but no enrichment must be obtained. If the party on whom the duty to repair rests, saves future repair costs, these will be deducted from the cost to repair the damages. Of course, *obsolescence* of any part of the building cannot fall under this rule.

The provisions in the Law on Commercial Premises Rent regarding repairs are very similar to the rules of the Law on Private Housing. The default rule is that the landlord (A) must keep every part of the rented premises in good repair (Law on Commercial Premises Rent Act, s. 16). This rule can be deviated from as is very often the case in practice. There are no standard contract provisions concerning the tenants taking on duties to repair, replace or renew. Although it is likely that the tenant will be responsible for the *dilapidated fence*, the *paintwork* and the *central heating system* becoming defective, it will depend on the terms of the individual contract. The damage on the *roof* will most likely be covered by an insurance policy taken out by the landlord and the *obsolescence of the central heating system* will also normally be the responsibility of the landlord.

If the damage is caused by a negligent act or omission, the party at fault can be held responsible in exactly the same way as is in the case of dwellings.

England

Generally speaking, it is for the parties to regulate the scope and existence of their respective repair obligations in express terms in the lease.[72] Further, commercial leases' repair obligations rest entirely on

[72] Though there may also be terms implied by the court – see *Liverpool Civil Code* v. *Irwin* [1976] 2 All ER 39.

the terms of the lease in question.[73] As to leases in general, the pattern is that the shorter the lease, the more burdens fall on the landlord.

There is some statutory regulation of the allocation of repair obligations in respect of short *leases of dwelling houses* under the Landlord and Tenant Act 1985 (LTA).[74] LTA, s. 11 applies where there is a lease (a) of a dwelling house (b) which is granted on or after 24 October 1961 (c) for a term of less than seven years (LTA, s. 13). There are some exceptions which will not be considered here (LTA, s. 14). The basic machinery of the Act is to imply terms in favour of the tenant into the lease under section 11(1).[75] These require the landlord '(a) to keep in repair the structure and exterior of the dwelling house (including drains, gutters and external pipes); (b) to keep in repair and proper working order the installations in the dwelling-house for the supply of water, gas and electricity and for sanitation (including basins, sinks, baths and sanitary conveniences, but not other fixtures, fittings and appliances for making use of water, gas or electricity); and (c) to keep in repair and proper working order the installations in the dwelling-house for space heating and heating water.' The terms imposed by statute may not be contracted out of, but can be dispensed with by leave of the County Court (LTA, s. 12).

In those *agricultural tenancies* still existing under the Agricultural Holdings Act 1986 (AHA), the Minister for Agriculture, Fisheries and Food has the power to create model clauses which specify the distribution of, among other things, repair liability in respect of 'fixed equipment' (AHA, s. 6). Although those model clauses may be contracted out of, there is a right to challenge any leases departing from their terms in arbitration (AHA, s. 8). In the current edition of those model clauses,[76] the liability for repair of various structures is divided between the landlord and the tenant.[77]

With those general points and specific qualifications in mind, and absent any express terms of covenant indicated, I proceed to consider

[73] See *Demetriou* v. *Poolaction Ltd.* [1991] 1 EGLR 100; *Mancetter Developments Ltd.* v. *Garmanson Ltd.* [1986] QB 1212.

[74] There is further regulation of very low rent accommodation under s. 8 of this Act, but given the rental market in England and Wales very few low rent leases are in existence.

[75] See too the extensions under s. 11(1A).

[76] The Agricultural (Maintenance, Repair and Insurance of Fixed Equipment) Regulations 1973, as amended by the Agricultural (Maintenance, Repair and Insurance of Fixed Equipment Regulations) (Amendment) Regulations 1988.

[77] See Schedule 1 to these regulations, in general.

the various matters complained of. The leading text on dilapidations law explores liability for repair by reference to five sequential questions:[78]

(a) Does the disrepair fall within the scope of the repair covenant?
(b) Is the subject matter of the covenant in damaged or deteriorated condition?
(c) Is the damage or deterioration such that it falls below the standard set by the covenant?
(d) What must be done to remedy the defect?
(e) Is there some other reason why the works should nonetheless not be carried out?

As to question (1), its aim is to ascertain the true scope of the repairing obligation imposed by the lease. Leases are over parcels of land called 'demised premises'. The key question is the true extent of the demise. Sometimes (as in free-standing residential accommodation) the whole land is simply passed over to the tenant. In other cases (as in a block of flats), shared areas ('the common parts' – staircases, lifts, receptions) may well be retained by the landlord and managed by him/her. In a block of flats, the roof is also frequently retained by the landlord to facilitate repair (given that a defective roof will harm a great number of tenants). Indeed it appears that the law presumes the roof is retained in such cases.[79] Applying the above to this case, one can say the following: defective central heating, roof damage and flaking paint (whether inside or outside) is in the first instance a question of construction of the express covenants. This is, however, subject to the special regime under the Law on Tenant Act 1985. In the case of tenancies qualifying thereunder, the central heating system would, if defective, be the landlord's obligation under, s. 11(1)(c). In respect of the roof (while governed by s. 11(1)(a)), there is no obligation to reinstate or rebuild the premises in the case of destruction by, among other things, tempest. This would be limited to complete destruction. The landlord will, however, still have to replace tiles blown away.

As to question (2), the issue here is the definition of 'repair'. As was stated by Atkin LJ in *Anstruther-Gough-Calthorpe* v. *McOscar*,[80] the word 'connotes the idea of making good damage so as to leave the subject so far as possible as though it had not been damaged'.

[78] These are simplified versions of the questions asked in Dowding and Reynolds, *Dilapidations Law*, chs. 7–11.

[79] See *Cockburn* v. *Smith* [1924] KB 119.

[80] [1924] 1 KB 716.

Similarly, 'disrepair' means 'a deterioration from some previous physical condition'.[81] This can have quite remarkable results. Thus parts of a house which are poorly designed (but in a good state of repair) will not be in 'disrepair', even if the flaw renders the house 'virtually unfit for human habitation'.[82] At this juncture one might consider the 'obsolescent' central heating unit. Obsolescence is not synonymous with disrepair – if the unit is in working order and in a good state of maintenance, there would be no breach of a repairing covenant here as there is no disrepair. In relation to the other issues which are raised, for example, fences or roof damage, those are likely to be dilapidations which a tenant would be required to remedy, though it may also be that as a matter of contract storm damage to a roof would be a matter under the insurance covenants, and could be excluded from a tenant's obligation. Whether or not flaking paint is disrepair or breach of decoration covenants is again a matter for the terms of a particular agreement, though it is possible for such a matter to amount to a tenant's responsibility under either.

The liability for damage caused by one party[83] is clearly a matter which can fall within the scope of a repairing covenant.[84] Leaving this to one side, however, it is useful to look at other doctrines the common law has developed to deal with the issue. The question of wilful or negligent damage by a tenant is dealt with by virtue of a duty imposed on the tenant to use the land leased in a tenant-like manner. The tenant is responsible for any damage caused by himself/herself, his/her family or guests in breach of that obligation.[85] A tenant is under the further obligation to remedy any breaches he/she has committed and to return the premises at the end of the lease with such damage remedied.[86] Further, the common law developed a doctrine called 'voluntary waste', signifying a deliberate act[87] which damages the value of the landlord's reversion. As against this, however, 'permissive waste', 'which has not come about by the [tenant's] own acts, but comes

81 *Post Office* v. *Aquarius Properties Limited* [1987] 1 All ER 1055.

82 *Quick* v. *Taff-Ely Borough Council* [1986] QB 809.

83 A particularly helpful guide here is Dowding and Reynolds, *Dilapidations Law*, ch. 21.

84 It is dealt with expressly by the model clauses in the Agricultural (Maintenance, Repair and Insurance of Fixed Equipment) Regulations 1973, see Schedule 1 Part 1 4(1)(b).

85 See, in particular, *Warren* v. *Keen* [1954] 1 QB 15 24; *Edge* v. *Pemberton* (1843) 12 M. & W. 187; *Regis Property Co. Limited* v. *Dudley* [1959] AC 370 esp. 407 and 409.

86 *Marsden* v. *Edward Heys Limited* [1927] 1 KB 1 8 (*per* Atkin LJ).

87 Probably not an omission, though see *Doe d Grubb* v. *Burlington* (1833) 5 B. and Ad. 507; *Mancetter Developments Limited* v. *Garmanson* [1986] 1 All ER 449.

about by a revolution, or by wear and tear, or by the action of the elements, or in any other way not being his own act',[88] is also not allowed by the law. An example will be destruction resulting from a failure to repair.[89] The deteriorating wall variant posited in this case would fall within this.

France

In the absence of a contrary stipulation in a *residential lease*, the tenant is only liable for routine maintenance and repairs in accordance with the use of the property that do not result from obsolescence or from an unpredictable *force majeure* which cannot be resisted (Civil Code, arts. 1754 and 1755). The tenant is responsible for the following routine repairs: repairs to fireplaces and mantelshelves, the plaster of the inside walls of apartments and other residences, glass panels, doors, windows, dividing walls, hinges, bolts and locks (Civil Code, art. 1754).

The repairs mentioned in the question are thus the landlord's (A's) responsibility as they are the result of obsolescence (the fences, the paint), or caused by *force majeure* (the roof) or do not amount to routine maintenance and repairs (central heating system, the roof). If the property is the principal residence of the tenant, the landlord is bound to provide a decent dwelling (Civil Code, art. 1719 1, modified by the Law of 13 December 2000 and Law no 2009–323 of 25 March 2009), which sustains the health and safety of the tenant and complies with the requirements for a residence. If the dwelling is not decent, the landlord cannot take advantage of the provisions on the nullity of the lease or of its termination to request the eviction of the tenant.

The Law of 6 July 1989 contains the same requirement (art. 20–1 amended in 2000 and in 2009), which applies to existing leases and empowers the tenant to require that the dwelling be brought into line with the minimal requirements for a decent residence. The routine upkeep of the property is borne by the tenant, who is also responsible for minor repairs as well as the repairs mentioned by a Decree of the *Conseil d'État*, unless they are the result of obsolescence, a fault or defect in construction, *force majeure* or a fortuitous event (art. 7 d). Again, the landlord A will be responsible for all the repairs mentioned in the question.

[88] *Davies* v. *Davies* (1888) 38 Ch.D. 499 *per* Kekewich J.
[89] *Herne* v. *Benbow* (1813) 4 Taunt. 764.

The Law on Agricultural Lease expressly provides that the *agricultural tenant* is not responsible for repairs other than routine maintenance or minor repairs (art. L 415–4 and L 411–12).

A *usufructuary* is only responsible for ordinary maintenance and repairs (Civil Code, art. 605). Major repairs remain the responsibility of the owner, unless they were caused by a lack of maintenance during the course of the usufruct, in which case the usufructary will be responsible for carrying out such repairs. Major repairs are repairs made to structural walls and vaults, the restoration of supporting beams and entire roofs of buildings, the renewal of dykes and constructions which lend support, and boundary fences (Civil Code, art. 606). All other repairs are ordinary repairs (Civil Code, art. 606, para. 3). Since this text contains an exhaustive list of major repairs, case law does not easily allow an extension of this list by analogy.[90] The nude owner will be charged with the restoration of the roof if it was destroyed by a storm, but not if it is only necessary to put a few tiles back into place. The owner is charged with the replacement of fences and other enclosing structures, but not with limited and specific minor repairs to such structures. The owner is also charged with the repair of structural, load-bearing walls but not with the repair of interior dividing walls. The usufructuary remains liable for the replacement of the furnace, repairs and repainting, and the redoing and repainting of the plaster of the outside walls, which are considered ordinary maintenance repairs.

Case law reasons that Civil Code, art. 605 (in the absence of a stipulation to the contrary in the contract) apportions the liability for repairs, but does not authorise the usufructuary, in the absence of a stipulation to the contrary in the deed constituting the usufruct, to take legal action to force the owner to carry out major repairs necessary for the preservation of the property.[91] The usufructuary is entitled to carry out the major repairs which the owner refuses to undertake and will be entitled to seek reimbursement from the nude owner for the amount that the value of the property will have been increased by on expiry of the usufruct. Neither the nude owner nor the usufructuary is bound to rebuild what has become dilapidated owing to ordinary wear and tear or has been destroyed by a fortuitous event (Civil Code, art. 607). If the property is destroyed by an earthquake and the cost of rebuilding is significant, neither party is bound to repair the damage.[92]

[90] Civ. 3, 27 Nov. 2002; Bull. civ. III, no. 235.

[91] Civ. 3, 3 May 1989; Bull. civ. III, no. 100.

[92] Civ. 3, 23 Oct. 1979; Bull. civ. III, no. 187.

Since the *rights of use and of habitation* are similar to a usufruct, the law applicable to usufruct also applies by analogy to these rights. The only difference is that these two rights confer less extensive rights of use and enjoyment on their holders.

Under a *hereditary building right* (*droit de superficie*) and a *hereditary land lease* (*emphyteusis*), the holder acquires a real right in the property. The holder of a *hereditary building right* must carry out the repairs mentioned above since he/she is responsible for maintaining buildings that he/she constructed in a good condition of repair (Law on Construction and Habitation, art. L 251–4). The holder is, however, not bound to repair the damage or to rebuild the building if the damage or destruction was due to a fortuitous event, *force majeure* or a defect in the construction of a building which already existed at the time the building right was granted. The holder must repair the damage if an existing building or the building he/she has built is damaged or destroyed by fire. In the absence of a stipulation to the contrary in the lease, the holder can demolish existing buildings with the view to rebuilding them. The holder of a *hereditary lease of land* (*emphyteusis*) has a similar obligation to maintain and repair existing and future buildings on the land.

The *borrower* of property is bound to exercise the care of a reasonable man (*bonus paterfamilias*) in the maintenance and preservation of the property since it is used gratuitously. If, during the term of the loan, the borrower is compelled to incur extraordinary expenses for the preservation of the property which were necessary and so urgent that he/she was not able to inform the lender thereof, the latter is obliged to reimburse the borrower (Civil Code, art. 1890). The borrower is not obliged to replace a heating system which is defective or obsolescent, but he/she cannot require the lender to replace the heating system either. If the borrower incurs this expenditure, as in the case of the roof, he/she will have to show that it was an extraordinary expense which was urgent and necessary for the preservation of the property. If the expenses are merely linked to the maintenance and use of the property (for example, painting and repair of the fence), the borrower will not be entitled to reimbursement. If the expenses became necessary due to his/her fault (for example, a deteriorated wall due to the lack of regular painting), the borrower will be responsible for the cost of repainting the wall. If the property has deteriorated, the borrower is presumed to be responsible for repairs, but the presumption may be rebutted by proof that the deterioration was caused by normal wear and tear or by an incident (such as a storm) for which he/she cannot be held responsible. The contract may provide that the borrower will be liable for certain expenses such as maintenance costs, provided that this does not amount to remuneration which may lead a court to reclassify the contract as a lease.

Since a *revocable permission* (*precarium*) is not regulated by any special statutory provision, the rules of the Civil Code must be applied, supplementing the will of the parties. The obligations under the contract are usually apportioned by the terms of the contract. A balance is often reached by requiring the *precarist* to assume the obligation for routine maintenance of the property. Here, as in the case of a loan for use, this counter-prestation must remain modest in order to avoid it amounting to the payment of rent and the reclassification of the contract as a lease.

Germany

The *landlord* is under a general obligation to maintain the property in a condition reasonably fit for the purpose for which it is let (Civil Code, § 535 (1)). Consequently, the landlord is liable to repair all defects that interfere with the proper use and enjoyment of the property. In the absence of contrary agreement, the landlord is not bound to repair small defects which do not interfere with the tenant's right of enjoyment.

The duty will therefore rest on A to repair all the defects mentioned in Case 5, with the exception of the situation where the central heating system becomes obsolescent without being defective. In that case, replacement will be regarded as an improvement (modernisation) rather than a repair, unless the tenant can show that the old central heating system does not operate properly. The relevant standard is, generally speaking, the one provided for in the lease agreement. The landlord is not bound to improve the property in accordance with rising standards unless the tenant can show that his/her health is in serious danger.

A will remain responsible for repainting the wall if, due to his/her omission, the wall is seriously damaged. The tenant (B) will only be liable for repairs if the defect can be ascribed to his/her negligence.

The default rule is somewhat different for *agricultural leases* (*Landpachtvertrag*). In an agricultural lease, the tenant is liable for ordinary repairs, whereas the duty to undertake extraordinary repairs rests on the landlord (Civil Code, § 586(1)). Ordinary repairs are those that arise in connection with normal wear and tear. Repairing the fences or repainting the walls will certainly belong to the category of ordinary repairs for which the tenant is liable. The same will be true for minor defects in the central heating system. If the central heating system becomes obsolescent without being defective, replacement is an improvement (modernisation) rather than a repair, and neither the owner nor the tenant will be obliged to do anything. If the roof is seriously damaged by an unusual storm, the repair needed will be regarded as extraordinary.

There is extensive case law on the issue of the extent to which parties may deviate from the default rules described above. As the default rule regarding leases in general (Civil Code, § 535(1)) is very unfavourable to the landlord, it is common practice that the landlord will attempt to shift certain duties of repair to the tenant under the lease contract. The courts have only accepted these practices to a limited extent in relation to residential leases. As a general rule, the tenant of residential property can only assume liability for minor maintenance repairs (such as repainting the walls of the apartment) and not for major structural repairs.[93]

In the absence of contrary agreement, the *usufructuary* must ensure that the property is maintained in a proper state. He/she is only obliged to make improvements and renovations to the extent that they relate to the ordinary maintenance of the property (Civil Code, § 1041). Extraordinary repairs and expenses are borne by the owner. However, it must be noted that the owner is not bound to carry out extraordinary repairs.[94] The underlying rationale seems to be that since the usufructuary is only entitled to the ordinary proceeds of the property (without transforming or substantially altering the property or excessive taking of fruits),[95] as a corollary, he/she is only responsible for the ordinary maintenance of the property.

Contractual provisions deviating from the *default rule* as described above are frequently used and often motivated by tax reasons.[96] The parties may stipulate that the usufructuary has to bear all costs, including those of extraordinary repairs.[97] Conversely, they may provide for the owner's obligation to bear the expenses of the ordinary maintenance of the property. Agreements on repairs and expenses are binding

[93] See Weidenkaff, in Palandt, *Bürgerlichen Gesetzbuch*, § 535, no. 44.
[94] See Bundesgerichtshof, *Neue Juristische Wochenschrift* (NJW) (1991), p. 837.
[95] See Case 6.
[96] See Frank, in von Staudingers, *Kommentar*, Vorbem, § 1030, no. 106–79.
[97] *Ibid.*, § 1041, no. 8.

on everyone who acquires the property or the limited right, provided it is registered in the Land Register (*Grundbuch*).

There have only been a few occasions where the courts have interpreted the relevant provision of the Civil Code (§ 1041). The repair of the *central heating system* will probably fall under ordinary repairs for which the usufructuary is responsible (unless stipulated otherwise by the parties). If the *central heating system becomes obsolescent*, the cost of its replacement will have to be borne by the owner.[98] Minor repairs of the *roof* are borne by the usufructuary.[99] The same is true if the *paint* of the building *flakes off*[100] or if the fences of the farm become dilapidated as these will typically be ordinary repairs. However, if any of the foregoing repairs involve major expenses, the repair will be regarded as extraordinary.

If the usufructuary *negligently caused the damage*, he/she will be responsible for the cost of repair.[101] Similarly, if the usufructuary's omission in not repainting the building eventually results in serious damage to the building, he/she will be liable to the owner for all the loss suffered through his/her neglect.

The German Civil Code (§1093(1)) provides that the rule concerning maintenance of the property applicable to usufruct (Civil Code, § 1041) applies *mutatis mutandis* to the *right of habitation*. Again, it is generally accepted that this rule is not mandatory. However, unlike in the case of usufruct, it is a controversial issue whether or not the parties can stipulate, with binding effect on third parties, that the holder has to bear the cost of extraordinary repairs.[102] The better view is to allow parties to deviate from the default position to the same extent as in the case of usufruct.[103]

The default rule is that the holder of a *permanent right of habitation* must maintain the property to the same extent as the owner would have done. This means that the holder of the right is responsible for most of the maintenance of the property (Law on Apartment Ownership, § 14

[98] See Bundesgerichtshof, NJW (1993), p. 3198.

[99] See Roth, *Reichsgerichtsrätekommentar*, § 1041, no. 1; Frank, in *von Staudingers, Kommentar*, § 1041, no. 10.

[100] See Frank, in *von Staudingers Kommentar*, § 1041, no. 10.

[101] The owner will be entitled to claim compensation for damages suffered on the basis of breach of *quasi* contract (*Positive Forderungsverletzung*) and tort law (Civil Code, § 823(1)). See Bassenge, in Palandt, *Bürgerlichen Gesetzbuch*, § 1041, no. 1.

[102] See Jerschke, *Beck'sches Notar-Handbuch*, no. 161.

[103] Mayer, in *von Staudingers, Kommentar*, § 1093, no. 47.

nos. 1 and 33(2)). This corresponds to the idea that a permanent right of habitation (*Dauerwohnrecht*) is in many respects similar to full ownership. Agreements on repairs and expenses deviating from the default rule are possible and binding on any third party acquiring the property or the limited right, provided that such agreement is registered in the *Grundbuch*. In practice, tax considerations are largely responsible for the frequent use of clauses which burden the holder of the right with an obligation to bear all costs relating to the ordinary and extraordinary maintenance of the property.

There is no statutory default rule regarding the maintenance of a structure which is subject to a *hereditary building right* (*Erbbaurecht*). The Regulations (§ 2 no. 1), however, clearly state that any stipulations on the erection, maintenance and use of the structure to be built on the land form part of the content of the right. Unless the parties have agreed otherwise, neither the landowner nor the holder is under an obligation to maintain the structure in a reasonable state of repair.[104] In practice, agreements on the creation of a hereditary building right often provide that the holder is under an obligation to maintain the structure and to bear all costs relating to ordinary and extraordinary repairs.

Greece

The answer to Case 5 depends on the kind of obligation each party has in the various situations.

Under the Greek Civil Code, the main obligation of the landlord is to deliver the property in a condition suitable for its agreed use and to maintain it in this condition during the entire period of the lease (Civil Code, art. 575).[105] This means that the landlord will be accountable for existing and future defects in the property which prevent it from being suitable for the purpose for which it was leased. If the parties agreed on a certain quality that the property had to conform to and that proved not to exist, the tenant will be entitled to demand reduction or non-payment of the rent (Civil Code, art. 576). The tenant will not be liable if the property deteriorates or is modified by the agreed use of the property (Civil Code, art. 592). The default position is therefore that the landlord is responsible for repairs necessitated by an existing defect in

[104] von Oefele and Winkler, *Handbuch*, no. 4.48.

[105] Rapsomanikis, in Georgiades and Stathopoulos, *GCC, Collective Analysis*, art. 575 (289–91).

the property or a defect which appears later which makes the property unfit for the purposes for which it was leased. However, Civil Code, arts. 575 and 592 are not mandatory: it is thus possible for the parties to agree either expressly or impliedly to shift the obligation for repairs to the tenant.[106]

If the *central heating system* of a leased residence becomes defective or the *fences* on the farm becomes dilapidated, it can either be the result of a defect that already existed at the conclusion of the lease or a defect that appeared later. This will certainly make the residence and the farm unfit for the purposes for which they are respectively leased. Since the tenant is not responsible for defects that result from deterioration of the property, the landlord will be under an obligation to repair the heating system and the dilapidated fences in the above two cases.[107] The position will be the same if the *paint* on the building *flakes off*. There can be little doubt that this will be the result of ordinary deterioration. If the *roof* is damaged in a storm, the residential property will certainly no longer be fit for the purpose for which it is leased. Here again the landlord will be responsible for the repair of the roof if the repair costs are not excessive. If the costs are excessive, the partial destruction of the property will be equated with total destruction and, consequently, dissolution of the lease.[108]

The replacement of the *obsolescent heating system* with a more up to date system will be classified as an improvement rather than a repair. None of the parties will be obliged to replace the heating system, and if the tenant does so, it will probably be classified as a useful expense (not a necessary expense since the old central heating system will still be able to function) for which the tenant can claim under the provisions on voluntary agency (*negotiorum gestio*) (Civil Code, art. 591).[109]

The Greek Civil Code contains two provisions which apply to the case *where one of the parties causes the damage*. First, it provides that the landlord is not responsible to the tenant for actual defects or the lack of agreed qualities known to the tenant at the time of the conclusion of the

[106] Rapsomanikis, in Georgiades and Stathopoulos, *GCC, Collective Analysis*, art. 575, no. 16 (291) and art. 590–2, no. 12 (315).

[107] Filios, *Obligations*, 209.

[108] See Athens Court of Appeal 5178/1998; EllDni (1993), p. 1097; 2771/2001, published at Nomos.

[109] Filios, *Obligations*, 212; Rapsomanikis, in Georgiades and Stathopoulos, *GCC, Collective Analysis*, art. 590–2, no. 6 (314); Athens Court of Appeal 7303/2000; EllDni (2002), pp. 227 ff.

contract or which were unknown to him/her due to gross negligence on the part of the tenant (Civil Code, arts. 579 and 580). The tenant seems to be personally barred from pleading defects or lack of qualities of which he/she had knowledge, or lack of knowledge on account of gross negligence.[110] Secondly, Civil Code, art. 592 excludes the tenant's liability only in cases of deterioration or modifications due to the agreed use of the property. From this it is implied that the tenant is responsible for damage that he/she has caused to the property.

If the landlord was *originally responsible for the repainting of the wall* which has flaked off, he will also be responsible for more serious damage to the wall caused by his/her omission to repair. However, the tenant has an obligation to notify the landlord of all defects that appear during the currency of the lease (Civil Code, art. 589). If the further damage to the wall can be ascribed to the failure on the part of the tenant to give timeous notice, he/she will be responsible for the repair of the wall.[111]

Several provisions of the Greek Civil Code deal with the *usufructuary's* maintenance obligations in respect of the property subject to the usufruct. First, there is a general obligation on the usufructuary to use and enjoy the fruits of the property while preserving (without impairing) the substance of the property (Civil Code, art. 1142). This is supplemented by the more detailed provision that the usufructuary is obliged to preserve the present economic purpose of the property and to exploit the property with due care and in an orderly way, without effecting substantial changes to the property (Civil Code, art. 1148). Finally, the usufructuary is specifically obliged to take care of the repair and renewal of the property. However, he/she is only bound to bear the expenses related to the usual maintenance of the property (Civil Code, art. 1152). Thus the nude owner is responsible for unusual and unforeseen repairs and expenses.[112]

In light of the above, the *default position* is that the usufructuary will be responsible for the usual maintenance and must pay the ordinary maintenance expenses while the nude owner is responsible for unusual maintenance and the payment of extraordinary,[113] in the sense of

[110] Filios, *Obligations*, p. 218; AP 768/1987 Efimeris Ellinon Nomikon (EEN) (1988), p. 308.

[111] Filios, *Obligations*, pp. 239, 240.

[112] Balis, *Property*, pp. 356–7; Georgiades, *Property*, vol. 2, p. 61.

[113] Extraordinary expenses are defined by business usage and must be understood as differing from the expenses related to the usual maintenance of the property provided, in Civil Code, art. 1152 (Karasis, in Georgiades and Stathopoulos, *GCC, Collective Analysis*, art. 1153, no. 3 (93)).

unforeseen, expenses. The repair of the defective heating system, the dilapidated fences and the flaked off paint relate to ordinary maintenance and expenses and are therefore the responsibility of the usufructuary. The repair of the roof of the building damaged in a storm will require unusual maintenance and extraordinary or at least unforeseen expenses and would therefore be the responsibility of the nude owner. If the renewal of the obsolete heating system can be classified under repairs, it will fall under extraordinary repairs and will therefore be the responsibility of the nude owner. However, if classified as a useful improvement, none of the parties will be under an obligation to replace the out-of-date heating system. In the latter case, if the usufructuary replaces the system, he/she will have a claim for compensation under the provisions governing voluntary agency (*negotiorum gestio*).

In principle, a usufructuary is not responsible for an alteration or deterioration of the property which resulted from an orderly exercise of the right of usufruct (Civil Code, art. 1158).[114] In practice, however, most damages result from an *omission on the part of the usufructuary* to comply with his/her obligation either to preserve the substance of the property (Civil Code, art. 1142) or to exercise his/her right in an orderly manner (Civil Code, art. 1148). In such a situation, the usufructuary will be considered to have caused the damage and will consequently be responsible.

If the party responsible for repainting the wall omits to do so, he/she will also have to stand in for any consequential damage. Thus the usufructuary will be responsible for his/her neglect in repainting the building. If, however, responsibility for repainting falls upon the owner, the usufructuary has a duty to notify the owner without delay of any deterioration of the property, or of a necessary extraordinary repair or preventative measure that must be taken to deal with an unforeseen peril. If the owner neglects or refuses to take measures to prevent deterioration or peril, the usufructuary may take such measures at the owner's cost (Civil Code, art. 1153).

The Civil Code, art. 1187 provides that the general provisions on the usufruct of immovable property shall be applicable by analogy to the *right of habitation* in so far as they are compatible with the nature of habitation. The answers to the above questions would thus be the same.

[114] Karasis, in Georgiades and Stathopoulos, *GCC, Collective Analysis*, art. 1158 (107–8).

Hungary

In the case of a *lease*, the landlord warrants that the object of the lease will be suitable for the use stipulated in the contract for the period defined therein and that it will comply with the provisions of contract law. Accordingly, the landlord has to maintain the quality of the property at the level agreed in the contract or, in the absence of such an agreement, in approximately the condition that the property was in when the contract was concluded.[115] The tenant bears the cost of minor maintenance of the property and other expenses relating to the ordinary use of the property, including taxes. The tenant is obliged to inform the landlord should the need arise for works that are to be performed by the landlord. Moreover, the tenant must permit the landlord to carry out these works and take whatever measures necessary to mitigate losses. The tenant is liable for any loss resulting from failure to inform the landlord of any problems (Civil Code, § 427).[116]

The Law on Residential Lease provides that, unless otherwise agreed, the tenant is responsible for the cost of maintaining and renovating the paintwork, doors, windows and equipment of the residential property, while the landlord is responsible for the cost of replacing or substituting them (Civil Code, § 13(1)). If the work to be performed in the residential apartment is due to the renovation of the building or the failure of mechanical systems, the costs are to be covered by the landlord (Civil Code, § 14(4)). On the basis of the above rules, the conclusion can be drawn that in the case of a residential lease it is the task of the landlord to repair the *defective heating system* and the *roof damaged in the storm*. It is the tenant who has to repair the *dilapidated fences* and to *paint the building if the paint flakes off*. Neither of them is obliged to replace the *obsolescent central heating system*.

In the case of an *income-producing lease* (lease for profit), including the lease of agricultural property, the tenant must bear the expenses that arise from repairs and renovations necessary for the maintenance of the property. Hence, it is the tenant who must repair the *defective heating system*, the *dilapidated fences* and the *flaked off paint* if these situations emerge after the coming into existence of the lease, as these are repairs

[115] Gellért, *A Polgári Törvénykönyv magyarázata*, pp. 1539–42.

[116] The tenant may claim recovery of the necessary expenses devoted to the property. Reimbursement for other expenses can be claimed according to the rules of representation without mandate (*negotiorum gestio*).

and renovations necessary for the maintenance of the property. The cost of extraordinary repairs and renovations are to be borne by the landlord. Thus the repair of the *roof damaged in a storm* is the task of the landlord. Neither of the parties is obliged to replace the *obsolescent central heating system*.

The *usufructuary* and the holder of *a right of use* are responsible for ordinary expenses and repairs in maintaining and using the property. Extraordinary repairs and expenses are the responsibility of the nude owner. The usufructuary and the usuary may effect extraordinary repairs if the owner does not respond to a request to do so. When the usufruct or use expires, the usufructuary or the holder of a right of use may claim reimbursement from the owner for his/her necessary expenses, less the decrease in the value of the property. If the value of the property has increased on account of the extraordinary repair, the usufructuary and the usuary will have a claim based on enrichment.

Accordingly, the usufructuary and the usuary have the duty to repair, replace or renew the *defective central heating system*, to *repaint if the paint on the building flakes off* and repair the *dilapidated fences* on the farm since these amount to ordinary repairs necessary for the maintenance of the property. On the other hand, the *replacement of the central heating system* due to its becoming obsolescent and *repairing the roof* damaged in a storm are extraordinary repairs which are the responsibility of the nude owner. Should the owner fail to carry out these repairs when requested, the usufructuary and the usuary may do this and claim reimbursement of the expenses, less the decrease in the value of the property from the nude owner upon termination of the usufruct or use. The replacement of the central heating system because it becomes obsolescent (without being defective) is not necessary for the operation of the property, but it increases its utility. Accordingly, this expense is not necessary, but useful. The fate of useful expenses is not expressly regulated but can be worked out with reference to the fate of necessary expenses and a possible claim for enrichment (cf. Civil Code, §§ 98(1) and 361). Repairs necessitated by the fault of one of the parties are the responsibility of that party and the additional loss suffered by the non-timeous painting of the wall must be borne by the usufructuary or the usuary.

These *default rules* can only be changed where a usufruct or a right of use is established by means of an *inter vivos* agreement. The Civil Code, § 584(4) provides that the parties may determine the content of the contract and deviate from default provisions unless there is provision to the contrary (Civil Code, § 200(1)).

In the case of a *loan for use*, expenses related to the maintenance of the property are to be borne by the borrower. All other expenses he/she may have incurred in relation to the property are to be settled according to the rules of representation without mandate (*negotiorum gestio*) (Civil Code, § 584(4)). Accordingly, repairing *the dilapidated fences*, the *defective heating system* and *painting the building* where the paint flakes off are the task of the borrower. The law does not impose any further obligations on either of the parties to repair, replace or renew the property or its components.

Italy

The *landlord* is obliged to carry out all necessary repairs during the term of the lease, with the exception of minor maintenance for which the tenant is responsible (Civil Code, art. 1576). The tenant is obliged to give the landlord notice of any repairs which become necessary during the term of the lease. Where such repairs are urgent, provision is made for the tenant to undertake the repairs and to claim reimbursement of his/her expenses (Civil Code, art. 1577). For urban leases, Civil Code, art. 1609 expressly states that minor maintenance repairs, which in terms of Civil Code, art. 1576 are the responsibility of the tenant, are repairs necessitated by deterioration through use and not those caused by decay (old age) or fortuitous events (events outside human control).[117] The lease of income-producing property is subject to a different rule: Civil Code, art. 1621 provides that the landlord is bound to carry out any extraordinary repairs, while all other repairs are chargeable to the tenant.

Thus, if the *fences* of a farm (which is income-producing property) are *dilapidated*, the tenant is obliged to repair them. The position is the same if the *central heating system* becomes defective or if the *paint on the building flakes off*. If the *roof* of the farm is damaged in a storm, the repair is chargeable to the landlord.

The answers are different for the lease of urban premises. While there is some debate on the criteria for distinguishing between the kinds of repairs, 'minor repairs' certainly do not include expensive repairs which cost more than a few months' rent or repairs necessitated by old age (decay). Repairing the *central heating system*, and probably also

[117] Some other minor modifications in the regulation of the lease of urban premises have been introduced by Law of 27/07/1978, n. 392, art. 9.

repainting the walls, will probably be considered repairs chargeable to the landlord. Repairing the *roof* is obviously the responsibility of the landlord. However, one must bear in mind that it is the tenant's duty to observe the diligence of a good *paterfamilias* in using the property leased for the purposes specified in the contract or for purposes which can otherwise be presumed from the circumstances (Civil Code, art. 1587). Consequently, the tenant has a duty to repair any damage *caused by his/her own actions or negligence* or resulting from abnormal use. If a wall is seriously damaged in consequence of non-timeous repainting, the tenant may be held responsible if he/she negligently omits to give notice to the landlord of the necessity of repairs. If the *central heating system becomes obsolescent*, replacement is an improvement rather than a repair, and neither the landlord nor the tenant is obliged to do anything.

The rules on maintenance and repairs are not mandatory, and the parties can deviate from them by agreement.

In the case of *usufruct*, the Italian Civil Code (Civil Code, art. 1004) provides that the expenses and obligations relating to the custody, management and maintenance of the thing are chargeable to the usufructuary. Repairing the fences or the central heating system and repainting the walls certainly belong to this category.[118] According to the prevailing opinion, unless some serious damage may result from the usufructuary's non-performance, the owner cannot enforce this duty during the usufruct: the usufructuary is only under an obligation to return the property in a state of good repair on termination of the usufruct.[119]

Extraordinary repairs are normally chargeable to the nude owner (Civil Code, art. 1005). If, however, they are caused by non-performance of the usufructuary's obligations of ordinary maintenance, they will be chargeable to him/her (Civil Code, art. 1004). If the owner refuses to carry out repairs, or delays their execution without justifiable reason, the usufructuary can undertake the repairs and claim reimbursement on expiry of the usufruct (Civil Code, art. 1006). The same provisions apply where, due to deterioration or accident, a building forming a necessary accessory to the land subject to the usufruct is partially destroyed (Civil Code, art. 1007).

118 According to Pugliese, 'Usufrutto', p. 515 the usufructuary must replaster the walls, repaint the doors and windows and paint the walls.

119 See Caterina, *I diritti*, pp. 145 ff.

Civil Code, art. 1005 defines 'extraordinary repairs' as 'repairs necessary to ensure the stability of walls and vaults, the replacement of beams, the renewal, in whole or substantial part, of roofs, ceilings, stairs, the banks of dams, water channels (aquaducts), and structural (load-bearing) or outer walls'. This enumeration is considered to be merely illustrative and thus the list is not exhaustive.[120] Several (non-mutually exclusive) criteria have been proposed to help draw a distinction between ordinary and extraordinary repairs. Amongst others, these include the amount of expenses incurred in carrying out the repairs and whether or not the repair was necessitated by normal wear and tear. Extraordinary repairs are those that do not arise from normal wear and tear.

There is little doubt that if the roof is seriously damaged in a storm, the owner will be responsible for its repair. If a wall is seriously damaged as a consequence of failure by the usufructuary to perform his/her obligations of ordinary maintenance, the usufructuary will be responsible for its repair. If the central heating system becomes obsolescent, replacement constitutes an improvement rather than a repair, and neither the owner nor the usufructuary will be obliged to do anything.

The rules on maintenance and repairs are not mandatory. It is not entirely clear, however, whether a different regulation would be enforceable against someone different from the original parties. In general terms, where the damage is maliciously or negligently caused by one of the parties, the person who has caused the damage will be responsible for the repairs.

There is no case law and little literature on the duty to repair or renew in the case of a *hereditary building lease* (*superficie*). *Superficie* usually involves the right to erect a new building and there is no duty to maintain the building in good repair in the absence of a contractual agreement. The holder of the building lease (*superficiario*) can even erect the building and then destroy it. However, it is doubtful whether the same rules apply where the building transferred is already in existence. Some scholars emphasise the fact that the holder of a building lease (*proprietario superficiario*) is an owner, and not the holder of a limited right. As 'owner', he/she should not have any duty to keep the building in a good state of repair nor have any right against the owner of the soil to carry out repairs.[121] Others submit that at least part of the rules

[120] See Trib Venezia, 25/01/1962, in 1962 *Giustizia Civile*, vol. 1, p. 392; Pugliese, 'Usufrutto', p. 512.

[121] See e.g. Natoli, *La proprietà*, p. 225.

pertaining to usufruct should also be applicable to the holder of a building lease.[122]

The Netherlands

The *landlord* of residential property has the obligation to do all major repairs to the property, unless it will be unreasonable to require this from him/her (Civil Code, art. 7:206). Minor repairs, which a handy tenant can reasonably do himself, must be carried out and paid for by the tenant (Civil Code, arts. 7:206, para. 2 and 7:217).

The tenant will not be responsible for any major repairs. The rules on repairs are mandatory (Civil Code, arts. 7:206, para. 3 and 7:242). The new Civil Code, art. 7:240 foresees the possibility of compiling a list of minor repairs in an Order in Council, which will be mandatory and from which the landlord will not be able to deviate.[123]

Law on Rural Leases (Pachtwet), art. 26, para. 1 reads: 'During the lease the landlord has the obligation to do all necessary repairs on the leased property, excluding minor and daily repairs which, according to local custom, have to be borne by the tenant.'[124]

In the case of *usufruct*, ordinary repairs must be carried out by the usufructuary (Civil Code, art. 3:220).[125] The *repainting* of the building where the paint flaked off, probably falls within the scope of ordinary repairs. In the case of extraordinary repairs, the usufructuary must notify the owner and allow him/her a reasonable period to carry out the repairs (Civil Code, art. 3:220). The owner is not, however, obliged to do so. If the owner does not repair the defects after being notified, the usufructuary may do so at the expense of the landlord. If the *roof* is damaged in a storm, the repairs will probably be regarded as extraordinary.[126] In the cases where the *central heating system* becomes defective and the *fences* on the farm become dilapidated, the position is unclear. If the extent of the defects requires the *entire central heating system* or *all the fences* to be replaced, it will more than likely be considered extraordinary repairs (this will definitely be the case where the heating system

[122] See Caterina, *I diritti*, pp. 145 ff.

[123] The list has been laid down in the Order in Council of 8 Apr. 2003, Stb (2003), p. 168, Decision: Small Repairs.

[124] In future this will be included in Civil Code, arts. 7:339 and 7:351.

[125] Asser, Mijnssen, van Dam and van Velten, 'Zakelijke Rechten', no. 279; Pitlo, 'Goederenrecht', no. 696.

[126] See, in general Pitlo, 'Goederenrecht', no. 696.

has become obsolescent). However, if defects require only a small repair, it will probably fall within the scope of ordinary repairs.

In the case of a *hereditary land lease* (*emphyteusis*), the holder is allowed to develop someone else's property (Civil Code, art. 5:85). Land leases are normally granted by public authorities which include the terms on which the lease is granted in a constitutive agreement registered in the Land Register.[127] The default rule is that the holder of the land lease is responsible for ordinary repairs and the landlord for extraordinary repairs (Civil Code, art. 5:96), but this can be changed in the constitutive agreement (Civil Code, art. 5:96 III). In the case of an extraordinary repair, the holder must notify the land owner of the need and allow the owner to do the repairs. The owner is not obliged to do so, nor is the holder of the land lease entitled to any compensation for damages incurred because of the defect (Civil Code, art. 5: 96 I).

The distinction between ordinary and extraordinary repairs depends on the circumstances of the case.[128] Thus it would really depend on the circumstances of the case whether the cases where the *central heating system* becomes defective or the *fences* on the farm become dilapidated would be considered ordinary or extraordinary repairs and thus the responsibility of the holder of the lease or the landowner. The *roof* damaged in a storm will call for extraordinary repairs, whereas the *repainting* of the building due to the flaking off of the paint and the defective heating system will need ordinary repairs. If an omission to repair results in further damages, this must be borne by the party who did not carry out the original repairs as in the case where the omission to repaint by the holder of the land lease caused serious damage to the walls.[129]

In the case of a *hereditary building lease* (*superficies*), B will become the owner of the construction on the land (Civil Code, art. 5:101). This implies that B has all the obligations and rights of an owner. It also means that it is for B to decide whether he/she will repair, renew or replace the object.[130]

Poland

Under a *lease*, the landlord is under a general obligation to maintain the property in a condition fit for the purpose for which it is let. However,

[127] Asser, Mijnssen, van Dam and van Velten, 'Zakelijke Rechten', no. 216; Pitlo, 'Goederenrecht', no. 647.

[128] Asser, Mijnssen, van Dam and van Velten, 'Zakelijke Rechten', no. 235.

[129] *Ibid.*; Pitlo, 'Goederenrecht', no. 648.

[130] Pitlo, 'Goederenrecht', no. 672.

minor repairs connected with the ordinary enjoyment of the property are the responsibility of the tenant (Civil Code, art. 662, § 1). The landlord is therefore liable for the repair of all defects that interfere with the proper use and enjoyment of the property. The landlord has no obligation to recreate the original state of the property where it has been damaged owing to circumstances for which he/she is not liable (Civil Code, art. 662, § 3). Repairing the *central heating system* will be the duty of the landlord, but he/she will not be responsible for the *replacement of an obsolescent heating system*. The landlord will also not be required to *repair the roof* damaged in a storm, even if this causes the property to be unfit for the purpose for which it is let. *Painting the building* will be the landlord's duty. If the tenant caused damage, the landlord will be obliged to repair the property but can seek redress from the tenant based on delictual liability.

In the case of *residential leases*, the Law on Protection of Tenants (POT) applies, and the above default rules change. The landlord is obliged to ensure the proper functioning of gas, water, heating, sewage, electric installations and lifts (elevators). This duty to maintain the property in a state fit for its purpose includes maintenance and cleaning of the common parts of the building. The landlord is obliged to restore the property to its original condition, even if the damage is due to circumstances beyond his/her control (POT, art. 6a). POT, art. 6b, § 2 places detailed obligations on the tenant, including the maintenance and replacement of damaged floor coverings, worktops, kitchen appliances, washbasins, sinks and faucets; the decoration of ceilings and inner walls; and the maintenance of the central heating system, fitted wardrobes and furniture.

In the case of an *income-producing lease* (*fruendi leases*), the tenant is obliged to carry out any repairs necessary to maintain the property in a proper condition (Civil Code, art. 696). This provision is understood to refer to repairs needed in the normal course of using the property, even if the repairs are not minor. They may not, however, amount to improvements. Therefore, *repairing the fences* or *repainting the outer walls* will be the duty of the tenant. The same will be true for *minor defects in the central heating system*, but if it becomes *obsolescent* without being defective, replacement would be viewed as an improvement. It is often the case that the parties fully accept these default rules. More-detailed contractual clauses will normally concern improvements. The general tendency is to place as much as possible of the obligations relating to repairs on the tenant.

Loss resulting from non-timeous painting can be the basis for a contractual or even a delictual claim for damages. The landlord is not responsible for repairs necessitated by damage caused by the tenant. The landlord can demand that the tenant repair the damage and if he/she does not respond sue the tenant in delict for damages. If the tenant causes damage through his/her inappropriate use of the property, the landlord is entitled to terminate the lease without observing the applicable notice periods (Civil Code, art. 667 and POT 11, § 2).

Under a *usufruct*, the usufructuary is obliged to use the property in a manner consistent with proper management (Civil Code, art. 256) and to carry out repairs connected with the ordinary use of the property. He/she must inform the owner of the necessity to carry out other repairs and improvements and allow him/her to do so (Civil Code, art. 260). The rationale is that since the usufructuary is entitled to use the property and reap its fruits without changing the substance of the property or its use, he will only be responsible for ordinary maintenance. The *repair of the central heating system* will probably fall under ordinary repairs for which the usufructuary is responsible, but not the *replacement of an obsolescent heating system*. The same applies to minor *repairs of the roof* or *repairing the fences*. *Painting* the outside walls can be the responsibility of the usufructuary if the usufruct was constituted for a substantial term.

If the usufructuary caused the damage, he/she will be responsible for the cost of repairs. Parties may change these default rules. The case of loss caused by non-timeous painting of the building will be addressed by general civil law rules concerning the performance of contracts and the right to demand damages when loss has been suffered through the fault of another.

The holder of a *hereditary land lease* (perpetual usufruct) is responsible for all the repairs mentioned as he/she technically owns the buildings and his/her other rights are similar to those of an owner. There is no possibility of shifting these obligations.

Portugal

Portuguese law on the maintenance of property subject to a *lease* is governed by provisions in the Civil Code as well as by Decree-Law 294/2009 on Agricultural Leases. Under the Portuguese Civil Code, the landlord's main obligations are to transfer the property to the tenant and to ensure that the property can be used in accordance with the purpose of the contract (Civil Code, art. 1031). The landlord must tolerate such use and is not allowed to act in a manner that will prevent or restrict it. If a building is leased, it must be delivered to the tenant in a good condition, unless the contrary is stipulated in the contract. There is a presumption in favour of the landlord that the building was in a good condition at the time of delivery in the absence of a document attached to the contract describing the condition of the building at the date of transfer (Civil Code, art. 1043 no. 2).

The tenant's duties include a duty to allow the landlord to inspect the building, to take care of the property and to exercise his/her rights with due diligence. The tenant must also allow the landlord to execute urgent repairs to the building (Civil Code, art. 1038). As long as the tenant exploits the property with the care of a *bonus paterfamilias* (Civil Code, art. 1043) and in accordance with the purpose of the contract, he/she is not responsible for any damage caused to the property and need not repair, replace or renew it before the property is returned to the landlord.

In the case of *residential or urban leases*, the tenant is entitled to make alterations to the building to suit his/her comfort or convenience. However, in the absence of a stipulation to the contrary, these alterations will have to be reversed on termination of the lease so that the building can be returned in its previous condition (Civil Code, art. 1072).

The landlord is responsible for both ordinary conservation (repair and cleaning, maintenance to keep the building fit for the purpose of the contract and work required by public authorities) and extraordinary conservation of the property (repair of defects in the building, and maintenance required as a result of damage caused by *force majeur*).

It is important to note that the tenant is not allowed to make alterations to the building except where authorised by the landlord or where that possibility is contemplated in the contract (Civil Code, art. 1074). The tenant is obliged (and consequently responsible for the repairs necessary) to maintain the dwelling in the same condition he/she received it, with allowance being made for fair wear and tear (Civil Code, art. 1043, no. 1 and 1044). The tenant is allowed to make urgent repairs where the landlord does not act within a reasonable time after being notified (Civil Code, art. 1036) and will be entitled to compensation. The tenant is also responsible for repairing damage caused by his/her negligence or the negligence of persons for whom he/she is responsible (Civil Code, art. 1043, *a contrario*).

The rules expounded above are also the default legal regime for urban leases used for commercial, industrial, professional and other purposes.

However, the parties may agree in a written deed that ordinary and extraordinary repairs as well as improvements to the property (*benfeitorias*) are the responsibility of the tenant (Civil Code, art. 1111).

In the case of urban residential leases, a *central heating system* constitutes a central part of the residential premises, and if the defect can be traced back to an inherent defect in the system, the landlord (A) will be liable under the obligation to deliver the building in a condition fit to be exploited in accordance with the purpose of the lease. A would thus be obliged to rectify the defect. Civil Code, art. 1030 expressly saddles the landlord with the obligation to carry out repairs necessary to maintain the building in a state fit for the residential purpose for which it is leased.

The position is different if the *central heating system becomes obsolescent (without being defective)*. If its replacement is classified as a conservation measure, it will fall under the responsibility of the landlord, but if, which is more likely, it is classified as an improvement, the landlord would have to carry out the improvement if agreed to by the parties in a written document. With regard to the *roof* being damaged in a storm, it is the duty of the landlord to keep the building fit for the purpose for which it was leased and he/she will be obliged to repair damages caused by *force majeur*, such as a storm. The repairs needed when the *paint on the building flakes off* will be classified as ordinary repairs necessary for the conservation of the building and will be the responsibility of the landlord.

Since the Law on *Agricultural Leases* does not contain specific provisions on the responsibility for repairs, the general legal regime on leases applies which places the responsibility of the landlord. If the *fences* on the farm become *dilapidated*, it may be considered an ordinary repair for which the landlord is responsible. Similar to the legal regime for residential leases, the tenant is obliged (and consequently responsible for the repairs necessary) to maintain the dwelling in the same condition he/she received it, with allowance being made for fair wear and tear (Civil Code, art. 1043, nos. 1 and 1044). It will be the responsibility of the tenant to repair the fences if dilapidation was due to his/her fault. The tenant is also allowed to make urgent repairs if the landlord does not act within a reasonable time after being notified (Civil Code, art. 1036) and reclaim the costs. Under an agricultural lease, both the tenant and the landlord are allowed to make improvements to the property (Decree-Law 294/2009, art. 21).

Since the landlord is responsible for repainting the building, he will be liable if *on account of his/her omission* the wall is seriously damaged. However, there is an obligation on the tenant to warn the landlord if the building is in need of urgent repair. An omission on the part of the tenant to warn the landlord timeously would shift the liability to the former.

The *usufructuary* is under an obligation to exploit the property like a *bonus paterfamilias* in accordance with its economic purpose (Civil Code, art. 1446) and without impairing the substance of the property (*salva rerum substantia*). In general, the usufructuary is not liable for ordinary wear and tear,[131] except where it is caused through his/her fault (Civil Code, art. 1452). The usufructuary is obliged to manage the property and to maintain it in a proper state of repair. He/she is responsible for ordinary repairs, namely those costing less than two-thirds of the annual net rent that can be collected from such property (Civil Code, art. 1472, nos. 1 and 2).[132] By contrast, any extraordinary repairs are the responsibility of the nude owner and the usufructuary only has a duty to warn the owner about these. However, if the need for repairs can be traced to inefficient management on the part of the usufructuary, he/she will be responsible (Civil Code, art. 1473, no. 2). If the owner refuses or postpones extraordinary repairs, the usufructuary can carry out the repairs and reclaim the cost from the nude owner. These expenses have to be reimbursed without it being necessary to wait for the termination of the usufruct (Civil Code, art. 1473, no. 2).

If the *central heating becomes defective*, the repairs needed are classified as ordinary repairs and the usufructuary will be obliged to repair it in order to preserve the property and keep it in a state of good repair (Civil Code, art. 1472). If the *central heating becomes obsolescent*, its replacement by a modern heating system will be considered an extraordinary repair and the cost of repair will have to be borne by the nude owner (Civil Code, art. 1473). If the replacement is classified as an improvement rather than maintenance, there is no obligation upon the owner to replace the central heating. If the usufructuary replaces the heating system, it will be classified as a useful improvement which would form the basis for a claim based on unjustified enrichment. If the *roof* of the house is damaged[133] in a storm, the repair may amount to an act

[131] If the usufructuary does not return the property in a proper condition, the owner can claim for damages: Court of Appeal of Porto of 30.03.2003 [Process 0030331], available at www.dgsi.pt.

[132] Decision of the Supreme Court of Justice of 02.02.1991 [Process 079975], available at www.dgsi.pt.

[133] The Court of Appeal of Porto of 13.12.2001 [Process 0131488], available at www.dgsi.pt, decided that if the roof of a house is damaged, the owner must bear the expense.

of extraordinary conservation of the property. Therefore, the nude owner will be responsible for the repair of the roof (Civil Code, art. 1472). If the *fences* on the farm become dilapidated, the repair needed would be classified as ordinary repairs which have to be carried out by the usufructuary. If the *paint of the building flakes off*, the usufructuary is obliged to carry out these ordinary repairs.

These rules are not mandatory and they can be changed by agreement between the parties (Civil Code, art. 1445).

Apart from his/her responsibility for ordinary repairs, the usufructuary (B) will also be responsible for extraordinary repairs *necessitated by his/her careless administration* of the property (Civil Code, art. 1473 no. 1). If the usufructuary, or a person for whom he/she is responsible, caused the damage, the usufructuary will be liable for the cost of such repairs.

If the major damage to the building can be traced back to the *usufructuary's omission to undertake ordinary repairs* such as the timeous repainting of the wall, he/she will be liable for the cost of the major repairs to the wall. If the nude owner refuses to carry out repairs for which he/she is responsible or delays their execution, the usufructuary may carry out the repairs at his/her own expense. These expenses must be reimbursed within a reasonable time and not only at the expiry of the usufruct (Civil Code, art. 1473 no 2).

If the *usuary* takes all the fruits of a property or the *holder of a right of habitation* occupies the entire house, he/she is responsible for all ordinary repairs, administrative expenses and taxes levied on the property as if he/she were a usufructuary (Civil Code, art. 1489). If the usuary only needs a part of the fruits or the holder of the right of habitation only occupies part of the house, his/her responsibility is reduced proportionately.

Scotland

Repairing obligations is one of the areas where the distinction drawn at common law between an 'urban' and a 'rural' lease is relevant.[134] This does not depend upon the location of the subjects, but on their nature. A rural lease is one where the main subject of the lease is the land itself, its produce and what is naturally on it or below it. An urban lease is one where the main subject is what has been erected on the land. The

[134] Paton and Cameron, *Landlord and Tenant*, pp. 70–1; Rankine, *Leases*, p. 174.

addition of an accessory to the main subject (for example, a garden to a house or a farmhouse to a farm) does not change the characterisation.

The *landlord* is under an implied obligation that the subjects are reasonably fit for the purposes of the lease.[135] In an *urban lease*, this translates into an obligation that the subjects must be wind and water tight and in a reasonably habitable and tenantable condition. 'Wind and water tight' has been defined as 'wind and water tight against what may be called the ordinary attacks of the elements, not against exceptional encroachments of water due to other causes'.[136] If the subjects do not meet this standard, the landlord is bound to repair the defect. This obligation is not, however, a warranty. The landlord is not in breach until the defect is brought to his/her notice and he/she fails to remedy it within a reasonable time.[137] The repairing obligation does not extend to defects which are the result of the tenant's own negligence,[138] the act of a third party or *damnum fatale*[139] (an 'act of God': 'a loss arising from an inevitable accident, such as no human prudence can prevent', for example, losses occasioned by storms or tempests, lightning, floods or over-blowing with sand).[140]

The common law is now subject to extensive statutory supplementation where the tenancy is of a 'house let for human habitation'.[141] The landlord comes under an obligation prior to the start of the tenancy and during it. He must ensure that the house meets the 'repairing standard' at the start of the tenancy[142] and must therefore inspect the house to identify any work necessary to comply with this duty and notify the tenant if there is any such work.[143] The landlord must also ensure that the house meets the standard at all times during the tenancy. This second duty only applies where the tenant notifies the landlord or

135 Paton and Cameron, *Landlord and Tenant*, p. 130; Rankine, *Leases*, pp. 240–1.

136 *Wolfson* v. *Forrester* 1910 SC 675 (IH) 680.

137 *Wolfson* v. *Forrester* 1910 SC 675 (IH) 680; *Dickie* v. *Amicable Property Investment Building Society* 1911 SC 1079 (OH) 1085.

138 Rankine, *Leases*, p. 242; *Hardie* v. *Black* 1768 Mor 10 133; *Maclellan* v. *Kerr and Irvine* 1797 Mor 10 134. The tenant would be liable for damage resulting from a failure on his/her part to take reasonable care of the property: *Mickel* v. *McCoard* 1913 SC 896 (IH).

139 *Bayne* v. *Walker* (1815) 3 Dow 233 238 243 245; *Little Cumbrae Estate Ltd.* v. *Island of Little Cumbrae Ltd.* [2007] CSIH 35, 2007 SC 525, para. 16. Parties can contract out of this rule: para. 17.

140 See the definition of *damnum fatale*, in Watson, *Bell's Dictionary*.

141 Housing (Scotland) Act 2006 Ch 4 (henceforth H(S)A 06). This applies to leases detailed at s. 12. Certain types of lease are excluded, such as a lease of a house on an agricultural holding. B's farmhouse would therefore not be covered by this statutory standard.

142 H(S)A 06, s. 14(1)(a).

143 H(S)A 06, s. 19.

where the landlord otherwise becomes aware that work requires to be carried out for the purpose of meeting the repairing standard. The landlord must then complete any required work within a reasonable time.[144] The 'repairing standard' is given a comprehensive definition, although – given the relative novelty of the statute – there is little case law expanding upon it. A house meets the repairing standard if:[145]

(a) it is wind and water tight and in all other respects reasonably fit for human habitation;
(b) the structure and exterior of the house (including drains, gutters and external pipes) are in a reasonable state of repair and in proper working order (in determining this, regard is to be had to the age, character and prospective life of the house and the locality in which it is situated);
(c) the installations in the house for the supply of water, gas and electricity and for sanitation, space heating and heating water are in a reasonable state of repair and proper working order;
(d) any fixtures, fittings and appliances provided by the landlord under the tenancy are in a reasonable state of repair and in proper working order;
(e) any furnishings provided by the landlord under the tenancy are capable of being used safely for the purpose for which they are designed, and
(f) the house has satisfactory provision for detecting fires and for giving warning in the event of fire or suspected fire.

This duty does not require the house to be rebuilt or reinstated in the event of destruction or damage by fire or by storm, flood or other inevitable accident.[146] These rules are mandatory. Contracting out is forbidden, apart from with the consent of a sheriff, who may make an order excluding or modifying the statutory rules only if he considers that it is reasonable to do so.[147]

In a *rural lease*, the landlord is obliged to provide sufficient means to enable the tenant to cultivate the land. He/she must put buildings and fences into tenantable repair at the date of entry so that they are capable of lasting the length of the lease if used with ordinary care by the tenant.[148] The landlord is not obliged to make 'ordinary repairs' during the course of the lease. Responsibility for ordinary repairs and maintenance falls on the tenant, who is required to leave the subjects at the end of the lease in the same tenantable condition as he received them,

144 H(S)A 06, s. 14(1)(b), (3) and (4). 145 H(S)A 06, s. 13(1).

146 H(S)A 06, s. 16(1)(c). There are various other limited exceptions.

147 H(S)A 06, s. 18.

148 Rankine, *Leases*, pp. 247–51; Paton and Cameron, *Landlord and Tenant*, pp. 134–5.

fair wear and tear excepted.[149] The landlord is, however, responsible for carrying out 'extraordinary repairs' to the buildings and fences. Where repair becomes necessary because of natural decay, it amounts to an extraordinary repair.[150] Neither party is obliged to repair damage resulting from *damnum fatale*.

Where the lease falls under the provisions of the Agricultural Holdings legislation, a specific statutory regime applies, which mirrors the approach of the common law.[151] The landlord is obliged, at the commencement of the tenancy or as soon as reasonably practicable thereafter, to put the 'fixed equipment' of the holding into a thorough state of repair. Fixed equipment is defined as including permanent buildings necessary for the proper conduct of the holding, permanent fences, water courses and access roads.[152] The landlord must provide such buildings and other fixed equipment as will enable an occupier reasonably skilled in husbandry to maintain efficient production on the holding. The landlord must, during the tenancy, replace or renew buildings or fixed equipment which is rendered necessary by natural decay or fair wear and tear. The tenant's responsibility regarding the maintenance of fixed equipment extends only to maintaining it in as good a state of repair (natural decay and fair wear and tear excepted) as it was in immediately after it was put into repair by the landlord.

These principles produce the following results in the individual questions. The landlord of a house is responsible for repairing the *central heating system* when it becomes defective.[153] If the central heating system has simply *become obsolescent* as opposed to defective, neither party is obliged to replace it. That will amount to an improvement as opposed to a repair.[154] A recent case concerning a commercial lease illustrates the point.[155] The lease provided that the tenant was to repair the subjects and keep them in good and substantial repair and condition. Various installations had reached the end of their 'economic life', although they were not defective and because of their age they no longer represented the least expensive way of performing their function. It was held that this did not mean the items were not in good

[149] See Caterina, 'A Comparative Overview', pp. 98–100.
[150] Paton and Cameron, *Landlord and Tenant*, p. 135.
[151] AH(S)A 91, s. 5(2) (1991 Act tenancies); AH(S)A 03, s. 16 (SLDT and LDT).
[152] AH(S)A 91, s. 85(1); AH(S)A 03, s. 93. [153] AH(S)A 06, s. 13(1)(c).
[154] On the distinction, see Rankine, *Leases*, p. 240.
[155] *Westbury Estates Ltd.* v. *Royal Bank of Scotland plc* [2006] CSOH 177, 2006 SLT 1143, paras. 34–7.

repair. The matter might have been different had the items been shown to be unreliable and prone to breakdowns and the same would be true here.

If the *roof* of a house or a building on a farm is damaged in a storm, neither party is bound to repair it because the damage results from *damnum fatale*. Depending on how serious the damage is, the tenant will be entitled either to abandon the lease (in the case of total destruction) or to claim an abatement of rent.[156] If the *fences* on the subjects of a rural lease or, more specifically, an agricultural holding become dilapidated, the tenant is obliged to repair them, unless it is the result from fair wear and tear or natural decay, in which case the landlord is obliged to repair.[157]

As for the *flaking paint*, there appears to be no discussion in the main Scottish texts of whether an obligation to repair includes an obligation to repaint.[158] Although English authorities are to be used with care in this field, it is difficult to disagree with the observation in the standard English text that 'painting which one is required to do in terms of a repairing obligation is limited to such painting as is necessary for the prevention of decay and does not extend to painting for mere ornamentation'.[159] That is consistent with the distinction which Scots law draws between repairing and improving. If the flaking was such that it could be said that the exterior of the residential house was not 'in a reasonable state of repair'[160] (as opposed to merely not looking smart), then the landlord will be liable to repaint.[161] The landlord of an agricultural tenancy will be required to repaint if the flaking is the result of natural decay or fair wear and tear. If the landlord fails to repaint when he/she is obliged to do so, he will be liable for repairing the resulting damage to the wall.

It does make a difference if *one of the parties caused the damage*. The landlord's repairing obligation does not cover defects which are the result of the tenant's own negligence. The party negligently causing damage will be responsible under ordinary principles of delict.

The *liferenter* is to preserve the subjects in as good a condition as when first received, subject to accident, *vis maior* and possibly fair wear and

156 Rankine, *Leases*, pp. 226–9; Paton and Cameron, *Landlord and Tenant*, pp. 142–3.
157 AH(S)A 91, s. 5(2), AH(S)A 03, s. 16(3)(b).
158 *Campbell* v. *M'cowan* 1945 SLT (Sh Ct) 3 6 does suggest that a tenant's repairing obligation could encompass repainting woodwork to protect against damp.
159 Lewison, *Woodfall's Law of Landlord and Tenant*, para. 13.044.
160 H(S)A 03, s. 13(1)(b). 161 H(S)A 03, s. 14.

tear. In the case of accident and *vis maior*, neither fiar nor liferenter is bound to repair. The scope of the fair wear and tear exception is difficult to ascertain, for it is also commonly said that the liferenter must carry out ordinary repairs and do what is necessary to preserve the subjects in a habitable and tenantable condition.[162] If the liferenter strays beyond repairs and improves the property, he/she is presumed to do so for his/her benefit.[163] It is thought, therefore, that the liferenter will be liable to repair the *heating system* if it becomes defective, but not to replace it if it merely *becomes obsolescent* (for that would be an improvement). If the *roof* is damaged in a storm, neither party will be bound to repair as it was caused by *vis maior*. Repair of the *dilapidated fences* falls, most likely, to the liferenter as would *repainting* (provided that painting was needed to maintain the property and not to improve it). On ordinary delictual principles, it will make a difference if one party *caused the damage*.

South Africa

The question deals with a general obligation on the part of the *landlord* to maintain the property in a condition reasonably fit for the purpose for which the property is let. The 'purpose' of a lease is determined by construction of the terms of the contract and the surrounding circumstances, including its previous and known intended use.[164] By considering the purpose of the lease, South African law effectively draws a distinction between urban and agricultural leases. Imperfections attributable to dilapidation or depreciation by reason of lapse of time, weather and normal use are regarded as rendering the property unfit for its intended purpose and are thus the responsibility of the landlord.[165]

Defective parts must be repaired or replaced by new ones, for example, new guttering,[166] and structural alterations[167] must be made if the defect is of such a nature that it interferes with the proper use and

[162] Caterina, 'A Comparative Overview', pp. 95–8. [163] Erskine, *Principles*, II. 9. 33.

[164] Pothier, *Obligations*, para. 23; *Weinberg* v. *Weinberg Bros (Pty) Ltd.* 1951 3 SA 266 (C) 272G.

[165] See Pothier, *Obligations*, para. 106; Voet, *Commentarius*, 19.2.14; Kerr, 'Lease', paras. 164–6.

[166] *African Theatres Trust* v. *Estate McCubbin* 1919 NPD 277 280 (new guttering).

[167] *Harlin Properties* v. *Los Angeles Hotel* 1962 3 SA 143 (A) 150.

enjoyment of the property. If the landlord is informed of defects, he/she is obliged to investigate the cause and make the necessary repairs.[168]

In the light of the above, a modern residential premises will no longer be considered fit for its purpose if the *central heating system becomes defective.*[169] Likewise, a farm will no longer be fit for its purpose if the *fences become dilapidated.* There will thus be an obligation on the landlord to repair the central heating system and the dilapidated fences and, if necessary, to replace them. Since the *replacement of an obsolescent non-defective central heating system* with a more modern system cannot be classified under 'repair', it will be considered an 'improvement', and will fall outside the landlord's obligations.[170]

From the above it is clear that, in principle, a tenant is only liable for small repairs or replacements. These are the so-called 'tenant's repairs' for which custom has made him/her liable.[171] The assumption is that these repairs are occasioned by the fault of the tenant or his/her servants and are not necessitated by age or the inferior quality of fittings (like doors, windows, shutters, hinges and locks) that have fallen into a state of disrepair. These items are presumed to have been in good condition if the tenants entered into occupation without complaint and without obtaining an acknowledgement from the landlord that certain fittings will be replaced or repaired.[172] Thus the tenant will only be liable for replacing or repairing a fitting if he/she ought to have had knowledge thereof at the time of entry.[173] Under the Rental Housing Act 50 of 1999 (s 5), the landlord and tenant are compelled jointly to inspect residential property before the tenant takes occupation to ascertain the existence of defects.

The principle therefore is that the landlord is liable for all major structural repairs and all smaller repairs occasioned by age or inferior quality of the fittings involved. If a defective state of affairs does not fall into any of these categories, the presumption is that the defect has been caused by the fault of the tenant and that he/she is liable for the repairs. Thus the *flaking off of the paint* on the building would be considered the result of ordinary wear and tear and within the landlord's duty to keep the property fit for the purpose for which it was let. If the *dilapidated*

168 *Salmon* v. *Dedlow* 1912 TPD 971; Cooper, *Landlord and Tenant*, pp. 98–9.

169 See *Poynton* v. *Cran* 1910 AD 205: a hotwater cylinder is an essential part of a hotel.

170 See Kerr, 'Lease', para. 162(b).

171 Cooper, *Landlord and Tenant*, pp. 111–12.

172 Pothier, *Obligations*, paras. 219 and 220, cited with approval in *Bresky* v. *Vivier* 1928 CPD 202 204–5.

173 *Shapiro* v. *Yutar* 1930 CPD 92 101.

fences cannot be ascribed to the negligence of the tenant, the landlord will also have to repair them. Where the *roof is damaged in a storm*, this will normally be considered damage caused by *vis maior* and not attributable to the fault of the tenant. The landlord will therefore be responsible for repairs and will normally take out insurance against such risk.

In the case of material defects which render the property unfit for the purpose for which it is let, the tenant can cancel the lease[174] and recover any foreseeable loss by way of an action for damages.[175] Alternatively, the tenant may request that the necessary repairs be made[176] and if the landlord delays claim damages for loss suffered; sue for a court order compelling the landlord to make the repairs; or effect the repairs and deduct the necessary expenses from the rent due.[177] In cases where it is unclear whether the work required amounts to repair, structural alteration or improvement, the tenant should seek the intervention of the court.[178] Finally, the tenant may claim a reduction of rent proportionate to his/her temporary or permanent deprivation of use, provided the inconvenience suffered is not slight.[179]

A landlord is of course not obliged to repair damage or defects *caused by the negligence of the tenant* or those for whom he/she is responsible.[180] The tenant is obliged to make reasonable use of the premises and exercise the same standard of care as a reasonable person would exercise with regard to his/her own property. In certain instances the tenant must take positive action to ensure that the property remains in a proper condition. The tenant of a vineyard must therefore work and manure it properly and in a timely manner and cultivate it in the manner of a good and careful winegrower.[181] The tenant of a hotel must exploit it in a manner that attracts and not discourages customers.[182]

Consequently, the tenant will only be liable if the damage or unfit state of affairs is attributable to his/her negligence.[183] He/she will not be

[174] See Kerr, 'Lease', para. 163; Cooper, *Landlord and Tenant*, pp. 98–110.

[175] Cooper, *Landlord and Tenant*, pp. 90, 108–10. The landlord is liable if he/she knew or, by reason of his/her trade or profession, ought to have known, of the defective condition.

[176] Cooper, *Landlord and Tenant*, p. 89. [177] *Ibid.* 107–8.

[178] *Poynton* v. *Cran* 1910 AD 205 227.

[179] Pothier, *Obligations*, para. 141; Cooper, *Landlord and Tenant*, pp. 100–7.

[180] *Brandt* v. *Kotze* 1948 3 SA 769 (C); Cooper, *Landlord and Tenant*, pp. 99, 223–33.

[181] Pothier, *Obligations*, para. 190; Voet, *Commentarius*, 19.2.29; *Manley van Niekerk (Pty) Ltd.* v. *Assegai Safaris and Film Productions (Pty) Ltd.* 1977 2 SA 416 (A) 423B-C.

[182] Pothier, *Obligations*, para. 189.

[183] Cooper, *Landlord and Tenant*, p. 223; Pothier, *Obligations*, para. 199; *North West Hotel* v. *Rolfes, Nebel and Co.* 1902 TS 324 336.

liable where the damage was caused through *vis maior*, a latent defect in the premises, or through the act of a third party for whose acts the tenant is not liable.

We have established that under South African law the landlord will be liable in the normal situation where the paint on the building flakes off owing to ordinary wear and tear. South African law, however, apparently expects the tenant to warn the landlord of the defect. Failure to do so will mean that the tenant is taken to have had knowledge of the consequences of the defect and is precluded from claiming costs for further damage on the principle of *volenti non fit iniuria*.[184] The courts have not, however, gone so far as to decide that the cost of repairing the more serious damage must be borne by the tenant. If, however, the tenant has complained of the unfit condition of the building, the landlord's knowledge of the unfit state of affairs will render him responsible for the more serious repair needed because of the delay. However, the landlord will only be liable for loss suffered by the tenant on account of the delay if the landlord knew or by reason of his/her trade or profession ought to have known of the defective condition.[185]

The *default rule* places the landlord under a general obligation to place and maintain the property in a condition reasonably fit for the purpose for which the property is let.[186] The 'purpose' of a lease is determined by the use of the premises as gathered from the terms of the contract and the surrounding circumstances, including its previous and known intended use.[187] This default rule is not mandatory and the tenant may assume a more extensive liability for repairs in the contract of lease. The burden of proving such an assumption is on the landlord and the clause embodying such an assumption is as a rule strictly construed in order to saddle the tenant with as little additional liability for maintenance as possible.[188]

The *usufructuary* (and the *usuary* and *habitator*) must exercise their rights sensibly (*arbitratu boni viri*) and exploit the property in accordance

184 Cooper, *Landlord and Tenant*, pp. 110–11.

185 *Heerman's Supermarket* v. *Mona Road Investments* 1975 4 SA 391 (D) 393D; Cooper, *Landlord and Tenant*, pp. 108–10.

186 See for usual clauses in leases, Kerr, 'Lease', para. 162; Cooper, *Landlord and Tenant*, p. 98 n. 1; *Proud Investments* v. *Lanchem Inter* 1991 3 SA 738 (A) 748A-C.

187 Pothier *Obligations*, para. 23; *Weinberg* v. *Weinberg Bros (Pty) Ltd.* 1951 3 SA 266 (C) 272G.

188 See Cooper, *Landlord and Tenant*, pp. 112–19 for the content and interpretation of various maintenance clauses, proof of breach and the landlord's remedies.

with its intended use or customary exploitation. The property must be restored in a proper condition without impairment of its substance (*salva rerum substantia*) excepting ordinary wear and tear[189] and loss and depreciation not caused by them. The usufructuary may not destroy the property, impair its value or change its character.[190] Consequently, the usufructuary is in principle obliged to make ordinary repairs and bear the expenses for maintaining the property in the state in which he/she received it.[191] Extraordinary repairs and expenses must be borne by the nude owner.[192] The usufructuary is responsible for temporary and the nude owner for permanent maintenance of the property.

If the *central heating system* becomes defective, the usufructuary will be responsible for repairs. If it becomes *obsolescent*, replacement will be a major item of maintenance to be borne by the nude owner. However, neither the owner nor the usufructuary will be *obliged* to do anything about it. If the usufructuary replaces the system, it will be classified as an improvement rather than a repair and no compensation can be claimed, except perhaps on the ground of *negotiorum gestio* (unauthorised administration). If the *roof of the house is damaged* in a storm, the major repairs needed will be the responsibility of the nude owner. Thus, if the usufructuary repairs the roof, he/she will be entitled to claim compensation from the owner.[193] If the *paint of the building flakes off*, the resultant ordinary repair must be attended to by the usufructuary. The same is true if the *fences on the farm* become dilapidated. However, if the repair involves major expenses, the nude owner will have to foot the bill,[194] unless the need to repair can be traced back to a lack of care by the usufructuary.

If the usufructuary or any person for whom he/she is responsible *causes the damage negligently*,[195] he/she will be responsible for the cost of the repairs. Consequently, if the major damage to the building can be traced back to the usufructuary's omission to undertake ordinary repairs (paint flaking off), the usufructuary will be liable for the cost of any resultant major repairs to the building. Similarly, if the

[189] See *Gibaud* v. *Bagshaw* 1918 CPD 202.

[190] See cases quoted by Van der Merwe, 'Servitudes', para. 434.

[191] Voet, *Commentarius*, 7.9.1.

[192] See *ibid.* 7.1.36–8; Van der Merwe, 'Servitudes', para. 436.

[193] *Philps* v. *Cradock Municipality* 1937 EDL 382; Van der Merwe, 'Servitudes', p. 437.

[194] See *Ex parte Borland* 1961 1 SA 6 (SR).

[195] By omitting repairs that a reasonable person would have undertaken in the circumstances.

usufructuary does not act as a sensible person in attending to his/her own affairs (by not repainting the building), his/her estate will eventually be liable to the owner for all the loss suffered through his/her neglect.

These are the *default rules*. They are mandatory in all cases where the usufruct is not established by an *inter vivos* agreement. If established by agreement, the default rules may be changed by the parties.

Spain

The *landlord* is under an obligation to maintain the property in a state of good repair during the currency of the lease (Civil Code, art. 1554–2, Law on Urban Leases, art. 21.1 and Law on Rural Leases, art. 18). The only exception is found in the Law on Urban Leases (art. 21.4), which holds the tenant responsible for certain specified minor items of repair. The landlord will be responsible for repairs affecting the habitability of the house or apartment such as a leaking pipe or defective electricity, whereas the tenant will, for example, be responsible for cleaning the house and for repairing holes made in walls for hanging pictures.

This principle can, by analogy, be extended to apply to rural leases. The tenant is obliged to notify the landlord when repairs are needed (Civil Code, art. 1559, para. 2 and Law on Urban Leases, art. 21.3). If urgent repairs are needed, the tenant (in case of an urban lease) can execute them and claim reimbursement from the landlord (art. 21.3). The Law on Rural Leases (art. 18.2) contains a special provision that grants the tenant four options where the landlord has been notified that certain repairs are urgent or necessary but the landlord delays in carrying them out. The tenant can:

- (a) approach the court for a judicial order that imposes a duty on the landlord to carry out the repairs;
- (b) sue the landlord for breach of contract;
- (c) obtain a reduction of the rent; or
- (d) execute the repairs, with a right of reimbursement through set off (*compensatio*) against outstanding rent (Law on Rural Leases, art. 18.2).

The tenant now has a fifth option, namely to resile from the contract (*resuelto*) (Law on Urban Leases, art. 27.3(a)). The amended Law on Rural Leases of 2005 added that the tenant is entitled to claim damages in any of the above cases if economic loss can be proved.

Necessary repairs are described as 'those required for maintaining the premises in a habitable condition and capable of being exploited for the purpose for which it is let' (Law on Urban Leases, art. 21.1 and Law on Rural Leases, art. 18.1). The landlord is not responsible for repairs necessitated by damage caused by circumstances not attributable to him (Law on Urban Leases, art. 21.1, para. 2) or by damage caused by the negligence of the tenant or his/her relatives (interpreted in Civil Code, art. 1564 as 'those who live with him') (Civil Code, art. 1563–4 and Law on Urban Leases, art. 21.1 *in fine*).

In view of the above, the repair of the *defective heating system*, the *roof*, the *fences* and *repainting the walls* to maintain the habitability of the house[196] will be charged to the landlord. If the *central heating system becomes obsolescent*, replacement will be considered an improvement for which neither the landlord nor the tenant will be responsible. The tenant can execute urgent repairs to avoid imminent damage and claim the cost from the landlord if he/she has previously notified the landlord that the repairs were needed (Law on Urban Leases, art. 21.3).

All the rules contained in Title II (residential leases) are *mandatory* unless the specific rule allows deviation from it (Law on Urban Leases, art. 6). Thus, the rule that imposes an obligation on the landlord to carry out all the repairs necessary for maintaining the habitability of the premises is definitely mandatory. The Law on Rural Leases (arts. 18 ff.) specifies that the repairs to be carried out by the landlord and the tenant are also mandatory. Law on Rural Leases (art. 21) allows the parties to arrange their obligations differently and to regulate their liability for future improvements (as opposed to repairs) of the property.

According to Civil Code, art. 500, the *usufructuary* is responsible for ordinary repairs,[197] interpreted as the duties of conservation and maintenance of the property.[198] Civil Code, art. 500, para. 2 defines ordinary repairs as 'those required to repair the damages and deterioration due to the natural use of property and that are essential to its conservation'. Authors consider that these comprise those regular and periodic repairs at moderate cost (the *modica refectio* of Roman law),[199] which do not exceed the notional rent for the property.[200] Where the usufructuary fails to make these ordinary repairs after being notified to do so, the

[196] See Law on Urban Leases, art. 21.1.

[197] Lacruz Berdejo, *Elementos*, vol 2, p. 128 considers that this is one of the differences between usufruct and lease. In the first case, it is the usufructuary and not the owner who is responsible for ordinary repairs. In the second case, we have already seen that the owner is charged with necessary repairs.

[198] Lacruz Berdejo, *Elementos*, vol. 3.2, pp. 29 ff.; García Cantero, 'Comment', p. 1331.

[199] García Cantero, 'Comment', pp. 1332–3.

[200] Lacruz Berdejo, *Elementos*, vol. 3.2, p. 32.

owner is entitled to do so at the usufructuary's expense (Civil Code, art. 500, para. 2 *in fine*).

The nude owner is responsible for all extraordinary repairs (Civil Code, art. 501).[201] If they are urgent, the usufructuary must notify the owner of the need to carry them out. If the usufructuary has notified the owner to carry out repairs which are necessary for the continued existence of the property and the owner fails to do so, the usufructuary may carry out the repairs and demand from the owner on termination of the usufruct an amount representing the increase in value of the property attributable to such extraordinary repairs (Civil Code, art. 502).

It is possible to regard the *repair of the heating system*, *repainting the walls* and *repairing the fences* as ordinary repairs for which the usufructuary is responsible. Where the *roof* has been damaged by a storm (and not by normal use), the repair will exceed the concept of ordinary repairs and will thus be the responsibility of the nude owner. The *replacement of the obsolescent heating system* can be considered as an improvement, which neither party is obliged to carry out. If the usufructuary decides to install it, it is regarded as an improvement, which he/she is entitled to remove if such removal is possible without damaging the property (Civil Code, art. 487).

Since usufruct is governed by the agreement which establishes the usufruct (Civil Code, art. 470), the above rules are not mandatory and can be deviated from if the usufruct is established by agreement.

The above principles will also apply if B holds a *right of use* or *a right of habitation*, also with regard to mandatory rules (Civil Code, art. 523).

The holder of a *hereditary building right* (*superficies*) becomes 'temporary owner' of the building or the plantation for the duration of the right. Accordingly, he/she will be responsible for all kinds of repairs, irrespective of their kind, unless otherwise agreed in the contract creating the building lease.

[201] *Ibid.* 33 specifies that the owner is not obliged to carry out the repairs since he/she is not in possession of the property. His/her duty is to pay for the repairs.

Case 6
Entitlements of the holder of a time-limited interest to fruits of agricultural property

With regard to the farm, to what extent is B entitled to:

- *cut plantations for timber, fruit trees, decorative trees, shrubs?*
- *open mines or quarries and/or continue mineral operations?*
- *harvest standing crops after the termination of his/her right?*
- *the proceeds, if a further right is created with regard to the object of the limited right (for example, if he sub-lets the farm)? What if the proceeds of the latter right become due on an annual basis, and the principal limited right expires six months before maturity of the sub-interest?*

Comparative observations

In general, the *agricultural tenant* may exploit the land by reaping natural fruits according to the ordinary standards of cultivation, with due care and in conformity with the property's intended purpose.[1] The tenant is therefore not allowed to impair the substance, economic or social function or the income-bearing capacity of the land and may not, without the consent of the landlord, change the existing method of cultivation to the extent that it substantially affects the future exploitation of the land.[2] The default position, subject to local custom and contrary agreement, is that the lessee must restore the property at the end of the lease to the condition in which it would have been had it been exploited in an orderly fashion during the term of the lease.

[1] See the German, Austrian, Greek, Belgian, Portuguese, Italian, South African, Danish, Hungarian and Polish reports.

[2] The tenant is, for instance, not allowed to convert orchards into pasturage or flower gardens into vegetable gardens. South African law allows an exception in the case of a long lease which will allow the restoration to the previous condition. See also the Scottish report.

The default rule in several countries[3] is that the tenant is allowed to cut *plantations* destined to be cut (*silva caedua*) at regular intervals in accordance with contractual arrangements and the accepted standards of exploitation in that particular locality.[4] In Greece, the *crop-sharing tenant* is given more control over the general management and exploitation of plantations, while English law vests the property in trees (and the eventual timber) in the landlord.

In principle, the tenant is entitled to enjoy the fruits, but not the substance, of *fruit trees, decorative trees* and *shrubs*.[5] In Poland, renewable trees such as bamboo are considered fruits and thus subject to appropriation by the tenant. England vests the property in trees and shrubs in the landlord and tenant respectively. In most jurisdictions,[6] the cutting down of trees and shrubs is allowed only in the interest of proper maintenance and management of the land concerned. The tenant may therefore cut down and replace old trees and shrubs, remove and replace dead trees and cut down dead branches and brushwood in the interest of proper husbandry. If a tenant is allowed a choice of crops, Spanish law allows him/her to cut down fruit trees and plant another crop as long as the land is returned in the same condition in which he/she received it.

The tenant is entitled to continue *existing mining operations* if this accords with the function of the property[7] and to collect the minerals mined on the land.[8] In principle, the *opening of new mines and quarries* will go beyond the agricultural purpose of the land and will be allowed only with the consent of the landlord[9] and the grant of a mining licence[10] or public concession[11] under applicable mining legislation.

In general, the tenant is not entitled to harvest *standing crops* after the termination of the lease, but some jurisdictions oblige the landlord (A) to compensate the tenant (B) for the value of the standing crops harvested according to accepted standards, with subtraction of harvest expenses.[12] Other jurisdictions allow the tenant to claim the production

[3] E.g. Germany, Austria, Greece, Belgium, Spain, Italy, Denmark and South Africa. But cf. England and Scotland.

[4] E.g. every seven years in Germany.

[5] In Portugal, for example, the tenant will be entitled to the cork from cork trees.

[6] E.g. Germany, Greece, Spain, Portugal, England, Belgium, South Africa and Hungary.

[7] A mining concession is usually required. See the Spanish and Portuguese reports.

[8] See e.g. the German, Greek, Belgian, Italian and Polish reports. In some of these jurisdictions, minerals are considered fruits of the land.

[9] See the English and Danish reports.

[10] See e.g. the German, Austrian and Greek reports.

[11] See the Spanish report.

[12] See the German, Austrian, Greek, Belgian, Portuguese, Spanish and Danish reports.

cost of crops left standing on the land,[13] while some jurisdictions oblige the tenant to leave a certain quantity of seeds, hay and fertiliser as required for the orderly cultivation of the land during the next season.[14] If the tenant unreasonably expected that the crops would be ready for harvesting on termination of the lease, the tenant, under South African law, is entitled to the cost of the seeds, ploughing, tilling and sowing the crops. If the expectation was reasonable, South African jurisprudence allows the tenant to re-enter and reap the crops on its maturity. Belgian law allows the tenant to harvest standing crops if *force majeure* prevented timely harvesting and English law restricts the time-limit for entering the land to reap matured crops.

In certain jurisdictions, the tenant is only allowed *to assign* his/her right in the property or *to sub-let* the land or part of it (for example, a house on the farm) with the landlord's consent. This rule applies to all leases in some jurisdictions[15] and to agricultural leases only in others.[16] The rationale for the Greek prohibition on assignment or sub-letting of agricultural leases without consent, is that an agricultural landlord entrusts the land to a particular tenant on account of that tenant's known expertise in cultivating the land. On assignment or sub-lease of the land without the landlord's consent, the latter may terminate the contract and sue the tenant for damages for breach of contract.

The Austrian law and the Spanish Civil Code dealing with ordinary leases entitle the tenant to sub-let the property or part thereof if it does not disadvantage the landlord and is not expressly forbidden in the contract. In contrast, the Spanish Law on Agricultural Leases allows assignment or sub-lease of the entire property only for a period not exceeding the term of the lease and in return for rent not exceeding the rent charged in the principal contract. The Spanish Law on Urban Lease allows the tenant to sub-let part of the premises with the written consent of the landlord and for a rent not exceeding the rent under the principal contract. If assignment or sub-lease is allowed, the tenant will be entitled to the *proceeds or rent* but will also be held liable for any damages attributable to the fault of the assignee or sub-tenant.[17]

13 See the Greek, Polish and Hungarian reports. But cf. the English and Scottish reports.

14 See the Greek report.

15 E.g. in Germany, Portugal, Denmark and Poland.

16 E.g. in Greece, Belgium and Italy. Standard form contracts in Greece contain a prohibition on the assignment or sub-letting of residential property, while Belgian law allows assignment or sub-letting without the landlord's consent to relatives.

17 See e.g. the Greek report.

Very few jurisdictions address the issue *where the proceeds under a sub-lease fall due on an annual basis and the principal right expires six months before the maturity of sub-interest*. Most jurisdictions accept that the sub-tenant cannot acquire greater rights than the tenant and that the sub-lease will be terminated automatically on termination of the principal lease and the loss suffered by the sub-tenant on account of the early termination of the sub-lease may be claimed from the sub-landlord but not from the principal landlord on the ground that the sub-landlord concluded a contract that was impossible to fulfil.[18] In England and Scotland, the termination of the principal tenancy also terminates the sub-tenancy, except in the case of merger and surrender where statute preserves the covenants under the lease so that rent becomes payable to the landlord. In France, the landlord can authorise the tenant to sub-let the property and redirect a percentage of the rent to the principal landlord.

Under a *usufruct*, the usufructuary is in principle entitled to the natural and civil fruits of the property when harvested as long as he/she respects the economic purpose of the property, takes reasonable care of it and exploits it in accordance with accepted standards of cultivation.[19] On termination, the usufructuary must return the property without impairment of its substance. In case of default, the nude owner can demand security against future damage and, on refusal, approach the court for suspension of the usufruct.

Most jurisdictions[20] consider *plantations* that are destined to be cut and used for timber as fruits and allow the usufructuary to cut them at regular intervals in accordance with good husbandry, local custom, regional statutes and regulations, on condition that the property is restored to its former condition. In Germany and Greece, the usufructuary must fell the plantation according to a harvest plan as agreed between the parties or according to a detailed harvesting programme, prepared by an expert appointed by the court on request of one of the parties.

18 See the Greek, Spanish, Belgian, Danish, Polish and Hungarian reports.

19 See e.g. the German, Austrian, Greek, Belgian and Portuguese reports. Under the Dutch Civil Code, the exercise must be in accordance with the nature of the property and local custom pertaining to the use and collection of fruits, and under the South Africa law, according to the judgment of a sensible person. If constituted by agreement, the terms of the agreement must be observed.

20 E.g. Germany, Austria, Greece, Belgium, Portugal, Spain, Italy, the Netherlands, South Africa, Hungary and Poland. But cf. Scotland.

In general, *fruit trees, decorative trees and shrubs* are not considered fruits[21] and may therefore not be cut or removed except in the interests of good husbandry and orderly exploitation. If removed, they must be replaced to comply with the requirement that the property must be returned without impairment of its substance.[22] While live fruit trees and decorative trees[23] may not be removed, dead shrubs, fruit trees and ornamental trees and undergrowth or trees uprooted or damaged by a storm[24] may be cleared subject to the obligation of replacement.

Most of the jurisdictions[25] consider stone and minerals as fruits and therefore allow the usufructuary to continue to work *existing quarries and mines* for stone and minerals. The only exception is South Africa, which allows the usufructuary to mine existing mines but to take only non-renewable minerals like salt and peat as fruits. Greek law requires an expert appointed by the court to prepare a plan for the exploitation of existing mines. Spanish law requires the consent of the nude owner to work existing mines and quarries and in the case of a legal servitude allows the nude owner (widow or widower) to take half of the proceeds of mining after the deduction of expenses. Under South African law, the usufructuary is not entitled to the minerals as such but to interest on the proceeds of mining, royalties payable on mining leases and moneys paid on options.

In general, the usufructuary will not be allowed to *open new mines* on the grounds that it would change the economic purpose of the land, amount to disorderly exploitation,[26] introduce substantial changes, and therefore substantially impair the property.[27] Under special mining laws in Austria,[28] Portugal, Spain and Italy, either the nude owner or the usufructuary, with the nude owner's consent, must obtain a licence to start mining operations.

[21] Poland makes an exception in the case of renewable trees and shrubs such as bamboo.

[22] See e.g. the German, Austrian, Greek, Belgian, Portuguese, Italian, Dutch, South African, Danish and Hungarian reports.

[23] Except according to the Belgian report if they are part of a nursery.

[24] See the Italian report.

[25] See e.g. the German, Austrian, Greek, Belgian, Dutch, Portuguese, Spanish, Italian and Scottish reports.

[26] In Germany and Portugal, the usufructuary is allowed to quarry for stone if this does not conflict with the ordinary exploitation of the land or does not alter its economic destination.

[27] See the German, Greek, Belgian and Spanish reports.

[28] Only stones from quarries belong to the landowner.

In Hungary, ownership of the land does not extend to the minerals below the land and minerals are considered the exclusive property of the State. Special Polish legislation permits the usufructuary to build and use mining equipment on the land in strict compliance with the provisions of the legislation. The usufructuary is obliged to inform the owner of his/her intentions and the owner is entitled to require security against future damage if the planned mining activity were to change the use of the land or conflicts with the proper management of the property.

Most jurisdictions[29] accept that *standing crops* belong to the nude owner on expiry of the usufruct as a *quid pro quo* for the fact that they became the property of the usufructuary when he acquired the usufruct.[30] Some jurisdictions achieve an equitable solution, by obliging the nude owner on expiry of the usufruct to reimburse the usufructuary for the cost of production of the crop up to the value of the standing crop.[31] Under Greek law, the usufructuary is further obliged to leave behind seeds, hay and fertilisers as required for an orderly cultivation of the next harvest. However, just as in the case of the tenant of agricultural land, the usufructuary's estate shall have a claim against the nude owner for compensation in respect of the quantity of produce that was left behind to the extent that he/she did not receive such items at the inception of the usufruct.

Italian law provides a more equitable solution. It divides the net proceeds of the crop between the usufructuary and the nude owner in proportion to the duration of their respective rights up to the time of harvesting. Hungarian law entitles the usufructuary to a portion of the standing crops proportionate to the labour and cost invested in their cultivation, which, interestingly, must be handed over to the usufructuary in kind. The Polish and the South African reports suggest that the usufructuary should have a claim on the ground of unjustified enrichment against a nude owner who becomes the owner of the standing crops on expiry of the usufruct.

In principle, the usufructuary is allowed to lease the property without the owner's consent and collect the rent as civil fruits until the expiry of the usufruct. Where the *usufruct expires six months before the next annual*

29 See the Austrian, Portuguese, Belgian, Spanish, Dutch and South African reports. But see the Scottish report.

30 Portuguese law achieves this by allocating fruits to the usufructuary on the date of harvesting (*iure corporis*) rather than the date of planting or sowing (*iure seminis*).

31 See the Austrian and Portuguese reports.

rent is due, most jurisdictions[32] will entitle the usufructuary to rent until the expiry of the usufruct and the nude owner thereafter until the termination of the lease. In Greece and Spain the nude owner is subrogated in such circumstances to the rights of the landlord (usufructuary) for the remaining period of the lease. If the lease is executed in a public deed or a private deed with a certified date, Italian law stipulates that if such lease comes to an end after the usufruct expired, the lease will continue for the remaining period of the lease up to a maximum period of five years with a division of rent as stated above. Hungarian law achieves the same result by providing that in such a situation the rent must be divided between the usufructuary and the nude owner in the same way as if the property was sold and transferred to the nude owner.

It is generally accepted that the holder of a *right of use* or of a *right of habitation* is allowed to use the property and to collect fruits for domestic purposes or to use the house on the property as a residence respectively. The fruits collected must be destined for immediate consumption by the usuary and his/her household and not for commercial exploitation. As evidenced by the Spanish and Italian reports, the right holder will only be allowed to collect wood, dead branches, dead trees and dead undergrowth from plantations and presumably also from fruit trees, decorative trees and shrubs as firewood for himself/herself and for his/her family. Because of the restricted content of the right, the usuary or the *habitator* will not be entitled to open new quarries or mines or even work existing ones. Spanish, Italian and Hungarian law does not allow either the usuary or the *habitator* to rent out the property. Traditionally, however, the usuary was allowed to rent out a room in the house, provided he/she occupied the rest of the house, and the *habitator* was allowed to rent out the entire house. Under the French Civil Code, a surviving spouse with a right of habitation is allowed to rent out the residential premises for which he/she no longer has any use (for example, because he/she has moved to a retirement home).

In principle, the holder of a *hereditary building right* (*superficiarius*) is entitled to improve the property by constructing buildings on the property, planting plantations and fruit trees, and sowing crops, but he/she is not entitled to open and work new mines and quarries on the land. In some jurisdictions,[33] the *superficiarius* is treated as the owner of the

[32] E.g. under German, Austrian, Belgian, Portuguese, Spanish, Italian, Scottish, South African, Hungarian and Polish law.

[33] See e.g. the Spanish, Belgian and Dutch reports.

improvements and can therefore exploit them for his/her own benefit if not restricted in the constitutive deed. The holder must maintain the plantations and trees which were on the land when he/she entered it. In some countries,[34] the holder is entitled to lease the land to a third person if it is not prohibited in the grant of the *superficies*. The tenant's right will be extinguished on expiry of the *superficies*.

If a *hereditary land lease* (*emphyteusis*) is granted by the state or local authority, Belgian law entitles the holder to exploit the property by carrying out standard operations in conformity with the purpose of the property and to reap its normal economic proceeds. The holder (*emphyteutor*) has at least the same rights as the usufructuary concerning plantations, fruit trees, ornamental trees or shrubs. He/she is further entitled to excavate stone, coal, turf, clay or similar substances from the soil if the landowner had already done so prior to the grant of the hereditary land lease. However, he/she is not allowed to open new mines or quarries. Standing crops left on the expiry of the land lease will belong to the owner on the model of usufruct. While the holder is in principle allowed to rent out the property, the expiry of the hereditary land lease will extinguish the lease also in Belgium and France.

Austria

In the case of an *income-producing lease*, the tenant is entitled to use the leased object and to enjoy its fruits. In principle, he/she is obliged to take due care when doing so and must not change the substance of the property. The exact extent of his/her rights depends on the contract, its purpose and local customs.[35] Hence, it is hardly possible to give an exact solution to the question of cutting plantations, trees and shrubs without considering the circumstances, the nature of the property and the contract concerned. As a general rule, the cutting of *plantations* and trees is only allowed if it is in accordance with local customs and not to an extent which will result in a substantial change of the property. It is probable that, generally, the tenant will have to prove why he is entitled to do so.

Mining activities are governed by the Law on Minerals (*Mineralrohstoffgesetz* BGBl I 38/1999, last amendment 84/2006). The

[34] France, Spain, Belgium and Italy.

[35] Würth, in Rummel, *Kommentar*, § 1098, para. 2; Iro, in Koziol, Bydlinski and Bollenberger, *Kommentar*, § 1098, para. 1; Binder, in Schwimann, *Praxiskommentar*, vol. 5, § 1096, para. 5.

requirements for prospecting and acquisition of minerals depend on the kind of minerals concerned. The Law on Minerals distinguishes between three types of minerals, namely those which can be acquired by anyone ('free minerals' (s. 3)), those which belong to the State ('state owned minerals' (s. 4)) and those which belong to the respective landowners (s. 5). In any case, prospecting, mining and acquisition of minerals require certain licences and/or approvals by the competent authorities. Parties to the respective public law proceedings are the applicant, the landowner, sometimes also neighbours, federal states and municipalities (ss. 30, 37, 76, 81 and 116).[36] If the tenant wants to continue existing mining operations he/she not only needs to conclude a contract with the landowner but also needs a mining licence recognised by the competent authorities (s 52).

Upon termination of the lease, the tenant is obliged to return the leased property in a condition conforming to the particular season concerned (Civil Code, § 1109). There is no regulation as to the distribution of the fruits if the agricultural lease expires before the fruits are harvested. It seems to be appropriate to apply Civil Code, § 519, which applies to usufruct by analogy. Accordingly, any fruits not yet harvested on termination of the income-producing lease becomes the property of the landowner. However, the landowner has to compensate the tenant for any expenses incurred in producing these fruits. Civil fruits (rents) of any sub-lease, on the other hand, must be distributed proportionally.[37]

According to Civil Code, § 1098, the tenant is entitled to sub-lease the land, provided that the sub-lease is neither to the disadvantage of the landlord nor expressly prohibited in the contract.

Under a *usufruct*, the usufructuary is entitled to use the land without any restraints as long as he/she does not interfere with the substance of the property (Civil Code, § 509). Hence, in principle, the usufructuary can cut trees of a *plantation*, but not to the extent that this results in the clearing of the plantation (*Kahlschlag*).[38] Proceeds from overexploitation must be returned to the owner.[39] There is neither express statutory provision nor case law which covers *decorative trees*, *fruit trees* or *shrubs*. However, from the general duty to maintain the substance and not to

[36] Randl, *Neuordnung des Bergrechts*, p. 248.

[37] *Binder* draws a similar conclusion in Schwimann, *Praxiskommentar*, vol. 5, § 1096, para. 21. For details as to sub-leases, see Case 9.

[38] Kletecka, in Koziol and Welser, *Bürgerliches Recht*, vol. 1, p. 425.

[39] Hofmann, in Rummel, *Kommentar*, § 511, para. 1.

change the type of husbandry, it follows that the usufructuary is allowed to cut them only if this is necessary for good husbandry.

In principle, minerals are deemed to be fruits. However, as mentioned above, some minerals are free (and can thus be taken by anybody) and some are considered state-owned. If the usufructuary wants to continue existing mining operations he/she not only needs to conclude a contract with the landowner but also requires a mining licence recognised by the competent authorities (Law on Minerals, s. 52).

After termination of the usufruct, the landowner has a proprietary right to get back his/her land in a condition conforming to the time of return (Civil Code, § 518). The distribution of the then existing fruits is subject to Civil Code, § 519. Consequently, the fruits not yet severed on return of the property belong to the landowner. However, the landowner has to compensate the usufructuary for all expenses incurred in producing these fruits to the extent of the value of the fruits. Civil fruits (rent) must be distributed proportionally.[40] Such rent may arise from leases which were taken over by the usufructuary from the landowner or created by the usufructuary himself.[41]

Belgium

The Law on Agricultural Lease applies to the *lease of a farm*. The agricultural tenant must exploit the property as a *bonus paterfamilias* according to the intended purpose determined by the provisions of the lease and the surrounding circumstances. The tenant may reap the natural and civil fruits. Upon termination of the lease, the tenant must return the property in the condition in which it was at the inception of the lease, or at least in the condition in which it will be after orderly exploitation. In general, the tenant is not entitled to encroach on the substance or the income-producing capacity of the property. Concrete questions regarding specific use and enjoyment by the tenant are determined by the contract: did the parties explicitly or implicitly allow such use?

The guidelines with regard to the *cutting of plantations*, *fruit trees*, *decorative trees* and *shrubs* are whether such acts are considered reasonable use (as a *bonus paterfamilias*) in accordance with the interpretation of the provisions of the lease contract. In principle, the tenant will not be entitled to cut plantations for timber, cut fruit trees, decorative trees or

[40] *Ibid.*, § 519, para. 1.
[41] For details regarding leases created by the usufructuary, see Case 9.

shrubs, unless this is regarded as a reasonable exploitation of the farm as a *bonus paterfamilias* or such exploitation has been agreed upon. However, cutting will be allowed if it is regarded as part of normal maintenance. Note that the Law on Agricultural Lease does not apply in case of forest trees or standard fruit trees.

The tenant may remove plants and trees that obstruct intended building construction with the owner's approval or by court order. The plants removed belong to the owner.

In the case of *mining and quarrying operations*, public law requirements must be complied with. In general, the tenant is not entitled to open mines or quarries and/or continue mining operations. He/she may not exploit the underground, unless it is considered reasonable use of the property in the manner of a *bonus paterfamilias* or has been agreed upon by the parties, for example, if the mine or quarry was opened at the inception of the lease. Note that the Law on Agricultural Lease does not apply in the case of exploitations of minerals on the property.

Standing crop which remains on the land on termination of an agricultural lease belongs to the landlord, who is under an obligation to compensate the tenant for expenses incurred in the production of the crop. However, if *force majeur* prevented the tenant from harvesting the crop before the term of the lease has expired, he/she will be entitled to do so for his/her own account (Law on Agricultural Lease, art. 45).

If the tenant creates a further right such as a *sub-lease* on the land, he/she is entitled to the proceeds of the sub-lease. The sub-lease will terminate automatically on termination of the principal lease.[42] The question regarding the fruits of such sub-lease after termination of the principal lease will thus not arise.

In the case of a *usufruct*, the usufructuary is in principle entitled to the natural and civil fruits of the property and becomes the owner thereof on collection. He/she must exploit the property as a decent owner, according to the judgment of a *bonus paterfamilias*. On termination of the usufruct, the usufructuary must return the property in the condition it was at the inception of the usufruct, or at least in the condition it would have been after orderly and normal use. The *rights of use* and *habitation* are restricted to the needs of the usuary and the *habitator* and their families and the usuary and *habitator* are entitled to collect fruits for themselves and their households.

[42] See Case 9.

The rights of the usufructuary with regard to *plantations*, *fruit trees*, *decorative trees* and *shrubs* are regulated in detail in Civil Code, arts. 590 to 594. In general, a usufructuary is only entitled to remove these trees in accordance with local customs and practices. Consequently, the usufructuary is entitled to *clear shrubs* (undergrowth) and clusters of bushes from the property, and *remove trees for timber from plantations* (Civil Code, art. 590–1). The time of removal and the number of trees removed must, however, accord with commercial custom and the practice of previous owners. *Decorative* and *fruit trees* must in principle be left untouched unless they were uprooted or damaged by accident. These trees and even undamaged trees may be cut and used to carry out repairs on the property for which the usufructuary is responsible. In such a case the usufructuary is obliged to replace the trees (Civil Code, arts. 592 and 594). In addition, the usufructuary may remove trees which are part of a nursery, provided they are replaced in order to maintain the value of the nursery.

The usufructuary may undertake *mining operations* on the property after he/she has complied with certain public law requirements. B may then continue operating mines and quarries that were operated prior to the inception of the usufruct (Civil Code, art. 598). He/she is not, however, entitled to open new mines or quarries which were not in operation at the inception of the usufruct (Civil Code, art. 598, para. 2).

Standing crops which remain on the soil on termination of the usufruct belong to the nude owner without any obligation on his/her part to reimburse the usufructuary for any cost involved (Civil Code, art. 585). This is based on the principle that allows B to retain the benefit of standing crops on the land on inception of the usufruct.

The usufructuary is entitled to the civil fruits (*burgerlijke vruchten*) of the property (Civil Code, art. 586). Civil fruits include the proceeds from the *lease of farms or houses* which is not possible in case of a right of use or habitation. Since these fruits are deemed to be acquired by the usufructuary on a daily basis, they belong to the usufructuary on a *pro rata* basis in proportion to the duration of the usufruct. Thus, even if the proceeds of the lease become due on an annual basis and the usufruct expires six months before such maturity, the usufructuary will still be entitled to his/her *pro rata* share of the proceeds, unless the parties have agreed otherwise.

B, the holder of a *hereditary land lease*, although entitled to the full use of the property, is not entitled to do anything that will diminish the value of the property. In general, B will be entitled to cut trees for timber in a *plantation* and cut *fruit trees, decorative trees and shrubs* which he planted himself. Trees that have fallen or died naturally belong to B, on condition of replacement (Law on Emphyteutic Lease, art. 4). Concerning the existing trees and shrubs, it is argued that the holder has at least the same rights as the usufructuary.[43] Certain public law requirements must be complied with before the holder may undertake *mining operations*. B is not entitled to excavate stone, coal, turf, clay or similar substances from the soil unless such excavation has already commenced prior to the inception of the hereditary lease (art. 3). In the case of standing crops remaining on the land on termination of the hereditary lease, the rules with regard to usufruct are applicable. If the holder leases the land or house, he/she may collect the rent for the duration of the hereditary lease but not beyond. The question regarding the proportionate division of an annual rent will thus not arise.[44]

Under a *hereditary building lease* (*superficies*), B is in principle deemed to have ownership of all improvements on the land, including the benefit of the fruits of the property. The hereditary building lease is rarely used in the context of a farm and the Law on Building Lease does not contain any provisions on the division of the proceeds of a farm between the owner and the holder of a right of surface. However, since the holder of the hereditary building lease is considered the owner of all improvements on the land, he/she is entitled to cut *plantations* for timber and cut *fruit trees* and *decorative trees* planted by him/her. The holder has no right to the soil beneath the surface of the soil as the land is divided horizontally leaving only the surface at the disposal of the holder. He/she is therefore not entitled to *work existing mines or open new mines*. In the absence of case law, the rules applicable to usufruct will probably apply in this case of crops remaining on the land on termination of the hereditary building lease. The holder will be entitled to the proceeds of a sub-lease granted by him/her for the duration of the building lease. The question regarding the proportionate division of an annual rent will thus not arise.[45]

Denmark

In Danish law there is no operative rule regarding the cutting of *plantations*. The answer depends on the interpretation of the *lease*. Usually the

[43] de Page and Dekkers, *Traité élémentaire*, no. 703. [44] See Case 9. [45] See Case 9.

tenant will be obliged to cultivate the land and keep it in a good agricultural state.[46]

A tenant will normally not be entitled to conduct *mining operations* on the land unless otherwise agreed, for example, if the contract contains provisions to that effect or if the rented area contains a quarry when the agreement is concluded.

B is not allowed to harvest *standing crops* after the term of the contract has expired.[47] If notice is given before the termination, B will be allowed to harvest the crops until the end of the notice period.

It is a commonly accepted principle (and an operative rule) that a person who derives rights from a time-limited contract, namely a person *sub-letting* land or buildings, does not obtain better rights than his/her contractual partner.[48] The owner (A) is entitled to regain possession when his/her contract with B expires even though B has sub-let the premises to somebody else and this person has a contract for a longer period. The latter may in fact sue B for damages caused by entering into a contract that is impossible to fulfil.

England

With regard to plantations,[49] the property in *trees*, or of that which is likely to become timber, is in the landlord, and the right as to *bushes* is in the tenant.[50] Until a timber tree is felled, a tenant can enjoy all fruits and benefits from it.[51] Felling a tree will amount to waste, but a tenant may remove *dead trees*[52] and chop down trees in the interests of maintenance.[53]

Whether or not leases *include the minerals* underground or not is a question of construction of the grant. Mines are land, and can therefore properly be the subject matter of a grant.[54] However, if a mine is not open at the date of the grant, then digging for minerals is actionable as waste without more. Once again, a tenant has the right to use certain

[46] This is not an operative rule but the most common clause in contracts. See Mortensen, *Landbrugsforpagtning*, pp. 375, 388.
[47] This is not an operative rule but will most probably be the default rule.
[48] See Jespersen, *Lejeret*, vol. 1, p. 83.
[49] See generally Heathcote-Williams, *Foa's Landlord and Tenant*, pp. 286–7.
[50] *Berriman* v. *Peacock* (1832) 9 Bing. 384.
[51] *Herlakenden's Case* (1589) 4 Co. Rep. 62a 62 b.
[52] *Doe d Wetherell* v. *Bird* (1833) 6 C. & P. 195.
[53] See Lewison, *Woodfall's Law of Landlord and Tenant*, para. 13–180.
[54] *Halsbury's Laws of England*, vol. 31, para. 321.

minerals – such as gravel – for reparations (as with trees). Again, the law is obscure, and ancient, and has not been the subject of recent litigation.

At common law, the tenant had the right to emblements, to '*reap what he has sown*'.[55] The right is restricted to entering to reap crops which mature within a year. This means that if the crop was planted during the currency of the term, the right to reap arises if the crop matures within a year of that date. The right is restricted to entering within a year to reap crops which mature after termination of the lease.[56]

The general effect of termination of the principal tenancy is that any *sub-tenancy* under it also ends.[57] The rule does not, however, apply to surrender or merger.[58] In the case of surrender, this is explicable by virtue of the fact that the landlord takes the tenancy he has granted to B subject to any valid interests which B has created, including a sub-tenancy to C.[59] Surrender may occur expressly by deed (Law of Property Act, s. 52)[60] or alternatively by operation of law.[61] Merger occurs where the tenant acquires the reversion from the landlord, or where a third party acquires both the lease and the reversion. In these circumstances, the lower estate merges with the higher. Again, the sub-tenancy survives. Statute preserves the covenants in this situation so that they continue to operate (Law of Property Act, s. 139). Rent is payable to the 'new' landlord.

France

If the tenant does not perform the stipulations under an *agricultural lease* and damage is caused, the Civil Code provides that the landlord can cancel the lease, re-enter the property and claim compensation for damages (Civil Code, arts. 1764 and 1766). The Rural Code, art. L 411–27 refers to this rule of the Civil Code, but provides in addition (Ordonnance no. 2006–870 of 13 July 2006) that the fact that the tenant engages, with respect to the leased land, in practices which have as their objective the preservation of water resources, biodiversity, landscaping,

[55] See also Schedule 8 to the Law on Agricultural Holdings 1986.

[56] *Graves* v. *Weld* (1833) 5 B. & Ad. 105. See generally *Halsbury's Laws of England*, vol. 1.2, para. 382.

[57] *Barrett* v. *Morgan* [2000] 2 AC 264.

[58] See Lewison, *Woodfall's Law of Landlord and Tenant*, para. 16–163.

[59] See Hargrave and Butler, *Coke upon Littleton*, p. 338a.

[60] This is so, irrespective of whether the lease was created orally or not.

[61] As to which, see Harpum, Bridges and Dixon, *Megarry and Wade's Property*, para. 14–174.

quality of produce, soil and air, or the prevention of natural risks and the battle against erosion, cannot be raised in support of a suit by the landlord for the cancellation of the lease. The tenant may remove embankments, hedges or trees to combine a number of adjoining parcels in order to improve the agricultural exploitation of the property, but only if the landlord, having been duly informed, does not object to such measures (Rural Code, art. L 411–28C). The provisions in the lease contract which set out the condition of the property at the inception of the lease (art. L 411–4) will determine, on termination of the lease, the improvements made and the deterioration caused by the tenant during the term of the lease.

The tenant will be entitled to *cut trees* if he is allowed to do so under the terms of the lease, or in accordance with Rural Code, arts. L 411–27 and L 411–28. The tenant is entitled to *open mines or quarries* and/or *continue mineral operations* only if he/she is allowed to do so under the terms of the lease or in accordance with Rural Code, art. L 411–27. The tenant is entitled to harvest *standing crops* after the termination of the lease if allowed under the terms of the lease. An oral lease of a rural tenement is deemed to have been concluded for a period which will allow the tenant to harvest all the produce of the farm (Civil Code, art. 1774). Thus an agricultural lease of arable land, a vineyard, or any other agricultural tenement whose entire produce is harvested during the course of a year is deemed to be concluded for one year.

Under the general law of lease, Civil Code, art. 1717 allows the tenant to *sub-let* the property unless it is forbidden by the terms of the lease. The tenant can collect rent from the sub-tenant, but only until the lease expires.

Since a *residential lease* typically turns on the identity of the tenant, the law forbids sub-letting, save in the case where the landlord assents to it in writing. If the landlord authorises sub-letting, the sub-lease is governed by general law by virtue of which the sub-lease is terminated on expiry of the principal lease. Thus, the tenant cannot collect rent after the lease has expired. The amount of rent due in terms of the sub-lease must be approved by the landlord and may not exceed the rent due from the tenant (Law of 1989, art. 8).

The sub-letting of *agricultural land* is forbidden (Rural Code, art. L 411–35). However, the landlord or a tribunal[62] may allow the tenant to grant sub-leases for leisure or vacation use for no more than three

[62] See Case 9.

consecutive months, or sub-leases of buildings meant for residential use. This authorisation must specify the portion of the rent which must be redirected to the landlord to cover the cost of the work which will ultimately have to be carried out on the property, and the manner in which the reimbursement due to the tenant at the end of the lease will be calculated. This provision of the Rural Code is mandatory.

Under a *usufruct*, the usufructuary is entitled to enjoy and use the property in the same way as an owner, on condition that the substance of the property is preserved (Civil Code, art. 578). With regard to *plantations*, the usufructuary is allowed to cut the trees in the plantation periodically, in accordance with usages of the locality and surrounding owners (Civil Code, art. 591). He/she is, however, under a duty to replace the trees. The same applies to underwood which the usufructuary is entitled under Civil Code, art. 590 to remove in accordance with the usage and customs of the locality and the surrounding owners regarding the time of cutting and the quota of underwood that he/she is allowed to appropriate. The usufructuary also seems entitled to cut thicket, staddles for supporting hay, props for supporting vineyards (Civil Code, art. 593) and forest trees, and to remove nursery trees as long as he/she replaces them in accordance with the customs of the locality (Civil Code, art. 509, para. 2). For the rest, the usufructuary is not allowed to interfere with wood or timber trees, except when using trees which were uprooted or broken by accident, to carry out repairs that he/she is bound to make on the property. For this purpose, the usufructuary may even cut down trees if the nude owner agrees that such action is necessary for the preservation of the property (Civil Code, art. 592).

The usufructuary may appropriate *dead fruit trees* and those which are uprooted or broken by accident, subject to the condition that they be replaced (Civil Code, art. 594). The usufructuary is entitled, in the same way as the owner, to *operate mines and quarries* which are being worked at the inception of the usufruct. Where the operation of the mines and quarries may not be carried on without a concession, such concession must be obtained from the President of the Republic before operation may commence (Civil Code, art. 598). The usufructuary is not entitled to *open new mines or quarries* or to extract peat from the land if it has not been done before. The usufructuary is not entitled to harvest *standing crops* after the termination of his/her right. Standing fruits and crops belong to the nude owner without compensation on either side for ploughing and seeds (Civil Code, art. 585).

Since the usufructuary is entitled to exploit the fruits of the property, he is permitted to *lease the property* and collect the rent as civil fruits. However, on expiry of the usufruct only the nude owner, having regained complete ownership of the property, is entitled to collect the rent emanating from the sub-lease.

The right of *habitation* permits B to reside on the property (along with his/her family), but not to sub-lease it or to collect income from it (Civil Code, art. 634). As an exception, a surviving spouse with a right of habitation (Civil Code, art. 764) is entitled to lease out the residential premises in order to draw the income necessary to move to other suitable accommodation (for example, a retirement home) if the premises in question no longer suits his/her needs.

The holder of a *hereditary lease of land* (*emphyteusis*) is entitled to develop and improve the land by planting trees or crops, or by constructing buildings on the land. The law only requires him/her not to diminish the value of the land. It must thus be determined whether or not the *cutting down of trees* has diminished the value of the land. The holder may sub-lease the land and collect rent until his/her time-limited interest in the property expires, with no stipulation to the contrary being possible. The sub-tenant of the holder of the hereditary lease has no right of renewal against the landowner of the property and cannot claim an indemnity from him/her if the holder of the hereditary lease is evicted from the property. On expiry of the hereditary lease, the title of the sub-tenant is extinguished.[63]

The holder of the *hereditary building lease* is entitled to sub-lease the buildings and collect rent with no stipulation to the contrary being possible (Code for Construction and Habitation, art. L 251–3). Every sub-lease or title of occupation of any kind which burdens the buildings is extinguished upon expiry of the building lease (art. L 251–6).

Germany

B will only be entitled to the fruits of the farm under an *agricultural lease* (*Landpachtvertrag*), which allows him/her to enjoy the fruits of the farm (Civil Code, § 585). As a general rule, the tenant of a farm must exploit the property according to the ordinary standards of cultivation (Civil Code, § 586(1) sent. 3) and may reap the benefits (natural and civil fruits) of such exploitation (Civil Code, § 585(2) referring to, § 581(1)). In order

[63] Civ. 3, 09.02.2005, Constr. urb. Apr. 2005, no. 73.

to avoid disputes over the original condition of the leased property, Civil Code, § 585b provides that the parties to this type of lease must agree on a description of the property at the outset of the lease.

Consequently, B is only allowed to *cut plantations* if such activity is in accordance with the accepted standards of exploitation of plantations in that area (allowing, for example, the felling of trees every seven years). Whereas plantations of timber are destined to be felled, fruit trees are meant to be exploited by reaping the fruit on a regular basis. Cutting down *fruit trees* will destroy the substance of the leased property and is thus not permitted. Similar considerations apply with regard to *decorative trees*. *Shrubs* can only be cut if they were originally intended to be cut.

Mining is subject to special mining legislation. Any person proposing to conduct mining operations falling within the scope of application of the German Federal Mining Act (*Bundesberggesetz*) must apply for a licence to mine. The holder of such licence (*Bergbauberechtiger*) obtains the right to appropriate minerals collected on the land (*Aneignungsrecht*). The tenant does not have the power to open new quarries, given that such exploitation will go beyond the agricultural destiny of the property (Civil Code, § 590(1)). The tenant may, however, exploit those quarries which were already in operation at the beginning of the lease.

B is not entitled to *harvest standing crops* after the termination of his/her right. However, if the lease expires before the end of the harvesting season (*Pachtjahr*), A must compensate B for the value of standing crops, which, according to accepted standards, have to be harvested by the end of the harvesting season (Civil Code, § 596a(1)), taking into account the usual expenses that B would have made in order to harvest the crops.

The tenant is not entitled to *sub-let* the property without the consent of the landowner (Civil Code, § 589).

Usufruct is the only real right which can be applied to this question. The usufructuary is entitled to the natural and civil fruits of the property (Civil Code, §§ 1030 and 99 ff.). He/she becomes owner of the natural fruits of the property on collection (Civil Code, § 954). However, the usufructuary must respect the typical (customary) economic destiny of the property and may only exploit it according to the accepted standards of cultivation (Civil Code, §§ 1036(2) and 1039(1)). After termination of his/her right, the usufructuary must return the property without substantial impairment of the substance (Civil Code, § 1055).

The usufructuary is only entitled to cut *plantations* which are meant to be felled. However, he/she may cut plantations for timber in accordance with the harvesting programme (business plan) agreed upon by the parties. Each party is entitled to claim at any time that an expert be appointed at a cost shared by both to work out a detailed harvesting programme (Civil Code, § 1038(1)). B may not cut *fruit trees, decorative trees* or *shrubs* unless they are dead.

The usufructuary enjoys the fruits of the *mines and quarries* already in operation at the beginning of the usufruct. He/she is also entitled to open up new quarries as long as this does not substantially alter the economic destiny of the property (Civil Code, § 1037(2)).

The usufructuary may *sub-let* the property in which case he/she is entitled to the civil fruits (rent) produced by the lease. The usufructuary's right to sub-let the property includes both ordinary and agricultural lease. The usufructuary does not need to obtain the owner's consent for sub-letting the property. Alternatively, where the usufruct expires six months before the proceeds of the sub-lease become due, the rent in terms of the sub-lease is divided between the usufructuary and the owner of the property in proportion to the duration of their rights (*pro rata temporis*) (Civil Code, § 101, no. 2).

Greece

The *agricultural tenant* is obliged to exploit the land in an orderly manner (Civil Code, art. 619), namely with due care and in conformity with the intended purpose of the land[64] and, in particular, to preserve the productivity of the land (Civil Code, art. 623).[65] Without the landlord's consent he is not allowed to change the existing method of exploitation in a way that may substantially influence the exploitation on expiry of the lease (Civil Code, art. 623, para. 2). He/she is obliged to restore the land, livestock and equipment to the condition in which it would have been if during the lease they had been exploited in an orderly fashion (Civil Code, art. 629). From other provisions (Civil Code, arts. 621, 624 and 625), it seems that this default position may be altered by special contractual provisions or by local usage. In the case of a *crop-sharing lease* where the rent consists of a share in the produce of the land, the landlord shall assume the general management for the exploitation of the leased land and the supervision of all relevant work in accordance with the conditions laid down in the contract or prescribed by local usage (Civil Code, art. 642). The

[64] Filios, *Obligations*, p. 327; AP 1225/1979; NoV (1980), p. 703.
[65] AP 898/1974; NoV (1975), p. 496.

crop-sharing tenant is further bound to notify the landlord before he/she starts harvesting the crop (Civil Code, art. 644).

Since the cutting of timber *plantations* at regular intervals would be considered orderly exploitation of agricultural land and in conformity with its intended purpose, the tenant may cut these plantations in accordance with the local customs of the area. This is, however, subject to the provisions contained in the contract of lease. By contrast, the cutting of *fruit trees* (where orderly exploitation exists and the intended purpose of the lease is the collection of fruits), *decorative trees* and *shrubs* will not be considered orderly exploitation except in so far as the cutting of dead branches and the replacement of dead trees are required to restore the land to the condition it was in when possession was assumed by the tenant. This position can again be qualified by differing local customs or a contrary provision in the contract of lease. In the case of a *crop-sharing lease*, the landlord is given more control over the general management and supervision of the exploitation of the land in accordance with local custom and conditions laid down in the contract of lease (Civil Code, art. 642).

The ownership of land extends to the space above and below the ground, unless otherwise stipulated in the law (Civil Code, art. 1001). The Legislative Decree 210/1973 on the *Law on Mining* (*Περί Μεταλλευτικού Κώδικος*) introduces an exception to this rule.[66] The Law divides minerals found in nature into two categories for the purposes of the law, namely (a) those listed in art. 2, which include, among others, copper, gold, silver, sulphur, and gems, and (b) those listed in art. 5, which include minerals used mainly for construction such as marble, limestone, chalk and gypsum.

The right of ownership of the land does not extend to the minerals of the first category, irrespective of whether such minerals are found on or under the surface of the land (art. 3). A person interested in extracting such minerals must first obtain a licence from the Prefect entitling him/her to search for such mineral deposits (arts. 15 ff.). If, after the granting of the licence and during its validity, mineral deposits are found, the person who conducted the search can submit a request to the competent Prefect to be granted the whole or a part of the land for which the licence has been issued (art. 44).

Minerals of the second category belong to the owner of the land where they are found (art. 6). The owner is entitled to exploit these minerals subject to restrictions of special provisions on quarries.

[66] For real rights provided by special legislation, see Georgiades, *Property*, vol. 2, pp. 51 ff.

Furthermore, Law 669/1977, art. 3 regulating licences for the exploitation of quarries grants the right to exploit quarries to the owner of the land or the person to whom the owner has assigned his/her right by notarial deed. For such exploitation, a licence granted by a ministerial decision is needed (Law 669/1977, arts. 4 ff.).

In the case of the lease of land for which a licence to extract minerals has been obtained, the tenant would be entitled to *operate the mine or quarry*. The lease of a mine[67] or quarry[68] has been characterised by the Greek Courts as belonging to the category of leases of other income-producing property. Civil Code, art. 638 provides that the provisions on the lease of agricultural land, with the exception of Civil Code, arts. 632 to 637, are applicable by analogy to these leases. The notion is derived from Civil Code, art. 961, § 1, which stipulates that fruits of property are its organic products as well as everything obtained from the destination (intended purpose) of the property. Consequently, minerals mined are natural fruits, as they are extracted from the mine or quarry in conformity with its destined use.[69]

On termination of the agricultural lease at the end of the harvest period, the tenant will be entitled to harvest the *crops remaining on the land*.[70] Termination of a lease before the end of the annual harvest period prevents an agricultural tenant from harvesting crops that are still on the land. He/she will, however, be entitled to claim for expenses incurred in the production of the said crops to the extent that such expenses do not exceed the value of the crops (Civil Code, art. 631). Furthermore, upon the expiry of the lease, an agricultural tenant is obliged to leave on the land such quantity of its produce, particularly seeds, hay and fertilisers as is required for an orderly cultivation of the land until the next harvest. To the extent the tenant had not received such quantities of produce at the inception of the lease, the agricultural tenant shall be entitled to claim compensation from the landlord in respect of the items he/she leaves on the land (Civil Code, art. 636).

67 AP 165/1964; NoV (1964), p. 610; Georgiadou, in Georgiades and Stathopoulos, *GCC, Collective Analysis*, art. 638, no. 3 (399).

68 AP 1033/1979; NoV (1980), p. 473; AP 816/1973; NoV (1974), p. 325; Patras Court of Appeal 670/1996 Arm. 1997 1121; Nafplio Court of First Instance 12/1987 Arm. 1987 750; Syros Court of First Instance 183/1967; NoV (1968), p. 435; Lamia Court of First Instance 214/1965; NoV (1965), p. 1092; Georgiadou, in Georgiades and Stathopoulos, *GCC, Collective Analysis*, art. 638, no. 3 (399).

69 Georgiades, *Property*, vol. 2, p. 116; Georgiadou, in Georgiades and Stathopoulos, *GCC, Collective Analysis*, art. 961, no. 6.

70 Georgiadou, in Georgiades and Stathopoulos, *GCC, Collective Analysis*, art. 631, no. 1 (393).

In an ordinary contract of lease (including the lease of a house), the tenant is entitled, in the absence of contrary agreement,[71] to assign his/her right of use and in particular to sub-let the property. In such a case, the tenant will be liable to the landlord for any damage attributable to the fault of the sub-tenant, even if the landlord has consented to the sub-lease (Civil Code, art. 593).[72] In the case of an agricultural lease, the default position is that in the absence of a contrary agreement or local custom, an agricultural tenant (tenant-farmer) is not entitled to assign the use of the leased land and particularly to sub-lease it, without the consent of the landlord (Civil Code, art. 624).[73] The rationale for this distinction is that the agricultural landlord entrusted the land to a particular tenant on account of the latter's known expertise to cultivate the property in a proper and orderly manner.[74] If the tenant-farmer sub-leases the farm without the consent of the landlord, the landlord has the right to terminate the contract immediately and to sue for damages for breach of contract (Civil Code, art. 620 applying Civil Code, art. 594).[75]

The terms of the sub-lease may differ from the terms of the initial lease. It is therefore likely that the duration of the sub-lease may extend beyond the duration of the lease.[76] In such a case, however, the sub-tenant's right to use the property is not enforceable against the landlord, who by virtue of Civil Code, art. 599, § 2 may claim the property from the sub-tenant upon expiry of the lease.[77] The contractual relationship between the sub-landlord and the sub-tenant would nevertheless still be valid and the rules of the Greek Civil Code on lease would be applicable. If the sub-tenant is therefore deprived of the use of the property by the landlord, his/her obligation towards the sub-landlord to pay the rent will no longer be sustained (Civil Code, arts. 583 and 576).[78]

[71] Note that, as a rule, the standard forms of leases, prepared by the homeowners' association and usually used in everyday transactions, include terms preventing the tenant from assigning the use of the leased land, in particular through a sub-lease, without the consent of the landlord.

[72] Athens Court of Appeal 9825/1979; NoV (1980), p. 1182.

[73] AP 898/1974; NoV (1975), p. 496.

[74] Georgiadou, in Georgiades and Stathopoulos, *GCC, Collective Analysis*, art. 624, no. 2 (388).

[75] *Ibid.* art. 624, no. 3 (388).

[76] Rapsomanikis, in Georgiades and Stathopoulos, *GCC, Collective Analysis*, art. 599, no. 8 (327); Dacoronia, *Sub-lease*, 89 n. 47 and 42 n. 89.

[77] Dacoronia, *Sub-lease*, 89–90; Athens Court of Appeal 7760/1985; EllDni (1985), p. 1384.

[78] Dacoronia, *Sub-lease*, 86–7.

In the case of *usufruct*, the usufructuary is entitled to use and collect the fruits of the property without impairing its substance (Civil Code, art. 1142). In exercising his/her right, the usufructuary must preserve the intended economic purpose of the property and exploit the property with care and in accordance with the rules of orderly exploitation[79] without introducing substantial changes to the property (Civil Code, art. 1148). In the case of the usufruct of a plantation, a mine or a quarry, either the usufructuary or the nude owner has the right to require that the land must be exploited according to a plan prepared at a cost shared by them (Civil Code, art. 1149). Any one of the parties may request the court to appoint an expert to work out a detailed harvesting programme at a cost shared by both parties.[80]

In accordance with the above principles, the usufructuary will be entitled to cut down the *timber trees* as they are considered fruits of the land if they are meant to be felled at regular intervals. If exploited in accordance with a management plan, the exploitation must follow the guidelines set out in that plan.[81] Since the fruits must be collected without impairment of the substance or economic purpose of the property and according to the rules of orderly exploitation, the usufructuary will not be able to cut down *fruit trees*, *decorative trees* or *shrubs* unless it represents an orderly exploitation. The removal of dead branches and the replacement of dead trees or shrubs in order to maintain the economic purpose of the property will probably fall into this category.

The usufructuary will be entitled to continue *mining operations* in accordance with an exploitation plan if required by one of the parties. The usufructuary will, however, not be allowed to open new quarries or mines as this would change the economic purpose of the land, will not be in accordance with its orderly exploitation and against the prohibition on introducing substantial changes to the property.

The usufructuary of agricultural property is not entitled to collect *standing crops* which are not harvested on termination of the usufruct. He/she may, however, claim reimbursement of the expenses incurred in connection with the production of the crop to the extent that such reimbursement does not exceed the value of the crop (Civil Code, art.

79 Georgiades, *Property*, vol. 2, p. 63.

80 Karasis, in Georgiades and Stathopoulos, *GCC, Collective Analysis*, art. 1149, no. 2 (87).

81 Balis, *Property*, p. 354; Karasis, in Georgiades and Stathopoulos, *GCC, Collective Analysis*, art. 1149, no. 3 (88). If the usufructuary does not follow the guidelines of the plan, the nude owner can file an action forcing him to do so and sue for damages, in appropriate cases.

1162). In addition, the usufructuary is obliged to leave such quantity of the produce of the property, in particular seeds, hay and fertilisers as is required for an orderly cultivation of the property until the next harvest. However, to the extent that he/she had not received such items at the inception of the usufruct, he/she shall have a claim against the nude owner for compensation in respect of the items he leaves on the land (Civil Code, art. 1163).

The usufructuary has the right to collect the fruits of the property, including civil fruits such as the proceeds of a lease entered into by him/her (Civil Code, art. 961). Where the usufruct comes to an end during the term of the lease, certain provisions on lease are applied by analogy (Civil Code, art. 1164). These provisions (Civil Code, arts. 614–16 and 618) deal with the continuation of the lease as well as the prepayment, assignment or attachment of the relevant rent when an alienation of the leased land takes place during the term of the lease.[82] The only lease that will survive the expiry of the usufruct will be a lease prepared in a deed which bears a certified date (Civil Code, art. 614).[83] In such an event the nude owner will, by analogy, be subrogated to the rights and obligations flowing from the lease subject to any agreement to the contrary in the lease.

Hungary

On the basis of a *lease*, the tenant may use the property in a proper manner and in a way prescribed by the contract (Civil Code, § 425(1)). Under an income-producing lease, the tenant can use the property and collect its natural and civil fruits according to the rules of ordinary management (Civil Code, § 453). The concepts of proper use and ordinary management certainly do not cover the *cutting of fruit trees*, *decorative trees* or *shrubs*, but will cover the cutting of *plantations* for timber if they are cut regularly according to the rules of ordinary management. By analogy to usufruct, the principle of ordinary management also applies to the *opening of mines* or *quarries* and the *working of existing mines* or *quarries*.

Again, Civil Code, § 125(2), pertaining to usufruct, applies by analogy to income-producing leases. The tenant will not be allowed to harvest *standing crops* on termination of the lease, but can claim a portion of the fruit in kind corresponding with his/her labour used and expenses incurred in the production of the crop.

[82] See Case 2. [83] Balis, *Property*, p. 374.

The tenant (B) is only allowed to *sub-let* the farm under certain conditions and with the permission of the landlord.[84] If the farm is sub-let, the tenant is entitled to the proceeds resulting from the sub-lease. The sub-let of the farm does not create a legal relationship between the principal landlord and the sub-tenant. Hence, if the principal lease *expires six months before maturity* of the sub-lease, while the proceeds of the latter become due on an annual basis, the principal landlord will not be entitled to the rent of the sub-lease, nor will he/she be obliged to continue the lease. At the same time, the sub-landlord will breach the contract concluded with the sub-tenant since the sub-lease is terminated before its term expired. Accordingly, the sub-tenant may terminate the sub-lease as a result of the tenant's breach of contract and claim damages.

The *usufructuary* and the *usuary* are entitled to possess and use the property and to collect its fruits. They must, however, exercise their rights according to the standards of ordinary management. Accordingly, the usufructuary and the usuary are not entitled to cut *fruit trees*, *decorative trees* or *shrubs*. They may, however, fell *plantations* for timber if the regular cutting of the plantation is in accordance with ordinary management and the custom of the locality.

As regards *mines and quarries*, the Civil Code, § 96 provides that ownership of the land does not cover underground resources or natural sources of energy, which are exclusively state property (Civil Code, § 172(1)). Hence, neither the usufructuary nor the usuary is entitled to open new mines on the property without a concession from the State. Since the usufructuary must exercise his/her right according to the principle of ordinary management, he/she will not be allowed to apply for a concession from the State to open new mines or quarries, but will be allowed to work existing mines.

The usufructuary will not be allowed to harvest *standing crops* after the termination of the usufruct, but under Civil Code, §125(2) he/she is allowed to claim a portion of the fruit in kind (Civil Code, § 125(2)), corresponding to the labour used and expenses incurred in the production of the crop. Consequently, the usufructuary is entitled to a portion of the harvest up to the extent of his/her labour and the money invested in the cultivation of the crop. Since the usuary is not entitled to collect fruits except for domestic consumption, he/she will not be allowed to do any of the above.

[84] See Case 9.

The usufructuary (but not the usuary) will be allowed to *lease* the property to a third person and to collect the rent. If the usufruct ceases to exist and the property is returned to the nude owner six months before the maturity of an annual lease, the future proceeds of the lease are to be divided between the usufructuary and the nude owner according to the rules that govern the situation of division of rent upon the sale of property.[85]

Italy

When the object of a contract of *lease* is the enjoyment of income-producing property, the tenant is under a duty to manage the property in accordance with its economic destination and he/she will be entitled to the fruits deriving from the property (Civil Code, art. 1615). If the land is normally cultivated for the *produce of timber*, which is cut periodically, the tenant can cut and sell timber in accordance with the rules pertaining to proper farm management. He/she cannot cut *fruit trees or ornamental trees*, since they are not destined for the production of wood.

The tenant can exploit *quarries already opened* and in operation but is not entitled to open up and exploit *new quarries*.[86]

The relationship between tenants succeeding each other is regulated by Civil Code, art. 1646. This article provides that the new tenant shall leave his/her predecessor adequate premises and other facilities required for using the fodder and for harvesting the remaining crops. This implies that the old tenant has the right to harvest the remaining crops. The prevailing opinion is that the relationship between a tenant and a landlord is regulated by the same principle.[87]

As a general rule, in the absence of contrary provisions in the contract of lease, the tenant is entitled to further *sub-let* the property and to collect the proceeds of the sub-lease (Civil Code, art. 1594). However, when the object of a contract of lease is the enjoyment of income-producing property, the Italian Civil Code expressly forbids the tenant from sub-letting the property without the consent of the landlord. If the landlord has consented to a sub-lease, the latter can never outlast the original lease.

[85] Benedek and Világhy, *A Polgári törvénykönyv a gyakorlatban*, pp. 108–11.
[86] See L'Aquila App. 22/11/1988, in *Guirisprudentia Agraria Italiana*, p. 423.
[87] See Carrara, 'I contratti agrari', pp. 453–4; Romagnoli and Germanò, 'Dell'affitto di fondi rustici', p. 467.

Under a *usufruct*, natural and civil fruits belong to the usufructuary for the duration of his/her right (Civil Code, art. 984). This means that the usufructuary may cultivate the land for the production of fruits and that all fruits, however produced, belong to him/her. However, the usufructuary cannot change the economic destination of the land and must return the property without impairment of its substance in the same condition as at the inception of the usufruct.

If groves or rows of trees suitable for periodic trimming for firewood or with tall trunks destined for the production of wood are part of the property included in the usufruct, the usufructuary can proceed with normal cutting, taking care to maintain the original density of the groves or rows, and providing, if necessary, for their restoration. In respect of the manner, extent, sequence and time of cutting, the usufructuary is bound to conform to the usual practice of the region as well as to statutes and regulations applicable to forests (Civil Code, art. 989). Although the usufructuary is in principle not allowed to remove *fruit or ornamental trees*, he/she becomes the owner of trees that perish, are uprooted or damaged by accident. In such a case the usufructuary is, however, under an obligation to replace the trees (Civil Code, art. 991).

In Italy, mines are part of the patrimony of the State (Civil Code, art. 826). The usufructuary can, however, obtain a concession for mining exploration and operation on the land. In such a case, he will be liable to compensate the owner for the damage on expiry of the usufruct (Civil Code, art. 987). The usufructuary is allowed to exploit any quarries already opened and in operation at the beginning of the usufruct, but he does not have the power to open new quarries without the consent of the owner (Civil Code, art. 987). Provided that the quarries are open and in operation at the beginning of the usufruct, the usufructuary can exploit them more intensively than before.[88]

The usufructuary can let the land (Civil Code, art. 999). Leases concluded by the usufructuary which have not come to an end at the time the usufruct expires continue for the term agreed upon, provided that the lease has been created with a certified date prior to the termination of the usufruct. Such leases are, however, not allowed to persist for more than five years after the termination of the usufruct.

Since 'natural and civil fruits belong to the usufructuary for the duration of his/her right' (Civil Code, art. 984), and 'civil fruits are those that are derived from the thing as compensation for the

[88] See Cass. Civ. 30/07/1951 n. 2258.

enjoyment that others have of it' (Civil Code, art. 820), the usufructuary is entitled to the proceeds of the sub-lease.

With regard to *standing crops*, if the owner and the usufructuary succeed each other in the enjoyment of the property before the end of the harvesting season (agricultural farming year) or in the course of a longer farming cycle, the crops are divided between them in proportion to the duration of their respective rights during that period (Civil Code, art. 984). Since civil fruits are acquired on a daily basis (Civil Code, art. 821), the same principle applies to them.

The holder of a *right of use* can collect the fruits to the extent necessary to meet his/her needs and those of his/her family. According to the prevailing opinion, the fruits must be destined for direct consumption,[89] with the exclusion of any commercial exploitation. While in principle the usuary can cut *timber trees* and even *exploit a quarry* (directly utilising the stones), this type of exploitation has very little practical relevance. Because of its highly personal nature, the *rights of use* or *habitation* cannot be leased (Civil Code, art. 1024).

The holder of a *hereditary building lease* (*proprietario superficiario*) may sub-lease the building. Lease contracts concluded by the *proprietario superficiario* cannot last beyond the year in which the building lease expires (Civil Code, art. 954).

The Netherlands

It must be noted that an *agricultural lease* must aim at farming the land professionally (Civil Code, art. 7:311 read with art. 7:312). Moreover, an agricultural lease cannot be concluded in respect of a forest (Civil Code, art. 7:312). Therefore, cutting plantations for timber does not fall within the scope of an agricultural lease. However, cultivating fruit trees does fall within the definition of an agricultural lease.

The agricultural tenant is expected to behave like a 'good' lessee (Civil Code, art. 7:347). This implies that the tenant is entitled to cut fruit trees, decorative trees and shrubs in so far as he/she is required to do so as a 'good' lessee.

Moreover, the tenant is only entitled to change the purpose of the leased object with the written permission of the landlord (Civil Code, art. 7:348). In so far as it concerns minor changes which can easily be undone at the end of the agriculture lease, the tenant may perform

[89] See e.g. Pugliese, *Usufrutto*, pp. 809–10.

them without permission in writing. Therefore the question whether the tenant may cut fruit trees, decorative trees and shrubs depends on whether it can be regarded as a duty following from Civil Code, art. 7:347 and as to whether it is regarded as a change to the purpose of either the contract or the leased object.

As stated above, an agricultural lease is aimed at farming the land professionally (Civil Code, art. 7:311). Mining minerals and quarrying stones do not fit this purpose, which is provided for in Civil Code, art. 7:312. Consequently, an agricultural lease cannot be concluded if the mining and quarrying of stones form the core of the contract.[90]

In the case of the termination of an agricultural lease, Civil Code, art. 7:360 provides that the new tenant must allow the previous tenant to harvest the crops sown and cultivated by the previous tenant.

It also follows from Civil Code, art. 7:347 that the tenant is not entitled to sub-let the property, unless the agricultural landlord grants permission in writing (Civil Code, art. 7:355).[91] In the case of a sub-lease, the tenant is entitled to the proceeds.

A *usufruct* entitles B to use the property and to enjoy the fruits of someone else's immovable property (Civil Code, art. 3:201). The usufructuary may use or consume the fruits in accordance with the rules stipulated in the constitutive deed (Civil Code, art. 3:207). In the absence of special arrangements, the use and enjoyment of the fruits must be in accordance with the nature of the property and local customs. In relation to the owner, the usufructuary is obliged to exercise the care of a prudent person (Civil Code, art. 3:207).

The usufructuary becomes the owner of all the natural fruits which can be separated during the term of the usufruct (Civil Code, art. 3:216). The constitutive deed can stipulate which goods are to be regarded as fruits. Thus the constitutive deed and the character of the property subject to the usufruct determine the natural fruits that can be collected by the usufructuary. Because the trees of a *plantation* are destined to be cut for timber, the usufructuary will be entitled to cut them. This is, however, not the case with *fruit trees* in an orchard and *ornamental trees*.

Where a usufruct is granted over an *existing mine or quarry* it seems apparent that good maintenance of the usufruct will involve the mining of minerals or the removal of stones. The usufructuary will, however, not be entitled to *open new mines or quarries* without the consent of the nude owner.

[90] Asser and Snijders, *Pacht* 7-III, nos. 35 ff. [91] *Ibid.* no. 134.

With regard to the entitlement of a usufructuary to *standing crops* on termination of the usufruct, the position is that the usufructuary loses his/her entitlement to the crops at the moment of termination and the nude owner becomes the owner of the standing crops. The latter will probably have to reimburse the usufructuary for his/her expenses in producing the crop.

If the constitutive deed does not provide differently, the usufructuary is entitled *to lease* the property subject to the usufruct to someone else (Civil Code, art. 3:217 I). However, if the property subject to the usufruct is not leased at the inception of the usufruct, the usufructuary is not entitled to lease the property without the consent of the nude owner or authorisation of the court of first instance (*Kantonrechter*) unless such authority is expressly granted in the constitutive deed (Civil Code, art. 3:217 II). On termination of the usufruct, the nude owner is obliged to maintain the lease, subject to certain conditions (Civil Code, art. 3:217 III).[92] There is no literature with respect to the situation where the usufruct expires six months before the rent under an annual lease is payable.

Under a *hereditary land lease* (*erfpacht*, *emphyteusis*) the holder is entitled to remove all trees and plants that he/she has planted as long as the property is returned at the end of the lease in the same condition as on inception (Civil Code, art. 5:89 III). The holder may thus remove the *fruit* or *ornamental trees* as well as the *plantation* that he/she has planted. Since he/she is not allowed to change the intended purpose of the land without the consent of the owner of the land (Civil Code, art. 5:89 II), he/she will not be entitled to cut existing fruit *trees* or *ornamental trees* without the permission of the nude owner, but may collect wood from *plantations* that are meant to be felled at the appropriate time.

If the holder of a hereditary land lease is granted the right to *mine* or to *quarry* stones on the land in the constitutive deed, prudent maintenance of the land will involve the continuation of the mining and quarrying operations. However, if such a right is not expressly granted in the constitutive deed, mining and quarrying will be against the intended purpose of the property concerned (Civil Code, art. 5:89 II). In the literature, mining is given as an example of a forbidden activity.[93]

After termination of the hereditary land lease (*emphyteusis*), the holder is entitled to compensation for *crops remaining on the land* on termination

[92] Pitlo, 'Goederenrecht', no. 692.
[93] *Ibid.* no. 647.

if the crops were sown by him or bought from the reversionary owner (Civil Code, art. 5:99 I). This default rule can be altered by the parties in the constitutive deed. According to Civil Code, art. 5:99 II, paras. (b), (c) and (d), the constitutive deed may provide that B will not be entitled to compensation where he/she has not paid for the seeds, where the land lease is terminated by B, or where B was not obliged to plant the crops and was entitled to remove them upon termination of the hereditary land lease.

If B *sub-lets* the farm, he/she is entitled to the rent, unless the sub-lease was forbidden in the constitutive deed (Civil Code, art. 5:94 I). After the termination of the principal limited interest, B is not entitled to the proceeds. There is no information in the literature with respect to the situation where the hereditary land lease terminates six months before the rent under an annual sub-lease is payable.

Under a *hereditary building lease* (*superficies*), B becomes the temporary owner of the buildings and plants on the surface of the land subject to the hereditary building right. As owner, B will be entitled to cut the *plantations* and remove *fruit* or *decorative trees* unless the constitutive deed limits his/her entitlements to these plants (Civil Code 5:102).[94] Since the mining of minerals and the quarrying of stones concern operations beneath the surface of the land, such operations will not be allowed, especially if they are expressly forbidden in the constitutive deed (Civil Code, art. 5:102).[95] Upon termination of the hereditary building lease, the ownership of the land and the crops remaining on the land revert to the landlord. In certain circumstances, the holder will be entitled to compensation for expenses in producing the crops (Civil Code, arts. 5:105 III and 5:99). The holder as temporary owner of the house on the property is entitled to sub-let the house and to collect the rent. On termination of the building lease, the reversionary owner will be entitled to the outstanding rent. There is no literature on a possible division of the rent if the building lease is terminated six months before an annual rent under the sub-lease becomes payable.

Poland

Under an *income-producing lease* (*fruendi lease*), B is entitled to the fruits of the farm (natural and civil) but not to constituent parts of the land. B can collect fruits, but not *cut the trees*, unless the farm is used as a nursery for

[94] *Ibid.* no. 672. [95] *Ibid.*

growing renewable sources of trees and shrubs, in which case they will be treated as fruits. Since *plantations* are cut at regular intervals of seven or eight years according to local custom, the timber is treated as fruits to which the tenant is entitled. In contrast, minerals are treated as constituent parts of the land and not as fruits. Consequently, B will not be entitled to *open new mines* or even to *work existing mines* on the land. Mining is further subject to special mining legislation. B is not entitled to harvest *standing crops* after the termination of the lease, but may claim compensation for the costs incurred in their production, unless he/she was also left with such crops at the onset of his/her lease (Civil Code, art. 706).

B may *sub-let* only with the owner's consent (Civil Code, art. 698, §1). He/she may collect rent which will be calculated according to the duration of the lease (Civil Code, art. 55, §2). For the last year of the sub-lease, B will therefore be entitled to receive rent for the first six months.

Under a *usufruct*, B is entitled to the natural and civil fruits of the farm but not to the stones and minerals which are constituent parts of the land. B can collect fruits, but not cut the *trees*, unless the farm is used as a nursery for growing renewable sources of trees and shrubs, in which case they will be treated as fruits. The same applies to *plantations* that are destined to be cut.

Under the Geological and Mining Law Act 1994 the *usufructuary* is entitled to build and use mining equipment in order to operate *new and existing mines and quarries* on the property. The only condition is that he/she observes all the rules laid out in the Act. He/she is also obliged to inform the owner about his/her intention to conduct mining operations on the property and the owner may require security for a potential claim for damages if the planned mining activity were to change the intended use of the land or conflict with the rules of proper management (Civil Code, art. 267).

B is not entitled to harvest *standing crops* after the termination of his/her right. He/she is only entitled to natural fruits collected during the existence of the usufruct (Civil Code, art. 55, §1). He/she may, however, have a claim based on unjustified enrichment.

The usufructuary may *lease* the property without the owner's consent, in which case he/she is entitled to the civil fruits (proceeds) of the lease (the rent). He/she may collect the rent which will be calculated on the duration of the lease (Civil Code, art. 55, §2). For the last year of the sub-lease, B will thus be entitled to receive rent for the first six months.

Portugal

These questions concern the *lease of agricultural land* governed by the Law on Agricultural Lease which covers the lease of a farm for the cultivation of crops or the farming of livestock (art. 2(1)). The lease pertains to the soil, the permanent vegetation on the soil and the buildings exploited either as residence or for other agricultural purposes (art. 4). Unless parties agree otherwise, the lease does not include timber, forest trees, cork produced by existing cork trees on the land or any other structures or produce on the land that are not normally exploited by a tenant for agricultural purposes or as the tenant's residence.

The agricultural tenant is under an obligation to return the property in the same state as he received it (Decree-Law 294/2009, art. 22(1)). The tenant is not allowed to affect the productivity, substance or the economic and social functions of the property, and his/her processes of cultivation may not prejudice the productivity of the property (art. 21(1)). The tenant is therefore only allowed to prune trees, remove dead branches from *fruit and decorative trees and shrubs* and clear undergrowth. The landlord is entitled to claim compensation for damage caused to the property through the tenant's fault or as a result of the non-compliance with his/her duties as an agricultural tenant.

The tenant under an agricultural lease is not entitled to *open mines or work existing mines or quarries*. He/she cannot prevent the landlord from carrying out works necessary to ensure that the normal production of the land is continued after termination of the lease during the final year of the lease (Decree-Law 294/2009, art. 22(1) and (4). The tenant is, however, entitled to harvest crops standing on the land when the lease expires and is allowed to enter the land when the crops are ripe to harvest them (art. 38(2)). The new farmer (a new tenant or the former landlord) cannot prevent the harvest and collection of the standing crops.

The agricultural tenant is not permitted to assign his/her right or to create a further limited right over the property. Consequently, the agricultural tenant is not entitled *to sub-let the land* without the consent of the landlord (art. 10). If the tenant does sub-let with the consent of the landlord, the tenant is entitled to the proceeds. There are, however, restrictions on the amount of rent that the tenant can charge, namely not more than 20 per cent more than the rent he/she pays without the consent of the principal landlord (Civil Code, art. 1062). If the tenant, for example, pays rent of 1,000 Euros, and then sub-lets the farm, he/she cannot charge more than 1,200 Euros without the consent of the principal landlord. It must be noted that the sub-lease expires with the termination of the principal lease. The question regarding the proportionate division of an annual rent will thus not arise.

In the case of *usufruct*, the usufructuary has the right to use and enjoy the fruits of the property without impairing its form or substance. He/she must exploit the property like a *bonus paterfamilias* and in accordance with its economic destination (Civil Code, art. 1446). This test must be applied in the exploitation of the property.

A usufructuary is entitled to the natural and civil fruits of the farm. *Plantations* that are destined to be felled are considered fruits and the usufructuary is therefore entitled to cut an appropriate amount of wood and clear undergrowth in the ordinary course of husbandry. He/she must exploit the plantation in the same way as in the past or according to the customs prevailing in the community (Civil Code, art. 1455). Since *fruit trees, decorative trees and shrubs* are not exploited ordinarily by cutting them down, the usufructuary is not allowed to remove them, for example, to be used as firewood. Moreover, the usufructuary has a duty to return the property without impairment of its substance. He/she therefore has a duty to replace cut plantation trees and dead fruit or decorative trees (Civil Code, art. 1453, no. 2).

Decree-Law 270/2001 of 6 October establishes a specific regime for the *exploitation of quarries and mines*. A concession to search for minerals (Decree-Law 270/2001, arts. 20 ff.) and to prospect for mineral resources (Decree-Law 270/2001, art. 27) is needed to open quarries and mines. The owner, or the person with whom he/she had concluded a search and prospecting contract or only a prospecting contract, is entitled to obtain such a concession (Decree-Law 270/2001, art. 10 no 1). This contract must be executed in a public deed (Decree-Law 270/2001, art. 12 no 2) and must specify the annual compensation to be paid to the owner (Decree-Law 270/2001, art. 14).

Under Portuguese law, fruits are the natural periodic produce of property without the impairment of its substance (Civil Code, art. 212). Minerals and stones are not considered to be natural fruits. However, if the owner has concluded a contract with a third person *to mine or quarry existing mines or quarries*, the usufructuary (and not the nude owner) is entitled to collect the income from the mining or quarrying operations for the duration of the usufruct (Civil Code, art. 1457 no. 2). The consent of the nude owner is required should the usufructuary wish to *open new mines or quarries* (Civil Code, art. 1458). Otherwise, a usufructuary is only entitled to take stone from the soil to carry out repairs and works on the property for which he/she is responsible. A usufruct can be created over a concession obtained for the search and prospecting of minerals. In that case, the usufructuary has the right to exploit existing mines or quarries according to the practice of the owner (Civil Code, art. 1457 no. 1).

As a general rule, the usufructuary only acquires natural fruits on actual collection of the fruits (Civil Code, art. 213). It is therefore accepted that the moment of the collection of the fruits (*jure corporis*) rather than the moment of sowing the seeds (*jure seminis*) is crucial. Consequently, the estate of the usufructuary will only be entitled to fruits already collected on expiry of the usufruct. After the termination of the usufruct, the *standing crops* are the property of the owner. However, in order to treat both parties fairly, the nude owner is obliged on termination of the usufruct to reimburse the usufructuary for the cost of production of the crop up to the value of the standing crop (Civil Code, art. 1447).

The question regarding the proportionate division of an annual rent where the lease of the property expires six months before the annual rent is due, deals with the sharing of civil fruits (income from a lease of the property by the usufructuary) between the nude owner and the usufructuary. Civil fruits differ from natural fruits in that they are shared according to the duration of the usufruct (*pro rata temporis*) (Civil Code, art. 213 nos. 1 and 2) and they are divided between the nude owner and the usufructuary in proportion to the duration of each person's right. B can thus collect the rent for the duration of his/her usufruct. This will also be the case if the usufruct expires six months before the lease expires. The rent for the last six months will accrue to the nude owner and not to the estate of the usufructuary.

Since a *usuary* is entitled to use the property and to collect fruits to the extent necessary to satisfy personal and family needs, none of the above situations would apply to him/her.

A *hereditary building lease* (*superficies*) entitles the holder to plant or maintain trees or plantations or to construct or maintain buildings on land belonging to another, either for a fixed term or in perpetuity (Civil Code, art. 1524). The grant of a building lease can take the form of an alienation of a building or trees separate from the soil (Civil Code, art. 1528). Where the building lease entitles the holder to plant or maintain trees or plantations on land belonging to another, the holder is not entitled to cut *existing plantations, fruit trees, decorative trees or shrubs*. The position would be the same with regard to new trees and plantations planted by the holder. If, however, the right to the *trees* and the *plantation* has been granted to him/her separately from the soil, it is commonly accepted that the holder has the same extensive rights as the owner of the property.[96] Therefore, B will have full discretion to exploit the plantation in his/her best interest. However, the right will expire if the trees or plantation are destroyed and the holder does not make an effort to restore it (Civil Code, art. 1536 b).

As in the case of usufruct, the provisions on fruits contained in the general part of the Portuguese Civil Code will apply to crops remaining on the land on termination of the lease. Under Civil Code, art. 213, the holder of a building right only acquires natural fruits on actual collection (*jure corporis*). The estate of the holder will therefore only be entitled to fruits already collected on expiry of the building lease. After the termination of the *superficies*, the (existing or planted) trees are the property of the owner. In order to treat both parties fairly, however, the owner is obliged to reimburse the holder on the ground of unjustified enrichment on termination of the building right (Civil Code, art. 1538 no 2).

Where B has the same extensive rights with regard to the plantation and the building as an owner, he/she is entitled to create a sub-lease in respect of the property and to collect the income therefrom until the building lease expires (Civil Code, arts. 1539 and 213, no. 2). This is the position even if the rent only becomes due on an annual basis and the building lease expires six months before the end of the year.

Scotland

A lease does not confer upon the tenant every right competent to the landlord.[97] It allows the tenant to enjoy the fruits or profits of the subjects of the lease,[98] but (with the exception of mineral leases) not to consume the substance of the subjects.[99] The landlord is deemed to have reserved the right to all products, whether above or below the surface, which do not, either by industry or nature, yield periodical returns within the duration of the lease.[100] There must be an express grant to the tenant to enjoy these rights.

[96] Pires de Lima and Autunes Varela, *Có digo Civil Anotado*, vol. 3, p. 539; Oliveira Ascensão, *Direito Civil*, p. 532.

[97] Erskine, *Institute*, II. vi. 22. [98] Stair, *Institutions*, II. ix. 1.

[99] Rankine, *Erskine's Principles*, II. vi. 9. What we call a 'mineral lease' is really an out and out sale of a portion of the land: *Gowans* v. *Christie* (1873) 11 M (HL) 1 12.

[100] Hunter, *Treatise*, vol. 2, p. 206.

A liferenter is entitled, for the duration of his/her right, to the use and enjoyment of the subjects, together with the fruits. However, enjoyment is to be *salva rerum substantia*, namely without encroaching on the substance of the subjects. In modern terms, the liferenter is entitled to the income, but not the capital.[101]

Without an express grant, the *tenant* is not entitled to any of the timber growing on the subjects. The tenant may not *cut down woods*. They are reserved for the landlord who may cut them down during the currency of the lease, as far as they are not necessary for the shelter of any farmstead on the subjects.[102] An exception is made for young willow trees, which may be cut as a crop. When of a large size, however, even willow trees may not be cut[103] and that remains the rule even if they were planted by the tenant.[104] The fruit from fruit trees may be harvested by the tenant, but the trees cannot be cut.

As for the *liferenter*, trees are not generally classed as *fruits*,[105] and thus the liferenter cannot fell them. They are the fiar's property. That extends even to trees which the liferenter has planted. There are some exceptions, for example, in respect of coppice-wood and similar wood which is regularly cut to grow again and to wood required for the purposes of the estate (for example, for fencing).[106]

Minerals are also reserved *ex lege* to the landlord. Any grant to the tenant must be expressly made and that is rarely done. Instead, minerals are almost always expressly reserved for the landlord.[107] The *landlord* retains the right, subject to payment of damages to the tenant, to search for and *work minerals* during the subsistence of the lease.[108] They may also be let to another party.

In a *liferent*, the *removal of minerals* is strictly inconsistent with enjoyment *salva rerum substantia* as it diminishes the subjects. However, a liferenter is entitled to take minerals for *domestic consumption and for the purposes of the estate*, even to the extent of opening mines or quarries.[109] The liferenter is entitled to minerals (or rents in respect of them) where

[101] Styles, 'Liferent', para. 1638; Gordon and Wortley, *Land Law*, para. 17–36.

[102] J. S. More, *Notes to* Stair, *Institutions*, cclv. [103] Hunter, *Treatise*, vol. 2, p. 208.

[104] J. S. More, *Notes to* Stair, *Institutions*, cclv. Once planted, the trees accede to the land.

[105] Stair, *Institutions*, II. iii. 74; Erskine, *Institute* II. ix. 58; Bell, *Principles*, s. 1046; *Macalister's Trs.* v. *Macalister* (1851) 13 D 1239 (IH).

[106] *Dickson* v. *Dickson* (1823) 2, s. 152 (IH) 154; *Macalister's Trs.* v. *Macalister* (1851) 13 D 1239 (IH) 1242.

[107] Gill, *Agricultural Holdings*, para. 2.04. [108] Rankine, *Leases*, p. 209.

[109] Gordon and Wortley, *Land Law*, para. 17–40; *Dickson* v. *Dickson* (1823) 2 S. 152 (NE 138).

the mineral fields were already being worked at the commencement of the liferent or they had already been opened for working although they were not yet being worked.[110] In these circumstances, the liferenter may grant new mineral leases as long as there is no substantial danger of exhaustion of the minerals.[111]

The general rule is that *one who sows a crop is entitled to reap it.*[112] The maxim is *messis sementem sequitur*: the harvest goes to the sower. This holds true even after the termination of a lease. The tenant's right is 'not merely to enter the land when the crop is ripe for the purpose of reaping it, but to attend to it during its growth, and to perform any agricultural operations which may be necessary'.[113] This right can be modified or taken away by contract between the landlord and tenant, but it has been said that the rights of the sower are so firmly fixed in law that an agreement to waive both the entitlement to reap the crop and to compensation for it will not readily be inferred.[114]

As with tenants, so for *liferenters*: the harvest goes to the sower. The liferenter is entitled not only to what he harvested during the liferent but to all of the produce of what he sows.[115]

In certain circumstances,[116] a tenant is entitled to *sub-lease* the property. B is entitled to the proceeds of the sub-lease as civil fruits and also, more simply, as a matter of contract law. As a matter of property law, it is not possible for the *duration of the sub-lease* to exceed that of the principal lease, because the sub-tenant's right derives from the tenant's.

A proper *liferenter* is also able to grant leases and is entitled to the rent therefrom as a civil fruit of the property and as a matter of contract law. Without special powers or the owner's consent, such a lease may not exceed the *duration* of the life interest[117] (although the tenant cannot be removed until the Whitsunday (28 May) following the termination of the liferent).[118] The allocation of entitlement to rent is possibly one of

[110] Styles, 'Liferent', para. 1638; Gordon and Wortley, *Land Law*, para. 17–40; *Wardlaw* v. *Wardlaw's Trs.* (1875) 2 R 368 (IH) 372; *Campbell* v. *Wardlaw* (1883) 10 R (HL) 65 66; *Nugent* v. *Nugent's Trs.* (1899) 2 F (HL) 21 23; *Naismith's Trs.* v. *Naismith* 1909 SC 1380 (IH).

[111] *Wardlaw* v. *Wardlaw's Trs.* (1875) 2 R 368 (IH) 373.

[112] *Chalmer's Tr.* v. *Dick's Tr.* 1909 SC 761 (IH) 769; *M'Kinlay* v. *Hutchis or Heron's Tr.* 1935 SLT 62 (IH) 64.

[113] *Chalmer's Tr.* v. *Dick's Tr.* 1909 SC 761 (IH) 770.

[114] *Cameron* v. *Nicol* 1930 SC 1 (IH) 16–17.

[115] Gordon and Wortley, *Land Law*, para. 17–42.

[116] Detailed, in the response to Case 9.

[117] Erskine, *Institute*, II. ix. 57; Gordon and Wortley, *Land Law*, para. 17–52.

[118] Stair, *Institutions*, II. ix. 9; Paton and Cameron, *Landlord and Tenant*, p. 50.

the most complex issues in lease law. The general principle is that the liferenter is entitled to civil fruits (of which rent is one) accruing during the subsistence of his/her right. The question of when rent accrues can cause difficulty.[119] In respect of most leases the answer is simple. By the Apportionment Act 1870, *rent accrues from day to day* and is apportioned accordingly.[120] Assume B is a liferenter and has granted a lease to C with the entire year's rent due at the end of the year. If B dies on 30 June, B's estate is entitled to half of the annual rent. The apportioned amount is, however, only recoverable when the whole amount of which it forms part falls due, or would have fallen due, had the right giving rise to the entitlement not been terminated.[121] In our example, if the liferent terminates, A is not able to remove C from the property until the following Whitsunday, namely 28 May. At the end of the year, the rent becomes payable to A as the landlord at the time the rent becomes payable. The rent received by A is apportioned proportionally between B's executor and A. B's executor only has a claim against A and not against C directly.[122]

Complexity arises in respect of certain *types of leases* (mainly agricultural ones) where the law allocates certain dates on which rent accrues, known as term dates. These are the 'legal terms'. So, for example, in an arable lease, where the tenant takes entry on Whitsunday (28 May) 2011, the first legal term on which rent is due is Whitsunday 2012 and the second is Martinmas (28 November) 2012. Parties may provide differently in their lease contract and stipulate 'conventional terms' on which rent is to become due. They may provide either for the rent to be paid earlier than the legal terms (a 'forehand rent') or later than the legal terms (a 'backhand rent'). If parties provide that rent is to be paid backhand, the rule is that the person who is the landlord at the time when the rent becomes due in accordance with the legal term is not deprived of his/her right to the rent. The right vests in the landlord in accordance with the legal terms, even if it does not become due in accordance with the conventional terms until some later point. If there is a forehand rent, the rent vests in accordance with the conventional terms. So if B has a liferent and grants a lease where the law allocates certain legal terms, with the lease providing for conventional backhand rents, and B dies between two term dates, the law provides that his/her

119 See generally Gordon and Wortley, *Land Law*, paras. 17–44 to 17–49.
120 Apportionment Act 1870, s. 2.
121 Apportionment Act 1870, s. 3.
122 Apportionment Act 1870, s. 4.

executor is entitled (a) to the rent which fell due at the legal term, even if conventionally paid backhand, and also, (b) by virtue of the Apportionment Act, to the rent for the proportion of the period which he/she survived beyond the term date.

South Africa

If the tenant under a *lease* exploits the property according to its intended use and uses it as a reasonable person would use his/her own property, he/she may reap the benefits of such exploitation.[123] Consequently, the tenant may cut *plantations* destined to be cut (*silva caedua*) as long as he/she does so in good time and skilfully. *Fruit trees*, *decorative trees* or *shrubs* may only be removed if they have perished or if it is in the interest of good husbandry.

Opening mines or quarries on the farm will only be allowed if it is consistent with the intended purpose of the farm and if such activity was carried out in the past. The tenant will therefore be entitled to work *existing mines*. The right to mine will of course be subject to applicable mining legislation.

If the tenant planted the crop with a reasonable prospect of maturity before termination of the lease, South African jurisprudence allows the tenant after termination of the lease to re-enter and reap the standing crop.[124] If the crops were planted without a reasonable expectation of maturity, the tenant is not entitled to reap the crop, but can claim the cost of 'ploughing, tilling, sowing and seedcorn' even if he/she acted without the landlord's consent,[125] probably on the ground of unjustified enrichment.[126]

In principle, the tenant (B) will be entitled to the proceeds if a further interest is created with regard to the property, for example, if he/she *sub-lets* the house or the farm, which is normally allowed.[127] Since the sub-lease only creates a contractual relationship between the sub-tenant and the tenant,[128] the principal landlord will only have a claim for the remaining proportionate share of the rent if he/she assumes both the rights and

[123] Pothier, *Obligations*, para. 190; *Manley* v. *Van Niekerk (Pty) Ltd.* v. *Assegai Safaris and Film Productions (Pty) Ltd.* 1977 2 SA 416 (A) 423B-C.

[124] *Latelle* v. *Crafford* (1909) 26 SC 426; *Japtha* v. *Mills' Executors* 1910 EDL 150. See *obiter contra Lessing* v. *Steyn* 1953 4 SA 193 (O) 200–1; *Bester* v. *Van Zyl* 1972 4 SA 580 (T).

[125] *Lessing* v. *Steyn* 1953 4 SA 193 (O); *Steyn* v. *Fourie* 1956 4 SA 458 (A).

[126] Kerr, 'Lease', para. 209; *contra* Cooper, *Landlord and Tenant*, p. 332.

[127] Kerr, 'Lease', para. 197. [128] See Cooper, *Landlord and Tenant*, pp. 243–5.

obligations of the sub-landlord under the sub-lease on termination of the principal lease.

Under a *usufruct*, a usufructuary is in principle entitled to the natural and civil fruits of the farm. He/she must, however, exploit the farm like a prudent person (*arbitratu boni viri*) and in the customary manner. He/she must also eventually return the property without impairment of its substance.

If *plantations* are meant to be felled (*silva caedua*), the usufructuary may cut them at the appropriate time and in accordance with the customs of the locality. He/she may further cut and appropriate wood and undergrowth in the ordinary course of husbandry. He/she may not cut *fruit trees*, *ornamental trees* or *shrubs* unless they have perished. He/she must replace dead trees.[129]

The Roman idea that all *minerals* and metals are self-renewing and thus natural fruits susceptible to collection by the usufructuary, was not accepted in Roman-Dutch and South African law. Only minerals that are actually self-renewing, such as salt from salt mines, are regarded as natural fruits which are due to the usufructuary. In respect of non-renewable minerals, the usufructuary is allowed *to work existing mines*, prospect for minerals and *open up new mines* in accordance with mining legislation. His/her entitlement to non-renewing minerals, however, is limited to the interest on the proceeds of the minerals, the royalties payable on a mining lease, prospecting moneys and moneys paid on options.[130]

In principle, a usufructuary only becomes owner of the natural fruits of the farm on collection. Until collection the fruits vest in the nude owner. Consequently, the estate of the usufructuary is only entitled to fruits already collected on expiry of the usufruct. His/her successors-in-title will not be entitled to enter the land and harvest *standing crops*.

A usufructuary is entitled to the rental flow generated by the lease of the property as the civil fruits of the property.[131] Although civil fruits (like rent) becomes the property of the usufructuary as they fall due, they are divided between the former usufructuary (or his/her successors) and the owner of the property in proportion to the duration of the usufruct.[132]

129 Van der Merwe, 'Servitudes', paras. 427, 429.

130 *Master* v. *African Mines Corporation* 1907 TS 925; Van der Merwe et al. *Property and Trust Law*, s. 714.

131 Voet, *Commentarius*, 7.1.30; *Ex parte Marks and Marks* 1926 TPD 1.

132 Van der Merwe, 'Servitudes', para. 426.

Spain

Neither the Civil Code nor the special Laws contain explicit reference to the tenant's entitlement to fruits under a *lease*. However, since the essence of a lease contract is the tenant's entitlement to use the property, one can include under use the enjoyment of the fruits which are produced during the exploitation of the property. This especially applies in the case of *rural leases* as the Law on Rural Leases, art. 1.1 defines rural leases as leases which consist in the transfer of the possession of one or more farms, or part thereof, for agricultural, cattle-raising or forest exploitation.

When the land is leased for agricultural or forestry exploitation, the tenant will be entitled to cut plantations for timber periodically. He/she will also be entitled to cut fruit and decorative trees should he/she decide to plant something else, as the Law on Rural Leases, art. 8.1 allows him/her to decide which kind of crops he/she is going to grow, as long as he/she returns the land in the same condition that he/she received it. Where the system of exploitation involves a change of intended purpose (for example, turning an orchard of fruit trees into a vegetable garden) or extraordinary improvements, express agreement between the parties is required (art. 8.2).

Under Spanish law, mines belong to the State (Law on Mines, art. 2.1).[133] This article stipulates that all kinds of geological deposits are in the public domain which the State can exploit itself or grant the right of exploitation to another person by public concession under the Law on Mines. The tenant will not be allowed to open mines, or to continue mineral operations, as leases subject to the Law on Rural Leases can only give the tenant the right to enjoy the land through agricultural use, cattle-raising or forest exploitation.[134] Where someone has obtained the public concession to open or to exploit a mine, this right can also be leased.

The tenant is obliged to return the entire property on expiration of the contract of lease unless otherwise agreed (Law on Rural Leases, art. 12.2). Any crops remaining upon termination of the lease will belong to the owner (landlord) as no special rules exist in the Law on Rural Leases, and Civil Code, art. 451–2 will be applicable in such a situation. The tenant is, in contrast to the holders of limited real rights, not entitled to any reimbursement (Civil Code, art. 480).

133 Law 22/1973 of 21 July.

134 Law on Rural Leases, art. 6 d 5 stipulates that a lease which does not envisage an agricultural, cattle-raising or forestry exploitation will not be subject to such law.

The tenant is entitled to *sub-let* the land if this was contemplated in the lease contract. The object of the sub-lease must concern the lease of the entire property for the remaining term of the principal lease (so that the sub-lease expires simultaneously with the principal lease), and the rent must not exceed the rent payable under the principal lease (Law on Rural Leases, art. 23). The landlord's express consent will further be necessary to sub-let the property (art. 23, para. 2). If the lease contract is not subject to the Law on Rural Leases, Civil Code, art. 1550 allows the tenant to sub-let the whole or part of the property if it was not expressly forbidden in the principal contract. In the case of a residential lease, the tenant may cede the contract or sub-let part of the premises (not the whole house) with the written consent of the landlord (Law on Urban Leases, art. 8).

Under a *usufruct*, the usufructuary is not only entitled to use the property, but also to enjoy its fruits. The usufructuary is entitled to all kinds of fruits (natural, industrial and civil) (Civil Code, art. 471). With regard to pending fruits, the Civil Code establishes two regimes, depending on the kind of fruits. If the fruits are natural or industrial, pending fruits at the beginning of the usufruct belong to the usufructuary, but pending fruits at the end of the usufruct belong to the owner (Civil Code, art. 472). The usufructuary does not have to pay for the pending fruits that he acquires at the inception of the usufruct, but the owner is obliged to reimburse the expenses incurred by the usufructuary for the pending natural fruits which he/she acquires on expiry of the usufruct. By contrast, civil fruits are acquired by the usufructuary proportionately to the duration of the usufruct (Civil Code, art. 474).

The Civil Code contains some special rules for *trees, bushes or shrubs* on the property subject to the usufruct. Authors distinguish between a usufruct of trees or bushes (*usufructo de árboles o arbustos*), a usufruct of fruit trees (Civil Code, arts. 483 and 484 include vineyards and olive trees), decorative trees and bushes, and a usufruct of a forest/wood (*usufructo de montes*), with the last including timber trees destined to be cut. In the case of a usufruct of trees or bushes, the usufructuary is granted the same rights as an ordinary usufructuary, except for the rules regarding dead, broken or uprooted trees. Consequently, since the usufructuary is obliged to preserve the property's form and substance (Civil Code, art. 467), he/she is not allowed to cut fruit or decorative trees or bushes.[135]

[135] Lacruz Berdejo, *Elementos*, vol 3.2, p. 26 states that the usufructuary cannot cut fruit or decorative trees, change the vegetable garden into a flower garden, change the façade of the house or divide its rooms.

However, if the trees or bushes are dead, uprooted or broken by accident, the usufructuary may remove them, subject to an obligation to replace what he/she has taken (Civil Code, art. 483).[136]

In the case of a usufruct of a forest/wood, the usufructuary has the right to enjoy all of the forest/wood's resources, according to their nature (Civil Code, art. 485, para. 1). *Timber plantations* are considered natural fruits (Civil Code, art. 485, para. 2).[137] The Civil Code allows the usufructuary to proceed with normal cutting, while taking care that the area subject to the usufruct will not suffer any damage. He/she has to follow the practice of the previous owner and, failing that, he/she must follow regional customs as to the manner, extent and time of cutting.[138] If a nursery is subject to a usufruct, the usufructuary is allowed to thin out the plants in order to optimise growth of the rest of the plants. Finally, the usufructuary is not entitled to cut trees unless it will improve the condition of the property subject to the usufruct (Civil Code, art. 485) and he/she has notified the nude owner of his/her intention.

As mentioned before, under Spanish law, mines belong to the State, and a public concession is needed to exploit them. The usufructuary can, however, enjoy the products of an *existing mine or quarry* if his/her title contains an express reference to the mine (Civil Code, art. 476).[139] In the case of a legal usufruct (granted by law to the widow or widower), the usufructuary is entitled to half of the proceeds of the mine after the running expenses have been deducted (Civil Code, art. 477). The other half goes to the nude owner. Finally, the usufructuary may obtain the concession for an existing mine in accordance with the general rules contained in the Law on Mines (Civil Code, art. 478).

It must be noted that the public concession of a mine can also be the subject of a usufruct. Authors consider that such a usufructuary is entitled to receive half of the proceeds of the mine after running expenses have been deducted.[140]

The usufructuary may lease the land to a third party (Civil Code, art. 480). Leases concluded by the usufructuary will terminate simultaneously

136 Lacruz Berdejo, *Elementos*, vol 3.2, p. 46 considers that this obligation to replace the trees constitutes ordinary repair and is therefore chargeable to the usufructuary.

137 Lacruz Berdejo, *Elementos*, vol. 3.2, p. 47.

138 Although the Civil Code does not mention forest statutes and regulations, it is accepted that the usufructuary is also bound by them. See Maluquer de Motes Bernet, 'Comment', vol. 1, p. 1300.

139 Lacruz Berdejo, *Elementos*, vol 3.2, p. 52.

140 *Ibid*. 53; Peña Bernaldo de Quirós, *Derechos reales*, vol. 1, p. 630.

with the expiry of the usufruct, except in the case of the agricultural lease of a farm which will continue until the end of the agricultural year (harvesting season) (Civil Code, art. 480 read with Law on Rural Leases, arts. 10 and 24g). This exception also applies where agricultural leases have been concluded by the holder of a hereditary lease of land (*emphyteusis*) or a hereditary building lease (*superficies*). By contrast, residential leases concluded by a usufructuary shall expire simultaneously with the expiry of the usufruct without any exception (Law on Urban Leases, art. 13.2).

Natural, industrial and civil fruits belong to the usufructuary for the term of his/her right (Civil Code, art. 471). Natural and industrial fruits which have not been harvested at inception of the usufruct belong to the usufructuary, whereas fruits not harvested on termination of the usufruct belong to the nude owner (Civil Code, art. 472). Since civil fruits are acquired on a daily basis, they belong to the usufructuary in proportion to the duration of his/her right (Civil Code, art. 474).

The *usuary* can collect the fruits to the extent necessary to meet his/her needs and those of his/her family (Civil Code, art. 524). According to the prevailing opinion, the usuary can even sell some of the fruits in order to satisfy these needs.[141] In principle, the usuary may, if necessary, cut timber trees as they can be considered 'fruits' of the farm.[142] Owing to its highly personal character, the *right of use* or *habitation* cannot be leased (Civil Code, art. 525).

As the *hereditary building lease* (*superficies*) is a long-term development right to build or to plant on someone else's land, its holder is not allowed to cut *trees* or *shrubs*, with the exception of a *plantation*. The holder will not be able to *operate a mine* as this activity is not a part of his/her right. The holder can *sub-lease* the building or the plantation and the lease contract will terminate when his/her right expires.[143] Since the Civil Code does not regulate the holder's entitlement to fruits, his/her rights as possessor of the property entitle him/her to obtain all kinds of fruits during the duration of his/her right (Civil Code, art. 451, para. 1),[144] and civil fruits will accrue to him/her on a day-to-day basis for the duration of his/her right (Civil Code, art. 451, para. 3).

141 Lacruz Berdejo, *Elementos*, vol 3.2, p. 81; Rams Albesa, 'Comment', vol. 1, p. 1386.
142 See Lacruz Berdejo, *Elementos*, vol 3.2, p. 47.
143 LRL, art. 10 provides this solution, in the case of a rural lease.
144 Art. 452, para. 1 provides that where natural or industrial fruits have not been harvested at the end of the term the holder of the time-limited interest has the right to claim his/her expenses as well as a proportionate part of the harvest.

Case 7
To what extent may the holder of a time-limited interest convert his/her interest in the land?

B has a time-limited right in a house/a farm. He/she wants to convert the house into a warehouse/the farm into a hotel. Is he/she entitled to do this?

Does it make a difference:

- *if the alteration enhances the value of the property?*
- *if the neighbourhood loses its residential character/the farm becomes incorporated within the city limits?*
- *if the warehouse or hotel can be changed back to a house/a farm at a low cost?*

Comparative observations

Most jurisdictions stipulate that the *tenant* must exploit residential property in a manner consistent with its nature and intended economic purpose and return the property on termination of the *lease* in the condition in which it was received. The tenant will thus not be allowed to convert the dwelling house into a warehouse.[1] In England, such alteration will only be possible if not restricted by 'alteration' or 'user' covenants. Consequently, alteration of a house or farm to a non-residential use will be caught and excluded by user covenants if it is not already caught by any alteration covenants. Although the French Law on Residential Leases allows residential tenants to use the residence for professional or commercial purposes as long as neither clients nor merchandise come onto the premises, the above conversion will still not be allowed. Such conduct will entitle the landlord to cancel the lease and

[1] The South African report adds the examples of a dwelling house being turned into a stable, a hotel or a blacksmith's workshop and a shop being converted into a bar, a restaurant or a dwelling house.

claim damages for breach of contract,[2] to use a special procedure to evict the tenant[3] or to obtain an injunction to stop the conversion.[4]

In principle, it makes no difference if such alteration will *enhance the value* of the property or if the property can be *converted back* into its former condition at low cost. The South African report mentions that Roman-Dutch law allowed alterations more readily in the initial period of a long lease, subject to the qualification that the tenant must not damage the property and be able to reconvert the land to its former condition at the end of the lease. The default position can obviously be changed by initial or subsequent contractual arrangements.

In England, there is a judicial jurisdiction to discharge any covenants which are obsolete or which obstruct some reasonable private use of the premises. Change in the character of the land or locality or economic changes which render the covenants obsolete or otherwise oppressive can therefore lead to the discharge or modification of these covenants. Leasehold covenants restraining the use of the leased premises are in practice challenged on that footing.

The default position under the Danish Private Housing Act is somewhat different: the tenant is not, without the landlord's consent, allowed to use the premises for any purpose not agreed upon. If the tenant proceeds with the alteration without the landlord's consent, the landlord can terminate the contract without notice. Conversion such as that discussed here would probably need the approval of the relevant public authorities even if the alteration enhanced the value of the premises, the character of the neighbourhood changed or conversion back to the original condition was possible at a low cost.

Although change in the manner of exploitation of *agricultural* as opposed to residential *land under a lease* without the landlord's consent is, on the whole, more readily allowed by most European jurisdictions, it is not permitted where the alteration is so substantial that it affects the manner in which the owner can exploit the property when the lease expires. The farm must be exploited consistently with its intended purpose and maintained in a good condition of productivity. Consequently, B will not be allowed to convert the *farm* (agricultural purpose) into a *hotel* (commercial purpose) without the

[2] See the Austrian, Portuguese and Spanish reports. [3] See the Spanish report.
[4] See the Austrian report.

landlord's approval.[5] Such conversion will be a ground for cancelling the lease.[6]

In most European jurisdictions, the fact that the *value* of the property is *enhanced* by the conversion or that the farm can be *reconverted* to its original state at low cost before expiry of the lease will not affect the situation. While Italian law, for example, expects the tenant to manage the property dynamically so as to increase its productivity and profitability, the agricultural purpose of the land must always be respected.

Change in the *character of the neighbourhood* will also not affect the situation except that the tenant may be required to obtain approval from public zoning authorities, in addition to consent from the landlord. If a radical and unforeseen change of circumstances were to render the original use of the property absurd, the tenant can demand dissolution of the lease in continental jurisdictions but he/she will still not be allowed to alter the purpose of the property.[7]

Under a *usufruct*, the usufructuary must exploit the property in an orderly fashion, preserve its economic purpose and not introduce substantial changes to the property. He/she is obliged to return the property without impairment of its substance. The usufructuary may improve the property but not change its economic purpose. *Converting a dwelling-house into a warehouse* or *a farm into a hotel* will be regarded as a substantial transformation of the property and is not allowed without the nude owner's consent.[8] In some jurisdictions, a change of purpose may be agreed upon in the constitutive agreement *inter vivos*, or with the permission of the owner or the court of first instance.[9] In France, case law allows a usufructuary to change a leisure residence into a place of business as long as this does not constitute an 'abuse of enjoyment'. Poland recognises an exception by allowing the usufructuary, which is an agricultural co-operative, to change the substance and use of state treasury land granted in usufruct.[10]

Most European jurisdictions will further agree that the mere fact that the alteration *enhances the value of the property* or that the property can be

[5] See e.g. the German, Greek, French, Belgian, Spanish, Italian, South African, Hungarian and Polish reports. But cf. the Scottish report.

[6] See e.g. the Belgian and Spanish reports.

[7] See the Greek, Italian and Spanish reports. But see the Scottish report which refers to a procedure to change the title conditions of the property.

[8] See e.g. the German, Austrian, Belgian, Portuguese, Italian, Scottish, South African and Polish reports.

[9] See the Spanish and Dutch reports.

[10] See the French and Polish reports.

reconverted at low cost will not change the situation.[11] Academic opinion in Portugal and the Netherlands supports certain minor changes, for example, the conversion of a garage into a restaurant if the property's economic purpose could be maintained,[12] while South African and Hungarian sources support the view that an enhancement of the value of the property will suffice to allow the usufructuary to change the purpose of the property as long as it does not alter the fundamental function of the property. Greek law will allow the conversion if the property can be returned to its former condition at low cost. [13]

Some jurisdictions accept that *radical changes in the neighbourhood* which interfere with the business foundation of a usufruct constituted *inter vivos* as an estate planning mechanism[14] may affect the legal position.[15] In Belgium, changing circumstances may qualify as a socio-economic factor outside the control of the usufructuary, which will justify altering the intended purpose of the property. The French report also hints at the possibility of changing the exploitation of a usufruct if the *zoning of the neighbourhood* changes. The Italian report states that circumstances that radically change the original use of the property may probably make a difference but that there is no direct authority on the point. An article in the Spanish Civil Code on forced sales provides that, in the event of a radical change in the neighbourhood, the nude owner may subrogate the property, either by providing the usufructuary with another property of similar condition and value or by taking over the property and paying the usufructuary legal interest on the proceeds of the property for the duration of the usufruct. A similar solution is found in South African law, not on the ground of changing circumstances but on the ground that exploitation of the property by a widow caused such severe hardship to her that it was financially prudent (and also to the nude owner's advantage) to sell the property and allow the widow a usufruct on the interest earned on the proceeds of the sale.[16]

Most national reporters reported that the holders of the lesser rights of use and habitation will not be entitled to do the above conversions under any of the circumstances mentioned above.[17]

[11] See the German, Belgian, Portuguese and Spanish reports.
[12] See the Portuguese and Dutch reports.
[13] See also the South African, Hungarian and Scottish reports.
[14] See the German report. [15] See the Belgian, French and Italian reports.
[16] See the Belgian, French, Italian, Spanish and South African reports.
[17] See e.g. the Greek and South African reports.

The default position in several European jurisdictions is that the *holder of a hereditary building lease* (*superficiarius*) has the same rights as an owner with regard to structures on the land, subject to restrictions in the constitutive deed. The holder is regarded as an owner *ad tempus* and therefore not subject to the same limits on the use of the land as a usufructuary. He may exploit the property to its fullest economic potential, even if this involves changing the property's economic purpose.[18] Some jurisdictions will restrict this power to the construction of new structures, without allowing the holder radically to change existing structures on the land. A portion of Italian academic literature supports this idea by applying rules pertaining to usufruct by analogy to *superficies*.[19] The *superficiarius* will therefore not be entitled to convert an existing *house into a warehouse* or an existing *farmhouse into a hotel*. Parties may, however, agree in the constitutive deed that the holder may alter the physical condition of structures on the land, or their purpose, with the landowner's consent.[20]

In principle, the holder of a *hereditary land lease* (*emphyteusis*) can alter the intended purpose (destination) of the property when the character of the neighbourhood changes, provided that this would enhance the value of the land.[21] In some jurisdictions such alterations are allowed only with the consent of the landowner on the ground that the landowner still owns the land and any improvements, while the holder of the *emphyteusis* is only entitled to share in the use and enjoyment of the land.[22] In Poland, the matter is primarily regulated by provisions in the constitutive grant which usually contains provisions on the erection of new, and the alteration of existing structures on the land, sometimes even including dates of commencement and completion of building operations.

Austria

In principle, the use and the purpose of the leased object are defined in the *lease* and may not be changed by the tenant without the permission of the landlord (Civil Code, § 1098). If the lease is, for example, restricted to a certain branch of business, the landlord may apply to court for an injunction prohibiting action by the tenant in conflict with such

[18] See e.g. the Austrian, Spanish and Dutch reports.
[19] See e.g. the Belgian, Italian and Portuguese reports. [20] See the German report.
[21] See e.g. the Belgian report. [22] See e.g. the Dutch report.

restriction. Furthermore, unlawful change of the purpose and use of the leased object constitute a compelling reason for termination of the contract without notice (Law on Tenancy, § 30, para. 1, no. 7). This applies irrespective of whether the change of use is an improvement or not. B is therefore not entitled to convert the *house into a warehouse* (store) or the *farm into a hotel* without the permission of A, unless the contract allows him to do so.

Under a *usufruct*, the usufructuary is not entitled to change the use, purpose or type of cultivation of the land without the permission of the landowner,[23] even if the property is improved by such change. If the usufructuary acts in conflict with this restraint, the landowner can claim for restoration to the former condition. If unlawful changes are imminent, the landowner can ask the court for an injunction prohibiting such change and for security against future damage under Civil Code, § 520. As a usufructuary, B is not entitled to change the *farm into a hotel* and neither is the holder of a right of *use* or *habitation* (which is even less extensive than a usufruct) entitled to change the purpose of the land without the permission of the owner.

As stated in Case 1, the holder of a *hereditary building lease* owns the building and has a right of use with regard to the land (Law on Building Rights, § 6).[24] The holder of this right is therefore allowed to do anything with the building and may even demolish it.[25] As to the land, he/she is subject to the same restraints as the usufructuary. This means that he/she cannot change the purpose for which the land is used without the permission of the owner. Normally, however, these matters are arranged either expressly or implicitly in the contract which establishes the building right.

Belgium

If the parties have not made special contractual arrangements in this regard, the following default rules will apply: The conversion of the house into a warehouse/store and the farm into a hotel is not allowed under *a residential or agricultural lease* since the tenant is obliged to use the leased property according to its intended purpose which is determined by the provisions of the contract or the surrounding circumstances

[23] 1 Ob 502/88; JBl (1989), p. 103; 5 Ob 569/78; MietSlg 30.057; 7 Ob 142/02m; NZ (2004), p. 73; Hofmann, in Rummel, *Kommentar*, vol. 1, § 519, para. 1.

[24] Spruzina, in Schwimann, *Praxiskommentar*, vol. 3, § 6; BauRG, paras. 11 ff.

[25] BauRG, para. 11.

(Civil Code, art. 1728 1). An *enhancement in the value* of the property is not in itself sufficient to justify the proposed change in the intended purpose of the property. Even if the neighbourhood loses its residential character or the farm becomes incorporated within the city limits, the tenant is not entitled to effect the proposed change in purpose. The fact that the warehouse or hotel can be *changed back* to a house or a farm *at low cost* is again not in itself sufficient to justify the change of purpose.

Under a *usufruct*, the conversion of the *house into a warehouse/store* and the *farm into a hotel* is not allowed since the property must be used in accordance with its intended purpose as determined by the owner or in the manner of a *bonus paterfamilias*. In two exceptional cases the usufructuary is allowed to change the destination of the property, namely on account of socio-economical factors outside his/her control requiring adaptation of the property to the new situation, and where the previous owner had exploited the property in an abnormal way. In the latter case, the usufructuary (B) is obliged to manage and exploit the property as a *bonus paterfamilias*, even if this effects a change of purpose.

An *enhancement in the value of the property* will not in itself be sufficient to justify the proposed change in purpose of the property. However, the loss of the residential character of the neighbourhood or the incorporation of the farm within the city limits may qualify as an objective and external socio-economic factor which might justify the change in purpose. The fact that the warehouse or hotel can *be reverted at a low cost* to a house/a farm will again not in itself justify the change of destination.

The holder of *a hereditary land lease* (*emphyteusis*) can in principle alter the intended purpose of the property, provided this does not result in the reduction of the value of the land (Law on Hereditary Land Leases, art. 3). Consequently, if the alteration *enhances the value of the property*, the change in purpose would certainly be allowed. The same will apply in the case where the neighbourhood loses its residential character or the farm is incorporated within the city limits or where the warehouse or hotel can be *reverted* to a house or a farm at a *low cost*, on condition that the value of the land is not reduced by such alteration.

The holder of a *hereditary building lease* (*superficies*) may in principle change the intended purpose of the constructions on the land if he/she has paid for the existing structures on the land or where he/she has built them. The holder may exploit these structures in any way he/she sees fit and may even destroy them upon termination of the building lease. If the holder has not paid for the existing buildings on the land, he/she may not destroy them. The holder may obtain compensation for improvement to the land. These principles also affect the right to change the destination of the property.

Consequently, alterations to existing buildings paid for and new buildings are allowed. The position will be the same if the *neighbourhood loses its residential character* or the farm is incorporated within the city limits. If the warehouse or hotel can be changed back to a house or a farm at a *low cost*, the rights of the holder will be affected if the hereditary building lease was granted in respect of existing buildings not paid for by the holder. In such a case the holder will be obliged to restore the property to its previous condition on termination of the hereditary building lease.

Denmark

Section 26(1) of the Law on Private Housing states that the tenant may not use the premises for any purpose not agreed upon without the landlord's consent (Law on Private Housing, s. 26(1) and Law on Lease of Commercial Premises, s. 34(1)). These rules are not mandatory, but deviations are unlikely to be inserted in leases. If the tenant proceeds with a conversion without the prior consent of the landlord, the latter is entitled to terminate the contract without notice (Law on Private Housing, s. 93(1)(b) and Law on Lease of Commercial Premises, s. 69(1)(b)). A conversion such as the one in question will most probably be prohibited without the consent of the public authorities.

The situation remains negative even though the alteration *enhances the value* of the property, although this may of course make it easier for the tenant to negotiate with the landlord in order to obtain his consent. A change in the *residential character* of the neighbourhood or the *incorporation of the farm* within the city limits will not alter the situation. It further does not matter whether or not the tenant could *revert* the premises to its original condition upon termination of the lease.

England

Common methods by which alterations to the premises can be prevented include covenants against alteration and certain uses.[26] It is not infrequently the case that a lease of a house specifies that it is to be used for residential purposes only, or, alternatively that it is not to be

[26] Planning issues of a public-law nature may well arise in this context.

used for certain specified purposes. Further, or alternatively, it may be provided that alterations to the premises are impermissible. The court may also restrain alterations in so far as they amount to waste. If the landlord's covenant against alterations is qualified (that is, requires his/her consent), the statute provides that consent cannot be unreasonably withheld if the proposed work is an improvement (Landlord and Tenant Act, s. 19(2)).[27] Thus it may be that, in a qualified alterations covenant, the mere fact that there has been an increase in value indicates that it is an improvement, thereby triggering the statutory mechanism for reasonableness in respect of consent.

A tenant is, however, free to engage in any changes which fall short of an 'alteration'. It has been held that the term 'alteration' means structural alteration.[28] Whether given works amount to this is a question of fact and degree. Cosmetic changes (which are easily reversible) or the installation of new wiring will, for example, not count as alterations.[29] The conversion of a house into business premises or a block of flats is, however, thought to constitute alteration and therefore a breach of covenant.[30] It is, of course, possible for the landlord to draft his/her covenant in such a way as to ensure that even cosmetic or slight changes are prohibited.

Alternatively, the landlord may choose to regulate the use to which premises can be put by means of a 'user covenant'. These are frequently encountered in leases, and often enumerate the permissible uses or list excluded uses, sometimes in extreme detail.[31] Further, public policy grounds may be invoked to prevent certain uses. In construing such covenants (in so far as they are open to construction), the character of the premises can be taken into account.[32] In cases where the lease imposes a consent requirement for change of use, the landlord may not demand money as compensation for change of use, unless the change of use also entails an alteration of the premises (Landlord and Tenant Act, s. 19(3)). It is highly probable that the alteration of, say, a house or farm to non-residential use will be caught and excluded by user covenants, if it is not already caught by any alterations covenants.

27 See Lewison, *Woodfall's Law of Landlord and Tenant*, para. 11–261.
28 *Bickmore* v. *Dimmer* [1903] 1 Ch 158.
29 For a list of examples, see Lewison, *Woodfall's Law of Landlord and Tenant*, para. 11–258.
30 *Bonnett* v. *Sadler* (1808) 14 Ves 526; *Duke of Westminster* v. *Swinton* [1948] 1 KB 524.
31 It is often the case that residential leases specify use of the leased premises as a single dwelling, for instance.
32 *City and Westminster Properties (1934) Ltd.* v. *Mudd* [1959] Ch 129.

As to changes in character of the land or the locality, or economic changes, which render the covenants obsolete or otherwise oppressive, there is a judicial jurisdiction to discharge or modify any covenants which are obsolete or obstructive to some reasonable private use of the land (Law of Property Act, s. 84). Leasehold covenants restraining use of the demised premises are in practice challenged on that footing, especially where these leases are long commercial leases. Similarly, restrictions on alteration may be attacked by these means.

France

If B's *lease* of the property is regulated by a specific statute, he/she is not entitled to change the intended purpose of the property even if this increases the value of the property. A contrary act renders a residential lease open to cancellation, as the tenant must peaceably use the leased premises in accordance with the intended purpose of the property as set out in the lease (Law of 1989, art. 7). The tenant may, however, use residential premises which constitute his/her principal residence for professional or commercial purposes as long as no clients or merchandise are allowed onto the premises. This entitlement may not be restricted by a contrary stipulation in the lease (Code on Construction and Habitation, art. L 631–7–3).

If a tenant under an *agricultural lease* puts the leased property to a use other than for its intended purpose, the landlord may cancel the lease and claim compensation for the loss suffered as a result of the change in the intended use of the property (Civil Code, art. 1766).

Under a *usufruct*, the usufructuary is entitled to use the property in the same manner as an owner, on condition that the substance of the property is preserved (Civil Code, art. 578). Case law, however, allows an exception where a leisure residence is converted into a business concern.[33] Moreover, art. 618 Civil Code provides that an 'abuse of enjoyment' can lead to forfeiture of the usufruct. Under case law, concluding a commercial lease with respect to premises which are destined for another use can constitute this kind of abuse.[34] Finally, the usufructuary is bound to respect the provisions of local planning laws if the property is situated in a residential or agricultural zone. Thus, only if

[33] Civ. 3, 5 Dec. 1968; D 1969 274. [34] Civ. 3, 4 June 1975; Bull. civ. III, no. 194.

the immovable is no longer within a residential or agricultural zone *and* the conversion does not affect the substance of the property (for example, if the property can easily and at low cost be restored to its former state), is B able to carry out such a conversion.

Germany

German law distinguishes between *residential and agricultural leases*. In the absence of a contrary agreement, the tenant of residential property (*Wohnraummiete*) may only use the property for residential purposes. B will therefore not be entitled to *convert the dwelling house into a warehouse*. It makes no difference that such alteration may enhance the value of the property or can be reversed at low cost. Any changes in the character of the neighbourhood will only affect the additional requirements of public zoning law.

Under an *agricultural lease* (*Landpachtvertrag*), the tenant is in principle allowed to change the manner of exploitation of the property without the landowner's consent unless the alteration is so substantial that it affects the manner in which the owner may exploit his/her property upon termination of the lease (Civil Code, § 590(2)). Moreover, the tenant is only entitled to abandon the agricultural purpose (*landwirtschaftliche Bestimmung*) of the property where this is authorised by the landlord (Civil Code § 590(1)). Consequently, B will not be allowed to convert the *farm* (agricultural purpose) *into a hotel* (commercial purpose) unless the landlord allows him/her to do so.

Under a *usufruct*, the usufructuary (B) is not entitled to transform or substantially alter the property (Civil Code, § 1037(1)). Converting a *dwelling-house into a warehouse* or a *farm into a hotel* will certainly be regarded as a transformation or substantial alteration of the property and thus cannot be achieved without the owner's prior consent. The mere fact that the alteration *enhances the value of the property* will not make any difference.[35] Neither will it be permissible to argue that the warehouse or the hotel can be *reverted* to a house or a farm *at low cost*.

Changing circumstances (such as the neighbourhood losing its residential character or the farm being incorporated into a town) can only be taken into account if they are so radical as to amount to an interference

[35] Petzold, *Münchener Kommentar*, § 1037, no. 2.

with the business foundation (*Störung der Geschäftsgrundlage*) of the entire agreement (Civil Code, § 313).[36]

Under a *hereditary building lease*, the parties are free to stipulate that the holder may only alter the physical condition or the purpose of the structure with the consent of the landowner. Contractual arrangements of this kind are very common in practice.[37] Accordingly, B will not be entitled to make the conversions referred to in this Case without the consent of A.

Greece

Article 1, § 3 of Law 1703/1987 on *residential leases* stipulates that the lease of residential property is regulated by the terms of the contract and the ordinary provisions on leases (Civil Code, arts. 574–618), unless otherwise stated in these provisions. Although a tenant is not liable for deterioration of or alterations to the property consistent with its agreed use (Civil Code, art. 592), the landlord is entitled to give notice of immediate termination of the lease if the tenant uses the leased property in a manner inconsistent with the agreement (Civil Code, art. 594). The tenant is furthermore bound to restore the leased property to the condition he/she received it on taking possession (art. 599, § 1). Consequently, unless the landlord agrees to the conversion of the *house into a warehouse*, the tenant will not be entitled to effect such conversion.

In the case of the *lease of agricultural property* (a farm), the agricultural tenant (tenant farmer) is bound to exploit the leased land with care and in conformity with its intended purpose. He/she has to maintain the property in a good condition so as to assure its continued productivity.[38] Furthermore, the tenant is expressly forbidden from changing the existing method of exploitation in a way that may substantially influence the property's exploitation on the expiry of the lease (Civil Code, art. 623). He/she may therefore not convert the *farmhouse into a hotel.*

36 Interference with business foundations or *Störung der Geschäftsgrundlage* is a general concept – primarily, but not exclusively applicable to the law of obligations – intended to take account of (radically) changing circumstances. Though *Störung der Geschäftsgrundlage* is similar, in some regards to the *clausula rebus sic stantibus*, it is commonly regarded as a concept of its own.

37 See e.g. the standard form contracts, in von Oefele and Winkler, *Handbuch*, pp. 487 ff.

38 Georgiadou, in Georgiades and Stathopoulos, *GCC, Collective Analysis*, art. 623 (386–7).

It does not make a difference if the alteration *enhances the value* of the property.[39] The conversion of a farm into a hotel cannot be regarded as an improvement which increases the agricultural productivity of the property (Civil Code, art. 622). If the neighbourhood loses its residential character or the *farm becomes incorporated within the city limits*, it can be regarded as an unforeseeable change of circumstances which can justify the dissolution of the lease by a court (Civil Code, art. 388) on the basis that the economic purpose of the lease can no longer be pursued.

Under a *usufruct*, the usufructuary is bound to preserve the intended purpose of the property and to use the property in accordance with the rules of orderly exploitation. He/she is not allowed to introduce substantial changes to the property (Civil Code, art. 1148). Converting a *house into a warehouse* or a *farm into a hotel* will not only be against the intended purpose of the property and represent non-orderly exploitation of the property but will also amount to a substantial change in the nature of the property.

Since the rights of *habitation* and *limited personal servitudes* restrict the holder to a specific use of the property, the holder of the right will not be entitled to change the purpose of the property. The rules governing usufruct are applicable by analogy to the right of habitation and limited personal servitudes (Civil Code, arts. 1187 and 1189 respectively).

The strict obligations on the usufructuary to preserve the substance and economic purpose of the property (Civil Code, arts. 1142 and 1148) do not allow for an exception in the case where the *value* of the property is *enhanced* by the change or where the *neighbourhood* of the property *changes*. Since the usufructuary has to restore the property upon expiry of the usufruct (Civil Code, art. 1161), the change may not be considered substantial if the substance and intended purpose of the property can be restored *at low cost*. The same applies to the holders of the right of habitation and limited personal servitudes (Civil Code, arts. 1187 and 1191).

Hungary

The tenant under an *ordinary lease* or an *income-producing lease* and the borrower in terms of a *loan for use* must use the property only in a proper

[39] Filios, *Obligations*, pp. 235, 236, 328; Rapsomanikis, in Georgiades and Stathopoulos, *GCC, Collective Analysis*, art. 594, no. 3 (318); Georgiadou, *ibid.* art. 623, no. 4 (387).

manner and according to its function (Civil Code, §§ 425(1), 453 and 457 (2)(b); Law on Agricultural Land, § 18(a)). Accordingly, the tenant and borrower cannot alter the major characteristics of the property, nor can they reconstruct the property irreversibly. Consequently, the tenant and borrower are not entitled to convert the property. It is irrelevant whether the alteration enhances the value of the property, the neighbourhood loses its residential character or the farm becomes incorporated within the city limits.

As regards *usufruct* and the *right of use*, the requirement of proper management does not mean that the usufructuary and the usuary must adhere rigidly to the situation that existed prior to the creation of the rights *in rem*. On the contrary, the requirement of proper management must be determined on the basis of the general function of the property and any changes in circumstances.[40] It will be lawful to improve the use of farmland or to enhance the comfort of residential property, but it is prohibited to effect changes that reduce the value or the utility of the property.[41] A purported change cannot alter the fundamental function of the property. Residential property can thus not be converted into a business centre or factory, a house cannot be converted into a warehouse nor a farm into a hotel. The fact that the alteration enhances the value of the property makes a difference only if it does not alter the fundamental function of the property. The fact that the neighbourhood loses its residential character or that a farm is incorporated within the city limits is relevant only from the point of view of the public authority which must give permission to build.

The fact that the warehouse or the hotel can be changed back to a house or a farm at a low cost is relevant. If the initial arrangement can be restored at a trivial or relatively negligible cost, the alteration will not be contrary to the requirement of proper use and proper management as the property can be restored before it is returned to the owner.

Unfortunately, the law governing these aspects of usufruct and the right to use is not entirely settled since they are closely intertwined with family relations and inheritance matters. The object of these rights are normally residential properties and smaller farmlands which are meant to satisfy the personal needs of the holder and which are usually

[40] Reasoning of the ministerial proposal for the Civil Code, interpretation attached to, § 159(2).

[41] Gellért, *Commentary Civil Code*, vol 1, p. 537.

incapable of large-scale production. These points will require clarification from the Hungarian courts.

Italy

As a general rule, the tenant under a *lease* must use the property for the purpose specified in the contract or for purposes which can otherwise be inferred from the circumstances (Civil Code, art. 1587). Normally, a tenant converting a *house into a warehouse* or a *farm into a hotel* will be violating the contract. The fact that the alteration *enhances the value* of the property or that the property can *at low cost be reverted to its original condition* does not make a difference.[42] Under Italian law, a contract cannot, however, be terminated if the non-performance by one party only slightly affects the interests of the other party (Civil Code, art. 1455). This provision should thus be borne in mind when considering the rights of the landlord to demand termination of the contract.

While the Civil Code and several special statutes[43] expect dynamic management from the tenant of the income-producing property, and particularly from the *tenant of rural lands*, and encourage him/her to take measures to increase the profitability of the leased property, the tenant must always respect the intended agricultural purpose of the land.

If a radical and unforeseeable change of circumstances were to render the original use of the property absurd, the tenant can probably demand dissolution of the contract, but cannot alter the intended purpose of the property. There is, however, no direct authority on this point. It must also be kept in mind that the rules applicable to the lease differ according to the nature and purpose of the property leased.

Under a *usufruct*, the usufructuary has the right to enjoy the property in accordance with its nature and intended purpose (Civil Code, art. 981). In principle, the usufructuary is not entitled to convert a *house into a warehouse* or a *farm into a hotel*. The fact that the alteration *enhances the value* of the property is irrelevant.[44] Circumstances which radically change the original use of the property may influence this rule, but there is no direct authority on the point. The fact that it is possible to *revert* the warehouse to a dwelling house or the hotel to a farm *at a low cost* is apparently irrelevant.

[42] See Cass. civ. 20/06/1961 n. 1460.
[43] Civil Code, art. 1620; Law of 11/02/1971; Law of 03/05/1982 n 203.
[44] See Pugliese, *Usufrutto*, p. 297.

Once again, there is no case law and little literature on the conversion of land subject to a *hereditary building lease* (*superficies*). If it involves the right to erect a new building, the holder will be free, in the absence of contrary provisions in the constitutive agreement, to use the building as he/she pleases, as there is no previous intended purpose to respect. The rules may, however, differ for the conversion of an already existing building. Some scholars emphasise the fact that the *proprietario superficiario* is an owner *ad tempus*, and not the holder of a limited right. As such, his/her right to enjoy the property should not be subjected to the same limits as those of a usufructuary and in particular, he should be free to alter the intended economic purpose of the property.[45] Others suggest that the rules pertaining to usufruct should apply by analogy to holders of hereditary building leases.[46]

The Netherlands

The alterations are not allowed under a *residential or agricultural lease* unless the landlord agrees. In the case of an agricultural lease, converting the farm into a hotel will take the lease out of the category of agricultural leases. The Law on Agricultural Leases (*Pachtwet*) will no longer apply. The contract will henceforth be regarded as a commercial lease. Similarly, converting the residence to a warehouse will require the landlord's permission and will turn the contract into a commercial lease.

In the case of a *usufruct*, the usufructuary cannot change the intended purpose of the property, unless either the owner consents or there is an authorisation by the *Kantonrechter* (Circuit Court judge) (Civil Code, art. 3:208 I). This rule applies if the purported change is to the benefit of the owner, for example, if his/her wealth is increased.[47] The rule will also apply where the neighbourhood *loses its residential character* or the *farm is incorporated into a town*. It may, however, be possible to obtain authorisation from the court for such a conversion. Some authors argue that where a prospective change of destination will be temporary and can be *reversed at a low cost*, such a change will be allowed.[48] This rule does not apply where the usufructuary is entitled to dispose of the goods which are encumbered with the right of usufruct (Civil Code, art. 3:212 II).

[45] See e.g. Natoli, *La proprietà*, p. 208. [46] See Caterina, *I diritti*, pp. 83 ff.
[47] Pitlo, 'Goederenrecht', no. 697. [48] *Ibid.*

In the case of a *hereditary building lease* (*superficies*), the holder is the owner of buildings and structures on the surface of someone else's land (Civil Code, art. 5:101). The right of the holder with regard to the use, construction and demolition of buildings, structures and plants may be restricted in the constitutive deed by which the hereditary building lease is established (Civil Code, art. 5:102). If there are no restrictions in the constitutive deed, the holder seems to be allowed to do whatever he/she pleases with the buildings on the land. There is no obligation on the holder to uphold the intended purpose of the land subject to the building lease.[49]

Without the consent of the landowner, the holder of a *hereditary land lease* (*emphyteusis*) cannot change the intended purpose of the land or effect changes to the land which will be in conflict with such a purpose (Civil Code, art. 5:89 II).[50] This is a mandatory rule.

Poland

Under both an *ordinary lease* and an *income-producing lease*, the tenant may only change the use of the property with the landlord's consent (Civil Code, arts. 667, § 1 and 696). If no such consent is granted, changes may not be made, regardless of their cost, added value, changes in land use or in the neighbourhood.

Under *usufruct*, the usufructuary (B) is obliged to preserve the substance and the existing use of the land (Civil Code, art. 267, § 1). The only exception concerns the right to mine (Civil Code, art. 267, § 2 and 3). Theoretically, if the usufructuary is an agricultural production co-operative, it may change the substance and use of State Treasury land if such change does not contravene the provisions of the contract with the state (Civil Code, art. 275). This provision is rarely employed in practice, as there are not many agricultural production co-operatives left and income-producing (*fruendi*) *leases* are more popular.

The content of a *hereditary land lease* (perpetual usufruct, *emphyteusis*) is to a large extent shaped by contractual provisions. Land is generally given in hereditary land lease for residential, recreational, industrial or cultural purposes (Civil Code, arts. 236 and 239; Law on Management of Real Property, art. 29). The contract furthermore contains provisions on the erection of new buildings or the alteration of existing ones, even

[49] Asser, Mijnssen, van Dam and van Velten, 'Zakelijke Rechten', no. 252.

[50] *Ibid.*; Pitlo, 'Goederenrecht', no. 647.

including the dates of commencement and completion of building works (art. 62). Consequently, the holder will be able to make alterations which are in conformity with the contractual provisions.

Portugal

Under a *lease*, the tenant is not allowed to exploit the property in a manner contrary to its intended purpose (Civil Code, art. 1038 c), which means that he/she will not be entitled to effect the conversions referred to. In fact, such action would entitle the landlord to terminate an *urban or agricultural lease* (Civil Code, art. 1083 c; Decree-Law 294/2009, art. 17 no 2(c)). The tenant is not entitled to convert the *house into a warehouse* or the *farm into a hotel*, even when the alteration would *enhance the value* of the property, the area is *zoned as an industrial area*, the farm is incorporated witin the city limits or the intended purpose of the property can be *restored* later at a *low cost*.

Under a *usufruct*, the usufructuary has the right to use and administer the property and to enjoy its fruits. He/she must, however, exercise his/her right according to the standards of a *bonus paterfamilias* in accordance with the intended purpose of the property and without impairing its form and substance (Civil Code, art. 1446). Therefore, even if a certain degree of freedom is allowed in the exploitation of the property, the usufructuary's power to alter the property is restricted according to traditional academic opinion to improvements which do not transform the intended purpose of the property.[51] B would therefore not be entitled to convert the *house into a warehouse* or the *farm into a hotel*.

Recently, Menezes Cordeiro[52] provided a novel interpretation of the provision by suggesting that the usufructuary has to respect the intended purpose of the property, but does not necessarily have to maintain it if it is possible to restore the property to its intended purpose on termination of the usufruct. Therefore, the usufructuary is entitled to transform a garage into a restaurant, if it was possible to restore the *status quo ante* (economically speaking). Only if restoration of the economic destination is not possible would the usufructuary have disrespected the intended purpose of the property. Again, Oliveira Ascensão[53] regards Civil Code, art. 1446 as a default rule which can be

[51] Carvalho Fernandes, *Lições de Direitos Reais*, p. 345

[52] Menezes Cordeiro, *Direitos Reais*, p. 654. [53] Oliveira Ascensão, *Direito Civil*, p. 475.

modified by an agreement between A and B allowing the usufructuary to change the intended purpose of the property.

In the light of these principles, the usufructuary cannot convert the *house into a warehouse* or the *farm into a hotel*, even if the alteration enhances the value of the property or the neighbourhood loses its residential character or the farm is incorporated within the city limits.

However, Menezes Cordeiro[54] feels that although the usufructuary has to respect the intended purpose of the property, he/she does not necessarily have to maintain it if it is possible to restore the intended purpose of the property on termination of the usufruct. Therefore, the usufructuary will be entitled to transform the house into a warehouse or the farm into a hotel if it was possible to restore the *status quo ante* (economically speaking).

Under a *hereditary building lease* (*superficies*), the holder will not be allowed to change the intended purpose of an existing building. If the right pertains to the construction of future buildings, the holder, being regarded as enjoying the same rights as an owner, will be free to convert the *house into a warehouse* or the *farmhouse into a hotel*.

Scotland

Under a *lease*, a tenant is obliged to use the property for the purposes for which it is let. A tenant who uses property in a manner inconsistent with the objects of the lease is said to 'invert' the possession, which is a breach of contract.[55] Typically, a lease will provide that the property can only be used for certain purposes, in which case B cannot use the lease for any other purposes without the landlord's consent. (The landlord can restrain any other use by interdict.) Even if the lease is silent, the common law adopts the position that leases are granted with a view to a particular sort of possession.[56] A lease of a dwellinghouse is said to envisage residence: B can therefore not convert the *house into a warehouse*.[57] It makes no difference that the conversion will *enhance the value* of the property, that it could easily be undone or that the *neighbourhood*

[54] Cordeiro, *Direitos Reais*, p. 654.

[55] Rankine, *Leases*, p. 236; Paton and Cameron, *Landlord and Tenant*, pp. 137–8; McAllister, *Leases*, para. 3.3.

[56] Rankine, *Law of Leases*, p. 236.

[57] This very example is given by Hume, in Paton, *Hume*, vol. 2, p. 76 as an instance of inversion of possession.

has lost its residential character.[58] There is a procedure by which title conditions can be varied on the grounds, *inter alia*, of the changing character of the neighbourhood in which the property is situated.[59] Only a term of a registrable lease (one which exceeds twenty years' duration) is, however, within the definition of 'title condition'.[60] As a lease of a property for use as a private dwellinghouse may not exceed twenty years' duration, this procedure will not be available.

The same common law rules apply to *agricultural leases*. In one case a tenant of a house and farm was held not to be entitled to trade as a publican from the property.[61] If the lease exceeds twenty years' duration, however, the tenant can apply to the Lands Tribunal to have its terms varied. One of the several factors which the Lands Tribunal will consider is *a change in the character of the neighbourhood.*[62] Tenants of a 1991 Act Tenancy or a Limited Duration Tenancy also benefit from a statutory rule which allows the tenant to diversify beyond agricultural use.[63] The tenancy does not cease to be an agricultural tenancy by reason of the diversification. The tenant must send a notice of diversification to the landlord, detailing the proposed changes and how they are to be financed and managed.[64] The landlord then has an opportunity to object or to impose reasonable conditions on the tenant,[65] but both powers are subject to judicial control.[66] The only substantive grounds upon which the landlord can object to the proposed diversification are:

(a) that the use will significantly lessen the amenity of the land or the surrounding area;
(b) that the use will substantially prejudice the use of the land for agricultural purposes in the future;
(c) that the use will be detrimental to the sound management of the estate of which the land consists or forms part;
(d) that the use will cause the landlord to suffer undue hardship or
(e) where the landlord reasonably considers that the notice fails to show that the proposed changes or the business will be viable.

58 But see *Skene* v. *McBrerty* (1822) 1 S 369 where, because the landlord had not for some time enforced a term of a lease restricting the tenant to a particular use, it could not later be enforced by interdict because the nature of the lease was said to have changed.

59 Title Conditions (Scotland) Act 2003 (henceforth TC(S)A 03), Part 9, especially s. 100(a).

60 TC(S)A 03, s. 122(1).

61 *Miln* v. *Mitchell* 1787 Mor 15 254 (apparently, use as an ale house was 'such as, in itself ought to be discouraged'); Paton, *Hume*, vol. 2, p. 77.

62 TC(S)A 03, s. 100(a). 63 AH(S)A 03, Pt. 3. 64 AH(S)A 03, s. 40.

65 AH(S)A 03, ss. 40(9) and 40(10). 66 AH(S)A 03, s. 41.

Depending on the precise circumstances, B may therefore be able to convert the *farm into a hotel*.

Although there is no explicit discussion of the issues in respect of *liferent* as the liferenter is not allowed to encroach upon the substance of the subjects, it is thought that he/she cannot change its character by converting the *house into a warehouse* or the *farm into a hotel*. It might make a difference, however, if it were possible to *restore* the original use quickly and at a *low cost*, leaving the subjects in exactly the state they were in beforehand, as that would suggest that the substance of the subjects had not been affected.

South Africa

In the absence of a contrary agreement, the tenant under a *lease* is only entitled to use the property for the purpose for which it has been let according to its previous use or a use to which the property lends itself.[67] Hence the tenant of a dwelling house is not allowed to turn it into a stable, a hotel or a blacksmith's workshop in the same way that the tenant of a shop cannot convert it into a bar, a restaurant or a dwelling house.[68] These Roman-Dutch and South African examples illustrate that the tenant will not be able to convert the *house into a warehouse*. Again, in the case of farmland, the tenant may not convert pastureland into arable land or orchards into pasturage or flower gardens.[69] Consequently, the tenant will not be allowed to convert the *farm into a hotel*.

The permissibility of such alterations is not affected by *enhancement of the value* of the property or a change in the *character of the neighbourhood*. Such alterations may be carried out only with the express or implied consent of the landlord. However, some Roman-Dutch writers allow alterations more readily in the initial period of a long lease with the qualification that the tenant must be able to reconvert the land to its former condition at the end of the lease.[70] Thus the initial conversion will be permissible if the tenant will be able to *reinstate* the warehouse as a dwelling house or the hotel as a farm *at low cost*. This corresponds with

67 Van der Linden, *Koopmans Handboek*, 1.15.12.

68 Pothier, *Obligations*, para. 189; Voet, *Commentarius*, 19.2.29; Kerr, 'Lease', para. 186; Cooper, *Landlord and Tenant*, p. 207.

69 Voet, *Commentarius*, 19.2.29.

70 *Ibid.*; Cooper, *Landlord and Tenant*, p. 210; *Houghton Estate Co.* v. *McHattie and Barrat* (1894) 1 OR 92 102–3.

the principle that the tenant should be allowed to exploit the property advantageously as long as he/she does not cause harm and can return it in good condition.[71]

The only *personal servitude* applicable is *usufruct*, since neither the *usuary* nor the *habitator* has the right to exploit the house or farm to the extent envisaged here. The usufructuary has a duty to restore the property *salva rerum substantia*, namely to exploit the property without impairing its substance. Originally, the usufructuary was not allowed to alter the physical condition of the house or farm. Later, the emphasis shifted to the intended purpose (economic destiny) of the property. Limited structural alteration of the property was allowed if this was in accordance with its intended purpose.[72] South African law will therefore allow a new mode of exploitation if this is the sensible course to take under the circumstances. In an extreme case, the usufructuary was even allowed to sell a farm and retain a usufruct on the proceeds of the sale in order to avoid excessive hardship and because it was clearly to the advantage of the nude owners (minor heirs).[73] Thus, in cases of extreme hardship and where it will be to the advantage of the eventual owners, the usufructuary will probably be able to convert a house into a warehouse or a farm into a hotel.

Since advantage to the eventual heir impacts on the question whether conversion should be allowed, the fact that the conversion will significantly *enhance the value of the property* will be an important factor in favour of allowing the conversion. Again, the *changed neighbourhood* may make it extremely hard to continue the previous exploitation and will make the conversion of the property a sensible option.

Spain

The *tenant of residential premises* cannot convert it into a warehouse. He/she cannot even alter the appearance of the premises or its fittings unless expressly authorised by the landlord (Law on Urban Leases, art. 23.1). Such an alteration of the premises will entitle the landlord to terminate the contract (Law on Urban Leases, art. 27.2f).

[71] See Cooper, *Landlord and Tenant*, p. 217; De Wet and Van Wyk, *Kontraktereg*, p. 316.

[72] See Voet, *Commentarius*, 7.1.21, 24 and 26.

[73] See *Fourie* v. *Munnik* 1919 OPD 73, 79, 86–7; *Gibaud* v. *Bagshaw* 1918 CPD 202, 205; *Ex parte Keth's Estate* 1919 EDL 61; *Geldenhuys* v. *CIR* 1947 3 SA 256 (C) where the usufructuary of a herd of cattle was allowed to sell the herd because extreme hardship made it impossible for the herd to be maintained.

The *tenant of a farm* cannot convert it *into a hotel*. Such conversion entitles the landlord to sue for termination of the contract because the farm is no longer exploited in accordance with its intended purpose and used for purposes other than those agreed on (Law on Rural Leases, art. 25.c).[74] If the farm is *incorporated within the city limits*, the planning authority will zone it as 'urban land' (*suelo urbano*) or 'building land' (*suelo urbanizable*). Since the operation of an agricultural lease would then be impossible, the landlord is entitled to terminate the lease (Law on Rural Leases, arts. 7.1.a and 25.e).

A lease governed by Civil Code, art. 1555.2, obliges the tenant to use the property for the purpose specified in the contract[75] or, where nothing was agreed, to use it according to the purpose inferred from the nature of the property[76] and in accordance with local customs. If the tenant changes the agreed purpose, the landlord is entitled to demand the rescission (*rescisión*) of the contract and to be awarded damages (Civil Code, art. 1556), or to use a special procedure (*juicio de desahucio*) to evict the tenant (Civil Code, art. 1569.4). Note that the Civil Code will apply only if the lease is not governed by the provisions of the Laws on Urban or Rural Leases.

The fact that the alteration *enhances the value* of the property or that it can be *changed back* does not make a difference. If the neighbourhood *loses its residential character* or the *farm* is *incorporated* within the city limits, there are no special provisions that entitle the tenant to change the destination of the property.

Under a *usufruct*, the usufructuary has to preserve the form and substance of the property in the sense of preserving its intended purpose,[77] unless the constitutive title of a usufruct created *inter vivos* or the Civil Code allow change of the use or intended purpose of the property (Civil Code, art. 467). The rights and duties of the usufructuary are therefore as stipulated in the constitutive deed, and, failing this, as stipulated in the provisions of the Civil Code (Civil Code, art. 470).[78] This means that the

[74] The Spanish Supreme Court of 31 Mar. 1926 held this in a case of a tenant of a wheat farm who built a factory to produce flour. The court decided that in such a case the tenant does not alter the use of the farm and does not cause damage to, or reduction in, the value of the farm.

[75] Decisions of the Spanish Supreme Court of 8 Apr. 1952, 24 June 1952, 27 Feb. 1995.

[76] Lacruz Berdejo, *Elementos*, vol. 2.2, p. 123 states that the tenant is obliged to use the leased property according to the use and purpose it was leased for.

[77] Lacruz Berdejo, *Elementos*, vol. 2.2, p. 25; decision of the Spanish Supreme Court of 27 June 1969.

[78] *Ibid*. vol 3.2, pp. 5 and 6.

usufructuary cannot convert the *house into a warehouse*, or the *farm into a hotel*, unless the change was allowed in the constitutive title of the usufruct or in the Civil Code. The fact that the alteration *enhances the value* of the property does not make a difference: the usufructuary may only make improvements to the property in so far as its form or substance is not altered (Civil Code, art. 487). Conversion of the house into a warehouse or the farm into a hotel, although an improvement, also involves an essential change of the property's substance and its intended purpose. Even though it is possible to *change the property back* to its previous form *at a low cost*, the usufructuary will still not be entitled to effect such alterations as they will amount to a change in the intended purpose of the property. The Civil Code contains no rules on the radical change of circumstances of property subject to a usufruct. However, article 519 dealing with compulsory purchase provides that, in such cases, the nude owner is bound either to replace the property by another property of similar condition and value or to pay the usufructuary the legal interest on the proceeds of the property for the remaining term of the usufruct.

Spanish law contains no rules on the content of a *hereditary building lease* (*superficies*), but it is understood that the holder of the right has very wide powers to achieve the purpose envisaged in the constitutive title of the lease.[79]

[79] *Ibid.* 187.

Case 8
Remedies of the landowner against misconduct by the holder of a time-limited interest

A is dissatisfied with the way in which B conducts himself/herself with regard to the property. Explain what measures of control and eventual remedies are available to him against B.

Indicate when such control and remedies can be exercised.

Comparative observations

Under a *lease*, the discontented landlord may demand that the tenant use the property properly and in accordance with the terms of the lease. If the tenant does not heed the demand, the landlord may claim specific performance of the contract.[1] If the tenant persists in violating the terms of the lease, the most important remedy of the landlord is cancellation of the lease for fundamental breach.[2] In most jurisdictions a claim for cancellation can in appropriate circumstances be supplemented by an eviction order[3] and a claim for damages.[4] In the alternative, the landlord can request a court order to restrain the tenant from activities which violate the contract, such as using the property for

[1] See e.g. the German, French, Greek, Belgian, Scottish, South African and Hungarian reports.

[2] Italian law, for example, regards the operation of minor commercial activities without substantial physical alterations under a residential lease as a minor breach. Under Danish law, the lease can even be cancelled on grounds that it does not amount to a breach of the contract under Unidroit Principles.

[3] See e.g. the German, Austrian, Greek, French, Belgian, Portuguese, Spanish, South African and Hungarian reports. Germany has a detailed set of rules, supplemented with extensive case law, to strengthen the position of tenants under residential leases and to make their eviction more difficult. See also the 'irritancy clauses' inserted into Scottish leases.

[4] See e.g. the German, Greek, French, Belgian, Spanish, Portuguese, Danish, Scottish, South African and Hungarian reports.

purposes not provided for, exploiting the property improperly, damaging it or substantially altering it.[5]

In some jurisdictions the landlord may claim for damages aimed at recovering the reasonable cost of repairs[6] on the ground of non-fundamental breach which does not entitle the landlord to cancel the contract.[7] Certain jurisdictions even allow a claim for damages in the case of a fundamental breach if the landlord desires to keep the lease alive.[8] By contrast, other jurisdictions do not allow a claim for minor damages prior to the termination of the lease in lieu of insisting on repairs.[9] In France, the landlord, in lieu of claiming damages, may retain the amount deposited by the tenant at the inception of the lease against damage to the property or have recourse to the liability insurance which the tenant is required to obtain.[10]

In England, the remedies for breach of specific or general covenants are injunctions and damages, or, in the alternative, damages may be awarded to compensate the landlord for any loss or in lieu of an injunction. If the landlord's lease contains a proviso for re-entry entitling him/her to forfeit it for the precise breach committed, he/she may be able to bring the lease to an end by forfeiting it. Furthermore, it may be possible for a third party (or landlord) affected by the tenant's conduct, to bring an ordinary common law claim for private nuisance. It is also possible that more egregious behaviour will fall foul of the criminal law (such as public order offences).

The most prevalent remedy of the nude owner under *usufruct* for neglect or unreasonable exploitation of the property is an injunction (interdict) against the usufructuary compelling him/her to refrain from serious or repeated violations of his/her obligations.[11] In the case of minor violations, the nude owner's right to redress is restricted by the fact that the usufructuary has a discretion in deciding how and when to comply with his/her obligations, which forces the prudent nude owner

[5] See e.g. the German, Austrian, Portuguese, English, Danish and South African reports.

[6] South African law restricts damages to actual patrimonial loss.

[7] See e.g. the Spanish and Danish reports.

[8] E.g. under the Belgian and Spanish Civil Codes.

[9] E.g. damage which can be repaired at small cost. See e.g. the Belgian and South African reports.

[10] See the French report.

[11] See e.g. the German, Austrian, Italian and South African reports. German law also allow an injunction if the usufructuary ignores a warning against certain activities issued by the landowner.

to wait until the expiry of the usufruct before requesting restoration of the property and compensation.

In cases where a usufructuary's conduct constitutes a risk of serious damage or poses a serious threat to his/her interests, some jurisdictions allow the nude owner to demand security against future damage to the property[12] as a supplement to an injunction.[13] In other jurisdictions, the usufructuary may be ordered by the court to co-operate with the nude owner in preparing an inventory of the property at the start of the usufruct and to provide personal or real security against future damage.[14]

In case of persistent serious damage to the land, the nude owner in some jurisdictions may demand that the administration of the usufruct be placed under the supervision of the court, a professional manager or even the nude owner.[15] Under Greek law, this remedy is also available if the usufructuary is unwilling or unable to provide security. The management of the property will be handed back to the usufructuary as soon as security is provided or the grounds justifying the appointment of the manager have disappeared.

Most jurisdictions allow the landowner to claim compensation on termination of the usufruct for damage suffered due to non-compliance with the obligation to return the property without impairment of its substance.[16] This can include, *inter alia*, compensation for the repair of the farmstead, outbuildings, fences and gates and for recultivation of neglected agricultural land. Under Belgian law, the landowner may claim compensation even during the term of the usufruct for damage if immediate and certain damage can be proved.

In principle, a usufruct cannot be cancelled or the usufructuary evicted before the usufruct expires owing to the death of the usufructuary or completion of the term of the usufruct.[17] However, some

[12] See the German, Austrian, Greek, Italian, Hungarian and Polish reports. Under Hungarian law, security can be demanded from the usufructuary if the latter, after a warning, continues to exploit the property improperly, impairs its value or endangers the return of the property without impairment of its substance. Exercise of the usufruct can be suspended until the security is provided. In Poland, security can be demanded only where the usufructuary is allowed to undertake mining activities.

[13] See the Dutch and South African reports.

[14] See the Portuguese and Belgian reports.

[15] See the German, Austrian, Greek and Dutch reports. Under Italian law, the court may instead order that the property be leased out.

[16] The Scottish report emphasises that this is only possible on expiry of the usufruct.

[17] See e.g. the German and Polish reports.

jurisdictions allow the landowner to demand the return of the property if a request for security is ignored or if the property is seriously damaged or devalued through gross neglect of maintenance.[18] Depending on the seriousness of the circumstances, the court may either order the complete termination of the usufruct or the return of the property to the nude owner subject to an obligation on the nude owner to pay a fixed annual amount of money to the usufructuary until the expiry of the usufruct.[19] In Portugal and Spain, the landowner must hand over the net income of the property to the usufructuary every year.

In most jurisdictions, with the exception of Italy and Belgium, the remedies available to the landowner against a holder of the lesser personal servitude of *use* or *habitation* are less extensive than those available against a usufructuary. The German report, for instance, only mentions a court order to stop interference with the rights of the landowner and an action for compensation for damage caused intentionally or carelessly to the property. Greek law expressly denies a landowner to claim security against the holder of the right of habitation for unconscionable use of the property or to order the holder to insure the property against damage.

However, under Spanish law, the right of use or habitation expires automatically if the holder seriously abuses his/her right of enjoyment and the Polish Civil Code provides that in case of a strained relationship between the parties either party may request the court to convert some or all of the *habitator's* rights into a fixed annual sum based on their value or, in an extreme case, to terminate the right of habitation.

Some jurisdictions by analogy extend the remedies applicable to usufruct or a hereditary land lease to the holder of a *hereditary building lease* (*superficies*).[20] It is generally accepted, however, that the constitutive agreement establishing a building lease prescribes the parties' rights and obligations in much more detail than that creating personal servitudes *inter vivos*. Consequently, the landowner's most important remedy in practice is an action for breach of contract. If, for instance, the holder has substantially altered the physical condition of the structure without the landowner's consent as required by the contract, the landowner may request the court to order the holder to restore the original structure, or claim compensation for damages suffered. Under German law, the landowner may in addition claim for the retransfer of

[18] See the Austrian, French, Belgian, Italian, Portuguese and Spanish reports.
[19] See the Belgian, French and Italian reports. [20] See the Belgian and Dutch reports.

the building right against payment of a fair compensation for improvements if the conditions for re-transfer set out in the contract are met.

A remedy is available to the landowner in the form of an action to terminate the *hereditary land lease* (*emphyteusis*) if the holder seriously fails to comply with his/her obligations,[21] grossly abuses his/her rights or causes serious damage to the property.[22] The holder of the hereditary land lease may stay the termination by repairing the damage caused and by providing security against future damage.

On termination of the hereditary land lease, the landowner under Belgian law is entitled to claim expenses and compensation for damage and loss of rent caused by the holder's negligence and lack of maintenance. Under Dutch law, the landowner is allowed to deduct his/her expenses as well as compensation that can be claimed from the amount he had to pay the holder for improvements to the property. Polish law provides that, before terminating the hereditary land lease, the landowner may set a new date for the completion of a building which was not completed within the agreed time against payment of an additional rent.

In Hungary, a loan for use can be terminated with immediate effect if, *inter alia*, the borrower damages the property, uses it improperly, abandons its use to a third person without the permission of the lender, or if there is a risk that the borrower will not return the property in a sound condition. However, the law does not confer an express right of control on the lender.

Austria

If the tenant under the *lease* uses the leased object in a way which contravenes the terms of the contract, the landlord can ask the court for a prohibitory injunction. If the unlawful use is due to negligence, the landlord can also claim damages (Civil Code, § 1111). If the unlawful use causes serious damage to the property, the landlord may terminate the contract (Civil Code, § 1118, Law on Tenancy, § 30, para. 2, no. 3).

Under Civil Code, § 520, the nude owner can claim security against future damage to the property if the *usufructuary* behaves in a way which objectively creates a risk of damage to the land. Furthermore, the owner

[21] Under Dutch law if the holder fails to pay the annual rent for two consecutive years, or under Polish law if the holder exploits the land contrary to the terms of the grant, for example, where he/she fails to erect buildings which he/she has undertaken to erect.

[22] See the Belgian and Polish reports.

may ask the court for an injunction prohibiting future damage.[23] If no security is provided, the owner can claim the return of the property (and thus the termination of the usufruct) or ask for the administration of the property by the court.[24] The same applies to the right of *use*, the right of *habitation* and the *hereditary building lease*.

Belgium

In the case of a *residential lease*, Civil Code, art. 1730 requires an extensive inventory of the property at the outset (prepared by both parties either before the tenant enters into occupation or during his/her first month of residence). In the case of an *agricultural lease*, one party can demand from the other to co-operate with the preparation of such an extensive inventory during the first three months (Law on Agricultural Lease, art. 45–6). In the absence of this inventory, there is a presumption in favour of the tenant that he received the property in the same condition as it is upon termination of the lease, unless there is proof to the contrary. The tenant must return the property in the same condition he received it, as recorded in the inventory, except for items which have been destroyed or damaged on account of fair wear and tear or *force majeur*. The landlord may request personal or real security from the (residential or agricultural) tenant guaranteeing his/her compliance with his/her lease obligations.

In case of non-performance, the landlord may ask for specific performance if possible and if not, may claim compensation or, in the case of sufficiently serious default, cancellation of the lease, if necessary together with compensation for the damage caused. A *pactum commissorium* or explicit resolutive clause is forbidden by law (Civil Code, art. 1762 bis; Law on Agricultural Leases, art. 29). Cancellation of the lease always requires the court's intervention (Civil Code, art. 1184).

These remedies (compensation, specific performance or cancellation) may be invoked by the landlord if, for example, the tenant changes the intended purpose of the property without the consent of the owner or the tenant acts contrary to the standards of a *bonus paterfamilias*. If the tenant causes damage to the property (for example, because of a lack of maintenance), the owner may in principle only claim compensation or repair on termination of the lease,[25] unless the tenant has caused

[23] 1 Ob 502/88; JBl (1989), p. 103; Hofmann, in Rummel, *Kommentar* I, § 520, paras. 2 ff.

[24] Hofmann, in Rummel, *Kommentar*, I, § 520, para. 3.

[25] See Supreme Court of 25 Feb. 2005, *Arr Cass* (2005), p. 481.

immediate and certain damage or where the repair is needed without delay. Some authors argue that the owner can compel the tenant to perform necessary repairs at any time. In the case of serious damage, the owner can ask for the cancellation of the lease. It is accepted that the owner is entitled to enter the property if there are indications that the tenant causes damage that justifies the cancellation of the lease.[26] Under an *agricultural lease*, the landlord can terminate the lease at the end of each lease period if he/she can prove that the value of the property has decreased due to serious negligence in the maintenance of the property (Law on Agricultural Leases, art. 7–6).

An inventory of the property must be created at the start of a *usufruct* (Civil Code, art. 600). In addition, the nude owner is entitled to request security from the usufructuary guaranteeing compliance with his/her obligations (for example, personal or real security, the appointment of a sequester (guardian) over the goods, and certain investment measures which benefit the usufructuary but does not amount to general rights of management) (Civil Code, arts. 601 ff.).

During the course of the usufruct, the nude owner may demand that the usufructuary complies with his/her duty to act as a *bonus paterfamilias* (regarding maintenance and repair of the property). If immediate and certain damage is suffered by the nude owner, he may claim compensation during the existence of the usufruct. Otherwise, compensation for damages caused by lack of maintenance may be claimed only on termination of the usufruct.

Should B abuse his/her rights, A may request the early termination of the usufruct (Civil Code, art. 618) to protect him/her against destruction or substantial decrease in the value of the property. This harsh remedy requires a serious and substantial failure on the part of the usufructuary, such as not acting as a *bonus paterfamilias*, changing the intended purpose of the property, not using and maintaining the property for a long period or causing dilapidation of the property through his/her negligence. The remedy must be claimed in a court. The judge has a certain margin of discretion and may order complete or partial termination of the usufruct, allow compensation for damages, request additional security or order that the owner shall be reinstated in possession provided he/she pays a certain amount of compensation to the usufructuary. The Belgian Civil Code does not provide for the possibility of placing the usufruct property under the administration of a guardian

[26] Dekkers, Verbeke, Carette and Vanhove, *Handboek van burgerlijk recht*, no. 1063.

or trustee. However, it is conceivable that a judge will appoint an administrator or sequester to supervise the management of the property. We are not aware of case law in this regard.

Under a *hereditary land lease* (*emphyteusis*), the owner on termination of the lease may claim costs, damages and interest caused by the negligence and lack of maintenance on the part of the holder, including damages for the loss of rights which the holder allowed to lapse under the rules on prescription (Law on Hereditary Land Lease, art. 13). The owner has the right to terminate the hereditary lease on the ground of extensive damage caused to, or serious abuse of, the property (cf. usufruct). The tenant may counter such a claim by effecting repairs and providing sufficient security against future damage (Law on Hereditary Land Lease, arts. 15 and 16). The parties may contractually extend or limit the grounds for such early termination, provided they relate to non-performance or non-compliance with obligations under the hereditary lease. Parties could agree on a *pactum commissorium*, an explicit resolutive clause allowing the owner to dissolve the contract automatically if the tenant does not comply with his/her obligations under the lease.[27]

Since it is disputed whether the provisions of Civil Code, art. 618 or the Law on Hereditary Land Lease, art. 15 can be applied by analogy to the holder of *a hereditary building lease* (*superficies*), the parties are advised to regulate their position in this regard in the constitutive contract. This leaves the owner, in the absence of contractual provisions, relatively unprotected compared with owners under a usufruct or a hereditary land lease.

Denmark

Under a *lease of land*, the landlord's remedies depend on a breach of contract by the tenant. If this is not the case, the landlord (A) may only terminate the contract on notice, except where the contract is irrevocable.

If the tenant (B) has acted in breach of the contract, the owner (A) may terminate the contract without notice if the breach is fundamental. An injunction can be issued if the restrictive requirements of the Law on Administration of Justice, s. 642[28] are met. A may also claim damages. If

[27] See Supreme Court of 30 Mar. 2006, Pas. 2006 I 720; TBBR (2008), p. 88 n. Waterkeyn; T Not (2008), p. 97 n. Sagaert and Somers; RW (2006–7), p. 678 n. Vanhove.

[28] Consolidated Act, no. 1069 of 6 Nov. 2008 and later amendments.

the breach is not fundamental, or if the owner so chooses, he/she may instead demand that B reverse the contractual breach by restoring the property. B can also be forced to pay damages even where the breach is not fundamental.

The same rules apply to the *lease of buildings*. If the breach is fundamental and is covered by the exhaustive list of reasons for terminating the contract in the Law on Private Housing, s. 93 and the Law on Commercial Premises Rent, s. 69 the landlord may terminate the contract.[29]

In case of non-fundamental breach the tenant (B) must return the premises to their original condition at the latest at termination of the lease. The tenant is liable for any damage caused by improper conduct on his/her part, by any member of his/her household or by any third party he/she has admitted to the premises (Law on Private Housing, s. 25(2) and Law on Lease of Commercial Premises, s. 33(2)).

England

In the first instance, the express and implied terms of the *lease* govern the conduct of the tenant. These duties may be very specific, such as an obligation to effect certain repairs, to run only 'high-class' establishments or to run only certain specified trades. The duties may also be more general, so as not to cause, or permit to cause, nuisance or annoyance, or illegal or immoral behaviour. Covenants of the latter type set a higher standard than that required to establish common law nuisance.

The remedies for breach of covenant of the above type are injunctions (which, being equitable remedies, are discretionary and subject to the usual equitable limitations, such as not being available where the claimant has delayed, acquiesced in the defendant's conduct or otherwise behaved inequitably). Further or alternatively, damages may be awarded to compensate for any loss or in lieu of an injunction. Finally, if the landlord's lease contains a proviso for re-entry entitling him to forfeit it for the precise breach committed, he/she may be able to bring the lease to an end by forfeiting it. Relief from forfeiture will be available in the usual manner.

[29] The lease may be terminated, for example, in case of default in the punctual payment of rent; in cases where the premises are being used in a manner other than that agreed upon and the tenant fails to discontinue such use despite the landlord's objection; in cases where the tenant has vacated the premises without any agreement with the landlord; and finally, in cases where the tenant neglects the premises and fails to repair the premises without delay upon notice by the landlord requiring the tenant to do so.

Furthermore, it may be possible for third parties affected by the conduct (or the landlord, if affected) to bring ordinary common law claims for private nuisance. It is also possible that more egregious behaviour will fall foul of criminal law (such as public order offences). In practice, however, leasehold covenants will be the landlord's primary avenue to a remedy.

France

Civil Code, art. 1184 provides that the remedies available to A under a *lease* in the case of non-performance by B are a claim for specific performance or cancellation of the contract by the court and the payment of compensation for damages caused by the conduct of B. These remedies can also be found in certain statutory provisions. The tenant is liable for deterioration or destruction of the property unless he/she can prove that it occurred without fault on his/her part (Civil Code, art. 1732). The condition of the premises is compared with the inventory of the property drawn up at the inception of the lease. If no such inventory has been prepared, the tenant is presumed to have received the property in a good condition (Civil Code, art. 1731).

Under a *residential lease*, the tenant is liable for destruction or deterioration of the property unless he/she can prove that this is due to superior force, fault on the part of the landlord or the act or omission of a third party allowed access to the property by the landlord. In the absence of such proof, the landlord may retain, to the extent of his/her loss, the deposit paid by the tenant at the inception of the lease as security for performance of this obligations (Civil Code, art. 22) or have recourse to the proceeds of liability insurance which the tenant is required to obtain (Civil Code, art. 7).

The landlord may, in appropriate circumstances, institute an action for the cancellation of an *agricultural lease* and the payment of damages (Civil Code, art. 1766).

A *usufruct* may be terminated if the usufructuary abuses his/her right of enjoyment by harmful activities or where he/she causes decay through lack of maintenance (Civil Code, art. 618). The court must decide whether the seriousness of the acts or omissions justifies the termination of the usufruct or the transfer of the premises to the nude owner on the condition that he pays a fixed annual sum to the usufructuary until the expiry of the usufruct.

Germany

Generally speaking, the landlord can demand either specific performance or cancellation of the *lease*, or compensation for damages suffered. He can also request a court order restraining the tenant from certain activities which violate the contract. In practice, the most important remedy is the landlord's right to cancel the lease and to evict the tenant. The conditions for cancellation differ according to the type of lease concerned. During the past twenty years, a detailed set of rules has been introduced, supplemented by extensive case law to strengthen the position of tenants under residential leases and to prevent their summary eviction (Civil Code, §§ 568 ff.).

Various remedies are available to the landowner (A) under *usufruct* if the usufructuary (B) exploits the property in an unreasonable manner or neglects his/her duties. A may request a court order compelling B to refrain from injurious activities if B has ignored a warning (Civil Code, § 1053). If A has reason to assume that B's conduct can cause him (A) serious damage, A can demand that security be given against future damage (Civil Code, § 1051). If, despite a warning, B continues to cause serious damage, A can demand that the management of the usufruct be placed under the administration of the court (*gerichtliche Verwaltung*) (Civil Code, § 1054). Where B collects more profits than he is entitled to, A can claim for the fair market value of all fruits not due to B (Civil Code, § 1039). Finally, A may claim compensation for damages suffered because of B's failure to comply with his/her obligations. However, it is not possible for A to cancel the usufruct and eject the usufructuary.

Compared to usufruct, fewer statutory provisions cover the remedies provided to a holder of a *limited personal servitude* (Civil Code, § 1090) and the holder of a *right of habitation* (Civil Code, § 1093). Generally speaking, the landowner (A) may obtain a court order to stop any interference with his/her rights and where damage is caused, A has a claim for compensation if fault can be proved.

Agreements to establish a *hereditary building lease* (*Erbbaurecht*) usually prescribe the parties' rights and obligations in much more detail than those creating personal servitudes. Consequently, the holder's most important remedy in practice is an action for breach of contract. Moreover, the landowner can request retransfer (*Heimfall*) of the building lease against payment of a fair compensation for improvements if the conditions for retransfer set out in the contract are met (Regulations, § 2 nos. 4 and 32). If, by way of example, B has substantially altered the physical condition of the structure without obtaining A's prior consent as required by the contract,[30] A can request a court order compelling B to restore the original structure. A may also claim compensation for damages suffered (the sum of money necessary to restore the original condition) or claim retransfer of the building lease. If, however, B has made only minor alterations to the structure which do not in fact significantly harm a justifiable interest of A, such a claim will normally be rejected as disproportionate.

The remedies available to the owner against the *holder of a permanent right of habitation* (Law on Apartment Ownership, § 31(1)) are similar to those available against the holder of a building lease (see Law on Apartment Ownership, § 36 regarding retransfer of the property).

Greece

If the tenant makes improper use of the property, the *landlord* is entitled to give notice of immediate termination of the lease and to claim compensation for damages.[31] Such conduct is present where the tenant, notwithstanding the protest of the landlord, uses the property without due care and in a manner inconsistent with the agreement,[32] or does not behave appropriately towards the other tenants (Civil Code, art. 594).[33]

Subject to contrary agreement, the *nude owner* shall have the right to demand security from the usufructuary where the exercise of the usufruct poses a serious threat to the nude owner's rights (Civil Code, art. 1159). If the usufructuary is unwilling or unable to provide security or if he/she has seriously harmed the rights of the nude owner, the owner may request a court order for the lease of the property to an outsider or for the management of the usufruct to be entrusted to a manager for the account of the usufructuary. The court may also decide to appoint the nude owner as the manager. The management of the property shall return to the usufructuary upon security being provided or when the grounds justifying the appointment of the manager disappear (Civil Code, art. 1160). If the rights of the nude owner are seriously harmed, the nude owner can claim for damages during or at the expiry of the usufruct.[34]

[30] See Case 7.

[31] Rapsomanikis, in Georgiades and Stathopoulos, *GCC, Collective Analysis*, art. 594, nos. 6–10 (319); AP 812/1979; NoV (1980), p. 73.

[32] AP 88/1973; NoV (1973), p. 767.

[33] AP 1658/1983; NoV (1984), p. 1526; AP 689/1970; NoV (1971), p. 170.

[34] Karasis, in Georgiades and Stathopoulos, *GCC, Collective Analysis*, art. 1142, no. 32 (58).

The above do not apply to the right of *habitation*. The Greek Civil Code (art. 1186) expressly provides that the owner is not entitled to demand security from the holder of a right of habitation. The *habitator* is further not obliged to insure the building against damage.[35]

Hungary

Under a *lease* and an *income-producing lease*, the landlord may control the use of the property if this does not cause unnecessary inconvenience to the tenant. He/she may demand that the tenant use the property in a proper manner and in the way prescribed by the contract. If the tenant does not comply with the above demand, or if, owing to the extent of the danger, it is pointless to demand that the tenant stop the improper use, the landlord can terminate the contract with immediate effect and claim damages. If the tenant performed an unlawful reconstruction without the permission of the landlord or a competent public administrative authority, he/she can be ordered to restore the property to its original status. The owner can also exercise the above rights against a sub-tenant (Civil Code, § 425(2)–(4)).

The owner is entitled to control the manner in which the *usufructuary* exercises his/her rights. The owner may claim security if the usufructuary, despite repeated warnings, does not use the property in a proper manner, damages the property or endangers its return on termination of the usufruct. If the usufructuary fails to provide security, the court, at the request of the owner, can suspend the exercise of the usufruct until security is provided. The owner is also entitled to these rights against any person to whom the usufruct was abandoned (Civil Code, § 161).

The *loan for use* can be terminated with immediate effect if, *inter alia*, the borrower impairs the property, uses it improperly, abandons its use to a third person without the permission of the lender, or if there is a danger that the borrower will not return the property in a sound condition (Civil Code, § 585(4)(b)). The law does not, however, confer an express right of control on the lender.

Italy

When the tenant fails to perform his/her obligations, the landlord can either demand performance or termination of the *lease*, reserving in

[35] Papadopoulou, in Georgiades and Stathopoulos, *GCC, Collective Analysis*, art. 1186 (196–7).

both cases the right to claim compensation for damages caused (Civil Code, art. 1453). Termination may, however, not be claimed where non-performance by one of the parties only slightly affects the interests of the other (Civil Code, art. 1455). For instance, if the tenant of a residential premises operates a small commercial or industrial concern without any important physical alteration of the property, the landlord is not usually entitled to demand termination of the contract.[36] If the landlord claims performance of contractual obligations, he/she may in addition claim for damages even before the end of the lease.

A *usufruct* can be terminated if the usufructuary abuses his/her right by transferring or damaging the property or by allowing it to deteriorate owing to neglect to undertake ordinary repairs (Civil Code, art. 1015). Instead of terminating the usufruct, the court may order the usufructuary to provide security against future harm, or that the property be leased or placed under administration at the usufructuary's expense. The court may even order that possession be returned to the nude owner subject to an obligation to pay the usufructuary a specified annual sum of money for the duration of the usufruct (Civil Code, art. 1015). According to prevailing opinion, these remedies should only be exercised in the face of serious or repeated violations by the usufructuary.

As a general principle, the owner can obtain a court injunction to interdict the usufructuary from continuing unlawful activities on the property and claim compensation for any damage caused. However, there is some authority for the view that the owner's right to immediate action in respect of minor violations is limited by the fact that the usufructuary's autonomous right of enjoyment affords him a degree of discretion in deciding how and when to comply with his/her obligations. For instance, if a lack of ordinary repairs does not endanger the property, the owner should wait until the expiry of the usufruct before requesting restoration of the property and compensation for damage.[37]

The literature on *hereditary building leases* (*superficies*), does not discuss this issue.

The Netherlands

Under Civil Code, art. 7: 352 and the Law on Agricultural Leases (*Pachtwet*), art. 28 the landlord can sue the tenant for any damage

[36] See e.g. Cass. civ. 20/06/1957 n. 2339. [37] See Caterina, *I diritti*, pp. 153–4.

which flows from a breach of an *agricultural lease* and which is imputable to him/her. Any damage to the property other than damage by fire is presumed to be the result of the tenant's breach of contract. Civil Code, art. 7:218 applies the above rule also to *residential leases* with the added presumption that damage caused to the outside walls of the residence is not damage for which the tenant can be held liable.

In the case of *usufruct*, the nude owner is entitled to ask the District Court for either an order to declare him/her the administrator of the usufruct or to place the property subject to the usufruct under administration in the case of serious non-performance of his/her obligations by the usufructuary (Civil Code, art. 3:221).

The owner may terminate a *hereditary land lease* (*emphyteusis*) in the case of fundamental breach of contract by the holder or if the holder has defaulted on the payment of ground rent for two consecutive years (Civil Code, art. 5:87 II). Notification of the termination must be given to the person registered as holder in the Land Register by means of a writ served by a bailiff within eight days from the date of non-performance (Civil Code, arts. 5:87 II and 5:88).

Civil Code, arts. 5:87 II and 5:88 apply by way of analogy to an independent *hereditary building lease* (*superficies*) (Civil Code, art. 5:104 II). Where the hereditary building lease is linked to another real right, the statutory rule does not apply.

Poland

In general, the landlord is entitled to terminate any kind of *lease* with immediate effect without observing the notice periods (Civil Code, art. 667, § 2). The Law on Protection of Tenants, art. 11, § 2 relating to *residential leases* is an exception, requiring a notification of one month for termination on account of non-payment of rent, misconduct resulting in damage and causing a nuisance. The landlord can only request ejection of the tenant for important causes (Law on Protection of Tenants, art. 11, § 10). Obviously, the landlord has contractual claims for damages based on breach of contract where the tenant uses the property contrary to the provisions of the contract or in a way which may lead to damage to the property or its loss. The landlord is not entitled to obtain an injunction to stop acts which may cause damage.

The nude owner (A) has no right to cancel the *usufruct* and to eject the usufructuary. He/she may claim damages if the land is not in a proper condition upon termination of the usufruct. A request for security to be given against possible future loss is only possible if the usufructuary informs the landowner of his/her intention to undertake mining activities. Consequently, the provisions contained in the constitutive agreement by which the usufruct is granted (which is the principal manner in which usufruct is created in Poland) determine the ways in which the usufruct may be terminated and the scope of liability if one party is in breach of the contract. It may also be argued that A may resort to an *actio negatoria* to interdict a usufructuary from conducting harmful activities on the land. A may claim damages according to general contract law rules.

The owner has a very distinct remedy against the holder of a *hereditary land lease* (perpetual usufruct, *emphyteusis*) who uses land contrary to contractual provisions, particularly if he/she has not erected the specified buildings. The owner is entitled to terminate the hereditary land lease immediately (Civil Code, art. 240). Where the holder of the perpetual usufruct has not erected buildings within the agreed time limit, the owner may set a new date and levy an additional fee on the holder instead of terminating the perpetual usufruct (Law on Management of Real Property, art. 63).

Civil Code, art. 913 provides that if for any reason the relation between a *lifetime habitant* and his/her host is such that the parties cannot be expected to continue direct contact, the court shall, on demand of either party, convert some or all the rights of the lifetime habitant into an annual lifetime pension based on the value of those rights. In extraordinary cases, the court may, on demand of either party, terminate the contract of lifetime habitation.

Portugal

Under a *lease*, the tenant must take care of the property and use it with due diligence (Civil Code, art. 1038). On termination, the tenant must return the property in the same condition it was received in, with allowance for fair wear and tear.

In the case of an *urban lease*, the landlord may ask for cancellation of the lease (Civil Code, art. 1083) and institute a claim for delictual damages according to general rules contained in the Civil Code (arts. 798 ff.) if he/she is dissatisfied with the way in which B conducts himself/herself with regard to the property. Meanwhile, the landlord can obtain a court order to restrain the tenant from harmful conduct. The landlord can evict the tenant after cancellation of the contract (Civil Code, art. 1081).

The tenant has three months to leave the property, unless the judge orders him/her to leave immediately or unless the parties agree otherwise (Civil Code, art. 1084).

In the case of an *agricultural lease*, the landlord is entitled to notify the tenant of the cancellation of the lease in the following circumstances: if the tenant does not pay the rent; if the tenant's non-compliance with his/her legal duties affects the productivity, substance or the economic and social function of the property; if the tenant's method of cultivation prejudices the productivity of the property; or if the tenant does not maintain the property in a good state of repair or causes damage to items brought onto the property that are not included in the contract; if the tenant changes the structure of the land; and, finally, if the tenant allows a third party to use the land. In addition, the landlord can claim compensation for damage caused to the property through the tenant's fault or as a result of the non-compliance with his/her duties as an agricultural tenant (Decree-Law 294/2009, art. 17). The landlord can evict the tenant after cancellation of the contract.

At the outset of a *usufruct*, the usufructuary is obliged to prepare, in collaboration with the owner, an inventory of the various assets included in the usufruct and the condition and value of each item (Civil Code, art. 1468). In addition, the owner may request that the usufructuary provide security in case of damage to the property (Civil Code, art. 1468, no. 2). The nude owner will only be entitled to terminate the usufruct and request the return of the property if the harmful conduct of the usufructuary seriously affects the value of the property.[38] In case of termination, the nude owner is obliged to hand over the net income of the property to the usufructuary every year (Civil Code, art. 1482).

The nude owner can obtain a preliminary and urgent court order to stop harmful acts which diminish the value of the property. However, the offending usufructuary cannot be placed under management of the court or a professional manager. The most effective way to defend the property will thus be to terminate the usufruct.

The abovementioned also applies to a *right of use*, a *right of habitation* (Civil Code, art. 1490) and a *hereditary building lease* (*superficies*) (Civil Code, art. 1536 no. 1a and no. 2).

[38] Decision of the Court of Appeal of Lisbon of 22.05.2001 [Process 00115367], available at www.dgsi.pt.

Scotland

As a *lease* is a contract, normal contractual remedies are available to the landlord to control the tenant's behaviour if it is not in compliance with the obligations under the lease. These include a decree of specific implement (an order compelling performance of a positive obligation), a decree of interdict (an order prohibiting conduct of a particular nature), a decree for payment or an action for damages (the primary measurement being such amount as will put the landlord into the position that he/she would have been in had the tenant performed his/her part of the contract).[39] If, for example, the tenant is using the premises for a purpose prohibited by the lease, an interdict will be available to the landlord provided that there is a reasonable apprehension that the wrong will continue were that order not to be granted. A party is entitled to specific implement *as of right* and not as a matter of the court's discretion (subject to there being certain types of obligations which courts will routinely not enforce by implement). Implement will not, however, be granted after the lease has come to an end to require the tenant to do something which he/she was obliged to do during the lease (for example, to put the premises into a good state of repair).[40]

Leases will commonly also contain an irritancy clause.[41] Irritancy is a right to bring the lease to an end on the occurrence of a certain event, which need not be a breach of contract. It can be enforced only by court action. There are both legal irritancies (implied by law) and conventional irritancies (provided for by the parties themselves). At common law, the only legal irritancy was non-payment of rent for two years. Conventional irritancies are obviously more important. Any term of the lease can be made the subject of a conventional irritancy. One would certainly expect to see the obligation to pay rent and the alienation provisions included, and also provision made for the lease to terminate in the event of the tenant's insolvency. Irritancy in an assured tenancy (of residential property) will only be effective if it mirrors certain statutory grounds for terminating the tenancy.[42] In respect of agricultural

[39] See, generally, McBryde, *Contract*, chs. 20, 22, 23.

[40] *Sinclair* v. *Caithness Flagstone Co.* (1898) 25 R 703 (IH) 706; *PIK Facilities Ltd.* v. *Shell UK Ltd.* 2005 SCLR 958 (OH).

[41] Rankine, *Leases*, ch. 20, pt. 3; Paton and Cameron, *Landlord and Tenant*, ch. 15; McAllister, *Leases*, paras. 5.2–5.38.

[42] Because an order for possession may only be made if one of the statutory grounds for possession is made out: H(S)A 88, s. 18. If, at the time the proceedings commence, rent is

holdings, there are no controls over irritancy clauses in a 1991 Act tenancy.[43] The provision is slightly more controlled in respect of SLDTs and LDTs,[44] but the regime is still fairly liberal.

Generally, Scots contract law allows the 'innocent' party faced with a material breach of contract to terminate the contract ('rescind').[45] If faced by a material breach of contract by the tenant,[46] the landlord can elect to rescind the contract, which brings it to an end from that point on, and claim damages, or affirm the contract, in which case the right to rescind is lost. There are uncertainties about the circumstances in which this remedy is available to the landlord, standing the existence of irritancy.[47] It cannot in any event be used to circumvent statutory rules about termination and the recovery of possession.

In the case of *liferent*, A's remedies are more limited.[48] During the subsistence of the liferent, the fiar's remedy is the *cautio usufructuaria*. The liferenter may be required to give caution (a payment guaranteeing performance of his/her obligations) to the fiar against damage to the property by waste and destruction, but probably only in the case of actual or likely damage.[49] The fiar cannot obtain an order while the liferent subsists compelling the liferenter to comply with his/her duties, or obtain an award of damages, except in respect of those parts of the property in which the fiar has a 'present beneficial interest', such as the woods and minerals. The logic is that any damage can be made good at termination of the liferent. The Inner House has recently confirmed that this is the position[50] and, although Gordon[51] describes the decision as 'unconvincing', it does reflect the authorities.

at least three months in arrears, the sheriff must grant an order (Schedule 5 Ground 8). For other breaches, the sheriff has a discretion whether to grant an order for possession (Grounds 12–16).

43 AH(S)A 1991, s. 21(6). Even if the lease is silent, the landlord can seek to have the tenant removed if six months' rent is due and unpaid (AH(S)A 91, s. 20).

44 AH(S)A 2003, s. 18(1). 45 McBryde, *Contract*, paras. 20–88 to 20–127.

46 Non-payment of rent does not count as material (Gloag, *Contract*, p. 618), nor does unauthorised sub-letting or assignation (Rankine, *Leases*, 180), although in both cases it is open for the parties to provide otherwise.

47 Hogg, 'To Irritate or to Rescind', 1; McAllister, *Leases*, paras. 4.22–4.28.

48 Gordon and Wortley, *Land Law*, para. 17–60; Styles, 'Liferent', para. 1660–1.

49 Gordon and Wortley, *Land Law*, para. 17–60, citing *Ralston* v. *Leitch* (1803) *Hume*, p. 293.

50 *Stronach's Exrs* v. *Robertson* 2002 SC 540 (IH). The court held that a fiar could not obtain an order of specific implement against a liferenter to compel him/her to perform his/her duty to carry out repairs.

51 Gordon and Wortley, *Land Law*, para. 17–60.

South Africa

Under a *lease*, a landlord is entitled to an interdict restraining the tenant from using premises for a purpose for which they are not let,[52] using them improperly[53] or damaging or altering them.[54] If the tenant neglects a positive duty (for example, to erect a fence on a farm), the landlord may apply for an order for specific performance.[55] If damage can be proved, an action for damages will be available.[56]

In the case of a major breach, the landlord may cancel the lease and eject the tenant (claiming damages for past misuse). Factors such as the seriousness of the breach, whether it was progressive or whether the landlord is threatened with irreparable loss will be considered.[57] In the case of a minor breach such as causing damage, repairable at small cost, or improper use of the property on an isolated occasion, the landlord will not be entitled, prior to termination of the lease, to recover the damages in lieu of insisting on repairs. At termination, the tenant must return the property in the same condition he/she received it, fair wear and tear excepted.[58] Consequently, an award of damages before termination will compel the tenant unjustifiably either to restore doubly or before the required time has arrived.[59]

If the tenant[60] has caused material damage, the landlord can, in addition to bringing the contract to an end, institute an action for damages to recover the reasonable cost of repairs or restoration.[61] The damage sought is restricted to actual patrimonial loss, namely the difference between the actual value of the premises on termination of the lease and what their value would have been had the tenant restored the property in its proper condition. Although the reasonable cost of repairs or restoration may be an indication of such difference in value, it may not coincide with actual loss. For example, where a house is due to be demolished, the cost of restoration may be wholly disproportionate

[52] *Fichardt* v. *Leviseur* 1915 AD 182. [53] *Burns* v. *D and G* 1949 4 SA 135 (T).

[54] *Temple* v. *Schroer* 1929 SWA 14; Cooper, *Landlord and Tenant*, p. 215.

[55] *ISEP Structural Engineering and Plating (Pty) Ltd.* v. *Inland Exploration Co. (Pty) Ltd.* 1981 4 SA 1 (A) 5A-B.

[56] *Spies* v. *Lombard* 1950 3 SA 469 (A) 488. [57] Cooper, *Landlord and Tenant*, p. 215.

[58] *Ibid.* 217. Fair or reasonable wear and tear mean deterioration owing to the ravages of time, age, the elements and normal use.

[59] *Ibid.* 215–16.

[60] He/she is not responsible for damage caused through *vis maior*, latent defects in the premises or an act of a third party. See *ibid.* 223–6.

[61] See cases cited by Cooper, *Landlord and Tenant*, p. 226 n. 60.

to the reduced value of the non-repaired or non-restored house. In such a case, the landlord's measure of damages will not be the reasonable cost of repairs or restoration, but the reduced value of the premises.[62]

At termination of the lease, the landlord may demand that the property is returned to him/her, that it has to be restored to its original condition, if equitable,[63] or demand compensation for the amount necessary to restore the property if he/she does not want to ask for specific performance.[64] If termination of the lease is appropriate, the landlord will be entitled to the damages indicated above in lieu of repairs. In addition to a claim for damages to the premises, there is also a claim for loss of rent due to non-rentability caused by the damaged condition.

If the usufructuary does not exploit the property subject to the *usufruct* in a reasonable manner or neglects his/her duties, the nude owner may, in appropriate circumstances, approach the court for an interdict to restrain the usufructuary from injurious activities.[65] In Roman-Dutch law this action could be combined with an order that security be provided against future damage to the property.[66] The interdict could also be combined with an action for damages.[67] It is thus possible for a substantial amount of damages to be claimed from the estate of a deceased usufructuary who neglected the property during his/her lifetime for, among other things, the repair of the farmstead, outbuildings, fences and gates and the preparation of neglected agricultural land for re-cultivation.

Spain

When the tenant does not fulfil his/her duties, the landlord is entitled to demand either performance or termination (*resolución*) of the *lease* (Law on Urban Leases, art. 27.1). The Law on Urban Leases (art. 27.2) enumerates the situations where the landlord may demand termination

[62] *Swart* v. *Van der Vyver* 1970 1 SA 633 (A) 648D; *ISEP Structural Engineering and Plating (Pty) Ltd.* v. *Inland Exploration Co. (Pty) Ltd.* 1981 4 SA 1 (A) 8C-G. This will be nonsensical in the case where the change from grazing to arable land has actually improved the value of the land.

[63] *ISEP Structural Engineering and Plating (Pty) Ltd.* v. *Inland Exploration Co. (Pty) Ltd.* 1981 4 SA 1 (A) 5 12 13 16.

[64] *Spies* v. *Lombard* 1950 3 SA 469 (A) 488–9.

[65] See e.g. *Olivier* v. *Venter* 1933 EDL 206.

[66] See Voet, *Commentarius*, 7.6.1, 3.

[67] *Re* praedial servitudes, see *Kakamas Bestuursraad* v. *Louw* 1960 2 SA 202 (A).

(*resolución*) such as non-payment of rent or a deposit, sub-lease without the owner's consent, intentional damage to the property, causing a nuisance or ceasing to use the premise for residential purposes. The Law on Rural Leases (art. 25) enumerates more or less similar reasons for the termination, adding failure to improve or change the property as agreed in the contract, or where the land is zoned as urban land. The landlord may resile from the agricultural lease (*rescisión*) if the tenant does not pay for expenses required for the conservation of the property or for improvements agreed upon (Law on Rural Leases, art. 26).

Failure by one of the parties to perform his/her obligations under a lease governed by the Civil Code entitles the other party to resile from the lease (*rescisión*) (Civil Code, art. 1556) or to cancel (*resolución*) (Civil Code, art. 1568 with reference to art. 1124) and to claim compensation for damages caused. Alternatively, he/she can elect to demand only compensation for damages, while keeping the contract intact. The misconduct of the tenant (for example, violating any of the contractual clauses, using the property for other purposes than agreed, causing damage to the property) entitles the landlord to evict the tenant (*juicio de desahucio*) (Civil Code, art. 1569).

Unlike in other jurisdictions, it is not possible for the landlord to obtain an interdict restraining the tenant from damaging the property. The only remedies available are eviction or termination of the contract.

When an abuse of the rights under a *usufruct* causes serious damage to the owner, the latter will be entitled to request transfer of the property to him/her in return for payment to the usufructuary of an annual amount based on the net profits derived from the exploitation of the property (Civil Code, art. 520). Authors interpret this article as referring to breach of the usufructuary's obligation to exploit the property as a good *paterfamilias*,[68] and breach of the usufructuary's custodial duty towards the property.[69] As an alternative, the nude owner can wait until the termination of the usufruct and then claim compensation from the estate of the usufructuary for damages suffered on account of the dereliction of duty on the part of the usufructuary or retain the deposit which may have been required from the usufructuary at the inception of the usufruct (Civil Code, art. 491.2).

As in the case of usufruct, the nude owner can sue for the termination of the right of *use* or *habitation* if the holder causes serious damage by

[68] Moreno Quesada, 'Comment', vol. 1, p. 1376.
[69] Lacruz Berdejo, *Elementos de Derecho civil*, vol. 3.2, p. 30.

abusing his/her rights (Civil Code, art. 529).[70] The nude owner can also wait until the expiry of these rights and then claim compensation for dereliction of the holder's duties.

There are no special rules on a *hereditary building lease* (*superficies*), but as the holder has a long term right, it may be quite difficult to grant the 'owner' any remedy.

[70] Serious abuse that has to be understood as 'bad use', following Rams Albesa, 'Comment', p. 266

Case 9
To what extent can a time-limited interest be sold or donated, burdened with a mortgage or a separate limited right, attached in execution proceedings and included in the holder's insolvency assets?

Is B entitled to transfer/burden his/her time-limited right by:

- *selling it;*
- *donating it;*
- *mortgaging it; or*
- *creating a separate limited right?*

If so, to what extent is the content and duration of the later interest determined by B's interest?

Can B's limited right be attached in execution proceedings against B?

Can B's limited right be included in B's insolvency or bankruptcy assets?

Comparative observations

Under a *lease*, tenants are in general allowed to *sell* or *donate* their interest. This can take the form of either an assignment of the right of use to a third party[1] or the transfer of both the rights and obligations of the tenant to a third party (*Vertragsübernahme*).[2] In the latter case the transferee becomes the landlord's creditor and by assuming the tenant's obligations the landlord's debtor in place of the original tenant.[3]

Apart from Germany and Austria, where the construction of an assignment automatically requires the consent of the landlord, most of the

[1] See e.g. the Greek, Belgian, Spanish and Scottish reports.

[2] See the German and Austrian reports.

[3] See the Belgian report for regulation of the rights and obligations of the assignee by agreement between the parties and see the South African report for the difference between assignment and assumption of a lease.

other jurisdictions generally require the landlord's consent for the assignment of residential[4] as well as agricultural leases[5] if not dispensed with by contract, local custom (Greece) or a special law (Portugal).

In Spain and Belgium, an agricultural lease may be assigned to the spouse or descendant of the tenant without the landlord's consent, and in France, with the court's authorisation, to the spouse, civil partner or descendant of the tenant who partakes in the cultivation of the land. In the Netherlands, the co-tenant (usually the husband or wife) is allowed to continue a residential lease after the tenant's death.

In the jurisdictions where a lease is regarded as a mere personal right, it is generally accepted that a lease cannot be *mortgaged*.[6] The German reporter mentions the possibility of pledge (*Verpfändung*) or an assignment in security (*Sicherungsabtretung*) of certain rights arising out of a lease agreement but warns that leases are not popular in practice as collateral because of their inefficient enforcement in execution proceedings.

In jurisdictions where a lease of land is registrable,[7] a lease can be mortgaged without the landlord's prior consent.[8] Spanish law allows the pledging of the tenant's movables on the land as collateral for a loan. In England, as in other jurisdictions, the tenant is only permitted to mortgage his/her own property, so that the reversion is unaffected by his/her dealings with the lease. However, a mortgage creditor's acquisition of an interest in a lease is frequently an event which triggers the operation of forfeiture, so that the landlord acquires a right to re-entry on the occurrence of that event. Modern restraints on the right to forfeit require a court order to retake the lease.

The default rule in most jurisdictions is that the tenant is not entitled to *sub-let* residential[9] or agricultural property[10] without the consent of

4 The rationale in France is that the personal identity of the tenant is important in residential leases. In South Africa the landlord is granted a say in the choice of the new tenant where the assignment seriously prejudices his/her interest.

5 See e.g. the Greek, French, Belgian, Portuguese, Spanish, Danish, South African and Polish reports. But cf. the varied approach adopted in Scotland. In England, landlords in practice impose covenants either to preclude any alienation in whole or in part or else to make such alienation subject to permission, which itself is made subject to a reasonableness requirement in the Housing Act.

6 See e.g. the German, Greek, French, Belgian, Italian, Danish, and Polish reports.

7 In Austria, it is also possible to mortgage an unregistered lease since it is accepted that all rights may be mortgaged.

8 See e.g. the Austrian, Spanish, Scottish and South African reports.

9 See the Greek and Polish reports.

10 See the Italian report. But cf. again the varied Scottish approach.

the landlord,[11] subject to local custom (Greece) and special legislation (Portugal). In Poland, residential premises may be sub-let without the landlord's consent if the tenant is obliged to pay alimony to the prospective sub-tenant. Under Belgian law, a sub-lease of agricultural property as a whole to specific relatives is possible without the consent of the landlord. Under special Danish legislation, the tenant is in special circumstances allowed to sub-let the whole of the apartment for a period not exceeding two years in the temporary absence of the tenant owing to illness, business, studies or job placement. Hungarian law prohibits the sub-lease of agricultural land except where a written sub-tenancy is concluded with the written permission of the landlord, for the sake of integrated cultivation of the land.

Some jurisdictions prohibit the sub-lease of a part of agricultural land and the whole of residential premises but allow the sub-lease of only part of residential property with the consent of the landlord, provided the tenant continues to occupy the other part of the premises.[12] South African case law, however, suggests that a tenant may not sub-let if the sub-tenant is more likely to damage the property or to use it for purposes other than those contemplated in the lease.

When authorised by the landlord or permitted by law, the tenant in Portugal is under an obligation to inform the landlord of the sub-lease, on pain of cancellation thereof. The rent charged for the sub-lease must be the same as, or not higher than 20 per cent of, the rent charged under the principal lease in Spain and Portugal respectively.

Although no contractual relationship exists between the original landlord and the sub-tenant, the sub-tenant's title is dependent on the title of the principal tenant. In England, a sub-lease is carved out of the principal lease and must therefore be for a term shorter than the principal lease.[13] In the other jurisdictions, the sub-lease will expire on termination of the principal lease[14] and the landlord can evict the sub-tenant. The tenant is liable for any damage caused by the fault of the sub-tenant, and the fact that the landlord agreed to the sub-lease will not exonerate the tenant.[15] Under special Dutch legislation, an

[11] See e.g. the German, Austrian, Greek, Portuguese, Spanish, Dutch, Italian, English, South African, Danish and Hungarian reports.

[12] See e.g. the Belgian, Dutch and Hungarian reports.

[13] If it is for an equivalent term, it counts as an out-and-out assignment.

[14] See the German, Belgian, Portuguese, Spanish and Danish reports.

[15] See the Greek and Belgian reports.

agricultural sub-lease does not terminate with the death of the tenant but may be continued by his/her heirs.

The majority of jurisdictions hold that a *usufruct* as such is *not transferable* on account of its highly personal character, but that the rights arising from a usufruct are transferable.[16] Consequently, the right to exploit the property and to collect its produce and income can be sold or donated until the expiry of the usufruct. The usufructuary, however, remains liable to the nude owner if the transferee causes damage to the property.[17] Other jurisdictions hold that a usufruct as such is transferable but that its highly personal character causes the rights transferred to expire on termination of the usufruct.[18] In Italy, any transfer of the usufruct must be intimated to the owner: if not, the usufructuary and the new holder will be liable *in solidum* to the nude owner for damage caused to the property. A usufruct or the entitlements under a usufruct can be transferred for a fixed term or for the duration of the usufruct.[19] If the constitutive transaction contains a prohibition against transfer, any alienation is null and void and the prohibition can also be enforced against the transferee.[20]

Owing to their highly personal nature (*intuitus personae*), most jurisdictions do not allow sale or donation of the servitudes of *use* and *habitation*.[21] These rights are established to fulfil the basic needs of the beneficiaries: a roof over their heads and the possibility to obtain food to cover their daily needs. They are so intertwined with the person of the holder that they cannot be alienated or transferred.

German and Polish law accept that a *usufruct* cannot be mortgaged because it cannot be transferred as such. However, Greece, Spain, Austria, Belgium, France and Portugal expressly sanction the mortgage of a usufruct or at least the rights under it with some stipulating that the mortgage will not be terminated if the usufruct is terminated early by a voluntary act of the usufructuary or when the secured claim is discharged.[22]

[16] See e.g. the German, Austrian, Greek, Portuguese, Italian, Hungarian, Polish, Scottish and South African reports.

[17] See e.g. the Portuguese report.

[18] See e.g. the French, Belgian, Spanish, Italian and Dutch reports.

[19] See e.g. the Belgian, Portuguese and Italian reports.

[20] See e.g. the Italian report.

[21] See e.g. the German, Austrian, Greek, Belgian, Dutch, Portuguese, Italian, Hungarian, Polish and South African reports.

[22] See e.g. the Austrian, Portuguese, Spanish, Scottish and Italian reports.

Owing to their highly personal character, it is generally accepted that the personal servitudes of *use* and *habitation* can neither be transferred nor mortgaged.[23] Curiously, South African legislation allows the holder of a right of habitation to mortgage his/her interest in the property.

In most jurisdictions, the holder of a *usufruct* is not entitled to *create a separate real right*, for instance, a right of habitation over his/her interest in the property, but he/she is entitled to create a personal right, such as a lease or a loan.[24] In Portugal, the nude owner is only allowed to claim the return of the leased or loaned residential property three months after the expiry of the lease or loan or at the end of the harvest period in the case of the expiry of an agricultural lease. In Austria, the rights of the tenant are not terminated automatically on expiry of the usufruct and the nude owner is bound to take over the sub-lease. Similarly, in Belgium, the owner must respect a lease with a certified date concluded for a term of less than nine years and leases concluded for a longer term for a period of nine years if the term has already started on termination of the usufruct.

Only South African and Italian law allow the holder of a usufruct to create a separate real right over his/her interest in the property, namely a long lease and a second usufruct, right of use or right of habitation respectively. The second usufructuary is not bound by the first usufructuary's rights and obligations vis-à-vis the nude owner and the first usufructuary remains liable if the property is damaged or its intended economic purpose changed. Furthermore, renunciation of the usufruct by the second usufructuary does not extinguish the first usufruct.

In Germany, the holder of a right of *habitation* (*Wohnungsrecht*) is in principle only allowed to use the property for himself, his/her family and for persons required for his/her service and care and may only let his/her interest in the property to someone else with the consent of the landowner. In Spain, Belgium and Italy, the holder of a right of use or habitation cannot create a second use or right of habitation over his/her interest in the property owing to its highly personal character. Interestingly, South African case law allows the holder of a right of use to let out rooms which he/she does not occupy and a *habitator* to let out the whole dwelling-house. A *habitator* may not, however, allow a

[23] See e.g. the French, Belgian, Dutch, Portuguese, Spanish, Italian, Hungarian and Polish reports.

[24] See e.g. the German, Austrian, Greek, French, Belgian, Portuguese, Spanish and Hungarian reports.

third party to live gratuitously in the house in his/her place. In France, the *habitator* is allowed to lease out the use of the house to his/her spouse, civil partner or descendants. Note that, by contrast, the German permanent right of habitation (*Dauerwohnrecht*) is freely transferable and transmissible and can therefore be sold or donated subject to restriction in the constitutive deed. Although the right cannot be mortgaged, the holder is allowed to create separate real rights such as a usufruct with regard to it and lease out his/her interest under the right.[25]

Since the holder of a hereditary building right under a *hereditary building lease* (*superficies*) acquires a right akin to ownership,[26] the holder can *sell* or *donate* his/her interest in the land and transfer the right to another[27] by registration in the Land or Special Register.[28]

Certain jurisdictions[29] also allow the holder of a hereditary building right to *mortgage* the right. If title to the building right and the land merge, the Italian Civil Code provides that mortgages over the land and the building right continue to burden each of them separately. Under Austrian law, a mortgage over a building right continues to exist as a mortgage over the land when the building right expires and ownership of the building passes to the landowner. If the constitutive agreement allows compensation for improvements when the right expires, Austrian and Italian law provide that such proceeds will be subject to a mortgage registered over the building right.

Moreover, the holder of a hereditary building right is entitled to burden the right with all kinds of *separate limited real rights* or to create a lease over the right.[30] Examples are a praedial servitude,[31] a usufruct, a second hereditary building right but not a hereditary land lease. Such interests are dependent on the title of the original holder of the right and expiry of the building right will extinguish the real or personal rights. In German practice, frequent use is made of the provision in the Building Rights Regulations which allows stipulations in constitutive agreements to transfer or burden the building rights with the approval of the landowner.

Since a *hereditary land lease* (*emphyteusis, erfpacht*) is recognised in Belgium, the Netherlands and Poland as heritable and alienable, the

[25] See the German report for further details. [26] See the Italian report.
[27] See the German, Belgian, Dutch, Portuguese, Spanish and Italian reports.
[28] In the *Erbbaugrundbuch* in Germany.
[29] See the German, Belgian, Dutch, Portuguese, Spanish and Italian reports.
[30] See the Portuguese and Spanish reports. [31] See the Italian report.

holder may *sell or donate* it if not restricted in the constitutive grant. In these three jurisdictions, the hereditary land lease can also be *mortgaged* and the holder is allowed to *create separate real rights* over the hereditary lease, such as a usufruct[32] and a hereditary building right, but not another hereditary land lease.

In most jurisdictions, the rights under a *lease* are considered personal, which cannot be attached *in execution proceedings* by the tenant's creditors. Rights flowing from the lease, such as claims against the landlord for improvements or repairs, or the rental income flowing from a sublease, may, however, be attached.[33]

The interest of the tenant can be attached in jurisdictions such as Austria, Scotland and South Africa, which regard a registered lease as a real right, and in Spain, England[34] and Poland, which regard the lease as an executable receivable.[35] In Austria, however, this is not allowed in the case of a residential lease, which is essential for the tenant and his/her family.

In most jurisdictions, a *usufruct* is regarded as an economic asset in the usufructuary's patrimony that can be attached in execution proceedings against the holder. Note, however, that the purchaser in execution will only acquire a contingent right which will expire on the usufructuary's death.[36]

The interests inherent in the right of *use* and of *habitation* are so intertwined with the person of the holder that they can neither be transferred nor attached.[37] This makes the right of habitation attractive for estate planning purposes. Nevertheless, German law provides for attachment of personal servitudes where the holder has obtained permission from the nude owner to alienate the entitlements of the particular servitude. The South African report suggests that since the *habitator* is allowed to sub-let the dwelling his/her interest can also be attached.

[32] The prevailing Belgian academic view is that only a usufruct may be created by the holder.

[33] See e.g. the German, Greek, Italian, Belgian, Dutch and Danish reports.

[34] In England, a creditor's acquisition of a lease is, however, frequently an event which triggers forfeiture of the lease and re-entry by the landlord.

[35] See e.g. the South African report which states that the Land Register must be notified of the attachment.

[36] See e.g. the German, Austrian, Greek, Belgian, Dutch, Portuguese, Spanish, Scottish and Italian reports.

[37] See e.g. the Belgian, Dutch, Portuguese, Spanish and Italian reports.

All the jurisdictions that recognise *hereditary building rights*[38] and *hereditary land leases*[39] regard them as valuable limited real rights which can be attached.

The considerations applicable to execution proceedings against B apply equally to B's bankruptcy. A usufruct, the German permanent right of habitation (*Dauerwohnrecht*), the hereditary building lease (*superficies*, *Erbbaurecht*), and the hereditary land lease (*emphyteusis*) will be *included in B's insolvency assets*. Spain's insolvency law, for example, provides that all goods and rights included in the debtor's estate at the date of insolvency are part of the insolvency assets, which would include a lease. By contrast, a right of use or habitation (*Wohnungsrecht*) will in principle not be included, except in Germany where the *habitator* has obtained permission to alienate the entitlements of the right of habitation.

In England and Scotland, property in a lease is included in the insolvency or bankruptcy assets of the tenant. As in the case of attachment, insolvency or bankruptcy is, however, frequently an event which triggers forfeiture of the lease and permits re-entry by the landlord, although this must now be sanctioned by the court. Apart from this qualification, a lease forms part of the bankrupt tenant's estate and may be disclaimed or sold by the trustee in bankruptcy or other relevant entity.

Under South African insolvency legislation, which generally includes a lease in the insolvency assets of the lessee, the administrator has discretion to continue or to terminate the lease. If the administrator elects to continue, all the benefits and liabilities under the lease accrue to the insolvent estate. A similar situation exists under Danish and Belgian insolvency law where the administrator may adopt any synallagmatic contract if justified in view of the estate's financial interest. If not adopted, the landlord is entitled to terminate the lease and evict the tenant.

Austria

Generally, a party to a contract may transfer his/her rights and obligations under the contract or only assign such rights. The *transfer* of all contractual rights and obligations to a third party results in the third party succeeding to the position of the original party and normally

[38] See the German, Austrian, Belgian, Dutch, Portuguese, Spanish and Italian reports.
[39] See the Belgian, Dutch and Polish reports.

requires the consent of both original parties.[40] According to these general rules, the tenant cannot transfer *a lease* without the consent of the landlord. However, there are some rules which facilitate the transfer of leases for buildings and residential premises.

The Law on Tenancy, § 12(a) provides that if someone acquires the business which is operated on leased premises, that person automatically succeeds to the lease without the consent of the landlord. However, the landlord is entitled to increase the rent to the statutory maximum. If the lease is not subject to the Law on Tenancy, the transfer of a lease in case of the acquisition of a business on the leased premises is governed by the Commercial Code, §§ 38 ff.[41] Farmers are subject to the Commercial Code if they are registered with the Companies Register (Commercial Code, § 4, para. 3). According to Commercial Code, §§ 38 and 39, the person who acquires an enterprise succeeds to any contracts of the entrepreneur with the exception of non-transferable personal rights. Therefore, the third party also succeeds to leases.[42] However, the landlord is entitled to protest against such succession within three months of receiving notice thereof (Commercial Code, § 38, para. 2). In this case, the only possibility for the entrepreneur is to create a 'split-lease contract' as described below. The Law on Tenancy, § 12 allows the tenant to transfer his/her rights and duties to certain family members who have been living with him in the leased property for a certain minimum period of time. If the tenant does so, the landlord is entitled to increase the rent up to the statutory maximum.

In contrast, *by assignment*,[43] the third party does not become a party to the contract to the extent that he/she succeeds to the position of the assignor because he/she only acquires the rights of the assignor. In principle, rights can be assigned without the consent of the debtor (Civil Code, §§ 1392 ff.). It is disputed whether and under which conditions the tenant is allowed to assign his/her right to use the leased property.[44] According to the Supreme Court, such assignment is only binding with

[40] Welser, in Koziol and Welser, *Bürgerliches Recht*, vol. 2, p. 135.

[41] As to the relationship between s. 12a of the Law on Tenancy and s. 38 of the Commercial Code, see Beig, 'Wohnrechtliche Aspekte', p. 40.

[42] Beig, 'Wohnrechtliche Aspekte', p. 37.

[43] The term 'cession' is used in other jurisdictions to effect such a relationship.

[44] Bydlinski, 'OGH Anmerkung' 90 (with further references); Mayrhofer, 'Abtretung', pp. 146 and 169 (with further references); p. Bydlinski, 'Zur Abtretbarkeit', p. 728; Ertl, in Rummel, *Kommentar*, vol. 1, § 1393, para. 6; 2 Ob 553/76; SZ 49/159; 1 Ob 13/73.

the express or implicit[45] consent of the landlord.[46] Thus, no direct legal relationship between the assignee and the landlord arises. The assignment is only valid between assignor and assignee. Hence, similar to a sub-lease, the assignee is entitled to use the object, but does not assume the duties of the original tenant. The Supreme Court identifies this legal relationship as a 'split lease'[47] or a 'moderated assignment'.[48] However, many law professors criticise this concept as incoherent.[49] In any case, a contractual prohibition of a sub-lease also prohibits the assignment of the right to use the object.[50]

According to Civil Code, § 1098, the tenant is entitled to *sub-let* the leased object unless the sub-lease is to the disadvantage of the owner or the lease contract stipulates otherwise. Under the Law on Tenancy, § 11, the landlord may rely on such prohibition only if he/she can put forth a compelling reason why the sub-lease shall not be allowed. The legal relationship between tenant and sub-tenant is subject to the rules governing 'normal' lease contracts. Thus, the sub-tenant, in principle, has the same rights towards the tenant as the tenant towards the landlord[51] and the tenant is entitled to be paid rent. The sub-tenant has no direct claims against the landlord. Hence, any decision of a court which terminates the principal contract of lease is binding and may be enforced against the sub-tenant as well.[52]

In principle, *personal servitudes* are not transferable (Civil Code, § 485). Special rules apply to a usufruct. Although some decisions of the Austrian Supreme Court hold that the usufruct as such is alienable,[53] the majority of academic writers and older decisions of the Supreme

[45] 6 Ob 177/98t; wobl (2000), p. 13.
[46] OGH 21.2.1973; 1 Ob 13/73; Bydlinski, 'OGH Anmerkung', 90; 2 Ob 553/76; SZ 49/159; 5 Ob 199/01b; Hausmann; wobl (2003), p. 22.
[47] 6 Ob 177/98t; wobl (2000), p. 13; 1 Ob 519/91; ecolex (1991), p. 455; Pittl, 'Das "gespaltene Mietverhältnis"'; wobl 123; Ertl, in Rummel, *Kommentar*, vol. 1, § 1393, para. 6.
[48] 2 Ob 553/76; SZ 49/159; Mayrhofer, 'Abtretung', pp. 146, 149.
[49] Bydlinski, 'OGH Anmerkung', p. 90; Bydlinski, 'Zur Abtretbarkeit', pp. 730 ff.; Mayrhofer, 'Abtretung', pp. 146, 148.
[50] Ertl, in Rummel, *Kommentar*, vol. 1, § 1393, para. 6; Neumayr, in Koziol, Bydlinski and Bollenberger, *Kommentar*, § 1393, para. 5; p. Bydlinski, 'Zur Abtretbarkeit', p. 735; OGH 17.12.1976; 2 Ob 553/76; SZ 49/159.
[51] Iro, in Koziol, Bydlinski and Bollenberger, *Kommentar*, § 1098, para. 6. [52] Ibid.
[53] 3 Ob 268/03y; JBl (2004), p. 637; similarly, 1 Ob 453/50; SZ 23/280 and OGH 16.6.1908; R. VIII, 66/8; GlUNF 4271.

Court only entitle the usufructuary to transfer the right to exercise the usufruct (*Übertragung 'der Ausübung nach'*) but not the usufruct itself.[54]

The transfer of the right to exercise the usufruct can be registered in the Land Register, which will protect the transferee against third persons.[55] Without registration, the transfer only has obligationary effects between the transferee and the transferor.[56] In any case, the right of the original usufructuary remains registered[57] and he/she must still fulfil his/her duties towards the landowner.[58] The rights of the transferee terminate at the latest with the death of the original usufructuary.[59] Before that, the original usufruct may be terminated only with the consent of the original usufructuary and the transferee. The original usufructuary is not entitled to renounce the usufruct unilaterally.[60]

Furthermore, the usufructuary is entitled to conclude both a tenancy and an income-producing lease with regard to the land.[61] In such a case, the tenant is deemed to be the primary tenant and not only a sub-tenant (Law on Tenancy, § 2, para. 1)[62] and the usufructuary is entitled to receive the rent (Civil Code, § 511). The rights of the tenant are not terminated automatically when the usufruct expires because, analogous to Civil Code, § 1120 and Law on Tenancy, § 2, para. 1, the landowner is bound to take over the contract.[63]

The holder of a right of *use* can neither transfer his/her right nor lease the property subject to his/her right.[64] The right of *habitation* is either subject to the rules of usufruct or those of the right of usage.

54 1 Ob 453/50; SZ 23/280; 5 Ob 114/91; NZ (1992), p. 155 (Hofmeister); 7 Ob 603/94; wobl (1995), p. 242; 2 Ob 99/97s; Kletecka, in Koziol and Welser, *Bürgerliches Recht*, vol. 1, p. 426; Hofmann, in Rummel, *Kommentar*, vol. 1, § 509, para. 1; Iro, *Sachenrecht*, para. 15/37.

55 1 Ob 453/50; SZ 23/280; 5 Ob 114/91; NZ (1992), p. 155 (Hofmeister); Kletecka, in Koziol and Welser, *Bürgerliches Recht*, vol. 1, p. 426.

56 7 Ob 603/94; wobl (1995), p. 242; 8 Ob 534/94; NZ (1995), p. 153 (transfer of a non-registered *ususfructus*).

57 7 Ob 603/94; wobl (1995), p. 242.

58 1 Ob 453/50; SZ 23/280; OGH 29.11.1995, 7 Ob 603/94; wobl (1995), p. 242; Hofmann, in Rummel, *Kommentar*, vol. 1, § 509, para. 1; Kletecka, in Koziol and Welser, *Bürgerliches Recht*, vol. 1, p. 426.

59 1 Ob 453/50; SZ 23/280; OGH 29.11.1995; 7 Ob 603/94; wobl (1995), p. 242; Hofmann, in Rummel, *Kommentar*, vol. 1, § 509, para. 1.

60 5 Ob 114/91; NZ (1992), p. 155 (Hofmeister).

61 1 Ob 453/50; SZ 23/280; 4 Ob 506/89; JBl (1989), p. 442; 2 Ob 99/97s; 7 Ob 142/02m; NZ (2004), p. 737; Ob 66/01h; JBl (2001), p. 585.

62 7 Ob 142/02m; NZ (2004), p. 73.

63 4 Ob 3/29; JBl (1928), p. 392; Kletecka, in Koziol and Welser, *Bürgerliches Recht*, vol. 1, pp. 425 ff. For details as to Civil Code, § 1120, see Case 2.

64 Kletecka, in Koziol and Welser, *Bürgerliches Recht*, vol. 1, p. 427.

According to Civil Code, § 448, all property which can be subject to legal relations and transfers can also be mortgaged. The term 'property' includes intangible property such as *leases*.[65] Thus, except for non-transferable personal rights, rights can be *mortgaged*, provided that it is possible to liquidate them by enforcement.

In principle, the rights of a tenant under a lease can thus be mortgaged,[66] provided that it is possible to *attach* them.[67] However, even if the lease is registered in the Land Register, the law does not allow the mortgage of such a lease to be registered.[68] The *attachment* of rights under a lease is subject to the Law on Execution, §§ 331 ff. An attachment is prohibited if the lease concerns residential premises which are subject to the Law on Tenancy and which provide essential accommodation for the tenant and his/her family (Law on Tenancy, § 42, para. 4). The *liquidation* of attached lease rights may be effected by means of forced administration and forced sub-lease.[69] If sub-lease is not possible (for example, because of a contractual prohibition) or economically inexpedient, the enforcement proceedings must be closed and no attachment will be effected.[70]

A *personal servitude* can be *mortgaged* and *attached*, provided it is not inseparable from a certain plot of land (real servitude) or dedicated to the personal needs of the holder.[71] Hence, the right of use can neither be mortgaged nor be attached.[72] By contrast, it is possible to mortgage a usufructuary right,[73] even if it concerns residential premises.[74] The mortgage of a usufruct must be registered in the Land Register and will expire at the latest with the death of the usufructuary. If the usufructuary renounces his/her rights, the usufruct cannot be cancelled in the Land Register without the consent of the mortgagee.[75] In

65 Civil Code, § 285; Hofmann, in Rummel, *Kommentar*, vol. 1, § 448, para. 1.

66 5 Ob 47/94; NZ (1995), p. 92 (Hoyer); Kletecka, in Koziol and Welser, *Bürgerliches Recht*, vol. 1, p. 375.

67 5 Ob 47/94; NZ (1995), p. 92 (Hoyer); Hofmann, in Rummel, *Kommentar*, vol. 1, § 448, para. 8.

68 5 Ob 47/94; NZ (1995), p. 92 (Hoyer).

69 Oberhammer, in Angst, *Kommentar*, § 331, para. 39.

70 3 Ob 90/70; SZ 43/135; 3 Ob 82/73; JBl (1974), p. 374; 3 Ob 12/78; EvBl (1978), p. 150; Oberhammer, in Angst, *Kommentar*, § 331, para. 43.

71 Hofmann, in Rummel, *Kommentar*, vol. 1, § 448, para. 8; Koch, in Koziol et al., *Kommentar*, § 448, para. 9.

72 Hinteregger, in Schwimann, *Praxiskommentar*, vol. 5, § 448, para. 11.

73 5 Ob 74/98p; NZ (1998), p. 408 (Hoyer); OGH 16.6.908; R. VIII, 66/8; GlUNF 4271; Kletecka, in Koziol and Welser, *Bürgerliches Recht*, vol. 1, p. 375; Hofmann, in Rummel, *Kommentar*, vol. 1, § 448, para. 8.

74 Hofmann, in Rummel, *Kommentar*, vol. 1, § 448, para. 8.

75 5 Ob 74/98p; NZ (1998), p. 408 (Hoyer).

enforcement proceedings, a usufructuary right can be liquidated in accordance with the Law on Execution, §§ 331 ff. Primarily, the usufructuary right shall be liquidated by forced administration or by a forced income-producing lease.[76] The usufructuary right may be sold in execution only if these proceedings are neither possible nor economically expedient.[77]

A *hereditary building lease* can be mortgaged and attached in execution as well.[78] On expiry of a building lease, the building passes into the ownership of the landowner. A mortgage on the building lease, in this case, continues as a mortgage on the land (Law on Building Rights, s. 9). Furthermore, the mortgage also encompasses the compensation which the holder receives from the land owner on expiry of the building lease (Law on Building Rights, s. 10).

Time-limited rights in land are included in B's insolvency or bankruptcy assets as far as it is possible to attach them (Law on Insolvency, § 1).

Belgium

A lease can be assigned gratuitously or for consideration. The assignment of a *residential lease* is subject to the consent of the landlord. In case of such consent, the tenant (assignor) is discharged from all future obligations, unless otherwise agreed.

The assignment of an *agricultural lease* is in principle also subject to the consent of the landlord. The tenant, however, remains liable to the landlord, unless the latter discharges him/her. However, an agricultural tenant can assign the entire lease to specific relatives without the landlord's consent. The tenant then remains jointly liable with the assignee to the landlord. However, if the tenant (or his/her heirs) notifies the landlord of the name and address of the assignee within a period of three months after the latter's occupation, the lease will be renewed automatically by operation of law unless the landlord's objection to such renewal has been accepted. The assignee becomes the holder of a new lease and the tenant is then discharged from future obligations to the principal landlord.

Since a lease gives rise to merely personal rights, the tenant cannot create separate time-limited rights *in rem*. For the same reason, he/she cannot mortgage his/her rights, although a pledge is possible.

[76] Oberhammer, in Angst, *Kommentar*, § 331, para. 39; 3 Ob 35/93; NZ (1995), p. 275.
[77] 3 Ob 268/03y; JBl (2004), p. 637.
[78] Hofmann, in Rummel, *Kommentar*, vol. 1, § 448, para. 8.

In a *residential lease*, the tenant is entitled to sub-lease. A sub-lease does not affect the relationship between the landlord and the tenant (sub-landlord). The tenant is liable for the damage caused by the fault of the sub-tenant. In case of a residential lease, sub-lease of the entire property is forbidden. With the consent of the landlord the tenant (sub-landlord) can sub-lease a part of the property if the tenant continues to occupy the other part of the house as his/her principal residence. It is not relevant whether or not the sub-tenant will have his/her principal residence in the sub-leased property. The duration of the sub-lease may not exceed the remaining term of the principal lease. There is no direct contractual relationship between the landlord and the sub-tenant. Termination of the principal lease for whatever reason, results in the termination of the sub-lease. Within these limits, it also seems possible for the tenant to create a loan for use.

In the case of an *agricultural lease*, the sub-lease of the entire or a part of the property is subject to the consent of the landlord. However, a sub-lease of the entire property to certain relatives is possible without the consent of the landlord. The term of the sub-lease is limited to the term of the principal lease. There is no direct contractual relationship between the landlord and the sub-tenant. Termination of the principal lease for whatever reason, results in termination of the sub-lease. A specific feature of an agricultural lease is that the exploitation of the farm can be exchanged without the landlord's consent, for example, the tenant can allow another farmer to exploit a part of the leased land in exchange for his/her exploitation of part of the land of the other farmer. This is a *sui generis* contract that does not impact the rights and obligations of landlord and tenant.

The lease as such cannot be attached in execution for the tenant's debts. However, it will be possible to attach certain personal rights flowing from the lease, such as claims for repairs to be effected by the landlord. By contrast, a lease is included in the tenant's insolvency assets. The administrator in bankruptcy (curator) has a discretion to continue the lease, in which case all the benefits and liabilities under the lease accrue to the insolvent estate, or to stop performance under the contract, in which case the landlord can demand the dissolution of the contract and vindicate the property.

In principle, the holder of a *usufruct* may sell, donate or mortgage it.[79] The usufructuary can also create a further usufruct on the right of

[79] Verbeke and Vanhove, *Actualia vruchtgebruik*, pp. 73–101; Vanhove and Baudoncq, 'Combinatie van beperkt zakelijke rechten', pp. 135–53.

usufruct (the creation of a usufruct on the property itself is also possible). Generally, it is not possible to create a *hereditary land lease* (*emphyteusis*) or a *hereditary building lease* (*superficies*) on the right of usufruct, although some authors are of the opinion that the creation of a hereditary building lease is conceivable. Although newly created rights are in principle limited by the entitlements of the holder himself, the usufructuary may burden the property with any lease (including a residential or agricultural lease), even if this would exceed the term of usufruct, on the understanding that it will expire on termination of the usufruct.[80] The usufructuary may also allow a loan for use. Additionally, he/she may allow or acquire servitudes which burden or benefit the property subject to the usufruct.

The usufructuary's rights are open to attachment for the holder's debts (Judicial Code, art. 1560–2). The rights may also be included in the insolvency or bankruptcy assets of the holder. There is one exception to this general principle. Owing to their strictly personal character, the holder of a right of use or habitation may not sell, donate or mortgage it (Civil Code, arts. 631 and 634). Furthermore, the rights are neither open to attachment nor included in the insolvency or bankruptcy assets. The holder cannot burden his/her time-limited right by creating a separate limited right. Even the possibility of burdening the property with a lease or loan for use is excluded.

In principle, the holder of a *hereditary lease of land* (*emphyteusis*) or a *hereditary building lease* (*superficies*) may sell, donate or mortgage it.[81]

The holder of a *hereditary land lease* is entitled to grant certain limited real rights over the hereditary lease such as a usufruct, but not a hereditary building lease (although it seems possible to create such a right over the property itself) or (according to the view of a majority of academics) a further hereditary lease over the existing one (although it seems possible to create a further hereditary lease of land over the property itself). He/she is entitled to burden the land with any lease (including a residential or agricultural lease) or a loan for use. Regarding

[80] Indeed, in the case of lease, there is an exception to the rule that the usufructuary may not create rights that exceed his/her entitlements to the property. The nude owner must respect a lease with a fixed period of a maximum of nine years, except in the case of fraud. If the lease runs longer than nine years, the nude owner is only bound by the current nine-year period at the time of termination of the usufruct (Civil Code, art. 595). Civil Code, art. 595 also deals with lease renewals.

[81] Verbeke and Vanhove, *Actualia vruchtgebruik*, pp. 73–101; Vanhove and Baudoncq, 'Combinatie van beperkt zakelijke rechten', pp. 135–53.

servitudes, the situation is the same as under usufruct. The holder of a *hereditary building lease* is entitled to grant certain limited real rights over his/her building lease such as a usufruct, but not a right of surface and (according to the view of a majority of academics) not a hereditary lease of land.

In general, the transfer, mortgage and creation of limited real rights are restricted by the content and duration of the time-limited interest of the holder (unless otherwise indicated) according to the maxim *nemo plus iuris transferre potest quam ipse habet.*

The holder's time-limited real rights are open to attachment for the holder's debts (Judicial Code, art. 1560–2). The rights may also be included in the insolvency or bankruptcy assets of the holder.

Denmark

Under a *land lease*, B is not entitled to sell, donate or create a separate limited right without the permission of the owner. Where the owner has given his/her permission, the right of the purchaser/beneficiary/holder of the sub-lease will not comprise more than B's right under his/her contract. It is not possible to mortgage the right.

As B's time-limited right is personal in nature, it cannot be *attached in execution proceedings* against B. However, if B has a monetary claim against A, B's creditors may supersede his/her right to the money. Time-limited rights can be included in B's *bankruptcy assets* as the bankrupt estate may adopt any synallagmatic contract (Law on Bankruptcy, s. 55).

The tenant cannot sell or mortgage a *lease of buildings for residential purposes*, but the right to use the premises can be transferred either in part or in its entirety. Any tenant of a flat is entitled to sub-let up to half of the rooms of the flat for residential purposes without any time limits (Law on Private Housing, s. 69). In addition, certain tenants are entitled to sub-let a flat[82] which is let exclusively for residential purposes for a period not exceeding two years where the absence of the tenant is temporary and is due to illness, business, studies and job placement (Law on Private Housing, s. 70). Neither of these provisions can be deviated from to the detriment of the tenant.

[82] Sub-letting the whole flat presupposes that the property comprises more than thirteen flats, that the total number of persons in the flat will not exceed the number of rooms and that the landlord cannot object to the sub-letting on any reasonable ground.

B's time-limited rights cannot be attached in execution proceedings. The lease may be included in the bankruptcy estate where such inclusion, in the opinion of the Bankruptcy Court, is deemed to be reasonably justified by the financial interest of the estate's creditors (cf. Law on Bankruptcy, ss. 37 ff.).

The tenant may assign a *lease of buildings for non-housing purposes* on identical terms to a sub-tenant carrying on the same kind of business unless the landlord objects to such assignment on substantial grounds, such as the proposed assignee's financial position or knowledge of the relevant line of business (Law on Commercial Premises Rent, s. 55). This provision can and will often be deviated from in order to deprive the tenant of this right. This right may be donated under the same circumstances. Mortgaging the right itself is not possible, but under s. 47a(2) of the Law on Registration of Property it is possible to pledge, for example, livestock and crops. The tenant is not entitled to sub-let the buildings unless otherwise agreed.

B's time-limited rights cannot be attached in execution proceedings. The lease can, as a synallagmatic agreement, be adopted by the bankruptcy estate if it is found to be profitable (Law on Bankruptcy, s. 55). This is often the case where B is entitled to transfer his/her right to another tenant. If the contract is not adopted by the estate, it may be repudiated by A.

England

Again, regard must be had to the nature of the lease and to its terms. Public sector residential tenancies may, as a general principle, not be assigned (Housing Act 1985, s. 95). In principle, private lettings are freely assignable though, in practice, landlords impose covenants to either preclude any alienation in whole or in part absolutely, or else make such alienation subject to permission. By statute, those qualified covenants (namely, subject to permission) are subject to a reasonableness requirement (Landlord and Tenant Act 1927, s. 19(1)(a) and Landlord and Tenant Act 1988, s. 19).[83] In English law, B is only permitted to assign (or sub-let or mortgage) his/her own property, so that the reversion is unaffected by his/her dealings with the lease. Any sub-lease

[83] The statute does not operate in absolute covenants against assignment (see *Bocaro SA* v. *S. and M. Hotels Ltd.* [1980] 1 WLR 17).

granted is carved out of B's lease, and will therefore be for a shorter term (if it is for the equivalent term, it counts as an out-and-out assignment).

B's lease is property, and can therefore be subjected to any procedure that any other property may be subjected to. It ought to be added, however, that creditors' acquisition of interests in a lease, or the bankruptcy or insolvency of a tenant, are frequently events which trigger the operation of forfeiture, so that the landlord acquires a right to re-entry on that event. There are now restraints on the circumstances in which a landlord may exercise the right to forfeit: as a rule, leave of the court is required in order to re-take the lease.[84] Aside from this qualification, however, leases form part of the bankrupt tenant's estate and may be disclaimed or sold by the trustee in bankruptcy or other relevant entity.[85]

France

Under the general law of *lease*, the tenant only acquires a personal right in the leased property. Consequently, he/she may not sell, donate or burden the lease with a mortgage. However, if the lease does not turn on the identity of the tenant, the tenant may sub-let or even assign the lease to another person unless he/she has been forbidden wholly or partially to exercise that faculty (Civil Code, art. 1717). The tenant can also allow the land to be used by a partnership or grant a loan for use of the leased property.

B's time-limited right can neither be attached in execution proceedings against B, nor be included in B's insolvency or bankruptcy assets.

Since a *residential lease* typically turns on the identity of the tenant, the Law of 1989 forbids sub-letting or assignment of the lease without the written consent of the landlord. Although this Law does not forbid a loan for use of the dwelling, this may be forbidden in the contract. By contrast, the contract cannot forbid the tenant from lodging people who are part of his/her close family in the residential premises (CEDH, art. 8–1).

B's time-limited right can neither be attached in execution proceedings against B nor be included in B's insolvency or bankruptcy assets.

[84] See the amendments to the Law on Insolvency 1986 and the Rules made by the Law on Enterprise 2002.

[85] See Berry, Bailey and Shaw Miller, *Personal Insolvency*, ch. 25 for the general procedures in respect of natural persons. See Bailey, Groves and Smith, *Corporate Insolvency*, paras. 15–32 ff. for the detailed rules in relation to legal persons.

In principle, Rural Code, art. L 411–35 forbids *sub-leases of agricultural land*. However, the landlord may permit the tenant to grant sub-leases for leisure or vacation use of no more than three consecutive months. In such a case, the holder of the sub-lease neither has a right to renewal of his/her lease nor a right to stay on the premises after the expiry of the lease. Where the landlord has refused to grant approval, and a special tribunal presided over by a judge with equal representation from landlords and tenants finds the refusal to be without sufficient cause, the tribunal can authorise the sub-lease and lay down what portion of the rent must be redirected to the principal landlord. The landlord can also authorise the tenant in writing to grant sub-leases of buildings meant for residential use, specifying what portion of the rent has to be redirected to the landlord.[86] This provision of the Rural Code is mandatory.

Apart from the case where the parties have entered into an 'assignable agricultural lease',[87] Rural Code, art. L 411–35 mandatorily forbids any assignment of a lease, of whatever duration, extent or purpose, unless the assignment is granted with the consent of the landlord or authorised by the court, in favour of the tenant's spouse, his/her descendants, or his/her partner under a civil solidarity pact, participating in the operation of the property. The tenant is, however, allowed to place the leased property at the disposal of a partnership engaged in agricultural operations or contribute his/her rights under the lease (Law of the 22 December 1979; Rural Code, arts. L 411–37 and L 411–38) to such partnership. This is not considered a forbidden assignment of the lease.[88]

Since the tenant only obtains a personal right, he/she cannot burden the lease with a mortgage. B's time-limited right cannot be attached in execution proceedings against B, nor can it be included in B's insolvency or bankruptcy assets.

Since the Law of 5 January 2006, it is possible to conclude an 'assignable agricultural lease' in the case where an 'agricultural fund' is established entirely out of parcels which its operator holds by virtue of assignable leases (Rural Code, art. L 418–1).

The *usufructuary* can transfer his/her right by selling or donating it (Civil Code, art. 595). He/she is also entitled to mortgage his/her right. This mortgage will extend to improvements made on the property (Civil Code, art. 2397 amended by Ord. no. 2006–346 of 23 March 2006). Since the *usufruct* is limited in time, the security offered by the object

[86] See Case 6. [87] See below. [88] Cass. civ. 3, 5 Mar. 2003; Bull. civ. III, no. 54.

of the mortgage (*hypothèque*) is not very sound as the asset expires on the death of the usufructuary or at the expiry of the term agreed by the parties.

The usufructuary is entitled to lease the property to a third party.[89] For the enforcement of such a lease against the nude owner, Civil Code, art. 595 requires that the lease or its renewal must not be for more than nine years, with the lease only being enforceable against the nude owner for the remainder of the nine-year period following the death of the usufructuary. The usufructuary is not allowed to grant a lease of an agricultural or commercial nature without the consent of the nude owner or the authorisation of the court.

B's usufruct can be attached in execution proceedings against B and can be included in B's insolvency or bankruptcy assets.

A *right of habitation* cannot be subjected to a lease (save for the exception in favour of the spouse, as mentioned in Case 6), nor assigned or hypothecated. B's right of habitation cannot be attached in execution proceedings against B, nor can it be included in B's insolvency or bankruptcy assets.

Since the holder of a *hereditary building lease* (*superficies*) obtains a real right in the buildings and other constructions on the property, he/she is entitled to sub-lease the buildings without a stipulation to the contrary being possible (Code for Construction and Habitation, art. L 251–3). The tenant is free to assign his/her real right or subject it to a mortgage (Code, art. 251–3). B's time-limited right can be attached in execution proceedings against B, or can be included in B's insolvency or bankruptcy assets.

The fact that the holder of a *hereditary land lease* (*emphyteusis*) obtains a transferable real right in the property, entitles him/her to sub-lease the land. The holder is also free to assign his/her real right or subject it to a mortgage. B's time-limited right can be attached in execution proceedings against B and can be included in B's insolvency or bankruptcy assets.

The borrower under a *loan for use* cannot lease, assign or mortgage his/her right. B's time-limited right cannot be attached in execution proceedings against B, nor be included in B's insolvency or bankruptcy assets.

Germany

Under a *lease*, a tenant is entitled to *sell* his/her right of use regarding the property to someone else with the landlord's consent (Civil Code, § 399).

[89] See Case 6.

The third party then assumes all rights and obligations arising out of the lease (*Vertragsübernahme*).

Since a lease merely creates contractual rights, B cannot *mortgage* his/her right(s). In theory, a pledge (*Verpfändung*) (Civil Code, § 1273) or a security assignment (*Sicherungsabtretung*) (Civil Code, § 398) of certain rights flowing from the lease will be possible. The inefficiency of practical execution against these rights renders them unacceptable collateral in practice.

As a general rule, the tenant may not *sub-let* either residential or agricultural property without the consent of the landlord (Civil Code, §§ 540 and 589). Special rules relating to residential leases prevent the landlord from withholding his/her approval to a sub-lease of *parts* of the property if the tenant can show a justifiable interest (*berechtigtes Interesse*) in sub-leasing these parts (Civil Code, § 553). A sub-lease does not create a contractual relationship between the original landlord and the sub-tenant. However, a sub-tenant's right to the property is dependent on and determined by the title of the original tenant. Consequently, the original landlord can eject the sub-tenant through termination of the original lease.

Because of its highly personal character, a *personal servitude* (*Nießbrauch, Wohnungsrecht, beschränkte persönliche Dienstbarkeit*) cannot be transferred from the holder to a third person (Civil Code, §§ 1059, sent. 1 and 1092(1), sent. 1).[90] Although these rights as such are inalienable, the entitlements under a personal servitude can, however, be alienated (*Überlassung der Ausübung*) (Civil Code, §§ 1059, sent 2 and 1092(1), sent 2).[91] The contractual right gained by the third party expires when the usufruct expires.[92] The right to a *dwelling* (*Wohnungsrecht*) is so personal that it cannot be transferred (Civil Code, § 1093). Civil Code, § 1059, sent. 1 is not applicable to the right to a dwelling.

Since personal servitudes are inalienable, they cannot be *mortgaged*.[93]

[90] There is a very limited exception regarding a usufruct held by a juristic person (cf. Civil Code, § 1059a ff.).

[91] With regard to usufruct, the default rule is that the entitlements of the usufruct can be alienated (Civil Code, § 1059 sent 2). The usufructuary's right to alienate the entitlements can be excluded by agreement between the parties. Conversely, the holder of a limited personal servitude (*beschränkte persönliche Dienstbarkeit*) or a right of habitation (*Wohnungsrecht*) is not entitled to alienate the entitlements unless otherwise agreed.

[92] See Palandt, *Bürgerlichen Gesetzbuch*, § 1059, no. 3.

[93] Ibid., § 1092, no. 6.

The holder of a usufruct is not entitled to create a *separate real right*, for example, to grant a right of habitation to a third party. The usufructuary may, however, lease out the property since a lease only creates contractual rights under German law. The holder of a right of habitation (*Wohnungsrecht*) is in principle only allowed to use the property for himself/herself and his/her family. He/she may only let the property to someone else with the consent of the nude owner.

The main difference between the permanent right of habitation (*Dauerwohnrecht*) and the *Wohnungsrecht* is that the *Dauerwohnrecht* is alienable and transmissible (Law on Apartment Ownership, § 33(1)). As a holder of a *Dauerwohnrecht*, B will thus be able to sell or donate it, usually only with the approval of the owner as stipulated in the constitutive agreement (Law on Apartment Ownership, § 35).

The *Dauerwohnrecht* cannot be *mortgaged*.[94]

The holder of a *Dauerwohnrecht* can *lease* the property to someone else with the lease expiring on termination of the *Dauerwohnrecht* (Law on Apartment Ownership, § 37(1)). However, if the landowner (A) makes use of his/her right to claim retransfer of the right (*Heimfall*) (see Case 8), he is substituted for B in the lease with the third party (Law on Apartment Ownership, § 37(2)).

In addition, the holder of a *Dauerwohnrecht* is entitled to create a usufruct as a *sub-interest*.[95]

A hereditary building lease (*Erbbaurecht*) approaches full ownership in the sense that it can be *alienated* and *mortgaged* (Regulations on Hereditary Building Rights, § 1(1)). Moreover, the holder is entitled to create all kinds of *separate limited rights* as sub-interests. Such interests are dependent on the title of the original holder. The Regulations on Hereditary Building Rights (§ 5) allow parties to stipulate in the constitutive agreement that the holder may only transfer or burden his/her right with the approval of the landowner.

As a personal right, a *lease* as such cannot be attached in execution. However, the rights flowing from the lease (for example, claims for payment for improvements effected by the tenant) may be attached.

While a *usufructuary* interest can be attached in execution proceedings against the holder,[96] the interests inherent in the *other personal servitudes* (for example, a right of habitation) cannot be attached unless the holder (B) has obtained permission to alienate the entitlements of the servitude

[94] See *ibid.*, § 33, WEG, no. 1. [95] *Ibid.*

[96] See Palandt, *Bürgerlichen Gesetzbuch*, § 1059, no. 5.

(*Überlassung der Ausübung*) (Code of Civil Procedure, § 857(3)).[97] The fact that it cannot be attached makes the right of habitation (*Wohnungsrecht*) attractive for estate planning purposes.

The interests of a holder (B) in a *permanent right of habitation* (*Dauerwohnrecht*) and a *hereditary building lease* (*Erbbaurecht*) can be attached and sold in execution.

The considerations applying in execution proceedings against B will apply equally to B's bankruptcy. The equity in a *hereditary building lease* (*Erbbaurecht*), a *permanent right of habitation* (*Dauerwohnrecht*) and a *usufruct* (*Nießbrauch*)[98] will be included in B's insolvency assets whereas the equity in a right of *habitation* (*Wohnungsrecht*) and *other limited personal servitudes* (*beschränkte persönliche Dienstbarkeiten*)[99] will not be included without the permission of the landowner.

Greece

The Greek legislator gives the tenant under a *lease* the power, in the absence of contrary agreement, to *grant* to another the *use* of the leased property, *and in particular* to *sub-lease* the property (Civil Code, art. 593), which means that the use of the property can be granted to another by the tenant even without remuneration. In agricultural leases, however, the opposite rule applies. In the absence of contrary agreement or contrary local usage, the tenant-farmer is not entitled to grant the use of the leased land (with or without remuneration) to a third party without the consent of the landlord (Civil Code, art. 624).

Only immovable property capable of alienation or a usufruct over such property may be the subject matter of a *mortgage* (Civil Code, art. 1259). What is actually mortgaged is not the immovable property but the real right on that property, namely ownership or usufruct.[100] The Civil Code only mentions the right of usufruct. It will not be possible to create a mortgage over the equity of the tenant under a lease of immovable property because it only gives rise to personal rights. The right of lease is therefore not considered to be mortgageable.

The tenant is expressly given the right, in the absence of contrary agreement, to *sub-lease* the property to another. In such a case the tenant will be liable to the landlord for any damage caused through the fault of the sub-tenant. Consent of the landlord to the sub-lease does not

[97] *Ibid.*, § 1092, no. 9. [98] *Ibid.*, § 1059, no. 7. [99] *Ibid.*, § 1092, no. 9.
[100] Doris, *Real Security*, pp. 49, 50.

exonerate the tenant from such liability (Civil Code, art. 593). In the case of an agricultural lease, subject to any contrary agreement or local usage, the tenant-farmer is not entitled to grant to another the use of the leased land without the consent of the landlord (Civil Code, art. 624).

Since a lease is not a real right, B's right to use the property cannot be *attached* by his/her creditors. It will, however, be possible for his/her creditors to attach possible pecuniary claims against the landlord arising from the lease (for example, claims of the tenant for expenses owing to repairs necessitated by an existing defect in the property) as well as from the stream of rental income flowing from the sub-lease. The Greek Code of Civil Procedure contains special provisions on the attachment of pecuniary claims (garnishment, see Code of Civil Procedure, arts. 982 ff.).

The same considerations apply in the case of *insolvency* proceedings as in the case of execution proceedings against B.

Unless otherwise agreed, a *usufruct* as such is not transferable owing to its highly personal nature (Civil Code, art. 116).[101] Under reservation of the provision in Civil Code, art. 1164, however, transfer of the rights and benefits under a usufruct is possible for a period not exceeding the life of the usufruct. This means that although the usufruct as such may not be transferable, the right to exploit the property and to collect its produce and income can be *sold* or *donated* by the usufructuary, subject to the proviso that such right will terminate upon expiry of the usufruct.[102]

Since the right of *habitation* is even more closely linked to the person of the beneficiary, neither the right of habitation nor the rights flowing from it may be transferred.[103] The right of habitation expires on the death of the holder (Civil Code, art. 1185).

We have already seen that a *mortgage* can only be established on immovable property that can be alienated or on a usufruct on such property (Civil Code, art. 1259). It is not the immovable property but the real right on the property that is mortgaged.

Owing to the fact that a usufructuary may transfer the exercise of his/her right to another for a period not exceeding the life of the usufruct

[101] Balis, *Property*, p. 376; Roussos, in Georgiades and Stathopoulos, *GCC, Collective Analysis*, art. 1166, no. 1 (125).

[102] Balis, *Property*, p. 377; Roussos, in Georgiades and Stathopoulos, *GCC, Collective Analysis*, art. 1166, no. 24 ff. (130–3).

[103] Balis, *Property*, pp. 394, 395; Papadopoulou, in Georgiades and Stathopoulos, *GCC, Collective Analysis*, art. 1185, no. 1 (196).

under reservation of the provision in Civil Code, art. 1164, he/she may lease out the exercise of his/her right or lend it for use. Since these transactions only give rise to personal rights, they do not create a *separate limited real right* with regard to the property.

The prevailing view in Greece is that only the rights flowing from the usufruct can be *attached* and not the real right of usufruct as such.[104] What can be attached is merely the right to exercise the usufruct as a transferable personal right. Owing to the non-transferability of the real right of the usufruct, only the rights flowing from the usufruct can be included in B's *insolvency* assets.[105]

Hungary

Since a *lease* only gives rise to personal rights, it cannot be *sold*, *donated*, assigned or *mortgaged*, at least not without the consent of the landlord.

The permission of the owner is always required for the *sub-lease* of the property, except in the case of leases of land (Civil Code, § 426 (1)). The significance of this exception is, however, limited since the Law on Residential Lease provides that the tenant of residential or non-residential property can sub-lease the property only with the permission of the landlord (Law on Residential Lease, §§ 33, 38(3) and 42) and if the sub-lease is reduced to writing (Law on Residential Lease, § 33(2)). The same rules apply to income-producing leases (Civil Code, § 461 (1)),[106] with the exception of an agricultural lease.

A sub-lease of agricultural property is null and void (Civil Code 452(3)). The Law on Agricultural Land, § 12/A, however, provides for an exception. The tenant of an *income-producing lease* can, with the permission of the landlord, transfer the use of the land to a person experienced in the cultivation of agricultural land. The agreement and the permission of the landlord must be reduced to writing.

[104] See Roussos, in Georgiades and Stathopoulos, *GCC, Collective Analysis*, art. 1166, nos. 4 and 5 (126); Athens Court of First Instance 14507/1981; NoV (1981), p. 1583. *Contra* Yessiou-Faltsi, *Forced Execution*, p. 115.

[105] Roussos, in Georgiades and Stathopoulos, *GCC, Collective Analysis*, art. 1166, no. 6 (126); Spyridakis and Perakis, 'Interpretation of the GCC', art. 1166, no. 3 (11); Rokas, *Bankruptcy*, p. 127.

[106] If the tenant sub-leases the property with the permission of the landlord, he/she will be liable for the conduct of the sub-tenant. If the tenant sub-leases the property without the permission of the landlord, he/she is liable for loss that would not have occurred in the absence of the sub-lease (Civil Code, § 426(2)–(3)).

No sources could be found dealing with the question whether a lease can be attached for the purposes of execution against the tenant or whether a lease forms part of the insolvency assets of the tenant.

The usufructuary cannot transfer the *usufruct* as such but can transfer the rights under the usufruct to someone else (Civil Code, § 159(2)). In other words, the right of usufruct as an *in rem* right cannot be conveyed as such but the usufructuary may, for example, cede the right to use the property and collect its fruits without affecting the usufruct or the person of the usufructuary as the holder of the right *in rem*.[107] The rights under the usufruct can be transferred to a third person for consideration only if the owner is not interested in exercising the usufruct subject to the same conditions (Civil Code, § 159(2)).

In contrast, the *right to use* is highly personal in the sense that it can only be used to satisfy the needs of the usuary and family members living with him/her. Consequently, neither the *usus* as such, nor the rights under the *usus*, can be transferred to third persons (Civil Code, § 165(1)).

Since the usufruct as a right *in rem* is not transferable, it cannot be mortgaged as such. However, since the rights of use and enjoyment of the fruits under the usufruct are transferable, these rights can be mortgaged. Because of its highly personal character, neither the right *in rem* of use nor the rights under the right of use can be mortgaged (Civil Code, § 252(1)).

The holder of the usufruct *in rem* or the right to use *in rem* cannot create a separate limited right. The usufructuary, through transferring the rights under the usufruct to a third person, can create a separate right *in personam* with regard to the object of the usufruct. Nevertheless, the latter arrangement may have contractual implications not only as regards the relationship between the usufructuary and the third person[108] but also concerning the relationship between the owner and the third person.[109]

Because of difficulty experienced in practice to levy execution against a usufruct for the debt of the usufructuary, a usufruct can neither be attached in execution nor does it form part of the usufructuary's insolvent estate.

[107] Gellért, *A Polgári Törvénykönyv magyarázata*, vol. 1, p. 539; Benedek and Világhy, *A Polgári törvénykönyv a gyakorlatban*, pp. 108–11.

[108] Gellért, *A Polgári Törvénykönyv magyarázata*, vol. 1, p. 539.

[109] Benedek and Világhy, *A Polgári törvénykönyv a gyakorlatban*, pp. 108–11.

The borrower under a *loan for use* cannot temporarily donate or lend out the use of the property or transfer the right to use the property under a lease to a third person without the permission of the lender.[110]

Italy

Under a *lease*, the tenant has the power to sub-let the property leased, but cannot assign the contract to third persons without the consent of the landlord (Civil Code, art. 1594). Since the prevailing view is that a lease does not give rise to a real right, a tenant cannot mortgage his/her right, the lease cannot be attached by the tenant's creditors and it is not included in his/her insolvency and bankruptcy assets.

The usufructuary can assign his/her right either for a fixed term or for its entire duration (Civil Code, art. 980). He is therefore entitled to sell or donate his/her right of *usufruct*. The owner must, however, be informed of the assignment and failure to do so will leave both the usufructuary and the assignee liable *in solidum* to the owner. The purchaser or donee acquires the same right as the original usufructuary and thus the duration of the right assigned will be limited to the life of the original usufructuary. The alienation of the rights under the usufruct can be forbidden in the constitutive deed (Civil Code, art. 980). Contrary to the general rule (Civil Code, art. 1379), such prohibition is effective against third parties and any alienation of the usufruct in contravention thereof will be void.

The usufruct of immovables can be mortgaged (Civil Code, art. 2810). Mortgages over a usufruct normally come to an end when the usufruct expires. However, if the extinction is due to renunciation or abuse by the usufructuary, or to acquisition of the nude ownership by him/her, the mortgage continues until an event occurs that will otherwise extinguish the usufruct (Civil Code, art. 2814).

The right of *use* or *habitation* cannot be transferred (Civil Code, art. 1024). It cannot be mortgaged either, because this can lead to the transfer of the right.[111]

According to the prevailing opinion, the usufructuary cannot constitute praedial servitudes over the object of the usufruct. This is inferred

[110] If the borrower does not comply with this prohibition, he/she will be liable for all loss that will not have occurred if the use of the property has not been abandoned to a third person (Civil Code, § 584(2)).

[111] See e.g. de Martino, 'Dell'usufrutto', p. 357.

from Civil Code, arts. 1077–8, which expressly states that servitudes can be constituted by the holder of a hereditary land lease (*emphyteusis*) without mentioning a usufructuary in this regard, while it expressly mentions that a usufructuary may constitute a servitude in favour of the land over which he has a usufruct (art. 1078). Some authors rely on art. 1077 as implicitly denying that a usufruct may be constituted over the land subject to the usufruct.[112] Other authors disagree, for they see no reason, in principle, for denying the usufructuary the right of constituting praedial servitudes in favour of the land, with such servitudes being extinguished when the usufruct expires.[113]

It is generally understood that a usufructuary can create a usufruct, a right of use or habitation on his/her usufruct.[114] The effect is different from that of transferring a usufruct. In the first case, the second usufructuary does not succeed the first one in respect of his/her rights and duties towards the owner. There is no direct relationship between the owner and the second usufructuary. As such, the first usufructuary remains liable to the owner if the property is damaged or its intended economic purpose is changed. In addition, if the second usufructuary renounces his/her right, it does not imply extinction of the first usufruct. On the other hand, where there is a transfer of the usufruct, the transferee succeeds the original usufructuary in his/her rights and duties towards the owner, and enters into a direct relationship with him. The original usufructuary loses all his/her rights and duties (even if the duration of the usufruct is still determined by reference to his/her life).

The holder of a right of use or habitation cannot create another right of use or habitation on his/her right. The content of the right is limited by the needs of the original holder.

The usufruct can be attached in execution proceedings against the usufructuary and is included in the usufructuary's insolvency or bankruptcy assets. Although there are no authorities on the point, the fact that the right of use or habitation cannot be transferred means that it cannot be attached or be part of the assets of the insolvent estate.

The holder of a *hereditary building right* (*proprietario superficiario*), as an owner *ad tempus*, can freely sell or donate his/her time-limited ownership. He/she can also mortgage it with the mortgage terminating on the expiration of the term of the holder. If for some reason (for example,

[112] See e.g. Pugliese, 'Usufrutto', p. 438; Bigliazzi, 'Usufrutto', p. 144.
[113] See e.g. Gallo, 'Usufrutto', p. 59. [114] See e.g. Pugliese, 'Usufrutto', pp. 436–7.

acquisition of the ownership of the soil by the holder) the ownership of the building and the ownership of the soil are merged in one person, the mortgages encumbering both rights continue to affect each of them separately (Civil Code, art. 2816). If the constitutive agreement provides that, on expiration of the term, the holder is entitled to some remuneration (for example, for improvements to the building), a mortgage registered over such a right applies to such remuneration (Civil Code, art. 2816). The holder of the building right can create a usufruct over the building or constitute praedial servitudes over it. The extinction of the building right by expiration of its term also leads to extinction of the real rights imposed by the holder (Civil Code, art. 954).

The hereditary building lease (temporary ownership of the building) can be attached by B's creditors and is included in B's insolvency or bankruptcy assets.

The Netherlands

A *lease* of *residential property* cannot be transferred to a third person, nor can it be attached in execution. However, after the tenant's death, the contract may be continued by a co-tenant, for example, the tenant's husband or wife (Civil Code, art. 7:266). In principle, a sub-lease is not allowed, but there is an exception for a sub-lease of part of a residence as long as the tenant continues residing in the premises (Civil Code, art. 7:244).

The rules on *agricultural leases* are highly complex in this regard. A sub-lease without the landlord's permission is not allowed (Law on Land Lease (Pachtwet), art. 32; future Civil Code, art. 7:355). Under certain conditions, the tenant can be replaced with a third person against the landlord's will (Law on Land Lease (Pachtwet), art. 49; future Civil Code, art. 7:363). The contract does not expire when the tenant dies but may be continued by his/her heirs (Law on Land Lease (Pachtwet), art. 54; future Civil Code, art. 7:366).

The right of *usufruct* is an independent limited real right. The usufructuary is entitled to dispose of his/her right of usufruct by either selling or giving it to someone else, but it does not last longer than the life of the usufructuary and terminates upon his/her death (Civil Code, art. 3:203 II).

The usufructuary, B, can mortgage his/her right of usufruct. If B becomes insolvent, the right of usufruct can be sold in execution.[115]

[115] Wessels, *Insolventierecht*, nos. 2059, 2060.

The right of use or habitation is a purely personal right which cannot be transferred or mortgaged.

A distinction must be made between a *hereditary building lease* (*superficies*) and a dependent building lease which is attached to a residential lease or an agricultural lease. Only the independent building lease can be transferred.[116]

An independent building lease may be sold, donated or sub-let. On expiration of B's building lease, the right of the third party will terminate as B cannot transfer more than he is entitled to (Civil Code, art. 5:96 and 5:104 II). B can also encumber his/her building right with a mortgage. Since B's building right is part of his/her assets, it can be attached in execution proceedings against B and is part of his/her assets in bankruptcy proceedings.[117]

A dependent building lease is mostly dependent on a right of hereditary land lease (*emphyteusis*). On transfer of the hereditary land lease to a third party or on transfer of the holder's death to his/her heirs, the building lease automatically follows.

The *hereditary land lease* (*emphyteusis*) is an independent limited real right and can be transferred to someone by a contract of sale or a donation. The possibility of transferring the hereditary land lease can, however, be restricted in the deed of creation (Civil Code, art. 5:91).[118]

The hereditary land lease may be encumbered with other limited real rights, for example, a mortgage, which entitlement cannot be restricted.[119] B's hereditary land lease can also be attached in execution and will become part of the bankruptcy estate in case B becomes insolvent.[120]

Poland

Under Polish law, it is impossible for either party to a *lease* to assign (gratuitously or for value) his/her entire legal entitlements (consisting of rights and obligations) to a third party. Each party would have to assign his/her rights (Civil Code, arts. 509–18, which states that as a rule consent of the debtor is not needed) and obligations separately (Civil Code, arts. 519–25, which states that consent of the creditor is a requirement). One may argue that a lease could be assigned (*cessio*) according to

[116] Pitlo, 'Goederenrecht', no. 674.
[117] Wessels, *Insolvensierecht*, nos. 2059, 2060.
[118] Pitlo, 'Goederenrecht', no. 653.
[119] *Ibid.*
[120] Wessels, *Insolvensierecht*, nos. 2059, 2060.

Civil Code, arts. 509 and 519, provided that the lease has a market value. In practice, however, it may be difficult to obtain the consent of the other party if it is needed.

Since a lease is a contract which gives rise to a personal right, it cannot be mortgaged (Law on Management of Real Property, art. 65).

If B has an income-producing (*fruendi*) lease, he/she may sub-let the property, but only with the landlord's consent (Civil Code, art. 698, § 1). B also needs the consent of the landlord to sub-let residential premises, except if the sub-tenant is a person to whom the tenant is obliged to pay alimony (Civil Code, art. 688, § 2). In other leases, B may sub-let without A's consent, unless the contract stipulates otherwise (Civil Code, art. 668, § 1). The sub-lease may not last longer than the main lease and will expire, at the latest, on termination of the lease.

In execution proceedings, a lease will fall into the category of executable (or receivable) debts and other non-personal rights (Code of Civil Procedure, arts. 895–912). Since the attachment will cover the rights of the tenant under the lease and not the rent due under the contract (Code of Civil Procedure, art. 900, § 2) it will be difficult to place a value on such rights. In bankruptcy proceedings, a lease will be included in B's bankruptcy assets on the assumption that the rights of the tenant under the lease will have monetary value. It does not apply to the rent due under the lease (Law on Bankruptcy, art. 331), which falls into the estate of the landlord.

Usufruct as such is neither transferable nor transmissible on death (Civil Code, art. 254). The usufructuary may, however, transfer the right to exercise the usufruct to another person by lease or another contract. Such right may not last longer than the usufruct. A usufruct cannot be mortgaged (Law on Land Register and Mortgages, art. 65). In execution or bankruptcy proceedings, the usufruct will form part of B's executable or bankruptcy assets if it has been established as a non-gratuitous right and was therefore a source of income to B. Since a usufruct is non-transferable, the usufruct as such cannot be sold in execution. However, the rights flowing from the usufruct may be sold in execution subject to expiry when the usufruct comes to an end.

Personal servitudes in the form of a right of habitation may not be transferred or even exercised by a person other than the beneficiary (Civil Code, art. 300) and cannot be mortgaged (Law on Management of Real Property, art. 65). Because personal servitudes in the form of a right of habitation is so closely linked to the person of the habitant, it cannot be attached in execution of B's debt and does not form an asset in his/her estate or part of his/her executable or bankruptcy assets.

Lifetime habitation is a strictly personal right, which is neither transferable nor transmissible on death of the holder. It may not be mortgaged (Law on Management of Real Property, art. 65). Because of the close link with the person of the holder, lifetime habitation does not form part of the executable or bankruptcy assets of B.

A *hereditary land lease* (*perpetual usufruct, emphyteusis*) is transferable (by, for example, sale, donation, exchange or contribution in kind to a company) and transmissible on death. It may be mortgaged (Law on Management of Real Property, art. 65, § 3) and encumbered by servitudes, usufruct or contractual rights without the consent of the landowner (Civil Code, art. 233). A hereditary land lease is a very valuable right, with a market value often as high as the market value of ownership. It is therefore an important asset in B's estate which can be attached and sold in both execution and bankruptcy proceedings. In both cases, the provisions concerning attachment and sale of immovable property are applied (Code of Civil Procedure, art. 1004).[121]

Portugal

Under a *lease*, the tenant is not entitled to grant anyone the total or partial use of the leased property or to cede his/her rights gratuitously or for consideration by sub-letting the property or lending it out for use except if permitted by the law or authorised by the landlord (Civil Code, arts. 1038 ff.).[122] When permitted or authorised, the tenant has a duty to inform the landlord within fifteen days that he/she has granted the use of the property to another (Civil Code, art. 1038g). Notification, but not in a specific form, is required. Failure to notify entitles the landlord to terminate the contract.

The rent under a sub-lease may not be more than 20 per cent above the principal rent (Civil Code, art. 1062). If a higher rent is contracted, the principal landlord may cancel the lease. The sub-lease will terminate with the expiry of the principal lease.

The commercial or industrial lease is considered an asset of the enterprise. As such it can be attached in execution proceedings and can also form part of the insolvency assets of the debtor.

[121] See also Case 3.

[122] Law on Agricultural Leases, arts. 13 and 21e and the Law on Forest Leases, arts. 23 and 17e.

The usufructuary is entitled to transfer his/her right in terms of the *usufruct* indefinitely or for a fixed term to a third party, subject to restrictions imposed by his/her title and the law. He/she will remain liable for damages caused to the property by the transferee (Civil Code, art. 1444). According to the general principle, *nemo plus iuris in alium transferre potest quam ipse habet*, the usufructuary is not allowed to transfer more rights than he/she has. Consequently, he/she is unable to transfer his/her right or create servitudes or burdens which endure for longer than his/her usufruct (Civil Code, art. 1460 no 1). The rights of any third party will therefore expire along with expiry of the usufruct.

The usufructuary is entitled to burden his/her usufructuary interest with a mortgage which will also be extinguished on termination of the usufruct. However, when the usufruct is terminated by renunciation, acquisition of ownership of the property by the usufructuary or assignation of the rights of the usufructuary to the owner, the mortgage remains effective until the usufruct expires for another reason (Civil Code, art. 699).

The usufructuary is entitled to create a sub-interest with regard to his/her usufruct in the form of, for example, a lease or a loan (Civil Code, art. 1444). However, the usufructuary cannot burden the property for a term exceeding that of the usufruct. Hence the lease (Civil Code, art. 1051b) or the loan (Civil Code, art. 1130 no 1) will normally expire when the usufruct expires. However, the nude owner may only demand possession of the leased property or the property on loan six months after expiry of the usufruct in the case of urban property and at the end of the harvesting season in the case of agricultural property (Civil Code, art. 1053). In two exceptional cases the sub-interests will not expire together with the usufruct, namely where the usufructuary acquires the nude ownership of the property or where the usufructuary renounces the usufruct. In the latter case, the sub-interest will remain until the usufruct expires for another reason or on the term initially agreed (Civil Code, art. 1052 read with art. 1130, no. 2).

Since a usufruct is an economic asset, it can be attached in execution proceedings against B and can be included in his/her insolvency assets.[123]

The *right of use* entitles the usuary to use the property and to take its fruits to the extent necessary to meet personal and family needs (Civil Code, art. 1484, no. 1). Owing to its close link with the person of the

[123] Decision of the Court of Appeal of Lisbon of 10.03.1995 [Process 0007481] and Decision of the Appeal of Porto of 22.01.2001 [Process 0051482], available at www.dgsi.pt.

usuary (*intuitus personae*), the usuary cannot sell, donate or create a mortgage or a further right in respect of his/her right of use (Civil Code, art. 1488). Similarly, B's right of use cannot be attached in execution proceedings and cannot be included in B's insolvency assets.[124] The same applies to a *right of habitation*.

Under a *hereditary building lease* (*superficies*), B is entitled to sell or donate his/her time-limited right. The right of *superficies* is transmissible both *inter vivos* or *mortis causa* (Civil Code, art. 1534). The owner of the soil has a right of pre-emption when the right of *superficies* is offered for sale (Civil Code, art. 1535). The right of *superficies* may also be mortgaged (Civil Code, art. 688, no. 1 C) or burdened with a sub-interest like a lease. The expiry of the *superficies* will cause the extinction of the mortgage or the sub-interest (Civil Code, art. 1539), according to the principle *resoluto jure dantis resolvitur jus accipientis*.

If a building lease granted for a fixed term expires for any reason before the term ends, real rights created during the course of the *superficies* remain effective. For example, if a mortgage was created over a building lease with the right set to expire in 2015 and that right actually expired in 2010 (for example, because the holder acquired the land), the mortgage remains effective until 2015 (Civil Code, art. 1541). If, for any reason, execution proceedings have to proceed against B, only the building lease will be sold in execution.

Since the right of *superficies* has economic value, it can be attached in execution proceedings against B and can be included in his/her insolvency assets.

Scotland

Sale or *donation* of B's *lease* will be given effect by an assignation: that is the mechanism by which an incorporeal right such as a lease is transferred. Assignation of a lease[125] transfers not only the tenant's rights but also the tenant's obligations under the lease. It is, therefore, the transfer of the contract.[126] The existing tenant is known as the assignor

[124] Decision of the Court of Appeal of Lisbon of 22.06.89 [Process 0002359] and Decision of the Court of Appeal of Porto of 03.09.1999 [Process 9850162], available at www.dgsi.pt.

[125] See generally Rankine, *Leases*, ch. 9; Paton and Cameron, *Landlord and Tenant*, ch. 10; Gordon and Wortley, *Land Law*, paras. 18–28 to 18–34.

[126] Hugo and Simpson, 'Lease', pp. 324–6, note that there may be room for Scots law to recognise a transfer of only the tenant's rights and not his obligations. This is, however, certainly not common in practice.

and the transferee as the assignee. The assignor is discharged from future liability,[127] but not from liability for arrears. The assignee assumes liability for arrears and for future obligations.[128] Assignation is possible if the landlord consents. Whether the tenant can assign without consent depends upon whether he/she has the power to do so. Typically, this will be addressed in the lease. If the lease is silent, then default rules apply.

At common law, there is a presumption in respect of certain types of lease that *delectus personae* exists, in which case the lease cannot be assigned without the landlord's consent.[129] When the doctrine of *delectus personae* applies, it is presumed that the landlord deliberately chose the tenant for his/her personal qualities such as his/her financial standing or agricultural skills.[130] *Delectus personae* applies to the majority of leases, namely all rural leases, furnished urban leases, sporting leases and mineral leases. It is not presumed to exist in respect of unfurnished urban subjects and rural leases of extraordinary duration (the distinction between usual and extraordinary length is probably drawn at twenty-one years).[131]

Statutory regimes augment this position. In respect of residential tenancies, it is an implied term of every assured tenancy that the tenant shall not, except with the consent of the landlord, assign the tenancy in whole or in part.[132] B can therefore not assign the tenancy in implement of a sale or donation if it is an assured tenancy or a short assured tenancy unless the landlord consents. There are also statutory rules regarding agricultural tenancies. A short limited duration tenancy may not be assigned.[133] A limited duration tenancy may be assigned, provided the landlord consents. There is a procedure which the tenant must go through in order to obtain consent (involving serving written notice on the landlord giving details of the proposed assignee and the terms of the assignation). The landlord may withhold consent if there are reasonable grounds for doing so (for example, where he/she is not satisfied

[127] *Lord Elphinstone* v. *Monkland Iron and Coal Co. Ltd.* (1886) 13 R (HL) 98, 102; Rankine, *Leases*, pp. 193–4. This was a marked change from the previous law, as Rankine notes.

[128] Rankine, *Leases*, pp. 194–5; Paton and Cameron, *Landlord and Tenant*, pp. 162–4.

[129] The doctrine applies even where the tenant is a body corporate: *Scottish Ministers* v. *Trustees of the Drummond Trust* 2001 SLT 665 (OH), para. 15.

[130] Rankine, *Leases*, pp. 172–6; Paton and Cameron, *Landlord and Tenant*, p. 149.

[131] Paton and Cameron, *Landlord and Tenant*, p. 151.

[132] H(S)A 88, s. 23.

[133] H(S)A 03, s. 6(1). Given the contrast with s. 10A AH(S)A 91, this seems to be the case even where the landlord consents.

that the proposed assignee will be able to pay the rent).[134] The procedure in respect of a 1991 Act tenancy is the same as for a limited duration tenancy but it may only be assigned to a limited class of persons, namely those who will be entitled to succeed to the tenant's estate in the event that he/she dies intestate. This category includes children, parents, spouse and other relatives.[135] This is a mandatory rule and provision to the contrary in the lease is void.[136]

Land can only be *mortgaged* by means of a standard security.[137] A standard security can only be granted over a right which is capable of being recorded in the Register of Sasines or registered in the Land Register. A security can therefore only be created over a registrable lease. In the examples being discussed, a standard security can therefore only be granted over a limited duration tenancy or a 1991 Act tenancy. The creditor will carefully examine the provisions of the lease concerning assignation as these will restrict what he/she can do if he/she enforces the security.

A tenant may also, in certain circumstances, *create a separate limited right* by sub-letting the subjects.[138] Unlike in an assignation, where he/she sub-lets, the tenant remains contractually bound to the landlord but enters into a separate contract of lease with the sub-tenant. (The original lease is from then on referred to as the head-lease and the tenant sometimes as the mid-tenant.) The head-landlord has no contractual right against the sub-tenant (unless one is specifically provided for in the sub-lease, which will be unusual). The circumstances in which this is permitted at common law mirror those regarding assignation. A prohibition in the lease of sub-letting will not, however, encompass assignation, and vice versa: each must be separately provided for. Again, there is a statutory overlay. A tenant of a short limited duration tenancy may not sub-let[139] and a tenant of a limited duration tenancy may sub-let only on such basis as the lease expressly permits.[140] The position in respect of the 1991 Act tenancies is unclear.[141]

[134] AH(S)A 03, s. 7.

[135] AH(S)A 91, s. 10A. Succession (Scotland) Act 1964, s. 2 lists those entitled to inherit.

[136] AH(S)A 91, s. 10A(5). [137] CFR(S)A 70, s. 9.

[138] See, generally, Rankine, *Leases*, ch. 9; Paton and Cameron, *Landlord and Tenant*, ch. 10; McAllister, *Leases*, ch. 6; Gordon and Wortley, *Land Law*, paras. 18–35 to 18–39.

[139] AH(S)A 03, s. 6. [140] AH(S)A 03, s. 7(7).

[141] The statutory provision which purports to cover sub-letting does not do so: AH(S)A 91, s. 10A.

In the case of assignation, the assignee acquires B's right: no more, no less (*assignatus utitur jure auctoris*). A security is a limited real right in B's right and is therefore only as good as the parent right. Similarly, as a matter of property law, B cannot confer on a sub-tenant a greater right than he himself/herself has. He/she can, of course, do so as a matter of contract law, but this will leave him/her open to remedies for breach if the head-landlord (A) takes steps to enforce his/her right against B in a manner which prevents B from fulfilling his/her obligations to the sub-tenant. Granting an incompatible sub-lease will probably also place B in breach of the head-lease. There is a statutory derogation from the general rule for assured tenancies: if an assured tenant sub-lets, termination of his/her lease will not bring the sub-tenant's right to an end. Instead, the sub-tenant becomes the head-landlord's tenant.[142]

B's right as tenant is one of his/her assets and can therefore in principle be *attached* by B's creditors by way of diligence. Two types of diligence are available against land. One is inhibition, which prohibits the party inhibited from any future voluntary act conveying the property or otherwise granting a right in property over which the inhibition has effect.[143] A transfer in breach of this prohibition may be reduced by the inhibiting creditor. Inhibition is, however, not an 'attachment' as it does not give the creditor a real right in the property. It merely preserves the existing position. Adjudication is the diligence by which B's creditors can actually attach the lease.[144] Both of these diligences only affect leases which are assignable. However, it is only an express prohibition of assignation which renders a lease unadjudgeable: default rules of lease law do not do so, as the doctrine of *delectus personae* only applies to voluntary and not to judicial assignations.[145] If the lease expressly prohibits assignation or provides that it cannot be assigned without consent, it cannot be adjudged and an inhibition will also be of no effect in respect of it. There are doubts about the treatment of a lease which qualifies the landlord's ability to refuse consent, typically by providing that it may not unreasonably be withheld.[146] If the legislation providing for land attachment is brought into force, these doubts will be removed and all leases which provide that they cannot be assigned

[142] H(S)A 88, s. 28. [143] Bankruptcy and Diligence (Scotland) Act 2006, s. 160.

[144] The effects are detailed in the response to Case 3.

[145] Paton and Cameron, *Landlord and Tenant*, p. 150; Stair, *Institutions*, II. ix. 6; Bell, *Principles*, s. 1216.

[146] See Gretton, *Inhibition and Adjudication*, pp. 73–4 and Maher and Cusine, *Diligence*, paras. 9.23 and 9.42.

without the landlord's consent will be attachable, regardless of whether it is a condition that this consent should not be unreasonably withheld.[147] It is unclear how the rules on diligence interact with the rules regarding transfer of statutorily protected tenancies.

In the event that B becomes *insolvent*, the lease will form part of his/her insolvent estate. Assuming B to be an individual, the relevant insolvency regime is sequestration. The bankrupt's estate vests in the trustee in sequestration and that includes leases. As with other contracts of the bankrupt, the trustee has the choice whether to 'adopt' the lease. Only if the trustee does so (which will be very unusual),[148] does he/she become personally liable for performance of the tenant's obligations.[149] If the trustee does not 'adopt' the lease, the landlord ranks in the sequestration as an ordinary creditor. If the lease contains an express exclusion of assignees, the landlord has an option to refuse to consent to a transfer to the trustee or his/her nominee.[150] As with diligence, an implied exclusion, resting on *delectus personae*, does not affect the position.

A *liferenter* cannot assign his/her right to another with the effect that the assignee becomes the liferenter instead of the assignor. The real right cannot be transferred.[151] However, a liferenter can assign his/her interest so as to allow the assignee the enjoyment of the subjects of the liferent, unless the constitutive deed prohibits this.[152] The assignee does not obtain title to the land in place of the liferenter. His/her entitlement endures only for the liferenter's life (or for whatever other shorter period the liferent endures). An improper liferenter may be assigned. The exception is an alimentary liferent (one created to provide for the maintenance of the beneficiary and to protect him/her against his/her own possible improvidence),[153] although even this can probably be assigned to the extent to which it exceeds a reasonable allowance.[154]

A proper liferent (as a real right in land) may be the subject of a standard security. A standard security cannot be granted over an improper liferent, for that is not a real right in land. Such a right can,

[147] Bankruptcy and Diligence (Scotland) Act 2006, s. 82.

[148] Paton and Cameron, *Landlord and Tenant*, p. 196.

[149] *Cuthill* v. *Jeffrey* 21 Nov 1818 FC. [150] *Elliot* v. *Duke of Buccleuch* (1747) Mor 10 329.

[151] Stair, *Institutions*, II. vi. 7; Erskine, *Institute*, II. ix. 41; *Ker's Trs.* v. *Justice* (1868) 6 M 627 (IH) 631; *Chaplin's Trs.* v. *Hoile* (1890) 18 R 27 (IH) 33.

[152] *Chaplin's Trs.* v. *Hoile* (1890) 18 R 27 (IH) 33, under reference to Pothier, *Traité du contrat de vente*.

[153] Gordon and Wortley, *Land Law*, para. 17–04.

[154] *Claremont's Trs.* v. *Claremont* (1896) 4 SLT 144 (OH); cf. *Cuthbert* v. *Cuthbert's Trs.* 1908 SC 967 (IH).

however, still be assigned in security, that is, an assignation to the creditor qualified by an undertaking that he/she will retrocess (re-assign) the right assigned when the debt secured is satisfied.

A liferent may validly provide that it is to terminate in the event of insolvency of the liferenter so as to deprive the liferenter's creditors of the benefit of the use of the property.[155] If the liferent does not so provide, it forms part of the liferenter's insolvent estate and vests in the trustee in sequestration. The only way to allow the liferenter to retain the benefit of the liferent after his/her insolvency is for it to be constituted as an (improper) alimentary liferent, which may only be attached by creditors for alimentary debts.[156]

A proper liferent may be attached by B's creditors. It is adjudgable.[157] The appropriate diligence in respect of an improper liferent will depend upon the exact structure of the trust and the nature of the liferenter's right.[158]

South Africa

Under South African law, a tenant under a *lease* is entitled to '*sell*' his/her limited right and then 'cede' or 'assign' the rights to a cessionary or assignee. By cession, the tenant-cedent divests himself/herself of his/her rights against the landlord and substitutes a third party (the cessionary) as the landlord's creditor while the tenant remains the landlord's debtor.[159] By contrast, assignment transfers both the tenant's rights and obligations under the lease to a third party, the assignee. The assignee becomes the landlord's creditor and by assuming the tenant's obligations becomes the debtor in place of the original tenant. It is trite law that the transfer of an obligation requires the debtor's concurrence and therefore an assignment of a lease by the tenant requires the agreement of the landlord, the tenant and the assignee.[160]

Agricultural leases can only be transferred by sale or otherwise[161] with the consent of the landlord. By contrast, urban leases can be freely

[155] Gordon and Wortley, *Land Law*, para. 17–62. [156] *Ibid.* para. 17–04.

[157] Stewart, *Treatise Diligence*, p. 600. [158] *Ibid.*

[159] *Floral Displays* v. *Bassa Land and Estate Co.* 1965 4 SA 99 (D) 100H-101A; De Wet and Van Wyk, *Kontraktereg*, p. 372.

[160] Cooper, *Landlord and Tenant*, pp. 245, 258–9.

[161] Art. 9 Placaet of 26 Sept. 1658; *Spies* v. *Lombard* 1950 3 SA 469 (A) 481; Cooper, *Landlord and Tenant*, p. 260.

ceded without the co-operation of the landlord,[162] leaving him with a choice of tenant (*delectus personae*) if the cession unreasonably affects his/her interests.[163] Under the Insolvency Act, a stipulation in a lease which restricts or prohibits the transfer of any right under the lease shall bind the trustee of a tenant's insolvent estate or his/her successor-in-title.[164]

Assignment effectively creates a new lease between landlord and assignee, and therefore requires the same formalities as for the conclusion of a lease.[165] The Deeds Registries Act requires that any cession of a lease shall be notarially executed by both the cedent and the cessionary and registered in the Land Register.[166] Registration protects the cessionary and assignee (new tenant) for the remaining period of the lease.

B may *mortgage* his/her registered lease or sub-lease by the registration of a mortgage bond over the lease or sub-lease.[167] This only requires the consent of the landlord if agreed in the lease.[168] The Land Registrar must endorse the lease or sub-lease to the effect that it has been mortgaged.[169] An unregistered long lease is valid *inter partes*, and the resulting personal right may apparently be utilised as security by way of cession without the need for registration.[170]

Roman-Dutch law allowed a tenant, in the absence of a contrary agreement, to *create a sub-lease*, subject to certain qualifications such as that the sub-tenant had to be a respectable person.[171] In South African law, the tenant of urban property may sub-let without qualification.[172] There is, however, authority for the view of Voet[173] that a tenant may not sub-let if the sub-tenant is so circumstanced (*eius conditionis sit*) that he/she is more likely than the tenant to damage the property or to use the property for purposes other than those contemplated in the lease.[174] For reasons of parity it must be accepted that the landlord has the same *delectus personae* with regard to a sub-tenant that he/she

[162] De Wet and Van Wyk, *Kontraktereg*, p. 329 n. 120; Cooper, *Landlord and Tenant*, pp. 258–9. In this context 'assign' means 'cede'.

[163] Cooper, *Landlord and Tenant*, p. 260.

[164] Insolvency Act 24 of 1936, s. 37(5).

[165] Cooper, *Landlord and Tenant*, p. 269.

[166] Deeds Registries Act 47 of 1937, s. 3(p), 77(1) and 80.

[167] Deeds Registries Act, s. 102 *s.v.* 'immovable property' and s. 81.

[168] In *re Ramasamy Chettee* 1902 NPD 289. S. 91 of the Deeds Registries Act 47 of 1937 forbids the registration of the hypothecation of a cession of any registered lease or sub-lease.

[169] s. 82. See in general Scott and Scott, *Wille's Mortgage and Pledge*, pp. 71, 78.

[170] *Smith* v. *Farelly's Trustee* 1904 TS 949.

[171] See *Codex* 4.56.6; Voet, *Commentarius*, 19.2.5; Cooper, *Landlord and Tenant*, p. 245.

[172] Cooper, *Landlord and Tenant*, p. 245 n. 19; De Wet and Van Wyk, *Kontraktereg*, p. 326.

[173] Voet, *Commentarius*, 19.2.5.

[174] See De Villiers CJ in *Henderson* v. *Hanekom* (1903) 20 SC 513, 518.

has with regard to a cessionary. Consequently, his/her right to object to a sub-tenant will not be limited to reasonable apprehension of damage to or misuse of the property by the prospective sub-tenant.[175]

A sub-lease does not affect the lease between the original landlord and tenant and does not create a contractual *nexus* between the sub-tenant and the original landlord. A sub-tenant's right to the property is dependent on and determined by the original tenant's (sub-landlord B's) title. The sub-tenant has no claim against the original landlord in respect of the property and the original landlord can eject him/her upon termination of the original lease.[176]

The highly personal nature of a *usufruct* prevents it from being transferred as such to a third person. In this sense, the Deeds Registries Act, s. 66 only allows cession of a personal servitude to the nude owner.[177] However, the entitlements under a usufruct are transferable and can thus be *sold*[178] or *donated*.[179] The right gained by the third party is, however, merely contractual and automatically terminates on expiration of the usufruct.[180]

A *usuary* is only entitled to use the property and enjoy its fruits for domestic purposes. He/she is not entitled to alienate the use of the property to a third party by sale, gift, hire or otherwise.[181] By contrast, the *habitator* is allowed to rent out the property or to allow a third party to live gratuitously in the dwelling.[182]

Under the Deeds Registries Act 47 of 1937, the personal servitudes of usufruct and habitation (but not use)[183] may be *mortgaged* separately from the land.[184] In practice, however, the enforcement of the mortgage of a personal servitude is problematic because the Deeds Registries Act, s. 66 allows transfer of the personal servitude only to the

[175] Cooper, *Landlord and Tenant*, p. 246. See further, pp. 249–57 for sub-letting regulated by agreement (e.g. permission to sub-let, prohibition to sub-let and that, if required, the landlord's consent should not be withheld unreasonably) and the consequences of breach of such provisions.

[176] Pothier, *Obligations*, para. 280; Cooper, *Landlord and Tenant*, p. 244.

[177] Deeds Registries Act 47 of 1937, s. 66; Nel, *Jones: Conveyancing*, p. 213.

[178] Van der Merwe, 'Servitudes', para. 432; Voet, *Commentarius*, 7.1.32.

[179] Voet, *Commentarius*, 7.1 32; *Ex parte* Wessels 1949 2 SA 99 (O) 104 (*fidei commissarius*).

[180] See Van der Merwe, 'Servitudes', para. 432; *Durban City Council* v. *Woodhaven Ltd.* 1987 3 SA 555 (A) 561.

[181] *Dreyer* v. *Ireland* (1874) 4 Buch 193 202.

[182] *Arend* v. *Estate Nakiba* 1927 CPD 8.

[183] Van der Merwe, *Sakereg*, pp. 523 and 616.

[184] Deeds Registries Act 47 of 1937, s. 50(1) read with s. 69(4); Voet, *Commentarius*, 13.7.2, 20.3.1.

landowner.[185] Apparently, these problems may be avoided by the simultaneous registration of a mortgage over both the land and the usufruct,[186] which would allow execution against the land, free from the servitude.[187] Since the mortgage creditor cannot have a greater right to the property than the mortgage debtor (the usufructuary), the mortgage is terminated once the usufruct is extinguished by the death of the usufructuary or any other mode of termination.

South African law allows a usufructuary to *create a separate limited right* in the form of a lease of his/her interest in the residential property or farm.[188] The lease will terminate upon the termination of the usufruct, for example, if the usufructuary dies.

Although a usuary is not entitled to lease out his/her interest in the property, South African law allows a usuary of residential property to let out rooms which he/she does not occupy.[189] By contrast, the holder of a right of habitation has from early on been entitled to sub-let the property.[190]

The holder of a personal servitude can never grant more rights than he/she has. The grantee is thus subject to the same remedies available against the usufructuary. Furthermore, on expiry of the usufructuary's right, for example, on death, the right of the grantee also expires.[191]

Since a *lease* is an asset which can be ceded, it can also be *attached in execution* without an application to court.[192] The Land Register, however, must be informed of the execution proceedings.

At common law, the insolvency of the tenant did not terminate the lease.[193] The Insolvency Act now provides that the insolvency administrator may terminate the lease by written notice to the landlord.[194] Until termination, the insolvency administrator must pay the rent which will be included in the cost of sequestration. On termination, the landlord has a claim against the insolvent estate for compensation

185 See *Estate Grabe* v. *Bornman* 1938 OPD 127.
186 Deeds Registries Act 47 of 1937, s. 69(3).
187 s. 3(1)(i) and reg 41(7) of the Regulations under the Deeds Registries Act. See further Lubbe, 'Mortgage and Pledge', para. 447.
188 Voet, *Commentarius*, 7.1.32, 19.2.4; *Armstrong* v. *Bhamjee* 1991 3 SA 195 (A).
189 *Setlogelo* v. *Setlogelo* 1921 OPD 161.
190 Van der Merwe, *Sakereg*, p. 524 n. 497; Van der Merwe, 'Servitudes', para. 446.
191 Voet, *Commentarius*, 7.1.32.
192 High Court Rules r 45(8)(a); *Ormerod* v. *Deputy Sheriff Durban* 1965 4 SA 670 (D) 672–3.
193 See *Norex Industrial Properties* v. *Monarch SA Ins Co.* 1987 1 SA 827 (A) 837D-838G.
194 Insolvency Act 24 of 1936, s. 37(1); *Montelindo Compania Naviera SA Bank* v. *Bank of Lisbon and SA* 1969 2 SA 127 (W) 140B-H.

for any loss suffered by reason of the non-performance of the terms of the lease. Termination of the lease also deprives the insolvent estate of any right to compensation for improvements to the leased property effected without the consent of the landlord. Although a stipulation in a lease that the lease will terminate upon the sequestration of the tenant is void, a stipulation which restricts or prohibits the transfer of any right under the lease binds the insolvency administrator. The administrator must inform creditors at their second meeting *inter alia* of any lease entered into by the insolvent as tenant. The creditors may direct the action to be undertaken by the administrator with regard to the lease.[195] Subject to these qualifications, the lease is included in the insolvency assets of the tenant.

A usufruct may be attached in execution proceedings against B.[196] The purchaser in execution will only acquire a contingent right which will expire on the usufructuary's death. Since the holder of a right of habitation can sub-let and mortgage his/her interest, this fairly insignificant right may also be subjected to execution and sale in execution.

Both at common law and in terms of the Insolvency Act, all property of an insolvent at the date of sequestration belongs to his/her estate.[197] Since a personal servitude over immovable property is regarded as incorporeal immovable property, the right of a usufructuary or *habitator* will *also form part of his/her insolvent estate*. This view is supported by the decisions that such rights are subject to execution and sale in execution. The insolvency administrator may therefore sell these rights as part of the process of realisation of assets. Since the entitlements in terms of a right of use are not subject to execution and sale in execution, it is submitted that a right of use does not form part of the insolvency assets.

Spain

Under Spanish law, the tenant can cede[198] an *urban lease* to a third party with the landlord's written consent (Law on Urban Leases, art. 8.1). If the landlord refuses to give his/her consent, the lease contract can be

195 See Insolvency Act 24 of 1936, s. 37(1)–(5); Cooper, *Landlord and Tenant*, pp. 323–5; Smith, *Insolvency*, para. 175.

196 High Court Rules r 45(8); Voet, *Commentarius*, 7.1.32; *Ex parte Barnado's Trustees* 1910 CPD 78.

197 Insolvency Act 24 of 1936, s. 20(2)(b); Smith, *Insolvency*, paras. 149, 153, 159.

198 The term 'cession' in both the Law on Urban Leases and the Law on Agricultural Leases encompasses both sale and donation.

discharged for breach of contract (art. 27.2.c). The third party (cessionary) substitutes the tenant-cedent in the relationship with the landlord, with the result that the cessionary's interest has the same content and duration as that of the cedent (art. 8.1).

B is also allowed to sub-let part of the residential property leased, with the written consent of the landlord (art. 8.2). The term of the sub-lease will be the same as the term of the principal lease and the rent payable may not be higher than the rent payable under the principal lease (art. 8.2, paras. 3 and 4).

In the case of *rural leases*, the possibility of cession must be provided in the lease contract and the exploitation of the entire farm must be ceded (Law on Rural Leases, art. 23). Express (not necessarily written) consent of the landlord is needed. If the latter refuses, the tenant is entitled to sue him for breach of contract (art. 25.d). The cessionary's right has the same term as the principal lease and the rent paid may not exceed the rent of the principal lease (art. 23). The tenant of rural land is entitled to sub-let the land if it was agreed in the lease contract or if the express consent of the landlord is obtained (Law on Rural Leases, art. 23, para. 2). The object of the sub-lease must be the entire property for the remaining term of the contract and the rent payable must not exceed the rent agreed under the principal lease (Law on Rural Leases, art. 23). An amendment to the Law on Rural Lease in 2005 provides that the landlord's consent is not required if the sub-lease is to the spouse or descendant of the tenant (Law on Rural Leases, art. 23, para. 3).

Where the lease contract is governed by the Civil Code, the tenant may sub-let the whole or a part of the property if it was not expressly forbidden in the principal contract (Civil Code, art. 1550). The relationship between the principal landlord and tenant remains intact[199] and the sub-lease terminates on expiration of the principal lease.

The Law on Hypothecs contains no rule on the possibility of mortgaging the lease or the tenant's rights, but some authors and some decisions of the General Direction of Registrars and Notaries (*Dirección General de Registros y del Notariado*) resolved that the lease can be mortgaged, as it can be registered (Law on Hypothecs, arts. 2–5).[200] It should be noted that the tenant's interest can be mortgaged if the lease contract includes the stock in trade of business premises (*establecimiento mercantil*) (Law on Movable Hypothec and Pledge without Transfer of Possession, art. 2).[201]

[199] Lacruz Berdejo, *Elementos de Derecho civil*, vol. 2.2, p. 127. [200] *Ibid.* [201] *Ibid.*

The usufructuary may cede his/her right of *usufruct*. He/she can therefore sell or donate it (Civil Code, art. 480). The cessionary will then be treated as the new usufructuary,[202] liable to the nude owner (Civil Code, art. 498). The right of the cessionary will continue for the term of the usufruct or for a shorter period agreed between cedent and cessionary.[203]

The usufructuary may also mortgage his/her right (Law on Hypothecs, art. 107–1).[204] The same article provides that the mortgage will expire when the usufruct is terminated by an act unrelated to the will of the usufructuary. It will, however, continue where the usufruct is terminated early by a voluntary act of the usufructuary. In the latter case, the mortgage will expire when the secured claim is satisfied or when the usufruct should have expired.

A *right of use* or *a right of habitation* is an extremely personal real right which is granted to a specific person as income to cater for his/her daily needs or as a place to live in during his/her lifetime. Such a right can therefore not be leased, transferred (Civil Code, art. 525) or mortgaged (Law on Hypothec, art. 108.3).

The holder of a *hereditary building lease* (*superficies*) may cede (sell), donate[205] and also mortgage his/her right (Law on Land, art. 41; Law on Hypothecs, art. 107.5), because it is a right *in rem*. The Law on Land, art. 41.1 also considers the possibility of creating other personal rights or rights *in rem* over the hereditary building lease. The right of the new holder will last until the expiration of the term of the building lease as agreed between the parties when the right was constituted (Law on Land, art. 41.4, para. 3), or until the expiration of a shorter period agreed between assignor (cedent) and assignee (cessionary). This is not established by any rule, but it can be inferred from the general rules on rights *in rem*.

Under the Code of Civil Procedure, it is possible to attach any object or right with a patrimonial content (Code of Civil Procedure, art. 605–3 *a contrario*). This means, at least in theory, that it is possible to *attach* B's right. This is quite clear and unproblematic in the case of a usufruct and a hereditary building lease (*superficies*). The rights of use and habitation,

[202] Lacruz Berdejo, *Elementos de Derecho civil*, vol. 3.2, p. 23. [203] *Ibid.*

[204] But the Law on Hypothecs, art. 108.2 forbids the mortgage of a legal usufruct, except when it is granted to the widow/widower.

[205] González Pérez, *Comentarios*, p. 2211, includes the possibility to donate the right of *superficies* with regard to the Law on Land 1992, art. 287–3. In my opinion, it is also possible to donate the right of *superficies* under the Law on Land 2008. Art 41.1 is quite flexible, as it states that 'the right of *superficies* can be transferred and burdened subject to the limits established in the constitutive agreement'.

however, cannot be attached, as they are so highly personal that they cannot be transferred. In respect of a lease, B's right can be attached, at least in principle, but if it is sold in execution proceedings, a problem arises, as the rules regarding the cession of leases generally require the landlord's consent for the cession of B's right.[206]

The answer is the same as for the previous question. It might be added that the Law on Insolvency, art. 76 considers all property and rights included in the debtor's estate when the *insolvency* is declared as part of the insolvency assets. Only the right of use or habitation will be excluded.[207]

[206] See also Case 3. [207] *Ibid.*

Case 10
Use of time-limited interests in land for land development

A owns a vacant plot of land and wants to develop a block of flats/a shopping centre/an industrial building/a football stadium. A neither wants to engage in the construction nor to manage the structure once completed. However, A still wants to retain some control over the structure and to have unburdened ownership of the land and the structure at the end of the period.

Briefly indicate the various ways in which this can be done, and point out which new mechanisms and mechanisms already discussed in the previous Cases are the most commonly used in practice.

Comparative observations

As a *first option*, the contracting parties are allowed to use any traditional or previously unrecognised *type of contract* or a *combination of contracts* to achieve their desired goal. The Austrian,[1] Greek, Spanish and Polish reports mention a combined contract of services and management whereby B undertakes to construct the building and also to manage the completed structure for a certain term in return for an undertaking on the part of A to pay the agreed remuneration.[2] This mechanism allows A to retain full ownership of the land and the structure.

Another classic contract – mentioned in the Belgian, French, Portuguese[3] and Danish reports – is the so-called 'turnkey' contract, a term used in the building trade to designate a contract in which a builder agrees to construct a building to the point of readiness for occupancy and where the builder assumes all the risk. In France, use

[1] See the Austrian report for the so-called *Baubetreuungsvertrag*.

[2] The Polish report suggests that the management contract can be sub-contracted to a licensed real estate manager.

[3] Under a Law of 2004.

of this type of contract seems to be limited to the development of industrial complexes where the builder undertakes to design and erect the complex. The Belgian and Danish reports suggest that such a contract can be supplemented with a post-construction management contract. The Danish report recommends using two independent contracts, one with a turnkey developer and one with an administrator, but warns that in both these contracts the owner bears the overall risk.

The English and Scottish[4] reports suggest a building lease of land for a long term, usually ninety-nine years, at a so-called 'ground' rent. The tenant covenants to erect certain structures on the land according to a particular specification and to maintain the structures during the term.[5] The long term of the building lease approximates the civil law hereditary land lease (*emphyteusis*).[6]

As a *second option*, a *limited real right solution* may also be used in order not to engage A in the construction and to have the construction financed by the developer (B). The latter must be granted a real right over the property which can be mortgaged as security for a loan. The German, Austrian, French,[7] Belgian, Spanish, Italian and South African reports mention the traditional hereditary building lease (*superficies, Erbbaurecht*) as the most common device for achieving this goal. Although special regulations were initially introduced in Germany in 1919 in order to promote the supply of affordable housing in urban areas, the institution became more flexible over time and is presently also used to provide for commercial, industrial and sporting facilities.

It is almost universally accepted that the hereditary building right not only gives B a limited real right[8] but (temporary)[9] ownership of the building which he/she has erected, coupled with a right of use with regard to the land. If registered, this lease is a valuable asset in B's estate, which can be mortgaged. On expiry of the building lease, the landowner acquires ownership of the building subject to the payment of compensation of the actual value of the building (Belgium), a quarter of the value of the

[4] The Scottish report suggests a lease of 125 years, supplemented by a management contract and agreements of lease with future occupational tenants.
[5] See the Hungarian report for a similar use of a lease.
[6] See also the special contract mentioned in the Greek report. The so-called trust contract introduced in France by the Law of 2007 seems unsuited for this purpose.
[7] The French report calls it a construction lease.
[8] See the South African report and the Italian minority view mentioned in that report.
[9] See the Spanish report.

building (Austria) or as agreed in the constitutive deed (Italy).[10] In France, the holder is sometimes rewarded with a fractional share in the building.

Since very few of the provisions regulating a hereditary building right are mandatory, parties are free to include a variety of clauses in the constitutive agreement, for example, granting the required level of control to A for the duration of the right (Belgium) or pertaining to the design of the construction (Spain). The shorter term of a hereditary building right (*superficies*)[11] as opposed to that of a hereditary lease of land (*emphyteusis*), renders it more suitable for the envisaged transaction, especially in Austria, Belgium and Portugal.[12]

The Belgian, French, South African and Polish reports mention the hereditary land lease (*emphytheusis, erfpachtrecht*) as a possible option for achieving this purpose. In essence, the hereditary land lease (*emphyteusis*) grants B (the developer) the right to develop the land by, among other things, constructing buildings on it. This right can endure for a fixed term and B is entitled to exploit the construction during this term. Since none of the provisions of the regulatory statutes are mandatory, the parties are at liberty to provide in the agreement for A to have the required level of control for the duration of the right. On expiry of the hereditary land lease, the land and the structures are returned to the landowner. Owing to its long duration (in Belgium at least twenty-seven years), the hereditary lease (*emphyteusis*) is not so popular in practice.

The Belgian and Hungarian reports suggest that this goal can be achieved by the landowner creating a usufruct in favour of the developer which will entitle him to exploit the land and the buildings thereon for a fixed term. The Belgian report states that this device is less commonly used than the hereditary building right (*superficies*) and the hereditary land lease (*emphyteusis*) and that it is only used when the developer intends to develop the building from scratch. The Hungarian report states that this device is not used frequently in practice because usufruct is mainly used in a family context.

A special French Law of 1967 permits the owner of land to grant a concession to B for a term of at least twenty years, permitting B to build on the land against payment of an annual rent. Although doctrinal writers

[10] If not, B will have a claim on the grounds of unjustified enrichment.

[11] E.g. between ten and fifty or 100 years in Belgium and Austria respectively and a minimum term of ten years in Portugal.

[12] See further the Portuguese Law of 2007 on underground structures and the Austrian report on the right of superstructure.

cannot agree on whether the right of B is personal or real, the constitutive contract must be executed notarially and registered in the Land Register. Unless otherwise agreed, the concessionaire may choose the purpose for which he/she wants to exploit the property. On termination of the contract, the owner must reimburse the concessionaire with the amount that the completed structures has increased the value of the property.[13]

The German report suggests a *third* option. A can agree to allow B to acquire *full ownership of the land* subject to *a right* in favour of A *to repurchase the land* (including the structure to be built by B) after a certain period of time (*Wiederkaufsrecht*), which can be made enforceable against third parties by registering a priority notice in the Land Register. Such mechanisms are commonly used in sale-and-lease-back transactions regarding commercial property where the seller wants to continue to use the property or to manage it in his/her own name.

The Danish report suggests a similar mechanism rarely used in practice: A sells the land to B subject to an option in favour of A to repurchase the land and the completed buildings. In the sale agreement, this option can be constituted as a right of first refusal, an obligation on B to sell on demand or an obligation on A to purchase on a certain future date and A can provide some control mechanism for himself/herself in the agreement of sale. A more frequent variation in Danish practice is the following: A does not transfer full ownership of the land to B but only ownership of the building once it has been erected. The basic transaction will be a lease of the land in which A can include any of the three options discussed above. Such an option must be registered in the Land Register to be afforded proprietary protection.

Hungarian law also allows a contractual arrangement by which B will become the owner of the building erected on the land, subject to a right of pre-emption of the building in favour of A and a right of pre-emption of the land in favour of B. On the facts given, the landowner must arrange for the future transfer of the ownership of the structure. The Hungarian report suggests the following: sale of the land to B with retention of title of the future building, which is registrable; a right of pre-emption of the building in favour of A, which is also registrable; an option which entitles the landowner to buy the building by unilateral

[13] The restoration lease mentioned in the French report for the restoration of residential property by public or *quasi*-public organisations is not suitable for the purpose envisaged in this case. See further the provisions of the French Code for Construction and Habitation.

declaration; or an instalment sale by which the landowner will pay instalments on the sale of the structure until the (normally long) term of the transaction expires. The latter option will be most unsuitable, because by law an option can last for five years at most.

Austria

A *contractual solution* can be provided by a contract for organising and overseeing a construction (*Baubetreuungsvertrag*). This type of contract has been developed in practice under the principle of freedom of contract without any specific statutory provisions regulating it. The parties to the contract are the organiser (developer) and the initiator. The organiser (B) is obliged to conclude construction and financing contracts in the name of the initiator (A) in order to have buildings constructed on land belonging to the initiator. A contract for organising a construction contains elements of a contract for services and a mandate.[14] If a contract for organising a construction is closely connected with the acquisition of land by the initiator (A), it is deemed to be a development contract (*Bauträgervertrag*), which is subject to special legislation (*Bauträgervertragsgesetz*).[15] After the construction of the building, B can manage the structure/buildings on the basis of an income-producing (usufructuary) lease.

A can grant B a *hereditary building lease* (*superficies*). Under the grant, B acquires ownership of the building and a right of use with regard to the land (Law on Building Rights, § 6, para. 2). The term of a building lease must be between ten and 100 years (Law on Building Rights, § 3, para. 1). On expiry of the building lease, the landowner acquires ownership of the building and has to compensate the holder for a quarter of the value of the building (Law on Building Rights, § 9).

The building can also be constructed as a *superstructure* (*Superädifikat*) on the basis of a legal relationship which entitles B to construct his/her own building on A's land. A superstructure is a building, which, in contrast to other buildings, is legally independent from the land on which it is constructed. Its ownership does not follow the ownership of the land (Civil Code, § 435; for other buildings, see Civil Code, § 297). Whereas ownership of the land remains with the landowner, ownership of the superstructure is acquired by the contractor who erected the

[14] Krejci, in Rummel, *Kommentar*, vol. 1, §§ 1165 ff., para. 24.

[15] Böhm and Pletzer, in Schwimann and Verschraegen, *Praxiskommentar*, vol. 2, s. 2; BTVG, para. 6.

superstructure.[16] Contrary to building rights, a right of superstructure cannot be established with regard to an existing building.[17]

A building may only qualify as a superstructure if the developer intends to construct the building for himself/herself and wants the building to remain on the land only for a limited period of time. A limited destiny for the building is inferred from the appearance of the building,[18] its purpose[19] and the contractual relationship between the developer and the landowner.[20] However, it is not relevant whether the building can be removed without destruction.[21]

Although a superstructure may be registered in the Land Register, registration is not obligatory and only has declaratory effect.[22] Its legal basis can be a lease, a loan, a *precarium* or a servitude.[23] Most frequently, the landowner and the developer conclude a contract of lease that falls under the Law on Tenancy if the superstructure serves as residential premises under this Law.[24]

The ownership of the superstructure is transferable[25] and it may also be acquired by the landowner.[26] The constructor originally acquires ownership simply by constructing the building.[27] However, the transfer of the property requires the deposit of certain documents with the court.[28] The superstructure can also be mortgaged,[29] for example, as security for a loan covering the cost of construction.[30]

16 See 3 Ob 158/93; JBl (1994), p. 250.

17 3 Ob 158/93; JBl (1994), p. 250; recently 2 Ob 242/05k; RdW 2007/626 600; Kletecka, Rechberger and Zitta, *Bauten*, p. 31, para. 33; Kletecka, in Koziol and Welser, *Bürgerliches Recht*, vol. 1, p. 434.

18 3 Ob 67/81; JBl (1982), p. 481.

19 7 Ob 71/56; EvBl (1956), p. 148; OGH 24.2.1982; 3 Ob 67/81; JBl (1982), p. 481; OGH 16.4.1987; 7 Ob 513/87; JBl (1987), p. 779.

20 3 Ob 76/86; JBl (1987), p. 179; 5 Ob 98/90; NZ (1992), p. 66 (Hofmeister).

21 4 Ob 533/91; wobl (1992), p. 7 (Würth); OGH 16.4.1987; 7 Ob 513/87; JBl (1987), p. 779.

22 3 Ob 17/88; JBl (1989), p. 119; 5 Ob 119/00m; NZ (2001), p. 499 (Hoyer).

23 Rechberger and Oberhammer, 'Das Superädificat', para. 60.

24 1 Ob 565/84; JBl (1985), p. 107; 1 Ob 704/85; MietSlg 37.223; 1 Ob 588/89; wobl (1989), p. 73; 4 Ob 533/91; wobl (1992), p. 7 (Würth); OGH 11.12.1984; 5 Ob 607/84; SZ 57/194; 6 Ob 517/85; HS 16.536; 6 Ob 565/95; JBl (1995), p. 715; 5 Ob 115/03b; *immolex* 2004/22; Bydlinski, 'Superädifikate'; Rechberger and Oberhammer, 'Das Superädificat', para. 60.

25 Cf. e.g. 1 Ob 565/84; JBl (1985), p. 107.

26 3 Ob 76/86; JBl (1987), p. 179; Rechberger and Oberhammer, 'Das Superädifikat', para. 59.

27 5 Ob 98/90; NZ (1992), p. 66 (*Hofmeister*); 5 Ob 116/91; NZ (1992), p. 243 (Hofmeister).

28 Law on the Deposit of Documents Regarding Non-registered Land and Buildings; 3 Ob 130/87; JBl (1988), p. 578.

29 See e.g. 3 Ob 76/86; JBl (1987), p. 179; Graf, 'Superädifikate', paras. 61 ff.

30 See e.g. 3 Ob 130/87; JBl (1988), p. 578.

Belgium

In practice, the major criterion in electing a legal structure for land development will often be the tax implications. Such considerations are outside the scope of this report.

The most common legal device used in a development framework (provided time-limited rights are given to the developer and the landowner does not elect to follow the route of a classical turn-key development/contractor contract with a possible post-construction management contract) is the granting of a hereditary building lease (*superficies*) or a hereditary land lease (*emphyteusis*). It is also possible, although less common, for the owner to grant a usufruct where the holder is prepared to construct a building from scratch.[31]

Both the *hereditary building lease* and the *hereditary land lease* will grant B (the developer) the right to construct a building on the land during the duration of the right and to retain ownership of the construction during this period. Since very few provisions of the Laws on Hereditary Building Lease and Hereditary Land Lease are mandatory, parties have the liberty to include in the agreements a variety of clauses granting the required level of control to A for the duration of the right. One reason to elect the hereditary building lease over of the hereditary lease of land is the fact that the latter lease by its very nature must last at least twenty-seven years (with a maximum time period of ninety-nine years), whereas the hereditary building lease may not exceed fifty years and may be as short as the parties agree. Parties are also free to decide on the duration of a *usufruct*, but it may not exceed thirty years if the usufructuary is a legal person (Civil Code, art. 619).

Denmark

Of the several possible legal constructions, a contract between A and a developer willing to take on responsibility for the construction (a turnkey contract) and the administration of the structure upon completion will yield results closest to those desired by A. In order to retain *full ownership*, A must be willing to pay for all expenses. Contracts like these are not very often seen in Denmark. A variant solution is to undertake two independent contracts: one with a turnkey developer and one with an administrator. This option is chosen more frequently. Neither of these solutions removes the overall risk from the owner (A).

[31] See Case 1.

The desired results can also be achieved by arranging for A to *maintain the ownership* of the building *site* and for the developer to acquire *ownership of the buildings* that are erected. The developer then leases the buildings to A. A can also include in this lease an option to purchase the buildings when the developer or his/her successors wish to sell them (a right of first refusal), or whenever A wishes to exercise his/her option (the developer has an obligation to sell on demand), or at a given time (obligation to buy). Such an option must be registered in the Land Register in order to obtain protection. The developer may register his/her rights over the buildings (Law on Registration of Property, s. 19) and the buildings may be charged separately. Contracts of this kind are frequently concluded.

A third possible solution is to sell the land and include an *option* for A *to buy* the land and the buildings at a later time. In the purchase agreement this option for A can be a right of first refusal, an obligation for the developer to sell on demand or an obligation on A to buy at a later fixed date. Of course, by choosing this method, A will not be able to control the erection of the buildings unless control mechanisms are included in the purchase agreement. These types of contracts are rare.

England

It is possible for A to grant B a so-called 'building lease', being a lease for which the consideration is the erection or improvement of buildings.[32] A is able to retain control over the structural work by stipulating in covenants the type, nature and style of such buildings to be constructed.[33] A building lease will incorporate repair and improvement as well as building from scratch (Law of Property Act, s. 99(9)). The effect of a building lease is usually that B is then able to enjoy the building, subject to repairing obligations, and so on.

France

Freedom of contract allows the parties to devise a *suitable contract* solely limited by mandatory rules. If A does not wish to undertake the construction, the developer of this structure will require money to finance the construction. The contract chosen must thus facilitate the

[32] See LPA, s. 205(1)(iii) for a statutory definition.
[33] See *Hill and Redman's Law of Landlord and Tenant*, pp. A1428 ff.

procurement of bank financing which will be the case if A grants the developer a real right limited in time in respect of the land, which can be hypothecated.

A *hereditary land lease* (*emphyteusis*) meets this criterion, even if it does not, in essence, comprise the obligation to build, as is the case with the hereditary building lease for construction. The holder of the hereditary land lease is obliged to improve the land and to tidy up existing structures and even to erect new structures. Since the holder has a real right, he/she can hypothecate it as security for a loan to finance the project. The expiry of the hereditary land lease brings with it the automatic and immediate extinction of the real right under the lease.

The *hereditary building lease* (*droit de superficie*), which obliges the holder to improve the land by the erection of buildings and other structures on the land, is even better suited for this purpose. Like the holder of a hereditary land lease, the holder of a hereditary building lease has a real right which can be hypothecated (Code for Construction and Habitation, art. L 251–3). The holder is, however, in a position to offer a more solid security to the source of his/her funding, since the hypothec which will be granted stays in force for the term set at the beginning of the construction lease even if the lease is cancelled before the end of this term (art. L 251–6). The obligation on the holder may consist in the landowner-landlord receiving the structures or fractional shares in the structures, or of titles giving the right of ownership in or enjoyment of such structures which ideally suits A's desire to recover, in the end, the full ownership of the land and the structures erected on the land.

The following possibilities must also be mentioned. Land concessions are regulated by the Law on Land Planning.[34] This statute allows the owner of land to grant a concession to B for a term of at least twenty years to build on the land in return for payment of an annual rent (art. 48, para. 1, read with art. 50). The doctrinal writers have not reached agreement as to whether this right of B is a personal or a real right. This contract must be executed notarially and, since it is subject to the provisions pertaining to registration, it must be registered in the Land Register. Unless restrictions pertaining to the protection of the land and its surroundings have been agreed upon, the grantor (*concessionaire*) of the concession may choose the purpose for which he wants to exploit

[34] See the Law on Land Planning (*Loi d'orientation foncière*), no. 67–1253 of 30 Dec. 1967, arts. 48–60.

the property. The *concessionaire* can change or develop the property with the consent of the person who granted the concession. The latter is only entitled to refuse his/her consent for a legitimate reason. On termination of the contract, the owner must reimburse the *concessionaire* with the amount by which the completed structures have increased the value of the property (art. 54).

The *contract to develop an industrial complex* which is allowed under the principle of freedom of contract is complicated. Under this contract, the developer undertakes to design and build an industrial complex and hand over the keys to the landowner on completion of the complex. It is therefore designated as a 'key in hand' contract. Its purpose is the erection of an industrial complex that the developer undertakes to design and build.

A *lease of land for restoration* (Code for Construction and Habilitation, arts. L 252–1 to L 252–4) permits public or *quasi*-public organisations to lease property from landowners with the aim of restoring the property and renting it out as residential premises for the term of the lease. The duration of this contract must be at least twelve years, and it cannot be renewed tacitly. Under certain conditions, this lease may be assigned. It confers upon the organisation a real right which can be made the subject of a hypothec. At the end of the lease, the tenant must return vacant possession of the premises. The landowner can offer the previous occupants a lease of the premises or offer them alternative accommodation.

The French *contract of trust* (*fiducie*) must be distinguished from the common-law trust. This institution was introduced into French law by the Law of 19 February 2007 (Civil Code, arts. 2011 to 2031) and amended by Law no. 2008–776 of 4 August 2008 and by Ordonnance no. 2009–112 of 30 January 2009. It permits the settlor to transfer part of his/her patrimony to the 'trustee', subject to the latter acting in favour of a beneficiary for a fixed period of time (no more than ninety-nine years since the reform of 2008) and a specified purpose (Civil Code, art. 2011). Despite its wide definition, it is doubted whether this contract suits the situation described, since, even though the beneficiary can be the settlor himself (Civil Code, art. 2016), the settlor must be a legal person subject to corporate taxation (Civil Code, art. 2014) and the trustee must be a financial institution (Civil Code, art. 2015). Since the reform of 2008, a lawyer (*avocat*) may also be a trustee (Civil Code, art. 2015) and since article 2014 has been abolished the settlor may now also be a natural person.

Germany

If A does not want to engage in the construction himself, it must be financed by the developer (B). In practice, B will only receive a loan from a bank if he/she can provide sufficient collateral. Thus it is essential for B to be granted a real right which can be mortgaged as security for the loan. Any time-limited right that cannot be mortgaged[35] will not provide a proper basis for financing the development. Therefore, B can either be granted a hereditary building lease (*Erbbaurecht*), as discussed in Case 1, or full ownership of the land with A reserving the option to repurchase the land and the structure.

The Regulations on Hereditary Building Rights (Erbbaurechte-Rangstellenverordnung (*ErbbRRVO*)) were introduced in 1919 in order to promote the supply of affordable housing (particularly in urban areas) and to combat speculative land transactions.[36] Thus the institution of the hereditary building right (*Erbbaurecht*) has always been a widely used mechanism in housing development, in particular by public institutions. However, the hereditary building right (*Erbbaurecht*) is also very flexible and thus suitable for a large number of other purposes as well. It is also used for commercial land development in the form of industrial buildings or sports facilities.

Alternatively, B will have to acquire full ownership of the land. A can be granted a right to repurchase the land (including the structure to be built by B) after a certain period of time (*Wiederkaufsrecht*). A's contractual right to repurchase the land can be made enforceable against third parties by registering a priority notice (*Vormerkung*)[37] in the Land Register (*Grundbuch*) (Civil Code, § 883). Such mechanisms are commonly used in sale-and-lease-back transactions regarding commercial property where the seller wants to continue to use the property or to manage it in his/her own name. However, according to the facts of this question, the owner does not want to manage the structure himself. Therefore, it will be much more common (and acceptable to the financing institutions) to create an *Erbbaurecht*.

[35] See Case 9.

[36] For a discussion of the historical background, see von Oefele and Winkler, *Handbuch*, no. 4.48.

[37] A priority notice (*Vormerkung*) is an entry in the Land Register to protect a claim to a registrable right (in this case, ownership) in the land. Any disposition that conflicts with such notice is void vis-à-vis the person in whose favour the notice has been registered.

Greece

The Greek Law of Obligations (Civil Code, art. 361) allows contracting parties the freedom to define the content of their contractual relationships and thus to conclude contracts, which, if necessary, deviate from the most frequently encountered contracts regulated in the Special Part of the Law of Obligations (Civil Code, arts. 496–945).[38] This freedom has resulted in a great variety of atypical and mixed contracts. Accordingly, A may create an *atypical mixed contract* with B, with the content desired by the parties: B undertaking to construct the building and also to manage the structure once completed in return for an undertaking by A to pay the remuneration agreed upon. This mechanism – a combination of a contract for work and a management contract – will allow A to retain full ownership over the land and the structure developed on it.

The most commonly used mechanism in Greek practice is, however, the contract by which the contractor undertakes to use his/her own materials to construct a building, usually a *block of flats*, on the vacant plot of land and the landowner in return undertakes to transfer the ownership of the majority of the units or apartments, along with the proportionate percentage of co-ownership in the land, to the contractor or to third persons indicated by the latter, while the landowner retains the rest of the units along with the proportionate co-ownership of the land. In this contract, the parties submit themselves to the provisions of Civil Code, arts. 1002 and 1117 and Law 3741/1929, which regulate apartment ownership in Greece.[39] The obligations of all owners are regulated in the model rules of the block of flats (Law 3741/1929, art. 4, § 1), which are contained in a notarial deed which is recorded in the Conveyance Records (Law 3741/1929, art. 13, § 1), thus binding successors-in-title. This form of contract is used when the landowner cannot afford to finance the construction of the building. It is a mixed contract combining a contract for work (Civil Code, arts. 681 ff.) with a contract of sale as far as the results of the work are concerned (Civil Code, arts. 520 and 562).[40]

[38] Georgiades, *New Contractual Forms*, pp. 7, 8.

[39] Law 3741/1929 remained in force after the introduction of the Greek Civil Code according to art. 54 of the Introductory Law of the Greek Civil Code. For an analysis, see, among others, Georgiades, *Property*, vol. 1, pp. 659 ff.; Karasis, in Georgiades and Stathopoulos, *GCC, Collective Analysis*, art. 1117.

[40] Filios, *Obligations*, p. 453.

Hungary

Hungarian law follows the principle of *aedificium solo cedit*, with some exceptions relating to the situation where a new structure is built on the land of somebody else. The owner of the land is, in principle, also the owner of the structure. The builder may, however, be the owner of the structure if the law or the contract concluded with the proprietor of the land provides so. The owner of the land has a right of pre-emption regarding the structure and vice versa, that is, the proprietor of the structure has a right of pre-emption regarding the land (Civil Code, § 97).

If the builder acquires ownership over the structure on account of an agreement or a court order, he/she has a right *in rem* to use the land as long as the structure exists. The builder is entitled to use the land and to collect its fruits (for example, by leasing out the building), and is obliged to maintain the property. If ownership over the structure is subsequently acquired via inheritance or transfer of title, the new proprietor of the structure is entitled to use the land under the same conditions (Civil Code, §§ 155–6).

The right to use the land is a limited right *in rem*, which is not restricted in time. The right does, however, cease to exist once the proprietor of the structure acquires title over the land or vice versa, that is, the owner of the land acquires title over the structure. Accordingly, in the above scenario, the owner of the land has to arrange for the future transfer of the ownership of the structure. The following contract law arrangements are suitable for that purpose: sale with retention of title, right of pre-emption, option, instalment sale and sale combined with lease.

The builder may sell the structure to the owner of the land with retention of title. The seller will retain title over the property in the contract of sale until the last instalment on the price is paid. While the title is retained, the buyer cannot alienate or encumber the property. This provision does not affect the rights of third persons who acquire the property in good faith and for value. However, it is to be emphasised that sale with retention of title can be entered into the Land Register according to the Law on Land Registration. The buyer of immovable property who enters into possession of the property can collect its fruits and must bear the cost of maintenance and the risk of damage (Civil Code, § 368).

The builder may establish a right of pre-emption over the structure for the benefit of the landowner. This deed constituting the right of pre-emption must be in writing.[41] Once registered in the Land Register, it has an *erga omnes* effect and will prevail over rights related to the property subsequently acquired. The right of pre-emption is not transferable or transmissible and thus cannot be transferred or inherited (Civil Code, § 373).

The owner of the building may grant a written option[42] to the land owner that entitles him/her to purchase the property by unilateral declaration. An option is not really suitable for the purpose stated in the present case since it can be established for at most five years (Civil Code, § 375).

The owner of the land may, at the outset, when agreeing with the builder of the structure that the latter can build the structure on the land, simultaneously conclude an instalment sale contract with the builder through which the owner of the land is able to buy the structure through an instalment system (Civil Code, § 376). Accordingly, the latter will become the owner of the structure at the end of the requisite period.

Finally, the owner of the land may conclude a building contract with the builder under which he/she will acquire title of the building. Moreover, the owner may combine this contract with a lease contract of the structure, which will allow the builder to use the structure for a fixed term. Instead of a lease contract, the owner of the land may establish a usufruct or a right of use on the structure for the benefit of the builder. This construction is not commonly used in practice as usufruct and right of use are usually closely linked to matters of succession within a family.

Italy

The most obvious option will be for A to create a *hereditary building lease* (*superficie*) (Civil Code, arts. 952 ff.). Art 952 provides that 'the owner can

[41] In this case, should the builder envisage selling the building, he/she must first transmit the offer received to the holder of the right of pre-emption, except where such a transmission would cause extraordinary inconvenience or delay due to the residence or other circumstances of the holder of the pre-emptive right. If the latter accepts the content of the offer in a declaration addressed to the owner, the contract is concluded. If the holder of the pre-emptive right does not accept the content of the offer within a period of time that is normally applicable to the acceptance, the owner may sell the property according to the conditions of the offer or on better conditions (Civil Code, § 373).

[42] The grant of an option must clearly determine at least the property concerned and the price.

constitute the right to erect and maintain a structure above the soil in favour of others, who acquire ownership of it'. If the agreement is made for a fixed term, the hereditary building right will come to an end on the expiration of the term and the owner of the soil will become the owner of the structure (Civil Code, art. 953).

The Civil Code does not provide for any compensation for the holder of the building lease (*superficiario*). However, it is possible that the contract constituting the building lease may contain provisions on remuneration for the holder that may be determined in different ways. There is some debate over whether, even in the absence of explicit contractual provisions, the principles of unjust enrichment may, in some circumstances, justify some remuneration for the holder, the amount of which will depend on whether and how much he/she has paid for the constitution of the building right. In normal circumstances, the acquisition of the structure may be considered an indirect compensation for the grant of the building right.[43]

The prevailing opinion is that the holder of the building right has a limited real right (*ius in re aliena*) over the land, but a right of ownership over the building, whereas a minority view is that he/she has a limited real right over both the land and the building. The agreement constituting the building right must be made public by means of registration (Civil Code, art. 2643). If A conveys the land to C some time after the creation of the building right, the time-limited right of the holder (*superficiario*) remains enforceable if the act that constitutes the building lease (*superficie*) was registered before registration of the transfer to C (Civil Code, art. 2644). It is irrelevant when the building is erected. If the act constituting the building right is registered before registration of the transfer to C, then the holder's right to erect and maintain a structure above the soil is enforceable against C. If the transfer to C is registered before the act creating the building right, then the holder's right is not enforceable against C, even if the building has already been erected and C acquires full ownership of the building.

The same criterion regulates the protection of the holder of the building lease (*superficiario*) against A's creditors. A building right constituted prior to but registered after the attachment has no prejudicial effect on the attachment creditors even if the building was erected prior to the attachment. If the act constituting the building right was transcribed prior to the attachment, then the holder's rights on the land (the

[43] See e.g. Pasetti Bombardella, 'Voce Superficie', *Enciclopedia del diritto*, vol. 43, p. 1483.

right to erect a building) and on the building (ownership or at least a real right on it) are protected, and only the nude ownership of the soil can be included in the attachment. If the building right is created for a fixed term, ownership of the soil will lead to full ownership of the soil and of the building vesting in A upon the expiry of the term.

After registration of the building lease, the land owner can only mortgage his/her reversionary nude ownership in the land. If the building lease is registered after the registration of the mortgage, the rights of the holder of the building lease on the land and on the building will be included in the assets of the nude owner on attachment of the land by his/her mortgage creditors.

Once registered, the holder of the building lease (*superficiario*) receives full proprietary and possessory protection and in fact he/she is considered to be the owner of the building during the term of the building lease.

Since, in our case, there is no existing building to provide a point of reference in the absence of contractual agreements, neither the owner of the soil nor the *superficiario* is bound to maintain it in good repair. For the same reason, in the absence of contractual agreements, the holder of the building lease (*superficiario*) is free to choose and subsequently alter the intended economic purpose of the building. It is disputed whether a contractual provision concerning the intended economic purpose of the building is enforceable against third parties (third party transferee if the building right is transferred). There is no case law on the point.

Civil Code, art. 954 provides that the termination of the building right by expiry of the term for which it was constituted results in the extinction of real rights imposed on the building right. Lease contracts concerning the building do not continue beyond the year in which the term of the building lease expires.

In principle, the holder of the building lease may freely transfer his/her right. He/she can also mortgage it. Mortgages granted over a building lease are extinguished upon reversion of such lease to the owner of the soil when the term of the building lease is completed. However, if the holder/owner of the building lease is entitled to remuneration, such remuneration will be burdened by mortgages registered against the building lease. If, on account of other causes, the rights of the owner of the soil and of the holder of the building lease are merged, the mortgages encumbering both rights will continue to affect each of these rights separately (Civil Code, art. 2816).

The Netherlands

This can be achieved by creating a hereditary land lease (*emphytheusis*) (Burgerlijk Wetboek, art. 5:85). Taking into account the financial crisis, *emphytheusis* has gained renewed interest. This can also be achieved by creating a usufruct, which, however, seems to be less frequently used than *emphytheusis*.

A hereditary building right (*superficies*) (Burgerlijk Wetboek, art. 5:101) can also be employed. It is, for instance, used in the case of a sports club that owns its club house, but is not the owner of the grounds.

Poland

In practice, A will simply conclude a contract with a building contractor to carry out the work necessary for the construction of the building. If A does not want to manage the structure, he/she can hire a licensed real estate manager for this purpose (Law on Management of Real Property, arts. 184–90).

Theoretically, there are other possibilities. A can grant B (the developer) an income-producing lease, which confers a title on B to apply for building permission and to begin constructing the building. If this right is entered in the Land Register, it will be effective against all subsequent purchasers of A's land. A similar possibility will be offered by employing the contract of leasing (Civil Code, arts. 709.1 to 709.18), which can additionally contain B's option to purchase. Again, if this right is entered in the Land Register, it will be effective against all subsequent purchasers of A's land. However, in practice, developers are either owners of land or have a perpetual usufruct registered over the land. If not, the whole investment process usually involves close co-operation between the owner and the developer, who sometimes obtains powers of representation from the owner.

Portugal

Portuguese law accepts the principle of freedom of contract and thus allows parties to use any contract or combination of contracts to achieve their intended goal.

A may employ a *hereditary building lease* (*superficies*) which entitles the holder to erect a building on another's property, perpetually or for a fixed term. The building lease will expire if the holder does not complete the building before the time limit set by the parties or the legal limit of ten years. Termination will occur on expiry of the fixed term. Decree-Law 257/91 of 18 July 1991 stipulates that the purpose of a contract creating a building lease may be the construction or the management of a building constructed below someone's land. The aim of this provision is to clarify the current legal regime of building leases by expressly including in its scope the construction of an underground car park. This solution does not, however, properly suit A's needs. B will become owner of the building and A will not retain control over the structure.

A can conclude a *building contract* (*contrato de empreitada*) with B to build a block of flats, a shopping centre, an industrial building or a football stadium. The contract must be concluded in writing according to the new regime dealing with construction activity (Decree-Law 12/2004 of 9 January, art. 29).[44] The contract must contain an identification of the parties, the licences required for the construction and the property (including a copy of the building or site plan), the contract price, the date for the completion of the building and the conditions of payment. If the contract does not comply with these conditions, it is void (Decree-Law 12/2004 of 9 January, art. 29). After completion of the block of flats, shopping centre, industrial building or football stadium, the owner (A), may conclude a lease, a management contract or a contract of services with B or with someone else to manage the property. A is the owner of the construction and he/she controls the structure.

Finally, a situation may be conceived where an enterprise, usually a *construction company*, takes the initiative to construct the building. These enterprises act as developers (*promotores imobiliários*) and the owner is offered to engage in a development project (for example, a tourist resort). In this situation, it is common that parties agree that the developer will be entrusted with the management of the building.

Scotland

There are no particular legal forms which A will have to use in order to achieve these goals. A may, subject to the general law, enter into any contract he/she wishes regarding the use of the property. The precise

[44] Some other formalities related to the construction company have to be complied with e.g. the identification of the company and the number by which it is registered (Decree-Law 12/2004, art. 24, n. 2).

structure of the transaction will depend upon the landowner's and the counter-party's commercial objectives. One possibility is for the landowner to grant a long lease to a developer.[45] It will oblige the developer to complete the development within a particular period of time. The developer will use the lease as security to raise finances and will therefore need to obtain a real right by registration so as to be able to grant a standard security over the lease to the lender.[46] In this context, 175-year leases are not unheard of: the shorter the lease, the more depreciating an asset it is and the less attractive as security to lenders. (The grant of a lease may be preceded by an initial agreement for lease which will be subject to suspensive conditions, such as that the developer obtains the necessary planning permissions. Once they are satisfied or purified, the landowner's obligation to grant a lease to the developer is triggered.) Typically, the developer will pay the landowner a substantial premium (a one-off payment at the outset) for the grant of the lease. The developer will enter into the various contracts required to develop the site, for example, with builders, engineers and architects. Many of these are standard form documents. The developer will also enter into agreements for lease with occupational tenants (for example, retailers in the case of the shopping centre and a football club in the case of the stadium). These will most likely be concluded before the building is completed. Indeed, a lender will probably wish to see that certain key tenants are lined up before agreeing to fund the project. These agreements for lease will have to strike a balance between the tenant's interests (for example, in ensuring that the development is completed on specification and on time to allow them to trade as envisaged) and the developer's interests (for example, in retaining sufficient freedom to react to unforeseen problems in the construction process). The developer may well enter into a management agreement in respect of the building so that he is not troubled by day-to-day management issues, selecting new tenants and the like. The lender may insist that all of these contracts contain a 'step-in' clause allowing the lender to step into the developer's shoes and complete the development if, for some reason, such as insolvency, the developer is not able to do so. Once the development is completed, the developer may well transfer the entire building to an investor as an income-producing asset. (The transfer will

45 On commercial leases generally, see Cockburn, *Commercial Leases*; Ross and McKichan, *Drafting and Negotiating Commercial Leases*; Gerber, *Commercial Leases*.

46 CFR(S)A 70, s. 9.

be by way of assignation of the lease.) The lease from the landowner to the developer may provide for the rent to be linked to rental income from sub-tenants.

The parties can provide in the head-lease for the degree of control which the landowner is to retain. This is particularly relevant when it comes to granting a sub-lease to an occupational tenant. The lease may require the landowner's permission in order for a sub-lease to be granted and may set down criteria in accordance with which permission will be granted or refused. If the landowner's income is dependent upon rental received by the developer from sub-tenants, it will be particularly concerned about the financial strength of any sub-tenant. A common clause is to provide that the developer may sub-let only with the landlord's consent which shall not be unreasonably withheld. The head-lease will probably also contain an irritancy clause, allowing the landowner to terminate the lease in the event of breach by the developer of its obligations, such as paying the rent or complying with its obligation to develop the building. Termination has potentially disastrous consequences for the developer, who will lose the value of his capital investment unless there are provisions in the lease for him to be compensated by the landowner for the value of improvements.[47] There are legislative controls over the use of irritancy.[48] If the breach is of a non-monetary obligation, the court may only enforce the irritancy if, in all the circumstances, a fair and reasonable landlord will do so.[49] If, however, the breach is of a monetary obligation, the only restriction is that the landlord must give fourteen days' notice to pay the arrears due. If then the arrears are still outstanding, the court must enforce the irritancy.[50] In *CIN Properties Ltd.* v. *Dollar Land (Cumbernauld) Ltd.*,[51] the House of Lords upheld the irritancy of such a development lease for non-payment of rent, despite the windfall that this will provide to the landlord, and in *Dollar Land (Cumbernauld) Ltd.* v. *CIN Properties Ltd.*,[52] held that the tenant had no claim in unjustified enrichment against the landlord.

[47] *Dollar Land (Cumbernauld) Ltd.* v. *CIN Properties Ltd.* 1998 SC (HL) 90.

[48] Law Reform (Miscellaneous Provisions) (Scotland) Act 1985, ss. 4 and 5.

[49] On which see *Blythswood Investments (Scotland) Ltd.* v. *Clydesdale Electrical Stores Ltd. (in Receivership)* 1995 SLT 150 (OH) and *Aubrey Investments Ltd.* v. *DSC (Realisations) Ltd. (in Receivership)* 1999 SC 21 (OH).

[50] *CIN Properties Ltd.* v. *Dollar Land (Cumbernauld) Ltd.* 1992 SC (HL) 104.

[51] 1992 SC (HL) 104. [52] 1998 SC (HL) 90.

South Africa

The institution of *hereditary building lease* (*huisgebouwrecht*), which had strong links with the Roman institution of *superficies*, was known in Roman-Dutch law. It entitled the holder to erect a building on the land of another and to retain and use the building until the owner paid the value of the building or an agreed sum. On account of the principle of accession, the holder acquired only a limited real right to the building, while ownership remained with the owner of the land. The right is treated as incorporeal immovable property and is acquired and lost in the same way as other incorporeal immovable property. The right was established primarily by contract between the builder and the landowner but could also be implied where the landowner allowed the builder to build on his/her land. The right had to be registered to gain proprietary effect and the registration had to be cancelled when the right was terminated. Unlike a personal servitude, this right could also be alienated, a process for which registration was required.[53] However, it seems that this institution was, even in Roman-Dutch law, superseded by the creation of *tijnsrechten*, which explains why other Roman-Dutch writers like van der Linden and van Leeuwen do not mention it. Grotius only deals with it very cursorily. This kind of right has never been utilised in South African practice for the above purpose.

The Roman-Dutch *erfpachtrecht* based on the Roman *emphyteusis* was a kind of perpetual land tenure which could be granted by the State or an individual. It was transmissible to heirs and freely alienable. The holder was only obliged to pay a small yearly quitrent and his/her right over the property was so extensive that it almost equalled ownership. However, if the holder defaulted for three consecutive years, the right of *erfpacht* could be retracted. This Roman-Dutch form of land tenure was subsumed under the English form of land tenure, *perpetual quitrent*, when a Proclamation of 1813 restricted the forms of land tenure at the Cape to freehold (full ownership) and perpetual quitrent. The quitrenter acquired extensive rights against payment of a quitrent, which was later abolished. However, it was mostly utilised in original grants of state land where the State wanted to reserve mining rights and the right to build public roads when needed over the land. Legislation expressly provides for the conversion of perpetual quitrent to ownership and although

[53] Grotius, *Inleidinge*, 2.46.8–11.

certain land is still held under 'quitrent title' today, this form of land tenure has never been used to resolve the type of situation envisaged by the question.[54]

Another English form of land tenure transplanted into South African law was leasehold, which could take the form of a perpetual lease, a ninety-nine year lease or a lease for an indefinite period coupled with a right of renewal. This institution was again mainly used where the State did not want to grant state land as freehold but as a lesser tenure. The tendency to equate leaseholders with owners led to the statutory conversion of certain leaseholds to ownership. Thereafter, leaseholds trickled down to a few isolated cases.[55] I have come across seaside cottages and timeshares being sold as thirty-year leaseholds, with the rights of the holders expiring after thirty years and the public authority or developing agency being entitled to sell or lease out the cottages on time shares anew.

The only manner in which the result envisaged in the question can therefore be achieved will be by a contractual arrangement between the parties. This will most probably involve a combined building and lease of land contract with the price being the exploitation of the buildings for a certain period of time.

Spain

The parties can create an *atypical contract* in terms of Civil Code, art. 1255 in order to achieve the result envisaged in the question. It may take the form of a construction contract (*contrato de obra*) to which certain special clauses are added, for example, granting A a certain measure of control over the structure and affording B the power to manage the structure during a certain period, after which the structure will return to A.

The *hereditary building lease* (*superficies*) may also achieve the required result. It has already been said that the hereditary building lease grants its holder (B) some form of 'temporary' ownership over the structure. There is therefore no need for the owner (A) to manage the structure. In such a situation, A recovers the land and receives the ownership of the structure at the end of the agreed term, but he/she usually has no control over the structure, unless it is agreed in the contract that constituted the building lease.

54 See in general Van der Merwe, De Waal and Carey Miller, 'Property and Trust Law', ss. 855–9.

55 See in general *ibid.* s. 860.

Case 11
The effect of an option to purchase and an obligation to maintain in land development

According to the original contract between A and B (the developer), B has an option to purchase. To what extent is this option enforceable against C, who purchases the property from A?

In the original contract, A binds himself/herself and his/her successors to maintain the gardens surrounding the development. A sells all of his/her land in the area to a third party. To what extent is the third party obliged to maintain the gardens?

Comparative observations

An *option to purchase* is regarded in most jurisdictions as either a personal right which cannot be enforced against third parties, or as a limited real right, especially in the form of a right of pre-emption, or as a personal right, which acquires proprietary effect on registration.

If construed as a mere personal right, the option cannot be registered and is not enforceable against third party purchasers and will only entitle the holder to a claim for compensation against A.[1] Some jurisdictions acknowledge that if C purchases the property with knowledge of the option, he/she can be sued for the return of the property on the doctrine of fraudulent third party complicity.[2]

[1] See e.g. the Scottish report. This is also the prevailing, though not the unanimous, view in Italy. It remains unenforceable even if included in a duly registered hereditary building right (*superficies*) or a hereditary land lease (*emphyteusis*), since the option is not considered part of these grants.

[2] See the Belgian, French, Scottish and Danish reports. See also the Portuguese report for the case where the option forms part of a lease or a hereditary building right.

If construed as a limited real right, and registered, some jurisdictions[3] make the option enforceable against C, while other jurisdictions[4] make them enforceable against C only if constituted as a right of pre-emption (*Vorkaufsrecht*). If registered, such an option will entitle the holder (B) to assume the rights and obligations of C as set out in any subsequent sale and transfer agreement concluded between A and C. In Austria, a right of pre-emption can only be exercised if the owner receives a binding offer from a third person and the holder accepts the conditions under which the third party buyer C would have bought it.

English law also recognises an option to purchase as a property right, which will run with the land if a prior notification is appropriately noted in the Land Register. It will therefore bind A's successors-in-title if the option has not yet been exercised. In order to create such an interest, the normal rules for the creation of a contract to purchase land need to be complied with. A's transfer to a third party (C) in breach of the terms of the option makes A liable in damages and such a transfer may be restrained by injunction. This differs from the position in civil law countries where a breach of the rights of pre-emption will entitle the holder to assume the rights and obligations of the third party purchaser (C).

German law recognises that an option which takes the form of a right held by B to purchase the property (*Ankaufsrecht*) is a personal right which can be given real effect against C by prior notice (*Vormerkung*) in the Land Register. The registration of the priority notice does not technically create a real right, but it protects B's right to purchase the property from A vis-à-vis third parties like C.

Most jurisdictions accept that the grant of a principal time-limited interest (such as a hereditary building lease or a hereditary land lease) may contain *maintenance obligations* relating to the buildings on the land which will be enforceable against the successors-in-title of the holder. Maintenance obligations relating to the land surrounding the development contained in the constitutive agreement will, however, only be effective between the parties themselves.[5]

[3] See the Spanish, Danish, Hungarian (where an option is valid for a maximum of five years) and Polish reports. The Danish Supreme Court will even order C to restore the property to its former condition.

[4] See e.g. the German, Austrian, Portuguese and South African reports.

[5] See the Portuguese, Belgian and Italian reports which attribute such consequence to the *numerus clausus* principle.

In England, this situation is covered by the law concerning positive covenants. The purchaser of the surrounding land (as opposed to the development site) will not be burdened by the duty to maintain gardens on the surrounding land because outside the leasehold context the doctrine of privity does not permit a third party to be burdened with positive covenants to which he/she was not privy because such covenants do not 'run with the land'.[6] Consequently, B cannot directly enforce the obligation against A. In practice, however, if A, in his/her contract with B has bound himself/herself and his/her successors to maintain the gardens, A will only sell the land to C subject to C's agreement to assume the obligations relating to maintenance of the garden. South African law will fortify a chain of conditions that burdens all A's successors to maintain the garden by the insertion of a penalty clause in case of non-compliance. Otherwise, A will be liable on the ground of breach of contract for damages suffered by B. The Belgian report notes that if A imposes the same obligation of maintenance on C, such a clause will, in general, qualify as a stipulation in favour of a third party (*derdenbeding/stipulation pour autrui*). In such a case, B has a contractual right against C to compel performance of the obligation.

English law encourages this result by holding A liable for the failure to comply with the positive obligation even after the transfer to C. If A is sensible, he/she will have entered into an indemnity agreement with C whereby C covers A's losses. This can amount to an indirect method of enforcement of covenants, albeit a highly cumbersome and unsatisfactory one.

Most jurisdictions doubt whether the constitutive agreement to create a time-limited interest supplemented by a praedial servitude consisting of a positive obligation on A to maintain the gardens surrounding the development, will be enforceable.[7] Exceptions are, however, recognised in the case where the positive duty can be construed as ancillary to a registrable right such as a hereditary building right or a hereditary land lease.[8]

6 Leasehold covenants are an exception. The position will therefore be different if the purchaser acquired the development site itself, where leasehold covenants could come into play.

7 See e.g. the Scottish report.

8 See the German, Spanish and Belgian reports. Depending on their exact phrasing, such rights and obligations constitute an integral part of the real right of *superficies* or *emphyteusis* if registered together with the principal right and are therefore effective against third party purchasers. See the Scottish report for further exceptions.

The Austrian report suggests that the maintenance obligation can be made effective against successors-in-title if it is registered in the form of a land charge (*Reallast*) in favour of B's land or a certain person. Once registered, it obliges the owner of the land to perform certain services. Danish law will allow the maintenance obligation to be registered as an easement which can then be enforced against A's successors-in-title. If unregistered, it will only bind successors-in-title who acquire the property in bad faith.

Austria

B's *option to purchase* can be made enforceable against third parties if it can be construed as a right of pre-emption in terms of Civil Code, § 1072. Accordingly, the seller may include a clause in the contract of sale which obliges the purchaser to offer the property to the seller if he intends to resell it. Despite the wording of Civil Code, § 1072, a right of pre-emption can also be created by other contracts and not only by a contract of sale.[9] Under Civil Code, § 1073, a right of pre-emption can be registered with the Land Register whereupon it becomes a right *in rem* and effective against third parties. A right of pre-emption can, however, only be exercised if the owner intends to sell his/her property and receives a binding offer from a third person (Civil Code, § 1079, sent. 2). In such a case, the holder of the right of pre-emption has the possibility to acquire the property by accepting the conditions under which the third party would have bought it.[10]

In order to allow B to buy the property whenever he/she wants, A and B can conclude an *option agreement*. An option agreement defines the terms of a prospective contract between the parties and entitles the holder of the option to exercise the option and obtain performance under the contract.[11] In contrast to a right of pre-emption, however, an option gives rise to a personal right which cannot be registered in the Land Register.[12] It cannot therefore be made enforceable against third persons.

[9] Welser, in Koziol and Welser, *Bürgerliches Recht*, vol. 2, p. 172. See also 1 Ob 653/83; SZ 56/96 (pre-emption right of tenant).

[10] Welser, in Koziol and Welser, *Bürgerliches Recht*, vol. 2, pp. 173 ff. See also 1 Ob 653/83; SZ 56/96.

[11] Aicher, in Rummel, *Kommentar*, vol. 1, § 1072, para. 33.

[12] See the exclusive list of rights which can be registered in s. 9 of the Law on Land Register; Ob I 455/25; SZ 7/184; District Court of Vienna 13.11.1948, 41 R 1427; EvBl (1949), p. 84; Aicher, in Rummel, *Kommentar*, vol. 1, § 1072, para. 33.

If the *maintenance obligation* is constituted as a contractual obligation only, it cannot be enforced against third parties. If A and B, however, create a land charge (*Reallast*), B acquires a right *in rem*.[13] A land charge is registered in the Land Register (Law on Land Register, § 12) and obliges the owner of the servient land to perform certain services.[14] A land charge can be for the benefit of a certain plot of land or a certain person.[15]

Belgium

It is assumed that the developer has been granted either a hereditary building lease or a hereditary land lease over the land, both of which are rights *in rem*. It is also assumed that such contracts have been properly prepared by a notary public and registered in the Land Register. To the extent that these formalities have been observed, the hereditary building lease and the hereditary lease of land are fully enforceable against C. However, an *option to purchase*, even when incorporated in the constitutive contracts of these institutions, is not enforceable, since it does not form part of the building or the land lease. An option is a mere personal right and does not create a real right over the property.[16]

In the first instance, the purchase by C from A will provide B with a contractual claim for breach of contract against A. A's claim against C will only be entertained if B is able to show that C purchased from A in the knowledge that B had a contractual option to purchase. This will be covered by the legal doctrine of third party complicity to a contractual breach (*derdenmedeplichtigheid/tierce complicité*). The fact that a hereditary building lease or a hereditary land lease is registered in the Land Register (including the option) can be an element indicating knowledge on the part of the purchaser. If C is held liable, the remedies available to B may be annulment of the contract and replacement of C by B, or compensation for damages.[17]

Were A to sell the property without either continuing to *maintain the gardens* or imposing the same obligation on the third party purchaser, it

[13] There was a similar land charge in the case 7 Ob 517/92 (obligation to plant and maintain a hedge).

[14] 7 Ob 517/92; OGH 8.4.1997; 5 Ob 81/97s; NZ (1998), p. 87 (Hoyer); 5 Ob 167/02y; NZ (2003), p. 247 (Hoyer); Kletecka, in Koziol and Welser, *Bürgerliches Recht*, vol. 1, p. 433.

[15] Kletecka, in Koziol and Welser, *Bürgerliches Recht*, vol. 1, p. 433; Hofmann, in Rummel, *Kommentar*, vol. 1, § 530, para. 2.

[16] Supreme Court of 12 Dec. 1991; RW (1992–3), p. 217 n. Carette.

[17] See Supreme Court of 27 Apr. 2006, ARC04.0591.N, available at www.cass.be.

will constitute a breach of contract (especially if it were expressly indicated that his/her successors will also have such an obligation). If A imposed the same obligation of maintenance on C such a clause will in general qualify as a stipulation in favour of a third party (*derdenbeding/ stipulation pour autrui*).[18] If this is the case, B has a contractual right against C to compel the latter to fulfil the obligation.

The garden maintenance obligation will only be enforceable against the purchaser of land adjacent to the development sold by A if it takes the form of an easement (servitude) benefiting the developed land and encumbering the neighbouring land. A mere obligation to maintain gardens will not be deemed an easement between two parcels of land since it is a personal obligation that binds an individual and does not encumber land. There is a *numerus clausus* of real rights and the parties will not be able to create new forms of real rights.[19] B will only have a contractual right for damages against A. If A, however, imposes the same obligation of maintenance on C and that clause qualifies as a stipulation in favour of a third party, B will have a contractual right against C to oblige the latter to fulfil that obligation.

The answer could be different if A sells the land under development in respect of which the real right under a hereditary building lease or a hereditary land lease was granted. To the extent that certain obligations are imposed on the grantor of the real right as owner of the property subject to the real right (*qualitate qua*), some academics have argued that such rights and obligations form part of the real right and are therefore enforceable against a third party purchaser of the property subject to the real right (if the contract is registered in the Land Register). It will depend on the exact phrasing of the clause whether or not the maintenance obligation can be considered an integral part of the real right under a hereditary building lease or a hereditary land lease of land, or merely a personal contractual undertaking (which can, for instance, be a separate garden maintenance contract). An additional element to consider is that garden maintenance will normally be the responsibility of the holder in the case of a hereditary land lease. This statement is not unanimously accepted. The majority viewpoint is that it is doubtful whether such an obligation can be regarded as anything more than a personal undertaking which does not bind the purchaser.

[18] See Carette, 'Het derdenbeding', nos. 44 ff.

[19] See Supreme Court of 16 Sept. 1966, RCJB 1968 116 n. Hansenne.

Denmark

The *option to purchase* can validly be registered as an easement in the Land Register. If registration has taken place before C submits his/her deed to be registered, the option is clearly enforceable against C. In a Supreme Court case,[20] a tenant's registered option to purchase was overlooked by a bank that transferred the property to a fund/trust within the bank group. As a result of the decision, the tenant was reinstated and the landlord was forced to reverse substantial alterations of the buildings.

B's right is also protected, even if it is not registered, where the purchaser knows or should have known about B's option at the time when C's deed was submitted for registration (Law on Registration of Property, s. 1 and 5). Extinction of prior rights presupposes good faith on the part of the assignee.[21]

If the provision of the contract between A and B regarding the *maintenance of the garden* is registered in the Land Register as an easement, it must be respected by any third party buying the property. If not registered, it must only be respected where the assignee is in bad faith, otherwise the right will be extinguished (Law on Registration of Property, s. 1). In order to be registered, all easements must contain a provision stating who is entitled to enforce the easement (Law on Registration of Property, s. 10 (6)). In this case it seems that neither A nor B has a real interest in whether the third party as a new owner maintains the gardens or not. If no one has an incentive in enforcing the obligation, then the third party will not be held responsible even where the easement is registered.

England

An *option to purchase*[22] is a property right under English land law, and will run with the land if it is appropriately noted in the Land Register.[23]

[20] Supreme Court decision of 6 Feb. 2002 (UfR (2002), p. 965). See also Supreme Court decision of 12 Oct. 2004 (UfR (2005), p. 194) where a buyer in a similar way was forced to respect a registered right to purchase. He could not even claim damages from the seller.

[21] See Buch and Møller, *Projektudvikling af fast ejendom*, p. 92.

[22] A different creature is the right of pre-emption, which is triggered by the volition of A as opposed to the intention to purchase by B. It is not considered here.

[23] *Ruoff and Roper Registered Conveyancing*, para. 42–004. See, though, LRA 2002, s. 91 for the proposed changes for electronic conveyancing. It may be registered as a land charge in unregistered land. See Land Charges Act 1972, s. 2(4)(iv).

It will therefore bind successors-in-title of A if the option has not been exercised yet. In order to create such an interest, the normal rules for the creation of a contract to purchase land need to be adhered to (Law of Property (Miscellaneous Provisions) Act, s. 2). A transfer to a third party in breach of the terms of the option makes A liable in damages,[24] and such a transfer may be restrained by injunction.[25]

In repect of the *maintenance obligation*, a third party interested in the surrounding land alone (as opposed to also the development site, where leasehold covenants arise)[26] will not be burdened with the duty to maintain gardens on surrounding land. This is because, outside the leasehold context, the notion of privity does not permit a third party to be burdened by positive covenants (or other agreements) he/she was not privy to, still less to let their burden pass with the land.[27] English law does recognise that the restrictive covenants (which prevent successors-in-title from doing things) may so run, however.[28] In the circumstances, therefore, B cannot directly enforce the obligation against A.

B can, however, hold A to be continuingly liable for the failure to comply with the positive obligation (Law of Property Act, s. 79). If A has been sensible, he will have entered into an indemnity agreement with the third party whereby the third party covers A's losses. This can amount to an indirect method of enforcement of covenants, albeit of a highly cumbersome and unsatisfactory nature. There are other methods for enforcing positive obligations of this kind, though these are not relevant in the present context.[29]

France

In order to determine to what degree B's *option* can be enforced against C, one must distinguish whether A granted a unilateral offer to purchase or a right of first refusal to B. These are examples of mechanisms used in practice, for example, in the case of a lease for construction.

The *Cour de cassation*[30] had to decide on the effect of including a unilateral offer to purchase in a heritable building lease granted

[24] *Midland Bank Trust Co.* v. *Green* [1980] Ch 590 611.

[25] *Churchman* v. *Lampon* [1990] 1 EGLR 211.

[26] As to which, see the Landlord and Tenant (Covenants) Act 1995.

[27] See *Rhone* v. *Stephens* [1994] AC 310. [28] See *Tulk* v. *Moxhay* (1848) 2 Ph. 774.

[29] See Harpum, *Megarry and Wade's Property*, paras. 16–019 ff.

[30] Civ. 3, 15 Dec. 1993; Bull. civ. III, no. 174.

to B.[31] The court held that if the landowner-promisor who is bound to allow the purchase rescinds the contract before the option is exercised, the beneficiary cannot claim specific performance of the offer to purchase. Hence the sale to C is valid, despite the option to purchase granted to B. B can, however, raise either an action on fraud against the third party purchaser or an action based on fault on his/her part based on actual knowledge that the property was subject to a unilateral offer to purchase.[32] In such circumstances, the trial judge may award a remedy which seems adequate in the circumstances to annul the sale that is challenged.[33]

Where a right of first refusal is granted to the developer, the *Cour de cassation* reversed the previous case law on the subject[34] and allows the holder of the right of first refusal the right to annul the contract concluded with a third party in defiance of his/her rights and allows the holder to be put in the place of the purchaser if he/she can prove that the purchaser acted fraudulently. Proof of fraud consists in establishing that the third party purchaser knew of the first refusal agreement and of the intention of the beneficiary to avail himself/herself of the option. Although previous case law allowed this remedy, it required proof of a fraudulent collusion between the third party and the previous owner before the holder of the option could be put in the place of the acquirer. It must be added that the notary concerned also incurs civil liability where he/she knew of the existence of the right of first refusal, but does not protect the right of the beneficiary if need be by refusing to execute the notarial deed of sale which violates the right of first refusal of the developer.[35]

Germany

If the *option to purchase* is constituted as a personal right in the contract between A and B (Civil Code, § 463), it will not be enforceable against C. However, it is possible to create a real right enforceable against third parties in the form of a right of pre-emption (*Vorkaufsrecht*) (Civil Code, §§ 1094 ff.). The right of pre-emption must be registered in the Land

[31] It is advisable that the promise of purchase should not be exercisable before a period of eighteen years has expired.
[32] Civ. 3, 8 July 1975, Gaz. Pal. 1975. 2. 781.
[33] Civ. 1, 12 June 1954, JCP 1954 vol. 2, 8225.
[34] Cass. Ch. Mixte, 26 May 2006, Bull. civ., no. 4; BICC 1 Aug. 2006.
[35] Civ. 1, 11 July 2006; Bull. civ. I, no. 389.

Register (*Grundbuch*) in order to be validly created as a real right. It entitles the holder (B) to assume the rights and obligations of C as set out in any subsequent sale and transfer agreement entered into between A and a third party (C). Consequently, B does not have the right to purchase the property at a fixed price. Instead, the price is dependent on the conditions agreed upon between A and C.

Alternatively, A can agree to grant B a right to purchase the property (*Ankaufsrecht*). This is a mere contractual right which entitles B to purchase the property at a certain price. Since it is not one of the recognised limited real rights in German law, a right to purchase (*Ankaufsrecht*) cannot be registered in the Land Register. However, it can be made enforceable against third parties by registering a priority notice (*Vormerkung*) in the Land Register (Civil Code, § 883). Although technically the registration of the priority notice does not create a real right, it protects B's right to purchase the property from A vis-à-vis third parties (Civil Code, §§ 883(2) and 888).

By virtue of the Regulations on Hereditary Building Leases (§ 2 no. 1), the contract to create a hereditary building right can contain *maintenance obligations* relating to the buildings which will be enforceable against the successors-in-title of the holder (B). Maintenance obligations relating to the land surrounding the structure contained in the contract will be effective only among the parties themselves.[36]

It is debatable whether A's duty to maintain the gardens surrounding the development can become enforceable if contained in a contract creating a personal (or praedial) servitude supplementing the *Erbbaurecht*. German law has adopted the maxim *servitus in faciendo consistere nequit*, which means that, in principle, a servitude cannot impose a positive duty on the owner of the servient land. It may only entitle its holder to do something in respect of the servient land or compel the owner of the servient land to refrain from doing something on his/her land (Civil Code, § 1018). Certain exceptions to this rule have, however, been recognised. A servitude imposing a positive duty on the owner of the servient land may be established if such a right is ancillary to a registrable right or duty.[37] It seems therefore that a servitude obliging A (and his/her successors) to maintain the gardens surrounding the structure will only be registrable if it were ancillary to a registrable hereditary building right.

[36] von Oefele and Winkler, *Handbuch*, no. 4.49.
[37] Schöner and Stöber, *Grundbuchrecht*, nos. 1133 ff.

In practice, if A has bound himself/herself and his/her successors to maintain the gardens in his/her contract with B, A will only sell the land to C subject to C's agreement to assume all obligations in that regard. Otherwise, A can be liable for damages suffered by B for breach of contract.

Greece

Under Greek Law, B's *option to purchase* gives rise to a personal right only.[38] Such an option is therefore unenforceable against C. B will, however, have a claim for compensation against A since the fulfillment of the option, namely the performance of the contract embodying the option, will no longer be possible.[39]

A's *maintenance obligations* in respect of the gardens surrounding the development may not be included in the title conditions of a servitude burdening the land. This is in accordance with the Romanist tradition that a servitude may not involve affirmative duties for the owner of the servient property (*servitus in faciendo consistere nequit*).[40] Such duties may only be undertaken by virtue of personal obligations,[41] which are not enforceable against third parties. Consequently, the third party to whom the land is sold is not obliged to maintain the gardens. Again, A will be liable for damages suffered by B on account of breach of contract. However, if the mechanism described above[42] is followed and the recorded deeds include such a term, all successors of the initial contracting parties are bound by such an agreement.

Hungary

If the *option to purchase* is registered in the Land Register, it can be invoked against anyone who subsequently acquires ownership or any other rights over the property (Civil Code, §§ 375(4) and 374(5) in conjunction with art. 373(3)). An option can, however, only be established for a maximum period of five years.

[38] Georgiades, *General Principles*, p. 412. [39] Georgiades, *Option*, pp. 173, 178.

[40] See also Banakas, in Georgiades and Stathopoulos, *GCC, Collective Analysis*, art. 1188, no. 15 (207).

[41] Yiannopoulos, in Kerameus and Kozyris, *Introduction to Greek Law*, p. 163.

[42] See Case 10.

The obligation of *maintaining the garden* can be established only as an obligation *in personam*. Hence, if A sells all of his/her land in the area, that obligation cannot be invoked against the acquirers of the property.

Italy

The prevailing, though not unanimous, view is that an *option to purchase* is not enforceable against third parties. While no case law in point can be cited, the option is probably not enforceable against C.

The duty to maintain the gardens cannot be construed as a praedial servitude, because a praedial servitude cannot consist of a *facere* (a positive obligation on the part of the grantor).[43] Furthermore, property *in rem* obligations constitute a *numerus clausus*[44] and cannot be freely expanded by the parties. The contractual provision concerning the duty to maintain the gardens therefore creates a mere personal obligation, and is not enforceable against third parties.

The Netherlands

An *option to purchase* is a personal right which does not have any effect vis-à-vis third parties. In so far as it is only included in the contract, the option cannot be enforced against C who was not a party to the contract.

In so far as an *obligation to maintain* is included in a contract, A, but not his/her successors, will be obliged to maintain the garden, since a contract does not bind third parties. However, A can stipulate in the contract that his/her successors be obliged to maintain the garden. This is secured by a penalty clause. The construction is designated a *kettingbeding* (a perpetual clause) binding all successors-in-title. If A's successors-in-title do not comply with this obligation to maintain the garden, A will be in breach of the contract with B as this construction gives rise to rights *inter partes* only, which are not enforceable against third parties.

Poland

If the *option to purchase* is registered, it will be effective against C.

[43] See e.g. Cass. civ. 26/06/1987 n. 5636; Comporti, 'Voce Servitù', *Enciclopedia del diritto*, vol. 42, p. 289.

[44] See e.g. Bigliazzi, 'Oneri reali', pp. 59 ff.

If B has registered his/her right to have A *maintain the gardens*, that right will also be enforceable against future purchasers. It is arguable whether a servitude consisting of a positive obligation on the part of the servient owner can be registered against the servient land. It is, however, possible for the owner of the servient land to commit himself/herself to a negative servitude to not allow the trees or bushes on his/her property to grow beyond a certain height. In theory, such a servitude can thus be established and will be enforceable against third parties, but, in practice, this device is rarely employed.

Portugal

If the *option to purchase* is established as a personal right in the contract between B and C, it will not be enforceable against C (Civil Code, art. 414).

It is possible to create a real right enforceable against third parties in the form of a right of pre-emption. The right of pre-emption must be registered in the Land Register[45] in order to be enforceable against third parties. It entitles the holder to assume the rights and obligations of C as set out in any subsequent sale and transfer agreement entered into between A and C. Consequently, if the right of pre-emption is registered, B has the right to purchase the property at the price agreed upon between A and C.

Alternatively, A can agree to promise B to sell the property to him. This contract (*contrato-promessa de compra e venda*) consists of a commitment of buying and selling, and is governed by Civil Code, arts. 410 ff. Provisions governing the option to sell contract also apply to the preliminary contract, except for the provisions relating to formalities.The preliminary contract has to be signed by the parties to be legally binding. If the future contract is for the acquisition or constitution of a real right over a dwelling, the notary must certify the signature of the parties and the existence of a permit authorising the utilisation or construction of the property. The party that promises to sell or to create the real right may only rely on the non-compliance with these requirements when it was due to the fault of the acquirer.

Once the promise to sell or to buy is registered in the Land Register,[46] it will be enforceable against third parties.

[45] Law on Registration, art. 2 (1)(f). [46] *Ibid.*

If A binds himself/herself in the original contract that he/she and his/her successors will *maintain the gardens* surrounding the development, this is only enforceable between the contractual parties and not against third parties. Thus C will not be obliged to maintain the gardens. The reason for this is that the Portuguese Civil Code, art. 1306 recognises a *numerus clausus* of real rights. The Portuguese system of property is characterised by a limited number of real rights which are not subject to contractual modification because this principle vetoes the establishment of new rights *in rem*.

In practice, if A undertakes to maintain the gardens in the contract he/she concludes with B, he/she can only sell the land to C subject to C's agreement to assume all obligations in that regard. Otherwise, A will be liable for damages on account of breach of contract.

Scotland

If included in a lease between A and B, an *option to purchase* does not bind C. It is not a real condition of the lease.[47] An option to purchase does not create in the option holder (B) a real right which binds C. The right of an option holder is not one of the real rights recognised by Scots law. Nor is C bound by the obligations incumbent upon A as grantor of the option. Contracts bind only the parties to them. A must, however, when transferring to C, oblige C to perform the option if it is exercised, otherwise A exposes himself/herself to an action for damages for breach of contract.

It is a topic of some debate whether the fact that C knew of the existence of the option or acquired gratuitously or for a manifestly inadequate consideration renders the option binding upon him. This will be an application of the 'offside goals' rule.[48] In the paradigm case, this rule protects the position of a buyer (X) who has contracted to buy property from a seller (Y) against a subsequent transfer by Y to a third party (Z), in breach of the obligation owed by Y to X. An unexercised option is one stage removed from this paradigm case. Prior to exercise, the option holder does not have a right that is 'capable of being made real', which is often said to be one of the requirements of the rule.[49] For that reason, some adopt the position that an option is not protected by

[47] *Bisset* v. *Magistrates of Aberdeen* (1898) 1 F 87 (IH); *The Advice Centre for Mortgages* v. *McNicoll* 2006 CSOH 58, 2006 SLT 591 [39].

[48] Discussed in more detail in the response to Case 2.

[49] *Wallace* v. *Simmers* 1960 SC 255 (IH).

the offside goals rule.[50] There is, however, also judicial support for the position that one who acquires with knowledge of an unexercised option is bound by it.[51] This writer prefers that position.[52] The point is not yet settled. For B to protect his/her position, he/she can seek to have A's obligations under the option secured by a standard security over the land.

C is not bound by A's *contractual obligation to maintain the gardens*, unless he/she has assumed it. C's knowledge of the obligation makes no difference. The offside goals rule does not apply to a purely contractual obligation such as this.

If A had previously transferred ownership of some land to B and retained ownership of surrounding land on which the gardens were built and A is now transferring ownership of the garden land, the maintenance obligation can be constituted as a real burden on the garden ground. The owner for the time being of the surrounding garden land ('the burdened proprietor') will be bound to maintain the gardens for the benefit of the owner for the time being of land currently owned by B ('the benefited proprietor').[53]

If A granted B a lease of the property (excluding the garden ground), undertaking in the lease to maintain the gardens, and A is now transferring ownership of all of his/her property to C, the obligation to maintain the gardens may bind C as A's successor-in-title in respect of the leased property. The law as to when an obligation in a lease in respect of neighbouring property can be a 'real condition' of the lease so as to bind a successor-in-title is undeveloped.[54] The test appears to be that if the obligation is sufficiently connected with the lease it will be a real condition. Whether a court will hold that an obligation to maintain surrounding gardens will be a real condition cannot be predicted with certainty. If the matter is sufficiently important to B, he/she must seek to protect his/her position by having the original contract of lease provide that A will oblige any successor-in-title to perform this

[50] *The Advice Centre for Mortgages* v. *McNicoll* 2006 CSOH 58, 2006 SLT 591, paras. 41–51; Steven, 'Options to Purchase', pp. 432, 436.

[51] *Davidson* v. *Zani* 1992 SCLR 1001 (Sh Ct); *Royal Bank of Scotland* v. *Gibson* [2009] CSOH 14, 2009 SLT 444, para. 50.

[52] Webster, 'Options for the Offside Goals Rule', p. 524. The *Gibson* case is also discussed by Anderson and Macleod, 'Offside Goals', p. 93.

[53] This would be an 'affirmative burden' (TC(S)A 03, s. 2(1)(a)).

[54] See generally Webster, 'The Relationship of Tenant and Successor Landlord', ch. 7.

obligation and, ideally, secure that obligation and the obligation to maintain the gardens by means of a standard security.

South Africa

South African law draws a distinction between an *option to purchase* and a right of pre-emption in favour of B. In the case of an option to purchase, A's right will be regarded as a mere contractual right which cannot be enforced against a third-party acquirer. B will thus be restricted to a claim for damages against A for breach of contract. If, however, the arrangement between A and B can be construed as the grant of a right of pre-emption (first refusal) there is authority for the view that this arrangement can operate like an *ex lege* right of retraction harking back to its Germanic predecessor, which allowed the holder to retract the consequences of the sale of the land in breach of the right.[55]

The crucial issue regarding A's *maintenance obligation* is whether A's contractual undertaking that he/she and his/her successors-in-title will maintain the gardens surrounding the development is enforceable against the acquirer of A's land. This will only be the case if the right concerned is a real right and is registered as such. Under South African law, rights which do not form a 'subtraction from the dominium of the land' are not registrable. Since the right to claim performance of another party is traditionally considered a mere personal right, it will not be capable of registration. Furthermore, owing to the fact that it involves a positive duty on the part of the 'servient' owner, the passivity principle which prevents positive obligations being placed on an owner of servient land will also prevent the registration of this right as a praedial servitude. The successors-in-title will only be bound if the original contracting party has created a chain of conditions fortified by a penalty clause to bind his/her successors-in-title in similar fashion.[56]

[55] This proprietary remedy developed from the notion that the holder had incomplete ownership that automatically expanded to full ownership on breach of his/her rights. See *Associated South African Bakeries (Pty) Ltd.* v. *Oryx and Vereinigte Bäckereien (Pty) Ltd.* 1982 3 SA 893 (A) 905. *Contra Owsianick* v. *African Consolidated Theatres* 1967 3 SA 310 (A). For a detailed appraisal, see Naudé, 'Rights of First Refusal', pp. 66–90.

[56] See Van der Merwe, De Waal and Carey Miller, 'Property and Trust Law', ss. 117–19 and 684–5.

Spain

The *option to purchase* is enforceable against C if it is registered in the Land Register, which is permitted in the Regulations on Hypothecs, art. 14 (*Reglamento Hipotecario*).[57]

There is no definitive answer with regard to the *maintenance obligation*. Where the obligation on the part of A is registered as a material provision of the limited right that has been established between A and B, the third party is probably also bound by such obligation. If it is not registered, B retains the right to sue A and his/her successors for specific performance. Such obligation is, however, not enforceable against the third party, as the obligation to maintain the gardens is a mere personal obligation between A and B.

[57] Díez-Picazo, *Fundamentos*, vol. 1, p. 319. He adds that, if one of the main characteristics of rights in *rem* is their enforceability against third parties, the right of an option to purchase can be considered a right in *rem*, even when it does not grant its holder a direct and immediate power over the property. In his opinion, only the right of option to purchase immovables/real estate, which is registered in the Land Register, can be considered a limited right in *rem*.

Case 12
Development of an existing building and land development by a public institution

To what extent will your answers to questions 12 and 13 be different:

- *if A owns an existing building and wants it to be used as a shopping centre? A does not, however, want to manage it directly but wants to retain some control over the structure and have unburdened ownership of the building at the end of the period;*
- *if A is a public institution (for example, a City Council)?*[1]

Comparative observations

The obvious manner in which A can achieve such a result is to enter into a commercial lease[2] or a management contract[3] with B. Since A will retain ownership of the land and the structure, he/she will still have unburdened ownership of the land and building on termination of the lease or management contract.

A can also achieve this result by means of the establishment of a *hereditary building lease* (*superficies*) or a *hereditary land lease* (*emphyteusis*)[4] in jurisdictions which allow the holder of the right to improve the land not only by the construction of new buildings[5] but also by the exploitation of existing buildings.[6] The Belgian report suggests that a *usufruct* of the land for a fixed term can also achieve the goal envisaged here.

[1] Only briefly indicate public law requirements.
[2] See the Austrian, Greek, French, Belgian, Portuguese, Spanish, English and Scottish reports.
[3] See the Belgian, Scottish and Danish reports. [4] See the Belgian report.
[5] Austrian, Belgian and South African law and apparently also Danish and Hungarian law only allow the holder to improve the land by the construction of new buildings.
[6] See the German, Portuguese and Italian reports. A minority Italian view will allow the owner to transfer ownership of the existing structure separately from the soil,

The Danish report suggests that the sale and purchase back device can be utilised to achieve this goal. A will sell the land with the existing building, subject to a proviso that A may buy it back from B at a later stage. This option can be created as a right of first refusal, an obligation on B to sell to A on demand or an obligation on A to purchase the land back on a fixed later date.

The institutions of a *hereditary building lease* (*superficies*) and a *hereditary land lease* (*emphyteusis*) were originally designed to help the State and other public institutions like local governments and city councils to conclude arrangements with developers to develop unimproved land in the public interest, subject to the proviso that the land and the improvements had to be returned to the State or other public institution after a fixed term.[7]

Presently, public institutions in Germany and Poland, for example, frequently make use of these institutions to promote the public interest.

A special Italian law of 1971 gives municipalities the authority to expropriate urban land and grant hereditary building leases (rights of *superficies*) to developers for a fixed term of between sixty and ninety-nine years for the purpose of constructing affordable housing units on the expropriated land. The town council must approve the building lease and a separate agreement between the municipality and the concessionaire must regulate their relationship. The agreement may organise the sale of the residences or apartments, determine their price or rent and must stipulate the design and characteristics of the construction, the time schedule for the erection of the building, the sanctions for violation of the agreement and the right to terminate the building lease in cases of serious violations. The use of these institutions has in the course of time been extended to private developers.

Apart from the fact that public institutions must comply with national and European Union public procurement provisions,[8] hereditary building leases granted by a public institution in Portugal must last at least seventy years, the grant must contain provisions against speculative transactions but need not adhere to time limits for the completion of constructions, and transfer may be made subject to prior authorisation or a right of pre-emption in favour of the public authority.

usually for a fixed term. On expiry of the term, the owner will become the unburdened owner of the structure.

[7] Before 1999, a hereditary building right could only be created in Austria in favour of the State or the church.

[8] E.g. public tender provisions.

Under Belgian, Spanish and Italian law, a public institution may grant a concession with regard to state or public land instead of a hereditary building lease (*superficies*) or a hereditary land lease (*emphyteusis*).[9] Public institutions enjoy contractual freedom to shape the concession according to their needs, including the right to terminate or alter such concession in the public interest. The Belgian and French reports contain details of recent legislation on Public Private Partnerships to facilitate the provision of public services and the construction of houses.

Austria

As a contractual solution, A and B can conclude an *income-producing (usufructuary) lease*. If the building already exists, the ownership of the building follows the ownership of the land. The landowner therefore owns the building. Legal separation of such a building is possible only by creating a *hereditary building lease*. An existing building cannot be converted into a *right of superstructure*.[10]

Before 1990, a building right could only be created on land owned by the State or the church.[11] The fact that A is a *public institution* is today relevant only as far as approval provisions of public law are applicable.

Belgium

The *hereditary building lease* and the *hereditary land lease* both provide the means to achieve the same objective. From a conceptual point of view, the hereditary building lease will ordinarily involve construction, which is not the case in the current scenario: the hereditary land lease or a usufruct will be more suitable. This structure is more in line with the original rationale of both legal structures, namely to allow a third party to exploit the land economically. The same result can also be achieved by entering into a management contract or a lease.

As regards the second question, although they will also require mandatory public approval, the same legal structures will be available to a *public institution*. Recently, some academics seem to accept that such legal structures may also be granted over property that is part of the

[9] In Italy, it is disputed whether the rights of the concessionaire are genuine hereditary building rights (*superficies*) or *sui generis* rights modelled on *superficies*.

[10] 3 Ob 158/93; JBl (1994), p. 250; Kletecka, in Kletecka, Rechberger and Zitta, *Bauten*, para. 33; Kletecka, in Koziol and Welser, *Bürgerliches Recht*, vol. 1, p. 434.

[11] BaurechtsG 1912; wichtige Nov: BGBl 1990/258.

public domain, in so far as they do not materially affect the public purpose of the property. The Belgian Supreme Court has expressly confirmed this view in the case of a *hereditary building lease*.[12]

A public authority may also grant the developer a *concession* to use the state property. Such a concession will leave the developer with rights similar to those he/she would have had if he/she were the holder of the hereditary building lease or the hereditary lease of land (though such rights are often more restricted). Yet again, the contractual freedom of the public institution to agree on specific conditions with the concession holder is important. If the concession is granted with regard to land owned by public authorities, the latter will always have the right to terminate or alter such concession in the public interest, subject to liability for damages flowing from such an alteration or termination.

On 9 July 2003, the Flemish Parliament adopted the Decree regarding Public Private Partnership, which was published on 19 September 2003.[13] In a Public Private Partnership (hereafter PPP), government[14] and industry – the public and private sectors – work together in the implementation of investment projects, each retaining their own identity and responsibilities. They collaborate on the basis of a clearly defined division of tasks and risks. The aim of PPP, a format which has become quite widespread in recent years, is to facilitate smoother co-operation between the government and private partners in a more flexible, efficient and commercial manner. PPP is therefore not a new legal institution, such as a joint stock corporation, an inter-municipal body or a non-profit organisation. PPP projects must be implemented within the existing statutory and legal framework, using existing legal institutions. The rights granted over public domain property may not be manifestly incompatible with its intended public purpose. One must also bear in mind that the government is not a normal contract party and is bound by certain rules regarding the choice of a private partner.

12 Supreme Court of 18 May 2007; RW (2007–8), p. 736 n. Sagaert.

13 On regional level this legislation has been followed by municipal and provincial regulations providing for the same concept in creating autonomous municipal and provincial companies. See the Municipality Decree of 15 July 2005, art. 191 and the Province Decree of 9 Dec. 2005 art. 185.

14 The Flemish decree provides for the possibility of the Flemish Government (art. 10) and internally autonomous agencies with legal personality or publicly or privately formed externally autonomous agencies making use of the PPP format. These are complicated variations with some differences in gradation as to the public or private character and the more or less autonomy of the agency.

Under Belgian law, the following must be taken into account:

(a) the public approval legislation (which is, of course, in each case dictated by Community rules);
(b) the principles of good governance, such as the equality principle, which requires the government to give 'equal opportunities' to the market players; and
(c) the principle of transparency, forbidding the government from covertly entering into partnerships with private partners that evade any form of control.

From a European Union law point of view, one must also consider the various directives in the area of government contracts (the scope of which is ever expanding) and competition law. At present, Belgium does not have specific PPP legislation.

Denmark

In Denmark, only two solutions are possible where A owns an *existing building*, namely those described in the answer to Case 10. A is not allowed to choose the procedure mentioned to sell the existing building separately, as land and buildings owned by the same person cannot be subdivided.[15]

If A is a *public institution*, the same rules as applied in the answers to Cases 10 and 11, apply here. Municipalities frequently sell land on terms that give them the right to buy back the land and buildings on a later date and they only very seldom choose the schemes described in the answer to Case 10.

England

In variation one, this will be a case for an ordinary *lease*. In the second variation, I see no difference between lettings by a public or a private body.

France

If A owns an already existing building, a *commercial lease* will achieve the envisaged result.

[15] See Willumsen, *Tinglysningsloven*, p. 215; Mortensen, *Tinglysning*, pp. 48 ff.; Supreme Court decision of 1 Feb. 1985 (UfR (1985), p. 305).

Certain legal persons recognised under public law, namely the State, local authorities and public institutions, may enter into a *Public Private Partnership contract* (Ordinance of 17 June 2004). The purpose of such a contract is to entrust a private partner with the task of obtaining financing for the planning and operation of public services, equipment and building constructions.

Germany

A *hereditary building lease* (*Erbbaurecht*), as a 'right to have a structure above or below the surface of a piece of land' (Regulations on Hereditary Building Rights, § 1(1)), can also be created with regard to an already existing building. The creation of an *Erbbaurecht* in respect of an existing building is in no way different from the situation where the structure is still to be built.

As stated above, public institutions very often make use of the hereditary building lease (*Erbbaurecht*) to promote the public interest while retaining some control over the property.

There are no material differences regarding the answers to Cases 10 and 11. Public institutions must obviously comply with national and EU public procurement provisions and other public law requirements.

Greece

A can conclude a *lease* with B in terms of which A will be obliged to provide B with the use of the building as a shopping centre against payment of the rent agreed upon. During the period of the lease, A's ownership on the land and the building will be retained.

Public legal persons like city councils[16] are governed by the rules of public law, except when they act as *fiscus* for tax purposes.[17] As long as public law requirements are complied with (for example, the provisions applying to public tender), the answers to Cases 10 and 11 will also apply in this case.

[16] Legal persons of public law are those established by the State for the promotion of a public or governmental purpose.

[17] Dagtoglou, *General Administrative Law*, pp. 8–10; Spiliotopoulos, *Greek Administrative Law*, p. 37.

Hungary

Hungarian law follows the principle of *aedificium solo cedit* with certain exceptions mentioned in the answer to Case 11.[18] Once the building has acceded to the land, the owner of the land becomes the owner of the structure: the two cannot be separated again. The separation of the ownership over the land and an *existing building* can only be accomplished in the event that a new structure is built upon the land, the parties agree to this separation or the law makes provision for this to happen. Otherwise, the answers to Cases 10 and 11 are applied *mutatis mutandis*.

If A is a *public institution*, some of its assets may be exclusive state property (Civil Code, § 172; Law on Local Self Governments, § 79)[19] and they may not be transferable (or their transferability may be restricted) (Civil Code, § 173). However, if the property does not fall under any of these special categories, no civil law provisions are applicable, particularly to public institutions.

Italy

Civil Code, art. 952 allows the owner of the soil to transfer ownership of an existing building separately from the ownership of the land. It can be transferred for a fixed term. On the expiry of the term, the owner of the soil becomes owner of the building.

Some scholars maintain that the transfer of an already existing building does not result in the creation of a hereditary building lease (*superficie*). According to Civil Code, art. 954, the destruction of the building does not amount to the extinction of the building lease (*superficie*), unless there is a contrary agreement. This means that when the owner transfers an already existing structure, the transferee does not obtain the right to rebuild the structure, unless the owner of the soil has expressly granted him/her such a right. According to this view, one must distinguish between three different rights:

(a) the hereditary building lease (*superficie*) proper, namely the right to erect a building above the soil of another;
(b) the *proprietà superficiaria*, that is the right on the building erected by the holder of the building lease (*superficiario*), with the right to rebuild in case of destruction; and

[18] Gellért, *Commentary Civil Code*, vol. 1, pp. 329–31.
[19] 1990 évi LXV *Törvény a helyi önkormányzatokról* (Law LXV of 1990 on Local Self-Government).

(c) the separate ownership of buildings transferred by the owner without the right to rebuild.[20]

The prevailing view, however, emphasises the unitary nature of the building lease (*superficie*) as a right to erect and maintain the building. Even if the ownership of an already existing building is transferred, the transferee acquires a building lease, which enables him/her to maintain the building above the soil. Consequently, whether the holder of the building lease has erected a building or acquired an existing building in terms of the building lease, he/she has the right to maintain the building and to rebuild it in case of destruction, unless there is a contrary agreement.[21] Thus, according to the prevailing view, the situation is not substantially different from the one described in the answer to Case 10.

Public institutions quite frequently grant a developer the right to erect and maintain a structure above public soil. The right arising from such a concession is usually regarded as a true hereditary building lease (*superficie*), but some scholars prefer to classify it as a different, *sui generis* right, merely modelled on the building lease.[22] Regulation of the right is dependent on the circumstances and on the applicable statute. Different public institutions have varying degrees of discretion to revoke the concession where public needs dictate that this is necessary. The right of the holder of the building lease to alienate and mortgage the structure is usually excluded or severely limited.

According to the prevailing view, the holder of the building lease has a genuine real right vis-à-vis third parties, and a weakened real right (*diritto affievolito*) vis-à-vis the public institution, which, by following the correct procedure, can revoke the concession and become full owner of the structure.

A statute enacted in 1971[23] provides that municipalities can create building rights over properties expropriated by the State. In the context of a strategy aimed at creating affordable housing for the general public, the statute provides that the municipalities can expropriate urban land and then grant hereditary building leases (*superficie*) for a fixed term of between sixty and ninety-nine years for the construction of affordable houses. The grant of the building lease must be approved by the town

[20] See e.g. Salis, 'La superficie'. [21] See e.g. Pugliese, 'Della superficie'.

[22] See, generally, Pasetti Bombardella, 'Voce Superficie', *Enciclopedia del diritto*, vol. 43, pp. 1474 ff.; Guarneri, 'Voce Superficie', p. 219.

[23] Law 865 of 22 Oct. 1971.

council and this is followed by a separate agreement between the municipality and the developer, regulating the details of the transaction. The agreement can authorise the sale or lease of the apartments and specify criteria for determining the respective price and rent that has to be paid. The agreement must further specify the characteristics of the building, the time schedule for the erection of the building and the sanctions for non-compliance with the terms of the agreement, including termination of the building lease for violation of the material terms of the agreement.

A series of statutes[24] was then enacted to trigger and indeed encourage owners to purchase the ownership of the land from the municipality, which will entitle them to convert their hereditary building lease (*superficie*) into full ownership without any time limit.

The Netherlands

The answer is the same as in Cases 10 and 11 in both situations.

Poland

It is important to note that if the State Treasury or a local authority owns land, it may establish a *hereditary land lease* (perpetual usufruct, *emphyteusis*) on the state land or land which belongs to a local authority.[25] This land lease is commonly utilised for land with development potential. It provides the grantee-investor with a real right that has a wide content, is transferable, transmissible, may be executed against for the non-payment of debt and may serve as collateral for a bank loan. In practice, this institution is frequently used by the State or local authority because at the end of the ninety-nine years when the investor has been able to realise his/her goal, unburdened ownership as a rule reverts to the state or local authority.

Portugal

A can create a *hereditary building lease* (*superficies*) with regard to the existing building, which will allow the holder to exploit the existing building for the agreed term. A may also *lease* the building for exploitation by the tenant.

[24] The most recent is legge 23/12/1998 n 448, art. 31.

[25] See Case 1.

Public institutions very often make use of a hereditary building lease (*superficies*) to combine advancement (promotion) of the public interest with retention of control over the property. The building lease granted by a public authority is regulated by Decree-Law 794/76 of 5 November. Some differences with the general regime of *superficies* may be pointed out:

(a) Article 19 of the Decree-Law requires that the building lease must last at least fifty years, and if it promotes housing development, more than seventy years.
(b) The contract must contain provisions against speculative transactions and must avoid setting time limits for constructions (art. 20 1).
(c) The public authority may impose a prohibition on transfer of the building lease or make transfer subject to prior authorisation (art. 20 2).
(d) If transfer is allowed, public authorities are granted a right of preemption (art. 20 3).

Scotland

A can enter into a management contract with management agents who will manage the shopping centre on his behalf. This is not a nominate contract and is not subject to a particular legal regime. It involves no grant of a real right to the management agents.

A can also grant a lease of the shopping centre to B to manage it on his/her behalf. B will be responsible for managing the centre and for granting leases to occupational tenants. A common arrangement will be for the lease to provide for A to receive the greater of a flat rent or a rent which reflects rental income received by B. If units of the shopping centre are already occupied under leases already granted by A, A can grant an interposed lease to B, inserting B in the contractual chain between A and the existing tenants.[26] Whereas previously A was the landlord and the retailer the tenant, A will from then on be the landlord, B the tenant and the retailers the subtenants.

Unlike in other systems, there are no special property rights which can only be granted by public institutions. Such bodies do, however, have public law duties to take into account when deciding how to exercise their property rights. There is, for example, a statutory duty that, as a general rule, a local authority must not dispose

[26] Land Tenure Reform (Scotland) Act 1974, s. 17.

of land for less than the best consideration that can reasonably be obtained.[27]

South Africa

Unlike modern European jurisdictions which also cater for the development and use of existing buildings under the institutions of the *hereditary land lease* (*emphyteusis*) and the *hereditary building lease* (*superficies*), these two institutions are underdeveloped in South African law to the extent that they do not cater for existing buildings. This is also true of the institution of *leasehold*, which replaced the two institutions in South Africa.

If A is a *public institution*, in particular the State, the institutions of hereditary land lease (*emphyteusis*) and hereditary building lease (*superficies*) would have found some application in Roman-Dutch law but was swamped by the common law institution of leasehold in early South African law because the State was not prepared to grant full freehold title (ownership) with regard to undeveloped land. I have come across seaside cottages and timeshares being sold as thirty-year leaseholds, with the rights of the holders expiring after thirty years and the public authority or developing agency being entitled to sell or lease out the cottages or timeshares anew. However, this device is rarely used in practice.

Spain

In the case of an existing building, A may conclude a *lease* (governed by the Law on Urban Lease) with B for this purpose. The building will be restored to A at the end of the lease, but he/she will have no control over the structure during the term of the lease, unless otherwise agreed.

A public institution can conclude a contract by which it grants a concession to B to construct public works (*contrato de concesión de obra pública*). Under this contract, the public institution (A) will have the right to recover the structure and the land at the end of the term of the concession. It must, however, be noted that such term cannot exceed forty years (*Ley de Contratos de las Administraciones Públicas* (Law on Contracts of Public Institutions) of 30 October 2007, art. 244).

[27] Local Government (Scotland) Act 1973, s. 74(2).

In such a case, B will build the structure and have the right to exploit the construction for the agreed term. A will be able to retain some control over the structure (he/she can, for example, specify the price to be paid by the users of the structure as provided for in art. 238.2). The right of the concessionaire can be ceded and mortgaged (art. 228.f).[28] Public institutions seldom use a hereditary building lease (*superficies*) for this purpose.

[28] Art. 98 of the *Ley de Patrimonio de las Administraciones Públicas* (State Property Act) of 3 Nov. 2003 also permits the possibility to transfer the concessionary's right (either through an *inter vivos* or a *mortis causa* agreement) or to mortgage the right. In this case, the express authorisation of the public institution is required.

PART III

Concluding remarks

Case 1

We have seen that the main time-limited interests in land which provide the holder with some sort of proprietary interest in the landed property of another are the lease, the personal servitude of usufruct, the right of use, the right of habitation, the hereditary building lease and the hereditary land lease. The aim of this chapter is to indicate the similarities and differences between these institutions, before summarising the main conclusions of the project. The chapter will be concluded with a brief attempt to indicate the modern practical significance of each of these institutions.

An important similarity between the time-limited institutions is that they split the exploitation of the land or residential premises between two persons, namely the landlord and tenant, the nude owner and the usufructuary, the landowner and the holder of a hereditary building right and the landowner and the holder of a hereditary land lease.[1]

A further obvious similarity is that this splitting of the exploitation of the land is time-limited in all these cases. Even in the case where a hereditary land lease is granted in perpetuity, the landowner still has the right to claim the return of the property on account of non-payment of rent (canon) or material breach of the terms of the constitutive instrument.[2] The period of the split exploitation differs among the various institutions. Whereas the personal servitudes of usufruct, use and habitation can be established for either a fixed term or for the life of the holder, they can never endure longer than the life of the holder. On the other hand, there is no limitation on the duration of leases, except that

[1] See also Johnston, *Roman Law in Context*, p. 67.
[2] See Rome, 'An Elegy for Emphyteusis', p. 9.

they can never be granted in perpetuity.[3] They can in principle be established for only a week, or, alternatively, for a very long period of time. Their duration only has an effect on the formalities required for their validity or their enforcement against third parties. As regards the duration of hereditary building leases and hereditary land leases, minimum time periods (for example, twenty-seven years in Belgium) are generally required for their validity. If these leases are terminated against the will of the parties before the minimum period has elapsed, this does not lead to reclassification of the lease to an ordinary land lease.[4]

Another self-evident similarity, at least between leases and usufructs, is that the same rules apply with regard to the gathering of fruit.[5] Under both institutions, the tenant and the usufructuary are allowed to exploit the property by gathering both natural and civil fruits.

An important difference between the various time-limited institutions is the scope of the entitlements or 'dismemberments of ownership' under each institution. Although the owner allows the tenant to cultivate the land or to reside in a dwelling and, in the case of an agricultural lease, to reap its crops in exchange for rent, the landlord does not relinquish any of the constituents of his/her right of ownership. Thus, in principle, a lease leaves the owner's real right in the property intact.[6] The usufruct, on the other hand, reaches all the way through into the owner's bundle of real entitlements and temporarily relegates two of them to someone else,[7] though without thereby depriving the owner of his *dominium*, if only because the residual right of disposal is seen as constituting the core of Romanist ownership.[8] Thus *ususfructus* replaces the original *dominus* with a nude owner and a usufructuary, the new owner being 'nude' because he has been stripped of the rights of use and of profits, leaving him/her only the legal title.[9] However, paradoxically, since the legal rules relating to

[3] If granted in perpetuity, the transaction will be classified as a hereditary land lease.

[4] See Vanhove, 'Note on the Decision of the Court of Cassation', p. 679.

[5] See already Justinian's Institutes 2.1.36.

[6] This differs from the *communis opinio* of Roman-Dutch writers of the seventeenth century that the holders of long-term leases acquired *dominium utile* in the property. See Bodenstein, 'Huur van huizen', p. 12.

[7] Feenstra, *Romeinsrechtelijke grondslagen*, 95 points out that during the feudal system the Roman texts on usufruct describing usufruct as a *pars dominii* were used to classify the right of the vassal as *dominium utile*. He indicates that this is different from the modern approach in civilian jurisdictions, which classify a usufruct as a limited real right.

[8] See Buckland, *Roman Law*, p. 273; Pugliese, 'On Roman Usufruct', p. 538.

[9] See Johnston, 'Successive Rights', p. 154.

personal servitudes are designed to preserve the rights of the nude owner to the greatest possible extent, we can safely conclude that the entitlements of a tenant in terms of a lease to the use and profits of the property are more extensive than that of a usufructuary. In the case of a hereditary building lease and a hereditary land lease, the holders do not only acquire the entitlements of use and enjoyment of the fruits but also the right to dispose of the property. They only differ from full ownership to the extent that the holders must continue to preserve the property in good condition, pay the rent charge on the property and may be subject to further restrictions as agreed in the constitutive instrument. These institutions thus result in an almost complete dismemberment of the entitlements of ownership,[10] leaving only residual rights in the landowner, coupled with the right to collect the land charge. The right to collect the land charge is a real right that 'runs with the land'.[11] An owner will have recourse to these institutions only in the event of a lack of capital, subjecting the land to the arrangement in order to better preserve and improve its condition and productivity, and to derive a small income by way of rent. Therefore, they are mainly used by public authorities or private landowners with vast estates who cannot otherwise improve the land themselves.[12] The main difference between the hereditary building right and the hereditary land lease is that the former is mostly concerned with the improvement of the land by the construction of buildings, while the latter also encompasses the improvement of the agricultural potential of the land.

A minor difference between these institutions is that a lease, a hereditary building lease and a hereditary land lease each involves the holder's payment of a determinate sum of money in the form of a rent or rent charge, whereas usufruct, even if constituted by conveyance, by its nature does not require any money to change hands. Note, however, that with crop-sharing agricultural leases, the tenant can contractually arrange with the landlord to supply him/her with a fixed proportion of the harvest (*colonia partiaria*) instead of a monetary payment.

A major difference between a lease and other time-limited institutions is that while the civil law institution of lease has its origins in the

[10] The Roman-Dutch writer Grotius refers to *emphyteusis* as *dominium utile* in a gloss (*Inleidinge*, 2.38.5).

[11] See Rome, 'An Elegy for Emphyteusis', p. 2.

[12] See Johnston, 'Emphyteusis: Perpetual Tenure', p. 338.

Roman law of obligations, and straddles both the law of obligations and the law of property in modern law,[13] the other three civil law institutions stem from the Roman law of property and are still generally regulated by property rules. In Roman law, lease and the three property law institutions were discussed separately and there was no land law as such to unite these institutions.[14] One important consequence is that although there are quite a number of, mainly statutory, default rules standardising the practical application of a lease, deviation of default rules and the imposition of new obligations in lease agreements are common in practice.[15] This is not the case with the other time-limited institutions which are regulated by the rules of the property regime.

Another major difference between lease and usufruct is that while a lease splits profits concurrently between the landlord and the tenant, with the use and fruits to the tenant and rent (or a proportion of the crops in certain agricultural leases) to the landlord, usufruct splits the profits successively between the usufructuary and the nude owner – first exclusively to the usufructuary, and then returning it in its entirety to the nude owner. Usufruct effects, in a certain sense, a division in time but hardly in content, of a single ownership.[16] Thus the position of the usufructuary differs from the position of the tenant, but also from that of the owner. The owner, whose property is subject to a usufruct, is a nude owner lacking the entitlements of the use and enjoyment of the fruits of the property until the termination of the usufruct. The position of the holder of a hereditary building or land lease is basically the same as that of the usufructuary, owing to the insignificance of the rent charge payable to the landowner.

The various institutions also differ as regards the types of social relationships in which they typically operate, and the kinds of economic concerns that they intend to address. Lease is commercially driven and usually entered into by strangers, while usufruct is usually set up in a husband's will to provide for his widow without depriving his children of their inherited title.

[13] See Guerts, 'Historical Development of Leases', pp. 357 ff. for the hybrid character of lease at common law.

[14] See Robinson, *Sources of Roman Law*, p. 118: 'Land was (in classical law) just one of the *res mancipi*; there were no special forms of conveyance for land, no special kinds of security over it, no special rules about succession to it.'

[15] See also Johnston, *Roman Law in Context*, p. 65 for the position in Roman law.

[16] See Nicholas, *Roman Law*, p. 145.

The obvious solution for the owner of agricultural or residential property who does not have the will or capital to exploit the property is to ensconce a tenant who has a financial or dwelling interest in the land or premises.[17] Ultimately, both landlord and tenant are to gain from such an arrangement. The agricultural tenant can collect the produce from the land, while the landlord benefits in that the economic condition of his/her property will be preserved and he/she will derive a monetary benefit from the property. Likewise, the residential tenant enjoys the luxury of a roof over his/her head, while the landlord collects a commercial rent from the property.

By contrast, usufruct and the other personal servitudes initially have a purely alimentary objective, namely to provide a means of subsistence for a family member.[18] These servitudes therefore have a social, as opposed to a strictly economic, target. They allow the holders to have the use of the property and to gather its natural and civil fruits for a set period lasting no longer than the holder's lifetime, provided the holder does not alter the basic character of the property. The holder is in effect the present beneficiary, who, for the time being, is allowed to exercise specific entitlements which will be transferred back to the nude owner on expiry of his/her rights.

The institutions of the hereditary building lease and the hereditary land lease, again, were initially closely linked to the development of unimproved land. The aim of the State and other public authorities were to develop wide tracts of wasteland for agricultural use and for the provision of housing. The holders were awarded with almost all the entitlements of ownership, namely the right of use, the gathering of fruits and even the right to dispose of the building or land lease. These extensive rights were granted in order to encourage the holders to construct buildings on the land or to develop wasteland into viable farming units. That land development was the primary aim of these institutions is evidenced by the fact that the rent charge or canon levied on the holders was minimal and not a commercial rent as in the case of lease.

At this stage it is appropriate to ask to what extent the various ways in which the profits are split between the parties increase the productivity

[17] See Johnston, *Roman Law in Context*, p. 63 who remarks that much is to be said for letting property to someone with a financial interest in it and not to have it administered by an administrator.

[18] See Johnston, 'Successive Rights', p. 155.

of the property. Under an agricultural lease, the tenant is obliged to exploit the property as the proverbial Roman *bonus paterfamilias*. In concrete terms, it means that the tenant must maintain the essential character of the property, only use it in ways authorised by the landlord, and return it in its original condition except for ordinary wear and tear. From this it is clear that the tenant is not allowed to develop the property to its full economic potential. The usufructuary is even more straitjacketed in his bid to generate the maximum profits. He/she is obliged, and can indeed be compelled, to exploit the property only in ways that have already been established. He/she is not only forbidden to use the property for commercial purposes (except if it was already so used) but, additionally, he/she cannot use it for any new purpose at all.[19] The underlying principle forbidding new forms of income is to preserve the property's agricultural productivity since other sources of revenue are perceived to be of only temporary benefit.[20] In principle, the usufructuary is moreover not allowed to improve the property, except in cases where it can easily be restored to its former condition.[21] Eventually, the usufructuary has to return the property at the expiry of the usufruct without impairment of its substance. This lack of interest in property development indicates that the aim of the institution of usufruct is not to allow the holder to develop the land to its full commercial or even agricultural potential.[22] By contrast, the explicit aim of the institutions of hereditary building lease and hereditary land lease is to develop unimproved land by the erection of buildings and the improvement of the agricultural productivity of the land. These institutions are thus the most suitable mechanisms for achieving land development.

A similarity between the institutions of lease and usufruct is that the parties involved in these institutions are treated unequally. Leases generally, though not always, exploit the tenant, while usufruct is carefully designed to protect the interests of the nude owner. The earliest agricultural tenants in Roman law were destitute persons who attached themselves to rich aristocrats (*patresfamilias*) for a living.[23] Although their difficulty in paying rent was relieved by the fact

[19] See in general *ibid.* 154–5, 166–7; Johnston, *Roman Law in Context*, p. 67.

[20] See Kehoe, *Roman Agrarian Economy*, p. 119.

[21] See in general Johnston, 'Successive Rights', p. 154.

[22] See Crook, *Law and Life in Rome*, pp. 152, 161.

[23] See also Guerts, 'Historical Development', p. 357 who states that at common law the tenant was originally regarded as the servant of the landlord. See, however, Johnston, *Roman Law in Context*, p. 62 who states that this did not apply to urban leases in Roman

that they could pay with a proportion of the produce of the land,[24] it caused landlords to push them to produce as good a crop as possible, thus prolonging their servile relationship with the landlord.[25] This could perhaps explain why tenants had no security of tenure and why they neither had a real right nor legal possession of the land but only detention.[26] Tenants were only given a remedy against the landlord for breaching his duty to provide them with undisturbed possession, and not directly against a third party who interfered with his occupation. If the owner had sold the property and the new owner failed to respect the lease, the tenant could not insist on continuing in occupation but could only sue the original landlord under their original contract.[27] Furthermore, in the event that the tenant did not wish to leave the property, the new owner was entitled to impose new and less favourable lease terms.[28] Because landlords and tenants were most often not equals, modern law regulated their relationship to prevent the more powerful party from abusing his position. We have seen that most of the modern jurisdictions have come to the aid of the tenant by granting him a possessory remedy against disturbance of his possession and by reversing the maxim 'sale breaks hire' to grant the tenant the right to stay on the land after the property has been transferred to a *bona fide* purchaser. Furthermore, most of the modern European jurisdictions have adopted tenant protection measures to make it more difficult to evict tenants who have no alternative accommodation.

Although the usufructuary was not recognised as the legal possessor of the property in Roman law,[29] he was accorded a real right. But the

law. There existed a substantial urban rental sector and the tenants were members of relatively high social classes who regularly hired residential premises for several years and typically paid their rent in lump sums at yearly or half-yearly intervals.

[24] According to Zimmermann, *Obligations*, p. 356, this was designed in Roman law to keep agricultural tenants (*coloni*) on the soil and thus to ensure, in the public interest, that the land continued to be cultivated.

[25] According to Zimmermann, *Obligations*, p. 353, the payment of rent in the form of a proportion of the harvest further worsened the position of these early agricultural tenants because slaves were appointed to supervise the tenants' cultivation of the land. This reduced the position of these tenants to that of tied serfs in late Roman law and caused them to run away or join a band of robbers.

[26] See Johnston, *Roman Law in Context*, p. 62 who states that it was held until recently that 'the law of lease was a paradigm of law forged in the interest of the landowning classes'.

[27] See Johnston, *Roman Law in Context*, p. 66.

[28] See Kehoe, *Roman Agrarian Economy*, p. 185.

[29] Watson, *Roman Private Law*, p. 90 plausibly suggests that the reason why usufructuaries were not accorded legal possession in Roman law related to the social context of

inherent conflict of interest between the usufructuary with a temporary interest in the property and the nude owner who will become the unrestricted owner of the property when the usufruct expires[30] was already carefully regulated in Roman law to prevent the usufructuary from substantially reducing the value of the property before it was returned to the nude owner. This is clear from the manner in which the usufructuary was restricted in his use and exploitation of the property as discussed above.

usufruct. The typical relationship between usufructuary and owner was that of mother and son, and woman had a very weak position in the eyes of the law.

[30] See Johnston, *Roman Law in Context*, p. 67.

Case 2

Most systems accept the maxim 'sale does not break hire' and acknowledge that a lease complying with certain formalities (which differ from jurisdiction to jurisdiction) is enforceable against third-party purchasers of the land. By contrast, personal servitudes, hereditary building rights and hereditary land leases are enforceable against third-party purchasers owing to the fact that they are recognised real rights and that their registration provides the necessary publicity to third parties. Interestingly, even though the Spanish Civil Code still adheres to the Roman law maxim *emptio tollit locationem* or *venta quita renta* and acknowledges in principle that sale supersedes lease, the Spanish Laws on Residential and Agricultural Leases entitle the tenant to stay on the property for various periods of time, depending on the circumstances. This is a good illustration of the functional approach of the Trento project: the eventual solution to the problem is more or less the same, no matter what route and arguments are adopted along the way.

Case 3

In all jurisdictions, the assets or patrimony of the owner (landlord) are strictly separated from the assets or patrimony of the holder of the time-limited right. Consequently, the equity of the holder of a limited real right cannot be attached by the creditors of the owner (A) and does not fall into his/her insolvent or bankrupt estate.

In a competition with other real rights, for instance, a prior registered mortgage, most systems follow the maxim *prior in tempore potior in iure* and accept that the limited real right that was established first (the mortgage) has priority over the limited real right that was only established later (the time-limited right). In some jurisdictions, however, there is still a drive to protect the rights of the tenant to the greatest possible extent on the grounds of legal policy considerations. In this regard, a Solomon-like solution is achieved by South African law, which provides that the land must first be sold in execution burdened with the lease and only free from the lease if the proceeds of the first sale were not sufficient to discharge the claim of the prior mortgage creditor. Similar legal policy considerations for the protection of subsequently established personal servitudes or contractual rights like that of the borrower or precarious holder, do not exist.

Case 4

In the course of time, most holders of time-limited interests were granted possessory remedies to protect their occupation. The modern civilian possessory remedies did not derive from the interdictal Roman system but from canon law which, in order to protect the order in society, required that the *status quo ante* had to be restored before going into the merits of the case.[1] Most modern civil jurisdictions shed the requirement that the dispossession had to be by force and eventually got rid of the distinction between possessors and mere holders and extended the remedy to most persons in physical control of the land. Previously, mere detentors such as tenants, borrowers for use and precarious holders of land had to rely on the owner of the land to institute a possessory action to restore their physical control. The modern extension of possessory remedies to these holders has the result that both the owner and the holder now have a possessory remedy to have the *status quo* restored. In such a case the action of the person in physical control of the land, for instance, the tenant, as opposed to the landlord, must be preferred and the latter will only be allowed to apply for restoration of possession if the former declines.

Some jurisdictions allow recovery from a third party (D) who acquired the property from the dispossessor (C) if it can be shown that D has to an extent participated in the unlawful dispossession.[2] In this regard, it is

[1] The historical source of modern possessory remedies is the *canon reintegranda* of the *Dectretum Gratiani* which entitled a bishop who has been expelled by a secular authority from his See to claim to be restored in his former position before the merits of his expulsion were considered. See Hahlo and Kahn, *Union of South Africa*, p. 454; Kleyn, 'Die Mandament van Spolie'.

[2] See the German, Greek, Italian and South African reports, Case 4.

preferable to accept that something more than knowledge on the part of D of C's unlawful dispossession[3] is required. This will be the case where, for example, as under Italian law, D was the 'moral author' of the dispossession.

Besides possessory remedies, some legal systems allow a *quasi-vindicatory* remedy[4] to holders with a better right to possession (*ius possidendi*) than the person in actual possession.[5] These persons derive their title from the owner, either in the form of a personal right (for example, as borrower or tenant) or a real right in the property (for example, as the holder of a personal servitude, a hereditary building lease or a hereditary land lease). This allows B to institute a vindicatory action against either C or D (whoever is in possession) for the return of the property. In case of competition of the two remedies, the swifter possessory remedy will be preferred.

[3] See the Austrian report, Case 4.

[4] It takes the form of an *actio Publiciana*, *vindicatio usufructus* or an *actio confessoria*.

[5] See e.g. the Danish, French, Portuguese and Austrian reports, Case 4.

Case 5

With regard to the duty to repair, there is a convergence between the default rule in leases and the duties of the parties under usufruct. The default rule in *leases* is that the landlord is responsible for major (extraordinary) repairs and for smaller repairs needed to render the property fit for its purpose,[1] while the tenant is responsible for minor (ordinary) repairs which fall outside this category[2] and which include repairs owing to wear and tear because the tenant is presumed to have caused these defects. In the case of *personal servitudes*, the nude owner is responsible for extraordinary repairs, whereas the holder of the personal servitude is responsible for ordinary repairs necessitated by his/her exploitation of the property in accordance with its economic purpose, again including repairs necessitated by ordinary wear and tear. A major difference is that the amount which the holder of a personal servitude can spend on repairs is limited to a total of two-thirds of the income of the land. Furthermore, unless serious damage may result from non-compliance with this obligation, the nude owner cannot force the usufructuary, subject to his/her obligation to return the property on expiry with the preservation of its substance, to carry out the repairs.

With regard to *specific cases*, some jurisdictions emphasise the fact that the property must remain fit for the purpose for which it was let, and

[1] The purpose is determined by the terms of the contract and the surrounding circumstances, including the previous and known intended use of the land. In Austria, for example, the condition of a residential property must not pose a risk to the residents' health.

[2] This corresponds to the English Landlord and Tenant Act 1954, which implies certain terms in favour of the tenant in respect of short residential leases. See also the repair clauses in the Agricultural Holdings Act 1986.

hold the landlord responsible for the defective *heating system*, the *dilapidated fences* and the *flaking paint*. Other jurisdictions, at least in the case of agricultural leases, characterise the dilapidated fences, flaking paint and minor defects in the heating system as defects arising from normal wear and tear, and place the responsibility for repairs on the tenant. In the case of personal servitudes, most reports interestingly classify these defects as minor defects which must be repaired by the holder of the personal servitude.[3] The reports, however, warn that if any repair requires extraordinary expense, the obligation to carry out repairs will shift to the nude owner. The French report, for example, shows that the nude owner will be responsible for replacing the fences, but not for limited or specific repairs to the fences.

In most jurisdictions, the landlord will be responsible for the repair of the *roof* in order to make the premises fit for the purpose for which it is used and also if the damage was caused by *force majeure*.[4] In the case of personal servitudes, most jurisdictions regard *minor* repairs of the roof necessitated by the storm (the restoration of a few tiles) as ordinary repairs for which the usufructuary is responsible, while major repairs needed for the conservation of the property are classified as extraordinary or unforeseen repairs which are the responsibility of the nude owner. Interestingly, the Belgian report concludes that if damage is caused by *force majeure*, neither the nude owner nor the holder of a personal servitude will be responsible for the repair of the roof and so, if either one of them does effect the repairs, he/she will be entitled to claim a contribution towards the cost of the repairs from the other.

Most jurisdictions[5] will not hold the landlord responsible for the replacement of an *obsolescent heating system* as they classify it as an improvement and not as a repair. However, a substantial minority tries to impose responsibility on the landlord by equating obsolescence with non-repair, by considering renewal as a form of repair, or by classifying the replacement as a conservation measure or necessary for the health of the residents. In the case of personal servitudes, some jurisdictions classify the replacement of an obsolescent heating system as an extraordinary repair and hold the nude owner responsible.

[3] In Austria, the liability for repairs is limited to the income from the property.

[4] In South Africa, the rationale is that the landlord is responsible for procuring insurance and paying the insurance premiums.

[5] E.g. Germany, Greece, Portugal, Spain, Belgium and Poland, Case 5.

Other jurisdictions classify it as an improvement which need not be executed by any of the parties. If carried out by the holder of the personal servitude, the latter will be entitled to claim reimbursement on expiry of the servitude.[6]

Most jurisdictions[7] accept that the *default rules are not mandatory* and that parties can either expressly or impliedly deviate from them in a contract of lease or in a separate contract. The tendency is to move as many repair obligations as possible to the tenant, but most jurisdictions strictly construe deviations in order to prevent the tenant being overburdened in this regard. In the case of personal servitudes, contractual provisions deviating from the default rules are only encountered in the case of personal servitudes created by agreement *inter vivos*, and mostly for tax purposes.[8]

In principle, each party is responsible for *loss caused by his/her negligent acts or omissions*. The tenant is therefore liable for loss caused by his/her own negligence and the negligence of members of his/her family. Conversely, the landlord is responsible for further loss caused by his/her negligent failure to repair as in the case where the wall seriously deteriorates on account of not being repainted on time. In contrast, most jurisdictions hold the usufructuary liable for the deteriorated wall on account of non-compliance with his/her duty to preserve the substance of the property – either for the cost of repair, or in delict for the economic loss suffered by the nude owner. Other jurisdictions classify the repair of the deteriorated wall as an extraordinary repair for which the nude owner is responsible.

[6] Reimbursement will probably be based on *negotiorum gestio*. See the Greek and South African reports, Case 5.

[7] E.g. Germany, Greece, Portugal, Spain, South Africa, Denmark, Hungary and Poland, Case 5.

[8] See the German and Belgian reports, Case 5. In Germany, contractual provisions to shift the obligation for extraordinary repairs to the holder of a right of use are not accepted.

Case 6

There is a convergence between the entitlements of a tenant and a usufructuary to the fruits of agricultural property. The default position is that the tenant's exploitation is subject to the obligation to restore the property on expiry of the lease to the condition in which it would have been had it been exploited in an orderly fashion during the currency of the lease. The tenant is not allowed to impair the substance, economic function or the income-bearing capacity of the land, and may not, without the consent of the landlord, substantially change the existing method of cultivation. In similar fashion, the holder of a personal servitude must cultivate the land in accordance with its economic purpose and accepted standards of cultivation and return the property without impairment of its substance.

Most jurisdictions, with the exception of England, allow the tenant to cut *trees destined to be cut* (*silva caedua*) at regular intervals in accordance with the accepted standards of exploitation in that particular locality.[1] Similarly, the usufructuary is allowed to fell plantations at regular intervals in accordance with good husbandry, local custom and regional regulations on the assumption that fruits destined to be cut are natural fruits. Other than in Poland, where certain trees or shrubs like bamboo are regarded as fruits, the *cutting down of trees and shrubs* is allowed only in the interests of proper maintenance and management of the land concerned. The tenant may therefore remove and replace old and dead trees, branches and shrubs. In the case of usufruct, fruit trees, decorative trees and shrubs are not regarded as fruits[2] and may only be removed in the interests of good husbandry and orderly exploitation.

[1] E.g. every seven years in Germany, Case 6.
[2] Poland makes an exception in the case of renewable trees and shrubs such as bamboo.

Undergrowth, dead branches and shrubs and trees uprooted or damaged by a storm may be cleared subject to the obligation of replacement. Some reports allow the *usuary* to collect wood, dead branches, dead trees and dead undergrowth from plantations (and presumably also from fruit trees, decorative trees and shrubs) as firewood for his/her own use and that of his/her family.

While the *tenant* is entitled to continue *existing mining operations* on the property, *the opening of new mines* and quarries go beyond the agricultural purpose of the land and will only be permitted with the consent of the landlord and the grant of a mining concession. Most of the jurisdictions[3] consider stones and minerals as fruits and therefore allow the *usufructuary* to continue to work *existing quarries and mines* for stone and minerals.[4] In general, the *opening of new mines* is not allowed on the grounds that it will change the economic purpose of the land, amount to disorderly exploitation[5] and substantially impair the substance of the property.[6] However, under special mining laws in Austria, Portugal, Spain and Italy, either the nude owner or usufructuary with the nude owner's consent may obtain a licence to start mining operations. Because of the restricted content of their rights, the *usuary* and the *habitator* will not be entitled to open new quarries or mines or even work existing ones.

Most jurisdictions allocate *standing crops* on expiry of a lease or usufruct to the landlord or nude owner respectively. Under both institutions, the landlord or nude owner is obliged to compensate the tenant or usufructuary to some extent for the cost of production of the crop. Furthermore, if harvesting occurred before the termination of the lease or usufruct, the tenant or usufructuary is obliged to leave a certain quantity of seeds, hay and fertiliser as required for the orderly cultivation of the land during the subsequent season. Interestingly, South African jurisprudence allows the tenant to re-enter the land to harvest standing crops if he/she reasonably expected to harvest the crops prior to expiry of the lease.

[3] See e.g. the German, Austrian, Greek, Belgian, Dutch, Portuguese, Spanish and Italian reports, Case 6.

[4] Greek law requires an expert appointed by the court to prepare a plan for the exploitation of existing mines.

[5] In Germany and Portugal the usufructuary is allowed to quarry for stone if this does not conflict with the ordinary exploitation of the land or alters its economic destination.

[6] See the German, Greek, Belgian and Spanish reports, Case 6.

With regard to the *capacity to create further rights*, the tenant is only allowed to assign or sub-let the land with the landlord's consent, whereas the usufructuary is allowed to let the property without the consent of the nude owner and to collect the rent as civil fruits until the expiry of the usufruct. In both cases, the sub-lease or lease will expire on termination of the principal lease or usufruct. Any loss suffered by the sub-tenant can be claimed from the sub-landlord. Where the lease or usufruct expires six months before the next annual rent is due, the rent is divided between the two parties proportionate to the time periods before and after the termination. Spanish, Italian and Hungarian law do not allow the *usuary* or the *habitator* to let the property. Under the French Civil Code, a surviving spouse with a right of habitation is allowed to let residential premises which no longer suit her (for example, where she has to move to a retirement home) and use the rent for necessities.

Case 7

Neither the *tenant*, *usufructuary*, *usuary* or *habitator* will be allowed to change, for example, a dwelling house into a warehouse, or a farm into a hotel without the consent of the landlord or nude owner because both the tenant and the holder of a personal servitude are obliged to exploit the property properly and in accordance with its nature[1] and to return the property in the condition that it was received. The French position that a residential tenant may use the property for either residential or commercial purposes, as long as neither clients nor merchandise enter the property, is no real exception. The prohibition on alteration seems to be the predominant position irrespective of whether the value of the property is enhanced by the conversion, whether the land can be returned to its former condition at low cost, or whether there is a radical change in the nature of the neighbourhood. Exceptions are, for instance, English law, where conversion is permitted where a blanket prohibition on a change in the character of the land can render tenant user covenants obsolete or otherwise oppressive and thus susceptible to judicial discharge or modification; French case law, which allows a usufructuary to change a private residence into a place of business as long as this does not constitute an 'abuse of enjoyment'; and some jurisdictions which hint at allowing minor changes or conversions that enhance the value of the property but only as long as the 'economic purpose' or the 'fundamental function' of the property is maintained.

Under Belgian, French and Italian law a radical change of the neighbourhood or a change in the zoning of the land subject to a usufruct may qualify as a socio-economic factor outside the control of the

[1] Or 'economic purpose'.

usufructuary, which justifies an alteration of the purpose of the property. In Spain, the nude owner is apparently entitled to replace the burdened property with an equivalent or to sell the property and pay the usufructuary legal interest on the proceeds of the sale for the duration of the usufruct. Where being forced to 'exploit' the property caused severe hardship to a widow, South African case law allowed the nude owner to sell the property and to allow the widow a usufruct on the proceeds of the sale on the grounds that this was financially sensible and also to the advantage of the nude owner.[2]

Most national reporters indicate that the *usuary* and *habitator* will not be entitled to effect the above conversions under any of the circumstances mentioned.[3] By contrast, the holder of a *hereditary land lease* can alter the destination of the property when the character of the neighbourhood changes, provided that this would enhance the value of the land. Similarly, the holder of a *hereditary building lease* is entitled to exploit new structures on the land to their fullest economic potential, even if this involves changing the property's economic purpose.

2 See the Belgian, French, Italian, Spanish and South African reports, Case 7.
3 See e.g. the Greek and South African reports, Case 7.

Case 8

Apart from claiming for specific performance, the most important remedy of the discontented *landlord* is cancellation of the contract which can in appropriate circumstances be supplemented by an eviction order[1] and a claim for damages.[2] Legislation and case law in Germany made the eviction of tenants under residential leases more difficult. Some jurisdictions do not allow a claim for minor damage prior to the termination of the lease in lieu of insisting on repairs.[3] Alternatively, the landlord can request a court order to compel the tenant to effect repairs or to restrain the tenant from activities which violate the contract, such as exploiting the property improperly, damaging the property or substantially altering the property.[4]

By contrast, the nude owner is not entitled to cancel a usufruct or evict a usufructuary prior to the expiry of the usufruct.[5] However, some jurisdictions allow the landowner to demand the return of the property if a request for security is ignored or if the property is seriously damaged or devalued through gross neglect of maintenance.[6] Depending on the seriousness of the circumstances, the court may either order the complete termination of the usufruct or order the return of the property to the nude owner, subject to an obligation

[1] See e.g. the German, Austrian, Greek, French, Belgian, Portuguese, Spanish, South African and Hungarian reports, Case 8.

[2] See e.g. the German, Greek, French, Belgian, Spanish, Portuguese, Danish, South African and Hungarian reports, Case 8.

[3] See e.g. the Belgian and South African reports, Case 8.

[4] See e.g. the German, Austrian, English, Danish and South African reports, Case 8.

[5] See e.g. the German and Polish reports, Case 8.

[6] See the Austrian, French, Belgian, Italian, Portuguese and Spanish reports, Case 8.

to pay a fixed annual sum to the usufructuary until the expiry of the usufruct.[7]

A major difference between usufruct and lease is that the most important remedy of the nude owner is an injunction (interdict) against the usufructuary, compelling him/her to refrain from serious or repeated violations of his/her obligations,[8] which in the case of minor violations is restricted by the fact that the usufructuary has a certain degree of discretion in deciding how and when to comply with his/her obligations. This forces the prudent nude owner to wait until the expiry of the usufruct before requesting restoration of the property and compensation.

Another difference is that in cases where the usufructuary's conduct constitutes a risk of serious damage, most jurisdictions allow the nude owner to demand either security against future damage to the property[9] or the placement of the administration of the usufruct under the supervision of the court, a professional manager or even the nude owner.[10] The management of the property is handed back to the usufructuary as soon as the grounds justifying the placement no longer prevail.

A third difference is that most jurisdictions allow a claim for damages *only* on termination of the usufruct. Exceptionally, in Belgium, the landowner may claim compensation for damages even during the term of the usufruct if immediate and certain damage can be proved.

The nude owner generally has fewer remedies in the case of misconduct by the holders of the lesser servitudes of *use* and *habitation*. Some jurisdictions allow a court order to stop interference with the rights of the nude owner and an action for damage caused negligently or intentionally. Generally, no security can be claimed against future unconscionable use of the property. Under Spanish law, the entitlements rights of use and habitation expire automatically in the event of serious

[7] See the Belgian, French and Italian reports, Case 8. In Portugal and Spain, the landowner must hand over the net income of the property to the usufructuary every year.

[8] See e.g. the German, Austrian, Italian and South African reports, Case 8.

[9] See e.g. the German, Austrian, Greek, Italian, Hungarian and Polish reports, Case 8. In Poland, security can be demanded only where the usufructuary is allowed to undertake mining activities.

[10] See the German, Austrian, Greek and Dutch reports, Case 8. Under Italian law, the court may order instead that the property be leased out. Under Greek law, this remedy is also available if the usufructuary is unwilling or unable to provide security.

misconduct and if the relationship is strained. The Polish Civil Code allows either party to request a court order to convert some or all of the habitator's rights into a fixed annual sum, or, in an extreme case, to terminate the right of habitation.

Owing to the fact that the constitutive agreement establishing a *hereditary building lease* prescribes the parties' rights and obligations in much more detail than those creating a personal servitude, the landowner's most important remedy is an action for breach of contract. If the holder has substantially altered the physical condition of the structure without the landowner's consent (as required by the contract), the court may, on request, order the restoration of the original structure or award compensation for damage suffered. Under German law, the landowner may in addition claim for the re-transfer of the building right against payment of fair compensation for improvements if the conditions are met.

In a *hereditary land lease*, the landowner may terminate the lease if the holder seriously fails to comply with his obligations,[11] grossly abuses his/her rights or causes serious damage to the property.[12] Under Belgian and Dutch law, the landowner is entitled to claim expenses and compensation for damage and loss of rent caused by the holder's negligence and lack of maintenance.

[11] E.g. under Dutch law if the holder fails to pay the annual rent for two consecutive years and under Polish law if he fails to erect buildings that he undertook to erect.

[12] See the Belgian and Polish reports, Case 8.

Case 9

Under a *lease*, tenants are in general allowed to *sell or donate* their interest in the form of either an assignment of the right of use to a third party,[1] or the transfer of both the rights and obligations of the tenant to a third party (*Vertragsübernahme*).[2] Most jurisdictions require the consent of the landlord, if not dispensed with by local custom (Greece) or a special law (Portugal). Exceptions include the Spanish system, which allows assignment of agricultural leases to spouses or descendants of the tenant without the landlord's consent; the French system, which allows their assignment to spouses, civil partners or descendants of the tenant with the court's authorisation; and the Netherlands, which allows a co-tenant to continue a residential lease after the tenant's death.

The default rule in the case of *usufruct*, a *hereditary building lease* and a *hereditary land lease* is that the holder is entitled to sell or donate his/her rights without the consent of the landowner. The highly personal character of a *usufruct* causes the right of the transferee to terminate on expiry of the usufruct.[3] If the constitutive instrument contains a prohibition against transfer, any alienation is null and void and the prohibition can also be enforced against the transferee.[4] Since the holder of a *hereditary building right* or a *hereditary land lease* acquires a right akin to ownership which is freely heritable and alienable,[5] the holder can sell or donate his/her interest in the land and transfer the right to another[6] if this is not restricted in the constitutive instrument.

[1] See e.g. the Greek, Belgian and Spanish reports, Case 9.
[2] See the German and Austrian reports, Case 9.
[3] See e.g. the French, Belgian, Spanish, Italian and Dutch reports, Case 9.
[4] See e.g. the Italian report, Case 9. [5] See the Italian report, Case 9.
[6] See the German, Belgian, Dutch, Portuguese, Spanish and Italian reports, Case 9.

Only the rights under the personal servitudes of use and habitation are considered so personal that they cannot be sold or donated.[7]

The majority of jurisdictions regard a *lease* as a mere personal right and therefore do not allow its holder to *mortgage* it[8] but only allow the rights under a lease to be pledged or assigned in security of a debt.[9] The jurisdictions that allow leases to be registered[10] allow leases to be mortgaged without the landlord's prior consent.[11] While some jurisdictions[12] accept that a *usufruct* cannot be mortgaged because it cannot be transferred as such, most jurisdictions[13] expressly sanction the mortgage of a usufruct, or at least the rights under a usufruct, with some stipulating that the mortgage will not be terminated if the usufruct is terminated early by a voluntary act of the usufructuary or when the secured claim is discharged.[14] While it is generally accepted that the *personal servitudes of use and habitation* can neither be transferred nor mortgaged owing to their highly personal character,[15] South African law, curiously, allows the habitator to mortgage his/her interest in the property. The holders of a *hereditary building lease* and a *hereditary land lease*[16] are entitled to mortgage their right. On merger of the titles to the land and the building lease, the Italian Civil Code provides that mortgages over the land and the building right continue to burden each of them separately. Under Austrian law, a mortgage over a building right continues to exist as a mortgage over the land when the building right expires and ownership of the building passes to the landowner. The Austrian and Italian law also subject the compensation for improvements awarded on expiry of the building lease to a mortgage registered over the building lease.

With regard to the creation of rights, the default rule in most jurisdictions is that the *tenant* is not entitled to sub-let residential[17] or

7 See e.g. the German, Austrian, Greek, Belgian, Dutch, Portuguese, Italian, Hungarian, Polish and South African reports, Case 9.
8 See e.g. the German, Greek, French, Belgian, Italian, Danish and Polish reports, Case 9.
9 See the German report which warns that leases are not popular as collateral in practice because of their inefficient enforcement in execution proceedings.
10 In Austria it is also possible to mortgage an unregistered lease since it is accepted that all rights may be mortgaged.
11 See e.g. the Austrian, Spanish and South African reports, Case 9.
12 See the German and Polish reports, Case 9.
13 See e.g. the Greek, Austrian, Spanish, French and Portuguese reports, Case 9.
14 See e.g. the Austrian, Portuguese, Spanish and Italian reports, Case 9.
15 See e.g. the French, Belgian, Dutch, Portuguese, Spanish, Italian, Hungarian and Polish reports, Case 9.
16 See the Belgian, Dutch and Polish reports.
17 See the Greek and Polish reports.

agricultural property[18] without the consent of the landlord.[19] Some jurisdictions allow the sub-lease of only part of residential property with the consent of the landlord provided the tenant continues to occupy the other part of the premises.[20] If concluded without the consent of the landlord, the tenant may not charge the sub-tenant a disproportionate rent[21] and, on termination of the principal lease, the landlord is generally allowed to evict the sub-tenant. In most jurisdictions, the *usufructuary* is not entitled to create a real right like a right of habitation over his/her interest but he/she may create a personal right like a loan, and in some jurisdictions a lease over his interest.[22] On expiry of the usufruct, some jurisdictions compel the nude owner to respect the lease concluded by the usufructuary to a certain extent.[23] Italian law allows a usufructuary to create a second usufruct, right of use or right of habitation over his/her interest in the property. As in the case of a sub-tenancy under a lease, the tenant or second usufructuary of a principal usufructuary is dependent on the title of the principal usufructuary. In Spain, Belgium and Italy, the holder of a *right of use* or *habitation* cannot create a second *usus* or right of habitation over his/her interest in the property owing to its highly personal character.[24] Interestingly, South African case law allows the usuary to let out spare rooms and the habitator to let out the entire dwelling-house. In France, the habitator is allowed to rent out the house to his/her spouse, civil partner or descendants. The holder of a *hereditary building lease* is entitled to burden the right with all kinds of separate limited real rights, including a praedial servitude,[25] a usufruct and a second hereditary building right. He/she may not, however, grant a hereditary land lease over his building right in tandem with a lease over the building right.[26] Interests granted over a hereditary building right will expire on termination of

[18] See the Italian report.

[19] See e.g. the German, Austrian, Greek, Portuguese, Spanish, Dutch, Italian, English, South African, Danish and Hungarian reports, Case 9. This is subject to local custom (Greece), special legislation (Portugal) and special circumstances (Poland, Belgium and Denmark).

[20] See e.g. the Belgian, Dutch and Hungarian reports, Case 9.

[21] See the Spanish and Portuguese reports, Case 9.

[22] See e.g. the German, Austrian, Greek, French, Belgian, Portuguese, Spanish and Hungarian reports, Case 9.

[23] See the Austrian and Belgian reports, Case 9.

[24] See the German report with regard to the permanent right of habitation (*Dauerwohnrecht*).

[25] See the Italian report.

[26] See the Portuguese and Spanish reports.

the building right. Similarly, the holder of a *hereditary land lease* is entitled to create separate real rights over the hereditary lease, such as a usufruct[27] and a hereditary building right, but not another hereditary land lease in tandem with a lease over his/her interest in the land.

In jurisdictions which regard the rights under a lease as mere personal rights, a *lease* cannot be attached by the tenant's creditors. Claims against the landlord for improvements or repairs or the rental income flowing from a sub-lease may, however, be attached.[28] In jurisdictions which regard rights under a lease as real rights or executable receivables,[29] a lease can be attached, with the exception of an Austrian residential lease which is essential for the tenant and his/her family. Most jurisdictions regard a *usufruct* as an attachable economic asset in the usufructuary's patrimony. However, the purchaser in execution will only acquire a contingent right which will expire on the usufructuary's death.[30] The rights of *use* and *habitation* are so inherently intertwined with the person of the holder that they cannot be attached,[31] which makes the right of habitation attractive for estate planning purposes. Nevertheless, German law provides that personal servitudes may be attached with the permission of the nude owner, and the South African report suggests that since the *habitator* is allowed to sub-let the dwelling, his/her interest is also attachable. All the jurisdictions regard *hereditary building rights* and *hereditary land leases*[32] as valuable limited real rights which are attachable.[33]

The same considerations applicable to execution proceedings against B apply equally to B's bankruptcy. A *usufruct*, *hereditary building right* and *hereditary land lease* will be included in B's insolvency assets. The rules applicable to attachment also apply to B's insolvency in the case of a lease. Under Belgian, South African and Danish law, the administrator in insolvency is entitled to adopt or terminate the lease. By contrast, a right of use or habitation will generally not be included in the insolvency assets of the holder.

[27] The prevailing academic view in Belgium is that only a usufruct may be created by the holder.
[28] See e.g. the German, Greek, Italian, Belgian, Dutch and Danish reports, Case 9.
[29] See e.g. Spain, England and Poland, Case 9.
[30] See e.g. the German, Austrian, Greek, Belgian, Dutch, Portuguese, Spanish and Italian reports, Case 9.
[31] See e.g. the Belgian, Dutch, Portuguese, Spanish and Italian reports, Case 9.
[32] See the Belgian, Dutch and Polish reports, Case 9.
[33] See the German, Austrian, Belgian, Dutch, Portuguese, Spanish and Italian reports, Case 9.

Case 10

The reports suggest four alternative mechanisms where the landowner does not want to participate in the construction and initial management of the structure, but wants to retain control of the structure and have eventual unburdened ownership of the land. The favoured solution is the mechanisms based on limited real rights,[1] with the hereditary building lease being the preferred mechanism. This solution is preferred to the combination of various traditional or new types of contracts that can achieve the desired goal. The limited real right solution is also preferred to the full ownership solution where full ownership is transferred to the developer with the landowner retaining a right of repurchase.

[1] Leasehold covenants are an exception to this. The position will therefore be different if the purchaser acquires the development site itself where leasehold covenants can come into play.

Case 11

With regard to the *option of the developer to purchase the land* from the landowner, we have seen that options can be construed as personal rights, limited real rights (mainly in the mould of a right of pre-emption), and personal rights which acquire proprietary effect on registration. If construed as a mere personal right, the option is only enforceable against the third party purchaser of the land if the latter had the required knowledge of the option. If construed as a limited real right, the holder of the option (the developer) will be entitled to assume the rights and obligations of C as set out in any subsequent sale and transfer agreement concluded between A and C. If the option takes the form of a right to purchase the property, German law construes this as a personal right which can be given real effect against a third-party purchaser by registering a prior notification in the Land Register.

Most jurisdictions accept that the *transfer of a maintenance obligation* to a third party successor-in-title will only be effective between the parties to the constitutive agreement. In English and Scots law the beneficiary (B) cannot enforce the maintenance obligation against the successor-in-title because the latter is not privy to the contract and because positive covenants do not 'run with the land'.[1] B's position can, however, be strengthened by fortifying an undertaking by A that his successors-in-title will be burdened with the obligation with a penalty clause. This will force A and his successors-in-title to transfer the land to a third party purchaser subject to a chain of conditions

[1] Leasehold covenants are an exception to this. The position will therefore be different if the purchaser acquires the development site itself where leasehold covenants can come into play.

or covenants burdening every third party purchaser with the maintenance obligation.[2] Such a maintenance obligation can also be enforced against a third-party purchaser if this positive obligation can be construed as ancillary to a right capable of registration, such as a hereditary building right or a hereditary land lease.[3]

[2] Belgian law construes this as a stipulation in favour of a third party.

[3] See the German, Spanish and Belgian reports, Case 11. Depending on their exact phrasing, such rights and obligations constitute an integral part of the real right of *superficies* or *emphyteusis* if registered together with the principal right, and are therefore effective against third party purchasers.

Case 12

If A wants to exploit *an existing building* as a shopping centre without managing it directly, but wishes to retain some control over the structure and still have unburdened ownership of the building at the end of the period, the obvious solution is to enter into a *commercial lease*[1] or a *management contract*[2] with B. In jurisdictions which allow the exploitation of existing buildings by the holder of a *hereditary building lease* or a *hereditary land lease*, the same result can be achieved by the grant of such rights to B. The Belgian report suggests that this is also possible by the grant of a *usufruct* of the land to B for a fixed term. The *sale and repurchase device* suggested by the Danish report might not give A the necessary proprietary protection.

The institutions of a *hereditary building lease* (*superficies*) and a *hereditary land lease* (*emphyteusis*) were originally designed by the State and *other public institutions* like local authorities and city councils to conclude arrangements with developers to develop unimproved land in the public interest, subject to the proviso that the land and the improvements must be returned to the State or other public institution after a fixed term.[3] This is evidenced by the special Italian Law of 1971, which gives municipalities the authority to expropriate urban land and grant rights of *superficies* to developers for a fixed term of between sixty and ninety-nine years for the purpose of constructing affordable housing units on the expropriated land.

[1] See the Austrian, Greek, French, Belgian, Portuguese, Spanish and English reports, Case 12.

[2] See the Belgian and Danish reports, Case 12.

[3] Before 1999, a hereditary building right could only be created in Austria in favour of the state or the church.

The use of these institutions has in the course of time been extended to private developers. Public institutions must comply with national and European Union public procurement provisions.[4] In Portugal, hereditary building leases granted by a public institution must last at least seventy years, the grant must contain provisions against speculative transactions, but no time limits for the completion of constructions, and transfer may be made subject to prior authorisation or a right of pre-emption in favour of the public authority.

Some jurisdictions allow public authorities to grant a concession instead of the above hereditary rights to a developer, which can be shaped to satisfy the needs of the public body, for example, by including the right to terminate or alter such concession in the public interest. The Belgian and French reports contain details of recent legislation on Public Private Partnerships to facilitate the provision of public services and the construction of houses.

[4] E.g. public tender provisions.

Modern significance of time-limited interests in land

We could gather only scant evidence of the modern practical significance of the various time-limited interests in land. However, our reporters were asked to give an idea of the importance of the respective interests by giving each a rating of between 0 and 10 (see Appendix, below). This rating gives an indication of the frequency with which each time-limited interest is used today.

First of all, residential and agricultural leases are important in most countries. On the other hand, loan for use and revocable permission to use land (*precarium*) seem to be of very limited significance in modern times.

Usufruct seems to be a popular time-limited interest, especially in a family context. In this context, the law of succession, by virtue of which usufructuary interests are still largely recognised, plays an important role. In certain jurisdictions usufruct is a popular device in the practical sphere of estate and tax planning.[1]

Use and habitation are much less frequently used. One notable exception is Italy, where the practical importance of usufruct was radically reduced by a change to the law of succession in 1975. Since then, the right of habitation seems to have superseded usufruct in practical application. In Spain, following trends in the law of succession, usufruct and use and habitation appear to be equally important.

Hereditary land leases (*emphyteusis*) and hereditary building leases (*superficies*) enjoy a mixed practical application. In Belgium and England (in the form of long leaseholds), they are still often used. In Poland, the same is true for the former, but not for the latter. Belgium

[1] See Part I, Ch. 4.

has experienced a revival of the use of the hereditary land lease (*erfpacht*) by public authorities as mechanism for the implementation of various welfare policies and other political objectives, especially in the sphere of land planning, the provision of housing and community financing.[2] In 2006, the court of Cassation had to pronounce on the minimum duration of a hereditary land lease granted by a private landowner to a private person.[3] Since 2003, certain Belgian municipalities granted hereditary building leases over their sewerage systems to American enterprises for a term of ninety-nine years, with an immediate retransfer to these local authorities for a term of twenty-five years with an option to purchase at the end of the twenty-five years. This cross-border leasing of public sewerage systems had fiscal benefits for American investors and helped local authorities to update their outdated sewerage works.[4]

In Italy, hereditary building leases (*superficies*) are sometimes granted to football associations by public authorities over public land to develop football stadiums, which gives *superficies* a qualitative rather than a quantitative importance in that country. The hereditary land lease (*emphyteusis*) has virtually disappeared in Italy owing to unfavourable legislation that significantly impedes its practical application. Instead, local authorities grant ordinary leases to developers for the development of unimproved land in return for a nominal rent.

There are also instances in which hereditary land leases (*emphyteusis*) have been utilised in the Netherlands. In 2000, the local authority of The Hague converted a temporary hereditary land lease (*erfpacht*) of seventy-five years for the construction of houses into a land lease in perpetuity, accompanied by a considerable increase in the yearly rent (canon). The sitting holders contended that this was in conflict with the general principles of orderly management and the general private law principles of reasonableness and equity.[5] Moreover, the Dutch Department of Public Works has in the past granted hereditary land leases for the development of river banks, channels and harbours. Recently, the Commissioners of Crown Lands granted hereditary land leases over agricultural plots in the reclaimed polders of the Ijsel Lake. If a public authority owns the land, the constitutive agreement usually makes

[2] See van Oevelen, 'Actuele ontwikkelingen', pp. 342–3. See also Vanhove and Baudoncq, 'Combinatie van beperkt zakelijke rechten', p. 135.

[3] See Vanhove, 'Note on the Decision of the Court of Cassation', pp. 678 ff.

[4] Verstappen, *Erfpacht, opstal en vruggebruik*, pp. 1–2.

[5] See Struycken, 'Erfpacht en redelijkheid', p. 91.

provision for the enforcement of conditions by public sanctions.[6] Presently, combinations of hereditary land leases (*erfpacht*) and hereditary building leases (*opstal*) are being granted at an increasing rate to municipalities and financial institutions over agricultural land for the construction of conduits for the transportation of gas and other chemical substances.[7]

[6] Pitlo, in Reehuis, Heisterkamp, van Maanen and de Jong, *Het Nederlands Burgerlijk Recht*, vol. 3, p. 496.

[7] Pitlo, 'Goederenrecht', pp. 511–12. While not a widely used device in Louisiana, it was suggested by Rome, 'An Elegy for Emphyteusis', p. 17, that hereditary land leases could be revived to restore public and private land devastated by Hurricane Katrina.

APPENDIX

The importance of the various time-limited interests in land in individual jurisdictions

Reporters in individual jurisdictions were asked to indicate contexts such as family, inheritance, real estate, corporate, commercial business etc. and to rate the importance for legal practice and use in society, with 10 as very frequently used and 0 as virtually non-existent.

Belgium

Reporter: Alain-Laurent Verbeke (Feb. 2011)

Time-limited interest	Context	Importance	Comments
Residential lease		10	
Agricultural lease		10	
Loan for use	Family real estate	4	
Precarium	Business	2	
Usufruct	Family	10	
Use and habitation	Family	4	
Hereditary land lease (*emphyteusis*)	Real estate	10	
Hereditary building lease (*superficies*)	Real estate	10	

Denmark

Reporter: Hans Henrik Edlund (Jan. 2011)

Time-limited interest	Context	Importance	Comments
Residential lease	Commercial business	10	
Agricultural lease	Commercial business	4	
Loan for use	Family and commercial business	2	
Precarium	Family and real estate	1	
Usufruct	Family and real estate	1	
Use and habitation		0	
Hereditary land lease (*emphyteusis*)		0	
Hereditary building lease (*superficies*)	Commercial business	4	

England

Reporter: Oliver Radley-Gardner (Feb. 2011)

Time-limited interest	Context	Importance	Comments
Residential lease	Family	10	
Agricultural lease	Business and family	10	
Loan for use	Business	3	This might occur, but in reality would be a lease or a mortgage.
Precarium		0	Not really known to English law, might be a 'licence'.
Usufruct	Business and also private	5	Really, English law knows only profits *à prendre*, which are not time limited.
Use and habitation		0	
Hereditary land lease (*emphyteusis*)	All contexts	10	This is probably as close as one gets to the concept of the English lease.
Hereditary building lease (*superficies*)	All contexts	10	Would again be akin functionally to the English lease.

Germany

Reporter: Michael von Hinden (Feb. 2011)

Time-limited interest	Context	Importance	Comments
Residential lease	Urban	10	
Agricultural lease	Agriculture	5	
Loan for use	Family	5	Pretty rare with regard to immovables
Precarium		0	
Usufruct	Family, tax, corporate	7	
Use and habitation	Family	7	
Hereditary land lease (*emphyteusis*)	Various	6	Hereditary building right (*erbbaurecht)*
Hereditary building lease (*superficies*)	Various	6	Hereditary building right (*erbbaurecht)*

Greece

Reporter: Eugenia Dacoronia (Jan. 2011)

Time-limited interest	Context	Importance	Comments
Residential lease	Real estate	10	There are no official statistic data on any of the categories. Rate of importance based on personal estimate.
Agricultural lease		6	
Loan for use		5	
Precarium			
Usufruct	Family	8	
Use and habitation	Family	6	
Hereditary land lease (*emphyteusis*)			
Hereditary building lease (*superficies*)			

Hungary

Reporter: Csongor István Nagy (Feb. 2011)

Time-limited interest	Context	Importance	Comments
Residential lease	Commercial, business	6	In Hungary, residential lease is less widespread as opposed to residential ownership.
Agricultural lease	Commercial, business	8	Very common, owing to restrictions on ownership.
Loan for use	Family	4	
Precarium		0	Virtually non-existent.
Usufruct	Inheritance, family	10	Very rarely commercial.
Use and habitation	Inheritance, family	3	
Hereditary land lease *(emphyteusis)*	Infrastructural leases (airports)	1	Exceptional.
Hereditary building lease *(superficies)*	Family, inheritance	3	Rarely corporate; standard for gas stations.

Italy

Reporter: Raffaele Caterina (Jan. 2011)

Time-limited interest	Context	Importance	Comments
Residential lease	Urban	8	In 2008, 18.9 per cent of Italian families resided in leased premises, particularly in apartments leased from local authorities.
Agricultural lease	Agricultural	7	
Loan for use	Various	6	In 2008, 12.6 per cent of Italian families resided in houses or apartments by virtue of a usufruct or a gratuitous loan

Time-limited interest	Context	Importance	Comments
Precarium	Various	5	
Usufruct	Family, inheritance	3	In 2008, 12.6 per cent of Italian families lived in a home in usufruct or gratuitous loan.
Use and habitation	Family, inheritance	6	The surviving spouse is granted the right of habitation over the house used as a family home and the right of use on the furniture in the house (Civil Code, art. 540).
Hereditary land lease *(emphyteusis)*	Agricultural	1	The Italian legislation is very hostile to the owner (Law 607 of 22 July 1966, Law 118 of 18 December 1970 and Law 270 of 14 June 1974). It limits the rent that can be imposed and allows the landowner *(enfiteuta)* to redeem the land by paying a modest sum.
Hereditary building lease *(superficies)*	Various	5	

Poland

Reporter: Magdalena Habdas (Jan. 2011)

Time-limited interest	Context	Importance	Comments
Residential lease	Family/ inheritance	7	Particularly with regard to urban apartments leased from local authorities.
Agricultural lease	Family/ business	6	Mostly public sector.
Loan for use	Family/ non-profit organisation	5	The public sector uses loans for use to make their land available to non-profit organisations. This practice, though problematic, does exist.

Time-limited interest	Context	Importance	Comments
Precarium			
Usufruct	Family/ business	5	Persons who are self-employed entrepreneurs prefer usufruct to being land owners, since usufruct cannot be seized or sold.
Use and habitation	Family	5	
Hereditary land lease *(emphyteusis)*	Real estate, corporate, commercial	10	Popular investment by private individuals in public land.
Hereditary building lease *(superficies)*			

Portugal

Reporter: Sandra Passinhas (Jan. 2011)

Time-limited interest	Context	Importance	Comments
Residential lease	Real estate	10	There are no official statistics on any of the categories. Rate of importance based on personal estimate.
Agricultural lease	Commercial business	6	
Loan for use	Family	2	
Precarium	Family	1	
Usufruct	Family, commercial business	6	
Use and habitation	Family	4	
Hereditary land lease *(emphyteusis)*		0	
Hereditary building lease *(superficies)*	Family, corporate, commercial business	6	

Scotland

Reporter: Peter Webster (Mar. 2011)

Time-limited interest	Context	Importance	Comments
Residential lease		10	
Agricultural lease		10	
Loan for use		0	Although Scots law recognises the nominate contract of loan, a gratuitous right to use land would probably be analysed as a 'licence' – an innominate contract granting a right to use land which did not amount to a lease.
Precarium		0	The right to use land until the owner requested its return would also probably be analysed as a 'licence'.
Usufruct		3	The real right of usufruct is now relatively rarely used to create a life interest. This is more commonly done by means of a trust.
Use and habitation		0	These two personal servitudes were not received by Scots law.
Hereditary land lease *(emphyteusis)*		0	Although parties can conclude a long lease with the characteristics of an *emphyteutic lease* (subject to the statutory maximum duration of 175 years), this is not a recognised nominate contract. Until the abolition of the feudal system, a close analogy to *emphyteusis* would have been the grant of a feu, but the feudal system, and with it the possibility of granting such a right, was abolished in 2004.
Hereditary building lease *(superficies)*		0	Although parties can conclude a 'building lease', this is not recognised as a distinct nominate contract.

South Africa

Reporter: C. G. van der Merwe (Mar. 2011)

Time-limited interest	Context	Importance	Comments
Residential lease	Urban houses and apartments	10	
Agricultural lease	Private persons and local authorities	6	Prevalent leasing of portions of farms – for example, for grazing.
Loan for use	Family	1	
Precarium	Family	4	Unsophisticated use in parts of country instead of more sophisticated use of usufruct.
Usufruct	Family and estate tax purposes	6	
Use and habitation	Family and estate tax purposes	6	
Hereditary land lease *(emphyteusis)*		0	
Hereditary building lease *(superficies)*		4	In the form of ninety-nine years' leasehold in certain urban areas.

Spain

Reporter: Elena Sánchez Jordán (Jan. 2011)

Time-limited interest	Context	Importance	Comments
Residential lease	Residential use by families	7	Spaniards prefer to own rather than to lease premises, and only lease premises if they cannot afford to buy.
Agricultural lease	Families and corporations	4	

Time-limited interest	Context	Importance	Comments
Loan for use	Families, corporations	3	
Precarium	Family	6	
Usufruct	Family inheritance	9	In Spain, widows or widowers have a legal right to usufruct. This explains its importance.
Use and habitation	Family	7	In Spain, the father or mother who remains with the children after a divorce is granted a right of use and habitation on the family house even if it is not his or hers.
Hereditary land lease *(emphyteusis)*		0	
Hereditary building lease *(superficies)*	Real estate	5	

Bibliography

Bibliographies for the individual countries can be found after the General bibliography

GENERAL BIBLIOGRAPHY

Aynès, L., 'Observation Cour Cassation 12 Novembre 1998', *Recueil Dalloz Jurisprudence* (1999), p. 168

Barbaix, R., *Het contractuele statuut van de schenking* (Antwerp, 2008)

Bashier, R., 'Disinheritance and the Modern Family', *Case Western Law Review* 45 (1994), p. 83

Berenschot, E. B., 'Enige aspecten van de plaats van vruchtgebruik in het vermogensrechtelijke systeem', *WPNR* 5730 (1985), p. 178

Bodenstein, H. D. J., 'Huur van huizen en landen volgens het hedendaagsch Romeinsch-Hollandsch recht' (doctoral thesis, University of Leiden, 1907)

Borkowski, A., and Du Plessis, P. J., *Textbook on Roman Law*, 4th edn (Oxford, 2004)

Bos, E. C., 'Vruchtgebruik op aandelen: over de grenzen van goederenrecht, erfrecht en vennootschapsrecht' (dissertation, University of Maastricht, 2005)

Bougle, F., and Gouthiere, B., '*Patrimoine*', in *Mémento Pratique Francis Lefebvre* (Paris, 2009–10), p. 134

Brault, J.-C., 'Un convention de quasi-usufruit généralisée après le décès?', *Defrénois* (1997), p. 480

Buckland, W. W., *A Textbook of Roman Law* (Oxford, 1966)

Caroni, P., and Dilcher, G. (eds.), *Norm und Tradition: Welche Geschichtlichkeit für die Rechtsgeschichte?* (Cologne, Weimar and Vienna, 1998), pp. 77–108

Chappert, A., 'La Donation avec réserve de quasi-usufruit: une possibilité à utiliser avec modération en matière fiscal' *Defrénois* (1997), art. 36617, pp. 907–8

Coke, E., *The Second Part of the Institutes of the Laws of England Containing the Exposition of Many Ancient and Other Statutes, 1590–1640*, 2 vols. (London, 1797)

Crook, J. A., *Law and Life in Rome, 90 BC–AD 212* (New York, 2006)

De Brabandere, A., '*Usufruit, Usage, Habitation*', *Répertoire du Notariat Defrénois* (Brussels, 1977), vol. 2, bk. 11, no. 127

de Page, H., *Traité élémentaire de droit civil belge* (Brussels, 1982), vol. 6

de Page, P., '*Le Quasi-usufruit*', in F. Ackerman-Van Ommeslaghe, J.-P. Bours, et al., *La Fiscalité des donations et ses incidences civiles: région de Bruxelles-Capitale, région flamande et région wallonne* (Louvain-la-Neuve, 2005), p. 157

'*Les Donations: actualités de certaines clauses*', in C. Biquet-Mathieu (ed.), *Liber Amicorum Paul Delnoy* (Brussels, 2005), p. 139

De Wet, J. C., 'Huur Gaat voor Koop (1)' *THRHR*, (1944), p. 74

'Huur Gaat voor Koop (2)' *THRHR*, (1944), p. 166

de Wulf, C., '*Schenking van roerend goed. Bedenkingen en formulieren*', in C. Castelein, A. Verbeke and L. Weyts (eds.), *Liber amicorum Professor Johan Verstraete* (Antwerp, 2007), p. 213

Dekkers, R., and Dirix, E., *Handboek Burgerlijk Recht* (Antwerp, 2005), vol. 2

Derine, R., Vanneste, F., and Vandenberghe, H., *Zakenreht* (Ghent, 1984), vol. 2

Dockes, E., 'Essai sur la notion d'usufruit', *RTDciv* (1995), p. 482

Du Mongh, J., *De erfovergang van aandelen* (Antwerp, 2004)

Du Plessis, P. J., '*The Hereditability of* Locatio Conductio', in J. W. Cairns and P. J. Du Plessis (eds.), *Beyond Dogmatics: Law and Society in the Roman World* (Edinburgh Studies in Law Series, 2007), vol. 3

Enneccerus, L., *Lehrbuch des Bürgerlichen Rechts* (Marburg, 1908), vol. 1

Ewald, W., 'Legal History and Comparative Law', *ZEuP* (1999), p. 553

Feenstra, R., *Romeinsrechtelijke grondslagen van het Nederlands privaatrecht* (Leiden, 1990)

Ferid, M., 'Review of the Louisiana Practice', *American Journal of Comparative Law* 22:3 (1974), p. 582

Fiorina, D., 'L'usufruitier d'un portefeuille de valeurs mobilières', *RTDciv* (1995), p. 48

Fitting, H., *Lo Codi – Eine Summa Codicis in Provenzalischer Sprache aus der Mitte des XII. Jahrhunderts* (Halle, 1906), vol. 1

Frier, B. W., *Landlords and Tenants in Imperial Rome* (Palo Alto, 1980)

Gordley, J., *Foundations of Private Law: Property, Tort, Contract, Unjust Enrichment* (Oxford, 2006)

Graziadei, M., '*Tuttifrutti*', in P. Birks, and A. Pretto (eds.), *Themes in Comparative Law: In Honour of Bernard Rudden* (Oxford, 2002)

Grimaldi, M., '*L'emploi des deniers grevés d'usufruit*', *Répertoire du notariat Defrénois* (Brussels, 1999), art. 36939, p. 493

Grimaldi, M., and Roux, J.-F., 'La Donation de valeurs mobilières avec réserve de quasi-usufruit', *Defrénois* (1994), art. 35677, p. 12

Grossi, P., *Locatio ad longum tempus – locazione e rapporti reali di godimento nella problematica del diritto comune* (Naples, 1963)

Guerts, T. G., 'The Historical Development of Leases in Residential Real Estate', *Real Estate Law Journal* 32 (2004), p. 356

Hahlo, H. R., and Kahn, E., *Union of South Africa: The Development of its Laws and Constitution* (Cape Town, 1960)

Hansenne, J., *Les Biens: précis*, Collection Scientifique de la Faculté de Droit de Liège, vol. 2 (Brussels, 1996), p. 1025

Jamar, J. F., *Les Novelles: droit civil* (Brussels, 1941), vol. 3

Johnston, D., *Roman Law in Context* (Cambridge, 1999)

'*Successive Rights and Successive Remedies: Life Interests in Roman Law*', in P. Birks (ed.), *New Perspectives in the Roman Law of Property: Essays for Barry Nicholas* (Oxford, 1989), p. 153

Johnston, W. R., '"Emphyteusis": A Roman Perpetual Tenure', *U Toronto LJ* 3 (1940), p. 323

Kehoe, D. P., *Investment, Profit and Tenancy: The Jurists and the Roman Agrarian Economy* (Ann Arbor, MI, 1991)

Kleyn, D., 'Die Mandament van Spolie in die Suid-Afrikaanse Reg' (LLD thesis, University of Pretoria, 1986)

Kluyskens, A., *Beginselen van Burgerlijk Recht*, vol. 5, *Zakenrecht* (Antwerp, 1940)

Laurent, F., *Principes de droit civil*, 31 vols. (Brussels and Paris, 1878), vol. 6

Lawson, F. H., and Rudden, B., *The Law of Property* (2nd edn, Oxford, 2002)

Lubbers, A. G., 'Vruchtgebruik naar huidig en toekomstig recht', *Preadvies Broederschap der Notarissen* (1959), p. 144

Mackeldey, F., *Lehrbuch des heutigen römischen Recht* (12th edn, Giessen, 1833)

Mayer-Maly, T., *Locatio Conductio: Eine Untersuchung zum klassischen römischen Recht* (Vienna and Munich, 1956)

McClean, A. J., 'The Common Law Life Estate and the Civil Law Usufruct: A Comparative Study', *International and Comparative Law Quarterly* 12:2 (1963), p. 651

Megarry, R., and Wade, W., *The Law of Real Property* (6th edn, London, 2000)

Mellema-Kranenburg, T. J., 'Twee buitenbeentjes binnen het vruchtgebruik', *WPNR* 6687 (2006), pp. 777–8

Mijnssen, F. H. J., Van Velten, A. A., and Bartels, S. E. (eds.), *Asser's Handleiding tot de beoefening van het Nederlands Burgerlijk Recht*, Part 5, *Eigendom en beperkte rechten* (Deventer, 2008)

Goederenrecht, Zakelijke Rechten in Mr. C. Asser's Handleiding tot de beoefening van het Nederlands Burgerlijk Recht (Deventer, 2008)

Motive zu dem Entwurfe eines Bürgerlichen Gesetzbuches für das Deutsche Reich (Berlin and Leipzig, 1888), vol. 2

Mühlenbruch, C. F., *Lehrbüch des Pandekten-Rechts* (2nd edn, Halle, 1840), vol. 2

Mugdan, B., *Die gestammten Materialen zum Bürgerlichen Gesetzbuch für das Deutsche Reich* (Berlin, 1899), vol. 2

Nicholas, B., *An Introduction to Roman Law* (Oxford, 1990)

Nijs, A., van Zantbeek, A., and Verbeke, A., 'Schenken met behoud van bezit: acht clausules', *Tijdschrift voor Estate Planning* 3 (2005), p. 197

Nudelholc, S., and Karadsheh, D., 'Réflexions sur une nouvelle définition de l'usufruit et ses rapports avec le droit des successions et des libéralités', *Rev Dr ULB* (2003), p. 409

Osler, D. J., 'The Fantasy Men', *Rechtsgeschichte* 10 (2007), p. 169

'The Myth of European Legal History', *Rechtshistorisches Journal* 16 (1997), p. 393

Otte, G., '*Die dingliche Rechtsstellung des Mieters nach ALR und BGB*', in O. Berendts, et al. (eds.), *Festschrift für Franz Wieacker* (Göttingen, 1978), p. 463

Patault, A.-M., *Introduction historique au droit des biens* (Paris, 1989)

Pitlo, A., '*Goederenrecht*', in W. H. M. Reehuis, A. H. T. Heisterkamp, G. E. van Maanen and G. T. de Jong (eds.), *Het Nederlands Burgerlijk Recht* (11th edn, Deventer, 2001)
Planiol, M., and Ripert, G., *Traité pratique de droit civil français, 14 vols.* (Paris, 1952)
Posner, R. A., *Economic Analysis of Law* (4th edn, Boston, 1992)
Pretto-Sakmann, A., *Boundaries of Personal Property: Shares and Sub-shares* (Oxford and Portland, 2005)
Prutting, H., *Sachenrecht* (Munich, 2008)
Pugliese, G., 'On Roman Usufruct', *Tulane Law Review* 40 (1965–6), p. 538
Radding, C. M., '*Reviving Justinian's Corpus: The Case of the Code*', in P. Andersen, M. Münster-Swendsen and H. Vogt (eds.), *Law Before Gratian: Law in Western Europe c.500–1100* (Copenhagen, 2007), p. 35
Raynaud, P., *Les Biens* (2nd edn, Paris, 1980)
Robinson, O. F., *The Sources of Roman Law* (London, 1997)
Rome, G. W., 'An Elegy for Emphyteusis', *Civil Law Commentaries* 1:2 (2008), p. 1
Sagaert, V., '*Oude zakenrechtelijke figuren met nut voor een moderne familiale vermogensplanning*'. In W. Delva (ed.), *Familiale Vermogensplanning XXXste Postuniversitaire cyclus* (10th edn, Mechelen, 2004), p. 212
Schrage, E. J. H., 'Emptio (nondum) tollit locatum', *Acta Juridica* (1978), p. 1
'Sale Breaks Hire – Or Does It? Medieval Foundations of the Roman-Dutch Concept', *TvR* 54:2 (1986), pp. 294 ff.
Scott, S. P., *The Civil Law Translation* (Cincinnati, 1932)
Stein, P. G., *Roman Law in European History* (Cambridge, 1999)
Struycken, T. H. D., 'Erfpacht en de redelijkheid en billijkheid in het goederenrecht', *Nederlands Tijdschrift voor Burgerlijk Recht* 3 (2000), p. 91
Swadling, W. J., '*Property: General Principles*', in P. Birks (ed.), *English Private Law*, 2 vols. (Oxford, 2000), vol. 1
Thomas, J. A. C., 'The Sitting Tenant', *TvR* 41:1 (1973), p. 35
van Gaalen, M. S., 'Vruchtgebruik' (dissertation, Vrije Universiteit Amsterdam, 2001)
van Laere, D., 'De civiel- en fiscaalrechterlijke grenzen van schenking met voorbehoud van quasivruchtgebruik', *Not Fisc M* (2002), p. 188
van Neste, F., *Beginselen van Belgisch Privaatrecht*, vol. 1, *Zakenrecht: Goederen, bezit en eigendom* (Ghent, 1990)
van Oevelen, A., '*Actuele ontwikkelingen inzake het recht van erfpacht en het recht van opstal*', in *Het Zakenrecht: absoluut niet een rustig bezit*, Kluwer rechtswetenskappen, 10:16 (1992), pp. 342–3
van Oven, J. C., 'Het Vruchtgebruik in het Ontwerp Nieuw BW', *WPNR* 4595 (1959), p. 361
van Sinay, T., '*Vruchtgebruik op een algemeenheid en quasivruchtgebruik: vergelijking en toepassing*', in C. Castelein and A. Verbeke (eds.), *Notariële clausules: Liber amicorum Professor Johan Verstraete* (Antwerp and Oxford, 2007), p. 736
van Zeben, C. J., and Dupun, J. W., *Parlementaire geschiedenis van het Nieuwe Burgerlijk Wetboek* (Deventer, 1990–)
Vandenberghe, H.,'Actuele problemen van het vruchtgebruik', *TPR* (1983), p. 59

Vanhove, K., 'Note on the Decision of the court of Cassation of 30 March 2006', *Rechtskundig Weekblad* (16 Dec. 2006), p. 678

Vanhove, K., and Baudoncq, F., 'Combinatie van beperkt zakelijke rechten: Over de interne grenzen van vruchtgebruik, erfpacht, opstal en erfdienstbaarheden', *Notariaat* (6 June 2004), p. 135

Veaux-Fournerie, P., 'Usufruit, caractères et sources', *Juris-classeur droit civil*, arts. 582–99, fasc. 10, no. 42

Verbeke, A., 'Alstublieft en dank u wel!', *Tijdschrift voor Estate Planning* 3 (2008), p. 183

'*Bevoegdheid Vruchtgebruiker/Voorbehoud van quasivruchtgebruik/Voorbehoud van interings- en vervreemdingsbevoegdheid: civiele aspecten*', in A. Verbeke, F. Buyssens and H. Derycke (eds.) *Handboek Estate Planning*, Part 2, *Schenking* (Ghent, 2009), p. 407

'Creatief met vruchtgebruik', *Tijdschrift voor Notarissen* 10 (1999), p. 530

'*Modaliteiten bij een schenking*', in M. Tison and J. P. Buyle (eds.), *Bank en Familie* (Brussels, 2006)

'*Quasi-vruchtgebruik*', in H. Vandenberghe (ed.), *Zakenrecht Themis, 2005–2006* (Bruges, 2006), p. 37

'*Schenking met voorbehoud van vruchtgebruik*', in W. Pintens and J. Du Mongh (eds.), *Patrimonium, 2007* (Antwerp and Oxford, 2007), p. 264

Verbeke, A., and Van Zantbeek, A., '*Succession Law in Belgium*', in D. Hayton (ed.), *European Succession Laws* (2nd edn, Bristol, 2002)

Verbeke, A., and Vanhove, K., '*Spelen met het voorwerp van vruchtgebruik*', in P. Lecocq, B. Tilleman, and A. Verbeke (eds.), *Zakenrecht: droit des biens* (Bruges, 2005)

Verbeke, A., et al. (eds.), *Handboek Estate Planning* (Brussels, 2009–10)

Verstappen, J., *Erfpacht, opstal en vruchtgebruik* (Brussel, 2004)

Vieweg, K., and Werner, A., *Sachenrecht* (4th edn, Cologne, 2010)

Watson, A., *Roman Private Law around 200 BC* (Edinburgh, 1971)

Wieacker, F., *Privatrechtsgeschichte der Neuzeit unter besonderer Berücksichtigung der deutschen Entwicklung* (Göttingen, 1952)

Yiannopoulos, A. N., *Louisiana Civil Law Treatise* (4th edn, St Paul, MN, 2000)

Zenati-Castaing, F., and Revet, T., *Les Biens* (Paris, 2008)

Zimmermann, R., *The Law of Obligations* (Oxford, 1996)

AUSTRIA

Aicher, J., in P. Rummel, *Kommentar zum Allgemeinen bürgerlichen Gesetzbuch* (KBB) (3rd edn, Vienna, 2000)

Angst, P., *Kommentar zur Exekutionsordnung* (Vienna, 2000)

Beig, D., 'Wohnrechtliche Aspekte des neuen Unternehmensgesetzbuchs', *Wohnrechtliche Blätter* (2006), p. 37

Binder, M., in M. Schwimann, *Praxiskommentar zum Allgemeinen bürgerlichen Gesetzbuch*, vol. 3 (3rd edn, Vienna, 2006)

Böhm, H., and Pletzer, R., in M. Schwimann and B. Verschraegen, *Praxiskommentar zum Allgemeinen bürgerlichen Gesetzbuch*, vol. 4 (2nd edn, Vienna, 2001)

Bydlinski, F., 'OGH 21.2.1973 Anmerkung', *Juristiche Blätter* (1974), p. 90

'Superädifikate und Kündigungsschutz', *Juristiche Blätter* (1984), p. 241

Bydlinski, P., 'Zur Abtretbarkeit der Rechte aus einem Mietverhältnis', *Juristiche Blätter* (1985), p. 728

Eccher, B., in H. Koziol, P. Bydlinski and R. Bollenberger, *Kommentar zum Allgemeinen bürgerlichen Gesetzbuch* (KBB) (2nd edn, Vienna, 2007)

Ertl, R., in P. Rummel, *Kommentar zum Allgemeinen bürgerlichen Gesetzbuch* (3rd edn, Vienna, 2000), vol. 1

Graf, G., '*Superädifikate als Kreditsicherheiten*', in A. Kletecka, W. Rechberger and R. Zitta, *Bauten auf fremdem Grund* (2nd edn, Vienna, 2004), para. 61.

Hinteregger, M., in M. Schwimann, *Praxiskommentar zum Allgemeinen bürgerlichen Gesetzbuch*, vol. 5 (3rd edn, Vienna, 2006)

Hofmann, K., in P. Rummel, *Kommentar zum Allgemeinen bürgerlichen Gesetzbuch* (KBB) (3rd edn, Vienna, 2000)

Iro, G., *Bürgerliches Recht*, vol. 4, *Sachenrecht* (2nd edn, Vienna, 2000)

in H. Koziol, P. Bydlinski and R. Bollenberger, *Kommentar zum Allgemeinen bürgerlichen Gesetzbuch* (KBB) (2nd edn, Vienna, 2007)

Kiendl-Wendner, D., in M. Schwimann and B. Verschraegen, *Praxiskommentar zum Allgemeinen bürgerlichen Gesetzbuch*, vol. 2 (3rd edn, Vienna, 2004)

Kletecka, A., in A. Kletecka, W. Rechberger and R. Zitta, *Bauten auf fremdem Grund* (2nd edn, Vienna, 2004)

in H. Koziol and R. Welser, *Bürgerliches Recht* (13th edn, Vienna, 2007), vols. 1 and 2

Kletecka, A., Rechberger, W., and Zitta, R., *Bauten auf fremdem Grund* (2nd edn, Vienna, 2004)

Koch, B., in H. Koziol, P. Bydlinski and R. Bollenberger, *Kommentar zum Allgemeinen bürgerlichen Gesetzbuch* (KBB) (2nd edn, Vienna, Springer, 2007)

Konecny, A., and Schubert, G., *Insolvenzgesetze* (Vienna, 1999)

Koziol, H., Bydlinski, P., and Bollenberger, R., *Kommentar zum Allgemeinen bürgerlichen Gesetzbuch* (KBB) (2nd edn, Vienna, 2007)

Koziol, H., and Welser, R., *Bürgerliches Recht* (13th edn, Vienna, 2007), vols. 1 and 2

Krejci, H., in P. Rummel, *Kommentar zum Allgemeinen bürgerlichen Gesetzbuch* (KBB) (3rd edn, Vienna, 2000)

Mayrhofer, H., 'Abtretung von Bestandrechten und Abtretungsverbot', ÖJZ (1973)

Neumayr, M., in H. Koziol, P. Bydlinski and R. Bollenberger, *Kommentar zum Allgemeinen bürgerlichen Gesetzbuch* (KBB) (2nd edn, Vienna, 2007)

Oberhammer, P., '*Das Superädifikat*', in A. Kletecka, W. Rechberger and R. Zitta, *Bauten auf fremdem Grund* (2nd edn, Vienna, 2004)

in P. Angst, *Kommentar zur Exekutionsordnung* (Vienna, 2000)

in A. Konecny and G. Schubert, *Insolvenzgesetze* (Vienna, 1999)

Pittl, R., 'Das "gespaltene Mietverhältnis" und, §46a Abs 5 MRG', *Wohnrechtliche Blätter* (1997), p. 123
Prader, C., *Wohnrecht Online* (2007), available at www.rdb.at
Prader, C., and P. Kuprian, 'Erhaltungspflichten (Aufwandersatz) im MRG/WGG nach der WRN 2006', *Immolex* (2006), p. 271
Randl, H., 'Die Neuordnung des Bergrechts durch das Mineralrohstoffgesetz (MinroG)', *JAP* (1998), p. 248
Rechberger, W., and Oberhammer, P., '*Das Superädifikat*', in A. Kletecka, W. Rechberger and R. Zitta, *Bauten auf fremdem Grund* (2nd edn, Vienna, 2004)
Rubin, D., 'Offenkundige Wohnungsdienstbarkeiten?', *Ecolex* (1998), p. 545
Rummel, P., *Kommentar zum Allgemeinen bürgerlichen Gesetzbuch* (KBB) (3rd edn, Vienna, 2000)
Schauer, M., '7 Ob 547/95: Critical Comment', *Wohnrechtliche Blätter* (1996), p. 240
'Die Unternehmensübertragung nach, §12 Abs 3 MRG', *Juristiche Blätter* (1985), p. 257
'*Zur Verbücherung von Bestandverträgen auf unbestimmte Zeit*', in H. Hofmeister, W. Ogris and W. H. Rechberger, *Gedüchtnisschrift Herbert Hofmeister* (Vienna, 1996)
Schulyok, P., in A. Konecny and G. Schubert, *Insolvenzgesetze* (Vienna, 1999)
Schwimann, M., *Praxiskommentar zum Allgemeinen bürgerlichen Gesetzbuch*, vols. 2–5 (3rd edn, Vienna, 2004–6)
Spielbüchler, K., in P. Rummel, *Kommentar zum Allgemeinen bürgerlichen Gesetzbuch* (KBB) (3rd edn, Vienna, 2000), vol. 1
Spruzina, C., in M. Schwimann, *Praxiskommentar zum Allgemeinen bürgerlichen Gesetzbuch*, vol. 3 (3rd edn, Vienna, 2006)
Welser, R., 'Die Erhaltungspflicht des Fruchtniessers', *Notariats Zeitung* (1982), p. 145
in H. Koziol and R. Welser, *Bürgerliches Recht* (13th edn, Vienna, 2007)
Würth, J., in P. Rummel, *Kommentar zum Allgemeinen bürgerlichen Gesetzbuch* (3rd edn, Vienna, 2000), vol. 1

BELGIUM

Carette, N., '*Financiële aspecten van de woninghuurovereenkomst. Herziening van de basishuurprijs*', in A. Van Oevelen (ed.), *Handboek Woninghuur* (Bruges, 2009)
'*Het derdenbeding: wanneer heeft een beding de strekking van een derdenbeding naar Belgisch recht?*', in I. Samoy (ed.), *Derden in het contractenrecht* (Antwerp, 2009)
Dambre, M., and Hubeau, B., *Woninghuur*, Algemene practische rechtsverzameling (Antwerp, 2002)
de Page, H., and Dekkers, R., *Traité élémentaire de droit civil belge, vol.* 6 (Brussels, 1953)
Dekkers, R., Verbeke, A., Carette, N., and Vanhove, K., *Handboek van burgerlijk recht*, vol. 3, *Huwelijksstelsels, erfrecht, giften* (Antwerp, 2007)

Derine, R., van Neste, F., and Vandenberghe, H., *Zakenrecht*, Beginselen van Belgisch privaatrecht (Ghent, 1984)

Nyckees, J., *Articles 1754–1756 BW*, in *Commentaar met overzicht van rechtspraak en rechtsleer*, Bijzondere Overeenkomsten (Antwerp, 2002)

Sagaert, V., Tilleman, B., and Verbeke, A., *Vermogensrecht in kort bestek* (Antwerp, 2007)

Vanhove, K., and Baudoncq, F., 'Combinatie van beperkt zakelijke rechten – Over de interne grenzen van vruchtgebruik, erfpacht, opstal en erfdienstbaarheid', *Not Fisc M* (2004), p. 135

Verbeke, A., and Vanhove, K., *Actualia vruchtgebruik, erfpacht, opstal en erfdienstbaarheden* (Bruges, 2003)

DENMARK

Buch, A. V., and Møller, J. (eds.), *Projektudvikling af fast ejendom – en håndbog for praktikere* (Copenhagen, 2005)

Gomard, B., *Obligationsret* (4th edn, Copenhagen, 2006), vol. 1

Krag Jespersen, H., *Lejeret* (Copenhagen, 1989)

Mortensen, P., *Landbrugsforpagtning* (Copenhagen, 1999)

Tinglysning (3rd edn, Copenhagen, 2001)

von Eyben, B., Mortensen, P., and Sørensen, I., *Lærebog i obligationsret. Personskifte i skyldforhold, Fordringers ophør, Hæftelsesformer* (3rd edn, Copenhagen, 2008), vol. 2

Willumsen, Hans, *Tinglysningsloven med kommentarer* (Copenhagen, 1997)

ENGLAND

Bailey, E., Groves, H., and Smith, C., *Corporate Insolvency* (2nd edn, London, 2001)

Berry, C., Bailey, E., and Shaw Miller, S., *Personal Insolvency* (3rd edn, London, 2001)

Bignell, J., and Harpum, C., *Registered Land: The New Law* (Bristol, 2002)

Dowding, N., and Reynolds, K., *Dilapidations Law and Practice* (2nd edn, London, 2000)

Halsbury's Laws of England (4th edn, London, 1990)

Hargrave, F., and Butler, C. (eds.), *Coke upon Littleton* (19th edn, London, 1658–9)

Harpum, C., Bridges, S., and Dixon, M., *Megarry and Wade: The Law of Real Property* (6th edn, London, 2000)

Heathcote-Williams, H., *Foa's General Law of Landlord and Tenant* (8th edn, London, 1957)

Hill and Redman's Law of Landlord and Tenant (London, 1988)

McClean, A. J., 'The Common Law Life Estate and the Civil law Usufruct: A Comparative Study', *Int and Comp LQR* 12 (1963), p. 649

Ruoff, T. B. F., and Roper, R. B., *Ruoff and Roper on the Law and Practice of Registered Conveyancing* (London, 2005)

Simpson, A. W. B., *History of the Land Law* (2nd edn, Oxford, 1986)

Woodfall, W., *Woodfall's Law of Landlord and Tenant* (London, 2005)

FRANCE

Baudry-Lacantinerie, G., *Précis de droit civil, 3 vols.* (Paris, 1919)

GERMANY

Bassenge, P., in O. Palandt, *Bürgerlichen Gesetzbuch* (65th edn, Munich, 2006)
Frank, J., in J. von Staudingers, *Kommentar zum Bürgerlichen Gesetzbuch mit Einführungsgesetz und Nebengesetzen*, Bk. 3, Sachenrecht, §§1012–17 (Berlin, 2002)
Jerschke, H. U., in G. Brambring and H.-U. Jerschke (eds.), *Beck'sches Notar-Handbuch* (4th edn, Munich, 2006)
Mayer, J., in J. von Staudingers, *Kommentar zum Bürgerlichen Gesetzbuch mit Einführungsgesetz und Nebengesetzen*, Bk. 3, Sachenrecht, §§1018–112 (Berlin, 2002)
Petzold, R., *Municher Kommentar zum Bürgerlichen Gesetzbuch* (KBB) (3rd edn, Munich, 1997)
Roth, G. H., *Reichsgerichtsrätekommentar* (12th edn, Berlin and New York, 1978)
Schöner, H., and Stöber, K., *Grundbuchrecht* (13th edn, Munich, 2004)
von Oefele, H., and Winkler, K., *Handbuch des Erbbaurechts* (3rd edn, Munich, 2003)
Weidenkaff, W., in O. Palandt, *Bürgerlichen Gesetzbuch* (65th edn, Munich, 2006)

GREECE

Antapasis, A., in A. Georgiades and M. Stathopoulos (eds.), *GCC, Collective Analysis of the Civil Code* (Athens, 1980), vol. 3, art. 614 (359–68)
Balis, G., *Property Law* (4th edn, Athens, 1961)
Banakas, S., in A. Georgiades and M. Stathopoulos (eds.), *GCC, Collective Analysis of the Civil Code* (Athens, 1980), vol. 6, art. 1188 (202–7)
Dacoronia, E., *Sublease of Property* (Athens, 1994)
Dagtoglou, P., *General Administrative Law* (5th edn, Athens, 2004)
Dimakou, F., in A. Georgiades and M. Stathopoulos (eds.), *GCC, Collective Analysis of the Civil Code* (Athens, 1980), vol. 5, art. 955 (61–6)
Doris, P., *Real Security Rights* (Athens, 1986)
Filios, P., *Law of Obligations* (7th edn, Athens, 2007), special part, vol. 1
Georgiades, A., *General Principles of Civil Law* (3rd edn, Athens, 2002)
New Contractual Forms of Modern Economy (5th edn, Athens, 2008)
Option (Athens, 1970)
Property Law (Athens, 1991), vols. 1 and 2
in A. Georgiades and M. Stathopoulos (eds.), *GCC, Collective Analysis of the Civil Code* (Athens, 1980), vol. 3, art. 623 (386–7); art. 624 (387–8); art. 631 (393–4); art. 638 (398–9); vol. 5, art. 961 (81–5)
Karasis, M., in A. Georgiades and M. Stathopoulos (eds.), *GCC, Collective Analysis of the Civil Code* (Athens, 1980), vol. 5, art. 1117 (707–38); vol. 6, art. 1142 (42–61); art. 1148 (83–7); art. 1149 (87–8); art. 1153 (92–5); art. 1158 (107–8)
Kerameus, K., and Kozyris, P. (eds.), *Introduction to Greek Law* (3rd edn, Deventer, 2007) (in English)

Kritikos, A., in A. Georgiades and M. Stathopoulos (eds.), *GCC, Collective Analysis of the Civil Code* (Athens, 1980), vol. 6, art. 1271 (477–9)
Nikolopoulos, G., in K. Kerameus, D. Kondylis and N. Nikas (eds.), *Code of Civil Procedure* (Athens and Thessalonica, 2000), vol. 1
Papadopoulou, D., in A. Georgiades and M. Stathopoulos (eds.), *GCC, Collective Analysis of the Civil Code* (Athens, 1980), vol. 6, art. 1185 (195–6); art. 1186 (196–7)
Rapsomanikis, M., in A. Georgiades and M. Stathopoulos (eds.), *GCC, Collective Analysis of the Civil Code* (Athens, 1980), vol. 3, art. 575 (289–291); arts. 590–2 (312–15); art. 594 (317–20); art. 599 (325–7)
Rokas, K., *Law of Bankruptcy* (12th edn, Athens, 1978)
Roussos, K. l., in A. Georgiades and M. Stathopoulos (eds.), *GCC, Collective Analysis of the Civil Code* (Athens, 1980), vol. 6, art. 1166 (125–33)
Spiliotopoulos, E., *Greek Administrative Law* (11th edn, Athens, 2001)
Spyridakis, I., and Perakis, E., '*Interpretation of the GCC*', *Property Law* (Athens, 1977), vol. 3, art. 1166 (11)
Stathopoulos, M., *Law of Obligations* (Athens and Thessalonica, 2004)
Yessiou-Faltsi, P., *Forced Execution* (Athens and Thessalonica, 2001)
Yiannopoulos, A., in K. Kerameus and P. Kozyris (eds.), *Introduction to Greek Law* (3rd edn, Deventer, 2007), chap. 7, 'Property', pp. 153–66 (in English)

HUNGARY

Benedek, K., and Világhy, M., *A Polgári törvénykönyv a gyakorlatban* [*The Civil Code in Practice*] (Budapest, 1965)
Besenyi, L., '*Fejezet: a bérlet XXXVII*' [Chapter 37 on Lease], in G. Gellért (ed.), *A Polgári Törvénykönyv magyarázata* [*Commentary on the Civil Code*] (Budapest, 2002), vol. 2
Gellért, G. (ed.), *A Polgári Törvénykönyv magyarázata* (Budapest 2002), vol. 1
Lenkovics, B., *A dologi jog vázlata* (Budapest, 1999)
Petric, F., '*Harmadik rész: a tulajdonjog*' [Part 3: Ownership], in G. Gellért (ed.), *A Polgári Törvénykönyv magyarázata* [*Commentary on the Civil Code*] (Budapest, 2002), vol. 1

ITALY

Bigliazzi Geri, L., '*Oneri reali e obbligazioni propter rem*', in A. Cicu, F. Messineo and L. Mengoni (eds.), *Trattato di diritto civile e commerciale* (Milan, 1984)
'*Usufrutto, uso e abitazione*', in A. Cicu, F. Messineo and L. Mengoni (eds.), *Trattato di diritto civile e commerciale* (Milan, 1978)
Carrara, G., '*I contratti agrari*', in F. Vassalli, *Trattato di diritto civile italiano* (4th edn, Turin, 1959)
Caterina, R., 'A Comparative Overview of the Fair Wear and Tear Exception: The Duty of Holders of Temporary Interests to Preserve Property', *Edinburgh Law Review* 6 (2002), p. 85

I diritti sulle cose limitati nel tempo (Milan, 2000)
Chianale, A., '*L'Ipoteca*', in R. Sacco (ed.), *Trattato di diritto civile* (Turin, 2005)
Comporti, M., '*Voce Servitù* (dir. priv.)', in *Enciclopedia del diritto*, vol. 42 (Milan, 1990)
de Martino, F., '*Dell'usufrutto, dell'uso e dell'abitazione*', in A. Scialoja and G. Branca, *Commentario del Codice civile* (4th edn, Bologna and Rome, 1978)
Gabrielli, G., 'Sulla legittimazione a domandare la cessazione di immissioni', in *Rivista di diritto civile* (1997), II, p. 627
Gallo, P., '*Usufrutto, uso abitazione*', in M. Bessone (ed.), *Trattato di diritto privato* (Turin, 2001)
Gorla, G., and Zanelli, P., '*Del pegno – Delle ipoteche*', in F. Galgano (ed.), *Commentario del Codice civile Scialoja-Branca* (4th edn, Bologna and Rome, 1992)
Guarneri, A., 'Voce Superficie', in *Digesto civile* 19 (1999), p. 206
Natoli, U., *La proprietà* (2nd edn, Milan, 1976)
Pasetti Bombardella, F., '*Voce Superficie (dir. priv.)*', in *Enciclopedia del diritto*, vol. 43 (Milan, 1990)
Pugliese, G., '*Della superficie*', in *Commentario del Codice civile Scialoja-Branca* (4th edn, Bologna and Rome, 1976)
'*Usufrutto uso e abitazione*', in F. Vassalli (ed.), *Trattato di diritto civile italiano* (2nd edn, Turin, 1972)
Romagnoli, E., and Germanò, A., '*Dell'affitto di fondi rustici*', in F. Galgano (ed.), *Commentario del Codice civile Scialoja-Branca* (4th edn, Bologna and Rome, 1990)
Rubino, D., '*L'ipoteca immobiliare e mobiliare*', in A. Cicu and F. Messineo, *Trattato di diritto civile e commerciale* (Milan, 1956)
Sacco, R., and Caterina, R., '*Il possesso*', in A. Cicu, F. Messineo and L. Mengoni (eds.), *Trattato di diritto civile e commerciale* (2nd edn, Milan, 2000)
Salis, L., '*La superficie*', in F. Vassalli (ed.), *Trattato di diritto civile italiano* (Turin, 1954)

THE NETHERLANDS

Asser, C., and Abas, P., '*Bijzondere Overeenkomsten, Huur 5-IIA*', in *Handleiding tot de beoefening van het Nederlands Burgerlijk Recht* (8th edn, Deventer, 2004)
Asser, C., Mijnssen, F. H. J., and de Haan, P., '*Algemeen Goederenrecht*', in C. Asser, *Handleiding tot de beoefening van het Nederlands burgerlijk recht* (14th edn, Deventer, 2001)
Asser, C., Mijnssen, F. H. J., van Dam, C. C., and van Velten, A. A., '*Goederenrecht, Zakelijke Rechten*', in C. Asser, *Handleiding tot de beoefening van het Nederlands burgerlijk recht* (14th edn, Deventer, 2002)
Asser, C., and Snijders, G. M. F., '*Bijzondere Overeenkomsten, Pacht 5-IIB*', in C. Asser, *Handleiding tot de beoefening van het Nederlands burgerlijk recht* (Deventer, 2001)
Berger, K. F. M., *Burenrecht, mandeligheid, erfdienstbaarheden*, in *Serie Recht en Praktijk* (4th edn, Deventer, 2001)
Davids, W. J. M., *Mandeligheid en erfdienstbaarheden*, in *Monografieën Nieuw BW B-27* (Deventer, 1994)

de Jong, J., *Erfpacht en opstal*, Monografieën Nieuw BW B-28 (Deventer, 1995)
de Vries, A. E., '*Erfpacht en opstal*', in A. J. H. Pleysier (ed.), *Studiepockets privaatrecht 33* (Deventer, 2002)
Kleijn, W. M., *Vruchtgebruik*, in *Monografieën Nieuw BW B-10* (Deventer, 1990)
Mellema-Kranenburg, T. J., '*Vruchtgebruik algemeen*', in J. P. M. Stubbé, T. J. Mellema-Kranenburg, C. A. Kraan and I. J. F. A. van Vijfeijken (eds.), *Vruchtgebruik Preadvies voor de jaarlijks Algemene Ledenvergadering van de Koninklijke Notariële Beroepsorganisatie* (Lelystad, 1999)
Pitlo, A., '*Goederenrecht*', in W. H. M. Reehuis, A. H. T. Heisterkamp, G. E. van Maanen and G. T. de Jong (eds.), *Het Nederlands Burgerlijk Recht* (11th edn, Deventer, 2001), vol. 3
Rodrigues Lopes, D. L., *Onroerende zaken: gebruik, financiering, belegging* (Deventer, 1995)
Pacht, in *Serie Recht en Praktijk* (Deventer, 1997)
Snijders, H. J., and Rank-Berenschot, E. B., *Goederenrecht*, in *Studiereeks burgerlijk recht* (4th edn, Deventer, 2007)
Wessels, B., *Insolventierecht, Gevolgen van faillietverklaring*, Part 2 (Deventer, 2000)

POLAND

Bieniek, G., (ed.), *Komentarz do kodeksu cywilnego*, Bk. 3, *Zobowiązania* (7th edn, Warsaw, 2006), vols. 1 and 2
Czachórski, W., *Zobowiązania: zarys wykładu* (9th edn, Warsaw, 2005)
Doliwa, A., *Zobowiązania* (Warsaw, 2006)
Gniewek, E., *Prawo rzeczowe* (6th edn, Warsaw, 2006)
(ed.), *System Prawa Prywatnego: Prawo rzeczowe*, 4 vols. (Warsaw, 2005), vol. 4
Gurgul, S., *Prawo upadłościowe i naprawcze: komentarz* (6th edn, Warsaw, 2005)
Ignatowicz, J. (ed.), *System prawa cywilnego: prawo własności i inne prawa rzeczowe* (Ossolineum, 1977)
Ignatowicz, J., and Stefaniuk, K., *Prawo rzeczowe* (9th edn, Warsaw, 2000)
Jakubecki, A., and Zedler, F., *Prawo upadłościowe i naprawcze* (Cracow, 2003)
Karnicka-Kawczyńska, A., and Kawczyński, J., *Postępowanie zabezpieczające i egzekucyjne* (2nd edn, Warsaw, 2002)
Kawala, E., *Kodeks postępowania cywilnego: postępowanie nieprocesowe, zabezpieczające i egzekucyjne; przepisy z zakresu międzynarodowego postępowania cywilnego: tekst, obszerne orzecznictwo* (Torun and Lodz, 2003)
Kordyasz, D. (ed.), *The Bankruptcy and Reorganisation Law: Two-Language Version* (Polish and English) (Warsaw, 2004)
Majewska-Jurys, A., *Prawo upadłościowe i naprawcze: vademecum dla przedsiębiorców* (Bydgoszcz and Koszalin, 2004)
Marciniak, A., *Postępowanie egzekucyjne w sprawach cywilnych* (Warsaw, 2005)
Panowicz-Lipska, J. (ed.), *Prawo zobowiązań – część szczegółowa* (Warsaw, 2004)
Pietrzykowski, K. (ed.), *Kodeks cywilny: komentarz*, 2 vols. (3rd edn, Warsaw, 2004)
Radwański, Z., *Zobowiązania – część ogólna* (4th edn, Warsaw, 2003)

Rudnicki, S., *Komentarz do kodeksu cywilnego*, Bk. 2, *Własność i inne prawa rzeczowe* (6th edn, Warsaw, 2006)
Świeboda, Z., *Komentarz do kodeksu postępowania cywilnego*, 2, *Postępowanie zabezpieczające i egzekucyjne* (2nd edn, Warsaw, 2004)
Wójcik, S. (ed.), *Podstawy prawa cywilnego: zobowiązania - część ogólna* (Warsaw, 2003)
Zieliński, A. (ed.), *Kodeks postępowania cywilnego: komentarz do artykułów 506–1217*, 2 vols (Warsaw, 2006), vol. 2

PORTUGAL

Amâncio Ferreira, F., *Curso de Processo de Execução* (11th edn, Coimbra, 2009)
Aragão Seia, J. A., *Arrendamento Rural* (4th edn, Coimbra, 2003)
Carvalho Fernandes, L., *Lições de Direitos Reais* (Lisbon, 1996)
Coelho, José Fernando Lutz, *Contratos agrários de arrendamento e parceria rural no Mercosul* (Curitiba, 2002)
Garcia, M. O., *Arrendamento Urbano e Outros Temas de Direito e Processo Civil* (Coimbra, 2004)
Arrendamento Plural - Quadro Normativo e Natureza Jurídica (Coimbra, 2009)
Lebre de Freitas, J., *A Acção Executiva - Depois da Reforma da Reforma* (5th edn, Coimbra, 2009)
Menezes Cordeiro, A., *Direitos Reais* (Coimbra, 1993)
Menezes Leitão, L., *Direito da Insolvência* (2nd edn, Coimbra, 2009)
Mesquita, M. H., *Direitos Reais* (Coimbra, 1967)
Obrigações Reais e Ónus Reais (Coimbra, 1990)
Mota Pinto, C. A., *Direitos Reais* (Coimbra, 1971)
Oliveira Ascensão, J., *Direito Civil: Direitos Reais* (5th edn, Coimbra, 1993)
Pinto Furtado, J., *Manual do Arrendamento Urbano* (4th edn, Coimbra, 2009), vol. 1
Pires de Lima, F., and Antunes Varela, J. (with M. H. Mesquita), *Código Civil Anotado* (4th edn, Coimbra, 1987)
Remédio Marques, J. P., *Curso de processo executivo comum à face do código revisto* (Coimbra, 2000)
Vieira, J. A., '*Arrendamento de Imóvel dado em Garantia*', in A. Menezes Cordeiro, L. Menezes Leitão and J. Gomes (eds.), *Estudos em Homenagem ao Professor Galvão Teles: Novos Estudos de Direito Privado* (Coimbra, 2003), vol. 4, p. 437.

SCOTLAND

Anderson, R. G., '"Offside Goals" before Rodger Builders', *Juridical Review* 3 (2005), p. 277
Anderson, R. G., and Macleod, J., 'Offside Goals and Interfering with Play', *SLT* (News) (2009), p. 93
Bankton, M. A., *An Institute of the Laws of Scotland in Civil Rights (1751–53)* (Edinburgh, 1993–5), vols. 41–3

Bell, G. J., *Commentaries on the Law of Scotland and the Principles of Mercantile Jurisprudence* (7th edn, Edinburgh, 1870)

Principles of the Law of Scotland (10th edn, Edinburgh, 1899)

Bell, R., *A Treatise on Leases* (4th edn, Edinburgh, 1825–6)

Brand, D. A., Steven, A. J. M., and Wortley, S., *Professor McDonald's Conveyancing Manual* (7th edn, Edinburgh, 2004)

Caterina, R., 'A Comparative Overview of the Fair Wear and Tear Exception: The Duty of Holders of Temporary Interests to Preserve Property', *Edinburgh Law Review* 6 (2002), p. 85

Chalmers, J. P., *Trusts: Cases and Materials* (Edinburgh, 2002)

Cockburn, D. W., *Commercial Leases* (Edinburgh, 2002)

Dobie, W. J., *Manual of the Law of Liferent and Fee in Scotland* (Edinburgh, 1941)

Erskine, J., in J. B. Nicolson (ed.), *An Institute of the Law of Scotland* (8th edn, Edinburgh, 1871)

Flyn, D., and Graham, K., '*Crofting*', in R. Black (ed.), *Stair Memorial Encyclopaedia* (Edinburgh, 2009)

Gerber, K. S., *Commercial Leases in Scotland* (Edinburgh, 2009)

Gloag, W. M., *The Law of Contract in Scotland* (2nd edn, Edinburgh, 1929)

Gloag, W. M., and Henderson, R. C., *The Law of Scotland* (11th edn, Edinburgh, 2007)

Gordon, W. M., and Wortley, S., *Scottish Land Law* (3rd edn, Edinburgh, 2009)

Gretton, G., and Maher, G., '*Diligence and Enforcement of Judgments*', in R. Black (ed.), *Stair Memorial Encyclopaedia* (Edinburgh, 1992), vol. 8

Gretton, G. L., *The Law of Inhibition and Adjudication* (2nd edn, Edinburgh, 1996)

Guy, W., 'Registration of Leases', *Juridical Review* 20 (1908–9), p. 234

Halliday, S., 'Tacit Relocation', *Juridical Review* (2001) p. 201

Hogg, M., 'To Irritate or to Rescind: Two Paths for the Landlord?' *SLT* (News) (1999) 1

Hugo, C., and Simpson, P., '*Lease*', in R. Zimmermann, D. Visser, and K. G. C. Reid (eds.), *Mixed Legal Systems in Comparative Perspective: Property and Obligations in Scotland and South Africa* (Oxford, 2004)

Hunter, R., *A Treatise on the Law of Landlord and Tenant*, 2 vols. (4th edn, Edinburgh, 1876), vol. 2

Lewison, J., *Woodfall's Law of Landlord and Tenant* (looseleaf) (London, 2010)

Lord Coulsfield, and MacQueen, H. L. (eds.), *W. M. Gloag and R. C. Henderson: The Law of Scotland* (12th edn, Edinburgh, 2007)

Lord Dervaird, and Usher, J. A., '*Agriculture*', in R. Black (ed.), *Stair Memorial Encyclopaedia* (Edinburgh, 2001)

Lord Gill, *The Law of Agricultural Holdings in Scotland* (3rd edn, Edinburgh, 1997)

Maher, G., and Cusine, D. J., *The Law and Practice of Diligence* (Edinburgh, 1990)

McAllister, A., *Scottish Law of Leases* (3rd edn, Edinburgh, 2002)

McBryde, W. W., *The Law of Contract in Scotland* (3rd edn, Edinburgh, 2007)

Paisley, R. R. M., 'Real Rights: Practical Problems and Dogmatic Rigidity', *Edinburgh Law Review* 9 (2005), p. 267

Paton, G. C. H. (ed.), *Baron David Hume's Lectures*, 1786–1822 (Edinburgh, 1939–58)

Paton, G. C. H., and Cameron, J. G. S., *The Law of Landlord and Tenant in Scotland* (Edinburgh, 1967)
Rankine, J. (ed.), *J. Erskine's Principles of the Law of Scotland* (1st edn, Edinburgh, 1911)
A Treatise on the Law of Leases in Scotland (3rd edn, Edinburgh, 1916)
Reid, K. G. C., et al. *The Law of Property in Scotland* (1996), a reprint of R. Black (ed.), *Stair Memorial Encyclopaedia* (Edinburgh, 1996), vol. 18
Robson, P. W. G., *Residential Tenancies* (2nd edn, 1998)
Ross, M. J., and McKichan, D. J., *Drafting and Negotiating Commercial Leases in Scotland* (2nd edn, Edinburgh, 1993)
Steven, A. J. M., 'Options to Purchase and Successor Landlords', *Edinburgh Law Review* 10 (2006), p. 432
Stewart, J. G., *A Treatise on the Law of Diligence* (Edinburgh, 1898)
Styles, S. C., '*Liferent and Fee*', in R. Black, *Stair Memorial Encyclopaedia* (Edinburgh, 1992), vol. 13
Viscount Stair, in J. S. More (ed.), *The Institutions of the Law of Scotland*, 2 vols. (5th edn, Edinburgh, 1832)
Watson, G. (ed.), *Bell's Dictionary and Digest of the Law of Scotland* (7th edn, Edinburgh, 1890)
Webster, P., 'Options for the Offside Goals Rule', *Edinburgh Law Review* 13 (2009), p. 524
'The Relationship of Tenant and Successor Landlord in Scots Law' (Ph.D. thesis, Edinburgh University, 2008)
Whitty, N. R., '*Nuisance*', in R. Black (ed.), *Stair Memorial Encyclopaedia* (Edinburgh, 2001)
Wilson, W. A., *Trusts, Trustees and Executors* (2nd edn, Edinburgh, 1995)
Wortley, S., 'Double Sales and the Offside Trap: Some Thoughts on the Rule Penalising Private Knowledge of a Prior Right', *Juridical Review* (2002), p. 229

SOUTH AFRICA

Cooper, W. E., *Landlord and Tenant* (2nd edn, Cape Town, 1994)
De Wet, J. C., and Van Wyk, A. H., *Kontraktereg en Handelsreg* (5th edn, Durban, 1992)
Du Bois (ed.), *Wille's Principles of South African Law* (9th edn, Cape Town, 2007)
Harpum, C., *Megarry and Wade's Law of Real Property* (6th edn, London, 2000)
Grotius, H., *Inleidinge tot de Hollandsche Rechtsgeleerdheid* (Middelburg, 1767)
Kerr, A. J., '*Lease*', in W. A. Joubert (ed.), *The Law of South Africa*, 1st reissue (Durban, 1999), vol. 14
Lubbe, G. F., '*Mortgage and Pledge*', in W. A. Joubert (ed.), *The Law of South Africa*, 2nd reissue (Durban, 2008), vol. 17
Milton, J. R. L., '*Nuisance*', in W. A. Joubert (ed.), *The Law of South Africa*, 1st reissue (Durban, 1997), vol. 19
Naudé, T., 'Rights of First Refusal or Preferential Rights to Contract: A Historical Perspective on a Controversial Legal Figure', *Stellenbosch Law Review* (2004), p. 66
Nel, H. S., *Jones: Conveyancing in South Africa* (4th edn, Cape Town, 1991)

Pothier, R. J., *Traité des obligations* (Paris, 1813)
Traité du contrat de vente (Paris, 1762)
Scott, T. J., and Scott, S., *Wille's Law of Mortgage and Pledge in South Africa* (3rd edn, Cape Town, 1987)
Smith, C., *Insolvency*, in W. A. Joubert (ed.), *The Law of South Africa*, 1st reissue (Durban, 1998), vol. 11
Turpin, C. C., 'The Right of Ejectment', *SALJ* (1957), p. 145
Van der Linden, *Rechtsgeleerd Practicaal en Koopmans Handboek* (Amsterdam, 1806)
Van der Merwe, C. G., '*Numerus clausus* and the Development of New Real Rights in South Africa', *SALJ* (2002), p. 803
Sakereg (2nd edn, Durban, 1989)
'*Servitudes*', in W. A. Joubert (ed.), *The Law of South Africa* (Durban, 2000), vol. 24
Van der Merwe, C. G., De Waal, M. J., and Carey Miller, D. L., 'Property and Trust Law', in R. Blanpain and A. Verbeke (eds.), *International Encyclopaedia of Laws*, Supplement 6 (2004)
Voet, J., *Commentarius ad Pandectas* (The Hague, 1698–1704)

SPAIN

Arangüena Fanego, C., *Comentarios a la nueva Ley de Enjuiciamiento Civil* (Valladolid, 2000), vol. 3
Ballarín Hernández, R., and Mas Badía, M. D., *Comentarios a la Ley de arrendamientos rústicos* (Madrid, 2006)
de Ángel Yágüez, R., '*Comment on Article 1740 Civil Code*', in R. Bercovitz et al. (eds.) *Comentario del Có digo Civil* (2nd edn, Madrid, 1993), vol. 2
de los Mozos, J. L., *Tutela interdictal de la posesió n* (Madrid, 1962)
Díez-Picazo, L., *Fundamentos del Derecho Civil Patrimonial*, 3 vols (4th edn, Madrid, 1995), vols. 1 and 3
Fínez Ratón, J. M., '*Comment on Article 14*', in F. Pantaleón (ed.), *Comentario a la Ley de Arrendamientos Urbanos* (Madrid, 1995)
García Cantero, G., '*Comment on, art. 500*', in R. Bercovitz et al. (eds.), *Comentario del Có digo Civil* (2nd edn, Madrid, 1993), vol. 2
García Valdecasas, G., 'La posesión incorporal del despojado y la posesión de un año', *Revista de Derecho Privado* 30 (1946), p. 341
González Pérez, J., *Comentarios a la Ley del Suelo Texto Refundido de 1992* (6th edn (ed. M. Albaladejo García) Madrid, 1993)
Jordano Barea, J. B., *La categoría de los contratos reales* (Barcelona, 1958)
Lacruz Berdejo, J. L., et al., *Elementos de Derecho civil* (4th edn (ed. M. Albaladejo García) Madrid, 1999–2001), vols. 2 and 3
Lucas Fernández, F., '*Comment on Article 1571*', in Albaladejo García (ed.) *Comentario del Código civil* (2nd edn, Madrid, 1993)
'*Comment on Articles 1571 and 1572*', in M. Albaladejo García (ed.), *Comentarios al Có digo civil y Compilaciones Forales* (3rd edn, Madrid, 1997), vol. 1-B
Maluquer de Motes Bernet, C. J., '*Comment on Article 485*', in R. Bercovitz et al. (eds.), *Comentario del Código civil* (2nd edn, Madrid, 1993)

Marín López, M. J., '*Comment on Article 13*', in M. Albaladejo García (ed.), *Comentarios a la Ley de Arrendamientos Urbanos* (4th edn, Pamplona, 2005), p. 287

Martín Pérez, A., '*Comment on Article 446*', in R. Bercovitz et al. (eds.), *Comentarios al Código civil y Compilaciones Forales* (2nd edn, Madrid, 1993), vol. 6, p. 299

Moreno Quesada, B., '*Comment on Article 520*', in R. Bercovitz et al. (eds.), *Comentarios al Có digo Civil* (2nd edn, Madrid, 1993)

Pasquau Liaño, M., *Ley de Arrendamientos Rústicos: Comentarios Doctrinales y Formularios Prácticos* (2nd edn, Pamplona, 2006)

Peña Bernaldo de Quirós, M., *Derechos reales: Derecho hipotecario* (3rd edn, Madrid, 1999)

Rams Albesa, J., '*Comment on Articles 524 and 529*', in R. Bercovitz et al. (eds.), *Comentarios al Có digo Civil* (2nd edn, Madrid, 1993)

Rojo Ajuria, L., '*Comment on Article 4*', in F. Pantaleón (ed.), *Comentario a la Ley de Arrendamientos Urbanos* (Madrid, 1995), p. 181

Vattier Fuenzalida, C., '*Comment on Article 22*', in *Comentario de la Ley de Arrendamientos Rústicos* (Madrid, 2004)

General index

Country index

Books in the series

Time Limited Interests in Land
Edited by Cornelius van der Merwe and Alain-Laurent Verbeke

Unexpected Circumstances in European Contract Law
Edited by Ewoud Hondius and Christoph Grigoleit 978 1 107 00340 8

Personality Rights in European Tort Law
Edited by Gert Brüggemeier, Aurelia Colombi Ciacchi and Patrick O'Callaghan 978 0 521 19491 4

Precontractual Liability
Edited by John Cartwright and Martijn Hesselink 978 0 521 51601 3

Environmental Liability and Ecological Damage in European Law
Edited by Monika Hinteregger 978 0 521 88997 1 Hardback

The Enforcement of Competition Law in Europe
Edited by Thomas M. J. Möllers and Andreas Heinemann 978 0 521 88110 4 Hardback

Commercial Trusts in European Private Law
Edited by Michele Graziadei, Ugo Mattei and Lionel Smith 978 0 521 84919 7

Mistake, Fraud and Duties to Inform in European Contract Law
Edited by Ruth Sefton-Green 0 521 84423 1 Hardback

Security Rights in Movable Property in European Private Law
Edited by Eva-Maria Kieninger 0 521 83967 X Hardback

Pure Economic Loss in Europe
Edited by Mauro Bussani and Vernon Valentine Palmer 0 521 82464 8 Hardback

The Enforceability of Promises in European Contract Law
Edited by James Gordley 0 521 79021 2 Hardback

Good Faith in European Contract Law
Edited by Reinhard Zimmermann and Simon Whittaker 0 521 77190 0 Hardback